ROLLIN' AND TUMBLIN'

ROLLIN' AND TUMBLIN'

THE POSTWAR BLUES GUITARISTS

Edited by Jas Obrecht

Miller
Freeman
Books

SAN FRANCISCO

Published by Miller Freeman Books
600 Harrison Street, San Francisco, CA 94107

 Miller Freeman
A United News & Media publication

Distributed to the book trade in the
U.S and Canada by
Publisher's Group West,
1700 Fourth Street, Berkeley, CA 94710

Distributed to the music trade in the
U.S. and Canada by
Hal Leonard Publishing,
P.O. Box 13819, Milwaukee, WI 53213

Cover Design: Saroyan Humphrey
Text Design and Composition: Saroyan Humphrey

Library of Congress Cataloging-in-Publication Data

Rollin & tumblin : the postwar blues guitarists / edited by Jas Obrecht
    p. cm
ISBN 0-87930-613-0 (alk. paper)
    1. Blues musicians United State s Biography. 2. Guitarists United
State s Biography. I. Title: Rollin and tumblin . II. Rolling & tumbling.
III. Obrecht, Jas.

ML399.R65 2000
787.87 1643 092273 dc21
[B]   00-028815

Printed in the United States of America

00 01 02 03 04 05   5 4 3 2 1

To Michelle and Ava Obrecht

POSTWAR BLUES:
AN INTRODUCTION

BY JAS OBRECHT America was in transition, and so was its music. Down South, Jim Crow was the law of the land during the years around World War II, and life had become difficult to nearly intolerable for field hands such as Muddy Waters, John Lee Hooker, Howlin' Wolf, B.B. King, and Otis Rush. All of these men grew up in tumbledown shacks near the fields they worked, as did Charley Patton, Son House, Robert Johnson, and many other great bluesmen before them. All of them knew the backbreaking labor of a crooked sharecropping system that kept their families in perpetual servitude. All of them were barred from using "whites only" facilities such as drinking fountains, restaurants, and rest rooms. They'd seen the signs warning them in their travels: "Nigger don't let the sun go down on you here." Chain gangs were common sights, men were being lynched for little more than reckless innuendo, and extreme poverty was the norm. "In Mississippi," remembered Johnny Shines, who witnessed these conditions firsthand, "it was open season on black folk." Life had become far more treacherous than it had been in slavery times. ¶ Outside of farming, the only jobs available to uneducated Southern blacks were mostly in hard labor—logging, turpentine production, levee grading, ditch digging. Little wonder that during the 1930s and early '40s, thousands escaped the shackles of "Southern hospitality" by fleeing North, where, it was believed, people could forge their own destinies amid sprawling cities of opportunity. "There was a big demand for steel-driving men and strong-backed women to come North and work in the steel mills and factories," explained Danny Barker, a veteran New Orleans bluesman. "Automobile industry was begging for help, the steel mills of Detroit, Gary, Indiana, Cleveland, Ohio, Cincinnati. All said, 'Come North. We need workers.' And that's where the Southerners went, because the pay was better and it was a different environment, especially for black people. Above the Mason-Dixon line, where there was less pressure on you, you could walk tall and walk free."

"There was more freedom," agreed Sammy Price, a fine prewar Texas pianist. "You could laugh if you wanted to. In the South, sometimes you'd laugh and the cop put you in jail, thinkin' you laughing at him. Or he put you in for any reason. But when you went to Chicago, you had places where you could actually go in, buy a drink, and drink it, and you didn't have to bow your head in order to get out of the place. It was a community feeling. People were meeting new friends. All of these things had a lot to do with the clubs in the North."

For the lucky few—Waters, Hooker, King, Wolf, and Rush among them—music became a passport to a new life. The story of postwar blues is the story of the men who made this journey and how they transformed the music they carried with them into something that's enriched us all. *Rollin' and Tumblin'* gathers their stories, letting the artists speak for themselves in their natural voices wherever possible.

THE PREWAR ERA Besides the migration to big cities, several elements were crucial to the development of postwar blues, the most essential being the music that preceded it, the emergence of amplified instruments, and the rise of independent record labels.

From the turn of the century through the Great Depression, virtually all blues songs were accompanied by acoustic instruments—just about every imaginable configuration of piano, harmonica, banjo, fiddle, string bass, horns, drums, washboard, and homemade instruments—but most often, at least in rural areas, by an unamplified guitar made by Stella, Gibson, Harmony, or National.

An astounding array of acoustic blues made it onto record during the years between Mamie Smith's breakthrough "Crazy Blues," waxed with a jazz ensemble in 1920, and Robert Johnson's stark, harrowing country blues of the late 1930s. Along the way, many incandescent guitarists left their mark. First was Blind Lemon Jefferson, the most famous bluesman of the Roaring Twenties, with his fleet-fingered, unpredictable guitar style and booming two-octave voice. A man well acquainted with booze, gambling, and heavy-hipped mamas, Blind Lemon lived the themes that dominate his songs, and his lyrics provide a stunning view of society from the perspective of someone at the bottom. Jefferson's 78s crossed racial barriers, inspiring country musicians and bluesmen alike.

Jefferson's Paramount labelmate, Blind Blake, specialized in syncopated ragtime blues played on his "famous piano-sounding guitar," and his mid-1920s records were especially influential in the Southeastern states. New Orleans-raised Lonnie

Johnson emerged soon thereafter as the most sophisticated of the prewar blues guitarists, having the dexterity and harmonic savvy to accompany Louis Armstrong and Duke Ellington, record unsurpassed jazz duets with Eddie Lang, and release stacks of blues, ballads, and pop records under his own name. Significant portions of Johnson's vocabulary have survived intact into the modern era, making him, as Ry Cooder describes, "one of the transcendental people who influenced *everybody*."

In Louisiana and Texas, convicted murderer Huddie Ledbetter sang his way to freedom and became famous as Lead Belly. He changed worlds in 1935, shedding chain-gang shackles to become a darling of New York intelligentsia. Many regarded him as little more than a clothed savage, but he could be charming, witty, and courteous, and he was a great musician. "He sang some of the greatest protest songs of all time," remembered his friend Pete Seeger. "He had the heart of a champion."

While Lead Belly reigned as the self-proclaimed "King of the 12-String Guitar Players of the World," blues fans in Atlanta, Georgia, would more likely have bestowed that title upon Blind Willie McTell, a Depression-era recording star with a phenomenal repertoire of blues, hillbilly music, spirituals, quick-fingered rags, minstrel fare, and pop tunes. He played with a slide and bare fingers on a big-bodied Stella 12-string, specializing in shifting rhythms and resonant melodies as distinctive as his clear, nasal voice. Other Atlantans concentrated on frantic 12-string slide, with brothers Barbecue Bob and Charley Lincoln ranking among the best.

Regional sounds developed elsewhere as well. In the Southeast's tobacco belt, Blind Boy Fuller, Blind Gary Davis, William Moore, and Willie Walker blended ragtime and blues. St. Louis and East St. Louis were the home of a thriving piano scene populated by Peetie Wheatstraw, Roosevelt Sykes, and Walter Davis; among its guitar stars were the Lonnie Johnson–influenced Charlie Jordan and Henry Townsend, who doubled on piano and guitar. The Central Tracks district of Dallas, with its rows of black-owned stores, saloons, barbershops, and brothels, was the gathering ground of Rambling Thomas, Blind Lemon Jefferson, Lead Belly, T-Bone Walker, and singer Texas Alexander, all of whom relied on tips for sustenance. Beaumont, Texas, was the fearsome stage for guitarist Blind Willie Johnson, a street-corner evangelist with a gravelly, emotion-charged voice. Gifted with an exquisite sense of timing and tone, Johnson used a slider to duplicate his vocal inflections and produce an unforgettable phrase from a single strike of a string. His spiritual 78s are intensely moving, and he's certainly among the greatest of the slide guitarists. Like many of his blues contemporaries, Johnson, blinded in his youth by his stepfather, lived and died in abject poverty.

In Mississippi, Charley Patton, Son House, Willie Brown, Bo Carter and the Mississippi Sheiks, Skip James, Tommy Johnson, Ishman Bracey, Bukka White, King Solomon Hill, and others were rocking house parties, fish fries, gambling joints, and jukes with powerful blues, just as Robert Johnson, Elmore James, Tommy McClennan, and Muddy Waters would in years to come. Blues allowed these musicians to express themselves with impunity, as Cedell Davis, who grew up on a plantation near Tunica, Mississippi, remembers: "I was a boy back in the time of the farms, and a lot of people was on the farms. They had them country 'breakdowns,' as they called it. The guys would sing *anything* and play just the plain old country blues. And they called that 'gut bucket,' because they could say anything they wanted. They'd make up songs, and sometimes songs would be passed down through the plantation."

Many Delta bluesmen specialized in bottlenecking melodic leads on open-tuned guitars. As Muddy Waters explained, "Me and my guitar, we have a conversation and talk together—that's from the Delta style." This style also thrived in nearby Memphis, home of W.C. Handy, the so-called "Father of the Blues." Along Beale Street, thumping country stompers commingled with Hawaiian sliders, fife-and-drum bands, jazz musicians, bluesmen, and jug bands led by Gus Cannon and Will Shade. Guitarists Frank Stokes, Jim Jackson, Furry Lewis, and Robert Wilkins were Memphis regulars, while Hambone Willie Newbern, Sleepy John Estes, Mississippi John Hurt, and many others journeyed there to record.

At the vanguard of a smoother, more urban sound in the North were India-napolis' Leroy Carr, a dominating force in blues piano, and his partner Francis "Scrapper" Blackwell. Their 1927 debut recording, the sentimental "How Long—How Long Blues," became a runaway hit and made them the most popular piano–guitar team in the country. On dozens of follow-up releases, the mournful-voiced Carr manned his ivories with an easy-rolling touch, while Blackwell backed him with ringing chords and inventive solos. In Louisville, Sylvester Weaver, the first blues guitarist on record, played slide guitar with a knife in black vaudeville shows, often backing singer Sara Martin.

Chicago had black entertainment ranging from ritzy night spots to house-rent parties and sawdust-floored dives. Early in the Roaring Twenties, King Oliver and Louis Armstrong brought New Orleans jazz to South Side clubs, while classic divas such as Lucille Hegamin and Alberta Hunter belted out sophisticated blues. By mid decade the city was the center of blues recording, with musicians coming in and out of town to record solo or with house musicians such as banjoist Papa Charlie Jackson and the city's first pre-eminent blues guitar stars, Hudson "Tampa Red" Whittaker and Big Bill Broonzy. Both guitarists found stardom in the late 1920s as high wizards of hokum, a zany style epitomized by jivey lyrics and good-time arrangements. A persuasive singer, Broonzy had an extraordinary facility for raggy, syncopated playing. He was exceptionally inventive working within a 12-bar for-mat, drawing on a seemingly endless variety of string bends, multi-string slides, and other flashy embellishments. Unlike most bluesmen raised in the South, Broonzy specialized in C, the most common ragtime key.

Among the galaxy of prewar slide stars, none shone brighter than Tampa Red. Bridging blues, jazz, pop, and jive, his urbane, light-hearted records drew listeners from coast to coast, and he released more 78s than any other artist in blues history. With his warm, sweet tone and dead-on intonation, Tampa Red was a master of single-string melodies and streamlined chords—so much so that he came to be known as the "Guitar Wizard." He was also a terrific singer, with a keen, sensitive voice and street-wise delivery reminiscent of Lonnie Johnson, his favorite guitarist. Tampa Red's early ensembles, as well as those of Big Bill Broonzy, were crucial to the development of the modern blues band, and several of the songs Tampa Red composed or popularized—"Love Her with a Feeling," "Crying Won't Help You," "Sweet Little Angel," "It Hurts Me Too"—have become blues standards.

"Tampa Red ironed out all the kinks," explains Ry Cooder. "He made it more accessible and played it with more of a modern big band feeling—like a soloist, almost. He changed it from rural music to commercial music, and he was very popular as a result. He made hundreds of records, and they're all good. Some of them are incredibly good. You gotta say, okay, that's where it all starts to become almost pop. And he had a great guitar technique, for sure. He put it all together, as far as I'm concerned. He got the songs, he had the vocal styling, he had the beat. It's a straight line from Tampa Red to Louis Jordan to Chuck Berry, without a shadow of a doubt."

By virtue of her professional name, Memphis Minnie Douglas is forever linked with the city of Memphis, although the most important years of her career were spent in Chicago. One of the great 1930s blues singers, she had a strong voice and an appealing guitar style that mixed country and city influences. The celebrated hostess of weekly Blue Monday parties, Memphis Minnie was prolific, recording alone, with piano accompaniment, or with her husband, Kansas Joe McCoy, who'd usually flatpick a simple "boom-chucka" rhythm for her single-line solos.

All of these musicians played acoustic guitars, but by the late 1930s that was about to change.

THE EMERGENCE OF THE ELECTRIC GUITAR While an acoustic guitar was relatively easy to record as a solo instrument or in a small combo setting, even the best-made archtops had trouble competing with the volume of horns, piano, drums, and other band instruments. Through the 1930s, most jazz guitarists were relegated to comping rhythm while other musicians took the solos. The notable exceptions— Nick Lucas, Lonnie Johnson, Eddie Lang, Carl Kress, Dick McDonough, Teddy Bunn, and several others—had to position themselves closer than the other instruments to the recording source—often a single horn or microphone—to ensure their presence in the mix.

But help was on the way. In 1924, executives at the Gibson company had begun designing electric instruments, causing a furor and resignations among management when the project was shelved as "too futuristic." Four years later, the Vega company unveiled an electric banjo that combined a portable amplifying unit and a radio loudspeaker. Then Stromberg-Voisinet developed a soundboard-mounted microphonic pickup. In 1932, the Ro-Pat-In Corporation, forerunner of Rickenbacker, innovated an electromagnetic pickup and was soon offering the first production-model electric guitar, the Rickenbacker A-25 "Frying Pan," which was marketed to Hawaiian steel guitarists.

The first to successfully achieve guitar amplification on record was likely Eddie Durham. Around 1933, Durham recorded single-string solos with Bennie Moten's band, using an acoustic guitar he'd outfitted with a pie-tin resonator and megaphone. Then, in September '35, Durham soloed on "Hittin' the Bottle" with the Jimmie Lunceford Orchestra; according to jazz historian Leonard Feather, this was "the first recorded example of any form of guitar amplification." "DeArmond came out with a pickup, which I got," Durham remembered, "but they didn't have sound amplifiers. So I'd get any kind of amp I could find and sit in the corner of the stage and run the cord to the guitar, and that was it. I'd just play the solo work, and I think that at the time I was the only guy playing that kind of guitar in a jazz band."

In 1935, National, maker of metal-bodied resophonic guitars, introduced the pickup-equipped National Electric Spanish archtop. The following year, the Gibson company unveiled the ES-150, an unadorned archtop outfitted with a single-bar pickup. By 1938, Eddie Durham had featured the Gibson electric guitar on memorable 78s with the Kansas City Five and the Kansas City Six. But it took Charlie Christian, a former student of Durham's, to fully demonstrate the new instrument's potential.

The most influential of all jazz guitarists, Charlie Christian bought an ES-150 in 1938, after woodshedding with Durham in Oklahoma City. The following year, he made his spectacular debut with Benny Goodman, leader of the era's top swing ensemble. On session after session, Christian had the tonal strength and improvisational ability to play long, flowing solos on a par with those of his Goodman bandmates. Christian's influence was immediate, causing countless acoustic guitarists to switch to electric. As Christian disciple Barney Kessel explains, "A lot of people think that Charlie Christian simply wanted to amplify the natural sound of the guitar—that's not true! That's a different sound entirely. The electric guitar as he played it had its own sound. Charlie was the first one to play single lines like a horn. And Charlie's tone was the concept for what is being used today in jazz." Christian's harmonic and melodic capabilities reached beyond Goodman's swing, and in after-hours jam sessions at New York's Minton's Playhouse, he helped create bebop before his tragic death in 1941. Soon the sound he pioneered would resound in a dynamic new blues style led by Aaron "T-Bone" Walker.

TEXAS AND THE WEST COAST Due to rationing, material shortages, and a ban on recording, few blues records were made during World War II. Soon afterwards, though, the long, lean, open-line sound of Texas blues guitar was crackling over jukeboxes and radios. Enter T-Bone Walker, whose sophisticated electric-guitar styling would bring Texas blues to swank nightclubs and concert halls around the country. Blending jump blues and jazz, Walker fronted swinging big bands, and his flamboyant showboating—playing guitar behind his head, dancing around, doing the splits—was later adapted by Guitar Slim, Buddy Guy, Jimi Hendrix, and Stevie Ray Vaughan.

The Texas-raised Walker was influenced by country, jazz, Western swing, and, naturally, Charlie Christian. He excelled at mournful, worldly blues, and his licks became part of the blues guitar vocabulary, echoing through Clarence "Gatemouth" Brown, B.B. and Freddie King, Albert Collins, and many others. As Johnny Winter tells it, "T-Bone Walker is pretty much the father of the electric blues style. He influenced everybody. He played syncopated, he changed the meter around, he knew a lot of chords, and he did things that nobody else did. He was the first guy who did it right, and he influenced everybody who came along after him. He really defined electric blues guitar."

The invention of magnetic tape allowed virtually anyone to make records, and during the 1940s dozens of independent labels sprang into existence. Los Angeles, with its community of jump blues honkers, shouters, and wailers, became the home base for Specialty, Aladdin, Modern, Imperial, and other indies dedicated to issuing the R&B music being ignored by the majors. During the early 1940s Walker moved to Los Angeles, where he recorded many enduring sides for Capitol, Black & White, and Imperial. Other Texas bluesmen followed: Pianist/songwriters Amos Milburn, Percy Mayfield, and Charles Brown moved to Los Angeles, while electric guitarist Pee Wee Crayton divided his time between Los Angeles and San Francisco. Lowell Fulson, from Texas by way of Oklahoma, moved to Oakland, California, where he hit big after the war with "Three O'Clock Blues" and "Every Day I Have the Blues." Just across the San Francisco Bay, Louisiana-born Saunders King was swinging for the Rhythm label.

T-Bone disciple Clarence "Gatemouth" Brown made his first records in Los Angeles in '47, but stayed in Texas, where he had a long association with the Houston-based Duke/Peacock label, which also recorded Big Mama Thornton, Junior Parker, and Bobby Bland. By the mid 1950s, another generation of Texas-raised blues guitarists began its ascendancy: Johnny "Guitar" Watson relocated to Los Angeles and signed with Federal, while Albert Collins and Johnny Copeland began making singles in Houston in 1958.

But not all postwar Texas bluesmen gravitated toward jumping, band-oriented blues. By the late 1940s, down-home traditionalists such as Lightnin' Hopkins, Li'l Son Jackson, Smokey Hogg, and Frankie Lee Sims were making bristling records. Years later, Mance Lipscomb, who was a generation older than any of them, would join their ranks.

Sam "Lightnin'" Hopkins was almost as downhome as Blind Lemon Jefferson, whom he'd seen and greatly admired. A natural-born storyteller, he had a genius for improvising and copied no one. "I play from my heart and soul," Lightnin' said, "and I play my own, own music." Supremely confident, Hopkins made his first 78s in Los Angeles in 1946, but mostly recorded in Texas after that. Andrew "Smokey" Hogg beat him onto record by nearly a decade, but never came close to rivaling his success. Influenced by Big Bill Broonzy and Peetie Wheatstraw, Hogg recorded stacks of 78s after the war, but seldom strayed from a simple, slow-hand approach. Melvin "Li'l Son" Jackson was a far more facile player, his countrified solo sides on Imperial moving to hypnotic bass-string thumps and treble fills. Frankie Lee Sims ensured his legacy with 1953's "Lucy Mae Blues," a raucous juke-joint revelry.

Still, until the rock era, most people would associate Texas blues with horn sections and T-Bone–style solos. "A lot of people ask me what's the difference between Chicago blues and Texas blues," Albert Collins observed. "Well, we didn't have harp players and slide guitar players out of Texas, so most of the blues guitars had a horn section. That was the difference. The bigger the band is, the better they like it in Texas. It's hard to go down through there with just a rhythm section and get good response."

SWEET HOME CHICAGO During and just after the war, Chicago's blues community was headed by piano giants Big Maceo Merriweather and Memphis Slim, harmonica ace John Lee "Sonny Boy" Williamson, percussionist Washboard Sam, and guitarists Big Bill Broonzy, Tampa Red, Memphis Minnie, Big Joe Williams, and Arthur "Big Boy" Crudup, all of whom recorded for producer and A&R man Lester Melrose. Occasionally exhilarating but often bland, Melrose's ensemble recordings of blues, jazz, and novelty numbers for Columbia and Victor's Bluebird subsidiary created a market-dominating sound that became known as the "Bluebird Beat." During the '30s, these records were based mostly on guitar and piano, with occasional support from clarinet, washboard, string bass, and harmonica or kazoo. By the end of World War II, drums and electric guitar had become part of the mix.

Tampa Red was among the first dedicated Chicago blues performers to acquire an electric guitar, which he featured on 1940's "Anna Lou Blues." Two years earlier, though, studio guitarist George Barnes had used an electric guitar on his Chicago sessions with Big Bill Broonzy, Hattie Bolten, Blind John Davis, Jazz Gillum, Merline

Johnson, and Washboard Sam. ("When I was young, I hung around Lonnie Johnson," Barnes recalled, "and he taught me how to play the blues. I made over a hundred records with fellows like Big Bill Broonzy, Blind John Davis, and a host of other bluesmen. I was the only white musician on these dates.") By the early 1940s, Memphis Minnie, Big Bill Broonzy, and Moody Jones also had electric guitars.

Playing sessions by day and taverns by night, Tampa Red and Big Bill were renowned for their graciousness in helping struggling musicians newly arrived from the South, even as the music of these newcomers began supplanting their own. Tampa Red's spacious home at 3432 South State Street was a haven for blues musicians, with its big rehearsal room, guest rooms, home-cooked meals, and steady supply of booze. Tampa's drinking buddy Big Bill was a frequent guest, as were Blind John Davis, Memphis Slim, and Big Maceo. His visitors included Willie Dixon, Jazz Gillum, Big Joe Williams, Sonny Boy Williamson I, Doc Clayton, Robert Lockwood, Jr., Arthur Crudup, Washboard Sam, Romeo Nelson, Little Walter, Elmore James, Muddy Waters, and Muddy's old friend Robert Lee McCollum, who began recording as Robert Nighthawk in 1948. Tampa influenced McCollum, whose potent electric slide merged his mentor's facile approach with a sustaining Delta whine.

Striking a resonant chord with former Southerners who congregated in Chicago's taverns and clubs, the band-driven "deep-bottom Mississippi blues" of Muddy Waters became the dominant force in postwar Chicago blues during the late 1940s and 1950s. "I came to Chicago and I had to work my blues up in there," Waters stated. "When I did get it through, boy, I bust Chicago wide open with 'em."

Waters had come to town in '43 with an acoustic guitar. In Chicago's clubs, though, his Silvertone could scarcely cut through the din. "I was banging my hand all up," he recalled, "so I went to a thumbpick. That still wasn't loud enough, so I started playing electric."

In 1947, brothers Leonard and Phil Chess bought a piece of Aristocrat, a local independent label that released mostly pop and jazz 78s. The raw, amplified blues of Muddy Waters had yet to be documented, and the following year the Chess brothers began exploring that market by releasing "I Can't Be Satisfied" backed with "I Feel Like Going Home," which became a minor hit. Muddy Waters' initial releases with the Chess brothers featured sparse Robert Johnson–style blues accompanied by stand-up bass. In clubs, though, Waters was forging acoustic Delta fare into electrified band blues. At the core of his band was harmonica ace Little Walter, co-guitarist Jimmy Rogers, and Baby Face Leroy (followed by Elga Edmonds, better known as Elgin Evans) on drums. In 1950, the Chess brothers finally allowed Muddy to record with his band for their newly formed Chess Records. Vastly different from the jumps and ballads dominating the R&B charts, the Waters band's surging, beat-heavy rhythms signaled the beginning of the greatest creative era of Chicago blues. Soon Chess and its Checker subsidiary were offering 78s by Little Walter, Jimmy Rogers, Howlin' Wolf, John Brim, J.B. Lenoir, Willie Dixon, Sonny Boy Williamson, Otis Spann, Eddie Boyd, Lowell Fulson, Bo Diddley, and Detroit-based John Lee Hooker. By mid decade, Chicago seemed littered with indies, with blues coming out on Vee Jay, Atomic H, Cobra, JOB, Parrot, United, Chance, Cool, and many other labels.

Elmore James and Howlin' Wolf proved themselves equally adept at framing Delta blues in a band context. Fronting the roaring Broomdusters, James slid in open *D* on a Kay acoustic with a soundhole pickup. Sung with vein-popping passion, his Chicago-cut sides for the Fire and Enjoy labels were nothing short of monumental. "After me there will be no more," predicted Elmore, but following in his wake came such ferociously talented sliders as Earl Hooker, J.B. Hutto, Johnny Littlejohn, and Hound Dog Taylor.

When Elvis Presley hit big, Chess turned to acts with more youth appeal, notably Bo Diddley and Chuck Berry, while its venerable bluesmen saw their fortunes wane. By 1956, though, up-and-coming young players on Chicago's West and South sides were developing an aggressive new style. Otis Rush, Magic Sam Maghett, Freddie King, Buddy Guy, Joe Young, Luther Allison, Jimmy Dawkins, and Lonnie Brooks were all born within a few years of each other, and during their teens or early twenties they'd all come to Chicago from Mississippi, Louisiana, or Texas. Their cathartic, vibrato-enriched vocals spoke of heartbreak and love gone wrong. Played over easy grooves, their story-telling solos were marked by visceral attacks with spiking tones and elastic bends. Their influences ranged from Waters and Wolf to B.B. King, T-Bone Walker, Bobby Bland, and Junior Parker.

With powerful guitar jabs and fever-and-chills vocals, Otis Rush was the first to arrive, scoring a breakthrough hit in '56 with a cover of Willie Dixon's "I Can't Quit You, Baby," released on Cobra Records. A southpaw who plays a flipped-over, unrestrung right-hand guitar, Rush was soon moving in progressive directions. His sultry moaning and groaning in "My Love Will Never Die," another Dixon composition, foreshadowed '60s soul ballads, while his magnificent "All Your Love (I Miss Loving)" became a blues standard. Unrelentingly dark, his "Checking on My Baby" and "Double Trouble" epitomize what's become known as the "West Side sound." (On the original recordings of "Double Trouble" and "All Your Love," Ike Turner played what would become Otis Rush's signature licks.)

On Rush's nod, Cobra recorded 20-year-old Magic Sam in 1957, drenching his "All Your Love" and "Everything's Gonna Be Alright" with sultry, tremolo-washed grooves. Freddie King, already a session player for Parrot and Chess, also released his first single that year, "Country Boy" on the El-Bee label. In '58, Buddy Guy cut "Sit and Cry" and "Try to Quit You Baby" for Cobra, with Rush on backup guitar. Even on his first Chicago sides, Guy displayed the pleading, gospel-influenced vocals and idiosyncratic solos that remain his stylistic hallmarks.

Within a decade of its creation, the so-called "West Side sound" had influenced a generation of blues-rockers led by Mike Bloomfield, Jimi Hendrix, and especially Eric Clapton, who recorded a scorching cover of Otis Rush's "All Your Love" with John Mayall's Bluesbreakers. While some of the West Side originators have retired or passed away, Buddy Guy, Otis Rush, Lonnie Brooks, and Jimmy Dawkins are still hitting it hard today.

BLUES WITH A FEELING While many bluesmen migrated to the big cities of the Midwest and West Coast, others continued to perform and record in the South. In New Orleans, Mississippi-raised Eddie "Guitar Slim" Jones was stunning audiences with his over-the-top showmanship. Earl King, an avowed fan of Guitar Slim, T-Bone Walker, and Gatemouth Brown, debuted on Savoy in 1953, and then struck pay dirt with his Ace release "Those, Lonely, Lonely Nights." Later in the decade, New Orleans–born Snooks Eaglin began a recording career that simultaneously straddled acoustic blues and band-generated R&B. Around Baton Rouge, Louisiana,

Slim Harpo, Lightnin' Slim, Silas Hogan, Lazy Lester, and Lonesome Sundown were playing relaxed, harmonica-and-guitar-driven "swamp blues," as heard on many fine Excello releases.

In the Mississippi Delta area, many aspiring guitarists heard Robert Lockwood, Joe Willie Wilkins, and other guitarists on KFFA's popular *King Biscuit Time* radio program. In Memphis, B.B. King and Rufus Thomas hosted vital blues shows on Memphis radio station WDIA. B.B. King, who first recorded for Bullet in 1949, jumped to RPM in 1950 and endured to become the single most influential bluesman of the modern era. During the early 1950s, Sam Phillips, a young white man with unassailable taste in blues, began recording musicians for his Memphis Recording Service. Phillips' earliest sessions with Howlin' Wolf, Rosco Gordon, and Ike Turner's Kings of Rhythm were leased to Chess and RPM. Phillips founded Sun Records in 1952, and by '55 had recorded blues regulars from Memphis, Mississippi, and Arkansas, such as Junior Parker, Walter Horton, Little Milton, James Cotton, Pat Hare, Earl Hooker, Joe Hill Louis, and Doctor Isaiah Ross. But he was soon turning most of his attention to up-and-coming rockabillies Elvis Presley, Carl Perkins, Johnny Cash, and Jerry Lee Lewis. In the decades to come, Stax and Hi Records would further document the Memphis blues scene. Meanwhile, Jackson, Mississippi, was the home of Lillian McMurry's Trumpet Records, the pre-Chicago proving ground for Elmore James and Rice Miller, as well as Johnny Vincent's Ace Records.

Other bluesmen from the South found success in St. Louis, where Ike Turner, Albert King, and Little Milton were active by the mid 1950s, and Detroit, where John Lee Hooker, Calvin Frazier, Eddie Burns, Bobo Jenkins, Eddie Kirkland, and Baby Boy Warren were regulars at the clubs along Hastings Street.

While guitarists such as B.B. King and John Lee Hooker found fame as band leaders and solo artists, others proved nearly as influential via their roles as sidemen. Among the first and most impressive of these was Oscar Moore, who'd played behind jazz legends Art Tatum and Lionel Hampton before the war and performed with the Nat "King" Cole Trio from 1937 through 1947, when he moved to Los Angeles and joined his brother, guitarist Johnny Moore, in the Three Blazers. In the early 1950s, Matt and Floyd Murphy, Willie Johnson, and Pat Hare exerted their influence in Memphis. Other notable postwar sidemen included Lafayette Thomas and Johnny Heartsman in California, as well as Eddie Taylor for his work with Jimmy Reed, Hubert Sumlin with Howlin' Wolf, Wayne Bennett and Roy Gaines with Bobby "Blue" Bland, and Jimmy Nolen with James Brown. There were also stalwart studio specialists such as Mickey Baker in New York, Steve Cropper in Memphis, Earl Hooker in Chicago, and Billy Butler, who played on Bill Doggett's "Honky Tonk."

As folk blues gained popularity during the late 1950s and early '60s, several bluesmen who'd made 78s before World War II were "rediscovered" by blues aficionados and coaxed into recording again. Some, such as Bukka White, Skip James, Black Ace, Furry Lewis, and Mississippi John Hurt, had been performing all along. Son House, who had quit playing, had to be reminded of his old style. Rev. Robert Wilkins had long since forsaken blues for gospel, but his style was also virtually intact. Testament, Vanguard, Arhoolie, Columbia, and Prestige/Riverside/Bluesville released new works by the old masters, while Origin Jazz Library and Yazoo Records reissued old 78s on LPs.

As elder bluesmen were being re-appreciated, some talented but previously unrecorded musicians were discovered. Robert Pete Williams was found in a

Louisiana penitentiary during the late 1950s. Fred McDowell, who'd lived in Memphis during the '30s, was the reigning slide king of north Mississippi's hill country, where his droning, highly rhythmic bottleneck style and eerie tones are still imitated today. He first recorded for folklorist Alan Lomax in 1959 and went on to make several influential albums of blues and gospel songs. Texas songster Mance Lipscomb, who began recording for Arhoolie in 1960, proved to have a considerable repertoire of early blues, pop, and folk songs.

TRANSATLANTIC BLUES "Now the story must be told," sang bluesman Brownie McGhee, "the blues had a baby, and they called it rock and roll." During the early 1960s, that offspring was the result of an international affair.

While Muddy Waters, Howlin' Wolf, John Lee Hooker, and other bluesmen were struggling to get by on their home turf, young British bands were imitating their records. To the Beatles, Rolling Stones, Animals, Yardbirds, and John Mayall's Bluesbreakers, the recordings of Muddy Waters, Howlin' Wolf, and Jimmy Reed were just as influential as those of Elvis Presley, Buddy Holly, and Eddie Cochran. In an ironic yet welcome twist of fate, most kids in America became aware of the great blues names via cover songs and songwriting credits on albums issued by their favorite rock bands.

Great Britain's love affair with the blues began during World War II, when the promotion of American folk blues—as played by Lead Belly, Josh White, and Big Bill Broonzy in particular—became a cause célèbre for jazz critics, who spun their 78s on the BBC. By the early '50s, Britain's trad jazz—a lite re-creation of Dixieland and other prewar American styles—was in full swing. One of its stars, Chris Barber, toured the U.S. with his jazz band and arranged for Big Bill Broonzy, Josh White, and Brownie McGhee to perform traditional acoustic blues in British jazz clubs. At his recital for the London Jazz Club in September '51, Broonzy played a mixture of blues, folk songs, and ballads. Lonnie Johnson's breakthrough solo set at Royal Festival Hall in '52 featured "Stardust," "Just Another Day," "Backwater Blues," and "Careless Love," and he reportedly made a backstage recording with Lonnie Donegan, whose jazz band appeared on the same bill.

These American bluesmen became musical touchstones for Britain's first pop guitar stars, Big Jim Sullivan and Hank Marvin. Idolized by young Jimmy Page, studio legend Sullivan was steeped in records by Lead Belly and Sonny Terry with Brownie McGhee. "When I was starting the guitar," he recalled, "we used to go out on the Thames in a big riverboat with people like Sonny and Brownie and Big Bill Broonzy. They would be playing, and I'd just sit there watching them. That was the highlight for me." Instrumental star Hank Marvin, who formed the Shadows with Cliff Richard in '58, likewise cited Broonzy and Lead Belly as his main influences for taking up guitar.

Before his death in August '58, Big Bill Broonzy recommended that Barber bring Muddy Waters over. Just back from a tour of raucous Southern clubs, Muddy, accompanied by pianist Otis Spann, opened his British tour with his Fender Telecaster and amp at full concert volume, causing aghast purists to proclaim the performance a musical catastrophe. At the time, Great Britain was enamored with skiffle, a folksy, bluesy, somewhat heavy-handed answer to America's folk boom. The movement got its name from Dan Burley's "Skiffle Boys," cut in 1946 with Sonny Terry and Brownie McGhee, and hit its peak with Lonnie Donegan's 1956 recording of Lead Belly's

"Rock Island Line." Dozens of future British stars got their start strumming skiffle. "Lonnie Donegan set all them kids on the road," remembers George Harrison. "Everybody was in a skiffle group. You only needed two chords."

By the early '60s, aspiring British musicians were avidly seeking American blues and rock and roll records. Jeff Beck was enraptured by Cliff Gallup with Gene Vincent's Blue Caps. Elvis' "Baby, Let's Play House" with Scotty Moore inspired Jimmy Page to play guitar, and Page rapidly made the progression through Elvis, Ricky Nelson, and Gene Vincent to the hard-core blues of Elmore James and B.B. King. Eric Clapton formed his first band, the Roosters, to play covers of Lightnin' Slim, Fats Domino, and T-Bone Walker.

Former boyhood chums Keith Richards and Mick Jagger were enthralled with mid-'50s Chess records. The instant they recognized each other on a train platform in 1960, Richards was as interested in Jagger's albums as he was in Jagger himself. "Mick had *The Best of Muddy Waters* and *Chuck Berry Is on Top* under his arm, which were very hard to get in England," Richards recalls. "I said, 'Hey, man, nice to see you, but where'd you get the *records?!'*"

Country blues reissues were also enthusiastically received. Columbia's first Robert Johnson LP had a profound impact on Clapton, who'd ultimately spearhead the British blues boom. "Both of the Robert Johnson albums actually cover all of my desires musically," Clapton explained. "Every angle of expression and every emotion is expressed on both of those albums." His other early favorites were *Ray Charles Live at Newport, The Best of Muddy Waters, Howlin' Wolf, Freddie King Sings,* Jimmy Reed's *Rockin' with Reed,* Chuck Berry's *One Dozen Berries,* and B.B. King's *Live at the Regal.*

A magnet for aspiring musicians, London's Skiffle Centre was transformed into the London Blues and Barrelhouse Club, where Long John Baldry and former Barber bandmates Alexis Korner and Cyril Davies held court. Mick Jagger, Brian Jones, Ginger Baker, and Jack Bruce all took turns in Korner's Blues Inc. "We'd all meet in this blues club, Alexis Korner's place," Richards recalls. "And Brian, he stunned us playing Elmore James shit on slide onstage with Alexis, along with Cyril Davies, Nicky Hopkins, and Jack Bruce on bass. All of those guys were gathering together in just a few spots in London." Jagger and Richards were soon sharing a flat with Jones. They named their band after Muddy's Chess recording of "Rollin' Stone," and in the months to come their hip-shaking covers of Bo Diddley, Jimmy Reed, Slim Harpo, Muddy Waters, and Howlin' Wolf tunes would lead a new generation to the blues.

Chess talent scout Willie Dixon, who first played in London in 1960, provided encouragement—and demos of his songs—to aspiring British rockers. In 1962 Dixon and Memphis Slim helped organize the first of nine annual American Folk Blues Festival tours of Europe. With front-row tickets for the London show, the Rolling Stones watched John Lee Hooker, T-Bone Walker, Sonny Terry and Brownie McGhee, and Shakey Jake from just a few feet away. Used to playing Detroit dives, Hooker was floored by the reception: "When I got to England in '62, it was like God just let Jesus go over there. That's all you could hear: 'John Lee Hooker!'" The real thing, amped and cathartic, had arrived.

The following season brought Sonny Boy Williamson, Muddy Waters, Lonnie Johnson, Big Joe Williams, Matt "Guitar" Murphy, Dixon, and Memphis Slim. The

Yardbirds, with Clapton on guitar, recorded with Williamson at the Crawdaddy Club. By 1965, Buddy Guy, Lightnin' Hopkins, Big Mama Thornton, Mississippi Fred McDowell, Sleepy John Estes, J.B. Lenoir, and Howlin' Wolf with Hubert Sumlin had also played overseas.

John Mayall's London-based Bluesbreakers became the testing ground for British blues guitarists, producing Eric Clapton, Mick Taylor, and Peter Green, among others. Clapton's fire-breathing tracks on Mayall's *Blues Breakers* LP brought him "Clapton Is God" cult status. No mere mimic, Eric used the sped-up licks of his idols Robert Johnson, Otis Rush, and Albert, B.B., and Freddie King to tap into an emotional reservoir all his own. Soon after the release of *Blues Breakers* in '66, Clapton formed Cream, which covered Dixon, Waters, and Skip James tunes on the first album.

Besides providing the soundtrack to an all-too-brief era, the British Invasion bands helped bring long-overdue fame to John Lee Hooker, Willie Dixon, Jimmy Reed, Muddy Waters, and other postwar blues greats. An often-heard anecdote holds that soon after landing in the U.S., the Beatles announced their desire to see Muddy Waters and Bo Diddley. "Muddy Waters," asked one reporter, "where's that?" An incredulous Paul McCartney is said to have answered, "Don't you know who your own famous people are here?"

But by the time the Beatles landed in America, there were already some savvy— and soon to be highly influential—young musicians woodshedding with blues masters. In Beaumont, Texas, Johnny Winter was playing along to the records of Son House, Robert Johnson, and Muddy Waters, just as John Hammond was doing in New York. In Seattle, Jimi Hendrix was copping licks from his dad's Muddy Waters and B.B. King 45s. In Chicago, Mike Bloomfield, Charlie Musselwhite, and other young white musicians were making pilgrimages to clubs to jam with Muddy Waters, Magic Sam, Howlin' Wolf, Otis Rush, and other bluesmen. Bloomfield joined harmonica ace Paul Butterfield on 1965's *The Paul Butterfield Blues Band,* which featured an integrated lineup playing the music of Elmore James, Little Walter, Muddy Waters, and Willie Dixon. America's blues-rock boom was on, and soon hepped-up blues songs were being played to stadium crowds by Canned Heat, Blues Project, Fleetwood Mac, Cream, Johnny Winter, the Jimi Hendrix Experience, Led Zeppelin, the Jeff Beck Group, the Allman Brothers Band, and others. And almost to a man, the postwar bluesmen were both gracious and grateful to those long-haired kids who helped bring their music center stage in the land of its creation.

Portions of ROLLIN' AND TUMBLIN' *were assembled from articles and interviews that originally appeared in* LIVING BLUES, GUITAR PLAYER, MOJO, *and other magazines. Wherever possible, this book's interviews feature the complete conversation rather than the edited version originally published in magazine format.*

I am grateful to the blues artists and journalists who have contributed to this book, as well as to Jim O'Neal, Ry Cooder, Keith Richards, and Ben Harper for their words and inspiration. And a very heartfelt thanks to Mrs. Rosedell Thomas for introducing me to the blues all those years ago. —*Jas Obrecht*

ANN ARBOR, MICHIGAN

TEXAS AND THE WEST COAST

T-BONE WALKER

BY CHRIS GILL T-Bone Walker struck the stormy world of the blues like a lightning bolt from the heavens. Infusing the blues with a sophisticated, uptown flavor, Walker helped redirect the course of the music, taking it from juke joints and roadhouses to swank nightclubs and large theaters. Favoring swing rhythms and big-band accompaniment, Walker blended jazz and blues and became a seminal figure in the development of urban blues and early rock and roll. ¶ T-Bone was a flamboyant entertainer whose wild stage antics were a sharp contrast to the more conservative sit-down performances of most of the country blues musicians who preceded him. Dancing, doing splits, and playing the guitar behind his head, T-Bone whipped audiences into a frenzy. Countless guitarists imitated his stage moves, including Chuck Berry, Guitar Slim, Buddy Guy, Jimi Hendrix, and Stevie Ray Vaughan.

But T-Bone's most lasting contribution was his pioneering electric guitar style. Walker was one of the first musicians to embrace the electric guitar, and his horn-inspired single-note lines helped establish the guitar as a featured solo instrument. His licks have become standard fixtures in the rock and blues guitarist's vocabulary and have influenced a wide range of guitarists, including Albert, B.B., and Freddie King, Otis Rush, Albert Collins, Billy Gibbons, Michael Bloomfield, Duane Allman, and Eric Clapton. John Lee Hooker, who became close friends with T-Bone, recently said, "He was the first man that made the electric guitar popular. Everybody was trying to sound like T-Bone Walker. The guitar players, you'd hear that fancy electric style. It's very up-to-date. That sound he was doin' then would be up-to-date right now in these late years."

BORN WITH THE BLUES   T-Bone Walker was born with the blues. "Man, I didn't start playing the blues ever," Walker remarked in Nat Shapiro and Nat Hentoff's *Hear Me Talkin' to Ya* [Dover]. "That was in me before I was born, and I've been playing and living the blues ever since. You've got to live the blues, and with us that's natural."

The son of Movelia Jimerson and Rance Walker, a laborer who stacked lumber for a mill, Aaron Thibeaux Walker entered the world on May 28, 1910, in Linden, Texas. The family moved to Lawrenceville, where Rance found work picking cotton. In the evenings, Movelia lulled young T-Bone to sleep with her guitar playing and singing. "The first thing I can remember was my mother singing the blues as she would sit alone," Walker said in *Hear Me Talkin' to Ya*. "I used to listen to her singing there at night, and I knew then that the blues was in me too."

When T-Bone was two years old, his father wanted to start a farm in Conroe, Texas. Deciding that farm life was not for her, Movelia set off with T-Bone for the city, moving into her sister-in-law's Dallas home. She found work cooking and cleaning for white families, and eventually got her own place in the Oak Cliff section of town. Soon she met Marco Washington, a musician who played several stringed instruments in Coley Jones' String Band, a group featuring several other Washington family members. Washington and T-Bone's mother eventually got married and established a household where music and musicians were always welcome.

"Mama played guitar—pretty good, too," Walker told Helen Oakley Dance in *Stormy Monday—The T-Bone Walker Story* [Louisiana State University Press]. "Good enough to fall in with Huddie Ledbetter more than once." Ledbetter, who recorded as Lead Belly, and Blind Lemon Jefferson frequently visited the household and participated in many high-spirited jams with Walker's mother and stepfather. By the time he was eight years old, T-Bone started hanging out with Jefferson, passing the cup for money and leading him around the rough dives lining Central Avenue.

Inspired by the music he heard at home, with Jefferson, and at Dallas' Holiness Church, Walker started singing, dancing, and playing a crude guitar that he made from a Prince Albert tobacco can, nails, and wire. When he was ten he began singing and dancing with his stepfather's band. On weekends the band would parade through the streets of South Dallas, young T-Bone and his cousin Casey leading the way doing flashy splits and spins. T-Bone admitted that he wasn't much of a musician at that time, but a few years later he was good enough to play the ukulele, and he worked out his own routine with the band.

Walker's mother let T-Bone play her guitar occasionally, showing him how to bend the strings. Soon afterwards, the 12-year-old saved some of the change that he picked up dancing in the streets and bought himself a banjo. Walker said that his experience playing the banjo later inspired him to play single-note lines on the guitar. T-Bone started making the rounds at downtown hotels where he danced and played for handouts.

Walker started listening to other musicians and imitating their styles. He was heavily influenced by pianist Leroy Carr's records, and he copied Carr's singing as well as the playing of his guitarist, Scrapper Blackwell. Later, T-Bone witnessed a performance in Dallas by Lonnie Johnson, which greatly impressed him.

At 14, Walker got his first taste of life as a traveling musician when he hooked up with Dr. Breeding's Medicine Show, where he helped gather crowds while Breeding pitched his phony elixir. T-Bone's next gig was with blues singer Ida Cox's band. Falling in love with a dancer named Dorothy, who was part of Cox's entourage, T-Bone ran away from home and dropped out of his freshman year in high school. He played banjo and danced in the show, but the gig was cut short when a sheriff in Albany, Texas, made him return home.

Back in Dallas, Walker played on street corners and at carnivals, social functions, dances, and parties to make money. By 16, he was accomplished on the guitar, banjo, mandolin, violin, and piano. He was hired to back up Ma Rainey when she appeared at the Coliseum in Houston for three days. Joining Lawson Brooks' 16-piece band, which featured many of his classmates from Booker T. High School, Walker dropped out of school for good. "I could always make money and figured there wasn't time enough for school," T-Bone told Dance. Around this time Walker purchased his first guitar, although he played banjo in the band since an acoustic guitar wasn't loud enough to be heard over the horns. Walker played with the band on and off for several years, playing around Texas and in Oklahoma City, where he met Charlie Christian. Not wanting to leave his mother alone while the band went on the road, Walker eventually returned home.

OAK CLIFF T-BONE T-Bone's next break came in 1929, when Cab Calloway's band passed through town. Winning first prize in an amateur contest, Walker was allowed to work with Calloway's band for a week. T-Bone performed his routine where he played banjo while doing the splits, and Calloway even let him sing "Minnie the Moocher." Walker went over well with the audiences—perhaps too well. "Calloway fired him because when my father did 'Minnie the Moocher' he got bigger applause than Cab," says T-Bone's daughter, Bernita Walker-Moss. "My dad used to tell that story all the time."

The stint with Calloway may have been brief, but it brought Walker to the attention of a talent scout from Columbia Records. The label paired Walker with pianist Douglas Fernell, and the two cut a 78 attributed to Oak Cliff T-Bone that featured Walker's compositions "Trinity River Blues" and "Wichita Falls Blues." Walker's singing style was similar to Leroy Carr's, and his country blues guitar playing showed little of the sophistication or distinctive style evident on his later recordings.

Towards the end of '29, T-Bone was working as a caddie at a Dallas country club, where he often spent his time shooting craps and gambling with patrons. Here he met Count Biloski, who offered Walker a job as a guitarist and dancer in his band. T-Bone was the only African American in the band, and in Oklahoma City a few men from the audience took objection to his "friendliness" with a female singer in the group. Walker ran off to Kansas City and lay low for a while with some friends, but his drinking and gambling was getting the worst of him. Broke and suffering from an ulcer that bothered him for the rest of his life, Walker returned to Texas.

In 1933, Walker ran into Charlie Christian again in Oklahoma City. The two were reportedly taking guitar lessons from Chuck Richardson, who helped shape both musicians' chord vocabulary. Walker and Christian started performing together. "We'd go dance and pass the hat and make money," Walker told *Living Blues*. "We had a little routine of dancing that we did. Charlie would play guitar while I would play bass, and then we'd change, and he'd play bass and I'd play guitar. And then we'd go into our little dance." Although they were playing acoustic guitars at the time, both later became seminal figures in the popularization of the electric guitar.

While playing with a small band at the Gem Hotel in Fort Worth, T-Bone met his future wife Vida Lee. "She was the love of his life," says Bernita. "My mother had seen him singing and wanted to know who he was. She asked my aunt, who told her to stay away from him because he wasn't any good. He saw her and fell in love with her immediately. He took her out, and one week later they ran off to the courthouse and got married."

The couple moved in with Walker's mother, and T-Bone supported the family by working on weekends with a four-piece band and during the week as a single performer. Although he was a proficient player and singer, T-Bone usually relied on his dancing abilities to make money. "In the show I'd be playing and singing," Walker recalled in *Stormy Monday*, "and then have to jump up right away because someone had called for me to dance."

Walker scraped together a living as best as he could, but it wasn't always easy going. His luck changed when Vida Lee decided that she wanted to move to Los Angeles. "My mother stayed in Texas until her father died," recalls Bernita. "When he died she came to Los Angeles to be with her sister, and my father came with her. Whatever my mother wanted, that's what she got."

T-Bone found jobs playing in clubs in Watts such as Little Harlem, the Club Alabam, and the Plantation. He joined Big Jim Wynn's band for a brief period, but soon T-Bone's popularity grew and he established his own following. Walker was unlike any performer Los Angeles club-goers had experienced. Sharply dressed in double-breasted suits, Walker cut a distinctive figure, and huge crowds came to see the performer who held his guitar in an unorthodox manner away from his body, parallel to the floor. T-Bone stunned audiences with bold stage moves that culminated with him playing the guitar behind his head and dropping to the floor in splits without missing a note.

"Things were always jumping," Henry "Phace" Roberts recounted to Dance about T-Bone's early L.A. shows. "The chicks would be excited. You'd see them crossing the floor, climbing the bandstand, and handing Bone money. Fives and even tens! When he went into the splits, they'd kneel beside him, counting out their bills, putting them in his pockets or guitar."

ELECTRIFYING THE BLUES   The atmosphere in these L.A. clubs was raucous and rowdy. To be heard over the commotion, Walker got himself a Gibson ES-250 electric guitar and an amplifier and started to develop his groundbreaking style.

Influenced by saxophone and horn lines and phrases, T-Bone played single-note solos and chord patterns that mimicked horn sections. He restrung his guitar with a plain, unwound *G* string that allowed him to bend notes.

"The way T-Bone played was fantastic," Marili Morden, who ran the Jazz Man Record Shop, recalled in *Stormy Monday*. "I hadn't expected to prefer the electric guitar to the acoustic. It was new to us all, and I was dumbfounded." Moved by his act, Morden helped T-Bone get booked at the plush Trocadero Club on Hollywood's Sunset Strip. Decked out in tails, Walker made a first-class impression on the club's upscale clientele and became the talk of the town.

Soon the money was rolling in. Walker dressed in the finest East Coast suits and drove around in a new Cadillac or Buick. He hired the best musicians he could find, with a preference for jazz players. T-Bone was always genial and easygoing in social situations, but in rehearsal he was painstakingly serious. "The one thing that really disturbed him was musicians who couldn't read music," notes Bernita. "You couldn't play in his band if you could not read music. He felt that if you were going to be a musician, you had to read. My dad had a third-grade education, but he read, wrote, and orchestrated music for every instrument in his band."

T-Bone joined Les Hite's Los Angeles Cotton Club Orchestra in 1940 and started touring as their featured vocalist. He also played guitar, but due to objections from the band's rhythm section, he put aside his electric and strummed acoustic rhythms. "All the time on the road he was backstage practicing and experimenting with the electric guitar," notes Vida Lee in *Stormy Monday*. "He had it in the dressing room, and it got so he could do just about what he liked with it. It was more exciting than when he played acoustic, and the sound was so new that people started talking."

When Hite's band reached New York circa June 1940, Walker cut "T-Bone Blues" with the orchestra. It was his first recording since his 1929 Columbia 78. Walker sang the lead vocals, but it was Frank Pasley who played the electric steel guitar accompaniment.

Walker usually performed ballads with Hite's band, but he soon found that his audiences responded more enthusiastically to the blues. "My dad was really a balladeer when he first started out," recalls Bernita. "He wasn't a blues person. He sung ballads, but they were not received as great as his blues. So then he rolled over into the blues field."

In '42 Walker left L.A. to take a headlining stint at Chicago's Rhumboogie nightclub. The lavish production featured choreographed dancing, elaborately designed sets, and fancy lighting. Walker's performances attracted capacity audiences, and the show enjoyed a three-month run. By now T-Bone's status as a front person was established.

Later in '42, T-Bone finally had the chance to record his electric guitar when he cut "I Got a Break Baby" and "Mean Old World" with Freddie Slack's band for Capitol Records. Walker's guitar playing dominates both songs, which begin with guitar solos that last more than a minute before T-Bone's vocal begins. His sophisticated, bluesy lines are distinguished by a loose, swinging sense of timing, slick, sliding adjacent-string unisons, jazzy chords, and bent diminished chord triads. "Mean Old World" became a hit, introducing many musicians to a new sound—electric blues.

Walker recorded a few other sides with Slack's band, but these songs were not released due to a recording ban that lasted for most of World War II. During this period, Walker worked with Marl Young's orchestra in Chicago. He recorded several outstanding compositions in '45 for the Rhumboogie label; these were the first records to feature Walker's name on the label. They didn't sell particularly well, but they were highly influential, especially the jump blues "T-Bone Boogie," which features a I-IV-V progression, upbeat rhythm, and stunning guitar solo that may have been the template for Chuck Berry's rock and roll music nearly a decade later. Some of Berry's "signature" licks are note-for-note duplications of Walker's solo.

"When they inducted my dad into the Rock and Roll Hall of Fame in '87, Chuck Berry was there also," Bernita reminisces. "After they presented me with my dad's trophy, he came over to me and said, 'Baby, I want you to know something. Your dad is the greatest musician that ever lived. All the things that people see me do on the stage, I got that from your daddy.'"

In '46 and '47, Walker recorded dozens of sides for the Black & White label. Most of these songs were blues numbers, but he also cut a few romantic ballads such as "I'm Waiting for Your Call," "I Want a Little Girl," and "I'm Still in Love with You." His biggest hit, "Call It Stormy Monday," was issued in late '47, and it made T-Bone Walker a household name from coast to coast. Unfortunately, Walker was robbed of thousands of dollars in royalties due to the existence of a similarly titled song that was recorded after T-Bone's version, but released earlier.

"Call It Stormy Monday" influenced many aspiring blues guitarists. "He was the first electric guitar player I heard on record," B.B. King told *Guitar Player*. "T-Bone Walker had a touch that nobody has been able to duplicate. He made me so that I knew I just *had* to go out and get an electric guitar."

Walker was at the peak of his career. He hit the road on all-star "Battle of the Blues" tours, sharing star billing with artists such as Ray Charles, Lowell Fulson, Wynonie Harris, Big Joe Turner, and Jimmy Witherspoon. Because T-Bone's energetic performance was such a hard act to follow, he inevitably closed the shows. He hooked up with booking agent Harold Oxley, who helped bring bigger, more lucrative gigs. Backed by Jim Wynn's band, T-Bone toured extensively from the late '40s until '55. Walker didn't do any recording during '48 and '49, but many of his Black & White sides were issued by Capitol Records during this time.

Walker signed with Imperial Records in 1950 and cut more than 50 songs for the label over the next four years. Although he never scored another hit as popular as "Call It Stormy Monday," his Imperial recordings helped him maintain his career throughout the early '50s. Riding high on his success, T-Bone bought himself a fancy new blond Gibson ES-5, which became his main guitar.

THAT MEAN OLD WORLD Although dozens of artists started imitating T-Bone's music and showmanship, he seemed unfazed by the competition. Walker was always generous with his music, and he shared his playing secrets with anyone who asked. "If you came to him," recounts Bernita, "and you were a musician and said, 'Bone, I sure liked that chord you hit,' he would say, 'Come here. Let me show you how to do it.' That's what Johnny Guitar Watson, Pee Wee Crayton, Wes Montgomery, and Eric Clapton did. My dad was always encouraging and supportive. It wasn't a big deal to him. Some people want to hide their particular style so nobody else can get it. My dad was very giving about everything, whether it was music or the food in our house."

By the mid '50s Walker's big band style started to fall out of fashion as newer artists such as Chuck Berry and Elvis Presley gained popularity. Working with Dave Bartholomew's R&B outfit and members of Fats Domino's band, Walker recorded songs like "Teen Age Baby," where prominent drums gave the music a rock and roll feel. However, these failed to win Walker the attention that the newer artists commanded. "Things hadn't exactly slowed at that time," Walker told Dance, "because guys like Muddy Waters and John Lee Hooker were doing okay, and B.B. was climbing fast. But for me the situation wasn't so hot."

Bothered by his ulcer and other health problems, Walker decided to break up his band. He still played shows around Los Angeles, and occasionally he hit the road by himself or with his nephew R.S. Rankin, a guitarist who was billed as T-Bone Jr. To keep costs down, Walker worked with local pickup bands in the cities he visited. When Walker was in Los Angeles, his friends often dropped by, and his home was the site of many star-studded jam sessions. "We had jam sessions on Sundays," Bernita remembers. "My dad played any instrument that you didn't have to blow into—drums, organ, piano, xylophone, bass, cello, violin, banjo. Lots of different people came in—Ray Charles, Johnny Guitar Watson, the Four Tops, Pee Wee Crayton, Jim Wynn, Guitar Slim, Jimmy Witherspoon, Louis Jordan, Roy Gaines, Leo Blevins, Percy Mayfield—all these individuals who were in the blues field. Big Mama Thornton was always over. They were real good friends. Even Stymie from the Little Rascals came over. He lived with us for a while."

T-Bone was still making records, with music from three sessions in '55, '56, and '59 coming out on the Atlantic LP *T-Bone Blues* in '60. This critically acclaimed album featured remakes of his early hits "Mean Old World," "T-Bone Shuffle," and "Stormy Monday," and Walker was joined by Rankin and Barney Kessel on three cuts. Although mostly ignored by blues fans, the album helped introduce Walker to jazz enthusiasts.

T-Bone got a chance at a comeback in 1960 when Count Basie asked him to join a package show featuring George Shearing and Ruth Brown. T-Bone accepted the offer, but he left halfway through the tour because he felt that his act wasn't living up to his standards. Basie went to Europe the following year and was a huge success.

Walker had a second chance in '62 when he ventured over to Europe as part of a tour package that also featured Willie Dixon, John Lee Hooker, Memphis Slim, Sonny Terry, and Brownie McGhee. "We had a ball," Walker recalled. "People there *listen*. You've got to be a showman back here. Over there, the first time I did the splits the fans booed! They came to hear the music." One performance was released on *Original American Folk Blues Festival,* which was successful on both sides of the Atlantic.

Walker returned to Europe in '65 to play with a group that John Mayall had put together and to perform four shows in France. "There was an audience for his music over there," Bernita comments. "He didn't like the fact that he had to stay over there as much as he did in order for us to eat over here. He didn't like to be away from us. That annoyed him, but he couldn't get any work here. He had no alternative but to go over there where he was received more."

During the mid '60s Walker started recording again, participating in sessions in

Chicago and Houston. In '66 he recorded a Jazz at the Philharmonic Series album featuring Duke Ellington and members of his band, as well as Oscar Peterson. Interest in Walker's music picked up again stateside, and he signed with ABC Paramount Records. Producer Bob Thiele attempted to update T-Bone's sound on the album *Stormy Monday Blues,* but the result was a misguided effort that didn't complement Walker's style. Thiele made several other ill-fated attempts to present T-Bone in a contemporary setting, as heard on *Funky Town, Super Black Blues,* and *Every Day I Have the Blues.*

Walker continued to tour Europe and the U.S., including an appearance at the 1967 Monterey Jazz Festival. While on tour in France in '68, T-Bone's treasured ES-5 was stolen. "He was totally devastated," Bernita remembers. "It was a special Gibson—a big guitar, not like these little things that they play now. He was thoroughly sick when that was taken. That was his pride and joy." Walker replaced the guitar with a Barney Kessel Regular archtop electric.

The National Academy of Recording Arts and Sciences awarded T-Bone a Best Ethnic/Traditional Recording Grammy in 1970 for his album *Good Feelin'.* In '71, the Allman Brothers Band included a cover of "Call It Stormy Monday" on their best-selling *Live at the Fillmore East* album, introducing T-Bone's music to a new generation of fans. T-Bone should have received a handsome royalty payment, but instead the money went to his label at the time.

"He got shafted by a number of agents and publishers," Bernita laments. "My dad was the type of person who took you at your word. He trusted you. If you said that was what was in the contract, then to him that was what was in the contract and he signed his name. He signed away a lot of things where he didn't realize he was doing. After he found out that that's what he did, he was very upset about it."

Through all the troubles, T-Bone never lost his passion for playing. "He played around the house all the time," Bernita recalls. "He practiced a lot without his amp, playing chords and doing his finger movements. During the latter years he suffered from arthritis, so he did that a lot for therapy."

T-Bone's management put him out on the road again, backed by a rock band featuring guitarist Paul Pena. Walker disliked the band's loud playing and inflexibility, but he endured the tours because they made him money. Walker still played well, but his drinking on the road began to take a toll on his health. In June '74 Walker played his last concert, appearing on a bill headlined by John Lee Hooker in Pittsburgh.

On New Year's Eve, Walker suffered a stroke. He was admitted to the West Vernon Convalescent Home, where he passed away on March 16, 1975. His funeral was held a few days later at the Angelus Funeral Home. T-Bone's friends, fans, and family pushed to the front of a standing-room-only crowd that spilled out onto the sidewalks. The sendoff was a fitting finale to T-Bone's long and illustrious career.

SAUNDERS KING

BY JAS OBRECHT Saunders King was the first postwar "King of the Blues." More than a half-century after buying his first Saunders King 78, another King, B.B., still beams
at the mention of his name. "Saunders King—I'm a big fan
of his! He was one of the first of the people that played
blues and had the beautiful sound of the electric guitar. He
was a great singer. In fact, he was one of the people I idolized. I especially liked 'S.K. Blues'—still do! There was a part
one and a part two to it. I also admired his 'St. James
Infirmary' on Aladdin. To me, Saunders King was one of the
greatest ever." ¶ Born in Staple, Louisiana, on March 13,

1909, Saunders King was raised in Oroville, California, where he sang in the church choir and studied music in school. He became adept with piano, banjo, ukulele, and violin. His first professional appearances were with the Southern Harmony Four, a gospel quartet that broadcast over NBC Radio in San Francisco for several years. Inspired by Charlie Christian's records with Benny Goodman, King took up guitar in 1938. After working with an ensemble led by Jake Porter, he organized his own impeccably rehearsed sextet, which accompanied him during his debut session for Dave Rosenbaum's San Francisco–based Rhythm label in June 1942.

On the earliest Saunders King 78s, smooth arrangements framed Saunders' mellow and wry vocals and riveting guitar solos. Written during a dinner break at his first session, the sultry two-part "S.K. Blues" became his biggest hit, inspiring covers by Big Joe Turner and Jimmy Witherspoon. The song began:

> *"Come here, pretty baby, and put your fine mellow body on my knee*
> *Come to me, baby, and put your fine mellow body on my knee*
> *I wanna whisper in your ear and tell you things keep worrying me"*

The lyrics took a memorable detour when Saunders described buying his girlfriend "some hair" because "the good Lord gave her none." Then, in a stanza that would echo in other blues songs, Saunders sang:

> *"Give me back that wig I bought you, baby, and let your head go bald*
> *Yes, give me back that wig I bought you, baby, and let your head go bald*
> *You keep on mistreating me, baby, ooh, you will have no hair nor head at all"*

As on many of his 78s, Saunders' voice projected a soothing tenderness, despite the lyrics' message. His guitar playing was strong and innovative. (A fine sight-reader, King still possesses his handwritten chart from the original "S.K. Blues" session.)

Other standouts from King's 1942 Rhythm dates were the unbeatably smooth "What's Your Story Morning Glory" and "S.K. Groove," during which Saunders paid tribute to Charlie Christian with his comping and elegantly paced solo.

During World War II, while performers such as Muddy Waters and Elmore James were thumping Delta-derived electric blues on Southern farms and in Chicago taverns, Saunders King was flying high, "giving out with the hot stuff" with one of the West Coast's hippest jump outfits. He was a regular at posh spots in San Francisco, Hollywood, and Chicago, toured the Southwest, and even worked the chitlin circuit.

Not long after World War II King recorded for Decca in Los Angeles, but legal entanglements prevented the session's release. He resumed cutting for Rhythm in '46, producing classic 78s such as the two-part "Lonesome Pillow Blues" and "After Hours" backed with "Why Was I Born," with its terrific guitar solo. "Write Me a Letter Blues" was paired with the bop-inspired "Swingin'," one of King's finest performances. Subsequent Rhythm sessions yielded further gems: "Stay Gone Blues"/"S.K. Jumps" and "Something's Worrying Me"/"2:00 A.M. Hop."

On record and stage, Saunders never restricted himself to blues, delving into swing, ballads, bebop, and revitalized readings of standards such as "Summertime" and "Danny Boy." In newspaper ads from the late '40s, San Francisco's Club Savoy billed him as part of "The Greatest Sepia Show on the Coast," listing the "suave rhythms of Saunders King" just below headliner Art Tatum. Billie Holiday came to town and shared the bill with "The Red Hot Rhythms of Saunders King," as did Sarah Vaughan and others.

Near the decade's end, the Bihari brothers purchased most of Saunders' Rhythm masters and invited him to cut new material for their Modern Records. King's first Modern offering was the ballad "Imagination" backed with "Empty Bedroom Blues," which features an early use of low-volume electric guitar distortion. Modern next paired "Danny Boy" with "Read the Good Book," which despite its title is far closer to a Louis Jordan jump than a gospel tune. The Biharis reissued the old Rhythm master of "S.K. Blues" as the two-part "(New) S.K. Blues." King's brief sojourn at the San Francisco–based Cava-Tone label produced a single 78, "September Song"/"Nobody Wants Me."

In March 1949, a *Billboard* ad proclaimed, "Here he is!!! The King of the Blues, Saunders King, and Aladdin got him!" Saunders' Aladdin debut was an unforgettable version of "St. James Infirmary Blues" backed with his original "Little Girl." With their smooth guitar tones and still-fresh solos, these sides are among King's most vital recordings. He continued to expand his solo style on subsequent Aladdin releases, bending strings with aplomb on "Misery Blues" and stretching out nicely on "Stormy Night Blues." Cut in a superior studio, Saunders regards his Aladdin releases as his finest-sounding 78s.

By the early 1950s Saunders King's recording heyday was drawing to a close. He was in top form when he cut his potent "Summertime Boogie," released on RPM. (Issued on the Ace LP *The First King of the Blues,* the unissued alternate take of "Summertime Boogie" is the more happening version: cascading horn lines bridge towards rock and roll, while Saunders' solo conjures the spirit of Charlie Christian.) In 1954 King produced a pair of memorable platters for the Biharis' Flair subsidiary, "My Close Friend"/"Going Mad" and "Quit Hangin' Around Me"/"Long Long Time." His final session as a leader, at Fantasy Records in 1961, produced stinging-guitar remakes of "S.K. Blues" and "What's Your Story Morning Glory," released on Galaxy.

During the ensuing decades Saunders continued to play blues in nightclubs around the San Francisco Bay Area, but he increasingly devoted himself to raising his children and composing and performing spiritual music. An '89 stroke has since slowed his musical activities.

Today Saunders King and his wife Jo share a spacious home in San Rafael, California. The stack of charts Saunders has saved over the years hints at the broad scope of his musical interests: Among the yellowing pages are tunes by Ellington, Gershwin, Strayhorn, Coltrane, Rodgers & Hart, Charlie Parker, and the Beatles, as well as a chart for "Silver Dreams," which King sang on longtime son-in-law Carlos Santana's *Oneness, Silver Dreams—Golden Reality* LP. Our interview took place on July 28, 1995, with a follow-up several weeks later. An edited version ran as "Saunders King: S.K.'s Blues," in the March/April '96 issue of *Living Blues.*

What attracted you to the electric guitar so early on?

The sound. I was trying to get a sound. I traded guitars, different types of boxes. I had an acoustic Epiphone first, and the Epiphone gave me good sound. I tried the electric guitar and got a better sound.

Were you aware of the electric guitarists who recorded before Charlie Christian, such as Eddie Durham with Jimmie Lunceford or Floyd Smith with Andy Kirk?

Yeah. I'd go and watch Eddie Durham play. Oh, yeah. I was intrigued by the sound.

Do you remember the first time you saw an electric guitar?

Yes. I don't remember the year, but I remember the idea. It was at the Golden Gate Theater in San Francisco. There was a big band there playing with Alvino Rey, and I was intrigued by the sound he was getting, but he wasn't getting an electric sound. He was getting an acoustic sound. He had a large-size box, and he sat on the stage and played. I could hear him with just an acoustic box from where I was sitting quite a ways back. He had all kinds of boxes. He played one box and got one sound, and then all of a sudden he'd put it down and play another one. Alvino Rey—loved him. He played all kinds of melodies, different intricate things, and he led the band. It intrigued me.

When did you become aware of Charlie Christian? With the first Benny Goodman records?

Yes. He came out with something new, something different. He had a different sound, a complete sound, a big sound. It was with the Sextet with Lionel and them guys. He was great.

Did you have a favorite song of his?

"Seven Eleven." But I liked everything he did. No kidding—I liked anything he did. I even liked how he'd grunt and groan. He was a good musician.

Did you learn any of his music note for note?

No. I didn't want to. But I loved him. It's hard to get the notes, get the sound, of what he played.

It's not in the equipment.

No, it's the hands. The hands is what's happening.

Was Christian's "Blues in B♭," related to the song you recorded with the same title?

No. My piece "B♭ Blues" was just a blues, and it had different hollers. I'd sing a verse, and the fellows in the band would sing a verse. We'd call them "holler tunes."

Was Charlie Christian the first guy who could hold his own alongside great horn players?

He was the first one. As a matter of fact, I was working at Jack's Tavern in San Francisco, and Charlie came in. He was here with Benny Goodman's band, playing with Lionel in the Sextet, and he came in and everybody asked him to play one. We were off the stand when Charlie came in. I said, "Well, what do you want to play, Charlie?" He said, "'Stardust,' man," and that was it. He played by himself—I'll never forget it—on my guitar, which had a very bad pickup. He was different. He was taking a solo by himself, and he made such changes—crazy changes. In these kind of clubs I was working, we sort of played it straight, but he made all those sounds and different changes. He was great. Charlie Christian didn't fool around.

Did you get a chance to talk to him?

Yeah. He was a great guy. At that time, quite a bit of drinking was going on, and he had been to different clubs. Club Alabam was around the corner, Harold Blackshear's Supper Club was happening too. So naturally he went with the fellas—wherever they'd go, he would go. Ben Webster was there. Ben Webster kept playing all night long. That's the first time I heard Charlie Christian in person, and he really could play. I was surprised. I'd heard his records—loved his records with the Sextet. But to see him play, see his action, was different. There was no one who could play like him.

What stood out?

He played rhythm, and then he'd go from rhythm into the solo, and he played by himself. That was different. It made all the difference in the world. The audience in Jack's Tavern was rather small, and all the big band guys who came through there came by Jack's and played afterwards—like a jam session—and it was great. More bands came to town then than they do now, from what I hear.

Were there other impressive electric guitarists around then?

There was none that impressed me.

A lot of cats built their careers around sounding like Charlie Christian.

Oh, yeah. Yeah.

Even today, if you can play Charlie Christian note-for-note, you can find work in jazz circles.

Right.

What's your opinion of the rumor that Charlie died after smoking reefer while he was a patient in a TB ward?

I don't think so. Maybe. I think it was alcohol. The night he was in Jack's, people were giving him drinks. When they wanted to hear him play, they sent a drink over to him, and he was just drinking one right after the other. I didn't drink at that time, and I was wondering why he drank all the time. He didn't need to be drinking. He started perspiring—the water was running off of his face. He was playing "Stardust," and I thought then that he's got to be sick. He was in bad shape. Ben Webster came around and played with him half the night, and Charlie was still playin'. Then he went out in the streets and danced on the sidewalk.

Was he a good dancer?

For a dancer, he was a lot of guitar player! [*Laughs.*] He could dance. That's what he was gonna be—a dancer. He didn't want to be a guitar player; he wanted to dance.

Charlie did?

Sure! As soon as the music started, he wanted to dance. I don't know if it was the alcohol or what, but that's what he did. The waitress at the place I was working urged him on. She'd buy him drinks, because he stood by the bar doing dance steps. I think the alcohol killed him.

Was the fact that Charlie was playing in an integrated band important at the time?

Yeah, very important. And the things that he played, you didn't hear it all the time. And when you heard him play within the greatest band, it was so different. Quite different.

That must have been inspirational.

It was, it was. I didn't have a good amplifier; I had a fair amplifier. I was working with the guitar that I wanted to get the sound that I wanted, but I didn't have the amplifier. So I hooked my amplifier up to the speaker, which was up in the back of Jack's Tavern, and the sound was coming all the time. It would cause feedback sometimes, and I didn't know what to do. But it was good—it kept me solid. I had a chance to buy a guitar, and I didn't buy it. The guy that owned Jack's Tavern saw what I was drivin' at, so he bought the Epiphone for me and gave it to me. That started me out getting into something.

Before then you'd played ukulele and banjo and studied violin.

Yes.

Did you study solfeggio?

No.

Were your folks encouraging of your career in music?

Oh, yes. My father was a great singer, and my mother was a great singer.

Did you know as a child that that was what you wanted to do?

Well, no. But I studied hard to learn what I wanted to be. I wanted an answer. And the answer was music.

Did you take up electric guitar first or acoustic?

Acoustic.

Did you quit playing violin once you acquired a guitar?

Yeah. Because of all the fights I got into with that violin. Every time I took the violin to school with me, I would be in a fight before I got home. So I learned how to throw rocks—then they didn't bully me. I had one friend in Oroville, Cy.

Were you aware of acoustic guitarists like Eddie Lang or Lonnie Johnson?

Eddie Lang, yeah. I wasn't aware of Lonnie Johnson. I'd heard of his name, but I wasn't aware of the things that he was doing. But I was aware of Eddie Lang—very much so. He was great. He did some great things. And it was funny—he played, but he wasn't aggressive like I wanted him to be.

He was more polite.

Yeah, really. I liked him. And I met him in person at the Fairmont Hotel. Louis Armstrong came to town also, and Louis and I were great pals, you know. I used to run with him all the time, and a lot of things would happen where I would have a little better insight into it than he did, and I could tell he wanted me around, you know. He was reading a radio script, and that's where I ran into Eddie Lang.

Did you see Eddie play?

No, no. I heard him, but I didn't see him play. I wanted to, but I didn't.

It's strange that he and Charlie both died so young.

Well, you can try to put a stamp on it, a reason they passed on, but you can't say for real.

During the '40s, what set San Francisco apart musically?

We had a lot of after-hour clubs over here, like Jumbo's Bop City, and that's where the San Francisco blues and jazz came from. You went in at one o'clock, and the music was just beginning to feel good. Peggy's Chicken Shack was right next to Jumbo's place, so there was good food—that was great. Jumbo was a great guy. We'd go there and jam the rest of the night, and that's where the jazz came from, mostly.

What attracted you to blues?

I really wasn't attracted to blues music. I came from the radio. Jack's Tavern was the first night club I played.

Who were some of the first bluesmen in San Francisco?

That really played the blues? I didn't know of any, actually, because San Francisco mostly had a lot of dinner clubs. And in a dinner club, you didn't hardly play the blues. Seemed like the club owners in the Fillmore was trying to get away from the blues. They wanted class.

They wanted the white shirt and tie crowd?

Yeah! That started at Jack's. It was around the time of the war, because he had drapes over the door due to the blackout. We never saw the planes, but they were supposed to come over. The siren would go off to pull the curtain closed, and he'd have music behind the curtain and no one could see the lights. That's the way that was. Going due west from the town area, there was Harold Blackshear's Supper

Club, Club Alabam, New Orleans Swing Club. And then there was another area going further away.

What do you remember about your first recording session in 1942?

The environment was very poor. One of the reasons was we did not have many places to record. We recorded at Sherman Clay, a music store at Kearny and Sutter in San Francisco.

Did they hold sessions in a room upstairs?

Yeah. A recording studio. As a matter of fact, that picture [*points to the cover of his Ace LP* The First King of the Blues] was taken upstairs. That picture was taken at my first session. That's Sammy Deane and Johnnie Cooper and Eddie Taylor and myself.

Eddie Taylor was a fabulous sax player.

Yes, he was. Marvelous. We were together a long time. We were the best of friends. Oh, he was wonderful. None better. I went to Los Angeles and got him. He came from Dallas to Los Angeles, and I went down to Los Angeles to play. I had to go to the union and ask to have a tenor player. The first tenor I had was Bob Barfield, a great, great horn man and arranger. Didn't need a piano to arrange by. We'd just sit down and talk arrangements.

You'd do head arrangements together.

Yeah. Barfield left. He got homesick and he came home. I went to Los Angeles and found Eddie and brought him back to San Francisco with me, and we played for years together. Beautiful, beautiful man. He could play.

Did you teach him parts or did he instinctively know what to do?

He instinctively knew what to do.

Who did the horn arrangements at your session? Some of them are so tight.

Yes. We had charts. I wrote some of them, and Cedric Hayward wrote some. He could write real well. And we used to talk things out, because sometimes, you know, you talk out an arrangement, and you want it to go one way and you run into a block. So you have to back up and do it all over again. And that's how Cedric and I worked. Cedric was a piano player, could play very well. Texas boy. He helped with the arrangements. Barfield could also write, like that arrangement for "Why Was I Born" with a big band.

You have a terrific solo on the "Why Was I Born" 78.

That was great. I thought it was a great arrangement.

Did you write "S.K. Blues" during your first session?

Yeah.

Now, your mom and dad were ministers, right?

Yes, they were.

In some ways, that's a pretty sexy song. Did they object to the lyrics?

No, no. [*Smiles.*] They didn't have any problems with it at all.

Is it true you wrote "S.K. Blues" on a challenge?

Yeah. After the session, the guys said, "We're going for a break to get something to eat." We were at the Sherman Clay, and we needed one more tune for the session. And Dave Rosenbaum asked me, "Can you bring another tune?" I said, "Yeah. Let me get something to eat." I was recording on Kearny and Sutter, and I left there and went out to the Fillmore District. While I was eating the food, I wrote the tune. And I had one verse too many for the tune.

You needed two three-minute sides?

Yes. I had about six minutes, so we filled in. And that's how "S.K. Blues" came about. I didn't even know it was gonna be a hit or anything when I wrote it. I came back and finished the session and I went home. Eddie Taylor came by and he told me, "Say, man, you know that tune might be a hit." I said, "Oh, man. What are you talking about?" "No kidding," he said. "That's a real downhome blues, and you might have a hit." Sure enough, later on we were in Texas, and when I got there it was a hit. Everybody was playing it in all those little clubs. Yeah, I was surprised.

You used that line "give me back the wig I bought you." Had you heard that before?
No, I'd never heard it before.

That's become a standard blues lyric. Lightnin' Hopkins used it . . .
I had never heard it before.

So maybe he swiped it from your song.
I don't know.

Did songs usually come to you in a quick flash of inspiration or did you labor over them?
They came in an inspiration.

Did songs ever come while you were sleeping or without an instrument?
Yeah. I like that. It happens quite often. The funny thing about it, when I wake up and get up, I sometimes lose it.

How was the band set up and miked at your 1942 Rhythm session?
Two mikes. One for me, and the other one would be off to the side, close to the piano setup. The horns were around the piano there. Sammy Deane was our trumpet player.

Did your mike pick up your voice and guitar amp?
Yes. I had the guitar across my lap, and the amplifier was down on the floor alongside me.

Did you distance the other musicians from their mike according to the volume of their instruments, so the horns would stand further back than the piano and the drums would be further back than the horns?
Exactly. That's right.

Was there a producer at the session?
Yeah, such as it was. I knew what I wanted to hear and how I wanted the setup, but the producers would never give it to me. The only time I got a good producer was on that "Why Was I Born," and that was a large band.

Same label, though.
Yes.

Do you remember the guitar and amp you used for the 1942 session?
I was using Gibson then.

That was an expensive guitar.
Yeah, it was expensive.

Yours was fancier than Charlie Christian's.
Yes. Charlie was using the one bar [pickup] on his, and so was I.

Did you play at a low volume?
Yes. That's how I got the sound. That was the sound.

You'd turn down the volume while comping and then turn it up when you soloed?
Yeah, that's right. Turn it down, turn it up.

Did you always use a pick?
No, no. I was experimenting all the time. I went up to Chicago, and the musi-

cians were waiting for me. So instead of using a regular pick, I used a felt pick and turned the volume up. I always used a new felt pick that was stiff and turned the volume up. That would get a good sound.

So you could crank up the volume and still get a soft, bassy tone.

Right. You got it right.

Could you burn through those picks pretty quickly?

Yeah, three or four a night.

Did you try tortoiseshell picks?

Yes. I kept getting too much sound.

Why did you hold your guitar body perpendicular to the floor like T-Bone Walker?

To get the sound from the box. Get all the action.

Could you hear yourself better in a club by holding your guitar this way?

In a way. To tell you the truth, that was like protection for me. At a lot of clubs you worked in, you might get into a beef. Some guy might come up to the stage and say, "Play 'Down Home in Dixie.'" If I don't play it and he gets mad, that box is part of my protection.

Another foot-and-a-half between you and that guy.

That's right.

Who did the arrangement on the 1942 Rhythm release of "What's Your Story Morning Glory"?

It was a head arrangement. We were sitting talking and had the idea for the sound for the tune while Barfield was playing the sax. He wanted to do a solo, and we had to find some way to get him in there, so that's how the arrangement came about.

Did you work out your solos in advance of recording them?

Sometimes I did.

What was the best kind of microphone to sing with? Did you have a preference?

No. Didn't matter.

Your song "S.K. Groove" really has the Charlie Christian influence.

Yes.

Especially the way you come into the solo . . .

Yeah. Could have been.

What did you think of Big Joe Turner's cover of "S.K. Blues"?

Well, I didn't like it. I thought he'd let me get a start, but New York boys, they didn't do it that way. If they heard something they thought would be a hit, they'd cover it. And that's what I didn't like about it. Joe and I finally met, and we talked it over. So it was alright.

Were you ever paid for the use of the song?

No. Nothing.

That must have hurt.

No. But it would have been nice.

What was your reaction the first time you saw a 78 with your name on it?

I don't know what my reaction was. We were running so much and cutting so many things, it never had any reason or rhyme. We just played. We didn't think about whether it was good or what was going to be good.

I never had any trouble, with Johnnie Cooper playing piano, Eddie on tenor, and two trumpet players—Sammy Deane and Eddie Walker. We never had any problems among ourselves. We wanted to work, we wanted to play, and we enjoyed music.

We enjoyed each other. We'd play our regular gig and then we'd play after hours. We never worried about whether this is good, this is bad—we just played. And we played *mostly* something for the musicians that come around, and that was sharp. It was tight. I'd call to the fellows, "How about this, how about that." Everything was uptight with musicians around, so we never had to worry about whether we were gonna be good or not or whether they'd like us or not. Just listen.

Not long after your first 78s came out, the recording industry ground to a halt.
Definitely. Shellac shortage and the war.
Did they re-press your records on recycled materials at one point?
Yeah.
Did that affect the sound of the records?
Yeah, it did. Made a terrible sound.
Like those old Paramount records.
Yeah. The OKeh sound—that's shellac. Bad sound.
Did you think OKeh records had a bad sound?
On certain artists they had a bad sound. Certain artists they worked on to better the sound.
What label put out your best-sounding 78s?
I thought Aladdin did a good sound. Nice sound.
Do you remember the session in Los Angeles where you recorded "Big Fat Butterfly" and "B♭ Blues"?
Oh, yeah. That was a strange story. We did 22 numbers. A musician here in San Francisco had a tune he wanted me to do, so I said, "Yeah, we can do that tune." As soon as we did his tune, Decca stepped in and put a hold on the session to clarify our usage of the tune. This killed the session and nothing was released.
One of the blues reference books lists Barney Bigard as playing clarinet on "C Jam Blues."
No, we did not record "C Jam Blues."
What happened with those records?
I don't know.
Was Rhythm threatening to sue Decca?
No. Decca was threatening to sue Rhythm. I did all those cuts for them, and they wouldn't put it out because of a suit they had.
Do the masters still exist?
I don't know.
Do you remember the year of the Decca sessions?
No. It was after the war.
Where were your 1946 Rhythm sessions held? Like for "Something's Worrying Me," "2:00 A.M. Hop."
That would be Sherman Clay again.
By then your guitar tone had changed—more bass and midrange. Was this due to new equipment?
Yes. New equipment, different equipment.
Bigger amp?
Yeah. And for quite a while I got a feedback from it. I couldn't get the right sound I wanted.
Would you have to record at a low volume to get rid of the feedback?
Yeah, and I couldn't get the good sound.

Sometimes you didn't play guitar on your records.

That was my choice. I was trying to get a driving rhythm behind it without amplifying—a solid rhythm. A beat.

At your second 1946 Rhythm session you had a different bass player, drummer, and pianist. This was when you did "Swingin'," "Write Me a Letter Blues," "Why Was I Born."

Yes.

This session has a lot more energy.

Yeah. A lot of drivin'.

Why?

Everything was written out.

So things weren't written out at the first 1946 session.

It was what we called a head session.

And the second one had charts.

Yes.

They framed your solos really well.

Yeah. I had a different drummer, a young drummer named Bill Douglas. He played in Los Angeles, a studio musician. That session took off in the Mark Hopkins Hotel—big studio, grand. I really enjoyed that session. Everything was written out, everything was according to sound. He got the right kind of sound. That's what it was.

What kind of machines were they recording with?

Disc.

So you could hear a playback right away.

Yeah. Right away. As a matter of fact, that was one of the reasons that session was so great. When we were about to get a bite to eat or anything, we could go outside the studio and sit down and listen to it.

And you could do another take if you didn't think it was good enough.

Yes. The thing about Rhythm Records was that Dave wanted just a couple of takes, and that's not enough.

He wanted to crank through it and save money.

Yes! [*Laughs.*] That was it. That's exactly what it was. But at this other session, the guy would say, "Come and listen to it, S.K." I'd go outside the studio and listen to the playback. If there was anything wrong, we would cut again. He never mentioned anything about money. Never once. But Dave would clamp down.

Who wrote "Swingin'"?

Head. It was another head arrangement.

That is unrelentingly swinging.

Yeah, it has a kick to it.

Did you play much bebop music?

No. I may have had one or two tunes in the repertoire, but we didn't play that much.

Do you hear a relation between bebop and the blues?

Yeah.

What do they have in common?

The timing and writing. With bebop you got guys that just played real fast—no taking their time. And it never stopped; it went on and on. In other words, say they were having a *C* turnback—they'd just keep going. They'd go to the *B♭*, and then it would stop and start over again. We never picked up on Charlie Parker because that's the way he was going. He wanted to play fast. And he did play fast. Speed, speed.

Was that a characteristic of bebop from the beginning?

Yeah, I think so.

Was there a sense that musicians were paving new ground?

Yes. I think so.

Did you consider yourself a bluesman during this period?

No. First and foremost, a musician. Always. I got a lot of trouble about that in different towns.

During your late-'40s tours, what percent of your repertoire on any given night was blues music?

It was according to what people ask for. If they didn't ask for it, before the evening was over I'd play something. When people were dancing and making a lot of noise, they'd say, "Ah, we don't want to hear that. Play some blues, man! Play some blues!" So you did—you'd either play it or you'd get out of there! Even in San Francisco. One of the biggest fights we ever had was behind some young girls wanting to hear the blues. And to tell you the truth, I didn't play too much blues, because most of the clubs I was working weren't blues houses. I played supper clubs, the Fairmont.

Were you gigging a lot?

Yeah. Five nights a week.

Most people don't associate San Francisco with having a thriving blues scene back then. You hear a lot more about West Coast swing, Oakland blues.

Yeah. Really.

Who was the most exciting blues musician you ever saw?

I don't know that I could answer that, because there weren't too many—certainly not in San Francisco.

How about on the road?

Roy Milton. He played the boogie-woogie blues. The house would rock when he played—really! He followed me into Harold Blackshear's Supper Club, and we thought we were doing pretty good—until Roy Milton came along! No way. He starts blues at the beginning of the evening, right straight through. He didn't stop for anything. Now there was a guy that played the blues.

Good band?

Yeah. A good band. And he sang and played. But they didn't advertise that this was a blues band. You went there and you got what was played.

Who was the most interesting musician you ever encountered?

[*Long pause.*] Eddie Taylor. Unknown to the public, but to me he was one of the finest and most interesting musicians I've ever met. Really was. I could be standing up playing, and he'd be next to me, and something would happen in his mind. There would be something he'd want to play, and he would play counterpoint to what I was playing. We'd play a duet together, and then he'd take a solo. I'd take a solo, and we'd cut back and do an ensemble together. He was the most interesting musician I've known. I played with a lot of musicians who said that he was not a very good tenor player, but to me he was the end.

Cab Calloway tried to steal Eddie Taylor. He came to the Backstage, which was a club in San Francisco where we had been about a year. Someone had told him about Eddie Taylor, and he came to catch our matinee. He was working downtown. I found out that he wanted to hire Eddie Taylor! But Eddie wasn't going anyplace.

When did Eddie quit being in the band with you?

When he moved to L.A. Beautiful guy.

How did you first run into Charlie Parker?

I was in Chicago. We were playing upstairs in the Cafe Society on 55th Street. We took intermission, and I went downstairs. When you're in a strange town you want to meet people, so I went on the street, and I saw a crowd of people across the street. It was like a park, and I heard some guy playing. He was standing on the bench. The crowd of people were hearing this wilting sound of this horn. As a matter of fact, he had as big an audience as we had upstairs. I didn't know who he was. I headed back upstairs and asked my trumpet player who that player was. He says, "Charlie Parker." The guy could play. Charlie had a strange feeling about him. The first time you heard him, he would attract your attention.

You'd either think he was great or the worst guy you'd heard.

Yeah, that's basically what it was [*smiles*]. And everybody was standing around hollering and screaming applause. He had his new shoes on, standing on the bench playing.

For tips?

No. Just blowing by himself. Nobody with him. That's how I first met him. By himself. He didn't have a coat on, in the park playing. I stood and listened to him, and then I had to go back to work and I *missed* him when he went back to work at a club across the street.

What a character.

What a man!

Did you like him?

Yeah, very much so. I liked him. If you're a musician and you play him, this feeling would happen for you. You'd get it from him. He didn't need a drummer, he didn't need a big band. He didn't need any of that. All he wanted to do was to play.

Were you a fan of Miles Davis?

Yeah. A buddy of mine. He would come to the apartment when he used to play at the Blackhawk during the '40s.

Was Miles famous when you first met him?

Yeah.

For the bebop stuff?

For whatever style he was playing. He changed often. You never could figure Miles out. One season he'd play something sweet, and the next season he'd be wild. He'd come back with a change of style. But as long as I can remember, he was always famous.

Was he respectful?

With me he'd be respectful. We got along fine, beautiful. He'd sit around my house and be respectful. He was crazy about my wife. He was always saying I married a "child bride." [*Smiles.*] My wife and I went to hear him at the Both/And on Divisadero Street, and during intermission he came out and picked me up—he was always strong!—and held me. He said, "You crazy man with a child bride!" Cicely

Tyson was upstairs, and when she came down he told her that my wife was "a young child bride and she shouldn't be in here. She's underage."

Was Miles' sound that different when he first came out?

Yeah, he had a different sound. He liked what I call the "wah-wah."

The mute?

Yes. He believed in it. He was weird, but he played. I loved him. I loved the music. He was different. He wanted different *sounds*. He wanted musicians to use certain things. Like today you listen to him, and tomorrow you hear different sounds. He played some weird stuff, and he was the only guy who could do it. And he was sincere about it. This boy doing it now . . .

Wynton Marsalis?

Yeah! They were starting to compare him to Miles.

They're in different leagues.

Right. You're right.

Miles changed music more than once.

Yeah. I saw Miles with just a trio, and he was swingin'! It was marvelous. Miles was playing bebop or whatever he called it, but it didn't sound like him. When he came the next season, a whole different Miles was coming across the concourse, as smooth as glass.

Who's the best swing drummer you ever saw?

Jo Jones. He was fine. He used to sell the fellas in the band chicken. He wanted to make some money off of them. He was fun.

Did you admire Jimmy Blanton?

Oh, yeah. The bass player. You can't touch that. I never did see anyone who could play bass like him. He was amazing.

Another cat before him was Pops Foster.

Oh, yeah. I saw him at a distance, never met him.

Was Wellman Braud in the same league as these guys?

No. No one was in Blanton's league.

Did you know Art Tatum?

I watched him play. I worked at NBC in San Francisco for four years, and I had the weekend off once when Mingus came to town. So I followed Mingus in town, down south. Same thing with Tatum. I followed Tatum around town and I followed him all over California. Marvelous man. He changed his music around every night. Every session, between numbers he'd change his stuff. I'd try to follow his thoughts, follow where he's going to go. He'd do those session head changes. He was a genius.

Did he have bad eyesight?

Yeah, but I don't think he was completely blind. Quite the fellow. Quite the musician.

Did you know Illinois Jacquet?

Yeah, he was in Toronto with Jo Jones and Milt Buckner. They had a trio together. It was the first time I had seen Jacky play baritone. Milt was on the organ. What a trio! We had fun that trip.

Were you a fan of John Coltrane?

Oh, yeah. When I first heard him, I couldn't understand him.

Too far out?

Yes. But then I sat down and listened to him, and he was alright. When I could get what he was saying, he was great. He came in Jack's too.

Ever run into Coleman Hawkins?

Yeah, but we never had anything in common.

Who was the most arrogant musician you encountered?

Ben Webster. Big attitude. He was a funny guy—he wouldn't ride in the car with you. He'd take a bus and go downtown to his job. He'd eat out of a paper bag— that's the kind of guy he was. He was weird.

Who was surprisingly sweet and humble?

Barney Bigard. Beautiful, beautiful.

When you were young, did you see any of the famous blues women, like Ma Rainey, Bessie Smith, Ida Cox . . .

Missed 'em all. I wasn't interested in them. Women blues singers—I don't know, just didn't move me. I listened to them, but they didn't move me.

Did you like Billie Holiday?

Oh, yeah. I loved her. I think she's everyone's favorite. We were listening to some records the other day, and I pulled out a Billie Holiday album. We worked together in San Francisco in three different clubs—Savoy, 90 Market, and New Orleans Swing Club.

Was she straight when you met her?

No. But she had just gotten herself together, and her manager was my manager at the time. When she came to town, she needed someone to work with her, so I worked with her. The same thing happened with Sarah Vaughan. She came to town and needed a band, and I worked with her at 90 Market Street.

How did you become associated with Louis Armstrong?

Satchmo, I always liked him. I always liked him as a person. I loved him as a musician, loved a lot of things about him. Whenever he'd play, I would go to wherever he was playing and listen to him. He just had certain riffs that he'd play. If you weren't a musician, you would miss it. He'd play the same thing over, the same lick, every tune he played. At the end of it, he'd have that one certain thing he'd do. He was really a great person. I met him when he was reading a script for the Bing Crosby show. It was for a radio show in San Francisco.

What kind of guy was he offstage?

Louis? Oh, he was just fun.

Was he a cut-up?

No. Just ordinary, natural fun. Natural with it. No, he didn't cut up.

As a young man, were you aware of his records with the Hot Five?

No, no. I heard of them in later years.

When you toured the chitlin circuit, did you play in the Deep South?

I played in Memphis—I guess you'd call that Deep South.

Was that during the Jim Crow era?

Yeah. And also I played at Mahara College, the black college. That was the Deep South.

Was it scary to travel through the South at that time?

My father moved the family to Los Angeles when I was young. We had lived in Louisiana and Texas, and Dad thought our opportunities would be better in California. Therefore I was aware of how things were in the South. We worked a dance in Nashville, Tennessee. The woman who ran the fan club was there, and during the intermission they wanted the whites to come down on the floor and dance with everybody. The people sponsoring the dance had a rope down the middle of the floor.

For whites on one side, blacks on the other?

Yeah! You understand. So somebody came to me and said, "Look at what is happening out here." So I went behind the curtain and looked, and there was this segregated deal. And I could tell that the Caucasian kids who were on the balcony wanted to come down and dance on the main floor. They wanted to dance with everybody. I asked the road manager about it, and he made some flippant remark. I always had a terrific temper, and he told me to quiet down and just play the gig and get out of there, and we did.

Were there many fights in the clubs you played?

No. The biggest fight I ever had in a club was in Tucson. I don't know what happened. The act started, and I was playing "Swanee River" in swing time with Charlie Mingus, and I looked and saw a bench up in the air! A whole bench! Broke up that club. I didn't like Tucson, but I met Charlie Mingus again there. Good gig being with Mingus, who wanted to fight all the time. And he got into it.

Yeah?

Oh, yeah! Oh, he was very mean.

Did Miles like to fight?

I never saw him fight. I heard him using foul language, but had never seen him fight. Mingus would fight.

When you toured, were you part of a package with other artists?

No, I didn't get into that at all. I carried an extra artist with me—a singer or a dancer with the band. My band was six pieces, so I could afford to carry one.

You must have been doing pretty well to afford to take six guys on the road.

Oh, yeah. We were doing very well.

Were you a strict band leader?

Never.

You'd let your guys stretch out?

Yeah. I believed in that. Back then, that's what was happening.

Did you invite people to sit in on the bandstand with you?

No, no.

Did you play places where they'd have a band set up on each end of the dance hall, so when one took a break, the other could start up?

Yes. Louis Armstrong played at Ocean Beach with us in Santa Monica.

Did you mostly tour by car or train?

We did car.

Did you visit New York's Swing Street—52nd Street—while it was flourishing in the '40s?

No. I was headed for New York when I met Bone [T-Bone Walker]. That was in Chicago. I'd heard about Bone from the West Coast and Texas. So my manager sent me to New York, and on my way to New York we were going to stop in Chicago a couple of weeks. It so happened we stayed in Chicago four weeks on 55th Street. Bone was up the street from me at a club, and I was in Cafe Society only a half a block away. Bone would take intermission and come down and visit me, and I'd go up and visit him. That's how we first met. Bone headed home, and so my manager says, "Before you get home, we'll go by Texas with Bone." I said, "Oh, that's great. Bone and I together—crazy." So we stopped at the Rose Room in Dallas, and Bone took sick—I don't know what it was. So I had to play the whole gig by myself. When I left, I left Bone there. That's how I first met him.

Didn't he give you advice about carrying a gun in Chicago?

Yeah! It was his doing, not mine. [*Laughs.*] Bone, he called me "K." He said, "Hey, K, do you have your pistol with you?" I said, "Ah, no. I don't have a pistol." He said, "I got mine." He had two, one this way [*indicates his belt*] and one that way [*points to his pocket*]. Chicago was pretty rough, and so Bone showed me his pistols.

Was T-Bone a hard-partying kind of guy?

Not necessarily. I never saw him doing that.

Was he pretty serious offstage?

Yeah. He was serious with me, because I wanted him to play the right notes and chords. We were at Blackshear's Supper Club, and he was playing a tune he had written, but it had the wrong chord changes. I got on him about it, and so he took me back into his dressing room and played the right chord changes. But evidently those were the chords he wanted to play.

Were you around for any of the guitar battles, like Gatemouth Brown versus T-Bone Walker?

No. Gatemouth Brown worked out at the Booker T. Washington Hotel in the City. The afternoon I saw him, I didn't know what he was playing because his chord progression was different. Hollering going on.

During the '40s, did many musicians want to become involved in cutting contests?

Yeah! That's what a jam session was about.

Headcutting?

Yeah.

What was your approach to surviving a situation like that?

Play, play, play. Call a head. We'd call certain head numbers that we knew they didn't have in their books, and that was it. I'd call out something like "Swingin'." We had certain outlays where if a musician didn't know when to come in, it was too bad.

You were gonna smoke him.

That's right. That's what the session was all about.

Did you always know which chords and notes you were playing? Were you thoroughly versed in music?

Oh, yes. I learned it as a violin player. I went to school in Oroville, my home in Northern California, and studied music there. Went to school, got it right. If it wasn't right, my music teacher, Mrs. Forsythe, would see to it that I'd get it right. She'd say, "You put that extra note there, Saunders. It doesn't belong there. It belongs here." She always saw that I'd get it right. I don't know where she is now. She's probably dead, like most of 'em.

What happened to Eddie Taylor?

He died several years ago. The last time I saw him, his sister took him to the doctor, and I could tell from her reaction that he was sick. It was very, very sad. A sad day for me.

Are any of your old bandmates still around?

Johnnie Cooper was the last one. A couple of years ago, he passed. They had his funeral at the Grace Cathedral.

Johnnie Cooper was really talented. He could lay back on a song like "What's Your Story," but when he needed to, he could really jam.

Oh, yeah.

Your band had a nice sense of dynamics.

Yeah, I thought so.

Did you require that your bandmates could read?

Yes. Everyone.

So a good trumpet player who couldn't read would be out of luck?

He wasn't with my band. He wasn't in my band at all.

Would you recommend that aspiring musicians learn to read and write music?

Yes, by all means, because that would put you on the right track.

Did you play on other people's records as a guest?

No. Because I had this band, and if I played with another artist on another record, they wouldn't like that. We had to stick together. And that was our forte.

What was it like when you switched over to the Modern label? Did they have a better budget, better studio?

They had a better budget—I'm sure of that. They had a marvelous big studio in Hollywood.

Do you recall cutting "Empty Bedroom Blues"?

Yeah. We did that session in my apartment.

You hauled a disc-cutting machine into your apartment?

Yes. We brought the cutting machine and everything right into the apartment. At that time it was possible to cut in the apartment if you had the right machine. We'd cut and lay back and wait and get a chance to play it over again. Sometimes they didn't sound too good.

Do you recall the make of the machine?

No, I can't.

Did you own it?

Yeah. But I don't know what happened to it.

On "Empty Bedroom Blues" you had a more distorted guitar tone. Were you hearing things differently?

Yeah. We took the cut to the studio and did it over again.

When did you first record onto tape?

I don't remember.

Your Aladdin 78s like "Little Girl," "St. James Infirmary Blues," and "Misery Blues" had a fine sound.

They were done in a new studio with excellent acoustics and good technicians. It was a good session.

During this session you started bending guitar strings.

Well, I think that's an association with someone else. Most of the blues players, they were bending strings.

The younger guys like B.B. King?

Yeah. They were bending strings and notes. And I could do it, but I didn't because I didn't want to at that time. And when I came home, I found out that some other musicians had moved in my spot. In other words, they got there by bending notes. Texas boys, Louisiana boys were bending notes. So I started. Tried that. I didn't care for it. It was a means to an end.

Were people bending before the war?

Not that much.

Charlie Christian didn't.

No. Charlie didn't have time. That's what I'm talking about: He didn't have time to bend. He gotta move!

Was it surprising to you when downhome guys like Muddy Waters became popular?

It was a surprise.

Did it seem like a musical step backwards?

Not really. I played with Muddy Waters in San Diego. It was in a big barn.

What were your sessions with the Bihari brothers like?

Nice. Joe was really nice. As far as the money was concerned, he was beautiful. He was great, anything I wanted. The only thing I didn't like about him was he wanted to compare me to B.B. King. He gave me a bunch of records and wanted me to listen to them and simulate them. But that wasn't my gig at all.

That's not who you were.

That's where we fell out.

B.B. King has said nice things about your music.

One year I went down to Oklahoma on a tour, and I had a little problem with a fella stealing our instruments. I had no idea B.B. was there—he was working the radio. That night he came to the club and said to me, "Don't worry about it. I'll get 'em back." Sure enough, the next day everything was right. B.B.'s a nice guy.

When you recorded "My Close Friend" for the Biharis, whose idea was it to pound the beat on the piano? That is so hip!

[*Smiles.*] Cedric.

That's almost like a T-Bone song.

Yeah. It was from the same time, so naturally it had that kind of connection.

Jerome Richardson played good sax on it.

Really. Great. He was a blower. He would blow most people off the stand. As far as reading and knowing the music, there was none better.

The title of your song "Read the Good Book" suggests a gospel connection, but the lyrics sure sound a lot more like Louis Jordan.

[*Laughs.*] Yeah. I liked Louis Jordan, but his wife changed my outlook on him. She had two or three Cadillacs and wouldn't let him have one. Oh, yeah. She was the boss.

Was he a pretty sweet guy?

Well, to the fellas outside of his band, he was fine.

You also did "Going Mad" for the Biharis.

Yeah! [*Laughs.*]

Wow! What's going on there? That's the first time I heard you sing and play fills at the same time.

Yeah. I don't know.

Was that cut all at once?

Yeah. It was done simultaneously.

By then were they using more than a couple of mikes?

Yeah. They'd mike everybody except for the drummer.

Was that a nice studio?

Yeah. In San Francisco.

At various times in your career, your name appeared as S.K. or Eskay.

I used to sign my name "Eskay."

Do you have souvenirs from your recording heyday, such as your charts?

Yeah. I have most of the charts I wanted to keep.

When you were doing all this stage work and recording, did you still practice?

Oh, yeah. My wife's mad at me now because I don't practice.

Unlike most blues artists, you were very broad-based, covering a wide range of styles.

Yes.

Even today, it's hard to imagine someone improving on your "St. James Infirmary Blues" solo. It's still very modern sounding.

Well, yeah. I hope so.

In terms of vocal performance, do you have a favorite of your own records?

Yeah. I have one or two. One is "Sometimes I Feel Like a Motherless Child." I recorded it, but they didn't put it out.

Was that with Decca?

Yeah. In the '40s.

Any other vocal favorites besides "Sometimes I Feel"?

[*Pauses.*] "Summertime."

What's the best guitar you've owned?

Gibson 300. I had two of them. I had one electric and I had one standard. The best guitar I ever had was the standard. I could sit and play with the band without amplifying, and it gave me tone—big tone. Big box, big tone. And it could sing! It would sing for you. And some of the greatest things happened in those times.

Did you ever own a solidbody guitar?

No. I had a Telecaster, but it wasn't mine. And I had a Dobro.

Did you play it slide or standard?

Standard.

Was it a metal-bodied guitar?

Yes.

Those things had good volume.

Yeah. I loved it.

Any favorites among your own guitar performances?

No.

Your solo in the 1961 version of "What's Your Story Morning Glory" sounds angry. It's like you're going for the jugular.

I was mad. I had one fellow on the piano, a fellow on the bass, and they weren't playing. I appreciated the fact that they were doing the session with me, but they were not playing, so I had to do something. So that's what it was.

Is that session a bad memory for you?

Yeah. It was a very poor session.

Did you enjoy recording "Silver Threads" with Carlos Santana?

Oh, yeah.

After "S.K.'s Blues," what were your most popular records?

"I've Had My Moments" and "Why Was I Born."

Do you have a collection of your own 78s?

No.

During your career, did any musicians give you good advice or look out for you?

I'd look out for myself, and I'd look out for other musicians.

You were the paternal figure?

Yeah! I guess you could call it that.

Did wanting to be with your children figure into your decision to leave the road?

Oh, sure. San Francisco is a weird city, a wicked city, and I wanted to be there with them.

You started playing for the church during the 1970s?

Yes. Holiness.

Is that Pentecostal?

Pentecostal.

Was there any problem with bringing an electric guitar into church?

None whatsoever. They liked for me to bring it in. They use them in most Pentecostal churches.

Do you still go to church?

Yes. Once a week on Sunday, the Sabbath. Once I get there for the church service, there's a certain calmness, a certain serenity, that I don't get any place other than the church.

When did you give your last blues performance?

I don't know.

Were you playing blues at the club in Sunnyvale where you worked during the '70s?

Yeah! I played blues.

Seeing all the charts and lessons you've saved through the years, it's evident that music has been a lifelong journey for you.

Yeah. I've loved my life.

Do you still play much today?

No.

You know how sometimes musicians try to copy their heroes note for note?

Yeah.

What would you encourage a younger musician to learn from you?

I'd like for them to learn music.

Thanks for the interview.

Beautiful. Beautiful.

LOWELL FULSON

BY MARY KATHERINE ALDIN AND MARK HUMPHREY

Raised in Oklahoma and steeped in Western swing and Texas blues, Lowell Fulson became one of the leading figures of postwar West Coast blues. Part Choctaw Indian, he was born in 1921 in Tulsa, Oklahoma, and did his first singing at church picnics and socials. By 1939 Lowell was working with Dan Wright's string band in Ada, Oklahoma, where he was spotted by singer Alger "Texas" Alexander. Impressed with his guitar playing, Alexander, who'd recorded with Lonnie Johnson and Eddie Lang, took the teenager to Texas to accompany him for a few months. In 1941, Lowell moved to Gainesville, Texas, where he worked as a dish washer and played Saturday night country balls. Drafted into the Navy in 1943, Fulson was stationed in Oakland, California, where he cooked for officers and entertained troops at night. Later on, he led a small combo entertaining troops on Guam.

Shortly after his discharge, Fulson settled on the West Coast, as did Texas bluesmen T-Bone Walker, Smokey Hogg, Pee Wee Crayton, and L.C. Robinson, all of whom played electric guitar, and pianists Charles Brown, Ivory Joe Hunter, Amos Milburn, and Percy Mayfield. Basing himself in Oakland, Fulson began playing clubs near the shipyards, which were employing thousands of African Americans who'd come in from Texas, Louisiana, and Oklahoma.

At first Lowell played downhome two-guitar blues with his younger brother, Martin Fulson, and then he formed a small group and began moving to a smoother, more urbane style suitable for ballads and blues. His pianists during this era included Lloyd Glenn, who'd played jazz in San Antonio and Dallas before the war, and Eldridge McCarty.

Fulson made his first recordings for producer Bob Geddins' Big Town label in 1946. Two years later he recorded "Three O'Clock Blues," on Down Town Records; an early-'50s cover by B.B. King became a big hit. In 1949, Lowell had a hit with "Everyday I Have the Blues," an adaptation of Memphis Slim's "Nobody Loves Me" recorded for Swing Time, and then struck the charts again with "Blue Shadows" and the Christmas favorite, "Lonesome Christmas."

During the early 1950s, Fulson began touring extensively; Ray Charles and Stanley Turrentine passed through his lineups. After a 1953 session for Aladdin, Fulson began his long association with Chess Records' Checker subsidiary with "Reconsider Baby," his most successful record. Fulson jumped to Los Angeles–based Kent Records in 1964, and scored his first major hits in a decade with "Black Nights" and the funky "Tramp." Fulson continued to record prolifically, cutting for United, Jewel, Granite, and Big Town in the 1970s, and seeing much of his old repertoire come out on Arhoolie, Night Train, Chess, Ace, and other labels. He signed with Rounder in 1988 and produced *It's a Good Day*, followed by *Hold On* on Bullseye Blues in 1992. His final new album, *Them Update Blues*, came out on Bullseye in 1995 and was nominated for a Grammy Award for Best Traditional Blues Album.

During the 1990s a number of awards and honors came Fulson's way. He was inducted into the Rhythm and Blues Hall of Fame in ceremonies held in Los Angeles in early 1993; he also received five W. C. Handy Awards in 1993, including induction into the Blues Hall of Fame for both himself as an artist and for "Reconsider Baby" as a song. His newer recordings for Rounder and Bullseye Blues garnered rave reviews, awards, and sales, and his compositions were often recorded by others.

The following interviews, which were put together for the June 1994 *Living Blues* cover story, were conducted in two main "chunks" at Tina Mayfield's home in Palmdale, California, where Lowell was living. Tina, the widow of blues songwriter Percy Mayfield, is a registered nurse, and it was thanks to her tireless care and supervision that Lowell's final years were made comfortable. For the ten years that he lived in her home, she cooked food that was appropriate for his diabetic needs, checked his blood sugar every morning, and traveled with him to the occasional appearances at festivals and concerts that he felt up to doing. When I asked David Nelson (then editor of *Living Blues*) to let me do a feature on Lowell, it was to Tina that I turned, first for encouragement and later for scheduling.

Lowell and I had known each other off and on since the mid 1960s, but until his wife Sadie died and he moved into Tina's home, we hadn't seen much of each other. For the last ten years of Lowell's life, my friend Mark Humphrey and I were more frequent visitors to his home, and consequently he was already used to telling me stories and felt relaxed when it came time to talk "on the record." I was assisted in the interview process by two close friends—Mark, who lives in Santa Monica, California, and Keith Briggs, of *Blues & Rhythm* magazine in England. Mark, himself a musician and writer, is, like Lowell, a native Oklahoman. Mark and Lowell spent many hours playing guitar together and talking about Oklahoma. Lowell was always glad to see Mark, and when we walked up to the door together he'd be sitting on the front porch waiting for us with the greeting, "There's my home boy again! Did you bring that guitar today?"

In later years, when his hands were too stiff to play, Lowell set the guitar aside; I'd watch as his hands tapped against his leg and his fingers formed well-remembered chords as he listened to Mark playing songs he recognized. Keith Briggs came out to Palmdale with us for one of the interviews and made a number of helpful suggestions about background questions to ask.

At the time of these interviews Lowell was in fairly good shape physically and mentally, and for the most part was able to give coherent, meaningful answers. However, there were one or two questions that produced, at the time, a more taciturn response, or none at all. To supplement the interview, therefore, I used two or three short excerpts from tapes of conversations we'd had in the late 1970s and early 1980s.

After these interviews were conducted, Mark and I continued our regular visits to Lowell, even as his health and memory began to fail. He was always glad to see us and still teased me and called me "Champ," but he was clearly declining and sometimes the three of us would just sit for long periods of companionable silence on his front porch. Eventually his liver and kidneys failed, and our visits were to hospitals and then nursing homes. Tina helped us stay in touch as he was moved from place to place.

We had to schedule our visits for the days he wasn't having dialysis, and that restriction, combined with the intensive work schedules of two busy writers, meant that we saw him less frequently than we wanted to. "Well, you found me again!" he'd grin when we walked into his room in the latest care facility with bags of fan mail, a thermos of the coffee he loved but the nursing homes did not provide, and an acoustic guitar. Mark would sit by his bed, playing softly, while I read him his mail. "Now, that's nice," he'd say, as I read him best wishes from folks around the world. He looked at the stamps and the postmarks, remembering when he had played a festival or a club in each city. Fans sent cassettes, CDs, drawings, postcards, blues festival programs, and get-well wishes to my post office box, and Lowell hoarded it all in a cupboard and a drawer, and on a bedside table. We went for short walks around the nursing home's block, and gradually things seemed to improve.

Right at the end of his life he was able to leave the nursing home to live in the home of fellow blues guitarist Terry deRouen and his wife Ruby. Both diabetics themselves, they were well able to cook and care for him. A medical van picked him up and brought him back on dialysis days, and he seemed to open up once he got out of the hospital environment and into a real home again, although his memory was still deteriorating. But he was only at Ruby and Terry's for a few short months; I think we had visited him there only twice when Tina called early one morning with the news I had been dreading. Lowell Fulson died a few weeks short of his 78th birthday, on March 7, 1999, of kidney and liver disease and congestive heart failure. His funeral was held at Angelus Funeral Home in Los Angeles, and he was buried just a few places from his friend Charles Brown's grave at Inglewood Cemetery.

When and where were you born?
I'm from Tulsa, born on March 31, 1921. When I was old enough to realize anything or know anything I was in Tulsa. But before then, my mother said that I was born up on Choctaw Indian strip. We used to call it the bush country, down there. My father got killed there and my mother left and went back down there. And when I was old enough to get listed in school there in kindergarten, I remember that pretty good. I don't remember my father so well, though. He got killed on the job working at an oil mill. That was 'long about 1925–'26.
There was a race riot in Tulsa in 1921, the year you were born.
Yeah. Mama used to tell me how she was runnin' and hidin' with me. I don't know what month that was going on, but she had to hide me to save my life.
What were your parents' names?
Martin Fulson and Mamie Wilson. I think my daddy was born about 1900.
How many brothers and sisters did you have?
By my real father, my mother had two children. That was me and Martin. Ten, twelve years later she came up with another boy and a daughter by another marriage. So I have one sister and two brothers.
Was Martin older or younger than you?
Younger.
Did anyone in your family play a musical instrument?
Yeah. They all hammered around on something. We had guitars, mandolins, violins. My grandfather played violin. He was in his mid-nineties and I was like 12 years old, in '35. The old man hung in pretty good. He played violin, and they say my daddy accompanied him—they called it "second on the guitar," you know. That was on my daddy's side. And on my mother's side they all played a little. My uncles—I had about four or five of them—they all played something. Some of them belonged to the Holiness Church and they played the guitars there. They all had a little music.
Do you remember when you were a child hearing them playing music at home?
Yeah. I was right under them, right in the way. And they just couldn't keep me away from them guitars. I didn't like the fiddle so much. I didn't like the sound draggin' that thing across there. So I taken up with the guitar. And I banged around on it. 'Course they didn't want me to play the guitar, the uncles didn't. 'Fraid I'd break it or something. That was their personal entertainment. But I'd

wait till they go, and when everybody leave and go to work, I would . . . Funny thing, I learned to tune the thing before I learned to really play it. 'Cause they would check to see if I had messed with it. They never did find out.

Well, later, when I got about 12–14 years old, they had a picnic out there, and two uncles were furnishing the music, mandolin and guitar. They went off and stayed a little longer than they were supposed to. And the people got restless, so I got up there and played an old song called "South Texas Blues." I learned that pretty good. A few Blind Lemon Jefferson licks, you know. And people were dancin' and I was playin'. I couldn't play but one song, but I must have been doing pretty good with it.

How had you heard Blind Lemon Jefferson songs?

On them old phonographs. RCA.

You had one at your house?

Yeah.

Did your folks buy the records?

The boys did.

Where did you go to school?

I went to school at something like a mission school in Atoka, between Tulsa and Atoka [about 130 miles south of Tulsa]. I was from Atoka. It is one of them country schools. You have everything in there—the church, the schoolhouse, the community center. It was all the way through to the ninth grade. You had Coalgate and Lehigh and Atoka. Atoka was the kind of largest one 'cause it held all the records for the Indians, the half-breeds, the Indian-born bloodline thing in there, and they claimed it caught afire and burned up a lot of the records. I know I went down there, and I couldn't find no records on my dad. I had seen records on some of the Fulsons, but not my dad. He was the youngest boy, the youngest kid period, out of a whole bunch of them. Grandpa had married an Indian woman. She was a Cherokee. But we went under the title of Choctaw Freedmen. And I think he was freed [from slavery] under the Choctaw Indians. So my grandpa was what you called a Choctaw Freedman, by the state of Oklahoma. I never did get the straight of how he got with the Indians and got a Cherokee wife, but he said he was 19 years old [when he fought] during the Civil War.

What was his name?

Henry Fulsom. He used to tell me quite a bit. He died in 1935 in September. And I think he was 90-some years old then. He was an Indian herb doctor, yeah. But he was a black man. He was from Africa. So he just brought what he learned from Africa over here, and by being with that ol' Indian chief and what they taught him down there, you know, he got to be pretty sharp with medicine and healing and curing things and people.

So your grandfather was actually born in Africa?

Yes. See, his last-born son was my dad. They tell me that my grandmother passed giving birth to my dad. She had had too many babies.

Your grandfather fought in the Civil War with the Indians?

Yeah, I don't remember whether he told me that or I just knew it, but it was an organized thing. He got away from them, then a man took my uncle Pres. They run him in there with the Indians and kept him. He didn't know where the rest of his people were that had come over with him on the ship. Some of 'em must have never lived 'cause he didn't see them. They took them out there to Oklahoma and changed their names.

What was the main thing that people did around there? Farming?

Yeah, but they mostly planted what they wanted; they didn't hardly market any stuff. Family raised, and used for the family. I think they raised everything down there, so that they didn't have to buy nothing but sugar, salt, pepper, stuff like that, you know.

People would have cattle and hogs?

Cattle and hogs and chickens and everything. They raised stuff to feed themselves. They get corn and they go to town. You'd give them so much of what you bring into town to grind your corn. You didn't see a lot of money, but there was a lot of trading. Guys would take and plant a little cotton, that was a little extra money. It wasn't a whole lot—your family could pick it all out in a day or two. They would sell it, and they would sell them the seeds and trade it for the cotton or the lint. So they'd make a little money off it, everything else was trade. You give me a bushel of corn, and I'll grind up the rest of it. So you don't see no money. So when I tell people that you could change a penny in those days, they look at me like I'm crazy. But you could change a penny. You call it mills.

Did your family have livestock on your land?

Yeah. Back in those days in that part of the country, there were no fences. It was open land. You would put your mark on your cattle, you would brand hogs, you would clip his ears a certain different way. So if it get too far and you would catch one, you better look at him because if he belonged to someone else over there, there would be trouble. They grazed together and stuff like that. We kept mostly all of the Fulsons' and the Wilsons' together. That community was half built upon just relatives. From Tulsa back to Atoka, and all between, was Wilsons and Fulsons. Half-breed, quarter-breed, eighth-breed, whatever.

Did you grow up on a pretty big place there?

Yeah. It was blocked off in 40-acre lots, you know. And everybody who was of age, like from my daddy's age on up, got 40 acres of land, but them that was younger didn't get anything 'cause they weren't old enough to be responsible for keeping it up. There were 600 acres of land down there, it was cut up and divided between the relatives from the government.

What did your family and neighbors do for entertainment? Were there dances out there?

Called 'em picnics. Now they call 'em festivals. And it wasn't no race barrier, everybody—Indians, white, black. We were playing music and dancing, but you knew who to dance with and who not to dance with. You danced with your own woman. And they would dance with their own, and it was a lot of fun. Nobody say, you brushed against my old lady or you pushed against my man. None of that went on. Wasn't nothing like that.

The community was pretty open and people knew each other?

Yeah. They knew each other. Everybody visited everybody. The Colberts and the Monroes, they were black-complected people, straight hair and stuff. And they were mostly Indians or part Indians, and they were the ones to give the dances. From the time I was 15 or 16, I would play all of them. I would make five dollars every time I would play one of those dances. I'd make five dollars, and it would take some of those guys a week to make five dollars, and I would make it in one night playing picnics. I guess you'd do what they do now, charge them to come in. You'd have it at home, sometimes you have it in Atoka, sometime you'd have a party in the country, and sometimes they'd have it closer up to where we lived, which was called the White Hall settlement, and further back north was Seely settlement, where the straight hair, black-complected lived. They were mostly Cherokees.

When you played at these dances, would you play solo or would you play with a little band?

Well, it would have sometime four or five on the thing. They'd build a platform, big, huge platform. And then they'd make their own alcohol, see. And it was no sale—when they looked at you, if it looked like you'd had enough, you would not get no more. They would dish it out to you in cups. I was too young; they would not give me none. I'd sneak me a little every once in a while, a little of that home-made beer. Choc-beer.

What was your first guitar?

I think it was a Kay, an acoustic. It wasn't no electric then. They would make their own lights to hang up on the fences. They were making like a clothesline or something all across there. Kerosene and they'd make wicks. Put them in Coca-Cola bottles, and at night they would light them and it would be lighter than it is in here. You did not see no electric guitar—I didn't—until 1936–'37. In Montgomery Ward, it was in there for $79. We thought, man, that's a year's work! They did not come up with no Dobro until I was about 17 or 18 years old. I bought one, paid five dollars for it. National, that was the name of it. They had a lot of their stuff down there that was pretty good.

What kind of tunes would the people like to hear at these picnics?

Well, some of them would like some of Bob Wills' stuff. He was a very famous man down through there. The boys would like "Shanty Town" or "Silvery Moon," "Beer Barrel Polka," and then later on in the night they would play the "West Texas Blues," "South Texas Blues"—it sounds the same to me. Fingering was about the same, but everybody had a style they played it in. The Hadley boys lived in town up there at Coalgate, so they were about the best around there. They would come out and play mandolin and guitar. Clarence and Frank Hadley. And we had a couple of pretty good harp blowers there, the Overton boys—they lived around Coalgate. Take a half a day and walk over there.

That was nothing for a young man, was it?

No, you were thinking about the fun you are going to have when you get there, and you are there before you know it.

When did you decide you wanted to play guitar professionally?

When I left home and went into Ada, Oklahoma, [at age] 17–18. A string band used to come through there once a year around May or June, and they were stay-ing all through the summer. And they set up housekeeping for mostly whites in town. Blacks would come, but they would be sitting over here, and I met old man Dan Wright. He was the banjo player, and that was his little carnival thing. [Dan Wright was a member of a large musical family from Texas, much like the Chatmons of Mississippi, and the Dan Wright string band played a wide variety of music for both black and white audiences. They never recorded.] He give me a job playing with James and the boys, first, second rhythm. He had a 17–18 piece string band, big band. That's when I really started making my change, playing my chords and accompanying. I would mix my rhythm with the songs I played. I catched on pretty good. I did everything but sleep with the thing.

What repertoire did that string band play?

Mostly country and western. They didn't play no blues.

Were they playing for dancing or for people to listen?

Mostly listen. You had something like a wagon for a platform. Great, big, old, long [platform]. Trailer, trailer, trailer, they'd put them together. Drop the sides off of it. Put steps up there. And the musicians all get up on that. And they had empty lots there, and people would put chairs out there. And you would start about one o'clock and play until about five–six o'clock every day.

Was this in a park?

No, it was just some vacant land they made a recreation thing out of. Dan Wright, he was a famous guy for big bands down in that country. He'd go down to Texas and stuff. I would just play with him when he would come to Oklahoma. I think he was a Texas man, 'cause he played a lot of Bob Wills and the Texas Playboys' records, you know what I mean. They would broadcast 'em. Blackstone Hotel, Fort Worth. That was all people listened to in the middle of the day is Bob Wills.

When did you move to Texas?

1940, I think it was. Yeah. I left with Texas Alexander. We had played for them with Dan Wright during the day. Then I would go with some of the guys in the big band. Come on down to a place we called Foggy Bottom, I think it was. They'd go down there and that is when you would hear the blues. And boy, them guys could play some guitar. And I got with Texas Alexander. He asked me, said, "Come on, join up with me." So I went playing behind him, you know, just sitting down there making a few changes as a sound. He said, "What you do?" and I said, "I don't do nothing but what I'm doing now, when I get a chance." And he said, "You ain't got no job?" and I said, "No." He said, "You could make some money with me, man. We'd split the kitty, and I know some places, make at least five dollars a night. And we got Friday, Saturday, and Sunday nights." So I said, "All right, sounds right to me." And I made enough money to send my mother money every week; she was a widow.

Was Foggy Bottom in Ada?

Ada, yeah. We went out in western Oklahoma and then I wound up in west Texas. He had an old car, and that car quit on him. He didn't have nothing but a little old suitcase to carry, and I had a few little old clothes and my guitar, and we would catch the bus and get into a town. As the boys would say, "Then go across the tracks. You'll find everybody who look like you." So we did pretty good. But my mother was kind of sickly, and it wasn't long before I came down there. Martin, he stayed with the grandparents. And I got me a pretty good job, and I got to thinking about getting married and I went back to Oklahoma and married Adena in 1939 in Oklahoma. I put my age up a little bit. I had one child with her, my first boy. Lowell Fulson, Jr.

How long did you stay with Texas Alexander?

About three–four months. I didn't stay long. Just a summer. When the winter comes, you aren't out there doing that. Not as cold as it gets in west Texas. You do the summer and spring. I just did one season with Texas Alexander.

Was Texas Alexander a hard guy to second behind?

No. He had it together. He would remind you of them old Baptist hymns people used to sing down there. Texas didn't have no guitar player with him. He just had that woman with him going as Bessie Smith and which I never did see her. I seen her pictures and she looked like the woman, all right. She could sing good. Tex had her with him. She didn't stay long. The time was going to be pretty rough out there, especially for a woman if you going through the type of one-night stands we was doing, you know.

Was Texas Alexander an easy man to be with?

Oh, yeah. He never talked to you, though, less'n you talked, 'cause we'd just go miles and miles, wouldn't say a word. 'Cause I wasn't no talker and he wasn't either.

A lot of miles between those towns out there.

Yeah. We'd go sometimes a day, half a day, depending on how he's traveling, how fast he was traveling.

Did he have actual bookings or did you just go from town to town and play wherever you could?

Just play wherever you could. No advance notice or nothing. Little town would be so small to when he come in sometime like this time [late afternoon], and start to singing in some of them juke joint places. He just go in and look around, and if things looked all right to him he'd start to singing. I had an old guitar like that, and we would just start strumming off, and the first thing you know, it's all over town and out in the country too. Within a couple of hours everybody would know around there.

Did you find his records in these towns? Were they on the jukeboxes?

Some places.

People knew who he was?

They knew who he was. He had one record they didn't forget called the "Boar Hog Grind." They didn't forget that. They pulled him off the air for that. I don't know why they wanna do him like that if RCA, which was Belltone, he was on, they the ones released it. They shouldn't jump all over the man if he get a few dollars to play the thing, well, he's going on and play the thing. He didn't know nothing about recording. He didn't care. They slapped it to him, a fine that he would never be able to pay. He had out a lot of records—he had out quite a few records, but he mostly would sing the stuff that would be happening on the plantations and in what they call them foggy bottoms and all them lowland places down in east Texas. He wouldn't play in Houston, stop in the big cities, or Beaumont. He'd go way down there to College Station or some towns I can't remember the names of but they was rural towns, you know. Just really country towns.

Was he in his forties, do you think, at the time that you were with him?

I would guess that. I'd guess that, because I was like 19 or 20, and he's old enough for my old man, you know. But he was a cool-living guy. He didn't drink, gamble, shoot dice, or nothing like that. Everybody knew Texas. They knew him by his singing, you know, and he wasn't a set-down man. He was a traveling man. He'd catch the Greyhound bus, just go to different cities and play, you know, and during that time they had cotton pickers. Maybe two or three truck loads of people would go from one farm to the other and pick cotton. Well, he didn't pick the cotton, but he would meet them because he sang the blues. They'd get in at night, you know. That's how I got to Altus, was with him. That's way out in western Oklahoma. I had never been 'cause I hadn't never been nowhere.

You've been to Sheffield, England. That is somewhere that Texas Alexander never got.

No, he would not have made it there. But if he had been living, he'd a been competition to a lot of them guys like Hooker and Lightnin' Hopkins. He'd a been in the middle of them guys.

Would people request songs or did he just have his own particular group of songs?

They would ask him to play some Blind Lemon Jefferson stuff.

He had to pick some in that style?

Yeah. I didn't particularly care about trying to play guitar behind him because they'd all change keys before time. They never would finish out a sentence. [*Sings "Ain't no more sweet potatoes/frost done killed the vine/Well the blues ain't nothing/but a good girl on your mind"*]. Now that's the end of that, but to me I'm in the half of that song. I'm playing 12-bar chords. I'm just halfway. And I got to skip all of this to catch up with him until I got used to what he was gonna do. Then when he got to that part, I'd just start on another verse, you know. Had it down and figured out it was 8-bar blues, was what that man was singing. But it had a good tone to it. It sound good. Yeah, it sound good, but trying to play it, you know . . .

Lonnie Johnson recorded with him, and he said it was like doing a week's work in a day if you worked with Texas Alexander.

Yeah. That was educational. That was a lot of work. But like if you would sing a song and you once sung it on a 12-bar blues style, he would sing it like that. He could sing it like you sung it. But if he was going to make it up hisself, he'd end it on an 8-bar. He just said two or three words and he's through with it and he ready to start on another something else. He would be telling his story his way in the songs, I guess.

When you got married to your first wife, where did you settle?

I went to Texas. I could make more money in Texas than I could in Oklahoma. Gainesville, north Texas. Close to the border of Oklahoma, 78 miles from the Oklahoma state line. I went to washing dishes. And I washed dishes—I wasn't a lazy man. If my job was washing dishes, I go in there and see something that needed turning over, a hotcake or bacon, I'd get the thing turned over. A boy named Billiken, he was the chef-cook, and he seen that I was paying attention, and he went to showing me about different things. And first thing you know I was preparing breakfast for the restaurant. I was what they called the breakfast man, get there early, early, early. I stayed there until I got drafted. I was 19 or 20.

What years were you in the service?

September 9, 1943, to December 5, 1945. Same thing—they got me out of a kitchen down there in Texas, and they put me in the kitchen when they put me in the service. They put me in the service with those stewards and bakers. And I did a little packing-house work in there. I didn't mention that I cut meat in Ada, because we were talking about music. I learned to cut meat. I was a pretty good butcher. I take a bone out of a chicken and the chicken still hold and all that stuff. I don't know if I could do that now or not. And I'd bone a chicken, bone a ham, whatever.

When I went into service, they'd get your record. I was in boot camp, when I got out of boot camp, which was Cambridge, Maryland, '43, they sent me to Oakland, all 400–500 of us. When we broke boot camp we went to California, and so they needed some cooks and stewards and things at the bachelor officers' quarters in Oakland, so they looked at my record and they seen that I had a variety of things that I do in the kitchen. They sent me there, me and about three more guys, and they had our job picked out for us. I didn't mind what it was, but getting rates, and I asked 'em, "Man, what can I do to get out of this uniform?" The Navy had them little ol' collars and the cap. and I didn't like that. So they say, "You want to get your blue jacket manual, then go up for a rating." And I did. I got that blue jacket manual, and went to my chief and he said, "Yeah, I think you're ready, Fulson. You been doing a good job, you haven't been late. When you do things, extra things, all that's good."

So I went up and I made my 3rd Class. And the price went up. I'm looking for the pay and the uniform. They bought me my first round of uniform. They give you a slip, I think it was $250 and a suit of clothes, cap, everything that the officers wore. We'd wear that but we'd have our insignia on it, but we wore the suit just like the officers. I like that; it was pretty good. Break my cap down, like General MacArthur. Some regulation stuff in there, you know. Those boys helped me pretty good 'cause I kept them woke most of the nights playing my guitar until the lights went out. And I didn't have no trouble. I had fun. I played all through the service—house parties there in San Francisco, they'd come get me. Sometimes they would be lined up at the gate. When I got through cutting meat Friday evening, I didn't have to come back until Monday morning.

Did you go overseas during your time in the service?

I went to Guam. I went over on the *U.S.S. Wayne* in '44. I did a lot of traveling in a short time. May '44 I was out there in the middle of the Pacific. *Wayne* didn't have much. We had 3,000 Marines on there, the last ones, going in there to do the cleanup. And we didn't have much. Little ol' ship sitting out there on that big ocean looked like a thimble in a lake or something. We didn't have no escort. We didn't have no big guns following us. We were bobbling out there and so we got to Hawaii. They figured it was too many mines. We didn't have no business there no way. 21 days I was on Guam, then they transferred me to the *U.S.S. Sparrow*— that was a submarine tender. All the submarines were coming in there and getting whatever they needed on their trip—torpedoes, food, and stuff. They had one called the *Red Fox*. People would say, "Man, I heard your name up there. I think you are going on the *Red Fox*." I say, "No, I don't want that."

So I go and asked the Filipino chief steward, "Whatta you got on the menu for the Captain?" And he said, "Well, he wants chicken, but he wants it baked whole. And a couple of these banties," and I said, "Let me fix them for him." He said, "I don't know about that, Steward, I don't know about that." And I said that I would be responsible for it. Now I talked with authority. You could hear me from here to the corner down there. He said, "You responsible?" and I said, "Say no more." So, man, I got in there and I did my special on him. He said that it looks so good that you can take it out there now. I said, "Not yet." You could smell the aroma from that chicken all over the top deck. Old man wanted to know, who cooked this? Well, he was glad to say I did, because he wouldn't get chewed out for it if there was something wrong. That old man, boy, he said, "Bring him here." He come got me and, "Where'd you learn to cook like this?" I say, in Oklahoma. I answered real fast, Oklahoma. He looked at me and said, "I think I'm gonna send you up to Admiral Lockett. Let you take this hut over. Think you can run it?" "Yes sir."

So they transferred me over there, and I missed that little ol' submarine that they were going to send me out on. That's what I was trying to get off! I wanted some more responsibility. I had my guitar and amplifier, I took that with me. And I got settled in and I relieved the chief. I was second class then. They'd say, "You done got three raises since you got in here, and you haven't even been in here a year." They offered me a chance to chef, but I didn't want to do that because I was playing pretty good and they give me six men who could play horns, and we went playing for the villages in and around Guam to give them some recreation. Then they would take and give them beer cards, and they was happy. And then Miss Lemon, she was the head Red Cross nurse, she'd be going down to Fleets Landing and the captain would say, "Take Lowell and his group down there. Give them entertainment."

When you were traveling around playing, did you teach these people songs?

They were better musicians than I was, see. I had one black boy playing with me, playing piano. So I would mold the white boys in with the black boy on my rhythm. And two or three times we would rehearse and two or three times they were playing rhythm just as good or better than anybody that I've seen. There was one little boy out of Boston. He could blow a horn. Then I was singing songs, Louis Jordan stuff, "Caldonia," and T-Bone Walker's "Bobby Sox Baby." I guess that's why I learned a little of this and a little of that. When you stop playing, you'd play the blues, you go with the Lightnin' Hopkins type music. And when then you get with your band, you have to switch off to more modern type music.

What kind of songs did you play for the soldiers on Guam?

I mixed it together. Some of the songs I sung with Dan Wright. I fared better throwing in a little country-western with it, mix that stuff up with Dan Wright stuff, "Beer Barrel Polka," "Silvery Moon," and "Tennessee Waltz." And the band was right in there. If I wanted to play "Caldonia," they were right there. I didn't sing none of Texas' songs. Not over there.

Miss Lemon would say, "Keep it jolly. They need to laugh—that is what I came for." "I ain't no comedian." She'd say, "You're doing fine." Boy, they sure was after me to ship over and stay. But see, I'd have had to take two or three years. I couldn't ship over for no one year. I said, "I'm going back to California and cut me a record." That is the only time that it ever really hit me that I was good enough to cut a record. Just mix all your stuff together and get you a style of your own, which you already have. 'Cause "Nobody played like you"—that's what the guys would be saying. I'd say, "Is that good or bad?" And they'd say, "I don't know, Fulson, but you sticks out more than anybody." And I said, "Well, great."

In October 1945, I was eligible for 44 points. I was ready for being discharged. But I am 6,783 miles from San Diego to Guam. I am way over there and they say, "Well, Fulson, you can get out now." I say, "When can I go?" They say, "We'll let you know when the ship comes in." I guess that was the longest two weeks. It took me two weeks to get a ship, get out from over there. We had an aircraft carrier coming back. They wasn't loaded. They were going back. They taken a bunch of us back to the States, and I was in the bunch. So after we got rolling, we were rolling pretty good. We rolled into the Great Lakes, and I got a train out of there. It took me longer to get from Great Lakes to Oklahoma than it did to come from Guam to the States.

But, anyway, I didn't tell you about my sideline, I'll tell you about that in a minute. Because I come back with more money than I went with. I let them play a little poker, and I cut the games. We had that going, and it was my money and I got to clean up after them in the barracks. And I had about $600 worth of change. And I didn't know that I had that much, because I'd just throw it in the foot locker, you know, just put my clothes on it. I ain't got enough time to be sitting in there countin' money. And I had all of that in there, and I'd be all worried, saying, "Where's my foot locker?" "Oh, it'll get there." And I finally got in to Oklahoma, to Norman. That is when I got mustered out. And I got paid. And they wanted my guitar and amplifier to put in the library. That is how they got their instruments, from different guys who played. They would leave their stuff, and if something would happen to one they would get their stuff and put it in the library. And they would issue it out to you; you couldn't leave with it.

So I got home and I had to sit around there. That's when I start working at this hotel [the Wade Hotel in Duncan, Oklahoma]. I sat around there for about a month. So you are always jealous when you come back—that's why there are so many divorces, because if you had a wife when you left, you didn't know if you had one when you got back or not. So I told my wife, said, "I'm going to California in a few months. I'll let you know when I get there." She said, "You always talking about going to California. Nobody knows you in California." I said, "They will when I get there."

So I got a job down in this cafe. I just went in there and went to work for $35 a week. They thought that was big dollars, and I did too. And my foot locker finally come in. It caught up with me. I said, "All right!" I said, "I'm not broke by a long shot." I give her some money, but didn't let her know what all I had in there. Wasn't none of her business. Said, "If you run through this, I'll just have to send for you." So that was around May, the spring of the year. So I worked up there about six months, pretty close, I go back out to California, and for two or three weeks I didn't know nobody. But I played there during the service, playing on street corners and police running me off, you know. So we went to playing parties up there. I got acquainted with those people, but I didn't know where they were at.

So I heard some music, and I knew what part of Oakland I was in, 7th Street. Maybe about the middle of the afternoon I heard music, and I followed the music, went on around there, and boy, there was Bob Geddins. So I said, that man looks familiar. He had promised me a record session. If I get out, come back. I didn't know if I was comin' back or not, so I throwed it out of my mind. But as you stand up there and look at this man, pressin' them records, things begin to come to you, you know. So there was an old guitar sittin' over in the corner. I picked it up, sat down, started messin' around with it, so he cuts the machine off. "Sing that again!" He talked through his nose, Bob Geddins. I did, so he said, "You want to make a record? You ever made a record?" I said, "Naw." He said, "You want to make one?" I said, "Yeah." He said, "You got that song finished?" I said, "Sure." "You got any more?" "Yeah." I was making them up as I go [chuckles]. "I got $100, you go over there and cut this record, I'd give you $100." I said, "Let's go." I went over there and cut "Three O'Clock in the Morning," and what else did I cut? "Miss Katie Lee," or something like that, I think it was.

I had to send and get my brother—see, we played together. He was in Florida.

They wouldn't put us together in the service 'cause we was too tight. One in the Atlantic and another in the Pacific. So I sent to get Martin. I said, "You come home now, man!" Bob Geddins was waiting. So we got there, Martin and I did, so I bought a Holiness preacher's guitar I had met, and he wanted to learn it. He didn't know nothing about it. He got it somewhere, but he wanted to learn it. He was one of those guys that couldn't learn. He couldn't get it. I said, "You want to play before you learn." But I cut my records with his guitar. So Bob had an old guitar, and he give that to Martin. And me and Martin cut three or four records together.

So I gets in from one of my evenings out with the boys, 'cause I'm staying with my stepdad, 'cause my mother had passed. The one who fathered the last two kids Mama had, I was staying with him. He was a farm man. He didn't know nothin' about no city work. I don't think there was anything he could do unless it was building something or tearing something down. Anyway, me and him and Martin, we stayed together. I still got that $100 in my pocket, burning a hole in it. So the government give me a house in Oakland, two-bedroom house out there. I say, my wife will be out here, she was on her way. I didn't know when. So anyway, I had got the house. People liked what I was singing; boy, they would just be gathered 'round me. I said, "Are we as good as they think we are?" Martin said, "Naw!" He was point-blank spoken. So I gets in one of them evenings, and who's sitting up in the house but Adena. Ain't say she was comin', but I was pretty smart—I wasn't a dumb dude. Everything was cleaned up for her. She was worse than I was when I came from overseas. She was checking around there, looking.

She thought you had a girlfriend hiding under the . . . ?

Yeah, she thought one had been there at least. Visiting or something. But I had too much room out there to be crowded up here. I started organizing me a group. I told Martin, organize me a group—just four guys, and I think we can do better. And he said, "You get the four guys, and I'll do the managing 'cause I ain't gonna play." I said, "You'll play if I need you?" He said, "Yeah." And I got me a band. Big Dad on bass. Eldridge McCarthy on piano. Who did I have on drums? I forgot now.

Were there a lot of clubs to play in?

No. Wasn't a whole lot of clubs where you would be recognized and make any money. So we'd go to places like Richmond. There were a bunch of country people. Them little country towns. Vallejo, Richmond, Rodeo. And in San Francisco, we had a lot of work over there too. Out of Double Rock Road and Redwood City and all of that. In Frisco they play downtown.

Tell us about Minnie Lou's Club in Richmond.

She didn't have no club when I first met her. I first played for a lady called Granny. I never did know Granny's name. But she is the one who had the Club Savoy then. But it wasn't Minnie Lou. Minnie Lou had a eat shop there. Specialized in all kinds of food. Well, it was next door to each other. Step out of one and step into the other. But they linked me to Minnie Lou, but it wasn't Minnie Lou I worked for, it was Granny. I started off at $10 a night and went up to $20 a night. That was around like '47, '48. That was when I went back and cut another record. I cut "Black Widow Spider Blues." Like to have jumped off too, if Bob Geddins had had any kind of record distribution like a lot of people, but he didn't trust nobody. He pressed his own records and everything. He wouldn't let nobody press them, thinking they were going to steal some: "They ain't gonna do none of that press ten for me and two for them. Before you know it, they'll own the place."

So he was a one-man operation?

One-man operation. And I done bought me a car. Next thing I know, Trilon called me and I did a session for them, which was with a full-length band. I wanted a strong rhythm section. And this boy was in school, Earl Brown, the one who blowed on the records, on "Every Day I Have The Blues," "Blue Shadows," he started playing with me. Me and my brother took all the Louis Jordan records we could find. He was 16, and we learned him to blow that, to sound the same, to blow that horn like that man, hold that horn up there. That's blues notes, long notes. So we got him down on that Louis Jordan style of holding them notes on that alto sax.

Who was Que Martyn?

Que Martyn was a Bay Area, semi-jazz and swing, you know. He was pretty well up to date on his music, you know. He figured he could make me sound a little better with his band if I trained. Which I put me in training—everything I would hear, if I couldn't play it, I'd learn it, you know. Que and I did some songs together. I think it was on the Trilon label ["Tryin' to Find My Baby"/"Let's Throw a Boogie Woogie"]. And they wanted to see if they could modernize Lowell, so we did the session all right, and it came out fair, far as I can remember. He was satisfied with me, throwed me a little money, and Que Martyn was one of the first black bands that went to Hawaii.

So then Jack Lauderdale [of Swing Time Records] came up there in 1948 and he wanted me to cut a record. I told him, "I don't know." He gave me his address and everything. And he said to come down, if I needed any money or anything. Well, "Three O'Clock in the Morning" ["Three O'Clock Blues," on Down Town] was selling so good. But the "Black Widow Spider Blues" really took off. I had more pieces. My wife wanted me to quit. We only had $300–400 in the bank, something like that. The girls were making a lot of noise. But if the womenfolk don't make no noise during one of your gigs, you don't have no gigs. You don't have no job long. The women makes the things happen. I had that little room just full of ladies. There'd be very few men, but a lot of womenfolk. So Granny liked that. She say, "I can make money with you. I'll give you a little raise—don't leave." Three nights a week, that was $60, and working in that shipyard, decommissioning them ships, it took me a month to make $60. And I'm making $60 a night just to sing every weekend.

It didn't take you long to figure out which was the better deal.

Yeah, going out there cold every morning. I quit, and Adena quit me. I didn't care. I wasn't going back out there. I'm going to Los Angeles and cut that hit record. I had "Every Day I Have the Blues" [on Swing Time]. Memphis Slim had "Nobody Loves Me," and the other side was "Angel Child." I didn't like "Angel Child," but I changed just one or two words. And I released it, got me a hit record out of it. And I went down and told her, but she didn't want to pay no attention. Me and Martin come on down here and cut that record. I cut "Sinner's Prayer" [on Swing Time]. I said, "I am going to bring my alto horn." Jack said, "Man, we got a million horn players." I said, "But you don't have none like this one." So he sent up and got him. Earl got on a bus, come on down there with his horn. And me and Lloyd Glenn, Billy Hadnott, Bob Harvey, we all got together, and I said, "Now I want you to put this smooth." So I sung it for them, and after a while Lloyd kind of tinkled on the piano. We went on and cut it, and it was a hit. But I didn't have nothin' worth a dime to go with it. So Lloyd Glenn sat down there and cut him an instrumental called "Old-Time Shuffle." So we put that on the other side of "Sinner's Prayer" until I could get another record. So we left that instrumental on one side. But I couldn't play the guitar in the modern style the way he was playing it well enough to put a solo in there. So they got Big Tiny Webb to put the guitar solo in there. He was kind of a jazz, blues-jazz guitar player. So I thought that was all right, long as it's a hit.

So you settled in Los Angeles then?

Yeah, but I just had to go back to Vallejo and show Adena what a mistake she had made throwing me out. 'Cause I had bought me a brand new Buick, '49. Metallic green, white khaki top. Laid all back. She quit the wrong man. "Whose car you done borrowed?" she said. I said, "Look on the steering wheel—it will tell you." Ownership slip have my name, you know.

So I moved down here. It wasn't too long before them booking agents had me on the road. About two or three months. After I got down there and cut that record, things going pretty good. And I go back in the studio, and they say, "We better get this before you leave because, boy, they get you out there and you never get back here, not with your group. So I say, "Good idea." So I cut "Blue Shadows" and "Lonesome Christmas, Part One and Two." So we left, 'cause they had that "Blue Shadows" for me to fall back on during the December months, from Thanksgiving on up. The Christmas things were going. They went big for years.

What was it like in Los Angeles as opposed to the Bay Area?

More countrified. Big ol' country town. San Francisco was more hip, sharp. Oakland was kind of country too. But in Los Angeles you'd get one street. Oakland had 7th Street, Frisco had Fillmore Street, and this town had Central Avenue. So you had to work off the main street, and you didn't go in another part of the city. You didn't have no reason to. You didn't live out there, you didn't have a job out there.

You didn't play in the clubs much around Los Angeles? You went right out on the road?

Well, I was too busy getting songs together and writing. And the record hit mostly in rural districts before it got to the city. So I played one club here, me and Smokey Hogg, and people didn't like him very much.

Did they think he was too country?

Yeah, they didn't like him. Not at that club. He sang silly stuff. "Possum up the simmon tree, polecat on the ground." He says, "Possum made a pass at the polecat, and they both went around and around." And stuff like that. They didn't like that. They'd say, "Get him off of the stage!" And they meant it. They had to take him off of the stage. And I had to play, and I ain't got but four songs that I could call and play 'cause I cut a lot of folk blues, and most of that stuff for Bob Geddins, you know, Big Town. But anyway, we played that. And my going-away dance was at the Paragon Ballroom then. Me and Bullmoose Jackson. He had out "Yes I Do." [*Sings "I love you, yes I do."*] Then we went on downtown and got uniforms, stage clothes, you know. So I bought me a station wagon, and I had my convertible. And I made my first tour like that. Me and Count [Carson] and that little Earl Brown, he had got a couple of years older. Year and a half. His mama said, "You take good care of my son, now." Treated him like he was my own.

Where did you tour that first time?

Oklahoma and Texas. Right back to Houston.

What other artists were on the scene?

My first tour during 1950 we ran into T-Bone Walker. He thought he owned Texas. And he just about did with that guitar and his style of playing. And there was Big Joe Turner and his group, Ivory Joe Hunter. The guys, we called it bumpin' heads. They would put us together, and they started making up those packages and putting three or four acts together, called the Big Show.

Did you work with Ivory Joe Hunter?

Yeah, we played a few spots, not a lot of spots. See, I had a pretty hot band after about a year on the road. I had about 10–12 pieces, and they were ready. There weren't that many large bands for the group singers to go out with. So they had the Moonglows and the Dominoes, Orioles. So when they sent me in the Apollo in '51, I come out, they went to putting the stars with my band. Everybody [sight] reads in the band, all except the band leader.

So they used your band to back up all the other groups?

So I got a lot of gigs that I probably wouldn't have gotten by myself. Even the Apollo Theater, even with one hit record. With one-and-a-half hit. But that band was good. Old Stanley Turrentine, and I kept Floyd Montgomery on bass, but I finally pulled him off and got a different bass, a different drums, and made the music modern, but swingin', you know. The onliest blues you would hear was when I went onstage. Even when I wasn't hauling the group singers, I could put myself where I wanted to, 'cause it was my band. But it happened that I was the type of guy who didn't like closing shows. And I don't care about that now, being the star of the show. I just want to give a good show whenever I get up there. I'd get up there, and the band would play, and then they would bring me up. And I'd do my little ol' thing and get completely out of the way.

Ray Charles and Turrentine, they worked together to put out the music charts. We didn't have no trouble. When I got to the Apollo is where Ray, being blind, that old man didn't want to take him. I said, "You have to take him because he is part of my band." He said, "Yeah, but he can't see." I said, "Well, he played that other stuff, didn't he?" Said, "Yeah." "Well, he can play yours." And Ray, he'd write it out in Braille and read it off to Stanley Turrentine. And then Turrentine would get it on paper for the rest of the group. Everything was to the minute. He was the most perfect man I have ever seen. And we were playing songs like "One O'Clock Jump," "Hazel Street Bounce," "35/30," and regular swing stuff you got in the late '40s. And they liked that. That went over pretty good. And then I'm through. Slip 'em to the group singers.

But on that first tour in 1951, it was just you and Earl and a drummer?

Five pieces. One horn was Earl Brown. No, I didn't have a rhythm guitar. I had four pieces. Alto, bass, piano, and drums. Very dull for the type audience I played. Boy played upright bass and no rhythm guitar, and I played rhythm and lead when it was my time onstage. But when the band was up there and they had to entertain the people, it was kind of weak 'cause the house was a big place, was full. But when I got back to California, I had ten pieces.

You had hired them on the road?

On the road. Yeah. Had guys from Pittsburgh. Stanley Turrentine and Billy Brooks and Lucky Nuble, out of Ohio, and Frank Ford out of Detroit, and the other trumpet player out of Virginia. I had two trumpets, alto, tenor, baritone. And that's what I kept till the Korean War snatched up two or three of my men. I wouldn't go through there to try to rebuild. But we was hot then, boy. We would rehearse every day and play the clubs that night. You'd think we just got together. And Ray would be writing that stuff down, you know.

You knew B.B. King when he was a DJ in Memphis?

Yeah, I met him.

He gave you some help when he was a DJ and you had given him, or somehow he had gotten, some of your publishing?

Well, that "Three O'Clock in the Morning Blues," I gave that to him to record. Well, one reason why, I didn't think he could sing that good, because I hadn't heard him singing. And he asked for it. I said, "You can go on. You can have it." Because the man I cut it for wasn't doing anything, just laying up there. And I cut it and it didn't do anything, 'cause he didn't have no distribution. Nobody knowed it but the people I know, and I don't know how he got anybody to find out about it. But I played at the Hippodrome down in Memphis, and it took me two days to get all the people in there. I had to stay over another day. B.B. was telling me about, "Peoples laughing at your music, but you the onliest one that ever been here to fill up this place and have to stay over another day to do it again. I pat my own self on the back 'cause I laid on your records." I said, "Well, now, glad to know that, man. Thank you very much." He said, "But tell you what you can do, you can let me do that 'Three O'Clock in the Morning.'" "Why sure, do the song."

Guy down there in Memphis named Papa Henry. He grabbed all up-and-coming musicians, you know. And I don't know what he, Papa, what he thought he'd get out of it. Anyway, he learned me how to come onstage. I never worked a theater.

What did he do?

Well, he would just say, "You just walk out there like you going to the bathroom or somewhere," he said. "Like you don't particularly care about coming onstage." He said, "We got to work on your attitude. Walk up a little fast. Be lively, smile." That was the hardest thing for me to do was, I call it, grinnin'. I would be think-ing about what I had to do, and all them people sitting out there looking. I didn't know whether I was gonna get run off the stage or not. I never did like theaters and shows to play, you know. It's a different atmosphere that you have when you walk out there. And you can hear a pin fall. Oh boy, I look back and Papa's saying, "Get on out there."

Did Lloyd Glenn go out on the road with you, or did he just record with you in L.A.?

He just recorded. See, he had kids in high school, and he was trying to get them ready for college and all that. He was a family man, and he had a nice-size family. And they were big kids. Big enough to need their daddy. So he stayed. That the reason Ray Charles and I got together.

Ray Charles would be on the road with you, but Lloyd would do the sessions?

Do the session, even when we were here in Los Angeles.

How did you come to record for Aladdin in New Orleans in 1953?

We never did have a contract. We just did a session. Cut some sides, but there wasn't no contract. I wasn't what you call with them, but I put some material with them.

Was that with your own band, or did they have a band there?

I had a band there. I used Guitar Slim for it, Lloyd Lambert.

How did you meet Joe Turner?

We was together at the Oakland Auditorium on the same bill, and that is how I met Joe. And we worked together ever since then. And they even toured us together more than a bunch of times. They would seem to think that our two styles of music went together for the public. I open it up; he close it down. So that suit me just fine. And I liked him. He would work with my band 'cause he didn't have no band. Had his Cadillac, driver, and valet, that was about it.

What do you remember about Pee Wee Crayton?

Me and Pee Wee go back a long time. When I first recorded, started in Oakland, he was up there at Slim Jenkins', and I'm trying to get a record. I had a record, but it wouldn't fit in Slim Jenkins' night club. It was the wrong type of music. He wanted more like the T-Bone Walkers, the Ivory Joe Hunters. Pee Wee and T-Bone sounded quite a bit alike, and I'm playing like Lightnin' Hopkins. I went struttin' in there one time. I was going to sit in on a jam session. So we got up there and Pee Wee says, "Lowell, if you are going to sit in with these guys, I think if it was me, now, I'd go back to school and learn a little more, and then come back 'cause these cats is pretty heavy." I thanked him for that advice. I said, "That is good. I think I will 'cause these guys is pretty sharp." So I sit around and listen all evening. "Come on, we play with you." I said, "No." My "Three O'Clock in the Morning" and my "Miss Katie Lee" and my "Black Widow Spider Blues" ain't going to fit this thing. So we didn't talk no more for a good while then.

He came out with "Texas Hop," and I put out a few things and I got my own band together. But I never did play for Slim. I didn't like the club. I didn't like the stars. I didn't like the attitudes. But I went right across the street to the Orbit Room. More cozy, but it didn't have the names Slim did. Well, I never did care to play there for a bunch of over-dressed, what you call them, snotty-nose people. When you first go out, they screen you to see what you was wearing. Well, I always was well-dressed. I watched the styles.

I come out with a couple hit records and I run into Pee Wee again, and I said, "Do you think I could make it into Slim Jenkins' now, Pee Wee?" He said, "The money you making, you could make it in there, but they ain't going to pay what you making." I said, "I ain't making all that much." I said, "How you know I'm making the money out here?" And about that time we put on a show out there in Oakland at the City Auditorium. Lowell Fulson and Big Joe Turner. And Pee Wee, he was still playing local at Slim's. He had a tour and went on the road somewhere. I don't know how Pee Wee came out on it. He was such a nice fellow. Always a nice guy. And he'd be trying to help you, you know, all he could. And he'd be more careful about playing a rhythm for you as you would play for yourself. Jump right up there and play that rhythm.

You had a heap of guitar players going around you then.

Yeah. Saunders King and Pee Wee Crayton and a lot of guys I didn't even get to know their names well enough. Back in them times people wouldn't pay to go see it. The other rural blues, some called it country blues. They wouldn't pay for that. But, it is a funny thing, they made more money than the guys doin' what we did, because they get one guitar set up and play that stuff all night and them white folks were eating it up, 'cause they wanted the real old blues that we started from, and we was playing in between, you know.

Tell us about "Reconsider Baby," which came out on Checker. You cut it for Chess, but it wasn't in Chicago at Chess.

No. Well, I couldn't find the musicians that I really wanted on the record, to be frank. I couldn't find my type of musician there at Chess. They had good musicians, but for themselves. And the type of music I played, they would play the changes, but that would be all. It was just different. We didn't fit together. So I'm playing in Texas with seven pieces. So when I would do a tour for Howard Lewis, we would go to Texas. So I told Howard, I said, "You get me a band." He said, "I got just the band for you." So we went down there and we rehearsed and went out on the road a week, ten days, something like that, come back in, everybody was happy. Things went well. So I said, "Could we do a session?" He says, "Yeah." So I said, "I don't have but one record. I may think of something else, but I just want to get this one down before I get to Chess, and I won't recognize it the next time I hear it." I said, "Let me see if I can get the Chess brothers together." So I called Leonard up, and Phil answered the phone. So I told Phil. He said, "Why don't you talk to my brother about it. To me that's a good idea, but you know how he is." Leonard said, "You got something?" I said, "Yeah, I got something." "Well, bring it on in, we'll cut it." I said, "No, this'n don't go like that. I want to cut it here. I got the band and everything." He said, "We got just as good a band." I said, "Not for this." I said, "We need boys done got acquainted. Now I don't want these strangers up there. I done went to a lot of trouble to write this thing and I don't want it messed up. I want it cut just like I want it cut."

He said, "Okay. Go in there and cut it. I'll call a studio." They called Studio Seven [in Dallas], and he said, "I'll have Stan Lewis to take care of the financial things." I said, "What, you think I'll take your money and go and spree with it and won't pay the band?" "Oh no, I didn't say that. See how you are talking, mother." That was Leonard's word. Sly way of cussin'. I said, "I want to do this thing tomorrow." So he set it up, and we went and rehearsed that evening, and I said, "I think we've got that thing just right." I had David Newman on tenor. I had Leroy Cooper on baritone. Worm on alto.

So anyway, I cut it, and Leonard said, "Look here, mother, let me tell you something. It better be something good, 'cause don't you be recording out of Chicago." I said, "Well, I'm already out of Chicago." "Just don't come back." We laughed about it. I forgot all about it 'cause I was satisfied. I done cut it. So in about two or three weeks they rushed it. No sooner they heard it than they went to work. They put it right on the masters. He said, "I think you got one." I said, "What I got?" Phil said, "Oh, you know, you done got you a hit." I said, "If you say so. You think it's a pretty good record?" He said, "It's going places." He said, "See if you can cough up a couple more of them, Fulson." I said, "How you think I'm gettin' them?"

I'd be fishing, me and my Coleman light down there. Wasn't nobody but me. So I would pull off my shoes. Had me a long cord string. I'd bait it down good. Throw it out in the water and I'd take the end of the cord and tie it around my toe, forget all about it, and fell asleep then. I would feel something shaking on my toe, and I said, "I got one!" I reached to get it and two or three big ol' catfish be on there. I don't do that no more. If one of them buffaloes had swallowed a catfish, then I'd have had to swim that big ol' river.

So you would get some of your inspiration when you were out fishing?

Yeah, you can get by yourself. If you do the things that you like doing, and then it's not no lot of people involved to attract your attention. I'd get out and fish every once in a while. Martin say, "Man, where you been?" I'd say, "Man, I been down there fishing." Then I'd say, "Man, I got that tune finished. I got to go in the studio now." He say, "Well, you finally finished it, huh?" I say, "Yeah." The melody, I got the songs. How was I going to play the guitar? How are you going to play the melody? What you going to say on it? You got your words all rhymed up? Your story's good. Now, how are you going to present it? Now, that is the problem. And I got that together. And that is how "Reconsider" was born.

Did you continue to just produce songs and send them back to Chess from wherever you were? Or did you finally go on and record in Chicago?

I did go on and record in Chicago, because Ray Charles done got out and took my band. He took the whole band from me, took all the boys.

When was that?

It was about '53–'55. Somewhere along in there. He had David Newman— Fathead—all of them, Cooper. The Fisher brothers. One bass and one drums. He had just about all them guys.

So you went to Chicago and recorded for Chess?

I went on and got with Otis Spann, and we sat down and talked and I'm seeing if I can get back to the ground floor and do like me and Lloyd Glenn did. He could play it, but he didn't have the imagination, see, towards my stuff, like Lloyd did. He'd lean part of the way, but I guess that he'd played for so many different people on different sessions until he had mixed emotions about some of my stuff on some sections. But he was a good piano player.

You did one session for Chess in Chicago with the Chess band, then you came back to L.A. and did some more tunes that were sent back to Chess and put out from there.

Yeah, I forgot about that.

And they were okay with that once you had the one hit with "Reconsider Baby"?

Yeah. Well, see, they used to do a lot of work, United Distributors, for Swing Time Records when I first started out over there. So as far as the music was concerned, I wasn't a stranger to them: "How can I get out of him what Jack Lauderdale got out of him on Swing Time?" But it wasn't so much as just I was lucky enough to get the band to blend in and kind of think my way. I got it here [*taps his head*], but I can't express it. I can't put it down on the paper, so I would be stuck with it. So a lot of times I would just get down there and put it on like that after I had seen a few mistakes made. But they kind of laid down on me a little bit on promotion.

Chess?

Yeah, Leonard was getting sick, you know. We tried some things, but I couldn't do that. Willie Dixon, those songs, I couldn't sing it. Not the way he wanted them. "Tolling Bells," I hate that thing. Oh boy, I hate that with a passion. If they'd have edited it, I could've got by some stuff. But they just put it out like I said on there, they left curse notes in there that I was using, the profanity. 'Cause I was saying pretty good. And for the key raise that he wanted to do, that throwed me too far away from baritone, and you go to screaming instead of singing. I am not a screamer. I do good to stay in the range of talking. 'Cause I am not one of them good singers, them boys with the old pretty voices and stuff. You got to do what you can with what you got to do it with. You don't try to be something that you're not. It's not a bad song. I'm singing it in the wrong key, so I can get way up there and get a preacher type thing singing. But they couldn't play it. I say, "Can't you follow me?" I said, "Follow me!" I said, "I'm making the chords, don't make nary a one until you hear me make one if we are going to mechanical this thing." When I think about that I get angry.

How did you come to sign with Kent in the mid 1960s?

Fats Washington introduced me to them. They had not paid me too much attention because B.B. made such a good swing for 'em until they kind of gave up hopes a little bit when B. left and went to another company. I think they just taken me because they really didn't have nothing else much going. And they figured since I already had a couple of pretty good records, they figured they had a chance on getting back. Which I did cut a hit for them. I got 'em a hit while I was there, and a good seller ["Tramp"].

That was a big record.

It's a funny thing. You talk with them guys, if you're right in the neighborhood and you can be around them sometimes, it helps. Sometimes it doesn't. But they backed off the promotion. I say, to get the record, you got to get it heard. And it may not catch on the first time around; some take a little more than others. I said, "You done made a little money on the thing, why don't you take some of it and put it back in this thing here?" "Black Nights" come to the verge of being a good record. But he sat down on the promotion. I said, "That's the reason y'all ain't got nobody. That's the reason why B.B. left." He wouldn't never say nothing to me. He would get that old cigar in his mouth and go on in the other room, old Jules Bihari.

Now, Saul Bihari, he died then, and I couldn't do nothing with Jules. Now Saul would listen, and he would give it a try, if I talked to him. And you show him to the point that you are the same guy that cut that other hit. Why can't we do this one, if you do like I ask him to do? Just let them play the records. Spend a few extra dollars and promote the thing, put somebody out there. "These promotion men aren't no good. They don't do nothing but run around and run up the expense on you." I would say, "Man, get on this one. We've got another one, and we can make enough money to cover this one. We can go with this one." Say, "Good idea, Lowell," and they'd get on it. If the record made sense enough and sounded good enough.

When you were promoting a hit, would you go around and visit the radio stations?

I wouldn't, no. Sometimes I would be invited. I got invited a lot of times, but I didn't go 'bout taking the job they were supposed to be doing. Because, one thing, I didn't have enough money to make no promises. You made promises that you are going to do this, you gonna do that, when the record get out, and then the man set on you and you can't do nothing. Then the guy's mad at you. So I didn't.

Sometimes we'd meet up at the bar or somewhere, and I would go around where they'd be hanging out. Accidentally on purpose, run into him. Being intending to all the time. Give 'em a good night. "No, man, I got that, I got that [the tab]."

Someone must have done something right in the promotion department because "Tramp" was a big hit.

Oh, he hated "Tramp," Jules did. Paw-Paw out of Birmingham and Bugs Scruggs, San Francisco [DJs]. They all met down there. So I was in there. So when they were talking, I was trying to hear what they were saying. I heard Bugs say, "What you got here on Fulson?" "Oh, he went down there and he cut some junk back there." He said, "Let me hear it." "Okay, but it ain't nothing to it. I wouldn't say nothing about it, but Fulson can do better than that." They played the record, and the man said, "Hush! Man, get me my copy, quick. You sitting on a gold mine, talking about you want to hear some blues. You better get that record out."

And they did, they followed his advice because he was a disc jockey. And so they took them some copies, and they just had a few pressed up, hadn't even thought about putting it out. But after I got with Bugs and Paw-Paw, we laughed and joked and the next thing I know that thing was making plenty of noise. And then Otis Redding jumped all over it, which I didn't mind a bit. But I said, "I wished you had given me another week." He took it right on to the pop field, you know.

I'm sure Kent didn't mind that either.

No, he didn't mind. Went to pay me off and he give me a check on five different days. "The third, you can run this in, the fifteenth, you can put this in, but . . . ." I said, "Just give me my money."

He was giving you postdated checks?

Yeah, postdated checks. They was something else, boy. But what you gonna do?

In general, what was it like getting record royalties?

They don't pay. No. They will run a tab on you to where you wouldn't draw any royalties in this century. They say, "Why it costs so much to cut this, costs so much for promotion." See, I knew better than this. In other words, if you don't get me a hit record, I'll starve to death because you ain't going to give me no royalties because the records won't sell. If I don't get a hit, it ain't going to sell, and if you don't promote it, I ain't going to get no hit. He said, "Oh yeah, we do good promotion. Everybody tell you we good for promotion." I said, "Tell you what you do: You just give me some money. I ain't talking about change, I want some money. And you don't have to promote it, you don't have to sell it. You don't have to do nothing. But if somebody sell it, it will still be me and my stuff." So I taken that attitude. So they call me in for sessions, but they didn't call me in with no bottles or no sweet talk.

You had to have an advance.

Advance money. All I could get. So it was left up to him to recoup his money and do his own promotion.

He had already spent the money, so he better get it back.

Yeah, he was going to want to get it back. So if that is what it takes, well, then he will spend some more money to . . . This is a pretty good item he is messing with, so they'd be satisfied if they could break even. They all said that. If you didn't get your money in personal appearances, you didn't get any.

When Otis Redding cut "Tramp," though, you got songwriter's royalties from his version?
Yeah.

Were some cities harder than others for you to play?
For me, the state of Ohio was the hardest state. Cleveland, Columbus, Cincinnati, Toledo. Yeah, hard for me to get in there. How I got there the first time, Moon Dog [Alan Freed] was in there, and he just broke "Everyday I Have the Blues" in New York. And that's the onliest one I had that they paid any attention to, 'cause Moon Dog liked it and he jumped all over it and then booked me into Cincinnati. I did very well. I played four or five times. The local promoters began to ask for me back.

Where is your favorite audience?
Texas, Oklahoma, Illinois, Kansas, Colorado.

How about Chicago?
Yeah, Chicago was good. And I did good in Florida, but something happened that they depended on one man getting most of the entertainers in my bracket down through there. I don't know whether he passed on or what happened to him, but we didn't have no promoters, less'n you want to drive way down there and play two towns and come back through Georgia and everything. And they had given us a little trouble. You know, here you come with a whole group, policeman call down there, "Where you going with this caravan, boy?" It was just a whole lot of stuff that you take along to keep yourself living [on the road]. It wasn't worth me going down there, so I didn't go back. I could play Louisiana, and come on back into Texas.

But like Mississippi and all them smaller towns in Mississippi, I played a lot of places. I played all over Mississippi. Dan's Playhouse in Biloxi and everything. But you didn't have any trouble if you say, yes sir, no sir, to the policemen when they stopped us. But if you didn't, you just may get jumped on. And I found that out. And I said, "Talk don't bother me." I said, "I'll say anything they want me to say. I come down here for money and get out of here. I don't live here." And I had to tell that man that. 'Cause he started to jump on one of my musicians. So I called him over there, and I said, "You know, he don't have good sense, sir." I said, "He's kind of retarded." He said, "Yeah?" I said, "Yes sir." So he said, "Well, I'm going to give him a little lecture." So he said, "Boy, you know how much it takes for me to kill you? Takes a nickel—that's what this bullet'll cost. And next time you meet an officer, you say yes sir or no sir. If you don't, you may just wind up with one."

That was in Florida?
That was in Mississippi. But you didn't have no trouble as long as you . . . And come to find out they used the same hospitality, yes sir and no sir, to they seniors or they bosses or somebody had a pocket full of money. One time they put me in jail in New Orleans. So I didn't go back to New Orleans after then. That was in the early '60s. No violation, nothing. I just happened to be in the place, Okadokee's Blue Room, after my show. If I'd have went on to the hotel like I usually do, I wouldn't have had no trouble. Well, they were giving me the party, you know, after-party. Me and Big Joe Turner had played down to, I can't think of that big ol' barn. The one-nighters was drawing pretty good, but they put him in there, you know. Now, I mean Joe could fill it up. I had a .25 automatic in my pocket. That's what sent me to

jail. And I am up there with a fresh process, black suit, white camel hair overcoat, you know, gloves. "What is this we got here?" He walked on my overcoat, kicked it all the way down the stairs. "That yours?" "Yes sir." "I'll pick it up." So I asked the captain, I believe it was. He had gold braids on him. So I went and throwed him a sign or two. He said, "Ain't no problem. Get out of here. But you sure don't be walking around with a pistol and you ain't got no permit." I said, "That's my ignorance." I went down there running with what they call "the school."

The guys that lived down there got in more trouble than anybody else and they knew better. Getting knocked down. They knew better than that. Go right upside his head. Jukebox man come down there, he knew the captain. Captain run a make on me, and found out that I was okay. He said, "You can get your gun back." I said, "No. Between where you at, assistant D.A., and where I got to go, they may stop me in between. And I'll be back here with the same thing, no permit." And he laughed. He said, "You know they wouldn't buy that." I knew it. "You can have it—I don't want it." I didn't have no business with it in the first place. More trouble than it's worth.

How did you meet Sadie?

[Guitar] Slim introduced me to her. He was playing here in Los Angeles at the Five-Four. And I just happened to come by. "This is my wife, Lowell. Now that is my wife. Don't mess with my wife." He talked crazy. I said, "She's too little for me. I don't want her. I ain't gonna bother her." He ain't never saw me with nobody that little. So we laughed about it, and he was satisfied. I didn't see Sadie no more until after Slim passed. And then the boy who used to drive for me, he said, "Do you remember this lady?" I said, "No." He brought her to my house. I had an apartment over there. West Los Angeles. And I had Ricky, my boy by Frances. He'd been staying with my stepdaddy in Stockton.

So we got to talking, and I said, "What do you do?" And she said she worked at City Hospital. She and her cousin had an apartment together. I said, "I've been trying to find me a baby-sitter for my boy." She said, "Well, we could keep him." I said, "I tell you what I will do. If y'all want to keep my boy for me"—he was about four—"then I will pay your rent here. You won't have no rent to pay." She said, "Sure, we'll take care of him." So I went and got Ricky and that is how we met, she was baby-sitting for me. They had different shifts. One would go to work, one wouldn't. It worked out just fine. And then she asked me, "I'm keeping your boy, suppose you send and get my boy." I said, "I can't send to get him, but if you get him out here, he can stay here. This is your house, not mine, do just fine. Raise him right along with mine." Start off as a baby-sitter, wound up as my wife. We got married in '60. [Sadie Fulson died in 1992.]

When "Tramp" was a hit in the mid '60s, rock and roll was out there getting bigger and bigger. What effect did that have on your career?

I had seen everything at a standstill for where the blues was concerned. So I put out a couple of things here, big band stuff like "Black Nights" and a couple of more things I got with Kent. But you had to make sure you got the right songs on the right stations. But they take it to them stations with the rock 'n' roll, so they pick it up, see, and they would see it said Lowell Fulson, and they would put it back, and reach and get the rock 'n' roll. But if you go to a station that played pops and stuff, you may get a chance to get it heard, whether they accept it or not. But I just seen all music standing still, but that. Nobody ain't gonna sell no lot of records.

Were you touring during that time?

Not a lot. Because I done got so disgusted with the bands and promoters and recording companies, and I'd been driving pretty hard since in the '40s. I said, "I am just going to take me a vacation." If you got a gig and band, I'll play it. If they don't have, I'll just go back to my pockets, live out of that. When your records go to dying down, boy, that's rough. When you go to living on past reputation, you don't get a lot of work. Musicians run up pretty high, get a seven-piece band, that's about a standard to travel with.

I guess the cost of living on the road had gone up.

It had gone up. Them guys would go and get them a bottle and get them some Muddy Waters or John Lee Hooker, Lightnin' Hopkins, Howlin' Wolf. They would sit at their house and listen to them blues and drink whiskey. And the Joe Turners and the Lowell Fulsons and the T-Bone Walkers, they'd kind of pushed us back a little bit. Pushed us back.

When was the first time that you went to Europe?

I think it was the last part of the '60s.

Did you go over there with a tour package, or were you a headliner?

My first time I went over there was mostly as a headliner. Like when I first went over there, I went to England, and I worked with the English band over there, which was pretty good. But then Phillip Walker and them had their band and they wanted a little stronger blues that they hadn't heard over there. So they put me headlining. And then everybody went.

Where have you gone besides England?

I been to Sweden and Switzerland. Japan. Brussels. Germany. The Scandinavian countries, Helsinki and all. They know who you are and they know what you are singing about. You talk about screamin', boy. Them people study their book about that music, and them singers, entertainers, they know who they's getting. And they might not know the words, but the way you deliver the melody, "Oh, yeah!" They know that record.

You were one of the last bluesmen to turn to a white audience. When all the others were playing for a white audience in the United States, you were still playing to your own audience. You held on to it longer than almost anybody. Do you think your sophisticated image had anything to do with it? The only time that you looked less than really slick was on the cover of Tramp.

Them kids sat up all night making up them jeans, sewing rags and things on 'em. They tried to make me just as ragged as they possibly could. I had a Dobbs hat. So I said, now, if they paying attention to my hat, they know I ain't a bum 'cause I couldn't buy this hat. One of my daughters, I said to her, "Now I am not wearing that hat. I am wearing my Dobbs." She said, "All right." 'Cause she had me fixed up looking worse than Moms Mabley with that hat on. So I talked 'em out of the hat; I wore my hat. I don't know whether the European tour had anything to do with me going to the white audience or not.

You were selling records to the white audience, but you were still playing pure

*blues to a black audience. Even B.B. started playing to white audiences in Europe
before he did in the States.*

I tell you what set B.B. up good—his recording company just pushed him on
TV. Just pushed him. I mean, they pushed that boy. They spent money to change
him over, not completely. Don't take him away from what he's got. Just spread
what he has, and recoup some of the stuff he didn't have and put it with what he
already have. I didn't get that. I wished for the audience, but I didn't get it until
later, which it came at a good time because my pockets was getting thin. And no
hit records on the market, and these smaller companies wasn't doing too much.
'Cause I don't guess they figured that I was delivering the type of stuff could get
over, you know. I don't know. I know when I did get to play for the white audience we had a ball. We had fun.

How did you start recording for Jewel?

Ferdinand Washington, he was acting as manager then, and co-writer on some
of my things, most of 'em. Him and Stan Lewis were both from Louisiana,
Shreveport. I met Stan Lewis when I cut "Reconsider Baby," so when my name
came up . . .

*You recorded in Dallas and in Muscle Shoals, Alabama, and in L.A., and all that
stuff came out on Jewel?*

Came out on Jewel. Stan Lewis, yeah. That was Stan's stuff.

How did Rounder Records come to find you?

I don't know. Ron Levy, I met him. I don't remember where, but I know we cut
in New Orleans. See, Ron played with B.B. King and so he knew quite a bit about
my work. And I wrote a song, Phillip Walker cut it with Rounder, "I'm Tough."
And I think between Phillip Walker and that record and hearing about me, is how
he knew me. I think we clinched everything on the telephone, and I don't think I
met him until I got to New Orleans. But it was between Phillip Walker and some
of those guys who were using some of my material.

And you did that first Rounder album in New Orleans?

Yeah.

You already had the material?

I had some stuff that I had been working on that year and some of it I had cut
it in '75. And this here is for my new LP which will be coming out whenever I get
into the studio, which I hope will be early this year.

How many albums have you done for Rounder so far?

Just two. This will be three.

Do they give you a fair amount of musical freedom?

Yeah.

Do you choose your own musicians?

Yeah, if it's necessary. They have a pretty good idea of what I need. Ron, he's a
musician himself. And a good piano man, organ and stuff. They always try to
work with the guy who has got the good ideas. He had good ideas. Sometimes we
debate on it, you know. Any real good musician has a chance to use notes and
things that are needed, then that takes some of the blues seasoning away from it,
you know. So we gets on, get on a balance, you know, and simple, make it good.
Not a whole lot of [*scats a fast scale*]. Pick a few good ones and left it with that.

LIGHTNIN' HOPKINS

BY JAS OBRECHT "I had the one thing you need to be a blues singer," Lightnin' Hopkins used to say. "I was born with the blues." The songs he created—"barrelhouse," he called them—were as sorrowful as a cottonfield holler and as earthy as the Texas bottom lands that swallowed his sweat. "You know the blues come out of the field, baby," Lightnin' said. "That's when you bend down, pickin' that cotton, and sing, 'Oh, Lord, please help me.'" ¶ Scars on his hands and ankles testified to stints on the chain gang and long days of driving mules and chopping cotton. But Lightnin' was indomitable, and like Lead Belly and Muddy Waters and other great bluesmen, he played his way to better circumstances, parlaying his anger and pain into tough, deeply felt music. "The blues is a lot like church," Hopkins explained. "When a preacher's up there preachin' the Bible, he's honest to God trying to get you to understand these things. Well, singing the blues is the same thing."

Sage, scoundrel, and natural-born storyteller, Sam "Lightnin'" Hopkins had a genius for improvised poetry, creating new verses or entire songs as the spirit moved him. He could sing about hairstyles, being broke, how his car was doing, goings-on in the club where he was performing, or the way things used to be. He damn near sang "Po' Sam" into an everyman of the blues.

Lightnin' was a supremely confident guitarist, keeping time with his left leg while swinging hard or traveling downhome. He often played a Gibson J-50 outfitted with a DeArmond soundhole pickup, and he also performed and recorded with a small Harmony flat-top and a Fender Stratocaster. Resting his pinkie and ring finger on the face of his guitar, Lightnin' played bass and rhythm with his thumbpick while plucking solos with his bare index finger. He thrived on first-position shuffles, especially in the key of *E* with the fat *A7* chord with the high *G*. "One of the most distinctive elements of the Lightnin' sound is that turnaround in *E*," observes ZZ Top's Billy Gibbons. "It's a signature lick that he did in just about every song he played. He'd come down from the *B* chord and roll across the top three strings in the last two bars. He'd pull the pick off those strings to get kind of a staccato effect, first hitting the little open-*E* string and then the 3rd fret on the *B* string and then the 4th fret of the *G* string. He would then resolve on the *V* chord after doing this roll. It's a way to immediately identify a Lightnin' Hopkins tune."

To accompany Hopkins meant doing things his way, as Gibbons quickly learned: "We were playing a traditional blues and we all went to the second change, but Lightnin' was still in the first change. He stopped and looked at us. Our bass player said, 'Well, Lightnin', that's where the second change is supposed to be, isn't it?' Lightnin' looked back and said, 'Lightnin' change when Lightnin' want to change.' And we knew—don't do that no more!"

"You had to know and feel Lightnin' and follow *him*," seconds Johnny Winter. "I guess he played a lot by himself, and he didn't worry about changes. It didn't hurt a damn thing, either. Lightnin' might not change on time all the time, but he was technically a damn good guitar player when he wanted to be. He could play his butt off, and he was always his own man. A long time ago Lightnin' was playing a local bar in Houston, and one of the frats came up and said, 'Do you mind playing something by John Lee Hooker?' And he said, 'I am Lightnin' Hopkins. I don't play nothin' else.'"

Even while covering well-known songs like "Trouble in Mind" and "When the Saints Go Marching In," Lightnin' inevitably swerved the arrangement to suit himself. "When I play a guitar," he said in the film *The Blues According to Lightnin' Hopkins*, "I play from my heart and soul and I play my own, *own* music."

"I WENT AHEAD AND MADE ME A GUITAR" Hopkins was born in the heart of East Texas Piney Woods country on March 15, 1912. "My family, we come up in Leona County," he told Sam Charters during a 1964 Prestige session. "It's just a little old country where they farm and raise cotton and corn and peas and peanuts, things like that. So that's where I grew up to know myself—back out from Centerville about 12 miles back in the country." Hopkins's grandfather was a slave who hung himself. His father, a hard-drinking gambler who'd done time for murder, was slain in an argument when Lightnin' was three. Sam's older brother John Henry fled the area soon afterward, leaving his mother on her own to raise Alice, Joel, A.B., and Sam.

Before he was big enough to work in the fields, Hopkins was drawn to music. "I heard my brother playing a guitar," he told Charters. "It was the first one I ever seen. He wouldn't let me play his guitar. I wanted to play it, so at last one day they come in and caught me with the guitar 'cause I couldn't hang it back up—see, I had to get in a chair to get it down. So he caught me fair. He said, 'Boy, I done told you—don't fool with that guitar.' He says, 'Can you play this guitar?' I say, 'Yeah, I can play it some.' He said, 'Well, go ahead, and let's see what you can do.' I went ahead and played him a little tune, and he liked it. So he said, 'Yeah, he can play some. Where you learn that from?' I said, 'Well, I just learned it.' So I went ahead and made me a guitar. I got me a cigar box, I cut me a round hole in the middle of it, take me a little piece of plank, nailed it on to that cigar box, and I got me some screen wire and I made me a bridge back there and raised it up high enough that it would sound inside that little box, and I got me a tune out of it. I kept my tune, and I played from then on. So I got me a guitar of my own when I got to be eight years old."

Sam toted his guitar to a Baptist church social in nearby Buffalo, where Blind Lemon Jefferson had him hoisted to the hood of a truck so they could perform together. "Boy," the great bluesman predicted, "you keep that up, you gonna be a good guitar player." Albert Holly, an old blues player who came around to court his mama, inspired Hopkins to sing. Sam played leads alongside his brothers and sister in the Hopkins Band and gathered with them around the organ to sing "them good old Christian songs."

During his teens Hopkins played with a fiddler, serenading and passing the hat. "When I got good, I went to find the places where they'd barrelhouse at," Hopkins said. "I didn't know—I just had to wander up on them places around Jewitt, Buffalo, Crockett. They had little old joints for Saturday nights, you know." In 1927 Hopkins began playing dances and jukes around the area with his cousin, blues singer Texas Alexander, who'd just done his first session with Lonnie Johnson on guitar.

By day Sam worked the fields, chopping cotton and driving a mule. "It was hard times," he told Charters. "I was trying to take care of my wife, me, and my mother. Six bits a day—and that was top price. I swear, I would come in in the evening, and it looked like I'd be so weak till my knees be cluckin' like a wagon wheel, man. I'd go to bed, and I'd say, 'Baby, I just can't continue like that.' Look like no sooner than I go to bed and I'm ready to go catch that mule again."

The hard-drinking Hopkins got into fights that landed him on the chain gang. "I had to calm down. Man, that ball and chain ain't no good for no man. From the '20s up until the '30s I was doing that. Getting cooped up and whomped around pretty good. Somehow or another, I'd always be lucky and managed to get out." He rode the rails and stayed in hobo camps: "I had some hard days travelin', but after I stopped in places and they found out I played that guitar like I do, they'd warm me up, feed me, and make me a big sack of food and tell me I can make it."

"A COUNTRY BOY MOVED TO TOWN" Sam Hopkins visited Houston for the first time in 1934 to broadcast with Texas Alexander and then returned home. Mance Lipscomb recalled seeing him playing an electric guitar in Galveston in '38. Hopkins finally moved to Houston for good and began playing on buses and in the dives along Dowling Street. Word of his performances reached Lola Anne Cullum, a talent scout who bought him his first amp and arranged his November 1946 debut session for Aladdin. Accompanying the 35-year-old bluesman on the drive to Los Angeles was pianist Wilson Smith. "When I gets in that studio," Hopkins recounted to Charters, "they said, 'Mr. Hopkins, we wanna see what you got to offer.' I walks up there and I grabbed that old guitar, and I ran back. I sang 'The Rocky Mountain, darlin', they way out in the West.' He said, 'He's sold,' right then and there. I didn't have to hit another note. Alright. I come on down. Smith was next. He said, 'Well, let's see what y'all got to offer on piano.' I gets up there and I play the same song—'The Rocky Mountain'—with Smith, and it sold him! [*Laughed.*] And boy, we tore the joint up. And so they named me Lightnin' and named him Thunder."

With its fearless bass licks and gripping solos, Hopkins' countrified style was fully evident on his first release, "Katie Mae Blues" backed with "That Mean Old Twister." The 78 became a hit and brought Lightnin' better-paying gigs around Houston. His second Aladdin session, held in L.A. nine months later, yielded another hit, "Short Haired Woman." Jumping from label to label, Hopkins record-ed prolifically in Houston during the next eight years, cutting nearly 200 selec-tions that would eventually come out on Aladdin, Imperial, Gold Star, Modern, RPM, United, Kent, Crown, Verve, Dart, Time, Mercury, Mainstream, Blues Classics, Decca, Herald, Arhoolie, and many other labels.

"Lightnin' liked to make records," says producer Chris Strachwitz, "and no wonder, when he could sit down a few minutes, make up a number, and collect $100 in cash. And local recording producer Bill Quinn had Lightnin' doing just that. Whenever Lightnin' needed some money he would go over to Telegraph Road and walk into the Gold Star studios to 'make' some numbers. And he had a fantastic talent to come up with an endless supply of these 'numbers.' Many were based on traditional tunes he had heard in the past, but all of the songs received his personal treatment and they came out as very personal poetry." Some songs presaged rock and roll, while others were as lonesome and sorrowful as Blind Lemon's old 78s. Hopkins's biggest Gold Star singles, "Unsuccessful Blues" and "Tim Moore's Farm," crackled over R&B radio and were spun on jukeboxes all along the Texas Gulf Coast.

Besides stripped-down guitar blues, Lightnin' recorded piano and organ solos—his "Zolo Go" was early Zydeco—as well as tap-dancing numbers. Bassist Donald Cooks and a variety of drummers accompanied Hopkins on records between '52 and mid '54, when Lightnin' played his last major session for Herald. Due to shifting tastes in R&B and pop music, Lightnin' produced only three singles dur-ing '55 and '56 and didn't record at all in '57 and '58. Then came a dramatic turn-around—educated white people became interested in folk blues.

On January 16, 1959, Hopkins recorded his first album, for Folkways. Sam Charters, who'd written about Lightnin' in his monumental book *The Country*

Blues, produced the session and provided the gin. "We recorded it in the shabby room he was renting," Charters wrote, "and I held the microphone in my hand so I could move it down toward the guitar when he was playing a solo, and then move it close enough to his lips for his singing." Lightnin' paid homage to Blind Lemon Jefferson with "Reminiscences of Blind Lemon" and covers of "Penitentiary Blues" and "See That My Grave Is Kept Clean." Subsequent 1959 sessions with Mack McCormack captured a wealth of improvised blues and traditional songs.

Chris Strachwitz made a pilgrimage to visit Lightnin' at a Houston tavern in 1959. "The songs I heard him sing were incredible improvised poetry, made up on the spot about whatever was on his mind that day or night," Chris observed. "Rhymed and underscored by the piercing sound of the amplified guitar droning over an ancient humming amplifier, Lightnin' sang about how he hardly got to the beer joint that night because it had been raining all day and his car hit all the chuckholes on the road since the water covered them all. He moaned about his arthritis bothering him on a humid night like that. He yelled out at several women jiving in front of him and pointed his long fingers at them while he told them a piece of his mind, always rhymed to the slow beat of his guitar and Spider, the drummer, who bashed out a powerful sanctified beat. Lightnin' hardly seemed to end one number—it was a continuous rap with his audience." The performance inspired Strachwitz to form Arhoolie Records, which has several top-drawer Hopkins albums in its catalog.

Lightnin', Sonny Terry, Brownie McGhee, and Big Joe Williams converged in a Los Angeles studio to record together for World Pacific in July 1960. In October, Hopkins joined Joan Baez and Pete Seeger onstage at Carnegie Hall to record "Oh Mary Don't You Weep." During the next two-and-a-half weeks, Hopkins recorded nearly four dozen songs at various New York facilities, including two Bluesville albums, a Candid LP, and the Fire release of "Mojo Hand," a compelling piece of voodoo imagery that became his signature song.

An instant hit on college campuses, Lightnin' crossed over to jazz audiences, being voted Best New Star—Male Vocalist in the 1962 *Down Beat* critics poll. Lightnin' explained his performance strategy to Charters: "See, here's the way I play songs. I goes on. If my first song don't hit 'em, my second one will, because I bring a feeling. And if they don't get the first feeling, they get the second feeling, and I got 'em and gone! Because I rocks the joint that way."

Lightnin' recorded prolifically during the '60s, with standouts on Arhoolie, Bluesville, Prestige, and Verve. He joined his brothers Joel and long-lost John Henry in Waxahachie, Texas, for a particularly memorable Arhoolie outing in '64.

Unlike his Lone Star contemporaries T-Bone Walker, Gatemouth Brown, and Lowell Fulson, Lightnin' did not want to promote himself by touring. He had an aversion to airplanes, refused to own a phone, and was known to refuse a $2,000-a-week tour to stay home and play in a dingy club for $17 a night. With his shades and shiny Cadillac, Lightnin' was a respected man about town who loved drinking, fishing, going to rodeos, shooting craps, and playing pitty pat. Most of all, he remained true to who he was—"a country boy moved to town."

"I always thought Lightnin' Hopkins was a real cool guy," remembers Johnny Winter, "because he could do big shows and then go out and play on the corner or on a bus or in a little juke joint. It didn't seem to bother him a bit. He could go from acoustic guitar to electric guitar or from playing by himself to playing with a band. Lightnin' was a real blues guy."

By the end of his life Lightnin' Hopkins was likely the most recorded of the postwar bluesmen. He exerted an enormous influence on other musicians—Albert, B.B. and Freddie King, Muddy Waters, Buddy Guy, J.B. Lenoir, Otis Rush, Albert Collins, Son Thomas, R.L. Burnside, and Jimi Hendrix all praised his records.

On January 30, 1982, Po' Lightnin' died of cancer of the esophagus in Houston's St. Joseph Hospital. "Lightnin' was one of the last of a dying breed," said Johnny Winter just after the funeral. "There are always going to be blues musicians, but it's just different with people who really lived the whole thing in the country and could talk about chopping cotton and pulling corn and riding freights. Lightnin' did everything the way you'd think a real blues player would do. He took care of the people he loved, and success never really seemed to go to his head. He did exactly what he wanted to do, and he sure gave us a lot of good blues."

GATEMOUTH BROWN

BY JAS OBRECHT Don't call Gatemouth Brown a
bluesman to his face. "I'm a *musician*," he'll growl, "not some
dirty lowdown bluesman. I play American and world music,
Texas-style. I play a part of the past with the present and just
a taste of the future." While Brown's rightfully regarded as the
greatest living exponent of the swinging, sophisticated blues
school once headed by T-Bone Walker, he's equally adept at
jazz and swing, Cajun, bluegrass, country, and folk.

Gruff, direct, and, fiercely individualistic, the Stetson-wearing, pipe-smoking Brown has a rich singing voice and spirited, horn-like approach to the electric guitar, which he plays bare-fingered. He's also adept on violin, viola, mandolin, bass, drums, and harmonica.

The oldest of seven children, Clarence Brown was born on April 24, 1924, in Vinton, Louisiana. At age one, he was bundled off to Orange, Texas, where he spent his youth. "I started strumming guitar behind my father when I was five," he says. "The kind of music I played then wasn't blues, wasn't jazz—it was country, Cajun, and bluegrass. That's what my father played, see. The guitar was bigger than me—it was one of those resophonic guitars with an all-metal body. We would play tunes like 'Boil Them Cabbage Down,' 'Bully of the Town,' and all that real heavy mountain music. Of course, that music means more to me than any other music because I am more familiar with it. Jazz and blues just came automatically."

Young Gate was soon experimenting with other instruments. "The first set of drums I played cost me a whippin'," he laughs. "I sneaked one of my mom's washtubs out and got me two tree limbs and put 'em to it. Man, I was wailing away, and my mom come out there and tore the tub all to pieces and, of course, she tore me up too. That was my first encounter with a set of drums. And my first fiddle—I tried to make it out of a cigar box and screen wire, and it didn't work."

Armed with his dad's advice—"learn to tune your instrument, don't overplay, and play some of everything so you don't get stuck in one bag"—Gatemouth embarked on his professional career at 16. His first band, the Gay Swingsters, was fronted by a mailman, Howard Spencer, who only knew how to blow sax in one key. "Everything he ever played was in B♭," Gate recalls. "I never will forget these guys taking me to Chain's Nightclub in Beaumont, Texas, and we'd play *hard* upstairs all night and got three nickels apiece, and the guy who was handling the thing took all the money. That's what you consider paying dues." The teenager toured with W.M. Bimbo and the Brownskin Models, an old-time traveling road show that left him stranded in Norfolk, Virginia. He found a job there at the El Dorado Club, drumming in the house band until the outbreak of World War II. After serving "five months, ten days, and a few hours," Brown headed to San Antonio, where he was billed as "The Singing Drummer" with Hort Hudge's 23-piece orchestra.

Producer Don Robey, who owned a club in Houston, was intrigued by Brown's act and invited him to Houston. The following morning, Gate was thumbing his way east to Houston, where he soon had a memorable encounter with T-Bone Walker: "T-Bone was the hot stuff on guitar throughout Texas at that time, and nobody knew I played guitar. So I went in this club—the Bronze Peacock—and sat down aside the bandstand. T-Bone was sick with an ulcer or something, and he laid his guitar down and ran to the dressing room. And so just out of nowhere I walked up on the stage, picked up his guitar, and invented a boogie—right there onstage. I started this tune with the words 'My name is Gatemouth Brown, I just got in your town, if you don't like my style, I will not hang around.' It was coming to me just out of the clear blue, and the women and men was just pouring money down my bosom and everywhere else. That tune happened to become my first recording, 'Gatemouth Boogie.' So all of a sudden T-Bone Walker recovered and come back and snatched his guitar from me, onstage. It kind of hurt my feelings, and he told me that as long as I live, never touch his instrument again. So I said alright. By that time Don Robey heard the commotion and the people screaming, and he came down and told me to come see him. The next day he bought me a Gibson L-5 for $700 and a uniform, and I've been going ever since."

Robey flew Brown to Hollywood to record his first four sides, cut on August 21, 1947, with the Maxwell Davis Orchestra. Gate's roots may have been in the fertile country blues territory of east Texas and southwest Louisiana, but his debut Aladdin 78s jump with progressive orchestrations and seasoned showmanship. "Robey knew nothing about recording," Brown says, "but he was a very smart man. After they recorded my first four sides and he learned more about the business, we formed the Peacock Record Company in Houston, and that was our company for 17 years." Brown's Peacock 78s featured piano, bass, drums, and a jumping horn section, and his exciting treble tone seemed to leap off of singles like "Boogie Uproar" and "Okie Dokie Stomp." By the late '50s, though, Gate's record sales were dwindling. After his final Peacock side in '61, he didn't record again until '64, making a single 45 for Cue.

In 1965, Gatemouth headed to Nashville to record C&W for the Hit Sound label. "I started easing back into what I always loved—country, Cajun, and bluegrass," he explains. "See, the clubs I was working was all Caucasian clubs, and so this music is what I started getting back to. I got to where I didn't want to play the rhythm and blues. I freelanced around for a while, and there was nothing happening because people at that time didn't want *music*. The old doo-wop bunch was out there doing acrobatics, and there was the hard rock and roll, so I just went to playing small clubs around Colorado, Nevada, and Texas. I decided to back off on recording in America."

Unbeknownst to Brown, French fans were raving about his Peacock sides. Promoters persuaded him to tour Europe in '71 with an all-star group. He recorded *The Blues Ain't Nothin', Clarence Gatemouth Brown Sings Louis Jordan,* and *Gate's on the Heat* for France's Black and Blue label and played the Montreux Jazz Festival. He was invited back to Montreux in '73, recording *Cold Storage* during the same trip. In 1977 Brown took his band on a tour of northeast Africa sponsored by the U.S. State Department. "It was one of the greatest chances of my life," he recalls. "We got to see the true grits of Africa, and it's a beautiful country." Returning stateside, Brown recorded *Blackjack,* a collection of jazz, blues, Cajun, bluegrass, country, and folk, followed by *Makin' Music* with Roy Clark. Hot on the comeback trail, Gatemouth cut several albums for the Rounder label during the 1980s, and since then has recorded critically acclaimed albums for Alligator and Verve.

This first interview took place in late 1992 at a San Francisco motel, where the outspoken Brown was alternately gruff, charming, and tender. James Rotondi accompanied me to the interview, an edited version of which appeared in the March '93 *Guitar Player* as "'Don't Call Me a Bluesman!' Gatemouth Brown Takes on the World."

"DON'T CALL ME A BLUESMAN!"

You've often said that you don't play guitar like guitar, but . . .

Like a horn. I play horn lines and horn kicks. You know how a horn would phrase different passages? Well, I do that with my guitar.

Do you always pick with just your fingers?

Always. I got control of my mind with my fingers. I got control of the guitar with my fingers. I can let them ring, or I can smother my strings in a snap and cut it just like a horn would do when your breath run out. The circle of breathing—I can do that by using my fingers. And of course another secret of mine, I pick with both hands. A lot of people don't understand that, and it's hard to explain.

Which fingers do you use?

Depends on what I'm playing. I might use 'em all, and I might use a thumb. I may use an index finger. I might use my ring finger. It's unexplainable. People ask, "How you do that?" I say, "Magic." When they say, "Show me how to do that," I say, "I show no one nothing." Years ago when I was playing along with my father, I said, "Dad, how you do this?" He said, "I'm not going to show you anything." I said, "How shall I learn?" He said, "Pay attention." It's as simple as that. I love my father more than life itself. Of course, I lost him in 1954, and man, that hurt me more than *anything* on earth. He was my life, and it was a great loss to me, but I kept my promise. I promised him that I would be the best in my field that I possibly could, and that's exactly what I'm doing.

When you arrange your music . . .

I head-arrange with the guitar. I put it on there, and then I got a guy that writes it—or they memorize it—and you got your take. Other guys in the band help with the filling in spaces too. And once we get them down, we write 'em.

What's the greatest satisfaction when it all comes together?

The greatest satisfaction to me is we don't have the same sound on everything. Most records you hear just strike one medium, and you can't even leave that. You have to stay with it, and that's bad, man, because if you can't grow, you're in trouble.

You've been making records longer than John Lee Hooker and B.B. King.

Why, sure I have. Notice the caliber of the music too.

It stayed high.

It stayed together. You see, friends are one thing, but I cannot shield a man if he's not musical, if he's not creative. And if you're gonna sound like you did when you first started, there's no point in keeping going.

Is it a compliment when guitarists try to figure out your tone or parts on the Peacock 78s?

Yeah, I think so. I'm not a blues player; I'm a musician. But all blues players, when they play the blues, their minds are in their work. It's what they want out of life—it's not what you need. But I'm different from that. When I walk on that bandstand, I'm giving myself to all of my kids. You are my child, you are too [*points to Jas Obrecht and James Rotondi*]—all of you. I have no color barrier. Period. And the message I'm trying to give to them will help them rather than make them try to live like these supposedly blues players do. That's why I hate the idea of people labeling me as a blues player, because I'm not.

Although you've played some really great . . .

I play blues, sure, but don't call me a bluesman. When the white society think of blues, they think further back. See my last album? *No Looking Back*. So forget it.

Don't look back to older musicians?

No. Forget it.

Why? What if that old music still brings pleasure to people?

That's fine if somebody else want to do it, but I don't want them to ask me to do it. I cannot talk for others, but I can always talk for myself. Mostly all you kids do is listen to the beat or listen to how sorrowful a blues is. And it is sorrowful, because it's very negative. And you notice that every white blues player that ever got out there to play what he thinks is the blues, if he tried to live that life, it killed him. I'm serious! That's what I'm trying to get to. Do not tackle something you don't know nothing about!

When you were a kid, how was blues music regarded in your neighborhood?

Well, son, I'm gonna be honest with you. When I was a kid, I listened to very little blues because it made me feel sick inside. It just made me feel physically sick.

Hearing a Lead Belly or Blind Lemon Jefferson record?

Yeah, man. I wouldn't listen to that stuff. I didn't like it. It made me see disastrous things facing me. You see, my father was a great, great, great musician—three "greats" to it—and I don't ever consider myself better than he. I took what he taught me—just like what the Japanese doing with our inventions—and added to it.

Blues and jazz is not my first music. My first music is country, Cajun, and bluegrass. My daddy sung Cajun, country, and bluegrass, and played it on fiddle, accordion, banjo, and mandolin. He was a heck of a vocalist. But he was a railroad man. When he was coming up, they didn't have nightclubs like they have today. They had what they called "house parties." People who had the biggest houses moved all the furniture back, they would cook a lot, and they would have all kinds of drinks—it was great days when I was coming up. And another thing—I never been an alcoholic. I drank twice in my life. I got drunk because I was going in the service, and I was scared. The second time was through a woman—it happens to all of us. And I said, "If I ever get over this sickness, I'll never do it no more because I can't stand to be sick of the stomach." I can't, man.

I learned the other person's downfall, but I took advantage of it and didn't do it. Like all the cokeheads and all them people back when I was growing up: They was acting very strange, and I said I would never want to do that, and I never did. I wouldn't even know what cocaine tastes or feels like. It only takes a weak person to want to kill himself. And you can see it kill other people, like Charlie Parker, Gene Ammons—oh, dozens and dozens of other artists. Alcohol and narcotics killed 'em. I knew that's what killed 'em—why should I do it?

Can I ask you something off the record?

You can print anything you want, because I'm not going to give you a negative answer.

Do you think reefer is bad for musicians?

No! It's not, and I've always said that. Marijuana is the only substance on earth that's grown by what we know as God, nature, or whatever, that don't really harm no one. But all this manmade chemicals—that's what killing them. Alcohol is killing us. Whiskey is the most deadly drug on earth; it killed my third brother. Great, great guitarist and vocalist, but he followed people like Lightnin' Hopkins and Guitar Slim, and you see where they all end up: six feet deep. Alcohol is one of the most *devastating* drugs there is. You get too many drinks and run out there and kill everybody including yourself. They're fighting the wrong substance—that's all.

Guys used to say they'd have to drink to play good.

What do you mean *used to*, son? Right now we have what could be some great musicians, but this alcohol and women get in front of it. When you try to go with all these women—you can't do that. I am one of the few entertainers that don't go out there womanizing just because I'm in a position to do it. It means nothing to me. What means something to me is trying to keep families together and trying to keep people with love and concern for each other.

Do you see your music as a positive healing force?

It is. I've stated that all over the world. I do positive music. Even just my music without me opening my mouth is very positive. It tells a story. It tells you something about life. I've had ladies and men come up to me and say, "You know, Brown, when I left the house I felt very bad. But now I feel so good from the inside out." Boy, that's a great statement for people to make to someone. That's a great thing to be honored for.

Can compliments be a distraction?

To some of them. Not me. If I was asked about my Grammy Award, I'd say it was alright, but it wasn't nothing that was going to make me flip out on. It was just a piece of metal. What's important is the people I can get to with my music, not the piece of metal that's going to get to me. What good is that piece of metal? I don't care if I ever got a Grammy, and I've always said that. But I've got one, and very seldom does it ever make it in my write-ups. I just don't bother naming it. I got four or five Handy Blues Awards. I've gotten many documents from mayors all over the country. I'm a deputy sheriff in Louisiana, where I live. I arrest no one, but I'm well bonded by the sheriff's department, and I carry my stuff with me all over the world where I go. And I'm real good with all the policemans that I meet because I became one of them and maybe I have some good influence on them.

Are there certain songs you have to play every night or else people will be disappointed?

Well, they don't say anything about it. [*Laughs.*] I can't possibly play everything that I know in the run of the night. Sometimes they request "Okie Dokie Stomp," but I have ways I can soft them down. I may use the excuse about the band hasn't rehearsed this, and I don't want to do nothin' unless it's rehearsed—that sort of stuff. But basically I keep people so well geared up they forget about what they might want to ask. You have to keep 'em occupied.

What have you learned about performing after being on the road for 50 years?

Well, son, I've learned a lot. I've seen a lot. I've seen failure after failure after failure. I can see why they have failed, but what I've learned beyond that is not to get up on a bandstand trying to please *me*. I get myself on that public. That's why I don't like a heavy spotlight on me where I can't see the public, because I work with my public. That's the name of the game. I want to get a visual of you, so I know exactly what to do to get your response, and I can't do that if I can't see you. Now when you're on TV, that's a different story. You have to think of getting to the people in a different way. And you have to be careful about not making mistakes, because too many out there know when you've made one. And if you happen to make one—as we all will do—be smart enough to cover it. Like a cat—cover up your mistakes.

Do you ever just repeat it, so it seems like that's what you were supposed to do?

That's exactly it a lot of times! And it works. "Okie Dokie Stomp" has one of the biggest boo-boos in the world in it—I made a note that I wasn't supposed to make in it—and it works because I play it over.

We recently saw an old photo of you playing a Fender Telecaster.

Yeah. Fender used to give me a Telecaster every year and a half, but I never could like 'em. But I loved their amplifiers. Now I use Music Man amps—one for my viola and fiddle, and the other one for my two guitars.

What's your all-time favorite setup?

Well, son, let's put it this way: My favorite guitar is the one that sounded good to me at the precise moment I was playing. I'm not cutting you short. Now, I got a Washburn guitar that I bought for $175 brand-new out of a pawnshop. I love pawnshops; I get good stuff out of there. Then, of course, my ['63 Gibson] Firebird has been with me for years. It's famous all over the world—the one with that leather pickguard. I use that with the Music Man, and that's my sound.

What does the fiddle give you that the guitar doesn't?

A different sound, a different feeling, a different avenue, and another planet. When I'm playing fiddle, I feel like my father is standing beneath it with me. It has been written that I'm the most unorthodox fiddle player and guitar player in the world—well, that's good because I'm all out there by myself. No one has ever been able to really copy my music. You can do the horn lines, but when you get to the guitar solo, that's when they all die off. I got my own individual style, and it's hard to explain. I can't explain my feelings to you.

Do you play rock and roll?

I play rock and roll a lot of times. You see, what they call rock and roll today is not rock and roll, son. It's a lot of noise. A lot of string bending and not even making a statement. Remember that tune of mine called "Chicken Shift"? That's rock and roll. "Dolly Got the Blues"—that's rock and roll. Louisiana Zydeco is a mixture of rock and roll and Creole music. Then I play straight-ahead Cajun that has nothing to do with nothing else but Cajun.

What can you say to young rockers?

If a guy's a heavy drinker or heavy dope user, don't follow him, because he's in misery in the first place. That's why he's playing that kind of music. And them hard rock players, well, all I can say for those kids is they're being brainwashed to brainwash others. Why play music that loud and ruin yourself before you hit 20 years old? And what they're playing is not understood—no way—because everything is so high volume. Why play something so loud where it's going to tear you up inside? I've seen guys that was so loud, my stomach was hurting!

What do you look for in a tone?

Dynamics. Just what I do. And there's four dynamics, all told: High volume, midrange, soft, and off. See, if you play in a high volume, you've got it goin'. Now, at a certain portion you drop it down and leave it to midrange. I go further than that: I go from a high volume to real soft, but just keep that drive going. And every time I do it, you can hear 'em scream all over the place because it feels good. I can rattle my guitar and almost tear out windows, and drop it to where you just barely hear it. Every man in my band knows when to do this. That makes music.

What should a Gatemouth Brown solo be about?

I don't understand the question.

A lot of guys show off during solos. They play fast licks over and over, but they don't tell a story in the way that you seem to on your records.

You asked that real nicely. In the first place, a guy who's doing that is not playing for people. He's on an ego trip trying to tell hisself he's the greatest guitar player in the world, and not playing nothing! Making a lot of nonsense. You can take a

five-year-old kid, give him a pick, and tell him just start hitting all them strings—
that's all they're doing. It's not making any sense.

Your solos work so well with the rhythm. If you're doing a nice shuffle, you move right into the rhythm.

Here's one secret about music—I don't care what instrument you're playing. If somewhere in the song you have a solo, every one that's playing with you needs to get *underneath* you—not even with you or over you. Then you do that for them when they solo too. I do nothin' I don't want my men to do. When the piano player is playing, I comp under him where he can be heard. Why? Because he's the one featured at the time. Not you. And every man in my band has got to be a good musician—if he isn't, he can't stay. Because I'm gonna damn sure make him solo. I give every man a chance for the world to hear him as well as me. That's what teamwork is all about.

What are your rules for the band?

Not a beer bottle, not a whiskey glass, or nothing on that bandstand—number one. I don't want no bullshitting and talking to each other on the bandstand unnecessarily. I want everybody to concentrate on his job. I don't want no scrambling about all over the bandstand.

Do you have rehearsals?

Never. I need to, but I don't. Son, I haven't had no time.

How many nights a year do you play?

About 300 or less.

You've been playing Ellington's "C Jam Blues" for a long time.

Yes. I just like the drive of the tune. I like the concept. I don't like all of Ellington's music, no, but that's one of the few I've liked. It's a different blues from the other kind of blues. I put myself into it and just keep the identification. That's the next thing. When somebody does somebody's music, don't do it note-for-note like that person—that's stupid. Use the head of the tune, and then when you come in, play it yourself. Don't try to play what that other person played, because you can't do it. I wouldn't even attempt to try. That's what you call a copier, and not a rearranger. I rearrange everything. I can kick any big band tune and rearrange it, but you'll know it's the tune because the idea is there. After that it's me, but it's all gonna fit. I used to do the theme from *Dr. Zhivago*, and I never knew that bridge. So I made a bridge up to go with it, and it was perfect. When somebody said that's not right, I said, "Look—what is right? You want me to copy? You want to hear every note that was done in this tune? I'm not going to do it. There's going to be some changes." I'm going to use his head idea, and after that it's me. That's how I'm successful in what I do.

Frank Zappa has said that you're probably his favorite guitar player.

Man, there's 100,000 guitar players around the world say this. But I don't hear me nowhere. Maybe I influenced them to get started. If you notice, a lot of people now are trying to use my type of arrangement, but they can't do it because I never do the same thing twice. All these musicians get right down in front of me. . . .

I'm going to be there tonight.

And I'm gonna get you, son. In concert I say, "How many musicians, guitar players, what have you, are here tonight?" Boy, they all stand up. I say, "I know why you're here. You're here to snatch some licks." Then my final word is, "Snatch on this," and I may come up with a jazz tune, man, and *burn* it. [*Laughs.*] They just sit there like, oh, no. I say, "This is a very easy tune to play." I love to tease the kids. Back in the '60s and '50s, you used to get guitar players from all over the world wanting to have what they called a battle of guitars. And I've never lost one.

What was your secret?

Being myself.

Would you be put up against guys like Guitar Slim?

No, man, they're not guitar players! See, that's what I said a while ago. When they think of blues, you all go right to the bottom of the barrel and scrape off the crud. And you expect me to go along with it, but I'm not. This man killed himself trying to be me. He was so frustrated. He tried to dress like me, he tried to walk like me, he tried to play like me, he tried to sing like me, and he didn't do none of that. But one thing he did that wasn't like me was being a heavy drunk. I played in Kansas City one time, and he come to town. And back in them early days, I was wearin' tails. And he went and bought him tails just like me and changed his Cadillac color every day to suit the tails that he was wearing—that was so stupid. But the ultimate of the story was he was real ignorant, and he went and opened his trunk right on the street with me and a bunch of people standing right there, and he had about ten gallons of wine in that car. And he died a young man—too young. I met his son, who said, "Mr. Brown, I want you to tell me something about my daddy, because I don't know him." And I said, "Son, I would rather you not know."

Which historical musicians would you most like to have seen?

Count Basie and Louis Jordan. Those were my idols as a child. Louis Jordan was one of the greatest gimmick singers in the world. Nobody has ever surpassed this man.

What would you have young players learn from your concerts?

Good question. Here's your answer: What the young people can learn from me through my concert is the positive music. Let's go back to the way that people lived in Mississippi, like with B.B. and all them. During their times, they wrote about the common life that was going on. It was about hardship and working, no money, and that sort of stuff. In Texas, T-Bone was writing about how no good a woman was. Now to me, if the man didn't like no woman, he must have hated his mother. Every song that he's got is against a woman. What caused him to be what he is was a woman.

Your music has a lot of love in it.

Thank you. That's the difference. Now you see what I'm talking about. I've had a few hard times, but no one ever had good times all their life. Somewhere back in your life you did somebody wrong, and you sure gotta pay—it's the truth, but I try to outlive that.

What records are the best introduction to your guitar playing?

Any one you pick will have a good message for you. That's all I can say.

What keeps you growing?

Positive thinking, positive living, treating you like I wished to be treated. I don't look at you because your skin is light. I don't want you to look at me because my skin is dark. We're all people. We need each other. If we don't have each other, what the hell we got? One shouldn't look at one because of the color of his skin. Because there's blacks I don't want around me, and there's whites I don't want around me. There's other nationalities I don't want around me, but I take people as individuals.

You've spent your whole career knocking down racial barriers.

That's right. And if I had to go back and do it all over again, it'd be a hard job. Still is. I turned down two movies because I didn't like what they wanted me to portray. I'm not going to be an Uncle Tom for nobody. I came this far by being me; I'll continue going by being me.

TEXAS GOLD In 1997, Gatemouth Brown celebrated his 50th year in the music business with the magnificent Verve release *Gate Swings,* cut live in the studio with his road band and a studio horn section. Brown revisited his favorite big-band classics—"Midnight Hour," "Too Late Baby," "Take the 'A' Train," "Caldonia," "One O'Clock Jump," and "Flyin' Home." The following interview ran in the October '97 *Guitar Player* as "Texas Gold: 50 Years of Gatemouth Brown."

How was it working with an orchestra again?

Real good feeling. I'll tell you what, man—it took my mind back to the '40s, when music was real music. All the horns—13 pieces—and my rhythm section was right there to do it.

Set up like on the bandstand?

That's right. I played the tunes and put them on tape, and Wardell Quezergue wrote the charts around those. Then we took the charts and the whole band into the studio and set them down just like I did in the old days. It went fine, man.

Did you cut your parts at the same time?

Oh, yeah!

Did you use old-time mikes or amps?

Oh, no. I used my regular amplifier. Your sound is in your fingers, and I've got an engineer who's quite sharp.

When you were making the album, did you have to do several takes of any songs?

Not a bunch of takes, no. Maybe a couple.

Recording like that is a lost art to people used to overdubbing.

Oh, man, they overdub so much and so heavy, until there's no way in hell that they can play it in public. Alright now, all the horn lines that you hear on my album, my keyboard player Joe Krown, my alto player Eric Demmer, and myself, we play the same lines with just the three of us. And then my bass player, Harold Floyd, knows my book, and David Peters, my drummer, he stays in the pocket. So those four pieces and myself can actually voice the instruments to where it sounds like a band instead of some little aggregation.

Did you do much rehearsing for the sessions?

No, because I played some of those tunes on the road all the time. And then some were fresh—I didn't do them at all. I imagine we rehearsed about an hour or two. They're very good musicians, and all of them were reading charts. That made the difference. See, all these horns was New Orleans musicians.

Are those jazz standards some of your favorite songs?

Yeah. Out of the whole barrel, that's some of the favorites. Now, like that "Gate's Blues Waltz"—I wrote that one. I've had it for a while, and we played it on the road. "Take Me Back, Baby"—that was a fresh one. That was an old Count Basie tune with Jimmy Rushing singing it. It come out real nice.

"Flyin' Home" too.

Yeah, that's Hamp—Lionel Hampton.

You're doing the Illinois Jacquet sax part.

Yeah, I'm doing his solo on my guitar—that's true. Man, I loved his way of playing.

You've said you like to approach the guitar like a horn.

I do.

How is that affected when you're working with 13 horns?

It's fine. I'm playing them horn lines, and I come in and play horn solos. I play the kicks with the band. It's just a magical thing.

It must give you a lot of energy having that big sound behind you.

Oh, yeah. You can hear a lot of guys—I won't name them—trying to have big band horns, but nobody knows how to voice their instrument. All them guitar players are just guitar players, as far as I'm concerned. They're not doing nothing that's any different. Even with different sounds, it's just the same up-the-middle road. They don't know how to end their tunes—they end them with the drummers making the last word—*ba-dum,* and a whole lot of crap on the ending. I just don't like the way bands are doing things anymore.

Besides Charlie Christian, who are some guitarists who've worked well with horns?

It's hard to say, man. I don't know. I'm gonna tell you: I don't listen to no guitar player, on the average, for my guidance. I don't do that, because I'll figure out my own way to play it.

Have you ever played with another guitarist in your band?

Oh, yes. I've had them, but they get in the way.

Tell us about your guitar and amp.

I use my Gibson Firebird, a real famous guitar. I also use my Washburn—I endorse Washburn. It's a hollowbody, like a Gibson D-35. I got two Music Man amps. They're just like a Fender, but I got them big speakers in them. I got one on my right for the guitar, and the one on my left is for my fiddle. Of course, I didn't play no fiddle on the new album at all.

Do you still own a Telecaster?

Nah.

Have you ever used a guitar pick on a record?

No. I never used a guitar pick in my life. The only time I use a pick is when I play mandolin.

This is your 50th anniversary of recording.

That's right!

What's the secret to long life in this line of work?

Well, you think positive. Don't do nothing to hurt yourself, like all these guys who get out there and get on alcohol. That's one of the worst killers in the world! Along with that, there's cocaine and heroin, speed, and all that crap. Nah. Trying to go with all the women every night—there's a lot of things that will take one down.

How do newcomers to the road tend to screw up?

Their first mistake is being on the ego trip. Egotistical people, they perish like the rest of them. That's deadly as well, man. You get out there thinking you're better than the people who made you, and then you fall by the wayside and you can't handle that. These record companies and news media take the person up that don't deserve it and put him on a top shelf, and he ain't gonna have nothing to stay up there with. And when he falls, he falls real hard. He can't take that. There's so many ways to mess yourself up.

Can a musician become so experienced that he doesn't need to practice?

Well, I can't talk for everybody, but I never practice. I do, but I practice in my head. I'll think of parts while I'm laying in bed or walking down the street or driving in my car or when I'm up on the bandstand playing. My solos are never the same thing, on the average. I'm always thinking of new things to do, but make sure that they fit.

Do you play guitar when you're off the road?

No! I never open my case. No, no! I want to relax, I want to go visit and do anything but hear music. Just to refresh my mind, I may listen to some of my old stuff on my car stereo.

Are you your own harshest critic?

Yeah, I am, really. And I got something else to say: This new record is starting to take me out of the blues scene. I hope so, man, because when they talk about the blues, the whites think of Mississippi and Chicago. Man, I can't stand that kind of stuff. I really can't.

No one who knows your music is going to mistake you for a Mississippi bluesman.

Yeah, but that's what's hung in people's minds. When they holler "blues," they want me to get down with "Good Old Home Sweet Chicago" or whatever that shit is [Robert Johnson's "Sweet Home Chicago"], and I don't play that, man. I just don't play that.

Some of them want you to be talking loud and having a bottle in your pocket too.

That's right! Now, I allow no drinking on the bandstand, I don't allow no risqué on the bandstand, I don't allow nobody to come up on the bandstand to mess with the musicians while they work. I got a dead law against all of that. My band is respectful to the audience and themselves, and that's the way it is. If they break the rules, I warn them, just like Clinton—"three strikes and you're out." That's right. See, people bring their kids—from infants up to teenagers—to the show. There's old folks, like Grandpa and Grandma. All ages comes to my show. Why? Because they gonna get a clean show and a good show and a show that got dynamics and is not harsh on their nerves. Of course, I have to hold my band down sometimes because younger people get excited and they get loud, but I tell them, "Looky here—this is not what my music is all about." We got four stages— loud, midrange, soft, and off. And that's the way I want it.

SWEET HOME CHICAGO

MUDDY WATERS

BY JAS OBRECHT Rolling his eyes skyward and shaking his head like a man possessed, Muddy Waters cast a powerful spell. His high cheekbones and Oriental eyes gave him a certain Eastern, inscrutable quality, and at times his face became angelic. He could easily work audiences into a frenzy, framing his urgent lyrics and otherworldly slide with electrifying band arrangements. ¶ A Delta-bred bluesman, Muddy instinctively understood the power in simplicity. Time and again, he transformed basic patterns into blues masterpieces. Decades after their introduction, hypnotic stop-time songs such as "Mannish Boy" still exhilarate listeners. Like the superstitions and voodoo images prominent in his best-known lyrics, Muddy's primal, earthy rhythms contain a deep, almost subconscious appeal.

More than any other performer, Muddy Waters was responsible for forging Delta acoustic music into electrified, band-oriented urban blues. And some of his bands were the stuff legends are made of. In the '50s alone, he performed with Jimmy Rogers, Pat Hare, Willie Dixon, pianists Otis Spann and Memphis Slim, and the top blues harmonica players—Little Walter, Walter Horton, Sonny Boy Williamson II, Junior Wells, and James Cotton among them. British groups copied his songs in the early '60s, one naming themselves after his "Rollin' Stone," and guitarists such as Buddy Guy, Mike Bloomfield, Eric Clapton, and Johnny Winter came to share his stage. But through the years and various sidemen, Muddy's music remained intensely his own. His vocals and playing patterns have often been imitated, but no one has ever quite captured his touch.

By the end of his life, Muddy Waters was hailed as the "Father of Chicago Blues." "It makes me feel very good to be called that," he said. "You know, I feel like I deserve it. I've been through quite a bit, and I've paid my dues."

Old-time bluesmen would insist that to really have an instinctive feel like Muddy's, you'd have to be raised in the Mississippi Delta. A flat plain of former swampland bordered on the west by the Mississippi River from Memphis to Vicksburg and on the east by the Yazoo River, the Delta has been predominantly African American since it was first drained and cleared by slaves. After the Civil War, its rich fields were worked by cotton sharecroppers who lived on tenant farms or plantations. Many found solace from their physical hardships and low social status in the church's promise of salvation and a joyous afterlife. Others turned to earthier remedies, such as drinking, gambling, and listening to "the devil's music" or, as it became more commonly known, the blues.

Bandleader W.C. Handy, the self-proclaimed "Father of the Blues," heard this form of music for the first time in 1903, when he was awakened in the Delta's Tutwiler train station by a ragged slide guitarist. By the late 1920s, Charley Patton, Son House, Willie Brown, Bo Carter and the Mississippi Sheiks, Garfield Akers, Skip James, Tommy Johnson, Ishman Bracey, Bukka White, and others were performing around the Delta. Patton, the most famous progenitor of the Delta style, sometimes cradled his guitar on his lap and fretted with a knife. The rough-voiced singer moved to Dockery's plantation in the heart of the Delta before World War I, and performed at house parties and local juke joints with two other influential guitarists, Willie Brown and Tommy Johnson.

A convicted murderer and failed preacher, Son House developed his ferocious slide style in the late 1920s and for a while played with Patton and Brown. For sheer finesse, Delta blues guitar reached its zenith in the 1936 and '37 recordings of Robert Johnson, who learned directly from Son House and Willie Brown. Johnson epitomized the Delta bottleneck style, executing poignant phrases against a steady bass beat. Of all the Delta bluesmen, Robert Johnson and Son House would have the most profound effect on young Muddy Waters.

DOWN ON STOVALL'S PLANTATION

"Well, my mother told my father
On the day I was born,
'Gotta boy child coming,
Gonna be a son of a gun'"
                    —"Rollin' Stone"

The second son of sharecroppers Ollie Morganfield and Bertha Jones, McKinley Morganfield began his Mississippi odyssey in the plantation settlement of Rolling Fork on April 4, 1915. The toddler loved to crawl in the standing water behind his father's two-room shack, so his grandmother nicknamed him Muddy. His sisters added Waters. Ollie Morganfield played blues guitar, but Muddy wasn't around long enough to remember it. With the death of his mother, the three-year-old was bundled off a hundred miles north to be raised by his maternal grandmother, Della Jones, who lived out in the country just northwest of Clarksdale on the Stovall plantation off Highway 1. Here Muddy grew up in a battered one-room cabin, less than a day's walk from where W.C. Handy first heard the blues.

The boy's earliest attempt at music consisted of banging on a kerosene can and singing. He failed at accordion and then took up Jew's harp. At seven, Muddy received his Christmas wish—a "French harp," or harmonica. After finishing the third grade, he was pulled from school to plow and chop cotton for 50¢ a day. Years later he described his field-hand days in Paul Oliver's *Conversation with the Blues* [Horizon]: "I do remember I was always singin', 'I cain't be satisfied, I be all troubled in mind.' Seems to me like I was always singin' that, because I was always singin' jest the way I felt. And maybe I didn't exactly *know* it, but I jest didn't like the way things were down there in Mississippi."

"From a kid up," Muddy told Jim O'Neal and Amy van Singel in *Living Blues*, "I wanted to definitely be a musician or a good preacher or a heck of a baseball player. I just had to. I had three choices. I couldn't play ball too good—like I hurt my finger and I stopped that. I couldn't preach, and well, all I had left was getting into the music thing." Even before he could pick "nary a note" on the guitar, Muddy jammed on harmonica with Robert McCollum, a popular musician who later recorded as Robert Nighthawk. Robert and his brother Percy played at Muddy's first wedding, to Mabel Berry, on November 20, 1932.

That same year, Muddy saved nickels and dimes until he had the $2.50 needed to buy a secondhand Stella guitar. "The first time I played on it," he told author James Rooney in *Bossmen* [Da Capo], "I made 50¢ with it at one of those all-night places, and then the man that runned it raised me to $2.50 a night, and I knew I was doing right." The first song he mastered was Leroy Carr's 1928 hit, "How Long—How Long Blues," while the first song he composed, he told Alan Lomax, was "I Don't Want No Black Woman Charley-Hamming My Bones." Muddy's next instrument, a Sears Silvertone obtained via catalog, cost $11. "I had a beautiful box then," he beamed. He watched his friend Scott Bohanner finger chords and taught himself to pick out little lead patterns. Muddy gave frequent performances, either as a solo artist or as the harp player accompanying Bohanner's guitar. Within a year Muddy surpassed Bohanner on guitar, and the teenagers formed an act patterned after the popular Mississippi Sheiks. Muddy played lead and harmonica, while Bohanner supplied rhythm and Henry "Son" Simms, a former Patton sideman, doubled on guitar and violin. The trio appeared at juke joints, country balls, and Saturday night fish fries around Clarksdale, earning a meal, moonshine, and half dollar apiece for playing blues and hillbilly tunes until sunrise. Muddy spent some of his money on 78s by Blind Blake, Blind Lemon Jefferson, Blind Boy Fuller, and Charley Patton. After hearing Robert Johnson's 78s of "Terraplane Blues" and "Walkin' Blues," Muddy said, "I always followed his records right down the line."

Whereas Robert Johnson fashioned his slide by chipping away at a broken bottleneck with a pair of pliers, Waters had another method. "First I'd get me a bottle that I'd think was going to fit my finger," he explained in *Guitar Player.* "I had the slide in the wrong place at first, on my second finger, and later I put it on my little finger. So I had to get the right pop bottle to fit. Then I'd wrap some string around the neck and soak it in kerosene and light it and let it burn till it go out. Then you just rap it, and it breaks off just right. It's a short slide, because I play single strings mostly."

The biggest influence on Muddy was Eddie "Son" House, who lived just north of Robinsonville and performed with his cigar-chomping pal Willie Brown. Unlike their sometime playing partner Charley Patton—a "clowning man" with a guitar—Son House took his music mighty seriously. Sitting on a straight-backed chair, he'd suddenly whip his head back, roll his eyes up inside his skull, and slide a bottleneck up his guitar strings. Veins bulging in his forehead, he'd moan, thump a bass note, and begin singing with the deep conviction of a sinner on judgment day. His guitar tuned to a chord, he propelled rhyming, strung-together verses with open-handed rhythms, bottleneck wails, and ringing notes pulled pistol-like with his index finger. In person or on 78, Son's blues were intense, anguished, and as powerful as any on record. Seeing him in rural Tunica County, Mississippi, had inspired Robert Johnson, and House likewise cast a lifelong spell over Muddy Waters, who first saw him perform in Clarksdale in 1929.

"One night we went to one of those Saturday night fish fries," Waters explained to *Down Beat* in 1969, "and Son House was playing there. When I heard Son House, I should have broke my bottleneck. Played this same place for about four weeks in a row, and I was there every night. You couldn't get me out of that corner, listening to what he's doing." In the O'Neal interview, Waters remembered, "I thought Son House was the greatest guitar player in the world when I heard him because he was usin' that bottleneck style, and I loved that sound, man." Big Joe Williams, who'd converted his guitar to a 9-string, reportedly taught Muddy "Baby, Please Don't Go."

While elements of Muddy's guitar tone and vocal style were drawn from House, some of his arrangement techniques and slide embellishments were closer to those heard on Robert Johnson's 78s. "I consider myself to be what you might call a mixture of all three," he explained to O'Neal. "I had part of my own, part of Son House, and a little part of Robert Johnson. I seen him at a distance a couple of times, but never actually seen him to play. I regret that very much, because I liked his style. I thought he was real great from his records, beautiful. Really, though, it was Son House who influenced me to play. I was really behind Son House all the way." Johnny Winter remembers that late in life Muddy still held House in high regard: "Muddy really did like Son House a lot; he seemed to think of Son kind of like a father figure. He learned a lot from him, and he always referred to Son House as the 'old man.'"

While living outside Clarksdale, Muddy supplemented his tractor driver income by providing musical performances and, in a way, community services. "I did it all, man," he confided to interviewers Robert Neff and Anthony Connor in *Blues* [Godine]. "I tried to gamble, and I made and sold whiskey. I didn't stick nobody up, but I was successful with my whiskey. I used to make that jive out on the Stovall plantation. Had me a little still back out in the bushes, man. I never did believe I would get over working, though, and I probably never would have but for music. I'd have worked to 105 years old and saved $10,000—*maybe!* Because they wasn't paying nothing. I made just as much as the guy who worked five days, 75¢ a day. I used to make $2.50 on Saturday night at a frolic or supper with my guitar, and you couldn't make but $3.75 for five days' work. So I laid back and hid from the bossman and made just as much as everyone and was just as rested as I wanted to be. You got to use your brain."

Muddy moved to St. Louis for a few months in '39 or '40, but found the city intimidating and unprofitable. He made pilgrimages to Memphis, which had long been a mecca for bluesmen, boatmen, levee workers, farmers, drifters, gamblers, musicians, hustlers, and whores, all of whom converged among Beale Street's saloons, gambling parlors, pawnshops, and chitlin joints. In Memphis, wrote W.C. Handy, "business never closed until somebody got killed." Sleepy John Estes framed it another way: "Memphis has always been the leader of evil things in the world." Muddy especially admired the Beale Street jug bands, which were precursors of the modern blues ensemble, having vocalists, a rhythm section, and solos on guitar and harmonica. Among the scene's spectacular harmonica players were Noah Lewis, Will Shade, Jed Davenport, Walter Horton, and Hammie Nixon.

Back home Muddy opened a roadhouse on the Stovall plantation, peddling moonshine, reigning over marathon gambling sessions, and performing music. On occasion he brought over talent from Helena, such as the night Sonny Boy Williamson played at Muddy's shack with young Elmore James on guitar. Sonny Boy returned the favor, featuring Muddy and Son Simms on his radio show. To lure heavyweight talent to his juke, Muddy sometimes drove to Friars Point, caught the Helena ferry, and headed to radio station KFFA, home of the popular *King Biscuit Time* show. The cost of hiring a better-known musician—$25 in advance, $25 the night of the show—was offset when the performers promoted their appearances over the airwaves.

Muddy had his own string band too, a raucous, drummerless, back-country outfit with Simms on violin, Percy Thomas on guitar, Louis Ford on mandolin, and a huge stand-up bassist named Pittypat. Their repertoire of waltzes and pop hits like "Sitting on Top of the World" and "Corrina" was similar to that of one of Muddy's favorite bands, the Mississippi Sheiks. ("Walked 10 miles to see them play," Muddy told O'Neal. "They was high time through there, makin' them good records, man.") Three or four times a year, bossman Howard Stovall hired Muddy's band to play white parties.

During the summer of '41, Alan Lomax and John Work, members of a field recording team sponsored by the Library of Congress and Fisk University, journeyed to the Delta to find Robert Johnson. By then Johnson was dead, and their second choice, Elmore James, couldn't be found. Locals directed them to a tough young field hand who, they said, played in a manner remarkably similar to Robert

Johnson's. He worked under the name of McKinley Morganfield, but everyone called him Muddy Waters.

Muddy had wanted to record since he'd first heard Son House 78s on the jukebox, but he was initially suspicious of Lomax, thinking he was there to bust him for making moonshine. Muddy eventually agreed to record a couple of songs in exchange for $20 and a copy of the 78. Muddy explained to Jim O'Neal that he led Lomax to his shack: "We went down there and we set his stuff up, got it out of the trunk of his car—all his long batteries—and set 'em up on my front porch. And I was in my front room with my guitar, my little microphone, and he ground his wire down through the window and we went to work. And when I played a song and he played it back, then I was *ready* to work. Never heard that voice before, you know, and I was *ready*."

His guitar tuned to open *G*, Waters slipped a bottleneck over his little finger and began with "Country Blues." With its deliberate pacing, dead-serious vocals, popping bass, and fierce slide chorus, the song was based on Son House's "Walking Blues," which Robert Johnson had also learned from House. Lomax interviewed Muddy on record immediately after he'd completed the take. Waters calmly described writing his version on or about October 8, 1938, while fixing a tire puncture: "I had been mistreated by a girl, and it looks like that run in my mind to sing this song. I just felt blue, and the song fell into my mind and just come to me just like that and I started singing my own." The song, he added, "come from the cotton field and the boy what put the record out—Robert Johnson. He put out 'Walkin' Blues.' But I knowed the tune 'fore I heard it on the record. I learned it from Son House." Asked whether Johnson or House was the better player, Muddy responded, "I think they both about equal."

The reason he took up guitar, Muddy told Lomax, was "I just loved the music. Saw Son Simms done playin', and I just wanted to do it and I took after it." He remembered practicing an hour-and-a-half to two hours every day when he first started, and described listening to a 78 of "How Long—How Long Blues," the first song he'd ever worked out on guitar: "I just got the song in my ear and went on and just tried to play it." He picked up his bottleneck style, he added, from Son House, and used three tunings—"Spanish" (open *G*), "the natural," and "straight *E*," which he also called "the cross-noting."

Muddy's second selection, "I Be's Troubled," was an original tune he'd made up while walking down the road after hearing a church song. The lyrics provided a good indication of his mental framework at the time:

> *"Well, I feel tomorrow*
> *Like I feel today,*
> *I'm gonna pack my suitcase,*
> *And make my getaway,*
> *Lord, I'm troubled,*
> *I'm all worried,*
> *And I never be satisfied,*
> *And I just can't keep from crying"*

Asked by Lomax how he wrote songs, Muddy responded: "I make up verses first. After I get my verse made up, then I come get my guitar and try two or three dif-

ferent tunings, see which one would be the better to play it in. Then I starts."
Muddy wrapped up the session with "Burr Clover Farm Blues," a song he'd composed at the request of his boss, who grew burr clover on the plantation.

Lomax kept his word and sent a $20 check along with the Library of Congress
78 of "Country Blues"/"I Be's Troubled," which stated "Sung with guitar by
McKinley Morganfield at Stovall, Miss., 1941" on the label. A testament to Muddy's
great musicianship, these tracks still sound as fresh and vital as the 78s Robert
Johnson had recorded just a few years earlier.

The following summer Lomax returned and recorded the Son Simms Four—
Simms, Percy Thomas, Louis Ford, and Muddy Waters. These raw, exuberant,
downhome cuts may seem out of tune to some listeners, but the peculiar tonalities
created by playing in improvised tunings on inexpensive instruments were exciting. In the years to come, Muddy would use microtonal excursions outside the
standard blues scale to conjure dramatic effects. Waters sang "Ramblin' Kid Blues"
and "Rosalie," while Louis Ford fronted "Joe Turner" and Percy Thomas handled
vocals on "Pearlie May Blues." Muddy and Simms both played guitars on a recutting of "Burr Clover Farm Blues" and the country swing tune "Take a Walk with
Me," which shares melodic similarities with Robert Johnson's "Sweet Home
Chicago." Charles Berry, Waters' brother-in-law, came in for a pair of takes of "I Be
Bound to Write You," essentially a dual-slide-guitar reworking of "I Be's Troubled"
with new lyrics. Robert Johnson's influence was unmistakable in Muddy's unaccompanied "You Gonna Miss Me When I'm Gone."

Muddy borrowed Lomax' Martin acoustic for his final session that summer,
probably held in a room off the commissary at Sherard's plantation in Clarksdale.
He recorded "You Got to Take Sick and Die Some of These Days" and "Why Don't
You Live Right so God Can Use You" and recut a tune from the summer before,
"Country Blues, No. 2." After another take of "You're Gonna Miss Me When I'm
Gone," Muddy wrapped up his Library of Congress recordings with "32-20 Blues"
featuring Charles Berry on second guitar.

According to Lomax' notes, Muddy's unrecorded repertoire at the time featured
pop songs ("Dinah," "I Ain't Got Nobody," and "The House"), country and western
faves ("Home on the Range," "Deep in the Heart of Texas," "Boots and Saddles,"
"Missouri Waltz," and "Be Honest with Me"), blues by Sonny Boy Williamson and
Walter Davis, and Muddy's original numbers "Ramblin' Kid," "Number One
Highway," and "Canary Bird Blues." Lomax noted that Muddy kept a table-model
Victrola record player at home, along with a few 78s by Arthur Crudup, Peetie
Wheatstraw, Tony Hollins, Sonny Boy Williamson, and Jay McShann. Muddy named
Fats Waller as his favorite radio star, Walter Davis as his favorite recording artist.

On December 18, 1942, Muddy made his mark—an "X"—on an application for a
marriage license in Coahoma County. Five days later, he took 27-year-old Sallie
Ann Adams of Stovall, Mississippi, as his second wife. The couple shared a four-
room shack in the middle of a cotton field with Muddy's grandmother and his
uncle, Joe Grant. Sharecropping eight acres, Muddy's family owned only a few
hogs and chickens and a small vegetable garden. After paying off debts at the plantation commissary, they hoped to clear between $100 and $300 at the end of the
year. Muddy's wife and grandmother were regular churchgoers, and on Saturday
nights everyone piled into Muddy's 1934 V-8 Ford to drive to country dances.
Waters told Lomax that besides blues, his band played love songs and breakdowns

at dances, adding, "I like to play the blues the best." The most popular non-blues numbers at these events, Muddy figured, were "Corrina," "Down by the Riverside," "Chattanooga Choo-Choo," "Blues in the Night," "Darktown Strutters Ball," and "Red Sails in the Sunset."

For Muddy and countless other African Americans in the Delta, life outside their own culture was often harrowing and brutal. The sharecropping system kept them in virtual peonage, while Jim Crow laws forbade them from using the same restaurants, drinking fountains, rest rooms, parks, train cars, schools, and hospitals as white citizens. "Uppity" black males who failed to step off the sidewalk to make way for a white person or who were accused of making a sexually suggestive remark to a white woman risked being beaten, castrated, or lynched, as thousands had since the turn of the century. After the outbreak of World War II, some of Muddy's pals fled to Chicago.

Muddy drove a tractor for another season, but more than anything he wanted to leave Mississippi and become a "known person." On occasion he sat in with traveling minstrel shows, and he blew harmonica for a couple of nights when Silas Green From New Orleans, the most famous of the Southern vaudeville carnivals still in operation, passed through Clarksdale. Sometimes he drove his band up to Memphis to perform for tips in Handy's Park. Waters was well liked by the plantation hands who came to toss dice or sip moonshine in his shack, and his blues performances had already made him a local legend. But the lure of what lay beyond the Delta was too powerful to resist: "I wanted to leave Mississippi in the worst way. I'd had a run-in with my boss on the plantation where I was working. I was driving a tractor and making some big bread—22¢ an hour—and I asked for a raise. He blew his top. I figured if anyone else was living in the city, I could make it there too."

CHICAGO BOUND Carrying only a suit of clothes and a guitar, Muddy Waters pulled out of the Clarksdale train station on a hot afternoon in May '43. He changed over to the Illinois Central in Memphis, and arrived in Chicago at 9:30 the next morning. It was a Saturday, but within hours he was hired to unload trucks on the afternoon shift at the Joanna Western Mills paper factory. Muddy stayed with childhood friends on the South Side for a couple of weeks, then moved in with his cousin. Within six months, he had his own apartment a few doors down at 1851 West 13th Street.

The most popular Windy City radio shows of 1943 broadcast big bands fronted by Tommy Dorsey, Harry James, and Glenn Miller. Bebop was making inroads among record buyers, and the rage in Chicago was love ballads by Nat "King" Cole, Billy Eckstine, and Johnny Moore's Three Blazers. The city's burgeoning blues community was headed by pianist giants Big Maceo and Memphis Slim and guitarists Big Bill Broonzy, Lonnie Johnson, and Tampa Red, who already owned electrics and favored a smoother, more urbane style than Muddy's deep-bottom Mississippi blues. Still, it was Broonzy who gave Muddy his start by introducing him around Sylvio's club as "a pretty good blues singer" from Mississippi. "My blues, I came to Chicago and I had to work 'em up in there," Muddy told Jim O'Neal. "When I did get it through, boy, I bust Chicago wide open with 'em. Memphis Slim was the big man, Tampa Red and Maceo, Big Maceo—them was the big dudes up in here then. Big Bill, that's the nicest guy I ever met in my life. He really say I had it. . . . Big Bill was my mainline man. He was one of the greatest in the business. He was just *great* comin' up."

Invitations to play house rent parties for whiskey and tips trickled in, and then Muddy found work backing Sonny Boy Williamson at the Plantation Club. Fingerpicking an acoustic, he could scarcely cut through the din. "I was banging my hand all up," he explained in *Guitar Player,* "so I went to a thumbpick. That still wasn't loud enough, so I started playing electric. I used to play with a metal thumbpick, but the sound is too tinny to me, so I use a plastic one now. No way could I use a regular flatpick.

"I had started with a Stella, and I had a Silvertone when I came North. First electric I got was in 1944. That's when I hooked into it, and it was a very different sound, not just louder. I thought that I'd come to like it—if I could ever learn to play it. That loud sound would tell everything you were doing. On acoustic you could mess up a lot of stuff and no one would know that you'd ever missed. So electric was really rough." Muddy explained that he started amplifying because "people were talking louder in the neighborhood taverns around Chicago, where I'd be sitting and picking my guitar. The people would be drinkin' a little booze and talkin' loud, and you couldn't get your sound over them. When I first got to Chicago, the first Sonny Boy [John Lee Williamson] would blow over the house mike sometimes. So the electric thing had started a little bit."

Muddy journeyed back to Clarksdale in 1945 for his grandmother's funeral. Meanwhile, another young Mississippi guitarist/harmonicist took a job at a radio cabinet company with Muddy's cousin, Jesse Jones. Upon his return from Mississippi, Muddy was invited over to jam with the new guy, Jimmy Rogers, and thus began an important Chicago blues partnership. Rogers blew harmonica in their earliest lineup, while Muddy and Claude "Blue Smitty" Smith, an acquaintance of Jesse Jones, handled guitars. Playing house parties, Muddy sang original tunes and covers of Robert Johnson and Leroy Carr 78s, concentrating on thumped bass notes and bottleneck slides until Smitty, who was adept with boogie-woogie and blues, taught him to finger-fret solos.

The trio moved on from one "five-dollar-a-night" club to another. Sonny Boy, who apparently liked Muddy's car as much as his playing, hired him for out-of-town dates, such as his weekly gig at The Spot in Gary, Indiana. When Sonny Boy got too drunk to sing, pianist Eddie Boyd would take over as frontman. One night Sonny Boy slumped into a corner and Boyd, too tired to sing, asked Muddy if he could take over. "I said, 'Okay, I can sing,'" Muddy described, "so I pulled the mike to me, opened this big mouth up, boy, and the house went *crazy,* man." The whiskey-loving Williamson eventually got the band fired.

Waters' first Chicago recording occurred in 1945 or '46, when he cut a hopping horn version of "Mean Red Spider" that was leased to 20th Century, a subsidiary of Philadelphia's Ballen Record Co. The side is credited to James "Sweet Lucy" Carter & His Orchestra, but the singer/guitarist is certainly Muddy Waters. According to Muddy, supervisor J. Mayo Williams also recorded Jimmy Rogers and Sunnyland Slim at the same session. Ernest "Big" Crawford played bass, while Lee Brown, who arranged the date, manned piano on Muddy's side. "When I actually started making records in Chicago," Waters recalled, "I had a Gretsch archtop with a DeArmond pickup on it."

Muddy's second commercial session, on September 27, 1946, was organized by blues recording czar Lester Melrose. Waters was there on the recommendation of James "Beale Street" Clarke. The musicians backed vocalist Homer Harris on three sides, and Muddy fronted on his own "Jitterbug Blues," "Hard Day Blues," and "Burying Ground Blues," which weren't released until the '70s. "That country stuff might sound funny to 'em," Muddy later speculated. "I'd imagine, you know, they'd say, 'This stuff isn't gonna sell.'"

Thanks to Sunnyland Slim, Muddy joined the roster of Leonard and Phil Chess' Aristocrat Records in 1947. He was driving a truck for a venetian blind company when Chess told Sunnyland to get him into the studio. Sunnyland called Muddy's supervisor and told him Waters was needed at home because his mother was sick. Waters played along. "I lied a big old lie that time," he would later smile. Muddy backed Sunnyland on "Johnson Machine Gun" and "Fly Right Little Girl," and then Chess asked him to play solo, "like Lightnin' Hopkins." Muddy fronted on "Gypsy Woman" and "Little Anna Mae" while Big Crawford, Memphis Slim's subtle sideman, thumped string bass. Amplification added new smoothness to Muddy's guitar tone, and perhaps a little of Blue Smitty's coaching echoed in the single lines of "Gypsy Woman." The entire date lasted less than a half-hour.

Unimpressed with Muddy's sides, Leonard Chess shelved them for several months. After all, he figured, who was interested in old-time Delta blues? Encouraged by Evelyn Aron, his business partner, Chess finally agreed to let Muddy record again the following year. With Big Crawford's backing, Muddy cut "I Can't Be Satisfied" and "Feel Like Going Home." Both were old-fashioned blues, essentially reworkings of his seven-year-old Library of Congress sides. But amplification added sustain to his searing, whining slide, and Muddy intensified his declamatory vocal style by emphasizing vibrato and running words together into quick phrases. Vastly different from the sax jumps and smoky ballads dominating the R&B charts, Muddy's surging Delta rhythms signaled the beginning of the greatest creative era of Chicago blues.

ROLLIN' AND TUMBLIN' "I Can't Be Satisfied" was released on a Friday afternoon in April '48. Distributed from car trunks to record stores, beauty salons, barber shops, and train porters, the initial pressing of 3,000 sold out by Saturday evening. Muddy enjoyed recounting how he went to the Maxwell Radio Record Company to buy a couple of copies and found they were charging $1.10 for the 79¢ record and limiting sales to one per customer. Even after exclaiming "But I'm the man who made it," he left clutching only a single copy. "All of a sudden," he recalled, "I became Muddy Waters, you know? People started to speakin', hollerin' across streets at me." With just a handshake, Muddy and Leonard Chess sealed their contract. On Muddy's recommendation, Chess signed Robert Nighthawk.

"I Can't Be Satisfied" sold well in Chicago and the South through the summer of '48. The hit's immediate result was to land Muddy and his band—Jimmy Rogers on harp and guitar, Baby Face Leroy Foster on drums and guitar—prestigious gigs at the Du Drop Lounge and Boogie Woogie Inn. "Baby Face Leroy was from Memphis," Rogers recalled. "He was okay. He'd enjoy being around us every day, wherever we was gigging at. He wanted to learn songs, different lyrics and whatever. We'd just jam. I was playing harmonica some, and Baby Face would sing, and

Muddy, he would sing and play the bottom on the guitar. That was our pleasure thing. That's what we'd really dig."

A superb, Delta-bred harmonica player, Marion Walter Jacobs—soon to be known as Little Walter—joined later in the year, permanently moving Rogers to guitar and Foster to drums. "I met Walter down in St. Louis the first time," Rogers explained. "He was just out from Louisiana. He'd been down in Memphis and Helena, places like that. He was a young dude, about 16 or 17, when we first met up. He was interested in playing harmonica, so he'd be around with Sonny Boy— Rice Miller—and Peck [drummer James "Peck" Curtis] and Robert [Lockwood] Junior. He was trying to learn every phrase he could get, and Rice Miller was pretty good at that type of situation. He would show him licks. And once Walter'd hear it, it would psych him up in his mind to practice on it. When he'd get off by himself, he would do it. He'd just hang around and play around and follow him around from one gig to another."

Barely 18 years old when he joined Muddy's band, Little Walter was already an inveterate street jammer. "That boy, I had to chase him out of Jew Town regular," Waters told Jim O'Neal. "He'd see me coming, and grab his mike and *gone!* He done made a lot of money down there. You know, sometimes Walter'd take in $35 or $40. That was good money then. More'n a club was payin' us."

Waters and Rogers, in particular, took the music very seriously. "Muddy and I would see each other every day," Rogers explained. "It was just something I wanted to do. If I got an idea about some lyrics or something, I'd put them together by myself. Then when I'd get it halfway lined up like you want to, then you consult with your partner about it and work on it. Muddy and I were *very* serious about it. It was the most serious thing that I had going in my life at that time. That's what kept me out of a lot of the different mischievous things that youngsters will get into. That kept me busy. That was more important to me than breaking a window or doing the dumb things like kids do.

"We'd meet over at Muddy's house. He lived on the West Side, over at 1851 West 13th Street, during that time. I was down on Peoria Street in what they called 'Jew Town.' It was walking distance—I could walk from my house to Muddy's in about ten minutes. It was a long ways to walk, but it wasn't worth paying a streetcar fare to ride down there. We'd have a guitar over at his house, and me and Muddy would be there arranging. That's where we got Walter into arranging songs. See, Walter wasn't much of a songwriter, but he was a good player. He would just be there, and he wouldn't interfere with us. And then he might get up and walk out or something, and we would still be working on arranging this stuff. That's what we would do all the time. Every day we would do that. I worked with Big Crawford too. He was the nicest guy. He was big and tall—weighed about 300-and-some pounds and stood about 6'5". He was a huge guy, like Willie Dixon. I'd see him all the time, and we would talk and crack jokes and fool around together. And man, we was concentrating on arranging, same idea as Muddy. We were all doing the same thing together. We was just really into music, man. We wanted to do it. And that's really what we did."

Once Walter was onboard, the band began looking for new turf. "There were four of us," Waters confided to *Down Beat,* "and that's when we began hitting heavy. Little Walter, Jimmy Rogers, and myself, we would go around looking for

bands that were playing. We called ourselves 'the Headhunters,' 'cause we'd go in
and if we got the chance we were gonna burn 'em. Sometimes we'd come in and
win the contest—they'd have an amateur contest with a prize—but the guy would
come up to me after he found out who I was and say, 'Uh, uh, Muddy—you's too
heavy. You can work for me if you wants, but you's *too heavy* to be in the contest.'
Of course, I ain't like that no more. I know different now. 'Cause you can't be the
best. You can just be a good 'un."

But with the possible exception of Elmore James' Broomdusters later in the '50s,
Muddy probably did front the era's best electric blues band. Their music was raw
and physical, each song a taut, emotional plea with Muddy's voice and slide guitar
its roaring heart. Playing for all-black audiences, they seldom strayed from the
structure of traditional 12-bar blues, outside of occasionally stretching out the
count. Muddy was unafraid to sing behind the beat, telling his men: "You don't
count it out—you *feel* it."

For transplanted Southerners, Muddy's sets in tiny sawdust clubs conjured the
joy and anguish of their own pasts. He was the downhome blues shouter amplified, a commanding presence who could transfix the rowdiest tavern crowd with a
patented bottleneck slide to the tonic and fifth and a few words sung in dark baritone. "I used to watch that guy, man," describes Buddy Guy, "and happy tears used
to fall out of my eyes when I'd see him play slide. Oh, yeah." Muddy took chances,
and his tone had more bite than a scolding shrew. His greatest appeal? "It was
sex," Marshall Chess insisted. "If you had ever seen Muddy then, the effect he had
on women. Blues, you know, has always been a women's market. On Saturday
they'd be lined up ten deep."

As tight as Muddy's musicians were, they were not allowed to accompany him
in the studio. "Chess wouldn't upset things," Waters explained to Pete Welding.
"He wouldn't mess with the harp or the extra guitar. He wanted to keep the combination that had made a hit record—just Big Crawford's bass and my guitar. It
was amplified, but I was playing old-style blues." Muddy's final 1948 session produced "Down South Blues," based on the Delta's popular "Rollin' and Tumblin'"
theme, and "Kind Hearted Woman," which was closely patterned after Robert
Johnson's recording.

Baby Face Leroy came in on second guitar for four of Muddy's 1949 Aristocrat
sides, while the ever-present Crawford played bass. Of special interest, though,
were two highly amplified cuts Muddy made with just Crawford: "Little Geneva"
blended unusual slide licks into a theme based on Robert Johnson's "Love in Vain,"
while the bottleneck in "Canary Bird" buzzed around like a bumblebee. Muddy
took Jimmy Rogers, Little Walter, and Baby Face Leroy on a tour of the South afterwards, centering around Clarksdale and Helena. For several weeks he performed
daily on KFFA radio, earning five dollars a week and getting bookings via listeners
who phoned in.

On his return to Chicago, Muddy stepped outside of his leader's role to record
behind his sidemen. Along with Big Crawford, he played on Chess-produced cuts
credited to Jimmy Rogers & His Trio. He also clandestinely met Baby Face Leroy
and Little Walter over at the Parkway studios to be part of the Little Walter Trio
and the Baby Face Leroy Trio. Muddy laid back on most tunes, but couldn't resist
tearing loose with slides and moans during Foster's wild two-part "Rollin' and

Tumblin'," one of the most powerful downhome sides ever recorded. The song was based on a traditional Delta slide riff. "To me, that track's an example of somebody who transcends anything we think we know about the guitar," says Ry Cooder. "I mean, that could've been a one-string there, it could've been a post with a string, it could've been any of my guitars—it wouldn't make any difference.

"What's great about when guys play like that is you don't feel frets and six strings and a scale length. It's beyond construction and principles. Muddy's playing where he knows those notes are, and they are locking into this spirit thing of playing, the movement of the song. And he goes past the note—the note isn't just there at the fret, because there are degrees of the note. It's like Turkish music in some ways—degrees. There's 5,000 notes. The great thing about this is it liberates you from these idiotic frets. So sometimes he's expressing some excitement by alternating between playing a note and going sharp. And that's where all those old guys hear that stuff. There are nuances—no phrases come down the same. When you need a lift, you go sharp, and when you need to sour it up and make it feel a little darker, you go flat. But you don't think about it. You just do it.

"It is staggering to have that quality of performance on a record, though, knowing what we know. If you listen to Sonny Boy Williamson's 'Little Village' with Leonard Chess, how did records ever get made when assholes like that were running the show? It's amazing to me. They made these records under such duress, conditions that ultimately we see all around us today. They talk about slaves singing code songs—it's hardly any different. But the really amazing thing is that you can get that kind of free expression and excitement and even joy, perhaps, in a white guy's recording studio. It takes a lot of power and amazing strength of personalities. These aren't wimpy guys. They're pretty heavy-duty characters, and it's coming out. They're just blasting away. We're very lucky this shit got recorded at all. It's a miracle that it did, when you look at the record business and the people that ran it.

"Baby Face Leroy's 'Rollin' and Tumblin''' is not chord-based. You don't feel chord in it. And it's greater than anything African. This is taken to another planet. This is the beauty of the American music. Listen to those big string bends—whoa! Slap bass. It's incredible. Nobody in Africa can do that. I mean, as great as African music is, it all comes together in this country. Mister Microtone. I guess that's what you'd have to say, finally, about Muddy: He's Oriental in his approach."

Upset at hearing his most prominent artist on another label's release, Chess firmly advised Muddy not to play slide for anyone else. He paired him with Big Crawford for two 1950 takes of "Rollin' and Tumblin'" designed to compete with the Parkway issue. Snappy drums and bass lifted the song into the new decade, while Muddy's verse of moans paid homage to its Delta roots. Around this time, Leonard and Phil Chess bought out their partner at Aristocrat and formed Chess Records.

Muddy provided the new label's first hit, "Rollin' Stone" backed by "Walkin' Blues." The potent, bare-bones guitar of "Rollin' Stone" had a powerful impact on Jimi Hendrix, who recut the song as "Catfish Blues." Even with Muddy's distorted guitar sound, "Walkin' Blues" retained the flavor of Robert Johnson's version. The 78 sold exceptionally well in the triangle covering St. Louis, Memphis, and Chicago, and ranks high among Muddy's performances.

Muddy's band consistently packed the house at the Du Drop Lounge, where they were often double-billed in blues contests with Big Bill Broonzy or Memphis

Minnie. Encouraged by audience response at these shows, Chess finally let Little Walter back Muddy in the studio. That they could lock so tightly on their earliest effort, 1950's "You're Gonna Need My Help I Said," portended good things to come. Pushed by Little Walter's harp swoops and wails and the drummer's easy rim shots, Muddy's slide stung even harder on "Sad Letter Blues," "Early Morning Blues," and "Appealing Blues." The lineup's final taping of 1950 produced Muddy's first Top-10 R&B hit: "Louisiana Blues," a variation of the voodoo mojo hand theme with a nice guitar-harmonica unison, backed by "Evans Shuffle," a boogie harp showcase with one of the most effective false endings imaginable.

In sessions that followed, Waters and Walter further forged their instruments into a seamless voice or created stunning call-and-response dialogues. Once Little Walter expanded his presence on record by using a good studio amp, he took over as the band's main soloist. Jimmy Rogers, whose supple bass runs and unerring fills were essential to the stage act, was finally brought in to appear on "Long Distance Call," a Top-10 hit that Muddy later cited as his favorite record. Two other steady sellers, "Honey Bee" (with its brilliant microtonal slidework) and "Still a Fool," featured Little Walter's downhome guitar. "Walter was practicing guitar and wanted to play," Rogers remembers. "He would practice along with what we were doing, take a guitar and play along with it. After he learnt a few chords on it—notes and stuff—he played on those records."

"Muddy's style of Chicago blues did not follow the standard 'rhythm' and 'lead' concept," points out former Waters bandmate Bob Margolin. "All the instruments interwove high and low parts, constantly complementing and answering each other. Jimmy Rogers called this 'filling in the cracks.' This interactive approach was much more musically rewarding than the 'play your part' approach and is part of the reason why so many of Muddy's sidemen went on to make names of their own."

"She Moves Me," cut with Leonard Chess on bass drum, became Muddy's biggest hit of '52. With gigs nearly every night and widespread black radio play, Muddy now reigned supreme on Chicago's South Side. His amplified Delta music had come to define Chicago blues, and imitators sprung up in the Delta, Memphis, Detroit, and on both coasts. Tours took him to the East and South. Understandably, the potential of success on their own began to attract Muddy's sidemen. After all, they were all fine soloists, and Waters let them prove it. "I give everybody a chance to play," he told them. "I'm not going to hold you back. I love you, but I can't make the people do that. *You* do that."

Little Walter was the first to leave. He scored a huge 1952 hit on Checker with "Juke" (essentially the Waters band's instrumental signature) and quit to take over Junior Wells' position in the Four Aces. Naturally enough, Muddy hired Junior Wells until the harmonica player's induction notice arrived. At Chess' insistence, Little Walter continued to back Muddy in the studio until '57. For a while, Little Walter's popularity eclipsed that of his former bandleader.

Walter Horton, master of a wide, sweeping harp style, joined the band in 1953, but Little Walter played on the next hit, "Hoochie Coochie Man," a Willie Dixon composition that became Muddy's signature song. According to Dixon, Muddy knew it was a hit the moment he heard it: "I brought 'Hoochie Coochie Man' to him when he was working along 14th Street, and he liked it so well he went in the washroom, practiced a few minutes on his intonation, and he come right out and done it. And he's been doing it ever since." "Hoochie Coochie Man" sold 4,000 copies the first week and became Muddy's biggest seller, spending weeks in the R&B Top 10. A few months later, Horton took a gig under his own name and sent Henry "Pot" Strong to substitute. A strict leader who insisted that his band show up on time, sharp, sober, and ready to play, Muddy fired Horton and hired Strong, whose style resembled Walter's.

Muddy finally actualized his dream of a blues "big band" when pianist Otis Spann joined him. Spann, whom Muddy lovingly referred to as his half-brother, was an unobtrusive sideman who could accommodate styles ranging from subtle fills to thunderous boogies. His admission into the band completed Muddy's move away from the intimate Delta-inspired sound epitomized by the Big Crawford–Little Walter trio sessions to a smoother, more uptempo style. The Waters lineup of two guitars, harmonica, bass, drums, and piano created an enduring blues band standard.

With the added support of Spann, Muddy quit playing guitar. "The band sounded so good to me," he figured, "I didn't think I had to play." Traditional 12-bar blues gave way to groove-oriented arrangements, and with the new emphasis on harp, drums, and piano, Jimmy Rogers moved into the background. For a while, the formula worked. Trailing in the wake of "Hoochie Coochie Man," "I Just Want to Make Love to You" remained Top 10 for more than three months. The band hit the road for one-nighters in St. Louis and Nashville, dates on both coasts, and a full-scale Southern tour with Sarah Vaughan and Nappy Brown. Back home, Muddy moved his family into a well-kept two-story brownstone in the heart of Chicago's South Side ghetto.

Just as the Muddy Waters band was riding high, tragedy struck during the summer of '54: Stabbed by a girlfriend, Henry Strong bled to death in the back seat of Muddy's car. The incident deeply affected Muddy, who eventually hired James Cotton for Strong's position, although Little Walter was brought in to record "I'm Ready," which added to the voodoo mystique spun in "Hoochie Coochie Man." "Muddy swings out," described a *Cash Box* review. "Lyrics are pretty potent, and Waters' delivery is Grade A. Beat is solid, and ork-ing [backing] is torrid. A great bet to make it." And make it, it did: right into the Top 10. It was Muddy Waters' last big hit.

Chicago blues record sales started out strongly in 1954, then dropped 25% during the summer. Some South Side execs blamed the depressed economy. Television was also drawing evening listeners away from radio, the most important medium for blues promotion. But something fresh and urgent was starting to come over the airwaves, a primal blend of R&B, blues, and country that was destined to eclipse the blues and every other popular style: rock and roll.

In Memphis, Elvis Presley paired the country tune "Blue Moon of Kentucky" with a pulsating R&B version of "That's All Right" and sold over 7,000 copies in one week. Bill Haley & The Comets scored million-sellers with "Shake, Rattle, and Roll" and "Rock Around the Clock." Alerted to the vast new audience of white teenagers, A&R men from black-oriented independent labels scrambled for rock and roll acts. Elvis' TV appearances seemed to seal the fate of older bluesmen: After all, how could 40-year-olds hope to compete with the hip-shaking gyrations of a teenage idol? Chess Records jumped on the bandwagon and, on Muddy's recommendation, signed Chuck Berry and Bo Diddley.

Waters still landed an occasional song on the R&B charts—"Mannish Boy" in
'56, "She's Nineteen Years Old" in '58—but his single sales would never approach
those of the rock and rollers. With dismay, he saw the new generation of city-born
blacks abandon blues. "Young Negro kids now, they're so used to what they hear
on the radio, they just turn away from the old blues," he told Pete Welding. "It's
not the music of today; it's the music of yesterday."

Muddy's first album, Chess' *The Best of Muddy Waters,* came out in 1958. He was
still living comfortably, but prime gigs were dwindling. Across the Atlantic, though,
youngsters like Keith Richards and Mick Jagger were hot on his trail, sending away
to Chicago for his Chess releases. Trad jazz—essentially a recreation of Dixieland
and Chicago styles of the '20s—and a folk–blues hybrid dubbed "skiffle" had
become popular in Britain. Chris Barber, a leading exponent of trad jazz, had
already arranged passage for Big Bill Broonzy, Josh White, and Brownie McGhee to
come over and perform traditional acoustic blues in little clubs. Broonzy convinced
Barber to arrange a tour for Muddy Waters, and in October '58 Waters and Spann
flew over. Expecting to hear acoustic folk blues, British audiences were shocked by
Muddy's tavern-level volume. One staid critic found himself retreating from the volume row by row until forced to seek refuge in the men's room. "I didn't have no
idea what was going on," Waters told James Rooney. "I was touring with Chris
Barber—a Dixieland band. They thought I was a Big Bill Broonzy, which I wasn't. I
had my amplifier, and Spann and I was going to do a Chicago thing. We opened up
in Leeds, England. I was definitely too loud for them. The next morning we were in
the headlines of the paper—'Screaming Guitar and Howling Piano.' That was when
they were into the folk thing before the Rolling Stones." Muddy lowered his settings
for the rest of the tour, which reportedly went well.

To his surprise, the English tour brought Muddy the attention of American folk
and jazz fans. In April '59 he played Carnegie Recital Hall with James Cotton and
Memphis Slim. To capitalize on his newfound audience, he was encouraged by
Chess to record *Muddy Waters Sings Big Bill,* a less-than-distinguished album of
Broonzy material. Meanwhile, the electrified power of Muddy's stage presentation
transfixed attendees, as Paul Oliver witnessed at a 1959 show at the F&J Lounge in
Gary. "His band was his instrument," wrote Oliver in *Jazz Monthly,* "and he sang
unhampered, stamping, hollering, his whole body jerking in sheer physical expression of his blues. He would double up, clench his fists, straighten with a spring like
a flick knife, leap in the air, arch his back, and literally punch out his words whilst
the perspiration poured down his face and soaked through his clothing." Muddy
was in a near-trance when he came offstage at four in the morning and spent most
of the next day lying in a dark room with an ice pack on his forehead.

The Newport Jazz Festival booked the full Waters band to headline its 1960
blues program. Muddy was a sensation, earning standing ovations and being
called back to sing "Got My Mojo Working" a second time. Chess issued the performance as *Muddy Waters at Newport.* Muddy returned to England in 1962, once
again misjudging his audience, as he explained to James Rooney: "I went back—
took my acoustic with me—and everybody's hollering, 'Where's your amplifier?' I
said, 'When I was here before, they didn't like my stuff.' But those English groups
had picked up on my stuff and went wild with it. I said, 'I never know what's
going on.' A bunch of those young kids came around. They could play. They'd

pick up my guitar and fool with it. Then the Rolling Stones came out named after my song, you know, and recorded 'Just Make Love to You,' and the next thing I knew they were out there. And that's how people in the States really got to know who Muddy Waters was." Muddy returned to England as part of the 1963 American Folk Blues Festival package.

Encouraged by Otis Spann, Muddy began playing the red Fender Telecaster he'd acquired in 1957, although his next Chess LP was the unadorned, all-acoustic *Folk Singer,* with Buddy Guy on lead guitar. Muddy's unaccompanied "Feel Like Going Home" hearkened back to his Stovall days, while "My Home Is in the Delta" featured his unmistakable slide.

When British groups began arriving in America circa 1964, they proclaimed Muddy and other black bluesmen their sources of inspiration. The Rolling Stones were stunned by their first encounter with Waters, as Keith Richards describes: "Muddy was my man. He's the guy I listened to. I felt an immediate affinity when I heard Muddy play the opening lick from 'Rollin' Stone.' You can't be harder than that, man. He said it all right there. So we went into Chess Studios in '64, the first time we came to America. Went to Chicago to record most of our second or third album at Chess, and we walked in. There's Phil Chess and there's Ron Malo, the engineer, and this guy in white overalls painting the ceiling. As we walked by into the studio, somebody said, 'Oh, by the way, this is Muddy Waters,' and *he's* painting the ceiling. He wasn't selling records at the time, and this is the way he got treated. My first meeting with Muddy Waters is over the paintbrush, dripping, covered in white paint. 'This is Muddy Waters.' *I'm dying,* right? I get to meet *The Man*—he's my fucking god, right?—and he's painting the ceiling! And I'm gonna work in his studio. Ouch! Oh, this is the record business, right? Mmmmm. The highs with the lows! Ooh, boy. In that one little meeting, in those few seconds, Muddy taught me more . . . [*Imitates Muddy speaking in a gentle voice*] 'It's a pleasure to meet you.' And the look in the eye was saying, 'Well, *you* can be painting the ceiling next year!' Because he had no idea that we revered him or anything. We were just another bunch of creeps."

As Muddy became more famous in the years to come, he often credited the Rolling Stones with helping to renew interest in his music. "Ah, he did, yes, and bless him," Keith continues. "When we started the Rolling Stones, we were just little kids, right? We felt we had some of the licks down, but our aim was to turn other people on to Muddy Waters. I mean, we were carrying flags, idealistic teenage sort of shit. There was no way we thought anybody was really going to seriously listen to us, but we wanted to get a few people interested in listening to the shit we thought they ought to listen to—which is very elitist and arrogant, to think you can tell other people what to listen to. But that was our aim, to turn people on to the blues. If we could turn them on to Muddy and Jimmy Reed and Howlin' Wolf and John Lee Hooker, then our job was done."

Soon Eric Clapton, Jeff Beck, Jimmy Page, and Alvin Lee were paying Muddy homage through imitation and praise, awakening even more American youths to the fact that the songs credited to one "M. Morganfield" on their favorite albums were by an active performer. "That's a funny damn thing," Waters told Rooney. "Had to get somebody from out of another country to let my white kids over here know where we stand. They're crying for bread and got it in their backyard. They

got some of the best blues singers that ever lived right here in the United States—
there's nobody else, you know. They sure ain't got no real good blues singers in
England. But they got some heck of a players there—guitars, every other thing."

Students from the University of Chicago made pilgrimages to nearby South Side
clubs and began duplicating what they heard. Harmonica student Paul Butterfield
and his guitar-playing pal Mike Bloomfield launched the Butterfield Blues Band,
while other Chicago blues acts were fronted by Charlie Musselwhite and Steve
Miller. Jimi Hendrix unabashedly admitted his debt to Muddy, telling *Rolling Stone:*
"The first guitarist I was aware of was Muddy Waters. I heard one of his records
when I was a little boy, and it scared me to death."

"THE LIVING LEGEND" As rock and blues became more integrated, Howlin' Wolf,
John Lee Hooker, Buddy Guy, and Junior Wells found bookings in white coffee
houses and clubs. For the first time, Muddy himself was welcomed full-scale onto
the turntables and stages of young white America. And with the possible exception
of B.B. King, no other bluesman made the transition so gracefully. His new fans
found him confident, articulate, and proud: "I wasn't a cat to come in with a big
bottle of wine in my pocket and talking loud," Muddy insisted. Billed as "The
Living Legend," he found his new audience appreciative of his original style, which
enabled him to drop some of the newer songs he tended to dismiss as "commercial
gimmicks." "If you like the blues," Muddy said, "I can get them over to you no
matter what color you are. I do the same thing for white audiences that I do for
black audiences. I get down and do real blues. I get the blues, and I just let go in
the middle of it."

After issuing *The Real Folk Blues,* a 1966 hits compilation, Chess attempted to
"update" Muddy's sound by casting him as a soul singer on *Brass and the Blues.*
Competing with heavy organ and honking, overdubbed horns, Muddy was painful-
ly out of character. Otis Spann's Bluesway album *The Blues Is Where It's At* contained more blues-approved Waters slide. Muddy and his band backed John Lee
Hooker on *Live at Cafe Au-Go-Go,* and in '67 Chess issued more early Waters sides
on *More Real Folk Blues.* Around this time, Muddy hosted *The Muddy Waters Blues
Show* on Chicago's WOPA radio.

For his next LP, Cadet's *Electric Mud,* Waters was submerged in psychedelic
fuzz-tones, wah-wahs, and overbearing drums. It troubled him that the tracks
couldn't be reproduced onstage: "If you've got to have big amplifiers and wah-
wahs and equipment to make your guitar say different things, well, hell, you
can't play no blues." In the *Guitar Player* interview, Muddy referred to the project
as "dogshit." He returned to a purer sound for Fathers and Sons with Spann,
Butterfield, and Bloomfield.

Muddy's popularity with rock fans grew to the point where, in '69, his appearance at Chicago's Auditorium Theater almost brought down the house. "For nearly
ten minutes after he left the stage," wrote Don deMichael in *Rolling Stone,* "the
audience roared its delight. They stomped, shouted, clapped, whistled, screamed,
jumped up and down the aisles and seats. Pleadings from the stage to calm down
were to little avail." Muddy and his band then undertook a tough series of one-
nighters at colleges and clubs. On their drive home that October, Muddy was in a
head-on collision that killed his driver and left him with a broken leg, fractured

ribs, sprained back, and paralyzed right hand. "They had to lift me out of the car," he described. "I was in the hospital for three months. I had numb hands, and they gave me lots of trouble."

For a while, it was rumored he would never play guitar again. "I went places in Europe with Muddy after the accident," recalls Buddy Guy, "and he was very particular about who was driving and the speed they went. To be in a car when the steering wheel gets pushed completely through the driver, I imagine that follows you up to your death. Muddy had all these iron pins in his hip. Before that, he used to sit down and jump up and do his little Muddy dances all the time." After nearly a year, Waters was able to discard his crutches and take up guitar again.

He toured Japan, Australia, and stateside with guitarists Sammy Lawhorn and James "Pee Wee" Madison, drummer Willie Smith, and Pinetop Perkins, the replacement for Otis Spann, who'd passed away in 1970. A collection of Chess sides, *They Call Me Muddy Waters,* won the 1971 Grammy Award for Best Ethnic/Traditional Recording. Muddy flew to England to record his next album with Chicago bluesmen and British rockers Rory Gallagher and Rick Grech. *The London Muddy Waters Sessions* won Muddy another Grammy and helped him land a headlining role at the '72 Montreux Jazz Festival. The following year he moved his family to suburban Westmont, Illinois. Muddy featured his touring band on *Can't Get No Grindin',* while *London Revisited* collected unissued tracks from the Gallagher-Grech project. Muddy cut the Grammy-winning *Woodstock Album* and *Mandingo* film soundtrack in '75.

On occasion, Muddy was still able to share billings with peers such as B.B. King, Albert King, and Bobby Bland. "Ain't too many left that play the real *deep* blues," he explained to Robert Palmer in *Deep Blues* [Viking]. "There's John Lee Hooker, Lightnin' Hopkins—he have the Texas sound, and Texas blues is very, very good blues—and, let's see, who else? Ain't too many more left. They got all these white kids now. Some of them can play *good* blues. They play so much, run a ring around you playin' guitar, but they cannot vocal like the black man. Now B.B. King plays blues, but his blues is not as deep as my blues. He play a type of blues that can work in a higher class place, like to a higher class of peoples—they call 'em urban blues. Bobby Blue Bland, the same thing. Albert King play a little deeper blues than they do. Otis Rush is deeper. I don't want to put down nothin' that'll make anybody mad, but it's the truth. There ain't too many left sings the type of blues that I sing."

Muddy's favorite instrument during this period was his '57 Telecaster, which had a replacement rosewood neck that was slightly wider than standard. Bob Margolin, co-guitarist in Muddy's band from 1973 to '80, observed that "in the '70s—and I presume earlier—Muddy used Gibson medium strings gauged .012 through .056, replacing the wound G with a .022 plain. He had a mid-'60s Fender Super Reverb amp that he said had been modified for a 'heavier' sound, but after it was stolen he replaced it with a stock late-'70s Super Reverb that sounded just the same. He ran his amps with all the knobs set on '9' and no reverb or tremolo, controlling his volume from the guitar.

"Most of the time Muddy played in standard tuning. Wherever his capo went, he played in E and A blues-scale positions. He wore a 1¹/2" metal slide that he'd had since 1947 on his pinkie, and he used a National thumbpick on his index finger. His wild, powerful slide playing used every technique to create a full range of musical emotion: wide and narrow vibratos, muted notes, and bold sustain. When playing backup, he ran walking patterns on the bass strings, creating ultimate swing with what he called 'delay time,' a behind-the-beat feel. A great example is Muddy's playing on Sonny Boy Williamson II's classic 'Don't Start Me to Talkin'.' Occasionally in the '70s, Muddy would tune to open *A*, remove his picks, and play some of his early songs, usually 'Walkin' Blues' or 'Rollin' and Tumblin'.' The first time I saw him do this, before I was in the band, it was literally the deepest, most powerful music I'd ever heard. It still is. As great as Muddy's early open-tuned slide playing is, he developed even more subtlety and depth as he aged."

HARD AGAIN　Thanks in part to Johnny Winter and bandmates such as Bob Margolin, James Cotton, Pinetop Perkins, and bassist Charles Calmese, Muddy Waters created some of his most moving records during his final years. Winter juggled the roles of friend, bandmate, producer, and protector of the classic sound, and near the end, Muddy came to regard him as a son. Their albums together recast classic material from the 1940s and '50s alongside tough new songs—in effect, reprising Muddy's career—and brought Waters three consecutive Grammy Awards.

The bluesmen first met in Austin, Texas, during the late '60s, and then again in '74 while filming PBS' *Soundstage*. A couple of years later, Winter became Waters' producer. "When I heard slide for the first time, on *The Best of Muddy Waters*, I couldn't believe it," Winter recalls. "It was unique, so original sounding. At first I thought it was a steel guitar, and then I heard one cut that I was sure was just one guy playing guitar. Muddy would fret the guitar sometimes, and other times he would use a slide. He almost always went for single lines. He wore such a short slide on his little finger that he couldn't get but about two strings with it at the very most. So I'd learned pretty much everything from just listening to the records for all those years, and it definitely was cool to be able to work with the guy.

"Bob Margolin said that Muddy would work on stuff with him, but I had studied and loved Muddy's records for so long that I pretty much had gotten everything down before we started working together. Muddy was always real supportive of me. I remember him telling me a couple of times that people talk about white people not being able to play the blues. He said, 'Man, you can play as good a blues as anybody I ever heard—just that good old lonesome sound.' That really made me feel good. Sometimes you could read interviews where some people were trying so hard to get him to say bad stuff about me, and he just wouldn't do it. I loved him, man, and it was real mutual."

For 1976's *Hard Again*, they chose a live, "back to mono" approach and booked a studio in Connecticut with a room large enough to accommodate the whole band. "We miked everyone," Johnny says, "but we mostly used this one big mike in the middle of the room. It caught a lot of the room's natural echo." Muddy displayed spine-chilling authority as he premiered exciting new material, recut one of his old field recordings, and roared through standards like "Mannish Boy" and "I Want to Be Loved." Cut in two days, the album got its title during playback, when Waters uttered that the music "makes my little pee-pee hard again!"

Since Muddy hadn't played slide for a while, it was up to Johnny to conjure the *Hard Again* bottleneck sounds. "Muddy didn't play a lot at the time," Winter recalls. "In fact, for a while he'd almost completely quit playing guitar. The blues revival in the late '60s convinced him that he ought to start playing more guitar. But he just had one guitar on the road, and if he'd break a string or something, then you wouldn't hear any slide. But he'd usually just pick a couple of songs a night and play some really burning leads on that, but he didn't seem to want to play all the time like he used to. Maybe it was because he was in that car wreck, and he definitely had pain if he played very long. But Muddy loved that real trebly Telecaster sound, and he got a great sound out of his treble pickup. Muddy would tune his guitar to an E chord and just put his capo wherever it needed to go. But on that first record, every time I'd pick up a guitar, Muddy would put his down and just sing. There weren't very many tracks where both of us played guitar at the same time, but there were a couple, finally. I played slide on all that record."

With Johnny bottlenecking a metal-bodied National resophonic, Waters journeyed to his Delta roots for "Can't Be Satisfied" and "I Feel Like Going Home," which was eventually released on *King Bee*. "Boy, he really didn't want to do that," Johnny recalls. "We did those two songs the same night, after the whole record was finished and he was ready to leave. I begged him: 'Please, let's just try a couple of acoustic things.' He did those two songs one time each, and that was it. It's too bad Muddy wouldn't do more takes. We could have definitely got a better cut on both of those, but it was that or nothing. He was real conscious about not recording too many songs. He knew how many songs it would take to do an album. The Chess people put out so much of his extra stuff on albums, and he wanted to make sure that that didn't happen. He wanted to get paid for everything he did, and he didn't want a bunch of extra things floating around. So he was real careful." Muddy was pleased with the album, declaring that "*The Best of Muddy Waters* and the first one I did with Johnny—*Hard Again*—are the two best albums I ever did." The release brought the band bookings across the U.S. and Europe.

Winter produced Muddy's 1977 album *I'm Ready*, with Walter Horton and Jerry Portnoy sharing harp chores and Jimmy Rogers coming in on guitar. Muddy himself played slide on "33 Years," "Mamie," and "Screamin' and Cryin'," the original version of which he'd recorded in 1950 with Johnny Jones on piano and Leroy Foster on drums. "Somebody once asked Muddy what his favorite was of the songs he'd written, and he mentioned 'Screamin' and Cryin'," observes Bob Margolin. "I think writing from his own experiences was his method. When he presented things to the band in the studio, he would just say something like, 'We're gonna play a slow blues in *G*' or maybe 'a shuffle in *A*,' and he'd sing his new words.

"In his listening, Muddy just wanted to hear the real deep stuff. If Muddy listened to a Robert Johnson tape, he would have someone fast-forward through 'They're Red Hot' and 'From Four Till Late' to get to 'Kindhearted Woman.' He just wanted to hear the real deep blues. That's what he went for in his writing too, although he did write some silly songs, like on *Unk in Funk* and the *Woodstock Album*. But at his best, he was carrying on from what Robert Johnson and Son House did."

"Muddy had that Mississippi thing and the Chicago sound all wrapped up together," observes Johnny Winter. "It's pure style. Muddy Waters *is* Chicago blues, which is electric and has that group sound to it. But he always kept the feeling of the Delta. And Muddy didn't really play a lot of stuff. He pretty much had one or two leads, and he would just improvise around with those a little bit. He had it down where it was good and didn't really need to be more than what he did. He definitely had his little licks that he used to play in just about everything. He had those signature licks, so you could always tell that it was a Muddy Waters song. Muddy was real modest about his own guitar playing. He didn't feel like he was that great. I remember him saying, 'Well, even an old man probably can outplay me, but I got something now that works.' He knew what he did was cool, but it wasn't about technique. He just had a way of putting it all together."

The band's tour crisscrossed the U.S., and Muddy was invited to perform at the annual White House staff picnic in August '77. President Jimmy Carter handled the introduction: "As you know, Muddy Waters is one of the great performers of all time. He's won more awards than I could name. His music is well known around the world, comes from a good part of the country, and represents accurately the background and history of the American people."

Muddy and Johnny sorted through concert tapes for their stunning *Muddy "Mississippi" Waters Live*. Waters bellowed past hits in fierce, declamatory style and threw cross-sections of his whole stylistic spectrum into amazing slide choruses. His tone was otherworldly. The album left no doubt that Muddy Waters was still at the height of his powers.

Winter produced Muddy's swan song, *King Bee,* in '81, recutting "Sad, Sad Day" and "(My Eyes) Keep Me in Trouble" and taping "Champagne & Reefer," a pro-marijuana song used to delight concertgoers. Waters toured in support of the album—his slide playing was unspeakably brilliant during his shows in Saratoga, California, where he and Johnny Winter met for their *Guitar Player* cover story interview. Holding court backstage, Muddy awed us with his ageless wisdom and warm humor; I've never encountered a more stately being. Asked about the future of the blues, he responded: "It may change around a little bit, but it won't die. See, the groove was here [*long pause*] before time."

Muddy was home preparing for another album when he passed away in his sleep on April 30, 1983. Cancer may have silenced the 68-year-old bluesman, but his spirit and influence live on everywhere electric blues are played. Buddy Guy speaks for countless others when he says, "Whenever you hear me play, man, there's a part of Muddy Waters, Howlin' Wolf, Little Walter—all those great musicians. The only hard part about it is trying to play as much like them as you can, because nobody will ever fill the shoes of Muddy Waters and Howlin' Wolf and those great people that did that music."

JIMMY ROGERS

BY JOHN ANTHONY BRISBIN There have been few forces in postwar Chicago blues more influential than guitarist and singer James A. Lane, better known as Jimmy Rogers. Rogers wasn't simply an early and enduring partner of Muddy Waters. He gave the slide-playing Waters pointers on fingerpicking and tuning. He taught himself how to brace Waters' rough, electrified Son House/Robert Johnson–style Delta sound with a light musical touch on rhythm guitar and well-articulated walking bass patterns. Similarly, Rogers not only brought the enormously talented Marion "Little Walter" Jacobs to play harmonica with Waters and himself, but he also trained the wild teenager to perform in a band context. Rogers deepened the band's sound by adding Otis Spann after he found the extraordinary blues pianist "sleeping in cars on the West Side." The best postwar Chicago blues band—and the prototypical Chicago blues sound—was in large part designed and defined by Jimmy Rogers.

And that's not the half of it. Rogers was a matchless '50s session player for Chess who on numerous recordings devised ways to aptly frame tough-to-back leaders such as Howlin' Wolf and Sonny Boy Williamson II [Rice Miller]. From his 1950 Chess pairings of "Ludella" and "That's All Right" to 1959's "Rock This House," Rogers also delivered his own solid recordings, many self-penned and featuring his lithe and pleasing vocals. Although they were modest sellers at the time ("Walking by Myself," from 1957, marked his only appearance on the *Billboard* R&B charts), many of his songs have become blues standards, earning Rogers income and acclaim through cover versions by rock stars such as Eric Clapton and Gary Moore.

Following his twilight at Chess in the late 1950s, Rogers, like many other blues-men, gave up music for an income sufficient to support a growing family. He drove a cab and then ran a clothing store on Chicago's West Side with his wife, Dorothy. The urging of longtime musical friends Sunnyland Slim and Willie Dixon and a good offer from concert promoter Willy Leiser moved Rogers to return to playing in the late 1960s. He toured nationally almost continually since that time until the mid 1990s, a tribute to both his stamina and to the hard work of his longtime manager and agent, Tom Radai.

Rogers returned to the recording studio in 1972 for Leon Russell's Shelter label to cut the album *Gold Tailed Bird;* the original LP plus additional cuts were reissued by Capitol as *Chicago Blues Masters, Vol. 2.* Through the auspices of Johnny Winter, Rogers reunited with Muddy Waters for a 1978 tour and the album *I'm Ready.* The best of Rogers' later recordings are 1990's *Ludella* and 1994's *Blue Bird.* A double-CD retrospective of Rogers' Chess sides, *The Complete Chess Recordings,* was released in 1997, while his classic Chess work with Muddy Waters is available on the MCA/Chess compilations *The Muddy Waters Chess Box, Rare and Unissued,* and *His Best 1947-1955.* At the time of his death in 1997, Jimmy Rogers was working on a star-studded new release for Atlantic, which was to feature Eric Clapton, Mick Jagger, and other guest stars.

As huge a presence in the blues as Jimmy Rogers was, he was interviewed rela-tively infrequently. Sections of Mike Rowe's masterwork, *Chicago Breakdown* [Eddison Bluesbooks] and a lengthy interview by Jim O'Neal and Bill Greensmith in an early issue of *Living Blues,* remain two of the most substantive accounts of Rogers' career. Suffice to say that Rogers, while gracious to his fans, was a guarded person. He prized his privacy and found a way to "give 'em a smile and bypass outta there" when "they bug you so bad with a million questions all at the same time." My thanks to Tom Radai and to Rogers' devoted children Angela and Jimmy Lane—his father's rhythm guitarist and a blues artist in his own right—for their help in securing the 1994, 1996, and 1997 interviews that went into this September/October 1997 *Living Blues* cover story, "Jimmy Rogers: 'I'm Havin' Fun Right Today.'" And most of all, thanks to the late Jimmy Rogers for patience with those million questions.

JIMMY ROGERS: "I'M HAVIN' FUN RIGHT TODAY." My mother was Grozie Jackson. My father's name was Roscoe. He was a Lane. They met at Ruleville, Mississippi, but he was from Georgia, around Atlanta. So he came up there in Mississippi, workin', I guess. They got together, and I was born in Ruleville, Mississippi, 1924—June the 3rd. My mother was only twenty years old.

Ruleville is a few miles away from Vance. There was a place called Doddville, Mississippi, around there too. From there, I went to Atlanta. My father taken my mother and us back to Georgia. Yeah, he taken us away. That's where we was for a long time. One of those what ya called groundhog sawmills is what he worked at, and he got killed at a scuffle somewhere there. So after Atlanta, we went back to the Delta in Mississippi, to the place where I had some relatives live at, which was Vance. Yeah, my mother brought us all back home.

Then she met Henry Hall. That's where my sisters and brothers came in later years. But I was young and my grandmother taken me in. She brought me on up. She brought me and her baby girl, Annie Lou, up there at her house in Vance. I was mostly around my grandmother's kids and my uncle's kids—that was my grandmother's brother. Most peoples that I'm familiar with is peoples on my mother's side. That's the side I came up through. Most people thought my grandmother was my mother and my Aunt, Annie Lou, was my sister. She was four years older than me. I spent quite a few years with my grandmother in Vance, Mississippi.

I was a Lane, but I was with my grandmother, the Jacksons. I had always been goin' under Lane. I got my Social Security card under that one and came on through that way. One guy that my mother stayed around with was Henry Rogers. That's a different person than Henry Hall. I grabbed his name when I became a professional musician. My wife was a Turner but, by marryin' me, she's been a Lane for forty years. So all my kids is born under Lane. You'll never untangle that one. [*Laughs.*]

My grandmother was all right, but she was set in her own ways. She liked the church and stuff. Nothin' wrong with that. Matter of fact, it helped me. It kept me clean of bein' with police records and stuff like the youngsters of nowadays. She taught me to respect the ladies too. It was Mrs. So-and-so, or Miss So-and-so. I didn't never get into too much trouble because she would get this hide [*laughs*]. No straps—uh uh. A switch, man. She'd use a switch. She'd break those switches together and get that butt, boy. And they hurt. She could hit, hit pretty hard, yes sir. I'd find that out if I threw a rock, somethin' like that, broke somebody's window, or go off and stay too long, she might put off the whoopin' till tomorrow. Then I'd pay for old *and* new [*laughs*]. So I was a pretty good guy. I would do anything she would ask me to, but sometime I would want to do it on my terms, ya know. That's when I'd get in trouble. 'Cause, see, I liked music. I liked to deal with music and musicians and what have you. And she wasn't for that stuff.

She'd take me and my aunt, Annie Lou, to church with her lots, but sometime she'd go and leave us home. When I was ten, my aunt was around fourteen. Boys started looking at her, and she'd be gone. Then I'd be at the house around there by myself. That's when I could really cut up. I'd leave my guitar around the corner of the house—with steels on it or a bottleneck, piece of bottle to get notes—somethin' to pass the time away and entertain myself.

My grandmother and me, we had fun. She'd try to entertain me the best she could, but she didn't like that blues guitar too much. I had a lot of fun durin' Christmas, eat cakes and pies and stuff, cook a turkey or chicken or goose or whatever. We'd have a nice time. Santa Claus would come to us, bring us toys, maybe bring me a cap gun or somethin', a stockin' full of apples and oranges, a pack of candy and some firecrackers. Not much snow in Mississippi, not like it is in Chicago. My grandmother was a mother and a grandmother for me. She did all she could for to bring me up, and she brought me up as a pretty good young man.

My grandmother had a brother, Walter Miller—they called him W. M.—that was workin' as a porter for the I.C. [Illinois Central] Railroad Company. He'd shift from Chicago, Detroit, go down around Memphis. That was his run. Wherever he was, he'd send my grandmother tickets. She'd take the train or bus or whatever and ride to where he was, but she would catch up with him mostly here in Chicago or St. Louis. He would be sendin' her a lot of places on cleaning jobs—cleanin' the train cars. He'd hook her up in that stuff. Back at that time, that was a pretty good job. So wherever my grandmother would go, I was right with her. If she was on the train, I would go too. If she would ride the bus, I would ride the bus. Wherever she would go, I would go. I got a chance to see quite a bit of the world like that.

When I'd have a chance to go to school, I would go. But I'd be movin' around so much from one place to another with my grandmother that I didn't really get the schoolin' that I deserved and wanted. That's the reason I scuffled so hard for my kids. I put 'em all through school because I had the privilege to do it. Same thing with farm work. I milked cows, got eggs a little bit when I was real young, but my grandmother would keep me with her most of the time, so I didn't really get what I wanted out of farm life. That kept me in a different life from Snooky Pryor and them. They was mostly farm boys. I'd be goin' and comin'. I would stay for a while, then they wouldn't see me for the next couple of years.

Some of the time when she'd travel off workin' on the trains, she'd leave me with my aunt or somebody, or my cousins. That's where I'd be at all the time. She'd drop me off there, give my instructions or whatever I'm supposed to do—and I didn't give her too much trouble. But I was interested in gettin' out and meetin' some of these musicians that I'd been hearin' about.

I met Snooky Pryor down in Vance. He was on a plantation. He had four years on me. When we met, I was about nine. He was 'round about 13, 14. He was thin then, wasn't too much bigger than I was. You know, it didn't take young boys, at that time, too long to get to be real good friends, because it's nothin' to do in the country but just listen to the birds and stuff. I was out of Vance a couple miles. He was round about four or five miles out in the other direction. He'd come to Vance, come on through, come out there where we was—and we'd have fun that day! Yeah. We'd see each other and play around at somethin'.

We was playin' harmonicas and guitars—that's what we was interested in. He didn't know a bunch of the other guys I knew that also played harmonica. After we met up, I introduced him. God, Snooky and me, it wouldn't be nothin' for us to walk five or eight more miles together after he got to my place. Man, we'd do it to get where the hot spot was! We'd have eight or nine hours to drift around. It was somethin' to do, man! The Levi boys, that's who we would fool around with most. Other times two or three of us—like Baron Lee, Kitten, the Levi boys, and Roosevelt—we'd be together and go where Snooky was. Or Snooky and his brothers would come over there where we were and we would get together. Sometime Snooky would spend the night over to my house or over to the Levi boys' house. Then the followin' day we'd go again! Then he'd go home. We wouldn't see him for a while.

So we had us like a harmonica trio. We was makin' fun out of what we would do. We'd get harmonicas, buy 'em up. They was makin' 'em better durin' that time than they do today. We just paid 50¢ apiece for 'em, that's all. Now they cost $12.50, $15. I used to get Hohners, Marine Band, American Ace. Well, I didn't fool with American Ace too much. It was a cheap harmonica. Eventually I would leave Vance with my grandmother. We'd come to St. Louis, come to Memphis or someplace like that. I wouldn't see Snooky and them till maybe the next year.

Sonny Boy, not Rice Miller but [John Lee] Sonny Boy Williams[son], we'd hear his records once in a while. He was on RCA Victor label, and we'd get those records down in there. Sonny Boy was "the man" then. That was the style we were playin'. "Good Mornin' Little Schoolgirl" and "Black Gal" and all kind of stuff like that. That's the way we learned our licks on harmonica. Snooky, he stayed with that style. He used to be jealous of me with the harmonica. I was pretty good with it. I don't know how good, but he said he wished he could play like me. But I was interested in guitar.

After we'd get away from that, we used to hunt together. All of us, me and Levi and Baron Lee, Roosevelt and Snooky. We'd go rabbit huntin' mostly. And boy, Snooky was good tappin' a stick. He had a doggone stick about three feet long. He'd put a tap on the end of it, see, like a tap that come off a wagon—big, iron, weighted. He would trim the stick down so he'd get the end of it to fit in that hole in the tap. And he would line it with staples and nails around the outside so it wouldn't come off. Man, he could throw that stick. He didn't need no gun. He'd be off out there by himself. We were all huntin' together, but he'd get off from us. Sometime when we'd meet up again, next three, four hours, his waist be lined. He'd have four, five, or six rabbits. Him and that stick. He could throw that thing like you could shoot a rifle, but it was quiet—no shots like we'd be doin'. That's why he like to hunt all by himself. He'd kill 'em runnin' sometimes.

I had a .22 rifle. I was good with that rifle, but he used to take that stick, man, and tap 'em. In the rough, wooded area he would turn them dogs loose out there. That'd get 'em started. They'd start to track. You'd just stay around the edges, make contact with people so you wouldn't get shot. They'd come out, be hoppin' along from the dogs. You get a chance to shoot 'em like that. Sometime you'd catch 'em sittin'. I killed maybe four, five rabbits a day, but Snooky was off right there with his stick. We called him "The Stick Man." He was good with that thing. We'd take 'em to my grandmother at home. I'd skin 'em, wash 'em out, do around. The scraps, you'd throw 'em to the dogs. They'd swallow that like nothin'. Take 'em in the house. She'd salt 'em, put 'em in a pan with a little vinegar and let 'em sit there for a few hours. She'd cook 'em, man. Taste better than chicken. You'd get home and, if you wanna eat, she'd fix ya up! Either we'd hunt or go fishin'. My grandmother loved to fish too.

Sonny Boy [Rice Miller] was from another little place out from Vance called Glendora. He'd come through Vance. He was young then, had to be in his twenties, I'd say. They'd call him "The Loafer," ya know. [*Laughs.*] He'd have some harmonicas around his waist. He'd get out there and play—sit on a corner, storefronts, anywhere he could make him a few quarters. His playin' sounded pretty to me. It was hard. It was somethin' strange. He was a friendly guy. If you was interested in harmonica or blues music, you could get with him. He'd have a bunch of us followin' him around, man. We was 13, 14, 15 at the oldest at that time. He was goin' as Sonny Boy Miller. That's what we knew him as was Sonny Boy Miller. Next thing he grabbed Williams. Then it was Sonny Boy Williamson. People thought he was just Sonny Boy: "There go Sonny Boy." That's the way people figured it out to be.

He got to dealin' around with old man Sam Anderson over there in Helena, KFFA in Helena, Arkansas, and that's where he met all those other bunch of musicians around West Memphis and Friars Point. That's where he met all those guys: Dudlow Taylor, Joe Willie Wilkins, and guys like that.

There was a guy named John Blissett I used to follow around. He was an albino fella. He was good. I got some strokes out of him too. Snooky knows about him. I also remember when Hound Dog Taylor was young. Nathaniel, that was his name, but everybody called him Nitter. He used to come through Vance, Minter City, Philipp, places like that. That's where I met all those guys at, around in there. Nitter, most everything he play then was with a slide. He couldn't pick too much, but he could play with that slide on a hollow-box [acoustic] guitar.

I saw Son House play, yeah, in Clarksdale. He didn't play too much in town. Out at Stovall's or some of them places like that, they'd throw a party and he'd play. Him and Houston Stackhouse was family folks some kind of way. I don't know whether they was cousins or what they was, but they was some relation. Robert Petway and Tommy McClennan, I met those guys. I didn't never know 'em too well, but I did see them. It was at Vance. They was playin' in the street. They was just guys that played by themselves, ya know. Sit down, play like Honeyboy Edwards do now. Tommy McClennan and this other boy what died, uh, Robert Johnson—they was hangin' around Greenwood down in there. Yeah. Tommy McClennan remind me a lots of Homesick James. He'd get his words mixed up. He would do that a lot. I'd just laugh at him and go ahead. Little Richard sneaked around there and stole "be-bop-a-lu-bop" and "be-bam-boom." That was Tommy. Little Richard, somewhere he saw him and he grabbed that and he kept that. He made "Tutti Frutti" out of that. Tommy McClennan, that's where he got that from. He wouldn't tell you that [laughs], but that's the truth.

I saw Honeyboy a few times down South. He was mostly in Mississippi, but he was way up there out from Memphis, around Friars Point and some of them places. Honeyboy was a drifter, but he was up in that part, which was maybe 120–130 miles from where I was. Yeah. I was like "in the forty-mile bend" around in that part down there. There's another guy down there at that time were playin'—they called him Buford. He was a good guitar player. I saw Buford a few times. That's where Howlin' Wolf come up with his style, a lot of his material that he played in his lifetime, from Buford. Sonny Boy helped Wolf out too, learnt him a lot about the ropes of the road, you know, and how to handle himself, 'cause Sonny Boy was older. In fact, they was family. Sonny Boy was with Wolf's sister there; they were brothers-in-law, like that. So they used to travel around together a lot.

Sonny Boy was the big drawin' card at that time. He'd come out of Helena. People would come from a long ways away to see him, 'cause he was on the air. KFFA had a pretty big feel for that stuff. B.B. King was on the air too, playing and announcing, doing commercials for Pepticon: [*sings*] "Sure is fine, Pepticon!" I remember all that stuff. Anywhere a blues musician were, if it was in my range where I could get to them, I would make it there somehow.

I would sneak to see the musicians or listen to the jukebox play when I was 12 or 13. Seeburgs is what they called jukeboxes at that time. I couldn't go in, but I would hear 'em. I would tell my grandmother I was gonna spend the night over to the Leroy's house. Leroy's mother, she was pretty nice. She had a bunch of kids and my grandmother found out that she was what you would say "okay" to be around. In other words, she was pretty strict. She had two boys along about my age. So we'd get along okay. Snooky, he didn't live too far from her, and the bunch of us would hang together.

First we'd go to hang outside the club or two we had in town that you could dance at, but they closed early. About 12:00 or 1:00 the town closed. Then we'd catch 'em out there at the juke joint. People would be there all night. They'd be gamblin' and drinkin' and doin' around out there. There was one on Lake. That was about a mile, two miles from my house out in the country, on a lake bank. We'd walk out there, but we couldn't come in because we was underage. We could hear what was goin' on. We'd be standin' around out there under the lights, just be practicin' our harps. They'd be playin' one record right after another. Big Bill Broonzy, he was on the jukebox then with "Truckin' Little Woman." Tampa Red was on with "She Wanna Sell My Monkey." Memphis Minnie was on with "Me and My Chauffeur" and "I Can't Afford to Do It" ["Can't Afford to Lose My Man"]. Sonny Boy came in with "Good Mornin' Little Schoolgirl." Walter Davis . . . Memphis Slim came out with "You Gotta Help Me Some." I liked his sound.

Inside people were doin' the jitterbug. That's a swingin' thing that you dance with a partner. The jitterbug was really the thing. Girls would be swingin' their frocks, man. Truckin'—that was popular durin' that time. There was a dance they called "Pullin' the Skiff." That one was a mess, but they was enjoyin' it. People be drinkin' home brew or corn whiskey. They'd be sellin' sealed whiskey too, but we'd have to go somewhere and buy it off of somebody. We'd mostly drink just corn whiskey. Didn't cost but 25¢ a half pint. [*Laughs*.] That's all it cost was a quarter. We'd pitch in and get it and all get a swallow or two. We'd get enough to get a buzz off of it. And we'd be *gone* then, man. We was havin' *fun!* It was the good old days, as they say. We'd stay out, bring in daybreak before we'd go home. My grandmother didn't know where I was. [*Laughs*.] Then I'd come home maybe 10:00, 11:00 the next day. She would never try to find out too much about that stuff.

Arthur Johnson was Luther "Guitar Junior" Johnson's uncle. He lived around Minter City. I went over to visit my aunt and uncle in Vance and that's where Arthur was, over in there. That's where I got a chance to meet him. He had heard that I could play. Different people, they'd talk, so he wanted to hear me. He brought his guitar over there. He was tryin' to teach me somethin' about the guitar. That's what he was tryin' to do, but I really knew more about it than he did. He was gonna show me somethin', but instead I showed him! [*Laughs*.] I had found my way how to tune it in different keys and stuff 'cause I'd been around some musicians back durin' that time—Nathaniel. That's Nitter. I'd heard him play. Musicians, it don't take 'em too long to get some connection.

We went over to Philipp, Mississippi, one time in 1939. Arthur Johnson had a pickup truck. We'd all get on the back, get on the fenders, everywhere. We were just hangin' on there, man, *ridin'*! Philipp was about eight or ten miles away. My cousin, Archibald, who was livin' around there in that part of the country, he was with us too. We rode that truck over there to catch this dance. That was about the first live musicians that I ever got a chance to meet. That was Rice Miller, Sonny Boy. It was a club right on the ground floor—and a space back there where they'd have tables and chairs and stuff like that. We just went in, got us a seat. It wasn't too much to get in, about 50¢ or a quarter. We went there and we partied, met people like we was—young, some of 'em. We mixed with 'em, danced with some girls and whatever.

Backin' up Sonny Boy was Robert Jr., Joe Willie, and Peck. Five By Five [Dudlow Taylor] was with him on piano. They was already on the radio, broadcastin' [on the *King Biscuit Time* radio show] at KFFA, Helena, Arkansas. Sonny Boy and Robert Jr. were teamin' good there. They was a good team together, but Joe Willie Wilkins was my favorite. He had a tone. He carried a good bottom, if you know what I mean. Him and Robert was my favorite guys on guitar. I got some licks off of Robert from that night. Joe Willie and Robert, those are two guys I got a lotta licks from. Robert Jr. could play in a lot of different keys—*A* and he'd go to *D, E* natural, and *B*. He was playin' close to Robert Johnson's stuff. That's where he got his style. It wouldn't take me too long to catch on to what they was doin'.

I knew how to tune a guitar. It was tuned with a harmonica. It wasn't no big problem, because I had a guitar made onto the house on the outside. I know how it sound. I would play it with my harmonica tuned up there. That's how I learnt Little Jimmy, my son, to tune his guitar years later. I could tune my instrument 440 [A=440, or standard concert pitch]. All that I would have to do then is find out what key that they was playin' in and go to it. It was very easy to catch on to that type of material.

Sonny Boy [Rice Miller] would leave the band and go back there with his gamblin' and the band would play. Joe Willie'd be back there gamblin' too. Robert Jr., he didn't gamble, but he'd go back and oversee it. They'd be shootin' dice or playin' cards or whatever it was. People was dangerous about fightin' and stuff around with the gamblin'. I didn't hang around in there too much. I didn't think about I could get killed. But I *would* think, "If my grandmother knew I was there, boy, I was in *big* trouble." [*Laughs.*] So I would stay out there where the dance was goin' on. That's where I would hang. I got to play Joe Willie Wilkins' [electric] guitar that night because of that. Yeah, the musicians went back to gamble, and we'd be on the stage just playin'—and I'd take Joe Willie's guitar. Freakiest sound I'd ever heard. I was game, ya know. [*Laughs.*] I wasn't afraid or ashamed to play it. Whatever they was playin', I was just jumpin' in and playin' what I knew about it and keep up with it. I had never played an electric guitar before, and I didn't play one again until I got to Chicago. But I wanted one. Then I got one when I got to Chicago, got me an electric guitar.

Arthur Johnson, he would take us back sometime before daylight. He'd bring us all back, drop this guy off and that guy. Then he'd go on home. That's the way I started hangin'. We started doin' this different times, goin' to Philipp a lots when they were throwin' a dance up there. That's where the party would be goin' on. If Sonny Boy and them wouldn't be able to be back across the ferry from Philipp and

Friars Point to Helena at night after the party, they'd just hang around till the next mornin' at 7:00 or 8:00 when the ferry started runnin' again. Then they'd catch the first ferry that come in and get in to Helena to do their show on KFFA.

The ferryboat was a ship, but it had a big flat part where you could park cars, trucks, and things on it. It take so many this time and when he get unloaded, he'd load up another batch. Then he'd go back across, then carry another load back across. That's the way we'd transfer from one side of the Mississippi River to the other, from Friars Point, Mississippi, to Helena, Arkansas. It cost 35¢ to walk on, 50¢ for a truck or a car. The ride take about ten, 15 minutes. We'd do that a lot, played slot machines while we was on there. Yeah, they had 'em on the boat—but they'd close 'em all down before they get to the river bank. They'd close the door, lock 'em off limits. If we'd ride back across, they'd open it back up when they'd pull off the other side. We could gamble again until they started to approach the other side. We'd just ride that boat sometimes, just ride that boat from one end to the other. I used to see slot machines in stores too when I was small, for a penny and a nickel. You'd win sometime five or eight dollars on the nickel one. Penny a slot on the other, just pull down. You could hit 14¢ if they line up across there. It'd pay that off. It'd make us glad. We was havin' fun then.

Back then we listened to *King Biscuit Time*. You'd be watchin' the clock. You'd be lookin', tryin' to make sure you could find that station. The guy who would announce it would be advertising Pittypat. Then Sonny Payne would say, "This is *King Biscuit Time*." You'd say, "Boy, we got it now!" *King Biscuit Time* over KFFA was only 15 minutes. It was 12:15 in the day. The guy was announcin', talkin' about whatever they wanted to talk about for a minute. Then they would play a record for about two minutes and 45 seconds. Then he'd talk another minute. Then Sonny Boy and them would track out. They'd come out playin', bangin' away. Didn't have but 15 minutes. They'd do three songs, maybe four. My grandmother wouldn't pay that no attention. She'd be in the back of the house, be outside or whatever she be doin'. The first time I heard Robert Nighthawk was on that station, KFFA.

Then I started messin' around there, playin' house parties and different things, me and Arthur Johnson. Arthur'd get to drinkin'. Those guys would drink heavy, most of those guys would, and he'd wanna try and gamble. Then he'd leave to do that. Me and Johnny Tucker would be in there where they was tryin' to dance at. I'd put down my harmonica and take his guitar and play it. It was a hollow-box. That's all we played at that time. It would sound through the house. You would get big enough sound to hear and play okay. If the party was in a nice-sized bedroom, they'd move all the stuff out, put it in another room somewhere, and they'd say, "Dance is gonna be in here." Then it's open in there, and when you'd sing some-thin', it would sound. You could hear it soundin' real good, an echo sound. The gamblin' would be like in the back in there somewhere. Johnny Tucker was a friend of mine. He didn't play no instrument, but he liked to hang with me, 'cause he was around where I was gonna get me some whiskey, somethin' to eat, and he'd get a chance to have all he wanted.

Then I'd get a chance to see Robert Nighthawk. We'd get together after the show was over. We'd talk. He'd tell us about places they had played or was going to. I'd get a phone number on the place, set up a few dates for what night that Arthur and me could come in and play. About Robert's slide playing, I always had him

pegged as soundin' mostly like Tampa Red, but he was playin' more openly. He'd
come more forward. Tampa would lay in the back, in the bottom. He'd do "Sweet
Black Angel" and "That Ain't the Way to Do It." He wouldn't have a chance to
play too many 'cause somebody else has gotta sing one.

Pinetop Perkins says it was rough in those days, 'cause people wouldn't get but a
dollar a day for workin' in the fields, but that would pay the rent. They weren't
chargin' but six dollars a week. Get your other little pennies to get your cigarettes,
get your half pint. But if you don't play tonight, you just about broke. That money
gone, but at least you got your rent paid. I would listen to a song for a sound, a
beat, what have you. Guitar, that's what I wanted to do—to get the girls, man.
That's what it was about.

I WAS IN MEMPHIS IN THE LATE '30S. Memphis was swingin', man. Yes, sir. Memphis
used to be one of the center points of the South—Memphis and New Orleans.
Well, Georgia too: "Young New York," they called it. Georgia's always been on the
ball. Memphis is kind of second in line, but it be pumpin' too. Memphis was the
shortstop in it all.

Yeah, we'd take the bus or ride in a car with somebody that we knew from
Memphis—that had a curfew—to West Memphis, that was wide open. We'd go
down to the Baby Grand or someplace like that. They'd have some bands over
there, Roscoe Gordon. B.B. King, he would play some of those spots. They had a
crap house down there too. The owner, she'd throw a few parties sometimes. And
the roller rink. I wouldn't skate. I was always afraid to get hurt, but I liked to watch
the other kids.

In West Memphis and over in "Big Memphis," me and Joe Willie Wilkins and
Howlin' Wolf would play. At this roller rink in Memphis and the Baby Grand in
West Memphis, we used to jam. Not too many places, but I remember those two.
The people, they enjoyed it. Sometime we'd get three dollars a night, five dollars at
most, a drink of whiskey and two dollars. [*Laughs.*] But this was somethin' I wanted to *do!* I wanted to learn, go from there to better. Willie Nix sometime would be
with us, with Wolf playin' on drums. Yeah, old loud Willie. He was like Captain
Wisecracker, always tellin' jokes, talkin' a lot of trash. Willie Johnson was a guitar
player in that group too. I liked what he was doin' real good. He'd listen. He'd
catch on real fast. He was what ya call a creative musician.

Wolf, he was all right. A lot of people didn't understand Wolf. He was a man
that let you know that he knew what he knew and you gotta deal with that or
you weren't gonna deal with him at all. I liked Wolf. Even then, he'd have blow-
ups with Willie Johnson, 'cause Willie was kind of wild. I've played with wild
musicians; you've got to run your race, man. Wolf didn't accept that. He wanted
you to be like he wanted you to be. That was his way. If you can deal with that,
you make it. Roosevelt Sykes was another one who was set in his own ways. I
understood. I respected those people very highly in what they was doin' and the
way they was doin' it. I'd reach in and pick out a few things in their styles and
use it—and it'd work.

Wolf's timin' was bad. Maybe mine wasn't the best in the world, but it was pretty good. His timin', he would try to lay on his pattern. He'd follow the pattern
through. If it were four-beat or six-beat, he would really try to lay as close to it as

he could, and it was up to the band to keep him straight. If they don't keep him straight and follow what he's doin', things are gonna goof up and then you got a problem out of Wolf. I found that out at a real early stage there. He was kind of a hard guy to try to get through to, because you didn't understand where he was comin' from and he couldn't explain to you where he wanted you to go. See, ya got too much to deal with with Wolf. The voice that he had, he fooled around and found a way that he could do with this type of voice. Like *E* natural and *G*, you'd get his voice and his harmonica style to fit there. He'd count from there. And you gotta lay right there. You gotta get under him and you gotta stay there. If you could do that, you could play with him.

Oh yeah, Wolf clowned all the time back then in West Memphis. He'd get down, crawl across the stage. That was his thing. He was a comical guy. He got that part of his style from that guy Buford too. They called him Foots. When I was young, I heard of Foots. He was a guitar player who clowned. He'd waddle and twist, turn his eyes and do stupid stuff. His record didn't go too big, but Wolf got it and, later years, he made it over: "The Natchez Fire." Like I said, Wolf got a lot of his stuff out of Buford.

I met Big Walter Horton just walkin' around at Handy's Park. Different guys would be out there playin' guitars, playin' harmonicas, just sittin' around watchin' the birds. And I met him, ya know, in conversation. I come to know him as a harmonica player in Handy's Park and down on Beale Street, all around. I was seein' Big Walter a lot. Honeyboy and Walter used to team up in Memphis at that time. I left there and the next time I saw him was when he came to Chicago. Forrest City Joe was another guy. He was wild. A harmonica player, he was really good. I met Lloyd Lammons. I knew Pinetop durin' that time. [*Laughs.*] Old Perk.

I was also in St. Louis many times from '38 to '45. I wasn't workin'. I wasn't goin' to school. I was just scufflin' around, dealin' around with musicians. I was still with my grandmother. Like I said, wherever she would go, I were there. I was 16 years old, swingin' between guitar and harmonica. I wasn't doin' too much musically, just driftin' around, scabbin' and messin' around like that. I'd walk across the bridge from St. Louis to East St. Louis where the clubs were. Cost a nickel. My grandmother gave up the switch by then. I was gettin' to be a pretty good-sized boy. She'd always say, "I better leave him alone, but he done sold hisself to the devil!" She would use that phrase. [*Laughs.*]

I didn't have no Saturday gigs, but there were clubs where I could go in there and maybe play for the kitty or somethin' like that. The guy would just let me play and they'd pass the kitty around, pick me up a few quarters, maybe somebody give me a dollar.

I met Walter Davis—Old Railhead—in East St. Louis. He was a piano player somewhere along the lines of Sunnyland Slim [Albert Luandrew]. He would come out for ya like Sunnyland did. He was a pretty nice guy. I liked his style real, real good, and I listened to him quite a bit: "Come Back Baby, Let's Talk It Over One More Time" and "B & O" and a lot of different slow songs. He was mostly a by-himself player. He would make his changes when he get ready, start singin' when he wanted to. A band would have a rough time trying to back him up. But he had some sweet songs. I think I recorded a couple of his songs down through the years.

Henry Townsend wasn't too big then. He was playin' on a different level. He was like Lightnin' Hopkins or Tommy McClennan or Robert Petway, people like that [who played solo]. They was on that kick, see, and I was thinkin' about big band stuff, at least bigger bands than playin' by yourself. But I knew about 'em. Henry Townsend stood out like a sore thumb. I'd just go around and listen, and keep movin'. I'd be listenin', suckin' up a little here and there, and keep on movin'. I didn't try to play with those guys at all. They would see me. If they would have a chance, they would talk to me a little bit. All of 'em respected me. It was the way I approached 'em, I suppose. People would take time out and deal with me on certain stuff. I didn't know why at the time. But later years, I found out that I had somethin' good, that I was a pretty good guy. But at the time I just thought, "These are nice people. They like me."

Little Walter came out of Louisiana and came up around Memphis and St. Louis. He was driftin' around with Sonny Boy and Joe Willie. He was foolin' around with all those guys from Helena, over to Friars Point, Mississippi, back up around Clarksdale. That's what they would do, and Walter was just driftin', like out by himself. He was on his own, wasn't around none of his people or nothin' like that, when I met him in St. Louis. He was about 18. I had to be about 21 or 22. Then I came on to Chicago and met him again. That was the one guy, after Sonny Boy, who was better than I was on harp.

I left St. Louis and came back to Chicago in '39. I was on my own then. So I played all around in the area—me, [a piano player named] King, Porkchop [drummer Eddie Hines], Moody Jones, and a bunch of guys. Yeah, me and Porkchop, we was just scabbin' around. We was jammin' around downtown. We were on State Street sometimes, would jam. I meet some musicians anywhere I go. If there was some blues players there, I would find 'em. Johnny Young and Good Rockin' Charles, the harmonica player, they was around then. A lot of places, I would take my guitar with me. I would put it in my car. Some places I would take it out. I'd always have a harmonica somewhere on me too.

Chicago wasn't as big in '39 and '40 as it is now. The suburbs and stuff wasn't here. The places where I'd hang around were in not too big an area—the Zanzibar and Earl King's, the Plantation, 31st and Giles, and the 708 Club on 47th Street. They had a club over there on Indiana, the Flame, at 3020 Indiana. Me and Tampa Red and Big Maceo, we used to play down there, in the basement like. That was a nice club. It wasn't too big, but it was a swanky club. Tampa didn't get around too much, but Maceo, he'd come around where we'd be jammin' at and sit in with us. Oh, man, that cat sounded great to me. He carried a lotta weight with that piano, and he could play real good. He had that sound. He was heavy, man, with that left hand.

Big Maceo was a nice guy, good piano player. Real good and he made some nice records too with Tampa Red. So Maceo would be around us. Then another piano player I knew that could sound close like Maceo—call him Johnnie Jones—he started playin' with Tampa. After Maceo got crippled in his hand from a stroke, Tampa got Johnnie to play piano with him. That was his steady gig. Tampa's home base was the Flame. That's where Johnnie played with him a lot. That's the way it went up until Tampa got sick.

I used to go over to Tampa Red's house with Johnnie Jones. Tampa was a quiet type person, but you go to his house, he would treat you real nice. He would give you points on what you were trying to learn. Him and his wife—he had a nice wife too—they'd treat you so nice over to his house. We used to go over there, and he would tell us stories about different places that he played and how to react in different situations. You know, the straight way how to take care of yourself and conduct yourself with the public. And that's what I did. Well, a lot of us, we did that, the same thing.

Some of us were kind of wild, wouldn't pay attention to anybody anyway. Tampa would tell us, "If you live fast, you get in trouble fast. So you soon get it over real fast." I would listen to him. I was a good listener for tryin' to learn what was goin' on. I guess that's why I don't get in too much trouble now, because I've learnt from good guys who would tell me how to conduct myself. Big Bill and Tampa, people like that would tell you.

Big Bill taken a liking to me. When Muddy came to Chicago, he taken a likin' to Muddy too. I didn't play with Big Bill, but he had time for me. He told me a lot of points about life and about the blues scene. Bill was here in Chicago and then he'd be over in France, those two places. He was makin' a nice buck.

The first time I heard Memphis Minnie in person was in Chicago at the Cotton Club on 63rd off of King Drive; 63rd used to have three or four clubs up and down. It was a hot spot for music, a lot of jazz. And there was some blues. Memphis Minnie was in that bunch. That's where I met her. She was singin' "Look the World Over"—that's one song she played a lot. She'd do "The Chauffeur" and "Can't Afford to Do It," a lot of different numbers. She'd make up her show, and it'd come out okay.

She'd wear some nice clothes. She was pretty sharp. She would design them herself. She liked earrings. She'd make you get her some earrings made up to her satisfaction. She had a bracelet with dimes in it all around her wrist. She hooked the dimes and made a wristband out of it with a quarter in the center, and then she had earrings that had silver dollars in each one of 'em. She'd make rings and have dimes in the center, and she was crazy about chains. She'd make up a lot of her jewelry. She'd be onstage with more money on her than she'd make at the club that night. I don't know where she was livin', but she had one old man—they called him Squirrel. He was a guitar player. Somethin' happened, I don't know. They broke up, and she got with [Little] Son Joe. She stayed with Son Joe till the end of her years, 12 or 15 years.

She mostly just played with she and Son Joe, a team of two guitars. They didn't have no bass or anything. They'd sit down and play. Everybody just about would sit down and play back at that time. But she'd mostly stand up to sing. She could sit down, but she'd mostly stand, the way she'd be performin'. The crowd would call out different numbers. She'd wisecrack at somebody or somethin'. They'd get it goin'. She was a pretty rough lady. Mama didn't take no mess. She was that type. Oh man, she had a sharp tongue. She'd tell you what time it was in a minute. I had fun listenin' to what they was doing.

I'd jam with Son Joe and Memphis Minnie. I'd hit those spots. I got along with her because I never knocked her. She'd say I was the quiet one, but I'd be thinkin' a mile a minute. I'd stay a step ahead of her along that way. I know how to stay out of the way. I didn't take too much advice from her, because I didn't like the attitude that she had. I'd stay my distance. We recorded some records together and stuff. Sure did. By the time we got to the recordin' studio, I knew just about what she was lookin' for, so she didn't bother me too much. She gave her husband, Son Joe, hell because I would understand what she wanted in a way better than he did. She was a tough old cookie, man. "Kid" Douglas was really her name, and then she changed it to Memphis Minnie and she went all over the country with that one. Mmm, I knew her well.

T-Bone Walker, we made records with him. He was a guy. He wasn't from around here. He was from Texas, but he would be in Chicago for gigs, recording sessions, and what have you. I met a lot of different people from different angles, and I had fun with those guys. I really appreciate what they did. They passed on—Memphis Minnie, Tampa, Big Bill, all those guys. They've gone on and left us here. They was out there, man, before I was. I was glad to have the privilege to be in those guys' company because they'd been around a long time. They could give me some points on what the road was like or what life was like in the music field. And that's where I was, where I carried myself. So they really would help me. All those old-timers were really in my corner. We all got along real good.

We'd hang with Memphis Slim too. There was a place on the West Side off Maxwell Street there—the Triangle. They had blues. John Lee "Sonny Boy" [Williamson] and we all used to hang around there. Sonny Boy was a guy that, see, he'd get drunk and then he'd clown. [*Laughs.*] Him and Memphis Slim wrecked that joint one night when we was over there. They got in a fight. Memphis Slim didn't like no harmonica really. He didn't care nothin' about no harmonica player. He didn't respect 'em. But he had Sonny Boy in there 'cause Sonny Boy could help draw. That's what it was. He didn't want to pay him like Sonny Boy thought he should have been paid, and they got into it. They had a big mess. I got back over with the biggest part of the crowd. I knowed how to keep myself out of the way there. I'd been around that stuff before. They didn't have no guns or anything, just knives and bottles. The boss or somebody got in there and broke it up. That was one time. Where I got a chance to really get up with Sonny Boy was through Bob Myers. Sonny Boy would get drunk. He would play awhile. He'd get him a few bottles there, man. He'd go on off somewhere. He liable to leave the club and go on home and leave somebody else up there playin'. He didn't care. That's the way he was. He didn't have no band.

EVENTUALLY I WENT BACK TO MEMPHIS and back down South. I went to Georgia, and then I left there and we came back in Chicago in '45, '46, and I been in Chicago then ever since.

I had an uncle, Willie Miller, lived over on Lake Street in Chicago. He had some boys along my equal. My cousins. That's where my grandmother put me—over with them, see. But I would be goin' other places, man, to meet people. That's what my mind was made up to do. From South Bend back to Chicago back to St. Louis, that was my stompin' grounds for a long time. I had uncles and aunts, cousins, my grandmother, and all of my relatives, they was all around that area—and up in Detroit, but I didn't ever get up there too much. So I had a pipeline, places to stay and a lot of turf to cover. I'd be catchin' gigs up and down the road. My cousins would come with me sometimes too. One of 'em turned out to be a gambler. One of my cousins is a preacher now. They did different things with their lives, but I put mine into music.

My wife, Dorothy, I met her in South Bend in '43 or '44. She was there with her old stepmother. Originally she's from Jackson, Tennessee. She had a brother lived in Chicago, and other family too. How did I meet Dorothy? Young bucks runnin' around, "tappin' trees" and stuff. [*Laughs.*] She was young and beautiful, much smaller than she is now. I was the brave one talked to her first, of course! We used to "shoot" at 'em, man. We'd go out gunnin' for 'em. Dorothy was kind of shy. Her girlfriend put it together for us. She was a blabbermouth. I went over and hit, man. We started talkin'. One word lead to another, and we fool around and start talkin'. Then ya get hooked up. Ya start talkin' on the telephone and all that stuff. As I say, we were driftin', one place to the other. Young guys, man. I was on the road then, and still out here.

I'd get a job back in Chicago. If it wasn't what I liked or somethin' I wanted, I'd quit and get another. I could get a job anywhere, any time I wanted. I'd walk right out of one and right into another one. Same day. Factory work, workin' at a packin' house. I worked at Swift Packing House. I worked in all kind of places, but I wanted to do what I'm doin' now, see. That's what I wanted to do.

To hear some good music at night, I'd come south from Lake Street to 35th and Indiana, 47th and South Park. Where I would hang out would be like around 47th and Cottage Grove. All around in there there were different places. I'd be tryin' to sit in, meet musicians. Tampa Red, Big Maceo was kickin' in. Lonnie Johnson. I had heard all their records growin' up. Big Bill Broonzy was one of my favorites. I liked his guitar, and I liked the way he played. Jazz Gillum did "Key to the Highway." Big Bill was playin' on it, but Jazz Gillum was playin' harmonica and singin'. Big Bill used to back up a lot of musicians around at that time. He didn't have no steady band. He'd just play with Memphis Slim, Cool Breeze [Joseph Bell]—whoever was doin' somethin', he'd back 'em up. If he needed a guitar player, he'd play with 'em.

Sunnyland Slim was a drifter around in Chicago. He'd be all on the West Side, all over Chicago. Him and Memphis Slim be playin' different clubs in Madison Street and around. The first time I saw Sunnyland was over there. I was a young buck. I liked what he was doin'. I'd see Bob Myers. He was a harmonica player, and he would hang out a lot around Memphis Slim and Sunnyland on Madison Street. I was playin' harmonica then too. I'd have a harmonica in my pocket somewhere, and Sunny wanted me to come up and do some jams with him. He gave me a steady job with him at the Club 21. Sunnyland always had patience with musicians. If a musician felt like or thought he had any ambition in the music field, Sunnyland was right there to help him any way he could.

I had an acoustic. I'd put a DeArmond pickup on it and made it electric. It was a metal gadget you could put on it there, mount it to the guitar on that end [the soundhole's rim] runnin' underneath the strings. It was just loud. Ya didn't have no treble or bass. You just had loudness. Ya get your tone from the amplifier, such amplifiers as you had back then. Gibson was makin' 'em. I was dealin' with Gibson. This was all before I met Muddy.

I was livin' in the Maxwell Street area durin' '45 and '46. That's where I'd see so many musicians and things, by bein' there down in that area. And I started joinin' in with 'em too, playin' on the street. Everything that would happen, it would be right there by my house. On Saturdays and Sundays, Maxwell Street was the place. Everybody was gettin' down there to around 7:00, 8:00 in the morning. Peoples was comin' out, gettin' in the streets. The streets was full of people. People shoppin'. People gettin' their little stands put up, all of 'em down the street there full of different things to sell. People start walkin'. Man, you couldn't hardly get through there. After 9:00, oh, man, that place was swamped with people, and it'd be that way until 5:00, 6:00 in the evening. It's full, man, like Mardi Gras.

See, we had a little street money-making thing on Saturdays and Sundays with all those people goin' by. We could go down there on Saturdays and Sundays and hook up. We'd have some guy, give him a couple of bucks if he'd drop a cord out of his window down on the sidewalk down there. Two bucks for some juice. Ya had your own cords. Junction boxes, they call 'em now. They come 35 foot long. This guy plug in his amplifier, the other guy too—like that. Then we'd get some crates or maybe he'd give ya a chair or box to sit on. You'd line you up a place there and sit out and play.

People had their own favorite place on Maxwell Street that they liked. Everybody liked Maxwell and Peoria, the corner. And they had one down on Halsted and Maxwell, or 14th and Peoria, a couple blocks down. About three or four favorite spots that you could hook up. Then that was your spot. Nobody would bother you. The guys wouldn't try to wolf you out of your spot. You'd sit there and play for maybe three or four hours, make you some money that way.

You could make pretty good money doin' that. Pass the kitty, they called it. We'd start around 10:00 and go from there until around about 5:00 or 6:00 in the evenin'. And when we'd split up the money—me and Porkchop and Walter and John Henry [Barbee] and all those guys. I'd have sometime $45, $46 to my part. Man, you was makin' seven, eight dollars in the clubs somewheres tryin' to be paid. We were doin' "Caldonia," boogie woogies, all kinds of stuff. That's where I made up "That's All Right," "You Don't Have to Go," and all that stuff. I was buildin' those songs up. We did that on the street. You don't worry about nobody tryin' to steal your stuff back then durin' that time. Later years they started that. Man, we'd just get some ideas and go on and do 'em.

For musicians on Maxwell Street, I'd see Ed Newman and Slim, who was a guitar player. Stovepipe [Johnny Watson]—he was a good showman, little short dude. He'd put on a funny striped suit, walk around in tap-dancin' shoes. He was the one that was leadin' us around. He'd been around a long time. He'd been in New York, in Detroit, different places. At that time, he was about 40, I'd say. He'd been doin' it since he'd been a youngster. We come along there. He'd get us hooked up because we was doin' somethin' he liked to do. See, he was a washboard player. He'd clown, crack jokes, tap dance, cut a rug. Then he'd pass the kitty and stuff. He was the man who collected the money for us.

Ed Newman was a bass player. He had one of those big boom-boom-boom upright basses—that's what he played. He'd be right there with us till we pass him off to somebody else or get tired and start movin'. That big thing was hard to handle. It could fill up a car. He wanted to play within walkin' distance of Maxwell Street where he could put that thing on his shoulder and carry it around. Then he'd carry it home, put it up. Sometime they'd just tune the guitar down, make a bass out of it, if you could get a big enough amp, and you wouldn't fool with Ed. Porkchop was down there, Floyd and Moody Jones, Snooky Pryor. They was jammin'. They was really the street players. They were the big ones.

I was livin' right down the street on Peoria Street right off of Maxwell, been down there for a long time livin' on the first floor. When they'd start hookin' up, you could hear the music goin'. I'd be up there at home in the bed. This particular time I heard it and I recognized the sound. I had heard it before. I said, "That sounds like Marion!" Marion, that's [Little] Walter's name. So I got up and put some clothes on and went on down the street, about a half a block from the house. I got in there, got a chance to see him, a little peanut-head guy sittin' up there. I said, "That's Walter." When I got his eye, he knowed me. I didn't know he was even in Chicago.

Well, Sunnyland had been gone. Those guys, they drift—St. Louis, Memphis, different places around like that. So he brought Walter and Honeyboy to Chicago. He went back South in 1947 and came back again. I met up with Sunny too over on Maxwell Street. He had Little Walter and Honeyboy with him. That's when I first met Honeyboy, but I knew Walter from St. Louis. I met him again right there.

Through Sunnyland, Walter had been around Floyd, Moody, Johnny Young, Uncle Johnny, all those peoples, and that's what put me in to know all those guys. Walter would hang around with them. Since Sunnyland brought him to Chicago, he'd always be around somewhere where he could put a hand on Sunny. But if he gets tired, if he meets somebody that he wants to get hooked in with, he's gonna go. Sunny might not see him again till Tuesday or Wednesday or somethin', maybe not see him till the next weekend. That's the way Walter was. We didn't worry about that too much [chuckles]—that was a wild guy. "He's out there somewhere, I don't know. He's lookin' out for himself, wherever he be." Whenever he'd get ready to come home, he'd come. That's the way he was.

I had lost contact on Snooky Pryor from young boyhood comin' up. When we were kids, I had the name Snooky. That's what they had called me around my home. Some of my cousins and my grandmother, they'd call me that. I never did go for it too much, but it was okay. His nickname when we were kids, they called him Bubba. Yeah, Bubba Pryor. He didn't like that. I saw him again in '48 in Chicago on Maxwell Street. That was after he got out of the army. He was always skinny, but he had put on a few pounds more than I looked for him to be. And he had recorded that "Snooky and Moody Boogie" [released as "Boogie" on Planet, 1948], and that's when I saw he had taken my name. I said, "What's this Snooky and Moody stuff comin' out here on this record? I'm Snooky." He said he always loved the way I played harmonica, so he took it and put it into his music thing. "So you gone on from Bubba and took my little old name, huh?" [Laughs.] I was just havin' some fun out of it. I let it go. I didn't like it for my name—no way. We laughs about it now sometimes. We played a little bit together every chance we'd get on Maxwell Street. "Your papa was a preacher, your mama was an alley cat. Why you gonna do me like that?" Yeah! I remember that. He used to do that when we were kids. On Maxwell Street, Floyd and Moody Jones couldn't really get him what he wanted on that tune, but they would mess around with it.

"Snooky and Moody Boogie," I heard it, got ahold of it when it did come out.

Walter and I heard it, and we tried to rehearse it. Sonny Boy brought that in years ago. That was the old school—so we did it. "Juke" came from that stuff. "Juke" is built out of that "Snooky and Moody Boogie." All that come in through there.

I went to Sunnyland's place on 26th and Prairie plenty of times. We was all in that basement a lot of nights and days. It was a little get-together thing, yeah. He had a crap house down there. Sunnyland was pretty slick. He could make dice, ya know, his own self. He could build dice and make 'em loaded. He could whittle horses. He could make all kind of stuff. Sunny was a pretty keen guy with a cue stick as well as with, uh, dice and cards. He'd have gamblin' down there all the time. He put in a pool table down there. People was shootin' crap, all kinds of stuff. I wouldn't gamble with him. I wouldn't ever, *never* gamble with him, but I'd bet on him. He didn't want *me* to gamble, didn't want me to even get involved in that kind of stuff.

Yeah, when we got off workin' after a gig someplace, we'd get home and we'd go to Sunnyland's house, and that's where we could eat. That's why we hung in there all the time. He'd give away more than he'd sell sometimes, but he'd sell whiskey and food and everything. He had a nice little house down there where we'd go party. Musicians was welcome. And I met a lot of 'em down there. That started way before any of us did any recording.

Big Maceo used to come in and play the piano. In fact, Sunny was doin' those things back durin' the times of old Doctor Clayton. Doctor Clayton used to come down to Sunny's place years ago. Willie Mabon would come in and Memphis Slim and Little Brother Montgomery and Floyd Jones, all the guys. Roosevelt Sykes, Otis Rush would hang out there and, oh, just a host of others. Me, Little Walter, Baby Face Leroy [Foster], Lee Brown, my friends Dan and Jesse Jones, a bunch of us used to hang around at Sunnyland's place after hours. We'd play cards, drink, and have fun. He used to pay off the beat cop and give him free drinks. Oh, yeah! [*Laughs.*] That would happen. Those were what they call the good old days in Chicago, back durin' that time. Yeah.

Sunnyland Slim and Sonny Boy Williamson—John Lee Williamson—lived down on 31st Street off of Indiana, three or four houses apart. They was buddy-buddies, see. Sonny Boy was real educated, but he would get drunk and try to fight. So he and Sunnyland, they would kind of bust in and let loose, but they couldn't stay mad. They still would be together during the day around there. We'd go to his house there on Indiana around 31st. Sunnyland would send his old lady out to the store and get some pork chops or chicken or chicken giblets or chicken livers. We'd be sittin' around drinkin', and she'd fix us food. She'd go in the kitchen and cook. And man, we'd go in there and eat. Sunnyland was just that type of person. He always would help you in any way he could. We would eat, and they would play some more. He had an old piano there. We would jam.

Time would be marchin' on. Later on in the evenin', we done had a few drinks and done ate. We're tryin' to figure out which way we goin' now, after we get out of there, to try and make some money. Sometime you'd go over on Lake Street or go up on the North Side, the Cotton Club or some little club like that, or down on State Street. You could go down on State Street at night and go in them clubs.

I had a piano player called King. He was a pretty good piano player, and he could fix a piano. Pinetop is pretty good at patchin' up pianos too—uprights, that kind. Sunnyland, he wasn't into that fixin' 'em. He bought him a little old Willet when that thing came out—I think he paid $200 for it. Got it at Lyon and Healy. It was kind of like my amplifier, the color of it, and the legs screw on. Portable, they called it. You take it down, put all of its legs together and close it up. Carry it like a suitcase, ya know. This was around '50, '51.

Hardly no pianos on Maxwell Street, but across the street, Goldberg, he had a tavern. He had one in there. We'd be out in the street playin', King'd go in there and make him a few quarters like that. He'd sit up in there and play by himself, but with that electric stuff out there, we had a crowd. He'd make him a little money like that, but he gonna throw it away anyway.

I WAS WORKIN' FOR SANORA RADIO and Cabinet Company. They moved us from one buildin' to another. The company carried the crews that it wanted to another location. First I was on Roosevelt Road, then they moved us six or seven blocks over on another street, Hastings. That was their big building. I met Jesse Jones there. He was like a little foreman there on that job. I'd pick my people that I would deal with, and he was a guy I could trust. You can't very well trust nobody too much now. He was born in Chicago, in 1905 or 1908, somethin' like that. He was along my mother's age. But, ya see, he liked what I liked—the blues and bein' around musicians—and that's how we got to be friends.

I was sandin' and sawin' cabinets. You'd take the saw, cut the bad part off, smooth it off as it comes through. Then you put it on the conveyor belt that carry it on someplace else. Jesse got me a position there that stopped me from cuttin'. He said, "You gonna fool around and cut your hand off!" He give somebody else that job and put me on sprayin' the first layer of spray on 'em, like a varnish. That's what I was doin'. I'd catch them and do so many, go on. Put it on another belt and get another one. Just passin' the time, man, makin' the day.

Jesse knew a lot of spots where the blues would be. So me and Jesse would get together and ride the bus to some of the clubs. He didn't have a car, but he had different people that he knew that had cars. We'd get with some of them and we'd go places too. Jesse come there and buy whiskey all night, just to be partying with us. Ya know, a lot of women around, and he would buy a lot of whiskey and stuff. Sometime I'd have my guitar with me and sometime I wouldn't have it. I'd use their guitars, like Bill's [Big Bill Broonzy's]. I played his. He had a big blond Epiphone, push button. I *loved* that big guitar, man. That guitar cost maybe a couple hundred dollars when he bought it. It was a nice one, compared to those $25, $35 guitars I'd been gettin' ahold to.

Jesse was tellin' me about his cousin was comin' up from down South. He wanted me to meet him. I said, "Okay." That was Muddy Waters. He was down South. He hadn't even come to Chicago. Jesse and Dan, those were Muddy's first cousins.

Finally, he did come to Chicago. It was last of '44, comin' into '45. A state senator called Green had a car. He taken Muddy, brought him over to my house. Wasn't too far, a five-minute drive. Brought him over there and he came in. He brought a guitar with him to Chicago from down South, but he didn't bring no guitar that day. He just wanted to meet me. We talked. He was kind of shy—Muddy was a very shy person. Chicago, that's a big city to him, and he's afraid of gangsters. Al Capone and all those guys was around, and he heard about 'em. They'll kill ya. Slick guys and hustlin' girls, ya know, in Chicago. He was tryin' to stay away from that stuff. He taken a liking to me, 'cause he met me through his cousin.

The next time I went out to his uncle's house, where he was staying. That's over on 13th Street, 1800 block. We was in walkin' distance from each other. I was on the West Side too. It took me about ten minutes to walk from my house to where Muddy lived. Everybody be gone. We had the house, and we jammed. We did that for a while.

Then his uncle finally got him an apartment right down the street from him in the same block—1851 West 13th Street in Chicago, up on the second floor. His uncle hooked that up so he could take care of Muddy. Thirty-five a month for four rooms, he got it for him, and Muddy pay his own lights and gas. So he had it made there, second floor. His uncle was like the caretaker for this particular buildin'. This was Muddy's mother's brother—Dan Jones, Sr. Muddy just taken up with him. He treated him good. That was just like my grandmother had me, and my Uncle W.M. Miller, we was close too. That's the way we came into this thing. I guess in some ways we had so much in common.

Muddy and I, we could get along together, I would say. We could understand each other. I understood what Muddy was tryin' to do, because I was acquainted with the style that he was comin' into. I could help him out to fill in. I could fit into what he was doin'. My timin' was pretty good too. That's why I could team so good, so easy with Muddy. We would just rehearse all the time. That's all we would do, just lay around and practice, run through songs and build songs and sounds and tones. And it wasn't too hard for either one of us to catch on. He was a good bass carrier and I could play the lead to fit in, and we just kept on buildin' that way. Finally we came up with somethin'.

Muddy got a car here in Chicago. He was workin', and when his grandmother died, he was a beneficiary. He had a few bucks left after her burial down South. Muddy brought that little money back to Chicago. He got his paycheck and, with that other little money he inherited, he paid the down payment on the car. It was a rust-colored Chevy, a '40 Chevrolet two-door. It was pretty clean. His uncle vouched for him, and he paid the rest of it off by the month. I think it was $45 a month for 24 months or 36 months. We could get around then.

He'd get in that car of his, fool around and grab me. We'd go on out to the club like that. And when we'd get off the gig, he'd drop me off at home or we'd stop and get some food or whatever it was. And we'd go on home like that. He'd come on back over maybe 10:00 or 11:00 the next day. We'd go to a music store or wher- ever we had to go, pick up some strings or whatever you needed. He'd bring me back home. We'd sit there and drink some more whiskey. [*Laughs.*] Then he'd put me off. He'd go on home, and he'd come on back that night. If we had a gig, he'd come on over around 8:00 and I be ready. We'd go on to the gig.

At first, we had Baby Face Leroy and Walter in the group. Walter, he'd beat us there. We didn't have to worry about him gettin' there, 'cause he always be there where somebody drop him off. Muddy had the car, so me and Muddy would hang together. And Elgin [Evans], the drummer, he had his own car. We'd meet up there, go in and do the night there. We wasn't makin' no money, man, but still we was cookin'. Shit, man, I love that sound right today. It stuck in my head, but it's hard to find guys who can cook it up, though.

But almost nobody didn't have a car. Eddie Boyd, he was in the clique with us too. Didn't any of 'em have a ride. Muddy was the onliest one. Muddy had that old Chevrolet then and we could just go different places. That's better than tryin' to hire somebody to take you or ridin' the CTA. He didn't know the city too well, but the people he was dealin' with knew the city. I knew it. Eddie Boyd knew it. And going out to Gary, Indiana, Sunnyland, he knew it real good. So we could get together and just go from one place to another. Go to Milwaukee and go to Gary— that was about as far as we would go. And then back: the East Side, West Side, North Side, and South Side of Chicago, around where the clubs were. See, that's the way Muddy started gettin' around meetin' musicians here.

We used to drive to Gary for gigs in the car of Muddy's. It was me and Muddy and Sonny Boy and Sunnyland and Baby Face Leroy. We used to play over in Gary—27th Row, way down at Simm's, 22nd and Broadway, and F & J. We'd get about $10 or $15 apiece when we'd get a night there. [*Laughs.*] That was about all we'd get out of it, but that was pretty good. Gettin' our foot in the door—that's what we was comin' for. And it worked. For years and years we'd go up there on weekends. We'd play Friday and Saturday or Sunday up there. John Lee Williamson would get drunk and go to sleep, and I'd take the harmonica and make the night. [*Laughs.*] Yeah, it was a lot of fun.

I was playin' pretty good by then. I had a Silvertone electric guitar, but I had a Gibson amplifier with a small Gibson 12-inch speaker. It stood out pretty good, but sometimes, like if you were near the police station or the fire department, that'd be louder than the guitar was. You couldn't get too much volume on it. A truck would come through and you'd lose the crowd, yeah. But we could make out with it.

Sunnyland Slim had brought Walter and Honeyboy to Chicago, so I got a hold of Little Walter from there and pulled him in. Then I introduced him to Muddy. Baby Face Leroy was in Chicago then. We was runnin' a trio with him. Walter came in and strengthened it a little bit. The only problem we had with that unit was gettin' Walter down, bringin' him down. He had been used to runnin' and playin' by himself or playin' with musicians who didn't know much. His timin' was real bad. Nobody wouldn't take too much pains with Walter, because Walter was kind of wild. He was a player, but he didn't know about playin' with no bands or anything. He used to play by himself like Sonny Boy did, ya know. But Sonny Boy could play with a band or play by himself. That's the way he was. And Walter, he was still makin' him a few nickels out there playin' by himself. He had some good licks, and some wasn't so good. But after he got with us, he listened to what we were doin', and I learned him his count pretty good and we could work out somethin'. Sure, after he started playin' with musicians like us, even if he wasn't playin' with us, he got attached to that sound and he wanted to have somebody with him if it wasn't nobody but just a guy with a guitar. He never was too fond of pianos, but he liked guitar players.

Walter used the harmonica like a saxophone. He had that sound, that swingin' sound of his with that harmonica rhythm. But we had to put him in shape because he'd get executin' and go on. He was worse than the Bird, Charlie Parker. But we kept on till we got him. He would run his thing and I would say, "Look, I don't care how far you range on the wall. Just meet me at the corner." That's where I got that from—teachin' him how to do it. And what it takes to meet me at the corner, it was a little thing we'd have to do—run it timin', see. It was hard to get him into that, but we got him pulled pretty close to the beat on timin'. Sometime he'd override it a little bit, but there was enough there to fill it in and smooth it out. He'd try it this time. Then he'd try it next time. He kept on doin' it till he finally learned pretty good how to stay in the groove there.

Me and him got to where we could really groove together. We could team together. Muddy, all he could do was pit-pat along in the bottom. He could bottom [play bass notes]. And that's the way we put it through. So we went on from there. He got to be one of the hard hitters and we had the hottest band that was around: me and Muddy and Walter. They called us the "Headcutters."

Most of the playin' I did then, it would be me and Walter and Muddy. Sometime I'd play harmonica till I got Walter hooked in. Then I turned the harmonica over to Walter and went to full-time on guitar. Through Sunnyland, we got a Monday night at the 708 Club. Me, Walter, Muddy, and Elgin. It was a pretty good-sized night club. Muddy, he'd make about eight dollars and I'd get about eight. You'd get you some whiskey. We was havin' fun back then. We wasn't makin' too much money, but it was fun. I enjoyed it. We all did.

We had a gig, but certain nights we wouldn't be workin' or maybe we'd get off early. We just went from one joint to the other one where live bands was playin' at. As soon as we would get in a place, somebody would want us to play. They would tell the boss or whoever it was—they didn't know who we were or anything. The band members knew us, so they would want us to play because we could help liven the house up, ya know. We would go to the car and maybe get an amp and quick bring it in there and set up and jam a few numbers. And [shrugs] when we leave, the crowd would leave too. [Laughs.] So then they start callin' us the "Headcutters." That was a funny thing. We did that at a lot of clubs—Brown's Village, the Squeeze Club, Ada's Lounge, and the 708—oh, I could just go on namin' different clubs we went to around Chicago.

There was a whole lot of clubs here in Chicago then that had live entertainment. That was a big thing during that time. Guys couldn't play too well, but they would give 'em a gig. Club owners wasn't makin' no money that amount to anything, but they had live entertainment. That's what's supposed to be gettin' them a crowd: They'd have somebody sittin' in there jammin'. That's better than just playin' the jukebox. People would go somewhere where they have some live music, and a lot of musicians in Chicago got breaks from doin' that way. Tampa Red and Memphis Minnie and Memphis Slim, people like that—they would be playin' in these clubs and places that didn't have the license. They'd just get a little three-piece band in there and give 'em a few dollars, five dollars, whatever it was apiece. And they would sit in there and jam all night, ya know. And give 'em some free whiskey. [Laughs.]

We didn't stand up in those days, the late '40s. We sat down when we played. It's more relaxed sittin' down playin'. All bands did that. They'd sit down and play. The bandstand would be here and you'd have chairs, two or three guys. You wouldn't have no big band. Drummer and piano gonna sit down. We'd have chairs lined around and we'd sit down. Put the mike up in front of you. That's the way we did it. You could keep your time that way, tappin' your foot. You can't do that standin'. Baby Face, oh man, he'd click 'em both—clap, clap, clap!

Baby Face Leroy followed us around for a pretty good little while, but one thing: If it got slow, he'd kind of slack off some. Leroy, he gone. Get him a gas station job, pumpin' gas or fixin' tires. Another thing he was bad on was leavin' his guitar in pawn. Had to go by the pawnshop and get it out when he ready to work. He wasn't really up on this stuff that we was up to. Finally, he got in bad health and went back South. "Rollin' and Tumblin'"—that was a thing both Leroy and Muddy was doin'. It was okay. They kept messin' around with it. One was tryin' to outdo the other one on that. Muddy Waters wanted to be top dog on that. Leroy figured he knew more about it than Muddy did. That's where their little hang-up started. Wasn't nothin' serious.

THE FIRST RECORDING THAT I MADE IN CHICAGO, it was me and Little Walter and Othum Brown for the Ora Nelle label, down on Maxwell Street. "Little Store [Blues]" and different things like that. Me and Little Walter made "Muscadine Wine" too. We made a couple records down there for that place, Ora Nelle [Records], yeah. [Ora Nelle owner] Bernard Abrams, if he'd a had the money he could have made it too *before* Leonard Chess put Muddy out there. He just didn't have enough money to push it, see. Othum Brown, he was drunk and tried to do somethin' with his "Ora Nelle Blues" [the earliest version of the "That's All Right" theme, cut in 1947 by Othum Brown with Little Walter]. He tried but it didn't work. Joe Brown, I think it was his JOB label who did "That's All Right" first for me there, with Sunnyland playin' behind me, yellin', "Glory hallelujah!" That's right. [Rogers' August 1949 recordings of "I'm in Love"/"That's All Right" are reissued on Sunnyland Slim's Delmark album *House Rent Party.*] But we kicked that groove around for a while before we got what we wanted and had Chess [re]record it [in 1950]. Come to think of it, I recorded on harp before I recorded for Ora Nelle—me, Memphis Slim, Sunnyland. That was about 1945 for Harlem Records, I believe.

Sunnyland is the one who put us all into the record business. Sunnyland did that, put us on Chess label. Muddy was the leader on one of the first Aristocrat records that was made, and Sunnyland Slim was the finder of that. He was goin' strong and he had good connections in the field, and he boost us on over. The Chess brothers pulled out and changed the name of their label from Aristocrat to Chess after that, and that's when he put us on records, Muddy and me. Chess went on and pretty soon it was a big thing. The ball started movin' then. Bernard and Ora Nelle didn't have enough money, see, but the Chess boys did—eventually they did. Not right away. And they spread us all over the country and all over the world.

How it happened: Muddy's Uncle Dan got him a job—Brush and Graves venetian blind company, on a truck, on a route where they go. That's what Muddy was doin' when Sunnyland got in and told him that we were supposed to record for Chess. He pulled him off that truck. Sunny called over at Muddy's house when he hear somethin' in the wind that Chess was lookin' for somebody on that kick. John Lee Hooker was doin' it. Lightnin' Hopkins was doin' it. So Leonard wanted somebody that was playin' that kind of stuff. So Sunny knew that me and Muddy and all of them was doin' that type thing. Muddy had that growly, rough, bluesy voice. He told Leonard, "I got the right guy. In fact, all I gotta do is write him up."

But when he called, he found out Muddy was workin'. Leonard was a son of a gun, man. He told Sunny, said, "Hell, man. Go get him. Tell 'em his mama died, anything!" He didn't care.

Sunny called Muddy's house and his wife Geneva answered the phone. She knew Sunnyland. He was tryin' to make that lie stand up. He said, "Can you get ahold of Muddy?" She said, "Yeah, he's at work." So she gave Sunny Muddy's number on the job he was out on the road. Sunny called and he talked to this lady that take care of business there. He said, "As soon as you get ahold of him, tell him to come home. His mother's real sick." Muddy knew that his grandmother that raised him was down South! So he didn't know what the hell was goin' on. He had heard about this Chess was lookin' for him to do this stuff, but when it hit him like that, it was a surprise. So they got Muddy back to the office then. He got the news. He picked up right away that's what was goin' on, had to be somethin' about that recordin'. So they give Muddy a break and he went on home. Sunnyland rode the bus over to Muddy's house on the West Side and when Muddy got home, Sunny was there. Then they got together and talked. Muddy had his old car. So they drove on out there to talk to Leonard.

Muddy told me about it. "Well, we talked to Leonard. He told me he want me to do some solos like Lightnin' Hopkins, by myself, but I don't know about that." I said, "Man, try it if you can. Go back to the way you did it down South. Just think back. Get by yourself and just think back and go on and *do it!*" So me and him, we started practicin' and messin' around there. Two or three days we was messin' with that stuff. He tried to play that song about "Woke up this mornin', feel like blowin' a horn" by Robert Johnson. He picked the verses and got it. Hey, we lined it up there and he kept messin' around with it. So he said, "Well, that's one." I think he got about two numbers or somethin' together there that he could mess around with by himself with Sunnyland pling-a-ling a little with the piano like that. He hadn't told 'em about me. He was tryin' to do Lightnin' Hopkins' style and stuff. That's what Leonard wanted.

So Muddy went on out there with Sunnyland, and he practiced and messed around with hisself. Leonard Chess, he wanted somethin' kind of different, and Sunnyland was right there boostin' it along. So they patched up some stuff and made a big hit out of that junk, man: "I Can't Be Satisfied" and "Woke Up This Mornin' Feel Like Goin' Home" ["I Feel Like Going Home"]. I knew it. We played it all the time. He didn't wanna play it by himself. Sunnyland kept urgin' him. At that time, Muddy's bills was kind of gettin' high, his car note and he had to pay his rent. Geneva, she was workin', but she wasn't makin' but $40 a week at a cleaner's, doin' pressin'. Muddy, he was makin' about $60. And we hustled around on the weekends, playin' these gigs. Muddy was kind of a tight guy with them pennies, man. He watched his pennies, sure would. He could sort of ski along, but Sunnyland was boostin' him on about he could do this and he could do that. So he tried it. He didn't get no money out of it, but it started to put him on the market then.

Then Leonard came around; we was playin' at the Zanzibar. He and his bunch, they came over one Friday night. We were there. Leonard, he didn't know nothin' about nothin', I'd say. But he was listenin' to the sound that we had there. And he picked me out, singin', plus the guitar and harp sound me and Walter was doin'. He wanted to put me on records. That was '50 or '49, one of 'em. That put a little pressure on me. I had a lot of songs. I would write and do all that kind of stuff. But I wanted the opportunity to have somebody that meant somethin' to take it. I didn't wanna just throw it away. Muddy, he didn't throw it away, but Chess, he wasn't comin' up with no money. Muddy couldn't pay his car note. We used to hide his old car around to keep the finance company from takin' it. Yeah, he'd run around with it, stay in it, and send somebody in the store to get what he wanted, his old lady or somebody. Then he'd come back over to my house and hide it in my garage and then he'd go on home. We wasn't livin' too far apart. Chess would dodge him. He would say he's not in or somethin', 'cause Chess was scufflin' himself. He couldn't pay Muddy what he owed him. He was tryin' to round up enough money to get his thing goin'.

But Muddy had to pay rent. With the car note, that was close to $100 he had to pay. Geneva had Charles, that was her baby. So he was pretty tight there. He'd say, "Damn! It's a wild goose chase there with Chess." Chess was tight and his dad had hooked him up with a tavern, Mocambo Lounge, a little old small beer tavern. It was okay, clean, but his dad dropped all that stuff on him. His daddy was a plumber, old man Leonard. He had a lot of old buildings around. He was scufflin' and Leonard was scufflin', tryin' to do what he did do. He got the label workin' after a while. So we sufferin'. 'Course I didn't have no overhead like that, but Muddy, he had that little car hidden.

So Sunnyland had told me how to do with Chess. He said: "Do what you're gonna do." That's the way he did it, I guess—Sunny. But he never did make no hit. But he made some sellers for Chess. And that's the way I handled it. I'd go along with him. He'd ask me somethin'. I'd say, "Yeah, well, I can do it like this or do this." We was goin' downtown then to Universal Studios. He didn't have no studio then. Chess was goin' down to Universal. That's where he would rent a studio. He was payin' that guy $75 to use that studio for a couple of hours. Then you had to come in and rush the shit out. Do the best you can. Box it up as quick as you can, man, and get out of there on time, 'cause he's clockin' him.

Like I say, we had kicked that stuff around a lots—"That's All Right." It wasn't gettin' the right groove with it, but I kept on and kept on waitin' and buildin' it. Finally I got it like I wanted it when I did it for Chess. Yeah, that was the big one [the Chess version of "That's All Right"]. Johnnie Jones, myself, Walter, and Elgin. What made people recognize Jimmy Rogers was that sound, from 1950. I made it a couple of times more for different companies but always, after that, I kept my groove, my foundation. I won't let nobody pull me too far from there. You got to basic identify yourself. So many people ask me what it is. Well, that's it. The bridge is built. Peoples, you can cross it now. You can go from side to side.

I KNOW THAT MUDDY LIKED THE STYLE OF Robert Johnson *through* Son House. See, Son House was down there in Clarksdale, Mississippi. I didn't know Son House back durin' that time. Muddy did. Son House, ya know, he was a good player for that type of stuff. So he showed Muddy some points on what he was doin'. That's the way Muddy got the idea about what he wanted to try and do. He was stuck off on Robert Johnson. He played as close to him as he could. But he needed some help. He was tryin' to play huge slide, see. But for his pickin', he knew about it, but he didn't know any style of playin' like he'd learnt by bein' around with me and Baby

Face and Blue Smitty [Claude Smith] here in Chicago. Baby Face Leroy learned him some licks without usin' the slide. Blue Smitty worked with us for a while too. He gave Muddy a few licks.

I knew just about what it took to fit him. Baby Face Leroy, he would do it where he was playin' a different style. He was makin' the right changes where they were supposed to be, but he couldn't fit in. Me and Muddy and Walter, we could fit in real good. So that's the way we started doin' it after a while.

Muddy had his own style of playin' but he was playin' Robert Johnson's material, see. There was a change on it. You couldn't compare Robert to what Muddy was doin' because Muddy had a big, rough-soundin' voice for blues. We could fit it real good, and we just drivin' it. That's where we got so much power over a lot of other musicians that were playin'. They would be copyin' after somebody else, and they didn't have the music right. They were playin' one thing and singin' somethin' else, and it just didn't work, ya know. But they would get by with it a little bit. Sometime they'd come up with a pretty good seller. But everything mostly we was makin', it fit together and had that drive. And we was tellin' a good story pretty well all the time. Peoples really liked that.

Me and Blue Smitty was neighbors. That's how we met. He was a pretty nice player, but he wasn't really into his music thing too deep. He was an electrician. He was from 8:00 to 4:30 and go home, see. That was the type of person he was. He would play music mostly for his weekend thrill at the time or to get high, whatever. Sometime he would, sometime he wouldn't. If Blue Smitty wasn't there, I'd have to play the guitar. If he was, I'd play harmonica. Anyway, Smitty just wasn't too interested, and so we had to let him go, ya know. I'd be out there till the rooster crowed—as long as I was around where some music was goin' on. That was my shot. Elgin Evans was also startin' to hang around us. He was a drummer, a quiet guy. He used to play jazz till he got with us. He was an old-timer, see, a nice old man. He knew some old licks. He was older than Muddy. He was born in Elgin, Illinois. He had a lot of brothers, cousins, and different things. We all was musicians. Wasn't any money too much, but we were learnin' how to play and gettin' connections and stuff. We just stuck with it, that's all.

Muddy couldn't play with a slide in natural, like 440. He'd have to tune his guitar in Spanish [open *G*] to play it. So he'd have two guitars he'd take with him all the time. Before we'd go to these gigs, he'd have one tuned cross—we called it Spanish. He'd have one tuned that way. He'd play one, play along with us for a while, and he had another one all ready, just sittin' there in a rack. When he'd put that guitar down, that bass part, and grab that other guitar with that doggone piece of slide—oh Lord, man!—that's when Walter would have a fit. Muddy'd be breakin' on that *reahy, reahy, reahy!* Walter hated that. He'd say, "He's just scratchin' on that guitar!" I wouldn't tell Muddy. I knew what he was doin', but to make them turnaround changes, that's what was hard. I didn't know how to go into those certain changes and stay with the pattern. That was the bad part. Walter, he would just go. So we got him in pretty close to the pattern. We made the gigs, made the nights. And we was comin' up with this pretty good sound.

We wasn't playin' like the average guy play. We was playin' with changes. We was playin' music with two-, four-, six-, eight-, twelve-bar blues, most of the stuff eight bars or twelve bars, and that was somethin' that the average guy wouldn't understand. He didn't understand nothin' about it. Other bands would be just playin' and singin', and they made one beat, one sound. Go someplace else next time, just throwin' it together. But we had drive with what we were doin'. It added up, and it turned out to be what it really was supposed to be. Yeah, we had a lotta fun in this little field here.

When I wrote a song with Muddy, I tried to put as much into it, into the music as well as the lyrics. Somethin' that's catchy. You have to have a hook on your stuff there. That's what I always work for all the time. That's why we always could come up with somethin'. I never was too much of a guy to copy after nobody. I always tried to deal my own lyrics in my own style.

WE HAD GOT IN THE UNION, and the union didn't want us to play down on Maxwell Street. But I went down there many days and pulled Walter up from there. The hardest job for us was to keep Walter out from down there. If they had found out about it, they would have stuck a fine on him or blackballed him, like they done to Baby Face. But on Saturdays, maybe on Sunday evenings, he'd be around there makin' him quarters and things. He could really make more money on the street than he could at a gig, 'cause you'd have thousands of people durin' the day walkin' up and down Maxwell Street there. They'd throw ya quarters and dollars, whatever. For three or four guys, you could make you maybe $40, $50, where you maybe end up with at least about $15 or $20 apiece. It was somethin' for nothin', considerin'. And he'd be down there makin' his money, 'cause you couldn't make too much money on a tavern job—eight dollars, maybe ten at most, unless somebody tip you. But down there, you could mess around on a Sunday and a Saturday and you could come up with your money. All depend on how they tip. So Walter liked that.

When you belong to a union, they don't want you to be doin' that, 'cause it's scabbin'. They can't get any money out of it. It's just like the government is about bootleggin' whiskey. Same thing. They wanna have their hands in everything. Harry Graves, that was the musicians' union president. He would have those field guys out there watchin' that stuff. If you were a local musician and he'd catch you down there on Maxwell Street, he'd put a fine on you, see. Yes! So that's why we was tryin' to keep Walter out from down there. We'd quick run down and tell him, "The hawk is out!" That's what they called it. I didn't want him to get caught 'cause the little money he was makin', they'd put a fine on you. They'd charge you maybe $25 fine, and you might have to play three nights to make up that money, see. They had a union scale, but most places at that time, they would get a contract, but the club would pay you under scale to have you in the place. We'd just go along with it, you know, 'cause you'd make $10, $15 a night for three nights—$45—and you'd get free whiskey and he'd take care of the union tax for you. That wasn't bad. We got our foot in the door. Then we got in demand, see. But you gotta crawl before you can walk, is the old sayin'. And that's what we were doin'.

We had the Zanzibar, 13th and Ashland, West Side of Chicago. That was a good spot. Lowell King's, 3609 Wentworth, down from the White Sox ball park—that was another good groovy spot we had. The 708 Club on 47th Street, we had that spot. Docie's Lounge was back on 5114 Prairie. We had a lot of different spots. We worked six or seven nights a week. We'd work a night here, a night there. Zanzibar we worked three nights—Friday, Saturday, Sunday. And then we could get in at old Sylvio's on special occasions. We could get in over there, call 'em cocktail parties or whatever. Sunday matinee, they hooked that in. Sundays we might have to double up. Like maybe it would start at 2:00 or 3:00. Then we'd go till 8:00. Then we gotta take down, leave, and go to the gig. Be there at 9:00 and go until 2:00 at the club where we was playin'. That's stallin', double day. Wasn't too much money nohow, but you'd make $25 in them two days.

MUDDY AND WALTER AND MYSELF, we went out on the road in 1949. And we got a spot on KFFA in Helena through old man Sam Anderson. That's the guy that was helping Sonny Boy Rice Miller. Muddy, some way he got hooked up with that guy in a conversation. He gave us this spot. But we was on at 6:00 in the mornin', man. That was rough—for 15 minutes?! That 15 minutes seem like two hours. You had to have your gear lined up at 5:30, 5:45. You gotta get up, get down the hill to the station and be ready to go at 6:00—not 6:01, 6:00. Got your guitar sittin' here. Got it tuned and everything. When that light kick on, it's time for you to start. We was advertising for Cat's Clothing. "Go to Cat Clothing. You get yourself some nice stuff." He didn't pay us, but he would talk about us on the air, where we was gonna be that followin' night. That's your crowd right there. That's why we was doin' it. That was fun. Pinetop says it was rough. I guess maybe it was.

One time Walter and me slept late. We came in late. The radio is what woke us up. Muddy and Baby Face was down there playin'. I sure enough grabbed Walter, shook him. He said, "Hmmph?!" I said, "They on the air. Get your clothes on. We can be there in five minutes." We got dressed fast, then we had to take the car and then run down the hill from the hotel we were stayin' at. In about four, five minutes we were there. I peeped around the corner. The door was right there, and Muddy was sittin' there where he could watch that door, boy! He was lookin' for us anyway. When the light go out after they finished playin' one tune, then we get inside. Plug the amplifier in, go over there and plug your guitar up. Muddy, he looked at us. Leroy's sittin' up there. He's mad too because he had to be up, but he was there. Muddy didn't raise too much hell. We didn't do it but one time.

But, man, in Chicago we used to live in the studio all the time. Them Chess boys had us in there for days, day in and day out. We worked hard there for the Chess boys. I made a lot of stuff—I hope they don't ever release it. I hear some stuff they released on Muddy Waters. It's terrible, man. Muddy's not here to back himself up. A lot of this stuff, they wouldn't release it while Willie Dixon was alive. But I see they're puttin' it out now. Some of it is terrible. Some of it is real good.

In the studio, it's a lot different than out here on these stages when you performin'. They capitalizin' on what you're doin' when you're in the studio. If you make a mistake, they can stop you right there and come back and you can detect it. They'll make it over again or they can dub something in. They done got modern with this type of stuff.

Phil and Leonard Chess was businessmen. They was about money. We was about money too, but we was tryin' to learn to play the blues and tryin' to get on wax like we did. Muddy and I got on records. Chess boys, they out of business now. They gone but they left somethin' here for me to survive off of and we still goin'. So I'm glad we did run up on the Chess boys. We didn't get too much money out of the deal but, later years, it's beginning to pay off. He made us some big names in this blues field. He made us giants in this blues field, and I'm proud of it.

I would do a couple of tunes of my own at the end of a session with Muddy. I made a hit that way, just like we made "Juke" for Little Walter that way. We made that number at the end of my session and Muddy's session. That made a hit for Little Walter. That's the way he came into the picture, that same identical way. We all ended up pretty strong in this field. In fact, we were the strongest out there at that time. Everything we were doin' would click because we were teamin' together. My records would come out under my name. I could've had "Juke" or Muddy too—either one of us could've had that record. Taken it. But we wanted Walter to be on record as well. We were trying to make an all-star unit out of the deal. So we give Little Walter the credit for "Juke," 'cause he was the harmonica player.

The song known as "Juke" was our theme song. We didn't have a name for it then, but we was usin' it for comin' up and goin' down off the stage. We kept on nailin' on it till we got a good groove out of it. And Chess wanted it. So we recorded it at the end of a Muddy session. Then we had to figure out somethin' to put on the back side of it. And I happen to think of an old song of Sonny Boy Williamson called "Black Gal," but you couldn't use [the expression] "Black Gal" at that time. Leonard said, "Oh, no, you can't use that 'black gal.' Ya gotta put somethin' else in there." So me and Walter went in the bathroom and was standin' there tryin' to figure out somethin' to say to keep from singin' black gal. I had to stay there with him. We was sittin' down, knee to knee, where I could nudge him when he get to that turnaround, to that black gal part. I would say, "No black gal—baby! I'm crazy about you, *baby*." I finally got that through to him, got him to say baby instead of black gal. We grooved it. Once you get across that bridge you okay till it come around again. Cross this other bridge and then you gotta shake him up when he get there, because he gonna go the other way. We kept on till we got him tightened up there and we made a big record out of it. That was the backup for "Juke"—called it "Crazy About You, Baby."

The record came out, and we was down in Louisiana. We hadn't really heard it. They didn't know how to name it. We didn't know how to name it. We went downtown in Shreveport, Louisiana, and got uniforms. It was so hot down there that we got little stuff you could wear and rinse out the shirt when you off work and come home. Hang it up for the next morning, it'd be ready to go for the next gig. We didn't have nothin' that thin for that part of the country where it was that hot in the summertime. You needed it. So we went down there to get this stuff measured up—seersucker suits and little yellow eggshell-colored shirts, short-sleeve, and a pair of some beige pants. Walter was pretty thin. You could find a shirt that would fit him. That was not too tough. But the pants, the waist, they had to alterate the hips to bring 'em down so you could fit him.

So we went down there, got the little stuff. The guy said, "Come back around 4:00 and they should be ready to go." Muddy and me left the hotel around 3:00, goin' downtown. I guess it take 15 minutes. When we got back to the hotel, oh man, the girl up at the desk said, "The little guy with the checkered hat on"—that was Walter—"he said for you to take care of his amplifier. He's sick. He had a terrific nosebleed. He's goin' back to Chicago." He must have left out right after we left. She said, "He got a cab and got on the train or bus." But he went on back to Chicago. He left us down there.

Groove Boy, he was the guy who was bookin' us down there, he got us another saxophone player to replace Walter. We made out with him, got through, picked stuff you could kind of handle pretty good to make the nights. We didn't have but a couple more nights to go.

We all was confused. We didn't know how Walter was doin'. We all thought he was sick. He was a guy who would have those terrific nosebleeds. We know that. We was worried about him.

The real story is that he had called Leonard, said we was making all the money and he wasn't makin' none, and he was goin' home. See, he had talked to Dave Myers and Louis Myers—they were called the Aces. They were together with Junior Wells. Junior was a harmonica player for them. So Walter got with Dave on the phone, told Dave he was comin' in. The job that Junior Wells and the Aces had, 39th and Indiana at the Flame, they kicked Junior Wells out of there and got Walter. Dave and Louis just switched harmonicas. They kicked Junior out and took Walter in that unit. They had signs made up and everything: "Little Walter and the Jukes."

We got back to Chicago. We was lookin' to hear if Walter was in the hospital or somethin'. We didn't know. My wife, she said, "Walter got the boys—Dave, Louis, and [drummer Fred] Below—and they got the gig at 39th and Indiana where Junior had it. Junior is in the street." That's the way they did that one. Anyway, "Juke" carried it over, made a big hit.

Walter wanted me to go with him too, but I couldn't deal with Walter like he wanted me to. I have enough problem out of Walter when we was with the big unit. Dave and Louis, they was good players, but the timin' and the changes, they was kind of hard. But there's a couple of numbers they recorded together, it sound pretty nice. They'd do those fast shuffles. We'd been doin' that, and they picked up a lot of stuff off of us. Fred Below, their drummer? Elgin, our drummer, was schoolin' him, see. Rolls and turnarounds. Below had been playin' jazz before he went in the army. He knowed a lot of rolls, crashes, and whatever, in the jazz foundation there. And Elgin showed him how to get to them turnarounds that we would make—and riffs. He helped him a lots. Below turned out to be a nice blues drummer.

What I mean by Walter was wild or was a problem is that Walter was likely to kill you or anybody else that crossed him. Then he died 'cause somebody knocked his ass off. He had a very, very high temper. A young buck with a lot of temper. He had more nerve than brains, I'll put it like that. But I liked him a lot. We made do. We got along okay. I would tell him what to do the best I could. But when he'd get off there by himself and leave me, he'd fuck up—and we end up havin' to get him out of jail and all that shit, me and Muddy. [*Laughs.*] Muddy'd call the lawyer that we had, then call Leonard and tell him what he did. By the time he get down there they got it all lined up for him. But they gonna give him hell down there.

After Walter left us, we had Henry Strong on harmonica. We called him "Pot" because smokin' pot was the thing and he was heavy on that. He was good and he was learnin'. We was gettin' ready to go on the road. We played at the 708 Club in Chicago that night and I taken him home after we got off workin'. We were sup- posed to go pick up our uniforms the next day after 10:00. I told him I'd be at his house around 11:00 and we'd go to the cleaners. We wasn't gonna leave until later on that evenin' anyway. We had to drive all night. We was goin' to Louisiana. But I didn't know his wife was as mad when she got home as she was with him. It was about some stuff he had goin' there, some woman. She was there in the 708 that night. He talked to her. His old lady was in the club too, watchin' what was goin' on, and she was angry.

So I got him home that night. They went in the house, and I guess shortly after they got home, the phone must've rung or somethin'. That's the way I heard it. Muddy was in the buildin' there. He wasn't livin' there, but he was there. That was Leonard's daddy's buildin' they were all in there. Muddy say he heard the rumblin' goin' on. Henry was runnin', comin' down the hall. Muddy said to himself, "Somebody fightin'." He heard somebody call, "Muddy!" He went to the door, opened the door, and looked out. Henry was in the lobby on the marble floor. He was bleedin' like hell, didn't have no shirt on. Had his pants on, didn't have no shoes on. He musta been gettin' ready for bed. Muddy got a quilt and wrapped him up in it and carried him out there and put him in his car. Didn't have time to wait for no ambulance to come and get him 'cause he was bleedin' like hell, man. Muddy was trying to get him to the hospital, but he died on the way there. I didn't know nothin' about it. Elgin, he came over to my house about 5:30 the next mornin' and told me he was dead.

I said, "Here I go again, back in this rat race." I got George Smith to replace Henry. I knew him. He was workin', cleanin' up those theaters right after they close. Him and a couple more guys, they worked together as a unit. They had two or three theaters they would clean up. I went to where he was workin' that particular night. He was out. A guy came to the door and told me he was out in the streets on break. Then I went to George's house, about 20 minutes from me. I asked his old lady did she know how to get in touch with him. She said he was at work. I didn't tell her I just had left there and he weren't there. But I left Muddy's phone number with her. I explained to her that it was very urgent. When he did come home, he went straight to Muddy's house and then Muddy explained to him what was goin' on. He was glad to go with us. He wore Henry Strong's uniform, sure did. I went to the cleaners and got it out. He wore that uniform different places we went on tour. Then we went through to California and George fell in love with California.

Big Walter did some gigs with us occasionally around different places. He never really worked steady with us, but he'd work in and out. I could get Walter to go with me recordin'. I got a funny story about that. Good Rockin' Charles Edwards was another harp player. He stayed with me a little while, about three months, I would say. He played around with my kids, liked to clown like that. He was a good harp player, but recording studios? Nah, he didn't like them. "Walkin' by Myself," he was supposed to have made that number with me, but he chickened out. He wouldn't go in the studio. He got lost. I don't know what happened to him.

I didn't see him for about a week after that. Then he said, "Man, I went downtown." He threw it off. But he was a good performer on the stage. He was a more experienced player than Big Walter was, but I had to go get Big Walter to record the number. Walter was on a painting job. Went over to the house, got him off the ladder. He had coveralls on, pants full of paint. He got so mad about that, didn't want anybody in the studio to look at him. I said, "Man, you're there to be heard, not seen." But he soon got over that. There wasn't no whole bunch of people in the studio that day. It was kind of a quiet day. He didn't know if there was gonna be a lot of artists in there or what, 'cause he was paintin'. He was concentratin' on what he was doin'. But on "Walkin' by Myself," Walter did a *good* job of it. Sure did.

The difference between Little Walter and Big Walter on harp, Little Walter, he would swing more. Big Walter had a big tone but Little Walter was more riffin', uptempo stuff, see. Harmonica players, if they can stick close to that pattern, you can groove okay. Big Walter was good with riffs, but he wasn't really too swift. He played mostly tone, but he was a *good* harmonica player. George, he was a good riff man. That's the reason why we grabbed him, 'cause he could riff lots. He was a swift player.

Henry Strong would try to hang close to [Little] Walter in his style. He was tryin' to learn, he was comin' in. I believe he was gonna make a good harmonica player. But he was stage shy—kind of like Hubert Sumlin, playin' with his back to the public sometimes.

I knew Forrest City Joe too. He was a swingin' harmonica player, but he wasn't really too clickin' in that pocket we were in. He wasn't too up on that. But he was a good player with what he was doin'. Him and Big Walter, they would hang up together a lot of times, jammin' at different clubs like the Tick Tock and at 22nd and State—there was a club over in there. We had to know where to find Walter, because if we had to go out of town and needed a harmonica player, we had to go get him. If he could make the trip, he was gone! See, the main point is keepin' a band under control where you can put your hands on 'em when you need 'em. That's what's hard to keep lined up. But Forrest City Joe, he didn't stay in Chicago very long. He went back South and got killed in a car wreck.

We needed a piano player. I told Muddy I knew one that, if we could keep him straight long enough, we'd have us a good one. So I found Otis Spann. I brought him to the unit, sure did. He was related to Johnnie Jones. Through Johnnie, I met him and he was playin' with some boys over on the West Side of Chicago—Morris Pejoe and Henry Grey and a bunch of those guys. He was playin' maybe Friday and Saturday this week, then play next weekend, then maybe wouldn't play no more then for the next two or three weeks. That's what he was doin', scufflin' around, sleepin' in cars. He was sufferin' pretty hard at that time, Otis Spann was. So I got over to him, told him Muddy needed a piano player. He said, "Yeah, man." He'd follow me to the end of the earth, as long as he get him a few nickels and get him some whiskey and get a girl to look at him. That was Spann. So I got him in there, introduced him to Muddy. I told Muddy Spann was a pretty good piano player. I could see it in him. Muddy didn't know anything about those people. I brought him to the union and into that group too.

His comin' on created more power and a bigger spread on the type of music we was playin'. He strengthened the unit a lot. He could help out, a lot of cracks he could chink with that piano he was doin'. Then we started to run the chords with him, to help him make the changes with us. And that was a big boost. Spann was mostly a feeder, a backup man. The harp, Muddy, and myself, we played off each other all the time. All we needed was some more strength, and the piano made it much stronger. We teamed up good. Wasn't too hard for us to rehearse and get the few corners tightened up. And we went from there. I just kept buildin'. I built that band. Muddy was the leader, but I was leadin' the band. When they'd ask me somethin' about the unit, I'd tell 'em, "Well, see that guy there, Muddy Waters there. Talk to him about it." Keep that part of the weight up off me. But I would tell him on the side what he should do, how he should work it. And it worked!

MUDDY WORRIED ME ABOUT SINGIN' ALL THE TIME. He wanted me to sing. Muddy, he said he didn't like his own voice. I don't know why. He sounded all right to me. I could understand where he was goin' and lay there and get under him and ride him in them curves and things. I knew how he was gonna come up there and come down. Drive, then lay under him. Ya call that feed. I knew how to feed him real good. After I left and he got other bands, I'd listen to 'em. They could groove pretty good. He learnt how to lay in the pocket, but the bands would override him a lot. I'd hear 'em how they do it, 'cause they didn't understand. They'd hear the records. Peoples didn't understand the count or how we's doin' that. That's hard for a straight guy to learn that stuff. We done hit it and gone to something else. We wouldn't stay in one place. You got a lotta different phrases and turnovers and channels. It's like puttin' up a buildin'—lotta stuff ya gotta do. You try to explain that to 'em, you disencourage 'em real quick.

Muddy was just a quiet type of guy. He didn't mix too much with people because he didn't know what was happenin'. Muddy was always kind of quiet in Chicago. He kind of feared being with people, and he would think about all these gangsters and the stick-ups and all that stuff. He was always shy. Muddy didn't really run around too much to different clubs unless he had us with him. We went as a group, otherwise Muddy would be someplace at home or somethin'. He liked women, though. You know how that goes. [*Chuckles.*] Yeah.

Wolf, he was another guy that didn't run around too much by himself. He was a lonely type of person too. He was kind of laid back. But he was okay with me. A lotta musicians, younger ones, they couldn't understand him and they would have problems. My wife and me, Wolf and Lillie, we always got along real good. He was a nice guy, as far as I'm concerned. He was set in his old ways and stuff. Like a lot of musicians, he'd always try to find somethin' to argue about to get some shit goin'. [*Imitates Wolf's gravelly voice*] "I'm gonna tell ya what I been thinkin' about." I'd laugh about it and go ahead. But a lot of people would take him seriously. If you had to be involved with him, it's a different story, but I didn't have to really be involved with him unless he would ask me to go help him on a gig or somethin' like that. No, he didn't ever bother me. He was a friend of mine, I would say. He knew where I was comin' from, and he would treat me with respect. But he could be mean to his musicians. He wouldn't take the time to explain to you what you were supposed to do, because he didn't really know what to tell you. He'd start a humbug with you. But he never did start one with me.

I didn't hang around with none of those guys in Wolf's bunch anyway. We didn't really mix with too many different people. You see the other sidemen out in the street when you get out there. You say "Hey!" or whatever. But when it come time to go, they wouldn't know which way we went out—the back door, side door. We'd just be gone. You'd see us the next day or the next week or somethin' like that. Catch us at where we'd be playin' at or somethin' like that. They didn't know our whereabouts. You can't let those guys know too much about what you're doin' anyway. You have to try to keep your business to yourself, and that's the way we did it.

I made a lot of records with Wolf, me and Muddy Waters both. I knew how to find the pocket and I'd ride right there. Maybe certain times I wouldn't know what steps to take to do certain licks on him, but he'd just be playin' with me. He'd go along with it. He didn't never give me no rough time. I knew how to feed a harmonica player because I used to play harmonica myself and I know what it takes. With certain licks that you hit in your changes, you can throw a harmonica player a flip. If you don't really know how to get by it, you can mess him up real bad.

We was tryin' to make it an all-star unit, Muddy, Walter, and myself. That's what we had planned, but Walter left as soon as he cut a single. That was the end of that part of it. Me and Muddy, we stuck together. We got different harmonica players behind us, kept on doin' that. When I left the band, Spann was still there. He was a fantastic blues piano player. I left Muddy in the '50s and formed my own unit.

My own style developed from Big Bill Broonzy and guys like that—Lonnie Johnson, Tampa. I liked the style and tone that Big Maceo carried in that group. I liked that! So I could fit all that stuff in there, get some guys in to hit it, *boom!* It was no problem for me to start my own band. I had Big Walter Horton on harp, for a bass player I had Poor Bob. Henry Grey on piano and S.P. Leary on the drums. He was in his prime durin' that time. We was kickin'. They fitted in. Not the best, but I could get by with 'em pretty good, and I just kept shoppin'. Ya have to keep shoppin' and finally you find somebody that can fit you, your tone. You don't really go around doggin' musicians. They'll do it themselves. I never tries to control no man, but I'll tell him the way I feel about how things is supposed to be goin'. I respects them and they respects me. We get along like that.

Me and Eddie Taylor used to do stuff together. He respect me a lots and I did the same for him. We got along real good. People have said that Eddie Taylor took his style from my style. It's a possibility. The last trip he went out, I brought him back, him and Hubert. We went to Austin to record for Antone's in August 1985, and he died in December that year. He was sick then when we went on that trip, but I didn't know how sick he was. Eddie would hold a lot of stuff within. His wife, Vera, she didn't have the slightest idea how sick he really was.

I got inactive in music in the '60s because the blues players wasn't really makin' too much money, wasn't doin' too much movin' around and tourin'. We weren't doin' that much strong giggin' even in Chicago. Things kind of went into a slump. But I had Little Jimmy here and his sisters and brothers, kids comin' in. And I had to kind of do somethin' I could depend on for my family. I was a family man. I tried livery cab business, and then my wife's daddy died. There were three children, and they split the settlement between the three of them. She wanted to invest in women and children's clothin'. That was the thing she wanted to do, so I stood behind her. I liked the business. I was, like, plumber, carpenter, different things like that around that store. She was right there behind me, pushin'. So we had a clothin' store on the West Side of Chicago and we just stuck there.

My son, Jimmy Jr., he got to the place he could help me out in the store like my baby girl do now, and Dorothy, she was right there. That's the way I put my kids through school until Martin Luther King, Jr., got killed. Fire got to that, burnt that whole West Side down. They got me in that. I lost quite a bit of money. It took a long time, but I finally got a settlement in later years. But ya takes a beating goin' through there, because they said the fires was intentionally started. They have to investigate. They have to go through a lot of changes there, but I finally got through and got a check in later years.

I started back playin' music in '68, '69. They was all worryin' me about hittin' the road again: Sunnyland, Dixon, all those guys. Willy Leiser from Geneva, Switzerland, he taken me to Europe, taken me over to Sweden, to France and Switzerland. I stayed over there for quite a while and I made out pretty good. Europe was somethin' I was wantin' to see anyway. I enjoyed it. That started me back up. I been movin' along pretty well ever since. I don't mind travelin' just as long as I got "my train fare home."

Me and Muddy got along okay. We'd fall out sometimes, but it didn't really mean too much. Naw! It didn't really mean nothin' too much. Nothin' in extremes. Nothin' we couldn't handle. We would come around to some kind of agreement and work it out too, you know. And he could understand my position. See, Muddy didn't have no large family. His old lady, Geneva, she was like Dorothy. They understood we had a pile of kids to care for.

Muddy and me got back together for some of that Blue Sky stuff with Johnny Winter. His band messed up, and he called me up, "You gotta come with me this time." He didn't have no good unit, but we made the cake, all right. He had John Primer, Lovie Lee, George [Mojo] Buford, a couple of others I had never heard of. So I turned down some gigs I had, and we got together and went off. We worked it out real good. We had kind of a good number too. I wrote some numbers there that he recorded for Blue Sky before that tour.

Before he died, maybe a month or two, I was gettin' ready to go back on the road and I talked with him. He was tellin' me he was plannin' to come back out when the weather broke. He was gonna be ready to come back out, start doin' some tourin', you know. Next thing, I was up in Canada when he passed. He didn't never get straight really after that accident he had, that car accident. He didn't never get straight behind that. He broke his pelvis and some of his ribs messed up, and he come down with first one problem to the next problem, and it was on and on.

He died when me and him were still friends—that's the good part about it. Regardless to circumstances, we got along real good right up until he passed. Yeah, I thought a lot of him, ya know. I still have some amps and stuff in my house that I got from Muddy back durin' the time Muddy was in his prime, right? I keep 'em for like a souvenir.

I got the guys now in my band that can groove it pretty good. I got David Crawl from St. Louis on piano. A damn nice guy. Johnnie Johnson give him a lot of points about piano, and there's Keith from St. Louis. Ted Harvey, he's just like a bad check—you can't get rid of him. That's my boy. He been with me for about 15, 16 years. My son, he with me all his life. Fred on bass, he's a young rookie. When I'm not workin', he works with Little Jimmy [Lane] in his band, Blue Earth. It's between the blues and rock and roll. It keeps them eatin', pays some bills. They plays some Jimi Hendrix and plays some whoever he can. They got a little groove goin'.

It's hard to find guys that can play my old sound, but I fight along there with 'em and we come up with somethin'. I'm not a guy that likes doggin' a musician. I can't do that. If you can't follow, you can't lead. You gotta learn how to follow first. I know about that stuff. Before a young musician learn what's goin' on, if a woman tell him, "Oh, man, you sound good," a couple of guys tell him the same thing, buy him a drink or something, it's gone to his head right then. He's a star now. Before their wing feathers have even sprouted out, they wants to be a star. They want to start at the top and go up. There's a bottom there you gotta do. You gotta learn that.

A lotta musicians feel bad about scolding young musicians. That don't help 'em at all. You throw 'em further from what you was tryin' to do. Different guys got different ideas automatically. They wants to fit. It's like a shoe. A guy, maybe he like the way a shoe is made, but it maybe don't fit his foot, see. It's not comfortable. That's the way it is. So you gotta get guys that really wants to get in that groove and fit. Then you gone. My son, Jimmy, he got a lot of execution ideas, but I keeps him in that pocket there and he grooves real good.

Young people that's tryin' to do somethin' in music, I'll pass off my time with 'em as long as they're nice. Well, that's the way it was done with me. That's the way musicians are supposed to do. There's a lot of young musicians comin' up now in these later years that's around, but there's been a changeover. They be playin' funk and soul and callin' it blues, ya know. So time goes on.

So I been through the good and the bad—and the ugly. [*Laughs.*] I tell any musician that I talk with that's comin' up how to try and conduct themselves to survive out here and take care of life. That's all—ya ain't got but one. Some guys take heed and some don't.

My wife Dorothy and I, we been dealin' together a long time. She always been right there behind me, and she's still pushin'. I don't have to worry when I'm gone. There's someone taking care of business for me here at home: Dorothy and my daughter Angela. Dorothy's cleaned up this neighborhood. She's in with the polices and neighborhood watch stuff. She's a scufflin' woman, man! I try to give her credit for that. She's not in the best of health, but she's done all right, I'll put it that way. She takes care of those kids, takes care of family. She's a great mother, a family woman. I guess that's how she hooked me. For a good marriage you gotta have an understandin' between two people. Ya gotta love and respect each other. Womens has got a different approach about life. They want things to go the way that they feel like it should go. The majority of 'em is right.

I don't have too much trouble out of my kids, even from the time they were little and growin' up. I had 'em all stair-steps, a couple of years apart. They all around where I can put my hands on 'em right now. [*Laughs.*] One live upstairs in my place here. He's got a family. His name is James. Little Jimmy, he plays with me in the band. He lives down around 79th and Western. He sticks with me real good too. Yeah, I have some good-lookin' daughters. But look—they a chip off the old block. They take it from the old man. Me and the wife, we did everything to bring them up the best that we possibly could. I think I got a bunch of fine kids. I appreciate 'em and I love 'em all.

I don't be around Chicago too much. I live there, but I just come through there, pay the bills, and get goin'. I stay on the road. When I goes to Chicago, I goes to rest there. I ease in, stay at home, man. Let somebody else answer the phone. "I'm not here" or whatever. Stay away from that stuff. I don't wanna even work in Chicago. I plays Chicago Blues Festival, McCormack Place, Buddy Guy's—I go in there and play. That's about it till I go back on the road.

I LOVE PEOPLE RIGHT TODAY. I'm me, and that's the way I was raised. I don't dog nobody out, don't contradict ya. I'm not that kind of person, can't do it. It's not my nature, man. I don't bother nobody too much. Out of a month's time, it takes me 20 or 22 days to take care of my business and the other nine days to leave other people's alone. I don't be tryin' to criticize nobody. They gotta live in their life. They can't live in mine. That's *your* business. That's the way *you* make it. That's *your* life. You do it *your* way. And I don't get into trouble that way.

As far as other musicians, whether it sound good to me doesn't matter. It sound good to *him* or *her*. Why should I take time out to criticize you? Hell, what I'm doin' might not be too hot, as far as other people are concerned, but I'm tryin' to look out for number one. So it's all right. There's plenty of space out there for you as well as myself.

I got enough judgments about myself and about life to know certain things. I always teach my children and anybody else that I be around: Know your left hand from your right, your hat from your glove. And I have pretty good luck in doin' it. I tell 'em to be respectful. You give it, and you will receive it. *Demand* that you receive respect if you have to! If you givin' respect and you're not getting it back, you know what's happenin'. The person that you talkin' to, he may not know. You gotta feel around and try to find out where he's comin' from. Some way there you'll get through unless he's a fool, and then you leave him where he is. 'Cause you get with a fool on a bridge, and you'll be in trouble. You gotta go on your own and get off. Get out of it, get away. That's the way I explain life to my kids.

I tell them, don't go to school and tell other peoples, "Jimmy Rogers is my father." They gonna try to get somethin' goin' with you on account of my name. You gonna stop concentratin' on learnin', and you goin' there to learn books and lots of stuff I didn't learn. So tell 'em your name is John Doe or Jabbo Who, and if you wanna deal with people from school, okay. Otherwise, don't you involve me.

I've tried to make a decent life for my children and the people that I'm involved with. That's what I try to do. A lot of people live in this block and in the next block. I talks to everybody, just "How ya doin'." Some says, "Ya got a pretty house." I says, "Well, okay. It's just a house. Keeps the rain off your head." That's all I get out of that. I don't be, "I got this, I own that." I don't care about that stuff. All that's material things, man. Life, inside, is what's important.

WHAT WE GOTTA DO NOW IS FINISH UP some stuff that we got lined up on this Atlantic superstars project. Mick Jagger, he's gonna be there with me to record some in L.A. I call him "the Wild Man." He's one of my old European partners too and has done me some pretty good deeds over there. We got through with Eric Clapton. He recorded two days with us over here. We've recorded before. We've worked together a looong time. I been knowin' all those guys over in England for years. Those guys treats me like brothers, man. They're good to me, very good. Sure is.

Johnnie Johnson is good with that left hand now. So he's the piano player that I used on the Atlantic stuff and whenever I'm recordin' now. Since Spann's gone, all those guys is gone. Pinetop, he's still around, but for the last couple of years Pine's been kind of in low cotton. I talks to him about every week. He come over to the house or call. He stay in contact with me. Me and my wife, we look out for him since his wife passed.

I still write songs. I get by myself and thoughts come to me. Sometime I'll be at home. I got a couple of machines there. I'll wake up durin' the night and lay down some lyrics, run it back and mess around with it. It builds from there. That helps me a lot. "Walkin' by Myself" came to me in a dream. It sure did.

Yeah, I just made some pretty big money on a cover of one of my tunes—"Walkin' by Myself"—by rock star Gary Moore. That type of thing has been a long time in comin', but it's welcome anyway. Eric Clapton did a couple of my numbers on his *From the Cradle* CD—"Blues" and "Goin' Away to Worry You Off My Mind." That was a nice one, money-wise. I been on and off with the Muddy Waters Alumni touring for a long time. I got more work than I can reach right now, but I'm doin' my best.

Chicago clubs in the '40s and '50s were like places I likes to play right now, but places I play are mostly all big stuff now. You can't really mix with the public like you could do back then. You could walk around and shake hands with 'em. They'd hug you and you'd talk, go around and have a drink together. They got it now so they keeps you kind of divided. They got backstage and stuff. They have to make a reservation to get to where you be. And people, they bug you so bad. They ask you a million questions all at the same time. You're tryin' to do what you're tryin' to do. You got a job to do and they be all over the place. You just bypass out of it. You give 'em all a smile, talk to 'em best as you can, and you go on. Sometimes guys gets out of hand and you gotta take care of 'em.

MUDDY'S SOUND WAS HIS SOUND and my sound. I didn't never have no doubts about it that way. I appreciate bein' a part of it. We helped each other through this roughness. We built a good style that's standard out there and it's out there goin' now and I appreciate still bein' here to be a part of it.

I think Muddy and me contributed quite a bit to the blues, more than a lot of peoples before my time. They didn't ever strike it like we did. I'm proud to be a part of it. I'm well pleased to be in history for this thing. I guess the timin' must've been right. Some people say we brought in the new wave of Chicago blues. I've heard that. That's okay. We'll call it the new wave but, I mean, I came up under Tampa and Big Maceo and Memphis Minnie. I take a little piece of them with me. Right now they're still with me.

I had fun comin' right on up, and I'm havin' fun right today. When it gets to the place it ain't no fun, I'll leave it go. I'll go and do somethin' else—get my pole and go fishin'. [*Laughs.*] Yeah. I'm the man who plays the blues. That's me.

ELMORE AND HOMESICK JAMES

BY JAS OBRECHT Elmore James jump-started "Dust My Broom" with what's become the most imitated of all slide riffs. Performed in open *D,* it's based on stringy glides to the 12th fret, played with the passion of the procreant urge. While the song's signature slide and pumping bass originated in Robert Johnson's "I Believe I'll Dust My Broom," it's a mistake to brand Elmore James a one-lick wonder or Johnson imitator. During his prime, he fronted the Broomdusters, Chicago's most incandescent blues band, and he authored the enduring "The Sky Is Crying," "The Sun Is Shining," "Madison Blues," and "Done Somebody Wrong." ¶ Using a radio tube cover as a slide, James played his amplified Kay acoustic with unstoppable body rhythm, and his ferocious, anguished vocals were as fearless as his solos. "He's the guy," says Ry Cooder. "Elmore is so in the middle of the music all the time, just covering the whole thing like a great horn player. Ain't no problem memorizing what Elmore plays—it's how he *doesn't* play. The killer shit isn't the notes themselves, it's the sympathetic stuff going on around the notes and that feeling that's strictly body rhythm."

"I'M ELMORE—AFTER ME THERE WON'T BE NO MORE" Born in rural Mississippi on January 27, 1918, Elmore James plucked his first notes on a diddley bow, and then fashioned a one-string guitar from a can, board, and wire. When his distant cousin Homesick James first met him in Canton, Mississippi, around 1930, the shy 12-year-old was going by the name Elmore Brooks. By his late teens Elmore had acquired a National resophonic guitar and was playing at Delta juke joints and restaurants. "He never wanted to work in the field," an old neighbor recalled. "He would just take off with his guitar and move from town to town." James took up slide after meeting Robert Johnson, who shared his penchant for drinking hard, womanizing, and disappearing without warning. (In the parlance of the rural South, "dust my broom" referred to leaving town in a hurry.)

Soon after Johnson's death in '38, Elmore James was leading one of the Delta's first progressive blues bands. After a wartime stint in the Navy, he returned home to work in his adopted brother's radio repair shop and convalesce from a heart ailment. He played jukes and radio shows with Willie Love and Aleck "Rice" Miller (a.k.a. Sonny Boy Williamson II), and in early '51 backed Miller at his Trumpet sessions. In August, Elmore inaugurated his own recording career with a stomping, jacked-up version of Robert Johnson's "Dust My Broom" with Sonny Boy Williamson II on harp. The single reached #9 on the national R&B charts and inspired future producers to request thinly veiled remakes.

James moved to Chicago in '52 and commenced cutting singles for Meteor, Checker, and Flair. Soon thereafter he was backing pianist Johnnie Jones when he reunited with Homesick James, with whom Jones was lodging. They began playing together, usually billed in the *Chicago Defender* as Elmore James—The Broomduster. Elmore often supplemented his income by moonshining, and his sidemen shared his fondness for drink. Fights between Johnnie and Elmore were reportedly a nightly occurrence, and during their station-wagon tours, Elmore often engaged in practical jokes such as clandestinely pawning his bandmate's property.

At their peak, the Broomdusters featured Odie Payne on drums, tenor saxophonist J.T. Brown, and Homesick James playing bass lines and occasional solos on guitar. As Robert Palmer pointed out in his liner notes for *The Sky Is Crying*, "The Broomdusters were one of the greatest *electric* blues bands. In terms of creating a distinctive and widely influential ensemble—and in terms of sheer longevity—the Broomdusters' only real rival was the Muddy Waters group that included Jimmy Rogers, Little Walter, and Otis Spann. And judging from the recorded evidence, the peaks of intensity reached by the Waters band in full cry were at a level the Broomdusters reached before they'd finished warming up."

Elmore James was fresh out of the hospital from his second heart attack when he cut for Chief in '57. "Coming Home" rolled to the "Dust My Broom" theme, with Elmore, Homesick, and Eddie Taylor all reportedly playing through the same amplifier. Wayne Bennett played the elegant lead on "The Twelve Year Old Boy," cut at the same session. The date also produced an astounding rendering of Tampa Red's "It Hurts Me Too." Elmore's bookings jumped when the Vee Jay label reissued the sides.

The following year Elmore returned to Jackson, Mississippi, and became a disc jockey, but he was back in Chicago by November '59, when Homesick played bass on the legendary Fire/Fury session that produced "The Sky Is Crying," "Dust My Broom," "Held My Baby Last Night," "Baby Please Set a Date," and an instrumental dance tune, "Bobby's Rock." Earlier that year, the label had a #1 hit in *Billboard's* pop and R&B charts with Wilbert Harrison's "Kansas City," and Bobby Robinson decided to produce Elmore's session in stereo. James' otherworldly slide tone on these records has yet to be duplicated. "Elmore's beautiful sound is the greatest thing in the world," describes Ry Cooder, "but it's only on the Chicago sides that he cut for Fire and Enjoy. Even the Fire and Enjoy sides from New Orleans and New York sound different. He had something else he used on those. I don't think it was his Kay with a pickup, because there's no way a Kay with a pickup can sound like those Chicago sides, like 'It Hurts Me Too.' I am sorry—I've been through everything, and it cannot. That 'unknown amp' is the real mystery." The first release, "The Sky Is Crying"/"Bobby's Rock," reached #14 in the national R&B charts.

Homesick James played guitar during Elmore's smoky, saxy April '60 Chess sessions for "I Can't Hold Out (Talk to Me Baby)," "The Sun Is Shining," "Stormy Monday," and "Madison Blues." He switched back to bass for their fourth session together, at Manhattan's Belltone Studios, which produced "Rollin' and Tumblin'," "Done Somebody Wrong," and eight other songs. Homesick did not play on Elmore's subsequent "big band" session in New York, nor at his final dates in New Orleans and New York.

During 1961 Elmore was blacklisted by Chicago's musicians union for nonpayment of dues, and in '62, his health fading, he returned to Jackson, Mississippi, with Homesick in tow. For a while they stayed with Johnny Temple in Jackson, and then Homesick headed back north. Elmore and Homesick shared their final dates when promoter Big Bill Hill intervened with the union and brought Elmore up in May '63 to open his new Copa Cabana Club. Elmore arrived in Chicago on a Sunday, dropped his luggage off at Homesick's house, where he was staying, and played the Copa that night with Homesick and a drummer. Afterwards, they stopped by Sylvio's to see Howlin' Wolf. The musicians played the Copa twice more, and later that week 45-year-old Elmore James suffered a fatal heart attack just after taking a shower at Homesick's house.

Soon after Elmore James' death, his music became a touchstone for British bluesrockers, notably the Rolling Stones, Fleetwood Mac, and Yardbirds vets Eric Clapton and Jimmy Page, who briefly joined forces to record "Tribute to Elmore." While the Allman Brothers Band, Stevie Ray Vaughan, Johnny Winter, and countless others have championed James' music since then, his favorite saying still holds true: "I'm Elmore. After me there won't be no more."

ELMORE'S COUSIN, HOMESICK JAMES To this day, the foremost advocate of Elmore James' music is his old bandmate Homesick James, whose throaty, bittersweet sliding still conjures images of Elmore and his Broomdusters rollin' and tumblin' in a sweaty Chicago nightclub, playing so damn hot that working-class people threw money at their feet. Homesick's distinctive tone is a combination of heart and hands, a hunk of conduit, a homemade guitar, and a battered amp. Now in his eighties, he sings with a vibrant, vibrato-drenched voice somewhat reminiscent of the second Sonny Boy Williamson's.

Blues references list Homesick's last name as Williamson, although during our meeting he stated, "I can't tell nobody what my real name is. I never uses it. But my passport says John William Henderson." He was born in Somerville, Tennessee, on April 30, 1910. His father, a cotton worker named Pluz Williamson, played snare in a fife and drum band, and his mother, Mary Cordelia Henderson, performed spirituals on guitar. His churchified mother forbade him to play, fearing he'd learn blues songs, but by age eight the youngster was hauling out her guitar on the sly. A neighbor named Tommy Johnson—not the famous one who made 78s—taught him to play lap-style slide with a pocketknife. Young Homesick met Blind Boy Fuller during a visit to North Carolina, while Mississippi sojourns brought him his first contacts with Howlin' Wolf, Johnny Shines, and Elmore James. Homesick James and John Lee Williamson (a.k.a. Sonny Boy Williamson I) also met as boys and may have been relatives.

By 1933, Homesick, Sonny Boy, Yank Rachell, and Sleepy John Estes were working the southwest Tennessee blues circuit, with regular stops in Jackson, Brownsville, Nutbush, Mason, and Somerville. Homesick moved to Chicago in '34 and stayed with Sonny Boy, who'd arrived months before, until he found work at a steel mill. At night he played covers of Memphis Minnie and Blind Boy Fuller songs with Horace Henderson's group at the Circle Inn. He was quick to electrify his sound; a photo of him at the Square Deal Club, his second extended booking in Chicago, shows him playing a Gibson ES-150, which had just been introduced in 1936.

On occasion Homesick rambled south to play with Yank Rachell, Sleepy John Estes, and Little Buddy Doyle. James claims that he was one of the uncredited musicians who played on Doyle's 1939 Vocalion sides. After serving in World War II, Homesick joined Sonny Boy, Big Bill, and pianist Lazy Bill Lucas at Chicago's Purple Cat, with harmonica ace Snooky Pryor sitting in whenever he could get a pass from nearby Fort Sheridan. Later on, Homesick and Snooky worked with Baby Face Leroy Foster in South Chicago. Called up from reserve status, Homesick was wounded during a Korean tour of duty.

Homesick made his first recordings under his own name during 1952. Cutting for Chance Records at the old RCA Victor studio on South Michigan in Chicago, he dialed in a thick, distorted tone and traveled downhome, humming and moaning "Lonesome Old Train" to Lazy Bill's rocking barrelhouse piano. With lines like "I ain't gonna chop no more cotton, I ain't gonna plow no more corn," the flip side's "Farmer's Blues" was aimed at ex-sharecroppers who'd migrated to the North. Homesick says his second Chance session, with Snooky Pryor, was unissued. His next session produced the hit "Homesick," a rollicking romp with Robert Johnson–style turnarounds and slide figures that reappear on Elmore's later recordings. Its B side, "The Woman I Love," featured Johnny Shines on second guitar. At subsequent '50s sessions outside of his collaborations with Elmore James and the Broomdusters, Homesick backed Lazy Bill on a Chance 78 and covered Memphis Minnie's "Please Set a Date" for Colt. He assumed the pseudonym "Jick and His Trio" for a 78 on the short-lived Atomic H label.

For a while after Elmore James' death, Homesick fronted his own group in the same South Side taverns where he'd begun. He recorded an early-'60s 45 for Colt with Hound Dog Taylor on second guitar, and his reading of Robert Johnson's

"Crossroads" backed with "My Baby's Sweet" came out on the U.S.A. label. During '64 James made the *Blues on the Southside* album for Prestige, with Lee Jackson on bass. Homesick James & His Dusters (bassist Willie Dixon and drummer Frank Kirkland) resurrected Elmore's spirit on the 1965 Vanguard anthology *Chicago/The Blues/Today!,* covering "Dust My Broom" and "Set a Date."

During the '70s Homesick played clubs and made forays into Europe, often in partnership with Snooky Pryor. Their 1973 American Blues Legends tours of Europe produced a pair of albums and a review in which a critic described James' "usual tricks—playing guitar behind his back, jumping up and down, laying on the ground while playing." At the time, Homesick was in his early sixties. James recorded *Ain't Sick No More* for the Bluesway label, and in '74 played a guitar-bass doubleneck on Roosevelt Sykes' *Hard Drivin' Blues* and cut *Homesick James & Snooky Pryor* for Caroline. He returned to his acoustic roots for Trix' *Goin' Back Home.* He and Snooky worked as a duet during the '79 *Sad and Lonesome* sessions.

Since then Homesick James has played the role of elder statesman of the blues, making appearances at blues and jazz festivals and recording several albums in the 1990s. He also builds electric guitars, drinks heavily, and takes credit for some of Elmore James' accomplishments. Our interview took place during the summer of 1993, when Homesick was living in Nashville.

HOMESICK JAMES: REMEMBERING ELMORE

Who are the best musicians you've worked with?

I'll tell you, the best I worked with was me and Elmore. See, I was Elmore's teacher. And when he passed away, he passed away on my bed. Oh, yeah, he died right there in Chicago at 1503 North Wieland Avenue. He just had come back, and he said that when he died, he was gonna die with me. I wasn't thinkin' nothin' of it. And about two weeks later, he was gone. He was stayin' with me. That was 1963, May the 23rd or 24th. We was gettin' ready to go to a gig too—Club Copa Cabana.

Elmore sure was a fine slide player.

Well . . . [*Laughs.*] He got all that stuff from the old master here.

From you?

Hell, yes! I give him his first guitar when he was about 12 years old. I knowed where he stayed in Mississippi. I worked down there. Him and a guy by the name of Boyd Gilmore was tryin' to play. Elmore had a piece of wire tied up on a coffee can and a board—it had one string on it. He was tryin' to learn so hard, but Boyd Gilmore, he had an old guitar.

People have speculated whether Elmore James knew Robert Johnson.

Yep. Sure, Elmore knowed Robert Johnson. Well, Elmore and all of them were down in the Delta together. Elmore and Rice Miller, who was Sonny Boy number two—all those guys, they know Robert. I met him. See, I knowed Robert very well. Robert Jr. Lockwood can tell you that. I also knowed another guy that nobody never said anything about—I knowed Charley Patton personally. Now, I ain't thinkin' that I know them, I know these people. I know Ishman Brady [Bracey] perfect. I would associate around together. When I used to come through there, that's what would be playing at the picnics and the barrelhouses and things. I was hoboin' with my guitar, a Stella 6-string.

Were these tough men?

No, no. Nope. They would just drink and gamble, that's all. They run 'round with women and drink and gamble. That's what musicians act. No, they wasn't no mean guys. All of us was drinkers. Every musician drink. Ain't but one time he'll stop—that's when he comes down diabetic. Yeah, then they'll quit because they have to.

Describe your first gigs.

I played many a country supper. I was out runnin' around—picnics and frolics like that, me and Yank Rachell, Sleepy John Estes, and Little Buddy Doyle. We'd play at a picnic right here outside of Oakland, Tennessee, out on Highway 647. Little Buddy Doyle was a midget and I knew him personally, because me and him recorded together. That's sure the truth. Yeah. It was in 1937. Big Walter Horton was on the harmonica. It was at the Hotel Gillsaw in Memphis, right across the street from the Peabody Hotel. It was wire recording machines. But that wasn't really the first song I ever did. I did some stuff back in '29, a song with Victoria Spivey. She's the first person that turned me on to studio stuff. See, I did "Driving Dog" in 1929. Victoria Spivey, she heard me play, and she said I played that "cryin' guitar." Elmore, now he had never started yet. See, I had been with the Broomdusters ever since 1937 myself. I had the Dusters.

The expression "dust my broom" means to get out of town in a hurry, right?

Uh, no. It never was "dust my broom." It was "dust my room." And people made a lot of mistakes by sayin' that.

A lot of people heard Robert Johnson's version, which was "dust my broom."

"Dust my room," that's what it was. That was around before Robert Johnson did it. That was around in the '20s—'29 or '30.

How did you and Elmore get back together in Chicago?

What happened, he had an uncle there named Mac. And Elmore had this one record out, and this was that "Dust My Broom" thing with Rice Miller. He didn't have but one side [of the Trumpet 78]. He didn't do the other side, that "Catfish." Another guy down in Mississippi did that. Elmore just had one riff on guitar. See, I can read music and write it too. And what happened, I sent Elmore a ticket to get him to Chicago, because he had this song out that was so popular. Me and Snooky Pryor were workin' together out of the south of Chicago in the Rainbow Lounge, and when Elmore come, I had to quit and go and get Elmore together, because he didn't have nobody.

On some nights, it's said, you and Elmore were so hot that people threw money at your feet.

Oh, yeah. Heck yeah! Aw, people just give us money, man. When we played, people just come in and throw a twenty or a ten—that's the way it was. We were pretty good musicians, though.

How did you end up playing bass with Elmore?

I always could play bass. Harmonica, bass, guitar—I can play any instrument. But that wasn't no bass with Elmore. That was guitar tuned low. Elmore played bass too. We had a way of playing these guitars that no man would be able to do these things. In the key of D, I would keep four strings tuned into that Vastapol [*D, F#, A, D,* from the *D* string to the high *E*], and we would run those other two strings, the *A* and *E,* down lower, just like a bass, so it sounds like a bass. A lot of time when we'd be playin', Elmore would be runnin' that bass like I did while I be runnin' slide. See, all he would do is [*sings the "Dust My Broom" riff*] and run back to the bass pattern. All he could do was go to *D*. But he wasn't able to go to *G* and *A* in the *D* tuning. I'd let him play his part when it got to it, and I'd catch those other chords. We was workin' so good together. We were just a team. He'd run that real high note and then jump to the bass, and I'd jump right there. You couldn't tell when one switched to the other. See, we studied this stuff together, how to come up with ideas. We was the hottest band in Chicago. That's the way we were.

Were you playing loud?

No, no. Never did it loud. I don't allow it now.

Would people be dancing?

Oh, man. That's all they did, was dance. Yeah. Those days were so sweet, man. Everybody come out to drink, dance, and have a good time. Yep.

Did you do much touring outside of Chicago?

We come down to Atlanta, Georgia. We had a station wagon from Chess Records. I'd taken my money and put half, and he'd taken his money and made the payment. We traveled to a country club in Georgia, we played around there, and then we played around Cleveland, Ohio.

Was Elmore pretty quiet offstage?

Well, Elmore was real quiet all the time—until he take a drink. He used to say, "I'm Elmore. After me there won't be no more."

What did he like to do besides music?

Me and him used to set around and tinker with electricity and mess with making guitar stuff. If we wasn't makin' them, I'd be putting them together for him. Did you see that big old Kay guitar he got? I fixed that. I wired it up. He bought that guitar, paid $20 for it at a pawnshop over on Madison Street. It wasn't no electric. He said, "Will you put some electricity on it?" I said, "Yeah." I always knowed about electric. Me and him used to sit together. He stayed at my house all the time. I used to live on 1503 North Wieland, and I used to live at 1407 Northwestern. This was in '59, when we did "The Sky Is Crying," "Bobby's Rock," and all this stuff. And that's where I built his guitar for him.

Bobby Robinson writes that Elmore composed "The Sky Is Crying" the night before the session.

Ah, no. No, no. I know direct, 'cause I was right there. Okay. That's my song. That don't belong to Bobby Robinson or none of 'em. See, it had been rainin' so hard, and we were sittin' alone at 336 South Leavitt in Chicago. See, me and Elmore came up with the idea "The Sky Is Crying," but I told him, "Don't say that. Say 'the cloud is cryin','' because the sky don't know how to cry. The rain come out of the cloud." And when he got in the studio, he forgot. When we got home, he said, "You know, I made a mistake. But it's good, wasn't it?" I said, "Yeah." But no, he didn't write that. "The Sky Is Crying" come out in '59, and then we did "The Sun Is Shining," the "Madison Blues"—all that stuff is mine. I can verify these statements. Ask Gene Goodman at ARC Music—that's the copyright on all those songs. Later on I made "The Cloud Is Crying" for the Prestige label.

Which is the best label you worked for?

Vanguard wasn't too bad.

Besides Elmore's, what are the best records you've played on?

I'll tell you, the best thing I ever did was "I Got to Move," number one. I love that tune. Oh, yeah. I did that for Columbia or Decca, a long way back. I like that, and I like "Set a Date," 'cause all the youngsters are doing it now, like Fleetwood Mac, George Thorogood. After I had did it, then Elmore did it. He asked me if it was all right. See, Elmore wasn't no writer.

If, as you say, Elmore was taking credit for songs you wrote, didn't that cause trouble between you?

Well, how? No. We had an agreement, man. Nooo. See, every time he would ask me did I have some songs, you know. He say, "Can I do any of your songs?" I said, "Look. You don't have to ask me. Let's do it." Didn't make no difference. Some people, you tell 'em one thing, they'll print another. I seen a lot of things that they said about Elmore, and I said, "No, no, no, no, no. This ain't right." Like when I come up with the "Madison Blues," I played it all up and down Madison Street. That's where I wrote that song. See, we worked on a partnership basis. Like if he were living today, whatever royalty come, we broke it right down. He never was paid no more on no job than I was. Me and him got the same salary. But now the sidemen didn't get what we get. See, that was the agreement with the owners. "Homesick was makin' records way before I was," Elmore would tell them. He said, "Now, you ain't willin' to pay two leaders, I won't be there." I would tell them the same thing. That's the way we worked it. We just shared together.

You must have been really close.

Tell me about it. I never have been that close to nobody, no musician, because we just stayed together. Me and him run into a lot of problems, but we never had a argument. We had problems with our station wagon one time. That was up in Cleveland, Ohio. They repossessed it; they come and got it. Yeah. We got stranded. See, what was happenin', we had an agreement: "I pay this month, you pay next month." So his month come, he told me he had paid, and he didn't. When my month come, I sent my payment in. He got way behind on his, because he loved to play cards. He loved to gamble—drink and gamble. He'd lost all his money. He was always calling me and asking me to give him money, and I'd give it to him. I didn't loan it to him, I just give it to him. I'd say, "Yeah, what you want?" We were just like that.

They come and got the wagon. We was playing at a Cleveland musical bar, and we went out, and he told me somebody else stole it. He wouldn't tell me the facts about it. I called the guy who was booking us, Bill Hill, and asked him. He said, "Didn't you see Ralph Bass?" 'Cause Ralph—you know, the engineer for Chess Records—and Philip Chess, they come in the same night. I thought they was comin' through from New York, but they come there to get that wagon. It was a 1960 Ford Catalina, nice station wagon. It had "Broomdusters" on the side of it.

Anyway, then we had to get a ride back. So what'd we do? Now, Elmore had a contract with Chess Records. He said, "I'm gonna call Bobby Robinson, and I'll see can we get a session." Bobby agreed with it, and we flew in from Cleveland, Ohio, to New York, and that's where we recorded that "Rollin' and Tumblin'" and all those other tunes. That was in 1960. And we take all our money, put it together, and bought another wagon while we were up there. Same model, but it was rust-colored or beige. The first one was solid white. We had chauffeurs to drive us. We wouldn't drive 'cause we be drinkin' too much, carryin' on, talkin'. Me and Elmore, we were just always together, man.

What was your favorite drink?

Scotch. We'd drink that, and then we'd drink Kentucky Tideman or anything we could get to get high off [*laughs*]. We'd just sit back and come up with ideas and talk it, how we want this played. I was the leader of that band. Oh, yeah. That was my band all the way. We had J.T. Brown on the horn, Boyd Atkins. That was the best band I ever have worked with. J.T. was good about arrangin' music too. All those guys is dead now.

What did you use for slides?

Before I started making them from conduit pipe, I used the metal slip that goes over the top of tubes in them old radios and old record players. I used to pull that out and put it on my finger and play. This was after I learned how to stand it up [hold the guitar in normal playing position].

What did Elmore use for slide?

The same thing. A tube cover. Elmore used a light piece of metal, and Elmore had some big fingers too. He'd take one of those slips—protector tubes—from an old amplifier and put it on his finger. If he got a smaller one, then he would split it open—take a hacksaw and saw it open. That's what we played with all the time. See, we used to mess with a lot of stuff. But I use that conduit pipe all the time now. I don't like heavy. I don't think no man should use them big old heavy slides. You can't. The sound ain't there. Like you go to a store and buy them—whew, that's too much weight on your hand.

What amplifier did Elmore use at the Fire session in Chicago?

Mine. A Gibson. A big one. A GA-53, I think it was. It's at my house in Flint, Michigan, in the basement. I own a little small farm up there, and a lot of my kids live there. I got it when I was in the Army. The amp is brown on top and gray tweed at the bottom. It had letters on it, but by travelin', someone done knocked them off. It's about two-and-a-half feet high, and it could fit one 10 and one 12 speaker in the cabinet. Elmore didn't have no amplifier, and he didn't have no good guitar.

So to the best of your knowledge, that's the amp "The Sky Is Crying" was cut on?

I know what it was cut on, sure! Yeah, that's what it was cut on. And I got the picture with Elmore standin' with the guitar with my amp right there. Everywhere I go I keep it, so somebody start to try to say something about Elmore, I just straighten them up right quick. Okay, I want to tell you this too: That was a studio sound that people try to figure out. They'll never get that. The people at the studio knew how to operate that stereo sound into it. That's what that is. That's an echo sound. And it's two slide players—that's me and him both.

Were you in a big room?

No, not too big. Small studio. Bob Robinson come down and produced that for Fire and Fury Records. Yeah.

Beautiful sound. Open tuning.

The only people I really know who played in open *D* was me and Elmore. He had it in open *D* when he made "Dust My Broom," because Sonny Boy was playing a *G* harmonica. I always told him, "Don't never tune that string up too high," because if you tune that thing up to open *E*, you got too much pressure on your guitar neck. So you just let the strings back down.

See, I can't play a guitar like a lot of peoples could do—I just don't like that sound. Elmore never did like that either. I always keep a mellow sound. Don't never press down on your strings too hard. Just glide the slide. Take your time slidin', and don't be mashin' down on 'em. See, some people play the strings too high. The slide guitar players, they got to jack the strings up 'cause they always mashin' down, and the slide hit the frets. But my guitar strings are right down on the neck. Muddy had a heavy touch, and Hound Dog Taylor. The sound was brighter; it ain't no mellow sound, man.

What's your favorite electric guitar?

I make my guitars. I build my own guitars and fix them the way I want. But my favorite parts for what's goin' inside the guitar are Gibson. My favorite sound is Gibson. I bought some of those Seymour Duncan pickups, said I was gonna try them, and I don't like 'em. Too bright. I make acoustic guitars—the big ones with f-holes—and then I put electric to it. And then I buy the pickups and the controls and whatever I need—the switches—and put 'em in there. My house is a work-shop. I got guitars all over the place. I make 'em, builds 'em. I can go out and see a nice piece of wood, and I'll just take it and make me a solidbody. I ain't made acoustics since I been here in Nashville because I ain't got my blocks what I make 'em out of. But they sound better to me than the ones I could buy.

What was your setup on the new record?

I made the guitar I was usin'. You never seen a guitar like that. Everybody won-der how I put it together like that. It got a paint job on it, it got a lot of designs all over it. That was a Twin Reverb amplifier. Yeah, but give me the Gibson.

Some players say that a smaller amp gets a better sound for slide, makes it sound more like a harmonica.

Aw, no. It don't have to be. It depend on the way you set it.

Do you use guitar picks?

No, I play with my hands. I never have in my whole life used no pick. You can't slide like that, no. Nobody will ever be able to get the sound what I get out of the guitar, because I'm usin' my fingers. I wear the slide on my little finger, and I be pickin' the slide too at the same time I'm making chords with my other fingers.

You've been playing music for 70 years . . .

Over!

What's your secret for longevity in the business?

My advice for all youngsters is have a nice personality—number one. Know how to treat people, and don't let nothing go to your head, because those people, they the ones buyin' your material. They the ones that helped you up the ladder. Just work with the audience, and don't never insult nobody. Be a gentleman about things. And don't hang out all night if you can keep from it. Always try to go home and get you some rest. That's what I do, and I don't age that much. I take it easy, and when I'm not playin', you'll find me right at home.

Thanks for the interview.

Oh, I'm glad to help out. Anybody want me to help out in any way or anybody ask me something, I'm not too proud to do it. I don't like to copy nobody. Everywhere I go, I leave a ball of fire.

ROBERT
LOCKWOOD, JR.

BY LARRY HOFFMAN Brilliant, sensitive, brash—
Robert Lockwood is a man of many contradictions. It is well
known that he is the stepson of Delta blues icon Robert
Johnson, who revealed to Lockwood the secret techniques
that he jealously guarded from other players of his time.
Today, however, Lockwood rarely plays in Johnson's style
and hardly ever exercises his mastery of the slide guitar.
Instead, he favors his self-honed brand of jazzy jump blues.
Although he is now an accomplished bandleader, Lockwood
spent years building a peerless reputation as a blues session
man. ¶ Lockwood's moods range from proud (when talking

about his four children) to awestruck (when remembering his grandfather) to iras-
cible (when discussing the blues business). He becomes solemn when speaking of
Robert Johnson, nostalgic when recalling close musical friends such as Roosevelt
Sykes, and eternally grateful when acknowledging his wife and manager, Annie,
who, he is convinced, has kept him alive all these years.

These days, Lockwood plays in a duo with his longtime bassman Gene Schwartz,
and with his group—a hand-picked, jazzy blues sextet featuring tenor sax, harp,
guitar, bass, and drums. It is not uncommon for Lockwood to sit in a corner of the
stage, appearing to be a sideman in his own band. He provides each of the musicians with generous opportunities to solo throughout every performance, and the
band has an ambience more of family than business.

Comments from Lockwood's band members emphasize that closeness. Schwartz
testifies: "He taught me just about everything I know. I've been with him for 23
years, and that should tell you something. We are just like a big, happy family."
Tenor saxman Maurice Reedus—veteran of the bands of such jazz greats as Jimmy
Smith, Sonny Stitt, Gene Ammons, and Miles Davis—is another loyal bandmate:
"We're talkin' about, I'd say, 25 years now. First time when I got hip to blues is
with Robert. I love him; he's the best in the West." Guitarist Charles "D.C." Carnes
has been with Lockwood for just three years, but already has learned to appreciate
him: "Mr. Robert Lockwood is the gentleman master of the blues guitar—to the
ninth degree. I'm honored to be playin' with him, and I'm havin' a ball."
Drummer Jim "Gator" Hoare echoes Schwartz's description of the band's family-
like atmosphere: "I've been with Robert nearly 20 years. He's my daddy, taught me
a lot of stuff. I take drum lessons from Robert by watchin' him play guitar. He's like
family." And harpman Wallace Coleman adds: "I been with Robert since 1987. I
had some trouble with the changes at first, but Robert had a lot of patience with
me, working with me at his home. This was my first professional gig. He's a real
pro. He is the blues. In Cleveland, they call him the Granddaddy of the Blues."

Robert Lockwood was born on March 17, 1915. His ever-evolving career in pro-
fessional music spans a full six decades, and his talent has taken him from the
Delta street corners of his youth to stages throughout Europe, Japan, and the
United States. He has played venues as diverse as Cleveland's Brothers Lounge, the
World's Fair, the King Biscuit Blues Festival, the Smithsonian Institution, and
Severance Hall, home of the world-renowned Cleveland Symphony Orchestra.

The following reminiscences, in Lockwood's own voice, were drawn from interviews conducted over four days at his home in Cleveland, Ohio. They first
appeared as the June 1995 cover story of *Living Blues* magazine.

ROBERT LOCKWOOD, JR.: IN HIS OWN WORDS I was born in Turkey Scratch, Arkansas,
about five miles from Marvell. There was an Indian settlement 'round close to
there—a lot of land. My father was a tailor. My grandfather had a mill that would
turn corn to meal. He had a mill that would turn sugarcane into syrup. He raised
black pepper and raised corn.

My grandfather was a red man. He was red, very decent hair. Never went to
school—and finished school. Studied his sister and brother's books. He got a better
education than they got. He was a 32nd-degree Masonic. And my great-grand-
mother, which was his mother, she look like a full-blood Indian. Barely five foot

tall. Used to scare her, lookin' for her pipe and her pipe be in her mouth; lookin' for her glasses, her glasses be pushed up on her head. She could sit on her hair. And she would try to whoop my grandfather Ben. He'd pick her up in his arms, take her in the house. She be just kickin'. My grandfather weighed about 180 pounds. That son-of-a-bitch was all man, boy. He was somethin'. Taught me a lot. Never could compete with him no goddamn way. He could pick five or six hundred pounds of cotton a day, by hisself. I could barely pick two hundred. He'd carry two rows. If he didn't carry two rows, he could pick seven hundred pounds of cotton—without wastin' the time goin' from one row to another. If he only carried one row, shit! I used to just look at him and call him every kind of motherfucker I could think deep down inside because I couldn't touch him. And he had one finger off. I used to wonder, "How do he beat me?"

We moved to Memphis when I was four or five. Then from Memphis—where my parents separated—my mother kept me to St. Louis, and then she came back home to Marvell. She left me with my daddy's brother, Emmett Reese. My daddy's brother kept me till I was around eight or nine, and then my mama come pick me up, carried me to Helena [Arkansas], and I started to be goin' to school. I was eight years old when I started organ—the old organ that you pump. I had a couple of cousins who played three or four songs. I just watched them do it, and I done it. I never really considered myself as playin'. I could play two or three things on the keyboard. See now, I grew up around my grandfather, and he was a preacher, so we didn't have no reels, as they call 'em. We didn't get a chance to listen to nothin' like that. And there was no spiritual records bein' recorded back at that time. Every once and a while we'd get a chance to listen to a choir, something like that, you know.

I got a chance to listen to Blind Blake records when I was with my mother. I had an uncle on my father's side that had Ma Rainey and all that kind of stuff, and I'd get a chance to listen to 'em: Ida Cox, Texas Alexander, Blind Blake, Blind Lemon [Jefferson]. I had two uncles: one on my mother's side who was a good music teacher—a piano player who never played a job—and one on my father's side who played guitar a little bit. I played at my grandfather's after I really learned to play. My uncle who lived up North used to just sit and listen to me. When my grandfather got sick, he came back and lived with us for a minute. He used to just look at me and say, "How can you play it by ear like that?" It was amazing for him to see somebody play it by ear. "Molly and Me Make Three" ["My Blue Heaven"] and all that crap was out at the time, and he had that in music.

I always did like the sound of big bands—Fats Waller, King Oliver, Count Basie, Duke Ellington, Fletcher Henderson—and I guess maybe that's where I got my ideas from. Didn't hardly no bands come to Helena because Helena was wide open like Las Vegas—they couldn't get no good salary. Where there's gamblin', normally musicians really can't get paid like they should because people come to gamble. They don't come to listen to no music. In a big city like Las Vegas it's different. Now gamblin' and music coordinates. They use music to draw the people in the clubs; but after the people gets in the clubs, they don't hardly pay the music too much attention—they be losin' their money and winnin'.

Louis Jordan was just a little older than me. I used to listen to Louis Jordan. He used to come to Helena and play. That's about the only somebody who was comin'

to Helena. I was about 16 or 17 when I first heard him. Louis Jordan started playin'
early—medicine shows and things at that time. He was very pleasant to listen to,
you know. I've always liked him. Always had a combo, never had over eight pieces.
He was the hottest thing in America for a long time. King Oliver had about nine or
ten pieces. I liked Dixieland—it was more Dixieland back at that time than it was
jazz. I always liked bands better than I did somebody tryin' to play an instrument,
always. But I was crazy about Leroy Carr. He had such lay-back stuff. Scrapper
[Blackwell] and Leroy was workin' together. Charley Patton was back there, and I
enjoyed his records too. At that time we didn't have all these things to listen to, so
they were soundin' okay. You know, Blind Blake—I loved him. And Lemon was
okay, but I loved Blake. We had a record player in the house when I was growin' up.

My mother wasn't black; she was damn near white. Robert Johnson followed her
home, and she couldn't get rid of him! [*Laughs.*] I don't know if that's the first time
he met her, but I never knew anything about no Robert Johnson till he followed
her home. I don't think she knew anything about him till that day. She couldn't
get rid of him. He'd leave, be gone two or three months, and come back home
with all kind of money. And he treated my mother like a queen—all the time. I
don't know what she done to him. And they say that Robert Johnson was a wom-
anizer! He didn't chase no women; women chased him. They did. Everybody
chased him but my mother. My mother didn't. And all these artists today that
claim to have run with Robert Johnson never ran with him—Robert Johnson never
ran with anyone. They may have followed him, but he wasn't runnin' with anybody. Robert wasn't runnin' and pullin' at everybody; everybody runnin' and
pullin' at him.

And Robert was lookin' so young! Robert Johnson was fully Indian, had a lot of
Indian in him. Never had a beard, never shaved. That's an Indian trait. They got
no hair on their body. I ain't never seen an Indian with a beard, and I been on all
kind of reservations and all kinds of shit. Well, Robert had a lot of Indian in him.
All of us got Indian in us. I got four kind in me. My mother got two kind. My
mother and my father both had Indian in 'em. My daddy had Blackfoot and black
Creek, and my mother had Choctaw and Cherokee.

I REALLY NEVER HAD A DESIRE to play the guitar until Robert Johnson came along. All
the guitar players at that time—it was always two of 'em, one playin' chords and the
other playin' melody, and I just didn't like that. Robert showed up playin' it all by
himself. That was really a thrill to me. I always wanted to play something that I
wouldn't really have to have no help, you know. I didn't think that could be done.
And when I seen him doin' it, I decided that's what I wanted to do, you know, so I
kept worryin' him till he finally started teachin' me. So I started tryin' to play the
guitar when I was about 13 years old, when I first met Robert. At first, he would tell
me where to put my fingers, but he didn't have to do that after the first three
months. If I asked him something, he'd sit down and show me. He'd set the guitar
down, and I'd ease in and pick it up. I'd go get it. He wouldn't hear me when I pick
it up. It's hard to move an acoustic guitar, you know, without makin' a sound.

He mentioned makin' a guitar for me one time, and I said okay. And I helped
him. We took the little thin vinyl part—the finishin' part of the wood that they
puts on furniture—we took that off the Victrola, and that's what we used to make

the guitar. We also used an old cheese box—what cheese used to come in a long time ago. Robert carved the neck out of some wood, and planed it out with a planer and put frets in it. I helped him do that. I was about 13. I practiced on that guitar, but I learned on Robert's.

Well, I wasn't hard to learn—I learned real fast. I learned so fast I excited both him and my mother. He showed me something one time and when he look around I be playin' the shit out of it. "Sweet Home Chicago" is the first thing I learned to play. I heard him tell my mama, something's wrong with me. I was learnin' too fast. "Don't know what's wrong with him—something wrong with him!" Robert come home, and I sit, listen, and look at him play.

I had a little problem playin' and singin' at the same time, but about six months later I was doin' it perfect. I see him do it, and when he come back—he'd leave and always come back—when he come back again I be playin' it! You know, he always knew that I could play good. But I wouldn't play my best and let him hear me play my best. I felt like that he'd get cold feet about teaching me. I am the only person he taught, and he didn't want to be bothered with me. Every time he come home, whatever he was playin' before he left, when he come back, I could play it. He just look at me and shake his head. I knew him pretty close to ten years, somethin' like that. I went about three places with Robert in Mississippi, and we played a couple places in Arkansas. He instructed me until he died.

Robert never done nothin' but play music. He never did no kind of work. What he gonna work for? Robert go downtown, sit down on the street corner, and make $100 and come on back home! I used to just look at him. When I heard that he was dead, I wouldn't go to Mississippi for nothin'. I didn't want to see him dead. My mother didn't want to see him either. Remember him like he was.

Robert Johnson was 60 years ahead of hisself. Robert was a master. He was a master, and I have always known that. Robert's stuff was really superb. And there has never been anybody else that come close to what he do, but me. Robert could sing his ass off too. Yeah, he could really sing. I never talked to him about no other musicians. I never talked to him about nobody. I wasn't interested in nobody— why should I ask about 'em? You hear people talk about they played with Robert. They lyin', ha! He definitely did not want nobody to fake what he played—didn't want nobody watchin' him play.

I met Johnny Shines when I was 13 or 14 years old—'bout the same time I met Robert. Johnny was living up in Arkansas, up in Hughes, near Forrest City. And we would cross each other. See, Johnny Shines and Calvin Frazier was first cousins. Johnny said that he played some with Robert, but I just can't understand how he did. I know he knew Robert, but see, Robert was a loner—Robert didn't want nobody around him. He wouldn't sit and face another guitar player and let him see what he was doin'. But I never said that to Johnny, but I know that's the way he was. The only reason he showed me what he did [was] 'cause he was living in the house with my mother. No other way could I have ever gotten anything from Robert Johnson.

The first time I met Sonny Boy Williamson [Rice Miller], Robert brought him to my mother's house. They would run across each other and stuff like this. So he came home with Robert one night. I don't know whether they ever played together or not. Both of them was pretty headstrong, outstanding people. After he brought Sonny Boy to the house, he and Sonny Boy come back and begged my mama to let me go to Mississippi with [Sonny Boy]. And she sure didn't want me to go. Sonny Boy had heard me play at home. He made it sound so good, so she finally say okay.

I left with Sonny Boy in 1936. I went to Mississippi with him. We caught a train to different places. I was young—wasn't nothin' but a kid. It was fascinatin' to me. We jumped right on the train, tore a guitar up catchin' a train one time. I think we was in Mississippi. Hopped a passenger train—the Panama Limited—a runnin' motherfucker too, boy. [*Laughs.*] The train was standin' at the station. We just went over to the blind side and just got up there on it between the cars. It went on while we was still climbin'. We got on a train one time and thought the damn thing was gonna stop, and the motherfucker didn't stop! [*Laughs.*] And the man made us come inside and carried us on in to Jackson. Aw, that was stupid. Take a chance on gettin' killed and all that kind of stuff. We didn't do it a lot. I imagine Sonny Boy had done quite a bit of it, though. Meantime, Robert was livin' with my mother.

Sonny Boy and I did a lot of travelin' together. We was playin' on street corners all over Mississippi, all over Arkansas, and a lot of places in Tennessee and Missouri. The towns was the same as far as I'm concerned. We'd get on the street corners and make 35 or 40 dollars. Didn't make no difference 'bout the size of the town, 'cause down in the Delta, in that time, the streets would be full of people, period! We'd get permission from the police to play; the police would choose us a place where we could go and play, and we'd go. There'd be a lot of people, and we'd play until we got tired. We just barely missed the Tupelo storm [of 1936]. We was on our way to Tupelo, and we was doin' so good in Clarksdale, Sonny Boy said, "Well, we'll wait till tomorrow." We woke up the next day, they had cows up in trees and shit!

Well, I played like that for ten years, with Sonny Boy and by myself. Other guitar players couldn't be no help to me. What could they do? I was playin' my own rhythm, my own bass, my own lead. I played by myself; I recorded by myself. When I was playin' by myself, I didn't want no help. Somebody helped me, they'd be in my way. I play the lead and the background and everything when I play that style.

I met Hacksaw Harney about that time, and I ran into him later on in Clarksdale. Really, I think that's where Robert [Johnson] got a lot of his ideas from. I think that Hacksaw was a big influence with Robert. He just played the guitar very well. He played the guitar very, very well. And what he was doin' was the same type of thing Robert does. When I finally met Hacksaw, of course, he knew Robert—and he knew all about me 'cause Robert talked about me. And I'd catch Hacksaw watchin' me play. I say, "What the hell you lookin' at me for?" You know, Hacksaw couldn't talk plain; he was lisp-tongued. "Do-doggone it, Robert! You interestin'!" I said, "You interesting too."

Hacksaw came to Helena, to Crawford's place, called the Hole in the Wall. It was in the '40s sometime. Willie Love, a piano player, was workin' there. Didn't nobody know Hacksaw. He always dressed in starched and ironed overalls and a good-name hat and good-name shoes, white shirt. Hacksaw come in and come over there where I was and start talking to me. He asked me, "Do you think he'd let me to play the piano a little bit?" I said, "Yeah, I guess he would, Hack."

And he walked over to Willie Love and asked Willie Love about playin'. Willie told him he couldn't blow his nose. [*Laughs.*] I say, "Hot dog!" I said, "Man, you shouldn't have done that." He said, "That motherfucker can't play." I said, "Man, what you talkin' about?" He didn't know him. And I told Willie, "That's Hacksaw!" He says, "Who's Hacksaw?" I said, "You gonna find out when you get up off that piano." And he got up to let Hacksaw sit down. Whew! Shit! Willie didn't want to play no more. Hacksaw could play that piano, boy! He could play the piano and that guitar! Play the hell out of both of 'em. And Willie ask me, say, "Hey, damn, man, why didn't you tell me?" I say, "You didn't give me no chance to tell you." Hacksaw could play. You know, he built pianos. He'd buy the material and build them. Hacksaw pissed a whole lot of folks off with how well he played. He wouldn't piss Robert off, though. I would have to say that Robert and Hacksaw probably played together, but I never heard it. He was the only somebody who could compete with Robert. And by Robert havin' such a good voice, Hacksaw would have a pretty hard time. Other influences to Robert was Son House, Willie Brown—them guys—'cause he used to go around listenin' to them play.

Sonny Boy was the beginning of the harp players. When I met Little Walter, he was just a kid, didn't really have a home. A lot of times he come down [to] my house and I was eatin'—the old lady be fixin' dinner, and I'd give him mine. I was the only person that could do anything with Walter. He wouldn't pay nobody else no attention. It was before 1940; he was just a boy. I used to go play in the plantations in the fall. They was pickin' cotton. I'd stay out there, and I'd come home with as much money as the farmer had made. I used to go out in the country to play. Walter was about 15 or 16 years old then. And he'd get on the spare tire. I'd get out there, and I start playin' by myself. I start to playin', and the house get full of people. After Walter brushes all the dust off hisself, he's in the house! Now I can't take him back to Marianna 'cause I done started to work. I can't stop workin' and take him home. He show up in there, and I let him play harp. I let him play, and I'd end up makin' the man give him some money. He always sound good. He tried to play that damn harp damn near all his life. It's just my guess, but I ain't never seen Walter without his harp. I knew Walter when he was about 12 years old, and he always loved to play that harp.

I had a jazz band in Helena. I started playin' electric guitar in 1939, and Charlie Christian was the only other one I knew that was playin' it. He was playin' [by] puttin' a mike in the guitar. Then they started talkin' about makin' a pickup for the guitar. I really think he's the first somebody who played electrified guitar. When they made a pickup—as soon as they made it, I bought one. I bought that De-Armond pickup when it first came out in 1939. So did Charlie Christian. Now Charlie Christian played with Benny Goodman, but he was around with all those black guys too. And the black guys didn't give him no play, but then Goodman let him do what he want to do. That's the reason why he started playin' with him. I didn't know anything about Christian back then. When I realized that he existed, we was usin' some of the same type of licks.

I LEFT HELENA IN 1939. I went to St. Louis with a piano player named Jesse Young, who I ran into in Helena. We played together a little bit around town and left together. When we went to St. Louis, I already had people there. We were under the impression that they was recording blues there, and they was not. After I got there, I met Doctor Clayton, and me and the Doctor played 'round in St. Louis in little taverns and things. Doc played the ukulele a little bit, you know.

I played with John Lee [Sonny Boy] Williamson in St. Louis, before I went to Chicago—it was in 1939. I think he just had done "Sugar Mama" and "Good Mornin' Little Schoolgirl." And I knew Robert Nighthawk; I played with him in Helena and Chicago. Played with Houston Stackhouse too. You see, I could play behind John Lee, and he wouldn't need no two guitars. I played with Sonny Boy, and he didn't need no two guitars. I played with Little Sonny Boy [John Lee Williamson] all around St. Louis. We'd go out hustlin' and divide the money and all that shit. I never helped him make no records, though. Big Sonny Boy [Rice Miller] play rings around Little Sonny Boy—and every damn body else that was playin' harp at that time! I never played with Jazz Gillum, but I knew him well. I never did fool with guitar players; I was so far ahead of everybody.

It was a guy in St. Louis named Charley Jordan, and Charley Jordan had connections with Decca and Columbia. He was something like a talent scout for these two labels, and he sent me and the Doctor to Chicago to record for Decca. When we got to Chicago, the guy from the company—Mayo Williams—was out of town. Me and Doctor Clayton came to record records for Decca, and Williams was out of town. We ran into Tampa Red, who was a very, very nice man, and Curtis Jones— and then up steps Lester Melrose.

Doctor Clayton start to singin', and Melrose had a baby. When he finds out we comes to record for Mr. Williams at Decca, he had a fit. He had to have Doctor Clayton! Yeah! Lester Melrose heard Doctor Clayton sing, and he went crazy. So the Doctor, seein' how anxious Melrose was, went on and put the screws to 'em. He said, "I didn't come to record for you no ways, so why don't you go on leave me alone? We'll wait till Mr. Williams come back; that's who I come to record for anyway." Doctor Clayton got more money out of Melrose than anybody ever got. He was real educated, and he asked that man, he said, "Who do you think I am?" He said, "Now you want me. I do not want you. I did not come here to record for you." I think the Doctor got about $2,000 that day—either $2,000 or $3,000. And $1,000 was a whole lot of money then.

When he got ready to record, Melrose had designated Big Bill Broonzy to play with him. Now Doctor Clayton, he didn't know nothin' about no Big Bill. So the Doctor asked him, "Now who is doin' these recordings?" Melrose said, "You." The Doctor said, "Well, you don't choose nobody to play with me, then. You don't get no damn body to play with me!" He said, "Now Robert come from St. Louis with me, and that's who gonna play." Melrose didn't like that, but he accepted it. He had to accept it. Decca and RCA Victor was fightin' over talent. So Bill say I could play his guitar if I wanted to. So I played on the first two sessions with Doctor Clayton.

I used to try and teach Bill things on the guitar; he didn't even try to learn it. He said, "Aw, you can't teach an old dog new tricks." He'd look at me play and say, "Hell, I'll never be able to do that." No, I didn't like Big Bill's style. I learned from Robert Johnson. How could I stoop down to Bill? Shit. I'd have to stoop real low to get to Bill, 'cause Robert was the boss. Robert was a mystery. Everybody wanted to know how he done things.

Also on the sessions were Ransom Knowling on bass and tuba horn and Blind John Davis on piano. There was also a boy playing a can. I can't recall his name, Leroy something. Everybody called him Andy Gump. He played a can for a bass. I didn't need no damn bass, and they had him playing that thing on my record.

That just show you about people. But he was pumpin' that can back there. He was gettin' by with it, 'cause it wasn't an instrument. Finally they made him join the union. You know a recording session then wasn't but four songs. Lester was paying $12.50 a side—$25 for a record, $50 for the whole session. That's what Lil Green got for "In the Dark." Doc made him give me $500 for playin'!

Somehow—some kinda way—during that recording, I grabbed Melrose and tried to pull him out the car and kick his ass. He was talkin' that prejudice shit. I tried my best to get him out the car. And Doctor Clayton pulled me and pulled me and kept on pullin' me and got me away from him, else I would've kicked this mother-fucker's ass.

Melrose wanted me to record solo for him, and he come up to my room and talked to me. The Doctor done told me what to tell him. Melrose say, "Your shit might not sell." I say, "Well, I didn't come to record for you." I say, "Now, I'm gonna tell you the same thing the Doctor told you: Why in the fuck don't you just leave me alone." He went on downstairs—we was livin' in a hotel—and he went on out, and in about five minutes he was back. He said, "I can't give you no $600." I said, "Well, that's the only way you're gonna get my shit."

And he wanted me to play my stuff at Tampa Red's—around Tampa Red, Memphis Slim, Memphis Minnie, Li'l Son Joe, Curtis Jones, and Big Maceo. He wanted me to play my shit around them! And all these people were recording artists. So it ended up to, he say, "I don't know whether your shit will sell or not." I say, "I tell you what you do." I say, "You line them motherfuckers up that you got, and I'll cut 'em down." Big Bill, Johnny Temple, Memphis Minnie—I says, "Go get the motherfuckers and bring 'em." Say, "I'll play what they play, then I'll play what they can't play!" That's the way I got the $600! [*Laughs.*] Doctor Clayton was just laughin' his ass off. Then I recorded "Take a Little Walk With Me," "Little Boy Blue," "Mean Black Spider," and "Train My Baby" for him. I told Lester Melrose he could take the royalty, and you know what? He gave me $600. I got $500 for recording with Clayton, and I got $600 for recording myself. Out of that recording session I done and that recording I done with Doctor Clayton, I got $1,100—that was a whole lot of money.

But anyway, after we recorded, I had to go back to St. Louis to get me a Social Security card. See, I couldn't get my money. So I came back to St. Louis the next three or four days. When I got back here, Doctor Clayton didn't have no shoes! What happened was, after the recording session, the Doctor had taken the money he had made and bought everybody drinks and food at the club that night. People were just dinin', dancin', having fun. And when Doctor Clayton went to sleep or passed out, they stole his money and everything he had. They took his shoes off, took his coat. And when he woke up, he didn't have shit. He had on a suit, they told me. He was a superbly educated person, but he was a winehead. I bought him a pair of shoes, and before I went back to St. Louis, he gave me my money back. He got about five or six thousand dollars out of Lester Melrose, and Lester Melrose was only paying $50 for a recording session. Melrose was crazy for that boy's voice, 'cause he could sing.

Big Bill and Memphis Slim took me to a nightclub in Chicago, and they ordered a pint of whiskey—a pint of whiskey cost about $25 there—with a set-up. They thought I was going to pay for that! [*Laughs.*] Slim and Big Bill look at me and shook their heads. I said, "I don't give a damn what you say; I don't pay no $25 for no pint of liquor." So I don't know which one of 'em paid for it. One of them paid for it. They laughed at me 'cause I wouldn't spend $25. I stayed around in Chicago about two weeks.

I got a chance to help Roosevelt [Sykes] do a lot of recording, and Little Brother Montgomery. Roosevelt Sykes was the greatest piano player who ever lived. I never did too much playing with Roosevelt until I started making records. He was running all over Mississippi and Arkansas. Roosevelt was down there when Helena was wide open. He was playin' all over the place. And after a while, in 1940, Roosevelt was already in Chicago and St. Louis. I got a chance to do some recording with him, recording with Roosevelt, Sunnyland [Slim], St. Louis Jimmy [Oden].

I WENT BACK TO ST. LOUIS and stayed there for a while. Not too long after, I went back to Helena. I got down to Tunica [Mississippi] and got off the bus like a fool. Looked like a little ol' city that would've had one hotel. It didn't have one. I couldn't find nowhere to sleep. So I went into the restaurant, and they seen the guitar, amplifier, and mike stand. I went in and ordered me a steak. He served me the steak dinner, and I got ready to pay him. He said, "That's all right." And I'm tired of ridin', and I sure don't feel like playin' no music. But that's the reason why he done it—he wanted me to play. I really got kind of mad with him about that, but I done ate the food. He went and give me a half-pint of whiskey—Black and White scotch. So I went over with the guitar and amplifier and start playin'. In come the jukebox man, and he got my records. The records I done for Melrose has just been released. When they released the first damn record, I was back in St. Louis. I had never heard the record till right then. They didn't even play them back for you in the studio at that time. I heard it for the first time down South, on that jukebox in Tunica, Mississippi.

He walked up to me and called me by my name. By him having my records, he know my voice. He stayed around in there for a minute and told me, "When you get through playin', come on 'round the corner to my store." And when I got through playin', he know I wasn't comin' to his store. He sittin' back there in the corner of the room and damn near carried me around to his store. Then he put me in the back room. He had a bed back there and a little kitchenette. Told me to go back there and go to sleep. I went back there and went to sleep. Next morning I got up and got out of there—went to Helena.

I found Sonny Boy [Rice Miller]. He had been on *King Biscuit Time* for one week by hisself. So I joined him. Later on, I hired Peck [Curtis] myself. He played washboard. I hired Peck and bought him some drums. He never paid me for the drums. We started giving Peck $10 a day. That was a lot of money—$70 a week. People was workin' for $18 a week. Peck couldn't keep money from one day to the next. The other musicians would come and go on *King Biscuit Time*. I put Joe Willie Wilkins in my place, and Pinetop [Perkins] came. Dudlow [Taylor] was there for a minute. Then Houston Stackhouse came. Sonny Boy left the scene, and Peck kept it for a while. I don't know if Peck ever had a harmonica player or not. But I know he played on *King Biscuit Time* awhile before he died. They was some good old days. Back in those days, Helena was poppin'. Helena was wide open—just like Las Vegas.

Me and Big Sonny Boy [Rice Miller] was together when Little Sonny Boy [John

Lee Williamson] came to Helena, and didn't a damn thing happen. Sonny Boy come down there and got that record and moved Lacey Belle [his wife] down there. He couldn't make no money there. He and Big Sonny Boy knew each other. I just don't know what he came there for. John Lee couldn't play no harp with Sonny Boy. Little Sonny Boy came down there and got a spot on the air—his own show on KFFA. He had Othar Williams on guitar and a drummer. They both was callin' themselves Sonny Boy at that time. Big Sonny Boy chased Little Sonny Boy away from there. He couldn't play with Rice. Rice Miller could play Sonny Boy's stuff better than he could play it! John Lee had to get the fuck away from there, couldn't stay. I don't know whether John Lee told him to stop using his name or not, but when this thing came to a point—when there was two of 'em there—the man who owned Interstate Grocery changed and spelled those last names different. See, Big Foot Sonny Boy is Sonny Boy Williams, and Little Sonny Boy is Sonny Boy Williamson. [John Lee] just made a ass out of hisself comin' down there. I think Little Sonny Boy was down there three or four months in 1942. By the time I left the next year and got my own program on KFFA for Mother's Best Flour Company, John Lee had already left. And he was the one makin' the records! The man's playing his shit better than he played it. Shit! That Big Foot motherfucker could play that harp, man. There wasn't no comparison to Sonny Boy then. And there ain't no comparison to Sonny Boy today.

I wasn't with Sonny Boy no long time. I was with him longer on *King Biscuit Time* than I was any other time, and I was on *King Biscuit Time* for two years. Me and Interstate Grocery couldn't get along. That damn little money that they was payin', and all of a sudden it would come up short and wrong and all that shit. Old man [Max] Moore's secretary was fucking up my time. But he didn't want me to say that, you know. He didn't want her to be wrong. Once or twice a month we almost get to fightin'. He wanted to come 'round the counter where I was, and if he ever reached around there I was going to kick his ass. Come runnin' 'round the corner like he's tryin' to get to me, and I tell him, "Come on! Don't stop!" The other brother would jump over the counter and get between me and him. I said, one of these days he ain't gonna be here to get between us. I left *King Biscuit*. I imagine Sonny Boy minded, but what was he going to do about it? We were good friends. I could get along with Sonny Boy, but I couldn't get along with Max Moore. Me and my wife Ann finally went down there to see that old man [Moore], and we couldn't hardly get away from him and his wife. Didn't think we was ever going to get away. He held on to us and he held on to us! And his wife, she act like I'm her son now! Shit!

AFTER I QUIT KING BISCUIT TIME, I was just messin' around in Helena, and I had quite a bit of money. The man who owned the station called me one day. The Mother's Best Flour Company wanted to talk to me, and I did a show for them. I went to Mother's Flour with my first band—a jazz band: the Starkey Brothers. It was a quartet consisting of three brothers who played piano and two horns. I always listened to horns—to guys like Louis Jordan. My method has always been to try to be a musician, to play anything. So I was playin' all of it all the time—as much as I could learn about whatever it was I was learnin'—and tryin' to exercise it. I kept Mother's Best for a little better than a year. They was draftin' people in the army, and I couldn't keep a band. They'd have drafted me too, but I had a ruptured eardrum, so I couldn't prevent gas from goin' in my ear.

Then Sonny Boy and me went to Little Rock for a while before I went to Chicago. We was on KXLR together between 1944 and 1948. Then Sonny Boy left, and I kept it for a while before I left for Memphis. I had seven pieces without a harp. I lived in West Memphis for a while, where Sonny Boy used to be on KWEM. Howlin' Wolf was on that station too. Right in that time I met B.B. King. Yeah, it was about that time that I ran into B.B. and Bobby Bland. That was in Memphis. I worked with B.B. better than a year in 1948. Goddamn, B.B.'s time was bad, as bad as John Lee Hooker's!

John Lee [Hooker] just don't know. He ain't never knew. He was talking about his band and talkin' about he didn't need 'em. I got that boy by the hand, said, "Hey, man, come here." He say, "Oh, oh, oh, oh." I say, "What the fuck you talkin' about, you don't need the band?" I said, "Motherfucker, you better keep them boys!" I said, "Those goddamn boys chasin' your ass and wrap you up and make you sound so good. Better keep 'em!" [*Laughs.*]

Anyway, I was helpin' B.B. out and was tryin' to teach him what timin' was, and he didn't have no sense of it. He didn't understand what was happenin' with his time. See, I'm the cause of B.B. havin' a band! He didn't have but three pieces then, you know. I was teachin' him—at least, I was trying to teach him. B.B. came from under me like Luther Tucker, Hubert Sumlin, and others did. When he got ready to record again, I told his sponsor, I said, "Put the boy with eight pieces—not under eight pieces—so he will have to listen to the band." B.B. didn't know that [I did that] either, till about two or three years ago. He was at Blossom Center here in Cleveland, and we were backstage talking. I brought that up, and B.B. looked at me. He didn't know where them eight pieces come from! I think he thought old man [Phineas] Newborn was the cause of that. Well, old man Phineas put that band together to back B.B. up, and the next band he had was Bill Harvey, and Bill Harvey had 11 pieces. Harvey wrote all them charts out. When Bill left, B.B. didn't have nothin' to do but to get musicians who could read and say, "Well, here the music is, fellas." At that time, I don't think B.B. could read, but he can read now. Yep, he kept Bill Harvey a good while.

B.B have always worked. The guys in the band would want a day off—couldn't spend their money workin' seven days a week! And B.B. bought everybody in his band a car. I don't care what anybody says, I know B.B.'s the best. The best bandleader that I've ever seen. The musicians swear to it. Hard to find someone that says they don't like B.B.

I would go out in the park in Memphis and play. When I'd come out and start to playin', there'd be these little bands all over the park. And when I'd go out there, everybody would leave them other little bands out there and get around me. Nobody else couldn't make no money. I start goin' in the park early and let them people make some money. I go out there 3:00 in the evenin'. When I leave out of there, I'd have $85 or $90. Well, I didn't know nothin' else to play but Robert's stuff. I had a couple things that I played myself, but I mean, it wasn't nobody's but Robert's.

THE JAZZ STYLE I DEVELOPED come from me. I done all that mostly by myself, but I did have some help. That band I had in Memphis was all jazz musicians. Struction

[William Johnson], who was the leader, put a straight pick in my hands and told me I was going to have to use that pick if I wanted to play that. Showed me how to play finger exercises so I would learn how to hit the strings with the straight pick. Struction played guitar, bass, drums, piano. He's one of the best musicians that I've ever known. Good musician. And I started playin' horn lines and stuff. That was about the best band I've ever had. Really, it was Struction's band. He asked me did I want a band. I told him no. Next day he was right back out in the park again, said, "Robert Lockwood, I got four months' work for us. Don't you want a band?" Me and him was going to be makin' $18, and I think the band was goin' to be makin' $12. So Struction was a lot of help to me. We were playing all old standards, blues and jazz. I was playing my Robert Johnson style with them too. We had seven pieces, including horns. Struction wanted me to lead the band because I had some records out.

Then this little girl got in the group, and she started to having sex with the different guys in the band. So the guys started to getting mad with each other about her and all that shit. We was on our way back to West Memphis, and a friend of mine was driving behind me. I stopped the car, and he stopped behind. I said, "Now all you all's in love with this little lady!" I says, "Sweetheart, you get out the car—there's a car right behind us that's going to pick you up." I says, "Now all you motherfuckers that's in love with this little girl, you all get out with her!" Didn't nary a one of those son-of-a-bitches get out of that car. [*Laughs.*] She got out and went on back there and got in the car with the other guy. I pulled off. Before I got to West Memphis, everybody say, "Well, man, I want to stay with the band! Man, I want to stay with the band! Man, I want to stay with the band!" I say, "You motherfuckers gonna have to stop this bullshit 'cause you can't play when you mad with each other. Now how the fuck we going to sound, you know?" So everybody stayed with the band until I got ready to go back to Chicago. I put her ass out.

I had my own band in Memphis for about a year. I never had nothin' but jazz bands. I ain't never had a blues band. Finally, I got homesick for Chicago, and in 1950 I went on back and stayed for about ten years. Got to Chicago, and the first somebody that I played with was Curtis Jones, a piano player. He made that song "Lonesome in My Bedroom." He was real nice—had a nice style. He went to Paris, and died there too. I never got a chance to record with him. Pretty close to that time, I met Eddie Boyd. Eddie had a guitar player named L.C. McKinley with him when I first met him. He also had a big boy on guitar for a while—I can never remember his name. Lee Cooper from Mississippi played, was with him also. He was a real good guitar player. And also another pretty decent guitar player that he had was named Lacy Gibson.

Me and Sunnyland Slim recorded for Mercury Records in 1951. Bobby Shad was the A&R person. He insisted that I do "Dust My Broom." It was me and Sunnyland and [drummer] Alfred [Wallace]. And I'll bet you ten times Shad asked me, he said, "Did Elmore James write it?" I say, "No. Robert Johnson wrote 'Dust My Broom.'" He said, "Well, hell! If he didn't write it, goddamn it, why can't you play it?" I say, "Elmore James done recorded 'Dust My Broom' on the Trumpet label," and I say, "now Lillian McMurry got it copyrighted—but it ain't none of hers!" I say, "Well, okay. I'll record it." And Mercury hold me responsible for it right now!

Then Sunnyland and I went to the West Side. We was recording for JOB, and I was playin' with Little Brother Montgomery, Roosevelt Sykes, Freddie King, Harold Burrage, St. Louis Jimmy, Willie Mabon for a while, Eddie Boyd, Little Walter, and just about everybody else. I was living on the West Side, playin' clubs like the Zanzibar and the Savoy Club. I also played Sylvio's a lot with Sunnyland, and Martin's Corner every once in a while with Curtis Jones. Those was some interesting days. Every time you change artists, your music changes; every time you change bandleaders, your music changes. I was not playing Robert Johnson style with Eddie Boyd or Sunnyland Slim. When I played Robert Johnson, I played by myself; I wasn't playing gigs like that at that time.

Sylvio had a big name for that West Side. He gave Elmore James a job playin' two or three nights a week and runnin' the place in the '50s. I used to play with Elmore. Me, Sonny Boy, and Elmore James. I never recorded with him, but we used to play together. I threw out a clamp [capo] over here that Elmore had on his guitar. I tried to make him learn how to play. I throwed his clamp away. He talked about my mama. . . . [*Laughs.*] Nobody wouldn't say a word. [*Imitating Elmore's high-pitched voice*]: "I know it was you, motherfucker! I know it was you." He had a little ol' high voice, you know. "Hey man, I don't know anything about your damn clamp, or your guitar either." [*Laughs.*]

Yeah, after I got to Chicago I started playin' and recording with different people. It happened fast. All the harmonica players wanted me to help them 'cause I would play chords for them; that's what they needed. All the other guys wanted to outplay the harp player. [*Laughs.*] That's how I ended up with Chess—I mean, I was recording with a lot of people, you know. And the piano players, they wanted somebody to play chords for 'em, big heavy chords. And I was playin' them big fat chords, and they could just show their ass, you know. I was layin' them fat chords down, and they was showin' their ass, the harmonica players too. [*Laughs.*] Yeah. I recorded [sessions] for Victor, JOB, OKeh, I don't know what-all labels.

I knew Junior Wells when he was 16. Sunnyland wouldn't let him sing or play the harp. I told Sunnyland to let him. I begged Sunnyland. I said, "Why don't you let the boy sing?" He started makin' more tips than we was salary. 'Course, he was a kid, you know. So people just would give him money. Young guys started to comin' in there from different places. I don't think Buddy Guy was there back at that time. I don't think so, but he may have been. I didn't know him then. I think Otis Rush was there. He was with Cobra. I think Otis Rush is a superb musician. I have always admired him. He sing and play his ass off. Willie Dixon was with Cobra for a while too. I didn't know too much about him then. I lived on the West Side, but I be on the South Side every day. I was playin' clubs pretty much every night. I was in Chicago for about two years and didn't work with no certain body. Local 208 would call me and tell me somebody needed a guitar player. And I worked almost every night in the week.

CHESS COME LATE FOR ME. Chess finally showed up. Everybody had quit Chess but Muddy Waters! That's how Mud got to *be* Muddy Waters. There wasn't nobody there but him. Wasn't nobody on Chess' label but Mud. I don't know why the others quit—I don't know nothin' about their business, I just know Chess didn't have nobody. He didn't have nobody to push but Muddy Waters. Mud was workin' for the city, time he started recordin' for Chess. Chess had a friend named Sam Evans who was a disc jockey, and Sam Evans was advertising Chess' products.

Chess had Muddy's records on the air every day—five days a week. That made Muddy Waters. Muddy Waters was the talk of the town. As far as I'm concerned, he never could play and he never could sing. I used to tell Mud that to his face! He got made by accident.

Anyway, Sam Evans was playin' Muddy Waters material every day. And anybody didn't know anything started sayin', "Muddy Waters! Muddy Waters is playin' all over Chicago!" This was in the '50s. I never really worked with Muddy Waters steady. I worked with him a short while, playin' clubs in Chicago. I helped record with Muddy Waters. I played on a lot of his recording sessions. While I worked with Mud, he had Otis Spann playing piano, and he had James Cotton playing harmonica. I don't know where Little Walter was.

One time I worked with Mud, they was playin' at Fitzgerald's. They go to the bandstand, and they be standing up there for 30 minutes deciding what to play. One of 'em called a number, the other one says, "No, let's don't play that—let's do so-and-so." Thirty minutes went by, and none of 'em played a motherfucking thing. So when Mud asked me to help him out, we went on the bandstand, and I don't know who it was called the song, and they started that same stuff. I said, "Hey!" They say, "Yeah, yeah, yeah, Brother Robert." I say, "What did he say?" He say, "Play so-and-so." I say, "Well, goddamn it, play it. It's only going to last but three minutes!" And we just played one song right behind another. Muddy Waters said, "Goddamn! What did you do to 'em?" Mud tried his best to get me to stay with him. I said, "You're too tight with your motherfucking money. No way in the fuck we can stay together."

Muddy was a millionaire! How the fuck do you think he got a $300,000 or $400,000 house? Muddy Waters' catalog was worth a lot of money. He made a whole lot of money on the highway, was selling for between five and ten thousand dollars. Shit! What's going to stop you from getting rich, making that kind of money? Payin' his men $100 a day, $125. Leonard Chess ran Muddy Waters and Walter. He would tell 'em: "Don't pay 'em too much money. If you pay 'em too much, you can't do anything with 'em." Leonard had told Walter he didn't need no bass. That's how come I left his ass.

When Chess came, I was already there just like everybody else. And a lot of the guys that he was recordin' wanted me to help back 'em up. They were some interesting days too. Very interesting days. I done something like an album with the Moonglows on Chess label one time. And Chess come in on the last song and tried to change it. And I got up and handed him the guitar. Chess said, "What you doin'?" I said, "Motherfucker, you gonna play this one!" We done worked on this shit all this time, and he gonna bring his goddamn ass in and change something? I got up and handed him the guitar. Milton Rector was the bass player, and Milton Rector played guitar on the last tune because I walked out.

Leonard Chess liked me and he didn't like me. There wasn't but one Chess, the owner. Phil was just there. He was helping his brother run the business, but Phil wasn't callin' no shots. It was always Leonard. That man come a long ways in a short time. I don't know how that man done that! He come from nothin' to a multimillionaire—fast! I remember when I went to a hamburger joint to get a hamburger, and I'd bring him one and he didn't have money to pay for it! That's the truth.

He was tryin' to get the business off the ground. That's when he had Muddy

Waters and Sunnyland. There was a time when everybody quit foolin' with him. He wasn't doin' too good at all. Give him about three years, and that son of a bitch was a millionaire. He was tryin' to get some of his acts into the Chicago Theater. He didn't even have enough money to get in and listen; they wouldn't let him in there. Shit! A few years pass, he talked about buyin' the theater. He said, "If you all don't let me in this time, I'm going to buy the motherfucker, and you ain't gonna get in." [*Laughs*.] Willie Dixon was working directly out of Chess' office. Willie was a good man, a very good man, very, very good. They was some good days. I played with Willie Mabon too, you know. Willie was nice. He was a ladies' man. The ladies always did like Willie Mabon.

That "Little Village" thing [a reference to the studio take of Sonny Boy Williamson's "Little Village," during which Sonny Boy calls Leonard Chess a motherfucker] was something that we did every day. Nobody was never presented with his name. Then, when you said, "Hi, Mr. Chess," he say, "What'd I do?" I said, "You ain't done nothin'." "Well, I mean something wrong. You called me Mr. Chess!"

Well, it was nothin' uptight with that system. Everything was hangin' loose. Everybody was free to say what they want to say, do what they want to do—didn't make no difference. That's the way everybody understood it. Sonny Boy would always wait until Leonard was around a large group of his distinguished people. Then he'd go up and ask him for some money! He would always get it. That Sonny Boy was really something. Leonard was a likable person. He had a very good mind, a genius. And he was a good person. He had a good ear for sound, you know.

All them blues records that was being recorded, he would be there and kind of helpin' out about the sound. He had these contraptions all around the studio. He put the speakers in something closed, to get a different sound—in a cabinet. He would put whatever speakers in there that he wanted to get to create a different sound, whether it was the guitar or whatever. Now they done created the echo chamber and all that stuff. They didn't have that then. For our part, it wasn't about no comin' back the next day. I mean, everybody was dependent upon me and Willie Dixon and Fred Below and Odie Payne to help 'em do them records.

I WAS LIKE A FATHER TO LITTLE WALTER. When he first done "Juke," the Myers brothers stayed with him for a while. They were giggin' all the time. Finally Louis quit. Walter come to me on his knees. "Please come help me!" Well, really, I don't especially care about a harp. I don't really like a harp that much. Walter's the first harmonica player I ever had—the very first. And I told Walter, I said, "Okay, man. I'm gonna help you till you find you somebody." That cost me two or three years. And I quit playin' with him 'cause he wouldn't hire a bass player. He never did hire a bass player. He had a guitar playin' bass—David Myers and Louis and Luther Tucker playin' bass on the guitar. Two guitars, harp, and drums. Me and Dave for a while, and me and Luther Tucker for a while. That's the way it was. That's what they done on the record, and on the road too. I wanted him to hire a bass player. And he refused. I told him, "It was nice workin' with you."

Just before Walter died, he got arrested 'cause he got shot. Him and his woman supposed to have some kind of little problem, and they was scufflin' over a gun. Gun went off and shot him in the leg. And when the police came to the scene, he had his hand closed up. And they pried his hand open. He had three sticks of marijuana in his hand. They rolls that real skinny, you know. They pried his hand open and got that goddamn marijuana—them three little sticks—out of his hand. So when they got him to the hospital, they chained him to the bed. And I went and asked Leonard to get them to take them chains off of him. I told Mud to do it, and he grumbled. Leonard say he don't want nothing to do with him. I didn't give a goddamn what he says, I went on down there and got on Leonard's ass. Leonard called over there and told them to take the chains off him; that's all he had to do. Leonard said just leave him go—that's all. He had a lot of power. I got over there, and Walter said, "My white father got them chains off of me." I said, "You god-damned lyin'." I said, "Your black father got them chains off of you!" He laid up there and looked at me just as funny. I said, "Leonard and Muddy was going to let your goddamned ass rot right here."

I never knew about Walter being a fighter. I knew he didn't get pushed around that much. I know he'd fight—I'd fight! But I don't think he tried to start fights. He always did get into stuff, though. Almost had a brain concussion in Chicago. A guy hit him on the head with a gun or something. He died from that. He got hit like—shit! And 20 years later it killed him. The goddamn place where the man hit him that day, as the years passed, it kind of fucked him up.

Walter had a different style. He was all alone. Like Albert King was with his style. He created it. Walter had an eight-speaker Sears Roebuck amplifier—four on each side. He wouldn't hire a bass player, and for some reason he was dumb enough to think I wouldn't leave him. Now on "My Babe," I played the melody and the bass. We had to overdub because we couldn't find Tucker that day. I don't know where in the hell Tucker was. I played the session by myself—me, Willie Dixon, and Below. Dixon was playin' bass, but you couldn't hardly hear what he was doin'— that happened all the time. The Fender bass was in, but they didn't want to use it. And I quit Walter 'cause he wouldn't hire one.

After I left Walter, I went with Eddie Boyd for a minute. I played the Million Dollar Palm in Hallandale, Florida, with him. That's the first time I ever saw some-body shoot hisself with heroin. The man had blood all over the bathroom floor tryin' to find a vein—a trumpet player, a good musician. I just stood there shakin' my head. That was also the first time I saw Jay McShann. Everybody played that Million Dollar Palm. They had a little kitchen concern, and they had a room 'bout the size of a medium-size little pantry back there. And that room would be full of precooked chickens—stacked up. And in a run of 24 hours they didn't have no chickens left to sell. I used to order one of those chickens every day.

You could get about 1,000 cars in that place. And it was only 50¢ to come in. But when you got in, you weren't where the band played. The club had shutters that you could raise up. If you go in the club, then you had to pay a cover charge; and if you got something, then you know you had to pay for that—set-ups and stuff like that. But they had a whiskey store in the Palm. And like I say, those chickens would be gone. Everybody would be in there listenin' to the music and partyin'. It hadn't gotten like it is now, you know, but you see some of everybody there. The entertain-ers were black; white folks didn't know anything about the blues then.

First one to be playin' the Fender bass in Chicago was Reggie Boyd. I been knowin' Reggie ever since he was a boy. He get married when he was about 19 or 20 years old. He married one of the Sweethearts of Rhythm. She was an alto player, and she is responsible for his career—for him bein' what he is. They had a little boy, and Reggie was baby-sitting the baby while she worked. Reggie started takin' lessons to play the guitar. I don't know who taught him, but I do know that he ended up bein' a motherfucker. He can play his ass off! None of the guys he taught didn't really do nothin' with it like they should have done. He taught a lot of peoples like Louis Myers and Howlin' Wolf, but none of 'em ever made it up close to him. Reggie almost lost his mind. He was too far away from everybody. He walkin' around a genius guitar player and couldn't get a job. Just a mean world, boy.

I also played with George Smith a little bit in Chicago. He left and first went to Kansas City, tried his best to get me and Luther Tucker to go with him. Then Tucker's mother signed him over to me when he was 16, and we was goin' to the 708 Club. There was a bouncer that used to be there—Lane—he worked as the little policeman for the house and didn't want Tucker to come in the club. I said, "Lane, he'll be workin' here the weekend, man!" "Don't make no difference; I can't let him in." I said, "Okay." So the weekend come, me and Tucker come to work. I put Tucker in the union. The man just looked at me and shook his head. I said, "Lane, he's got a union card. And I'm his guardian." He said, "He's not comin' in here!" Tucker came in and played because the owner, Ben Gold, went over and told Lane to let him in. We didn't have no more trouble like that.

I went to Milwaukee once with Shakey Jake. Where we played at, the man paid everybody, then he put Jake in the freezer. I got in my car and pulled away, I saw Jake's car still sittin' there. And you know, I went back in the club and I said, "Where's Jake?" The guy from behind the bar says, "Shit, go down there and let that motherfucker out." [*Laughs.*] Lord have mercy, that boy came out of there, his eyes was shinin' like glass. Me and Jake laughed about this in California.

Jake was the best crap shooter I ever seen in my life. I seen him throw from two to twelve on them dice—square dice. I seen him bet ten dollars to two dollars and make ten and four! Shakey Jake—best crap shooter I ever seen, and I seen a whole lot of 'em. We used to come to a place what they call a barrelhouse. I think it was on the line of Indiana and Illinois. They wouldn't let Jake play. They wouldn't let him shoot dice. The man who owned it would give him $15 or $20 and tell him to go get him something to eat. Wouldn't let him play.

Freddie King was in Chicago then. Now I forget who he was recording for, but I played on his first session [for the El-Bee label, 1956]. I met him in Chicago. We was all livin' there. I think he played the 708 Club. I played on Harold Burrage's Cobra record—a thing called "Red Light." I got no credit for playin' with Walter— shit! Well, the Aces was takin' the credit for that.

AMONG THE PEOPLE WHO I REALLY ADMIRED the most was Roosevelt Sykes. Roosevelt was one of the nicest men I've ever seen. Sometime it gets me kind of emotional, you know. So I try to keep my mind off of them guys that I been knowin' a long time like that. There were quite a few guys who I know—we had no kind of disagreement. I think that's real good. Little Brother Montgomery and Memphis Slim were two others. Eddie Boyd wasn't too versatile, but he was tasty. And I really liked Willie Mabon, but he wasn't quite versatile enough either. Sunnyland know how to play chords to let you play.

I missed playin' with Louis Armstrong by an hour. Armstrong was paying from

$100 to $150 a day. He was playing an exclusive place downtown—might have been the Brass Rail or something like that. The Brass Rail was in the Loop in Chicago. A hundred dollars a day then in Chicago was a lot of money 'cause the scale was $18 for a sideman, $24 or $25 for a leader. And I think Lee Cooper got that job. Me and Lee Cooper had a trio for a year. He was a great guitar player.

I met Gatemouth Brown before that—somewhere in Texas. I been knowin' Gate a good long time. I was down in some parts of Texas just a little before Robert Johnson died—Texarkana, Texas—where Texas and Arkansas joins each other. I was in Orange and I was in Midland. I admire Gatemouth, although I really don't call him a blues player—I call him a musician. I known T-Bone Walker for a long time too. T-Bone was recording records when we were in Texas on the same package. I was workin' with Walter, and we was all playin' the same place.

Before I ended up coming to Cleveland with Sonny Boy, I recorded an album in New York City for Candid Records with Otis Spann. That really was not my job. I went there to help Spann and St. Louis Jimmy. I wasn't supposed to sing nothing. And after I got there, Spann ran out of material. And the man ask me, he say, "Robert, don't you want to put something on this album?" I say, "Okay." We were in New York only a few hours. We was there just long enough to come from the airport to the studio and record, and go back to the airport and go back home. That's where I seen Erroll Garner play—in the same New York studio. He sat down, got a balance, and played 14 tunes one right behind the other. Get up and walked out. He got paid $2,000. Nobody do that but him and Oscar Peterson. Nobody else. That little man was bad. I still get royalty checks from Candid for the Spann record. After we went to New York and recorded that, we went back home to Chicago and played a job that night. The next week or next couple of weeks Sonny Boy come to Chicago to record too.

You know, all them clubs and places I had been playin' with everybody else—all them club owners that knew me, they didn't want to accept me as a leader. Ain't that something? All the guys I played with: Eddie Boyd, Roosevelt Sykes, Muddy Waters, Willie Mabon, all them guys—I was the leader of the band. They was the star, and I was the leader. But the club owners didn't accept me as a leader. So I said, well, I guess I'll go back to New York.

And about five or six days before I got out of there, Sonny Boy come to town. He came to Chicago to record records, and I always played with him. So I help him do "One Way Out"; I played on the record. When he got through recording it, he begged me to come back here to Cleveland with him. I told him I was fixin' to go to New York, but I come here with him. And I didn't get no farther. Sonny Boy said, "Why don't you just stop and live and work with me a little while in Cleveland, and make you some money—then go to New York?" Fucked me up—I been here ever since. Cleveland was supposed to be on my way out of there on my way up to New York.

But I really think if I had not stopped—if I had gone on to New York, I'd proba-bly be dead right now. I probably would be, 'cause I wasn't takin' no kind of abuse from nobody. Again, I was carryin' a gun sure enough every day. Sometime I go out of here now and forget about it. When I was in Chicago, I carried one every day. I don't know why I didn't get caught with a gun. And as the years passed, I ended up with three brothers on the police force in Chicago! I got a brother there right now on the police force who's a detective—one of six younger stepbrothers. My mother raised 'em all.

ANNIE IS THE ONLY WIFE I EVER HAD. I met her in 1960 when I moved to Cleveland. We came here about a couple days apart. She came from Warren, Ohio, and we met at Lovings Grill. Sonny Boy and I played there for two years—six nights a week. I don't know why Sonny Boy was in Cleveland. Well, I had played Cleveland four or five times a year. They had a place called Gleason's, and they had a place called the Shadowbox. I had played here with Muddy Waters, Willie Mabon, Eddie Boyd, Little Walter, think that's about it. We was comin' to Cleveland through an agent named Shaw.

Elmore came to stay with us about a month, died shortly after. Stayed around here with me and Sonny Boy in the last part of '61, I think. We were living in the same place when Sonny Boy first brought me here. Elmore was pretty tasty, although I can do without the slide, period. I feel just about the same way about the slide as I do about the harp. Sonny Boy left Cleveland and went to Detroit, and from there to Europe.

When Sonny Boy left, I put my own trio together around 1964. I taught Gene Schwartz how to play the bass; so I had guitar, bass, and drums for four or five years. Finally, I added a horn and changed drummers. I had four pieces then. The next time I recorded since Chicago and New York was for the Big Star label—that was a joke. Then on Delmark with the Aces.

Jimmy Reed came here and played, stayed around here about two or three days. And we went to Leo's Casino, and he had me carryin' his guitar so I could get in for free. The owner said, "Goddamn it, Lockwood, you don't have to carry nobody's guitar to come in here." That flipped Jimmy. He thought he was doin' me a favor gettin' me in for that. And you know, I've always walked through the kitchen anyway.

I went to Detroit in 1972 and stayed there a short while. I went down and recorded for Motown. They never released it. It was my session. I had the Motown band. I think I done 14 tunes on the Tri-Fi label run by Berry Gordy's brother-in-law, Harvey Fuqua, who was the lead singer of the Moonglows. I played a little while there with Washboard Willie. See, Calvin Frazier was playin' with Washboard, but Calvin was workin' in the steel mill, so he gave me his job. That was an experience. Washboard was pretty interesting, pretty interesting. "She got a knee-action, baby, and hydraulic hips. Every time she walked, her honey dripped." I used to laugh at him. In Detroit I also met Baby Boy Warren, Freddy Butler, and Robert White.

THE BLUES IS PRETTY BIG NOW, but I think the wrong people's controlling it. Well, the people who is controlling the blues, they really don't know what the blues consists of. Putting the wrong people in the driver's seat, giving the wrong people credit. The blues ain't what the audience thinks the blues is—the musicians know what the blues are. The blues comes in all forms. So how can you not like the blues? They say they don't like certain type of blues. Blues comes in jazz, calypso, mambo—it comes in every conceivable form. Now the people say they don't like the blues, they don't know what the fuck the blues is. Glad I learned what I know.

The record companies try to change everybody's shit when you go to 'em. You got to satisfy him [the record exec]. Nine times out of ten his ideas are bad. I sit up here and put something together, then you going to tell me, "Well, I don't like what you got." Well, write your own then; let me play yours. Don't fuck with mine. Let mine stay like I got it. That's the real reason I got my own label. I don't have to go by nobody. Nobody'll have to pass no decisions for me to release it. I made more money off of [the self-released] *What's the Score* than I made off anything I ever recorded. When they get through gettin' theirs, and everybody else gettin' theirs, and everybody get through gettin' a piece, I come out the same way. Now, time comes to gettin' my publishing money, I get all of it. I don't have to share that with anyone else. I wish I had done it 40 years ago. If I had done it 40 years ago, right now I'd be a millionaire.

I tried to do what Muddy Waters done, and I got with Trix and different other small companies I recorded for. I thought maybe they was gonna try to go somewhere. If they went somewhere, they'd be carryin' me too. That was wrong. Yeah, it was wrong. Still ain't got no money! I got as much talent as B.B. got. I got as much talent as Bobby Bland got. And I got as much talent as Little Milton got. And I still ain't got no money. Anybody I had anything to do with has ripped me off. Everybody, everybody. I think I got a better shake in Japan than I got from anybody else.

I want to do something with my record label, Lockwood Records. I'm just tryin' to get my wife secured where if something do happen to me, she'll have a way to make a livin', so she won't have to be worried about nothin'. That's how come I'm still workin'. Get all these bills paid off, I might just stop running down the road. Just record records and stay home.

I have been exceptionally lucky—exceptionally lucky. Lord knows that without my wife, I wouldn't be around—not this long. Not after all the shit that's been happenin' to me. She kept me from gettin myself in jail, from killin' somebody. Damn, I know I wouldn't have made it.

When the old guys like me is gone, I don't know what's going to happen to the blues. They gonna be done lost a whole lot of different arrangements that they would have had. People [who are playing blues] don't have the wisdom to do things that I do and that a lot of other guys do who have been messin' with this stuff a long time. And I ain't got no goddamned advice for them! Why should I tell him something? Why? He ain't going to give me no advice, so I ain't going to give him none. And I wouldn't change nothin'. I'd just do what I'm doin'—express my ideas. Explore new ideas.

JIMMY REED

BY DAN FORTE   The nation's Bicentennial year, 1976,
was relentlessly harsh on one of America's few unequivocally
indigenous musical forms, the blues. The year started off with
the deaths of three of the idiom's longtime leaders in rapid
succession—Howlin' Wolf, Jesse Fuller, and Mance Lipscomb.
All this while the deaths of T-Bone Walker and Hound Dog
Taylor a year earlier were still fresh in the blues fan's mind.

Still, Wolf had been suffering from kidney trouble for several years (in fact, his death had been reported prematurely more than once), and Fuller and Lipscomb were 79 and 80, respectively.

But perhaps the worst shock came in August, when the blues world lost a veritable institution, Jimmy Reed. Born in Leland, Mississippi, Reed was not quite 50 years old and seemed to be at the beginning of a strong comeback when he died of respiratory stoppage apparently caused by an epileptic seizure during his sleep.

After having spent several years hospitalized due to problems of epilepsy compounded by alcoholism, Jimmy had returned to performing with regained health and an optimistic attitude. By this time the Reed repertoire sounded like a "Greatest Hits" album (or two or three). Songs like "Bright Lights, Big City," "You Don't Have to Go," "Baby, What You Want Me to Do," "Take Out Some Insurance," "Caress Me Baby," "Honest I Do," "Going to New York," "Ain't That Loving You, Baby," and "Big Boss Man" poured out, one after the other, all with that immediately identifiable shuffling, walking bass—relaxed but heavy on the backbeat. (As guitarist Albert King, who played drums behind Reed for a short time, once said, "All I could play was a shuffle with a backbeat"—which was about all that was required for the gig.)

Jimmy's guitar playing was primitive, to say the least, but nonetheless bluesy and as recognizable as his whining, nasal vocals. While repeating his usual song formula, in every possible variation, Jimmy Reed provided countless rock, jazz, pop, and R&B artists with a good portion of their material. The Rolling Stones, Elvis Presley, Count Basie, Muddy Waters, the Animals, Chuck Berry, Johnny and Edgar Winter, Charlie Rich, the Grateful Dead, John Hammond, Jerry Lee Lewis, the Blues Project, James Cotton, the Persuasions, Sonny James, Hot Tuna, Jimmy Witherspoon, Etta James, Bill Cosby, Ike and Tina Turner, Aretha Franklin, and others all turned to Reed's simple but effective music.

Here, in an account taped just two months before his death on August 29, 1976, "The Boss Man" reflects on his early development on guitar, his recordings, his career-long partnership with blues guitarist Eddie Taylor, his years in a V.A. hospital, and his subsequent short-lived comeback.

THE BOSS MAN: IN HIS OWN WORDS Didn't nobody teach me how to play the guitar. I just started off trying to fool with a box ever since I was about nine or ten years old. I wasn't making too much progress at it then, but I just kept on trying to do it. Eddie Taylor and me were raised up in the cotton patch together in Mississippi, and we'd fool around with guitars when we got off work in the fields.

But I really didn't get interested in it till after I'd done been up in Chicago. When I was 18 I went into the service, and when I come out, at about 20, I wanted to try it all over again. I was working in the steel mill and listening to that old Muddy Waters, Little Walter, Howlin' Wolf, the Aces, all of them. There was a tavern—it wasn't no "club"—across the street from my house when I was living out in South Chicago. I never did worry about going in the place or nothing; I would stand out there and listen to them playing a little while—but *I* couldn't play nothing. I said to myself, "Well, if these guys can play in here—I don't see too much that they're doing—I think I could do some of the same thing."

I went and bought me an old piece of guitar and just sat out in the alley right in back of my house. I bought me a little amplifier and plugged it in on the patio where I could hear myself.

And at that time you could buy them old 78-size dubs [blank recording discs] that didn't have nothing on them; and I bought one of these old record players where what you was playing on the guitar, you could take this dub and turn it over, and it would play back to you what you had just got through playing. I tried a couple of those, and it seemed like the junk sounded pretty good to me. But it didn't sound like I was getting enough in there—you know, just *me.* So this friend, Willie Joe Duncan, had this piece of wire. Him and me used to get together and just fool around in the alley, drinking and going on.

Then it got around to the point where after I cut about two or three of these old crazy dubs into records, I took them down to Leonard Chess. I asked him what he thought about them. He said, "Well, I tell you what: They sound nice. But I'm so tied up now with Muddy Waters and Walter and Wolf, I can't accept nothing else right now. You're going to have to catch me again later." This was around 1953.

And Vivian Carter was a DJ in Gary, Indiana, and she had a record shop on 16th and Broadway in Gary. Her old man, Jimmy Bracken, was working for Leonard Chess, and he was taking all this in when he heard those dubs, and he told her what he'd overheard. She sent me a telegram that I had an appointment with her for that coming Sunday. So I went over there and took these dubs along with me and my little piece of guitar and little old amplifier too. I played a couple of the records for her and got my guitar and amp, so she could see me do it. She said, "How would you like to cut some records for me if I could get you started?" I didn't know anything about cutting no records; I just wanted to hear myself either over the radio or in the jukebox. So we arranged to do a session, but I didn't have no band. She said she'd get the musicians to play behind me and asked me if I wanted pianos or horns or what in there. I never did bother about having piano on no records; it just didn't sound right to me. At the speed of the background I had, it seemed like it was always betwixt and between—wasn't fast enough or slow enough, either.

And when I got to the studio the next week, she had Eddie Taylor there to play background behind me! So on some of them records there was him, me, [guitarist] Lefty Bates, a drummer—and my son [Jimmy "Boonie" Reed, Jr.] had been fooling with my guitar and got pretty good himself. So I had something like four guitars, and the drums made five, and I was blowing harmonica too, just like I do it now. The one that made me want to get a harmonica was old man Sonny Boy Williamson —the original [John Lee Williamson], the one that did "Good Morning Little Schoolgirl." He could play some stuff! I was fooling with it in Mississippi and started playing with a harness in about '52.

So we did the session, and it sounded pretty good. The first record was "Found My Baby Gone." They named the company Vee Jay—"V" for Vivian and "J" for Jimmy Bracken. Their first records was mine. When I first started making records, I thought everything was going to be all right. And everything *was* all right until the thing started making money. I was supposed to be getting royalties, but I didn't get none.

But anyway, back in 1954 Vee Jay put out this thing I had cut about "You Don't Have to Go" with "Boogie in the Dark," a stone instrumental, on the reverse side. One evening I was coming home from the Armour Packing Company—I'd quit the iron foundry and was working as a butcher—and I heard this old number about "You Don't Have to Go" over the air. The guy on the radio said, "That's Jimmy

Reed; he's going to be out in Atlanta, Georgia, this Friday and Saturday night"—
and this was Thursday evening! I didn't know that I was booked in Atlanta. I headed home, grabbed my junk, headed to the studio to cut a couple of numbers, and
told Eddie Taylor, "Eddie, I'm supposed to be in Atlanta, Georgia. You going down
there with me?" He said, "Yeah, wherever you want to go!" So we bought a little
jug and struck out driving to Atlanta.

And I never did go back to the packing company to even give them back my knife
or my clothes or to get my check or nothing. That was the first time I had went on
the road or played *anywhere* before the public. I'd just been playing up and down the
alley or at friends' houses. I went to see *other* guys in Chicago playing in clubs—go
by just to holler at them. I didn't want to play or see the show either; I just wanted
to speak to them. Muddy Waters, B.B. King, all of them big cats—"Oh, you're Jimmy
Reed? I'm so glad you come down here to see me. How much they charge you to
come in?" "Oh, they let me come in for nothing." "Well, come back in the dressing
room." And I'd go back and listen to them talking about this, that, and the other,
but it didn't mean too much to me; I didn't know nothing.

I was working one-nighters mostly in Texas, Alabama, Florida, Louisiana,
Georgia, and out on the West Coast—while I was still living in Chicago. I might be
playing in California one night and have to be in Washington, D.C., practically the
next night. I had a little stage fright about playing before the public, but I was
drinking liquor at the time. I wasn't never no pot smoker, and I never did fool with
any of that cocaine or junk or crazy pills, but I'd drink me some liquor.

Then in the '60s some time I started having these [epileptic] seizures. I remember one time I went on the stage, and I didn't even know when I came off. I must
have collapsed on the stage, and they carried me off. After they found out I had
been in the service, the V.A. hospital in Downey, Illinois, accepted me in 1969.

The doctor said my nerves had got shook up, and the liquor I was drinking just
kept *pushing* me. He said he thought it would be a good idea for me to quit playing
music for a while, quit cutting records and everything. He said, "You need to just lay
down and rest a while; let your nerves get together." Used to be I could feel those
things coming on, and I'd go sit down. But then they started coming on me in my
sleep; then I'd have a heck of a time. Because you're capable of coming out from
under them things, and you're capable of not coming out. If there ain't nobody there
to stick something in your mouth, you might swallow your tongue or something.

Then I left the hospital and lived in one of these registration [convalescent]
homes until the doctor said, "Jimmy, you can go home when you get ready." So
they'd mail me a supply of medicine about once a month after I left in '72. I gave
up music for about four or five years; I didn't cut no records or do nothing.

I played guitar a lot in the hospital, though. They had a big old music center up
there where I would go and get me a guitar and amplifier and just lock up in a
room all day. And I didn't have nobody to help me out and back me up. See, during my first two or three records I wasn't doing nothing but blowing the solo on
the harmonica and starting off the intro on the guitar. Then the rest of the band
would haul off and head into it. But after I got in the hospital, my style changed in
a way. I started trying to play my intro part, as much of the lead part as I could get
in, do my singing part, blow the solo on the harmonica, and play the bass part all
the way through too. I started doing all that myself, which was a pretty hard thing.

But it got me to the place where if I *ain't* playing the lead part, it don't sound right now, since I been doing it a few years.

I used to do all my numbers with a $B\flat$ harmonica, which would cause the guitar to be in *F*. But after so long it started to strain my voice, so I started playing *A* harmonica, which caused the guitar to be *E*. I put a clamp [capo] on the fifth fret when I blow on the high part of the harmonica, and the band will be playing in *A* then. Of course, you don't *have* to put a clamp on it—there's a whole lot can be played up there without one. Eddie Taylor, he don't fool with a clamp. He's played with everybody, and you don't ever catch him putting a clamp on. I imagine if I hadn't tried to play the harmonica and done nothing but play guitar with everybody, I'd probably have been like him. Eddie, I don't care how many records he's made or who he's played with, when he plays somewhere with me, he don't worry about playing nothing he ever did on anyone else's junk. He helped me on all my records but about two.

I can't play behind anybody else. I have to start my own thing and let everybody push me. You can put me up there with somebody else playing, and I can't get in tune or keep up with them. But let me start *my* stuff, and I can go ahead on.

My son also played on all my records, except the first couple and the last couple. He's a stone musician. I ain't nothing, but he can play music, write music, read music, arrange music—he's just long gone with it. But he can't sing worth nothing, and he don't like the blues. He's a rock and roll type. He learned the guitar just from being around me—I ain't taught him nothing. Sometimes I'd go down in the basement and be up all night, trying to see what I could play on the thing. He wasn't nothing but a little kid, and he'd sit down there with me till him and the dog would fall asleep in the corner. I think he was, I should say, 10 or 11 years old when he first played on a record of mine. He plays rock and roll, but me, myself, I play the blues. I don't play no rock and roll stuff, but my records made it on the rock stations, because the background just had some kind of a beat to it that just got everybody to moving.

When me and Eddie used to fool around in Mississippi, they wasn't making no electric guitars. I started off with one of those folk boxes with the hole in the middle. But when I got to recording I had me an electric. I played some of everything—I never did have no special brand. Then in '72, after I got out of the V.A. hospital, I was at a music shop getting some picks and strings, and I saw this guitar [a Japanese Les Paul copy made by Ariel]. It had the type of feel I like in a box. So the guy let me have it for $42 or $52—I thought it was a pretty good deal.

My amp is an old Fender Concert; I think it was one of the first ones they made. I had a newer Fender amp, but I got this Concert for $90. The average cats on the bandstand, they turn their box wide open and have them blasting. I don't call that music; you can't hear what the other guy's doing. I can see them doing that if they're reading everything off sheet music, but when you're just playing by ear, you have to listen to who's doing what.

When I started out, I used a flatpick. But with the straight pick, in my style, the wrist will get tired. So then I started using the fingerpick and thumbpick, so there ain't nothing to get tired out but just my thumb. If I wanted to come off the bass with the lead notes, that's when the index finger comes in. This song I made about "Big Boss Man," I've tried to show a lot of guys who was stone musicians, pretty well professionals, how to play the intro to that, and they can't do it so it sounds right.

I just do my one straight thing. But it seems to work out pretty good like it is.

J.B. HUTTO

BY DAN FORTE Paul Oliver's book *The Story of the Blues* [Chilton] is probably as close to a definitive source as has been written about the idiom. But almost as valuable as the painstakingly comprehensive text is the extensive selection of photographs—each offering a rare insight into the lifestyle and environment surrounding the people who played or listened to the blues. For example, there's a 1966 glimpse of slide guitarist J.B. Hutto playing at Turner's Blue Lounge on 39th and Indiana in Chicago's South Side, a club which Oliver describes as "a rough joint." ¶ Judging by the picture, the late author must have been a master of understatement. Hutto, in short sleeves and sunglasses, sits on a tiny stage

J.B. Hutto was still alive when Dan Forte's profile, "J.B. Hutto: Keeping Chicago Blues Aflame with Electric Slide Guitar," ran in the March '79 issue of GUITAR PLAYER. *Hutto passed away on June 12, 1983, in Harvey, Illinois.*

barely a couple of feet higher than dance floor level. The reason he's not standing is obvious: If he did, his head might bump the low ceiling. Next to him a middle-aged black couple, dressed as informally as the musician, is dancing the boogie woogie. On the stark back wall hangs a burned-out Schlitz sign next to some crude ventilation system. Hutto doesn't seem to be too excited about whatever he's play-ing on his cheap Kay electric; his expression is more like that of a graveyard-shift fry cook flipping hamburgers—just someone doing his job. But in spite of his weary countenance, J.B. Hutto was and is one of the most inventive and individual slide guitarists to emerge from the school popularized by his chief mentor, the late Elmore James.

ELECTRIFIED MISSISSIPPI DELTA BLUES The blues has been J.B.'s occupation off and on for nearly 30 years. Born Joseph Benjamin Hutto in Blackville, South Carolina, on April 26, 1926, J.B. was raised in Augusta, Georgia, from the age of three. With his three brothers and three sisters, J.B. formed a gospel group, the Golden Crowns, and sang at the local Galilee Baptist and Holy Trinity churches; J.B. sang lead or second lead. Hutto recalls, "I listened to the majority of the blues records out then, but I wasn't playing that. I guess I was too young, anyway. I listened to them and liked them, but I wasn't really attracted to no kind of music until I hit Chicago." This is evidenced by the fact that J.B.'s resultant style sounds basically like electri-fied Mississippi Delta blues—whining guitar, percussive attack, and hollering vocals—and reflects none of the qualities found in the sort of ragtime blues played on the Eastern Seaboard.

When J.B.'s father died in 1949, the family moved to Chicago, and it was there at the age of 20 that Hutto became involved with the blues. "I was kind of young," admits J.B., "and I didn't know about people playing in clubs and things of that nature—so I was still looking for house parties, fish fries, and things like that. But there wasn't nothing happening. I began to make a few friends and began to talk, and they showed me around, and I started going to the clubs, seeing bands."

Hutto's first instrument was drums, which he played with Johnny Ferguson and His Twisters. "I played drums, but I was singing too," he reminisces. "Johnny was the leader, and he had a guitar. But when he'd lay it down I had it." J.B. met one-man band Eddie Hines, better known as "Porkchop," and the two (with Hutto on guitar) played on Maxwell Street at the open-air flea market known as Jew Town.

From the very start, J.B. played strictly electric guitar. Asked to describe his early style, he shrugs, "I can't explain it; I'll have to show you. [*He plays a dirge-like blues in standard tuning using a lot of open strings and sounding a bit like Lightnin' Hopkins.*] I didn't know how to come up here and maybe bend a string, then get back down here to catch it. But that's where I was coming from."

After hearing Elmore James, Hutto became enchanted with the sound of the electric slide guitar and set out to play it almost exclusively. "He was the cat who made me see what I wanted to do," declares the pupil. "He raised me. He could pick some, but he didn't do too much picking. I think he was like me—he liked that slide. If I could make this thing slide and cry like I want to, maybe I wouldn't do so much picking."

Hutto and Porkchop soon formed a band, and during the early '50s they played clubs like the Globetrotter and the 1015 Club. As Mike Rowe describes it in his book *Chicago Breakdown:* "J.B. blew upon the Chicago scene with one of the noisiest and toughest bands ever. Singing in the fierce, declamatory style of his idol, Elmore James, and backed by the heavily amplified guitar of Joe Custom, the crude harp of George Maywether, and the elemental percussion of Maxwell Street's Porkchop, they sounded ready to devour anything in sight!"

J.B. spent a lot of time with James, listening and learning, but while virtually every blues slide player owes a huge debt to Elmore, Hutto soon found his own voice—with a more varied single-note guitar approach and a more primitive, wild vocal style. In 1954 Hutto got his first opportunity to record, for the Chance label, under the name J.B. and His Hawks, a moniker his various groups have carried over the years. With his first 78, "Now She's Gone," the guitarist established himself as a powerful bandleader and a highly personal lyricist.

But almost as quickly as he had appeared on the scene, J.B. vanished from it around 1954 after recording a mere nine sides for Chance, only six of which were ever issued. The reason for his hiatus can perhaps be found in an anecdote related in Mike Rowe's book: "J.B. lost his guitar when a woman broke it over her husband's head, and he quit music for the quieter life of an undertaker."

Not until the mid '60s did Hutto re-emerge, but he seemed none the worse for the ten-year layoff. Producer Sam Charters recorded the Hawks—Hutto, bassist Herman Hassell, and drummer Frank Kirkland—in 1965 for Vanguard Records' *Chicago/The Blues/Today!* The session featured J.B.'s composition "Too Much Alcohol." Recordings for Testament, Delmark, and other independent labels followed, and the early '70s found Hutto touring blues festivals across the country and overseas, where he also recorded a couple of albums.

A number of different guitars have gone through J.B.'s hands over the years, and he doesn't seem overly concerned with model names and numbers. Until recently J.B.'s main ax was a Fender Telecaster with the finish worn away at the top frets, near the cutaway, due to Hutto's habit of riding the slide up past the neck to near the rhythm pickup to obtain higher notes. That problem was partially alleviated with J.B.'s most recent change in guitars, when he purchased a solidbody Epiphone with a longer neck and deeper cutaway. The two-pickup model is usually set with just the treble pickup or both pickups on.

After some experimentation, Hutto settled on an open-*D* tuning. "I used to be a one-key man," he confesses. "Tuned it in open *E,* and for anything else I used a clamp, a capo. But I had to tune it *up* to *E,* so now I tune it down to *D* [same as open *E* but one whole-step lower on each string]. I don't like my action too high; I don't move the strings up or down. If they're too high, I get a kind of grating sound; if they're too low, naturally you're going to hit the frets."

J.B.'s current amp is a Fender Super Reverb, and as for his slide, he explains, "I used to cut off a piece of pipe with a hacksaw. Now they're selling slides all over in music stores, so I bought one. I tried playing with a glass slide, but it didn't work. I play with it on my little finger, and now I've got two metal slides, a thin one and a heavier one that has a great tone—that really brings the sound out; it almost sounds like two notes. I can't find any as heavy as this one."

Unlike Elmore James, who used a flatpick, Hutto plays with a plastic fingerpick on his index finger, along with a thumbpick. "Elmore played with a flatpick," J.B. explains, "but he could use anything—flatpick or finger and thumb. But I think playing slide is good for playing with the thumb—Hound Dog Taylor used to play with the thumb. You can always catch the strings better. If I play very long without a pick, a knot will swell up on that finger. One night overseas our stuff was late, and we had to play a college gig with new instruments—no picks, no nothing. The next day I had to stick my finger in alcohol to cool it off."

"I LEARNED TO PLAY LIKE NOBODY" J.B.'s current repertoire includes many of his old favorites, new tunes (which he's writing all the time), and blues standards—all played with Hutto's indelible stamp. "I learned to play like nobody," he boasts. "And anything I play, I have to play my way because that's how I learned. Now, you can play just like the other man—that's fine—but in this open tuning it ain't gonna sound the same. So I just kick off my songs in my beat. Like 'Thrill Is Gone'—it's a beautiful song by B.B. King, and I can do it B.B.'s original way, or I can do it in my version. I'll tell you something about me—I just do my thing. Now, when I play with someone else, what the other man do, I got nothing to do with that. I don't try to outdo him, because we're playing together, making music for the public. When you get overanxious trying to outdo somebody, you always mess up."

Since the death of Hound Dog Taylor, Hutto has been one of the leaders in a very select group carrying on the Elmore James tradition. J.B. and Homesick James are the obvious keepers of the flame. Of his rival, Hutto feels, "Well, Homesick is a good slide player—or he would be if he played in time, let's put it that way. Time means a whole lot in music. And Homesick James has no time [*laughs*]. I've seen Floyd Jones sit up on the bandstand with Homesick and *sweat*. You got to jump in here and here and here. Homesick's all right by himself. When he can play like he wants to, he's a good guitarist, but put him with a band . . . [*laughs*]."

Of J.B.'s admiration for Hound Dog Taylor, there is no better indication than the fact that for a time after Taylor's death, Hutto inherited his band, the Houserockers, which was the only time J.B. traveled under a name other than the Hawks.

As for current favorites, though, and younger blues-rock sliders, Hutto sighs, "You hear one, you just about heard them all—the way they're playing now. Black musicians are trying to slip into the disco, trying to put the blues into something else and give it another name. They're carrying the same beat, the same sound, and you got nothing. The older blues, you can hear the changes and feel the changes, you know."

As for J.B. trying to update *his* style or cash in on current trends, purists have little to worry about. Today Hutto is playing the blues in the same loud, raucous, beautifully simple style that has been his trademark since the beginning. "When I got this here guitar," he states, "I loved it. This is what I liked; this is what I wanted. I have to have it with me. Sometimes you can wake up in the morning, and you'll find it laying right there on the pillow beside me."

WILLIE JOHNSON

BY **JOHN ANTHONY BRISBIN** Aside from the tale of
how Sunnyland Slim got young Muddy Waters off a venetian blind truck and into a recording studio with the Chess
brothers in the spring of 1948, there is probably no postwar
blues story more memorable than the one in which, during
the spring of 1951, a young Memphis disc jockey named
Sam Phillips followed up on a tip from a West Memphis
radio announcer and invited Chester Arthur Burnett into his
Memphis Recording Service to wax the hard, hauntingly
primitive "Moanin' at Midnight." Phillips, who later founded Sun Records and discovered Elvis Presley, has always
called that first session with Howlin' Wolf his greatest thrill.
¶ The best accounts of that date also praise Wolf's guitarist
on "Moanin' at Midnight," Willie Lee Johnson. Chris Morris,
in the notes to MCA/Chess' *Howlin' Wolf* boxed set, aptly
calls Johnson "the linchpin of Wolf's group," adding that

he "formulated the dense, distorted style that propelled Wolf's live and recorded work through the mid '50s." British writer Charlie Gillett describes Johnson's playing as sounding "as if he was twanging barbed wire with a six-inch nail." Dave Rubin, author of *Inside Blues Guitar, 1942–1982,* was similarly struck: "Johnson played like a bull in a rut on these jumping jaunts, pounding out comp chords and molten lead lines. . . . One of Willie Johnson's many attributes was his ability to combine jazzy, dominant chords with basic blues licks. Like a good short-order cook, he tossed it all together with sizzling distortion, making seemingly disparate elements blend into a satisfying culinary stew for the ear."

To the astonishment of Burnett and Johnson, "Moanin' at Midnight" and its flip side, "How Many More Years," rocketed to #10 on the *Billboard* charts as a two-sided hit for Chess Records in 1951. But a dispute raged immediately between Chess and Los Angeles–based RPM Records over the rights to Howlin' Wolf's material. The entrepreneurial Ike Turner was at the bottom of it. He had hired on with Sam Phillips to play piano on "How Many More Years" and other sides, while at the same time serving as an A&R man for the Bihari brothers' RPM enterprise. While Phillips was offering Wolf's recordings to Chess in Chicago, Turner was sending alternate versions of some of the same tunes to RPM. The tension was ratcheted up a few notches when subsequent recording sessions were held by Phillips in Memphis and by Turner across the Mississippi River in West Memphis, Arkansas. The rights to Howlin' Wolf's material were finally assigned to Chess in 1952 (in exchange for Chess' giving RPM the rights to promising young R&B singer Rosco Gordon), and in 1953 or possibly '54, Wolf sold his stake in the family farm to his brother-in-law and went north to Chicago to try music full time.

Willie Johnson had played with Wolf since he was a teenager, but he didn't make that trip north. Instead, he kept busy in West Memphis performing with Willie Nix, Junior Parker, Bobby Bland, Elmore James, Sonny Boy Williamson [Rice Miller], Rosco Gordon, and a harmonica player named Little Sammy Lewis. Johnson recorded with Nix for Checker and RPM and under his own name, with Lewis, for Sun. Two or three years later, however, Howlin' Wolf drove down South to collect Johnson and bring him to Chicago to replace the recently departed guitarist Jody Williams in his band. Johnson thrived for several years as a member of the Howlin' Wolf Band, playing with the group at the 708 Club, Sylvio's, the Zanzibar, and a host of other places. In the studio, Johnson brought his primitive Memphis fire to Wolf's "Smokestack Lightnin'" in 1956 and provided understated support to the hypnotic "Who's Been Talkin'" in '57.

A hard taskmaster, Howlin' Wolf expected band members to abide by his rules— no drinking on the bandstand being the cardinal one. Multi-instrumentalist Lester Davenport drummed for Wolf during the early '60s but was following him in the late '50s, partly because his cousins, Otis and Abe Smothers, played guitar in the band. Davenport remembers the tempestuous relationship between Howlin' Wolf and Willie Johnson: "Well, both of 'em had quick tempers. They couldn't get along on account of that. Willie Johnson, he wouldn't back down. Well, you know Wolf, he's not gonna back down. Wolf didn't want no drinkin' in his band and Willie, he had to have a drink. That was the main issue."

Muddy Waters made the same assessment: "Willie Johnson did play two or three weeks for me. He was good guitar player, but his head was baaad! He got, what you call it, evil. He wanted to fight and that kind of thing. I don't like the band fightin'." Muddy tried another of Wolf's guitarists, Hubert Sumlin, for a while and sent him back to Wolf as well: "Then me and Hubert didn't get along. Hubert went with me. And he went back to Wolf. Then he had Willie and Hubert and he had two bad boys up there too, boy. Two bad boys!"

In 1959, after a gig at Theresa's Lounge, Johnson left Howlin' Wolf's Band for the last time. Wolf was succinct when Dick Shurman asked him about Johnson's departure: "I didn't mind the fights, but he wouldn't give me no rest." Guitarist Jimmie Lee Robinson, who was on the scene at the time and who kept up with Willie in later years, adds an intriguing postscript to the story: "Willie and I went out ridin' together not long ago, ridin' around. He was drinkin' a lot. He'd be sittin' there in the car, drinkin' and talkin' about the old days, the past, you know. He was tellin' me that Wolf had slapped him. Wolf slapped him and they got into it. He said he took that razor and he cut Wolf all around his back with that razor. That broke 'em up, and then Mighty Joe Young took his place in Wolf's band."

Hampered by his drinking, Johnson was musically inactive during much of the rest of his life. As Robinson sums it up, "Willie didn't have nothin' goin' for long. Whatever it was he'd pick up, it was just a fly-by." The periods when he played well were more frequent during the 1960s than they were later on. "He played at Blanche's Lounge on Congress and Francisco with Calvin Jones, the bass player who used to be with Muddy," Lester Davenport remembers. "Willie played pretty much all around the West Side, you know, local clubs. He played with J.T. Brown, the saxophone player, at 16th and Homan, the Squeeze Club. He played the Happy Home when it was going. The Swing Club, he played there a few times. He was all around, you know, and he could play it all, from rock-bottom blues, Elmore James and all that, up to the late modern blues. He was a versatile player."

For a while, Johnson played in the house band at drummer Kansas City Red's club, Johnny Do Wrong's, at 5400 W. Madison. And on many weekends during the early and mid '60s, Johnson performed at the Rock Tavern in Rockford, Illinois. Jimmie Lee Robinson vividly remembers the Rock Tavern gig: "Willie Johnson was with us longer than he was with anybody, I guess: me, Kansas City Red, and Sunnyland Slim. We had a real nice, good, tight band. Robert Nighthawk used to come in there and play with us too. Pinetop Perkins came up there with us for a while. Rice Miller come up there and stayed with us for a while. We had another harmonica player used to play with us there named Little Ernie. He still lives up there, but he can't see too good. Me, Sunnyland Slim, and Red, we stayed there. But Willie came back to Chicago during the week. He had a wife and job.

"We stayed there for quite a few years. We all had girlfriends there. Sunnyland stayed with a girl named Big Rose. We'd gamble and play cards, but I never seen Willie Johnson gamble. Willie Johnson more or less enjoy hisself laughin' and talkin' and drinkin'. Red was the funniest thing. He always teasin' around. He would call me baby or honey sometime, pretend like he was gonna kiss me. One time he slipped and kissed me dead in my mouth. Boy, all of 'em fell out. Sunnyland, Willie Johnson, they all fell out laughin', you know. We'd play in Beloit, Wisconsin, too. And for Briggs and Briggs, a resort up in Kenosha, Wisconsin. I left out of Rockford in '65. I had to go to Europe. Sunnyland didn't go. They stayed around there. Now, when I came back from Europe, Willie was in Chicago. He was out west there someplace, out there 'cross Pulaski somewhere and south of Harrison Street. I seen him and I said, 'How you doin', Willie Johnson!' And he told me his name wasn't no longer Willie Johnson. He said, 'My name now is Willie Torch.' I said, 'What?' He said, 'Willie Torch. I'm an organ player now.' Ha ha. He was playin' organ. Then I seen him again, and he was back on guitar."

Living Blues founding editor Jim O'Neal, who was fresh out of college in 1970, picks up on Johnson's whereabouts at that time: "He was playing a little bit right when *Living Blues* started, at the Washburne Lounge with Sunnyland and Roosevelt Broomfield around 1970. I remember him sitting in with Kansas City Red at the Poinciana and with John Brim when he had the Broadway Night Club. That was probably the best night I ever heard him. He played with a couple of the young guys: Johnnie Mae Dunston's son, James Smith, and George somebody. And occasionally he'd play at B.L.U.E.S. He showed up at one or two of the *Living Blues* cookouts we had.

"Sometimes I'd just go check on him. I'd find him hangin' around some guys at a garage, shooting dice and drinking. We always wanted to hear that rough, raw guitar that he played with Howlin' Wolf but he, like Pat Hare, had progressed toward a more polished, jazzier kind of sound, which is maybe what they were trying to get when they were young guys playing on cheap equipment. The other thing that wasn't on record was the slide guitar playing. He wasn't known for that, but that was some of the most impressive stuff I heard from him in the later years. It was kind of in the Robert Nighthawk style."

Earwig Music's Michael Frank got to know Johnson in the late 1970s through Kansas City Red and Sunnyland Slim. He heard him at Al's Place and at the Delta Fish Market, where Johnson would play an occasional set with Red or Slim. In 1989, Frank produced five tunes with Johnson for Wolf Records that remain unreleased. Frank also arranged a handful of guest spots for Johnson at Rosa's during the late 1980s and 1990s. For most of those, Johnson either didn't show up or was too drunk to play. Still the believer, Frank booked Johnson for Earwig Music's 15th Anniversary Party at Buddy Guy's Legends on June 2, 1994. Frail but impeccably dressed in a suit and tie, Johnson showed that he could still unleash his talent, playing beside old friends Sunnyland Slim and Homesick James. His chording was complex but swingingly right. His picking was precise and clean, and it had Memphis written all over it. The date was talked about in blues circles for months. A series of rehearsals with Sunnyland Slim that would have led to an Earwig recording date were scheduled. But Willie Lee Johnson died at home on February 26, 1995, a few days shy of his 72nd birthday. Sunnyland Slim died shortly thereafter, on March 17.

The following recollections were collected in 1994 on a steamy June afternoon in Johnson's humble room at 57th and S. Indiana on Chicago's South Side. It was several days after Johnson's impressive performance at Legends, and he was still very excited about it. His girlfriend Diane napped comfortably on a double bed, and a pot of red beans boiled slowly on the stove as we talked. A considerate host, Johnson filled my glass of ice water many times and adjusted the window fan to suit me. I had heard Johnson described by so many as obstinate, angry, and hard drinking, but I found him shy and soft-spoken. I saw him three times that week: once briefly in a vacant lot at 57th and State by the newsstand where he liked to sit in the shade with his buddies, again on the night he played Legends, and once more for the interview at his home. He was sober all three times.

Toward the end of the interview, we moved outside and found a spot of shade.

Johnson sat on the stoop and played some neat licks on his guitar. As he did, his face lost its defensive tightness. The look of slightly pained distrust in his eyes melted away too, and he broke into frequent smiles. Diane woke from her nap and came outside to join us. The two of them laughed and joked as they told me about their relationship. The sound of that laughter, riding on the sunny breeze as my cab arrived, is the last memory I have of Willie Johnson.

WILLIE JOHNSON: IN HIS OWN WORDS I'll tell you, I had some good days with Wolf. I had some nice days with Wolf, and then I had some tough times with Wolf. Well, I don't say he was all that tough to get along with. Some of that was my fault 'cause I was a heavy drinker at that time. I was a heavy drinker, and he would try and tell me how he wanted it. I just got to the place I wouldn't listen. I'd let drinkin' over-power me. So sometimes we'd have difficulty.

I met Wolf in the [late] '30s at Dooley's Spur, Mississippi, near Lake Cormorant. That's right out from Robinsonville. Him and Son House and Willie Brown was playin' together. I was young, 13 or 14 years old, drivin' my dad's car. I slipped off to go down there. My dad had let me have the car to go to the show. Instead of me goin' to the show, I slipped off where Wolf and them was. Wolf told 'em, say [*imitates Wolf's gruff voice*], "I got this boy in here. I wants him to come up and do a few numbers. He can play it pretty good." I tuned the guitar my way, and I struck out on a tune. Son House and Willie Brown, you know, backed me up and all like that. They said, "This kid is good! He gonna be all right one day."

Then Wolf would let me play with him every Saturday night down there, you know. Son House and Willie Brown was playin' together, and me and the Howlin' Wolf was playin' together. Son House's style on guitar was kinda some style like Elmore James put out. Son House is the first guy I heard that started that slide stuff. Wolf taught me how to tune my guitar and everything. He set me on his lap. You know, he was a big man. I would set on his knee and he would reach over me like this and put my hand on the guitar, show me different chords. Oh man, he had long fingers. I used to play in Spanish [open-*G* tuning] all the time. But I would play everything they play 'cause I'd know where to go on it, you know. But he taught me how to tune it from *E* natural on up. And then I could play in every key. I learned the chords and everything. And I got terrific with him. I got to where I could go into every joint without anybody, you know, protectin' me. I got grown then so, yeah, he regard me as a guitar player then. Then he went to harmonica.

I was born in Mississippi, Lake Cormorant, 1923, fourth day of March. There were four brothers and two sisters among us. I was the youngest of the six. I was just a boy, runnin' around there, you know. I always had music on my mind. Ever since I been big enough, I been tryin' to play. My parents were Cora Lee Johnson and Cleveland Johnson. They were farmin' people. They worked hard on the share-crop. That work was pretty rough. You had to go out in the fields early every mornin', come in late every night. You quit work in the field, come to the house, and cook dinner. Then when it get cool enough, you'd have to go back and work till dark. Cotton and corn, yeah. That's Monday through Friday and till noon on Saturday. We had different kinds of animals—dogs, cows, chickens, hogs.

Mother was a church-workin' lady. She would take me to church on Sunday. Sunday school too. I sang there. They called that church two things: Lakeside Church and Lake Cormorant Church. But I started singin' at home. Daddy bought me a guitar. First guitar he bought me didn't cost but, I think, $1.75. It had a raggedy back on it and everything. So I learned how to strum that thing pretty good, you know. I started from that, just started playin'. There was a dude down there called Asa Bradford, and he learned me right smart about it. I learned what Asa Bradford had to offer. My mother never did interfere with what I wanted to do in music. She'd say, "There ain't nothin' I can do to stop you, so go ahead." Other than music, well, my mother'd tell me to do somethin', and I'd go on and do it. I wouldn't argue about it. I'd just work hard and do it. So that made a man out of me, and it helped me get through life.

My father, he would work! Sometime he'd plow all Saturday evenin'. But if we be caught up plowin', well, then he be gone fishin' Monday mornin'. He'd tell me, "See, if I hadn't a did that plowin' Saturday evenin', then I couldn't go fishin' Monday mornin'." He liked huntin' and fishin'. He never did take me huntin' with him, but fishin' and stuff like that, yeah, I'd go with him. What he taught me, well, it didn't turn out so good. He taught me how to drink booze. He got me on the booze kick. That wasn't so good. He used to drink whiskey, corn whiskey. He'd make it himself. He'd get corn, mix it, and let it sour. Then he'd put yeast cake in it, put him a little sugar and rye. Then he'd sit up, just let it get as sour as he'd want it to be. We had a big old stove we set it up on, and we had a copper coil, you know. Let it come through that copper coil and have a trough to cool it. He'd put a string in the copper coil, a little old pipe, and when it started drippin', that white liquid was clear. Then after a while, it'd start to runnin'. We'd run it off and make that corn whiskey. When it cooled off, we'd start drinkin' it then. Yeah, started livin' crazy then. He'd sell it too, for about nine dollars a gallon. He'd run off 15 or 20 gallons. It didn't take long. The law would catch my daddy. They didn't keep him long. He'd pay a fine, come right back out, and go to makin' it again. My daddy was somethin' else, I swear he was.

We had quite a few country suppers. They wouldn't let the kids in on the drinkin'. They'd have soft drinks for 'em and ice cream. Sandwiches and stuff like that. But you take the grown-ups and teenagers—they'd be swallowin' that booze down. Findin' somebody to hang onto tight. Yeah, that was the size of it.

I'd slip off and go to them juke joints on Saturday nights. Wolf would come down there too. He had been active a good while when I met him, playin' and doin' about, singin' and goin' on. Foots, that's what they called him. Yeah, he'd come in there with his old guitar swung over his back, stuff like that. And he'd get up and clown and do about with his guitar. Oh, he just get up and be dancin' while he playin' the guitar. He sang the same way he was singin' later on in Chicago. He got that tail dragger name—he used to sweat a lot. He would get one of these big towels and put it in his belt back here. And when he would swing his hips, that was a little show-thing like. And everybody would go to hollerin' and clappin' their hands, you know. And he'd just be waggin' and goin' on, tellin' 'em he the tail dragger and he drag his tracks out as he go. In those days, he would just make up songs—but he would make 'em rhyme. A song has gotta hit somebody, you know. The truth is told somewhere in that song that it hits somebody. So that's the way Wolf was. He was the kind of guy that he could make up a pretty good song. It wouldn't take him long either.

I never did know Wolf's family. He never did let nobody know. He was a plantation guy. He would work and so would I. I was a truck driver. I would drive the boss man's truck all the week haulin' cottonseed and stuff he had on there. Then I'd go down and play with Wolf on the weekend. We'd pack 'em in, just the two of us. I carried bass and lead. This was '39, '40, '41, somethin' like that. Sometime we make $5 a night, sometime we make $10. You'd be scared sometimes that somebody was gonna take your job, and if they was good enough they could take the job too.

Sonny Boy [Rice Miller] would come in there to Dooley's Spur. Now he would blow harp—he didn't give us cause to be scared. All of us played with him, see. Everybody would gather around him and play. He had a good thing goin'. He would tell me: "You got a good style, see. You gonna give somebody trouble with that guitar!" I taken him at his word. He'd leave there, play on the porch of them grocery stores in the evenin' time, like for Saturday evenin', and he'd draw a crowd. They'd be pitchin' them nickels and dimes and quarters and things at him, man. He'd make good money. He played by himself mostly, or with Joe Willie Wilkins and all of 'em. They played with him over in Helena. Sonny Boy wouldn't stay in no one place. He would come by my house sometime. It'd be hot and we'd be sittin' out on the porch. And he'd sit there and blow the harp. I'd get my ol' guitar and strum along with him.

I stayed with Joe Willie Wilkins and them a little while in Helena. Elmore, he had quit [the King Biscuit Boys]. You know, they called him "Mr. Clean," and he was playin' with 'em a little while. So I went over. Me and Joe Willie played with Sonny Boy maybe half a year or something like that. I never did play on the air with them. [The daily *King Biscuit Time* radio show aired for 15 minutes at noon-time over KFFA in Helena, Arkansas.] I just played around different places with them boys wherever they played at. I used to play with Sonny Boy over on Broadway [in West Memphis, Arkansas]. He was advertising the Broadway Furniture Company at that time. Played over at a place called the Hole in the Wall too. It's almost downtown in Helena. Yeah, we used to play down there right smart. We'd get over there and have a Saturday night thing: Sonny Boy, Joe Willie, me, Houston Stackhouse. Stackhouse, he could play. He played more like Joe Willie than anybody else. Joe Willie and Stackhouse, they was both pretty good. Then I played with Peck [Curtis] and Dudlow and Joe Willie Wilkins. Willie Love was playin' with Sonny Boy then, you know. Things started bloomin' good then.

Robert Nighthawk, he was livin' and playin' in Helena then. Robert Nighthawk, he had a right good thing going for hisself. He could play—and the women used to hang at him now. That Robert, he was bad with that slide. Yes sir, he had a devil of a tone. I tried to play like him, but I never did get that sound right. It mighta been in his electric amplifier, 'cause he was playin' electric guitar through it at that time. Joe Willie was terrific, but he never did make it to Chicago. Robert Jr. [Lockwood] would go down there and try and get him to come here, and he wouldn't come. He didn't wanna leave his family.

I tell you, what I liked about Joe Willie's playing is that he could play the blues the way that he developed it, and he could back you up in anything. He's like Robert Jr. Lockwood: He could play chords, and then he could turn right around and if you were playing lead, he'd play bass! Or else he'd play lead and you could play bass. Him and I played pretty much alike in a way, 'cause he could play bass on his guitar and lead all at the same time. He'd stretch them fingers, man. Joe Willie, he was a terrific guitar player.

Willie Nix was somethin' else. You know, I stayed with him a little while, played different places through Arkansas. We played Forrest City at the White Swan, Blackfish Lake, oh yeah. Sammy Lewis, he played harp for Willie Nix a long time. Willie played drums and sang. But you never could get along with him. He just fussy, that's all. He'll get drinkin', and he'll want to argue. And if we didn't pay him no attention, he'd want to fight. He'd just start in on anybody. He got to where he couldn't even get nobody [who] wanted to play with him. He would be all right sometimes. Sometimes when you yelled at him, you know, he'll mind. He wasn't just really a bad guy. He just have his ways, that's all.

I was with Wolf ever since I was 14 up until '59. All through the Memphis days, yeah. We had a spot on KWEM, we broadcast 15 minutes a day. We'd play different songs. A lot of people would turn us on, and Wolf would announce where we was gonna be that Friday night and Saturday night. People would be there waitin' on us when we get there, if they done heard us on the radio. This is 1950, '51. West Memphis was an open town. They didn't bother you too much there. They'd let you have your fun. Little Brown Jug, it was open. The White Front was open. Big Andrew Bass'. It was about four good places you could go to, all night joints. It was all on one street, Eighth Street. Go out of one door and go in another.

I'm the one written out the first number for Howlin' Wolf. I printed it, and put the words in his mouth. He couldn't hardly read. He didn't have too much schoolin' and I didn't either. I got a tablet, taken a pencil, and printed the first number that Wolf made. He could make the letters out. He just went to singin' it and playin' it. Later he went and had it printed, you know, on a machine, and copyrighted. That was at Sam Phillips' at Memphis, Tennessee. 'Cause Sam Phillips was workin' with Chess at that time. Sam Phillips, he had done talked with Wolf, but he wanted to come out for an interview, you know. We were playin' at the Brown Jug that night, but we didn't know that Sam Phillips had done slipped in the house. And he had taped us while we's there. Then he called Wolf off, went to talkin' with him about an appointment, when to come over. He say, "Well, you bring the band over on a Saturday. We'll run it down. Y'all come back in two weeks. Y'all go home and rehearsal."

So we would rehearsal this number "How Many More Years." We'd rehearsal that on the bandstand. We'd play that particular number a few times in a two-hour show. Then we'd play Friday night, Saturday night, Sunday night. So we'd do that, and it become a tight, together thing, you know. Willie Steel was on drums, Ike Turner on piano, Wolf on harmonica, me on guitar. No bass. Just like I tell you, I was playin' the bass part and the lead on my guitar.

So we went on over, went in the studio. We set up our things. And Wolf sung the number. Sam Phillips said, "Let's run it down two, three times. I want to hear it." While we's runnin' it down, he's listenin', but he was settin' at the switchboard all the time. He said, "Hold it right there. I'm gonna roll you now. I want you to put your best in it." And sho 'nuff, he rolled it. And first thing we knowed, he had done recorded "How Many More Years," "Cryin' at Daybreak," "Moanin' at Midnight," "Do the Guitar Boogie," all that stuff. You'd think there was two guitars in there, see. I was playin' all that chords and stuff. I didn't know what I was doin', but I just did it. That's all. I wasn't nervous. When you already used to performin' in a big group of peoples, you don't be nervous. You used to that.

Then Sam Phillips dubbed horn players in between that after we done a couple numbers. I don't know yet how he did it, but he did. Yeah, he hired two or three horn players. I voiced the horns with my guitar, string by string. I'd tell the horn player, "You take the third," and, "You take the fourth." If a trumpet player was there, I'd say, "You take the first." And it come up a lyrical thing, like harmony! I say [to Phillips], "Now, you just say one thing: the key you want it in, and let that harmony buzz out they horns." And it worked. Later he done put some bass to it. How he do this, I never did find out. Then Wolf hired a bass player called Rogers. Tall, black-skinned guy. He was from Memphis. Rogers used to play with Tuff Green.

When I first heard "Moanin' at Midnight" on the radio, I knowed who it was. But it was funny to me. I say to myself: "Listen at me!" [*Laughs.*] Yes sir. I said, "That's us playin' that!" Then all my friends and family heard it. Wolf went to gettin' bookings, oh man, all over then. We played in Little Rock a lot of times. McGehee, Arkansas. Now that was the best club for us. I forget the name of it but it was in McGehee. I just liked the way the place was lined up. It was in the summertime. They had fresh air goin' through there and everything. The tables were sittin' way out, they wasn't backed up to the bandstand. Bandstand revolved, go around, and the lights come on. It was nice. It was a widow lady's place.

A guy named Struction [William Johnson], he played piano with Wolf and us back in Memphis. He was a music writer. He went to writin' for Wolf, writin' his music. Wolf put the harp down for this number that he wrote, "Oh, Red." He recorded that with alto, tenor, and baritone. Good honkin' sax, yes sir! Struction, he didn't stay with us too long. He traveled with us three or four times on the road. That was it. Then he'd go back with this boy, he was a hell of a musician, Phineas Newborn. They banded up together. Hosea Kennard played piano with Wolf too, in Chicago. He was a nice little young man. He wasn't hardly old enough to be goin' in places, but Wolf got him in, you know, so he could play with him. Hosea stayed with us a good while. He got along real nice with Wolf. See, he didn't drink. He didn't drink, smoke, or do anything.

Wolf came up to Chicago before I did 'cause I and Sammy Lewis was playin' together in Arkansas. Wolf came to Chicago and he had a little band hooked up here. So Chess and Wolf's guitar player, Jody Williams, got into it or somethin'. I don't know how exactly it was but anyway, Jody couldn't record with Wolf no more—for Chess. And Wolf came back down and got me. Yeah, he drove all the way back down there and got me. Brought me here, and we was playin' at the 708 Club on 47th Street. We played there that Saturday night. And Monday morning, he got up, come and got me and taken me down to Chess, down to the studio. We set there and talked. Leonard Chess said, "You with Wolf now. I cuts a lot of records. You gonna be my guitar man in the studio." He said, "All of them that want a guitar, we'll just use you on every set." 'Cause he knew I could play. And so he hired me. I was on Willie Mabon's numbers. I was on a few of Eddie Taylor's numbers, playin' bass.

It wasn't hard gettin' used to city life. I'll tell you one thing: I was more interested in my music when I got here in Chicago than I was all the time before. 'Cause I had more music people to meet, and jobs were regular. Guitar players, I met some tough ones. Guitar Red and all them, Sammy Lawhorn—he was a tough guy. Wayne Bennett. Reginald Boyd—he was a teacher, you know. Zeb Hooker—Earl

Hooker they called him. Some of 'em would want me to teach 'em. They'd hang around with me when I lived over on Greenwood. See, we was livin' in Chester's [Howlin' Wolf's] buildin' over there on Greenwood. They'd come around and try and steal your notes and stuff. They'd be watchin' and they still couldn't do it. [*Laughs.*] We mess around. Sometimes we ride around all day. Sometime we set up in the house all day, playin' and foolin' with the guitar and things. Sammy Lawhorn used to come over like that. Eddie Taylor, he used to come over. Homesick James, he used to come around. Elmore James. I never was jealous about showin' what I could play. They would ask me, "How did you do that?" I'd say, "I don't know, man. I'd just think about it and go and do it. That's all." [*Laughs.*]

We never did have cuttin' contests, never did battle at one another like that. Like, if one was playin' some place and the other one walked in, he'd invite you up to play a number or two. We'd go in, play a number or two with 'em, then get down off the bandstand. We wouldn't want to take the crowd away from 'em. No. We'd just have some fun like that.

Who would I rate as top guitarist? I really don't know. That's hard to say. Zeb Hooker, he was tops with that slide. But you take him off that slide, he wasn't nowhere. He didn't know no chords. Louis Myers, now you could say that he was tops 'cause he knowed them chords. Yep. He knowed them chords. Now me and Hubert Sumlin used to stay together. I learned him right smart about guitar.

With Wolf in the '50s, we used to play the Green Door on 63rd, at Sylvio's on Kedzie and Lake, at Walton's Corner on Roosevelt and Fairfield. Oh, a lot of places we used to play—Blue Monday parties or whatever. Out of town too. St. Louis, Rockford, back down South. Everywhere he went, I was there. Never did get too much sleep at that kind of playin'. You'd have to be up all the time. And he'd entertain 'em. He'd crawl around on the bandstand or the bar with his harp, blowin' and singin'.

Wolf was a very strict guy. He didn't want no smokin' on the bandstand, and he didn't want no drinkin' on the bandstand. But when you come down on intermission, you could smoke. We'd come down. We'd sneak in a drink anyway. He'd be laughin' and talkin' with somebody else. We'd be tastin', you know. But he'd rather for you to wait till you get off work. He'd buy it for you when you get off work.

Me and Hubert played together with him a long time, and Earl Phillips. They would fight Wolf. He'd just get mad and go to cussin' and doin' about. I seen him slap Earl Phillips for drinkin', gettin' drunk on the bandstand, and messin' up his music. I would stand up there lookin' at them, 'cause he knowed not to hit me. He knowed not to hit me! One time the union put a $1,000 fine on Wolf. He stopped his fightin'. [*Laughs.*] Then he started fining his men. That's what they talked to him about. They told him, said, "When your mens do wrong, fine 'em. That's your job to put a fine on 'em." And he would give you some days off from playin' too. That hurt badder than anything, you know. That hurt badder than hittin' you and all that kind of stuff. You'd miss that money.

But Wolf had a great sense of humor. He'd laugh at the funny things that people would do in the band. He'd just laugh at you, some things that you do. But some things he'd get mad about. He'd pout all the week, man. I never did dodge him. I'd go to him and ask him for what I wanted. I'd tell him that if he was mad at somebody else, he didn't have to take it out on me. Sometimes he'd get on me. He'd say, "You didn't do like that when you was down there choppin' cotton. You done got up here now in these bright lights in the big city. It's done turned you crazy." He'd make them cracks now.

For a while he had us wearin' a tux. Yeah, we was wearin' tuxedos. And if you wore the wrong color tux for a night, you got fined for that too. And you couldn't talk to Muddy Waters' band. That'd be a fine. See, Muddy was jealous of Wolf recordin', and Wolf was jealous of Muddy. But they finally got together. They got together on that. I talked to 'em [Muddy's band members] anyway. Some of 'em were my best friends. I used to hang around with Jimmy Rogers. I used to hang around with Little Walter right smart. He could be a fighter, but me and Little Walter never had words. Walter had funny ways, but he had respect for entertainers. He was a nice guy. He wouldn't act stuck-up like, not too much.

I left Wolf in '59. I had weaned away from drinkin' when I quit. I left the band and got me a job. I just got tired of music and went on out and got me a job in a factory. This was out west, Bellwood, Illinois. Well, I didn't give up music entirely. Me and Kansas City Red and them went to Rockford. We'd play in Rockford every weekend. We'd go up there and play Friday and Saturday night. Sunday evenin' I'd leave and come back home. Then I'd go to my job and work all the week. I was the lead man. And Slim was on piano, Sunnyland Slim. Roosevelt Reed was the bass player. And Jimmie Lee Robinson on guitar too. We had a good show up there. We'd have some crowds. Red would sing some. Everybody in the band would sing. Jimmie Lee, he sing. And, you know, Sunnyland, he'd sing. We was real easy. One didn't try to put the weight on the other one. We did all right. After Rockford, I didn't fool with playin' with too many people. I just stuck to my job.

I practice regular. Sometime I keep my guitar in my hand as much as an hour and a half or two hours a day. As you can see, I'm still a ladies' man. That girl in there, Diane, I been goin' with her since she's 14 years old. And you know how old she is now? She's 44, and I'm 71. I've been at it just that long. I met her at her mother's house—and she still live with her mother. Yeah, she crazy about her mother. See, they moved into the buildin' I lived in on Wabash. She found out I was a musician. That's how she got to like me. She do's things that I like. I don't have no problem with her. Right now she's cookin' up some beans and stuff for me.

My advice about it? Don't be too tight on a woman. She's already grown. Let her go when she want, and come back when she get ready. Just as long as she have respect for you—that's the way I see it. 'Cause if you too jealous of her or you're too tight on her, she gonna slip and do somethin' anyway. I can't let the guitar worry me and let her worry me too.

JODY WILLIAMS

BY LARRY BIRNBAUM   Jody Williams is hardly remembered today, but in the 1950s he was a Chess studio guitarist; led Howlin' Wolf's band; toured with Charles Brown, Bobby Bland, and Memphis Slim; and cut sessions with Bo Diddley, B.B. King, and a host of others. The record-ed evidence suggests that he strongly influenced Otis Rush (and, by extension, Eric Clapton and Carlos Santana), and if you believe Williams himself, he even made an impression on Elvis Presley. Billy Boy Arnold, with whom Williams recorded classics like "I Wish You Would" and "I Ain't Got

You," says Jody was "the number-one guitar player in Chicago at the time. He was the most creative guy."

In the '60s, however, Williams gave up on music, frustrated over a failed lawsuit (claiming that Mickey & Sylvia's hit "Love Is Strange" was adapted from his work on Billy Stewart's "Billy's Blues") and bitter that he had never shared in the profits he made for so many others. He took classes in electronics and became a Xerox engineer, retiring in 1994 after 26 years. While lesser players of his era were redis-covered and rerecorded, Williams steadfastly avoided the blues scene, although he's remained at the same address on the South Side of Chicago for three decades. "I don't go to no clubs," he says. "Nobody knows where I am 'cause they don't see me hangin' out in those joints. I'd rather keep my distance."

Williams recorded a number of singles as a leader, singing on some, but these have never been collected on one album. Four tracks appear on a Relic CD, *Cool Playing Blues,* and six can be found on a rare Red Lightnin LP, *The Leading Brand.* Another Red Lightnin compilation, *When Girls Do It,* includes two cuts recorded under the name Sugar Boy Williams and attributed to Jody in the liner notes, but though the songs sound like him, Williams disclaims any knowledge of them and denies having recorded as Sugar Boy. As for his sideman credits, Williams simply can't remember them all. "It was a whole lot of changes back in them days," he says. "Things was happenin' so fast over a short period of years, it's kind of hard to say what took place when."

"I GOT HUNGRY FOR KNOWLEDGE" Born Joseph Leon Williams in Mobile, Alabama, on February 3, 1935, Jody moved to Chicago at the age of five. "When I started off I used to play the harmonica," he says. "My favorites was the Harmonicats—'Peg o' My Heart' and stuff like that. I was on the radio on the amateur hour in Chicago, and then I started doin' some of the theaters, talent shows and stuff, and that's how I met Bo Diddley. He had a guitar, and somebody was playin' a wash-tub with a clothesline and a plank on the side with the tension drawn on it nice and tight. It sounded like a bass fiddle. I did my thing at the theater there, and they came out with their guitar and the washtub. I liked that, so we got together backstage. I was playin' harmonica with the guitar and washtub, and it sounded pretty good together.

"I had never been up close to the guitar like that before, and I began to take interest in guitar playin'. The next week I spotted a guitar in a pawnshop, an elec-tric Silvertone, so I told my mother about it. It was $32.50, so she bought it for me, and the following week Bo showed me how to run the bass line. He was playin' out on the street corner, passin' the hat, and so we had two guitars and a washtub, and I played the bass line. This guy Casey Jones, he trained chickens—he had chickens jumpin' through hoops and everything—and he performed on the street corner. He'd be on one corner with the chickens, hollerin', 'No dime, no show!' and Bo Diddley and I, we'd be on the other corner playin'.

"Word got around, and there was a guy who did the shows at the old Indiana Theater. Come Saturday, the theater would close up at 12:00, and then they'd have what they called the *Midnight Ramble.* They'd have a six- or seven-piece band, and Muddy Waters would appear down there with the band. So the guy gave Bo Diddley and I a chance down there. That's one way we got some exposure, and after that we did a thing at the Rhumboogie Lounge. We were like an added attraction, and when the band had an intermission, that's when we'd go play.

"After I started playin' the guitar, I really got hungry for knowledge. I got me a teacher, and he wanted me to run the scales and stuff, but I wasn't interested. I just wanted to play some music. I had hung around in clubs, and I met Muddy Waters and James Cotton. So I finally got myself a group, and I was playin' the blues. I did background stuff, and then I learned how to accompany myself while I sang. I learned one blues song—I forgot exactly which one it was—and I would wait till everybody got about half-stoned and then I'd do my one song and sit down. I was the only one in the band that was sober all night long. I was the only one directly in the money come pay time, 'cause everybody else drank up the money.

"There was a harmonica player we called Pot; his name was Henry Strong. He was Muddy Waters' harmonica player, but we all used to play together—me on the guitar, Otis Spann on the piano, Pot on the harp, and another harmonica player we had occasionally who was Little Walter's uncle. All four of us had a flat together at 38th and Wabash, and in those days we played at the Tick Tock Lounge. And little by little, the band started to scatter. Otis Spann, he went with Muddy Waters, and you're not gonna find a piano player like Otis Spann. But at one time we all played together, and then we gave it up."

Through Spann, Williams began doing session work for Chess, and when Howlin' Wolf arrived in Chicago, leaving most of his band behind in Memphis, Jody backed him on such all-time blues classics as "Evil" and "Forty Four." "That's how I met B.B. King," he says. "Wolf and I was in the studio, recording. I'm sittin' there doin' 'Forty Four' or somethin', and the guy come in the studio. I didn't know who he was. He came in, and he stood there at the door, and I noticed he kept watchin' me. I just kept on playin'. I was playin' B.B. King all over the place; I could play just like B.B. King. So we stopped after we finished recordin' a couple of tunes and started listenin' to the playback, and Wolf called me over. He said, 'I want you to meet a friend of mine from West Memphis—B.B. King.' And I almost fainted.

"But B.B. said that rarely had he seen someone play his stuff and play it right, and we became good friends right away. And a couple of days later, him and I did some recordings." Released in 1954 under Spann's name, "Five Spot" (spun off from Roy Milton's "Junior Jives") bears out Williams' claim, as he follows King's solo with a strikingly similar one of his own. "I could adapt very easily to certain styles," says Jody, "and B.B. was one. Another style that I adapted to was Johnny Moore, the guitar player with Charles Brown. I can play all of that type of stuff. I first met Charles Brown just when he was makin' a comeback, so I got the call, and we did a bunch of one-nighters together. That was one of the first big-name groups that I went on tour with."

The jazzy, sophisticated influence of Brown and Moore is apparent on one of Williams' first solo recordings, "I Feel So All Alone," which remained in the can until Relic issued *Cool Playing Blues*. But Al Benson's Blue Lake label did release one Williams single—"Easy Lovin'," backed with "Lookin' for My Baby"—under the name of Little Papa Joe. By that time Williams had parted with Wolf, whose band he'd led for two years. "Back in those days, union scale was low enough as it was," he says, "and then he wanted to start messin' with the money. I did some singles with Memphis Slim after I met Wolf, and I closed up with Howlin' Wolf one Sunday night at Sylvio's cocktail lounge on the West Side. And the following Wednesday I was up in Asheville, North Carolina, with Memphis Slim. Then we went down in Florida and played a dance on Saturday night."

STEPPING OUT While still in Wolf's band, Williams recorded with harmonica player Billy Boy Arnold, who had played with him in Bo Diddley's street-corner group and without him on Diddley's first Chess sessions. Behind Bo's back, Arnold recruited Williams to cut half a dozen tracks for Vee Jay in 1955, including the irresistibly vibrant "I Wish You Would" and the comical "I Ain't Got You." "Matter of fact," says Williams, "I wrote the first song he did, "I Was Fooled." I don't know if I got any money out of it, but back in those days they was really rippin' us off." Leonard Chess, feeling double-crossed, saw to it that the records got no airplay, and the following year Williams rejoined Bo Diddley's band, without Arnold.

"Bo Diddley and I did tours with Roy Hamilton," he says. "Him and Bill Haley were headlinin' the show, and then there was Frankie Lymon, the Platters, Shirley and Lee, the Five Keys, Clyde McPhatter, the Drifters, Joe Turner, and the Teen Queens. Back in those days, you got a show for your money. I did the guitar work behind Joe Turner because no one else could play all those tunes, and I played guitar with the Teen Queens." Back in Chicago, Williams recorded on such Diddley classics as "I'm Lookin' for a Woman" (based on his own "Lookin' for My Baby"), "Hey, Bo Diddley," "Mona," "Say, Boss Man," and the scorching "Who Do You Love." If you listen close to the records," he says, "you'll hear me switchin' back and forth between lead and rhythm."

Bo Diddley has been credited with the discovery of soul singer Billy Stewart, but Williams insists that he was Stewart's sponsor. "Thanks to me, he became the big recording artist that he did before he died," Jody says. "I called him up on the stage and let him do some tunes. I saw he had a nice voice, good entertainer, good stage presence, so I wrote some songs and went down to the record company with him." Stewart's first record, "Billy's Blues," featuring Williams' winding, stinging guitar over a calypso beat, bears a remarkable resemblance to Mickey & Sylvia's pop smash "Love Is Strange," also released in 1956. Alleging that Bo Diddley had given the song to Mickey Baker, Williams engaged Benny Goodman's brother Gene as his attorney and filed suit.

Meanwhile, Williams toured with Bobby Bland and Junior Parker, played locally in the bands of Billy Boy Arnold and Otis Rush, and recorded with such artists as Rush, Floyd Dixon, Jimmy Rogers, and even white big band leader Buddy Morrow. In 1957 he cut a single under his own name—"You May," backed with the instrumental "Lucky Lou"—on Chess's Argo subsidiary. Otis Rush, accompanying Buddy Guy on Guy's first Chess single, "Sit and Cry," copied Williams' solo from "You May" virtually note for note and, to all aural appearances, transformed "Lucky Lou" into his own minor-blues masterpiece, "All Your Love." The latter was covered by Eric Clapton with John Mayall's Bluesbreakers and adapted by Fleetwood Mac's Peter Green into "Black Magic Woman," later a hit for Santana. This time, however, Williams did not sue, contrary to published reports.

In 1958 Williams was drafted into the army and sent to Germany, putting his suit against Mickey & Sylvia on hold for a year and a half. "Elvis Presley and I went in at the same time," says Jody. "He was in an armored cavalry outfit, and I was in Special Services. I was stationed in Dachau, where they had the concentration camp, and we would patrol up at the German–Czechoslovakian border, and when I'd come back, I'd go to the service club. So I'm on my way up there one day, and sure enough, Elvis was sittin' right in front of the club in a jeep, because they made him a jeep driver. So I walked over to him and introduced myself, and he knew who I was. He told me he caught my act with Bo Diddley at the Apollo Theater and also at a theater in Brooklyn. He did like Michael Jackson; he'd go out in disguise."

Discharged, Williams finally got his day in court, but a jury rejected his case. He picked up where he had left off, recording with Bobby Davis, Bobby Charles, the Daylighters, and others and cutting his own singles for obscure labels like Herald, Raines, and Yulando. But by the mid '60s he had had enough. "As the years passed, I thought about all the money I had lost, and it left a bad taste in my mouth," he says. He went to school and became a radio and television technician, then moved on to computers and photocopiers. Today he runs a copy shop in Chicago and recently opened another one in Nashville. "With my video equipment," he says, "I can capture any frame or individual scene, and my printers print a picture of this that I can put on a greeting card or a button or on a clock. I can also put that same picture on a T-shirt or a cap or a mug." Asked if he has any plans to go back into music, he replies, "Not really. Not less'n I could get lucky and win big money on the lotto where I could just live a life of ease."

HUBERT SUMLIN

BY JIM KENT For 23 years Hubert Sumlin played gui-
tar behind Howlin' Wolf. His classic parts in "Spoonful,"
"Smokestack Lightnin'," "Wang Dang Doodle," "I Ain't
Superstitious," and other modern standards influenced a
generation of blues-rockers, notably Jeff Beck, Duane
Allman, Peter Green, Stevie Ray Vaughan, and the Rolling
Stones. Jimi Hendrix once cited him as his favorite guitarist,
and Eric Clapton told *Guitar Player* in 1976: "For a long time
I'd really wanted to meet Hubert because he did some things
that freaked me out when I was picking up the guitar—that

ow,' just the weirdest playing. He's truly amazing."
are good summations of Sumlin's style. He responded to
ing songs around a single droning chord by creating
....tra-like riffs, and jagged, staccato fills. His solos were
, ...common vibrato and unexpected twists and turns.

Hubert Sumlin was born November 16, 1931, in Greenwood, Mississippi, and raised in Hughes, Arkansas. He took up guitar at age 11, and was soon sneaking out to juke joints to hear Chester Arthur Burnett, a.k.a. Howlin' Wolf, who befriended him. Working by day as a plantation hand, Sumlin was inspired by Robert Johnson and Charley Patton 78s. He formed his first musical alliance with James Cotton, and in 1954 he joined Howlin' Wolf for a short Southern tour. A few weeks later, he accepted Wolf's invitation to move to Chicago and become his co-guitarist. (Pat Hare, Jody Williams, and Willie Johnson also played guitar in Wolf's various lineups during the early to mid 1950s.)

During his first months in town, Sumlin attended the Chicago Conservatory of Music, studying scales and learning to read music. He soon abandoned using a guitar pick in favor of the fingers-only approach that became a hallmark of his style. Sumlin accompanied Wolf on "Forty Four," "Evil Is Going On," "Smokestack Lightnin'," and other tracks, and then in 1956 quit to tour with Muddy Waters. That association lasted about a year, and then Hubert rejoined Wolf. He stayed at Wolf's side until the end, playing everything from segregated Southern roadhouses to New York's Apollo Theater. In 1959 he appeared on Wolf's first album, *Moanin' in the Moonlight,* and the following year recorded "Wang Dang Doodle," "Back Door Man," and "Spoonful." He recalls using a Gretsch electric and an early Gibson Les Paul during this period and describes his stylistic hybrid of lead and rhythm as "'twixt and between."

The early 1960s brought such Sumlin-fueled Howlin' Wolf hits as "The Red Rooster," "Down in the Bottom," "Shake for Me," "Goin' Down Slow," "I Ain't Superstitious," "Do the Do," and "Built for Comfort." The band's mid-1960s European tours brought Sumlin the opportunity to record as a leader, and one of his final projects with Wolf, *The London Howlin' Wolf Sessions*, featured the Rolling Stones rhythm section and Eric Clapton, who presented him with a Stratocaster that he's used for many years.

With Wolf's death in 1976, Sumlin continued playing with the band. He worked clubs with pianist Sunnyland Slim and recorded the solo album *Groove* for Europe's Black and Blue label. In 1978 he played on five standout tracks with Eddie Shaw for Alligator Records' *Living Chicago Blues, Vol. 1.* By then, his original Les Paul was enshrined in a glass case in his living room, and he was favoring a Gibson ES-335 and a recent-model Les Paul.

Since then, the quiet, bespectacled bluesman has concentrated on playing under his own name. For a while he was reluctant to cover Wolf's tunes, but by the late 1980s he was playing "Down in the Bottom," "Hidden Charms," and others. As Jon Pareles noted in a *New York Times* review from that era, Sumlin was still hitting it hard: "Mr. Sumlin is a guitarist of few notes, masterfully placed. With his raw tone and an extraordinary variety of attacks, he mixes singing blues phrases and slashes of sheer texture—plunking out low riffs, squeezing out delicate sighs in the upper register, making single notes moan, or suddenly swooping down for a metallic shriek. Melodically, his solos are almost abstract; against the chugging rhythms of the band, they are terse and cutting."

In 1987, Sumlin released his first American album under his own name, Black Top's *Hubert Sumlin's Blues Party.* "I'm 55 years old," Sumlin said upon its release, "and I ain't never had a record out in the United States since I been playing all these years with Wolf. I'm very happy about it—it's been too long." The guitarist was soon the subject of a film, *Hubert Sumlin: Livin' the Blues,* shot by Juke Joint Films in Chicago, Boston, Texas, and Mississippi. Along with extensive Sumlin interviews and archival photographs and film clips, the documentary features guest appearances by Ronnie Earl, Stevie Ray Vaughan, and James Cotton. Since then, Sumlin has released *Heart & Soul* on Blind Pig and *Healing Feeling* on Black Top.

The following recollections, presented in Hubert Sumlin's own words, were gathered by Jim Kent during the filming of *Hubert Sumlin: Livin' the Blues,* and were first published as *Living Blues'* September/October 1989 cover story, "My Years with Wolf."

—*Jas Obrecht*

HUBERT SUMLIN: "MY YEARS WITH WOLF" I was born in the Delta, down in Mississippi, Greenwood, right beside the Yazoo River. My daddy was a sharecropper—a pusher—who used to work the other men on the farm, but he could work anybody there under the ground. He could pick 600 pounds of cotton in a day, way before sundown. He also made a living selling moonshine, which he made himself in his own still. He had three stills in a swamp—nothing but him and rattlesnakes and crocodiles. I followed that dude one morning, man, and he caught me. So he learned me how to make whiskey. The boss man knew he was doing it, but he left him alone because he was such a good worker; my people were good workers. There were 13 of us in this family; everybody had to contribute, otherwise we never would have made it. When we got around the table to eat, we ate a whole mountain of food.

My whole family was musically inclined. My sister sang gospel music—all my family sang in the choir. Mama was sanctified Baptist and she put us all in church. That's the first time I ever played on a guitar, in that old Baptist church, with this old Deacon: me on guitar, him on guitar, everybody else singing. My brother, A.D., who was about ten years older than me, he played the guitar. He made him a one-string, upside the wall, with a snuff bottle in it. These brooms used to have this baling wire wrapped around the straws, and cost, at that time, I guess about 35¢. We had three or four of 'em. So my brother taken that broom, unwind the damn wire off it, and drove him a nail in the wall, put another at the bottom and tied that wire up to the wall. Stuck my mama's snuff bottle in there and pulled it down till he got this tone off the wire. When he got ready to change the tone he raised the bottle up, get back to *C,* raise it up to *G,* and only one string.

I'm looking at him playing, and I'm just a little dude; and I'm watching what he's doin'. My mama bought him his first guitar after he learned this one wire upside the wall. He could play that so good—even had him a slide. She paid a whole week's pay for that guitar. She was working for these white folks at the funeral home and was making eight dollars a week. At that time for eight dollars you could go to the grocery store and you had t o have a mule wagon to bring the groceries home. So my mama bought my brother this guitar with all her money.

I didn't say nothing, I'm playing these strings on the wall. Since my brother done got the guitar, he left them alone. He done got promoted. He figured he done got to the flower bed of ease. He started to making notes on this guitar and started to put them together. I said, "Son of a gun, I'm hearing something now, and it's beautiful." About four months later, he's playing this guitar. And he got a couple of tunes sounding real good.

Now, I'm getting tired of these strings upside the wall, so I figured I'd go to him and ask him, "Hey, learn me one of these songs that I been hearing you playing." And he told me, "You better get back to those strings on the wall, 'cause I ain't gonna learn you nothing."

Later my mama come walking home from the job and she saw me—I was just a little dude, seven or eight—and she saw me crying and said, "What's the matter?" I said, "Well, I asked him would he learn me, and he hit me, knocked me across the yard." She called him in the house, and he got smart with my mama. She said, "You mean you won't learn him? Pull off you clothes." And she tied him to the bed. She went out and got some shingles off the house and tore his ass up. Then, later, my daddy come, he wanted to know what happened, and so then he give him a whipping too. After he done did what he did, my mother went to town and bought me my own guitar, just like his. So I notice him, watch what he did, where he placed his fingers, and so I got the shit together. I had me one tune, one of his'n; I still know it today. I stayed on that one tune until I learned how to get me another note, and another note, another string. That's how I learned.

I liked it so well, I carried it to the field where I was working. By this time, I got promoted from mules to tractors. But I'm still in the fields and I had plowed, I guess, about 40 acres that day with a big old John Deere. I had brought the guitar to the field with me. I parked that tractor but I left it running. I got on over under a shade tree and start to playing that guitar. So the boss man, he rode up on his horse, slipped up on me. I didn't hear him no way, 'cause I was playing, the tractor was running. "Bap, bap." This big old John Deere. He saw me down there and he got mad. "What the . . . You supposed to be plowing." He grabbed that guitar away from me and broke it across the tractor wheel. I flew upside his head, and I hit him—I'm big enough to be plowing, I figured I'm big enough to hit him.

I didn't do no more work that day. I went home and told my mama and she went and blessed him out. My mama sanctified too. So the man came back the next day and brought me a $16 guitar. He said, "I don't want to see this guitar in that field." I said, "Yes, sir."

So then I say, "I think I'm good enough now to play with somebody." Here come James Cotton. He used to come over to my house. He wasn't doin' anything and I wasn't doin' anything, but we was trying to learn. He used to come over to the house and bring his harp; me and him would sit around. My mama used to throw us out of the house and put us out in the yard, 'cause she didn't like that, you know. She was religious, sanctified. She said, "Get out of here with that stuff— y'all playing the blues. Get out there in that yard." We had to get out in the yard, and we got together. I went from Cotton to Wolf, Wolf to Muddy, back to Wolf, and that's where I stayed. All this in three years' time. I'm the only one in the family that got out. I ended up workin' with the people I wanted to work with, that I admired all them years: Howlin' Wolf, Muddy Waters, Jimmy Reed.

The first somebody I was listening to was Charley Patton, and all these guys, old guys, I ain't never met. But they inspired me, by listening, and I said, "Oh, my, one day, if these guys be living, I'm gonna be playing with some of these guys. I gonna be doin' some of what they doin'." All this good music, all this good stuff. People didn't understand what the blues was until they found out it's a thing we born with. In other words, I had 'em all the time and didn't know it. Somethin' about 'em; I didn't feel right unless I was around these guys.

The first time I saw Wolf he was playing at this juke joint, this big old honky tonk up on cement blocks, right down besides the Mississippi River, called Silkhairs. That was after we had moved to Arkansas. I was still a boy, maybe 11, 12 years old, in the town of Seyppel. You could crawl up under the pilings, man, and hear everything that was going on. I heard a lot of those musicians that way when I was still a boy. I knew he was playing there, but they didn't allow no youngsters in that club, 'cause they had booze and gambling going on in there.

So the first night I got up under the house, next to the band, where Wolf was playing—only they didn't call him Wolf then, he was known as Chester in those days—"Bigfoot Chester." I heard so much music that night, I couldn't believe it. I done got interested now. I had got by—slipped in, heard him, and slipped back home. My mama and them ain't noticed. By this particular time I'm getting bold. I been over there long enough to know now. I said, "I'm going over here and see these folks. I got to see the Wolf." They was lining up at the door; you know how they stand up at a door trying to get in, some of those ladies just stand like that— men too. So I just crawled between their legs and ain't nobody know nothin'. I had just made it inside and the man caught me, crying, "Get him out, get him out."

So then I went around to the back of the club, where they had all these Coca-Cola cases piled up. I climbed up to the top of that stack to where I could see everything that was going on, 'cause there was a window right behind the drums. Well, these Coke cases started to come unbalanced, and I fell through the window into the club, in the middle of a song. Over on the old Wolf's head I landed—right on the dude's head. He said, "Let him stay, let him stay. Bring him a chair." That's right, I sat there. The lady brought me a chair. I sat between Willie Johnson, Pat Hare, and Junior Parker, which he had at this time. He didn't buy me nothin'; he had the lady bring me a glass of water, and I sat there. I stayed with him that whole night, and when the show was over he said, "You live around here, boy?" and he took me home in his car. When he got there he made me wait in the car while he went in to see mama. And he told her, "Don't punish him, mother. He just wants to hear the music." That's the first time I saw the Wolf, and I followed him ever since.

Next time I saw him, I was almost grown. That was in about 1948. Wolf was just out of the army, and he was playing around there and still farming during the day. Ike Turner caught up with him and took him to the studio and he recorded "How Many More Years" [in Memphis, 1951], which was a big hit in the South at that time. He had got him this show on the radio [KWEM, West Memphis] where he could sing. And he was also farming; he always did farming. He was about 40 years old at this time and had been working on his daddy's farm since he was a boy. He was called "Bullcow" then because even as a boy he was bigger than any-body else. Charley Patton used to come around there in those days, and he showed Wolf some guitar. Sonny Boy [Rice Miller] was married to Wolf's sister, and he showed him how to blow harp.

Sonny Boy was a kind of drifter, and Wolf used to travel around with him some-times, scuffling for money on the streets. He told me about the last time they played together, somewhere in Mississippi, pass the hat stuff. Wolf playing guitar and Sonny Boy on harp, with the money in a bucket between them. They had played a while and made a few bucks, and Sonny Boy start to looking at that money. He told Wolf he had to use the bathroom, and he said, "Look here, there's too much money in here. You can't watch the money and play the guitar both." So Sonny Boy took the money and left Wolf with the empty bucket. Wolf, he kept playing for a while and made a few more pennies. But still Sonny Boy didn't come back. So he started to wondering what happened. Wolf got up and went into the washroom and saw the window was up, Sonny Boy was gone, the money was gone, and Wolf had the empty bucket. He said he looked for him for a year to kill him.

Anyway, Ike Turner got together again with Wolf to play on a record for RPM Records called "Riding at Midnight," with Willie Johnson and Pat Hare on guitar. This was along about 1951. Wolf's radio show had done run out. He started to thinking that making records might be easier than farming. So he left his band and went up to Chicago.

When he first got there he stayed at Muddy Waters' house for about two months. And Muddy introduced him around. Muddy was on the road a good bit in those days, so he took Wolf and introduced him to Sylvio, Booby and Mutt at the Zanzibar, and Ray and Ben Gold at the 708 Club. When Muddy went on the road, Wolf just stepped into his shoes in the three places where he was playing. He didn't have a band at that time, so he picked up some musicians to fill the gig. He had Henry Gray on piano, Sam Lay on drums, sometimes he got Jimmy Rogers to play guitar. But he was hooked up with Muddy and Little Walter, so he got with Johnny Littlejohn. Sometimes he'd have Eddie Taylor with him. Later he got together with Jody Williams.

Wolf had a problem getting musicians to stay with him. I'm the only one that lasted all those years. He was hard on a man, particularly if he'd catch 'em high; he'd pull 'em down off the bandstand and tell them, "Sit down, sit down, you ain't doing it." He always did like to give a good performance, and he was bad about firing a guy. He'd lay a man off for two, three weeks. Then he'd bring them back if he thought they'd got their mind right. So he had a hard time keeping musicians. They'd work for him at first because they liked the music, but they didn't like him.

So Wolf sent down to West Memphis to get me to come up to Chicago and play in his band. I was playing around with James Cotton at that time. We had a little outfit, and we were playing the jukes, fish fries, and wherever we got some people together. They'd put in some money—sometimes 50¢, a dollar. When we got up to makin' $2.50, that was top salary. We had Pat Hare, the guitar player that later got together with Bobby Bland, and Willie Nix on drums. We didn't have no bass player. Cotton had got him a show on the radio and recorded "Cotton Crop Blues" for Sun label.

I asked Cotton should I go, and he said I'd make more money with Wolf than I would with him. So I caught that train, and Wolf met me at Twelfth Street Station, which ain't no more in Chicago—they tore it down. But he met me at the station. Willie Johnson came up at that same time, so we made the band. When I got there my room rent was paid up and my union card and everything, so we went to work.

At first I was scared, nervous, but I shouldn't have been after playing with Cotton. All them name musicians which I had heard about and read about and heard on record was there, such as Little Walter, Eddie Boyd, Elmore James, Memphis Slim, Big Bill Broonzy—all these guys was working. I said, "Man, what am I getting into here?" After all, I say, "Oh, my, so what? You with Wolf. You as good as they is." The first somebody I played with in Chicago was Harmonica George Smith. We had us two weeks before we started to play, so I started out in his group. Then we went to work. The first week that we went to work—the first month— Wolf had Chicago sewed up, in the palm of his hand. That's how hot he was.

I played a couple of weeks with my back turned to the public, but the Wolf got me out of that. He got tired of it, and one night he said, "Ladies and gentlemen, let's give the drummer a nice round of applause." And he introduced the whole band—piano player, bass—and I knew he was saving me for something. So he said, "Now this is my guitar player, this is Hubert. Let's give him a nice round of applause for playing with his butt turned to the people." And everybody there fell down screaming and carrying on; you should have seen me turn around. He sure fixed me, man. But I come to thank him for it; he shamed me out of my nervousness—sometimes you have to do people that way.

Sometimes I'd mess up on changes and things, 'cause I was new with the band, and Wolf, he got tired of it. One day he sent me to school [Chicago Conservatory of Music] just to learn my keyboards and scales and so forth, so I could know what I was doin'. The man I studied under was 66 years old, and he played opera guitar. But he could play anything, the blues, and I got to love the man. So after he passed, I just quit and said, "Well, I know enough anyway."

You could walk down the street, out of one club into another, there was so many. Elmore [James] here, and Muddy Waters down there. It was great. We had a band going every night until four o'clock in the morning. Sometimes they'd just get up and close the fucking doors, and play all night long. After the gig was over, five o'clock or so in the morning, we'd go into the studio. That's when we'd go to record.

The first time Wolf took me down to Chess studios, we did "All Night Boogie," with me and Jody Williams on guitar. We got in there, and I heard this guy screaming at me. "He didn't do that right. Take it again." I said, "What's this? I ain't gonna like this guy." Wolf said, "That's the man. He's up in the booth behind the glass." That was how I first met Phil Chess. Wolf told him right from the beginning, "Don't talk to him no more. You want something done, you ask me. I'll tell him what to be doing." From then on he always asked Wolf; he didn't speak to me no more. We did "No Place to Go," which started Wolf off pretty good. But the next record we did was "Evil," and that really took off all over. We had the Chess rhythm guys, Otis Spann, Willie Dixon, and Earl Phillips behind us. Then we did "Forty Four," which also did well.

I had heard a lot of records, and I was playing so close to that sound. But I got tired of hearing that and I wanted to be me. I never was able to find myself being

Albert King or find myself being B.B. or find myself being Bobby; I played with a straight pick for about eight years, but it didn't sound right to me. I got down in the basement of my house, although I had been playing all that while, had already recorded with Cotton and Wolf, and tried to get my own style. I felt like I was just running all over myself, and I said, "I just want to be me." I got down on my knees and I prayed; I did some serious praying. It come to me all at once— throw the damned pick away and be yourself. That's when I discovered I had a tone of my own. You ain't gonna miss with your fingers.

I found out I was closer to Wolf than a lot of musicians are to each other. I was by him like Spann was to Muddy Waters. I said, "Hey, this is the man's voice, this is me." The music and the voice. We got to be so close, like father and son, the way Eddie Taylor was with Jimmy Reed. Hubert was Wolf, Wolf was Hubert. That's the way we had it, that's the way it was. I got to where I knew what he wanted before he asked for it, because I could feel the man. I just did what came natural and it seemed to fit.

We used to have our falling outs, though. He would try to talk to me and keep me from getting a swelled head. He would say, "Look here, Hubert, I think you're good. I like you, but you ain't great. Don't never let nobody tell you that you're the best in the world, 'cause, in my book, you all right, but guitar players are a dime a dozen with me. You know that, don't you?" I said, "Yeah, well, I know that." I said it, but I didn't believe it. I thought now he really done got down to the nitty-gritty with me. I be the next one to go. Now at this time, I could get anything, anybody I want. I made my name in that town; I was very famous. That's what I thought.

So I guess it got around that I wasn't satisfied playing with the Wolf. Muddy Waters happened to be looking for a guitar player to go on the road with him; he was a star and they were always traveling. Muddy offered me twice as much money as Wolf. He sent his chauffeur to the club, over to the Zanzibar where we was playing. Muddy was playing over at Sylvio's and his chauffeur came over and told me Muddy wanted to talk to me. They had four o'clock license at Sylvio's, so after we finished, about two o'clock, Wolf said, "Come on, let's go." And I said, "No, I'm going over here to see Muddy." Man, he offered me a $15 raise. So I didn't say nothing, but I went home and thought about it. Two days later, Wolf started to telling me I wasn't playing right and such, and I said, "Uh huh. Well, I'm steppin' down and going on the road with Muddy Waters." He said, "What? All right, man. Leave my guitar. Go on, git out." Man, he was changing colors. I knew he was mad. I left to go with Muddy. Wolf hired Willie Johnson back to replace me, like he was back in Mississippi.

Every day at 12:00, I'd get together with Otis Spann in Muddy's basement, and he'd show me Muddy's stuff. I wasn't playing too much lead at this time. Other words, my time was bad too, because I was playing with different people that didn't have time too good. Otis would show me notes, what guitar players do—what Muddy was doin'. And when I wasn't placing my notes right, he showed me on that piano. He would hit those notes, and I learned. We were right up under Muddy Waters' bed. Muddy, he'd come down and see we was doin' all right, so he'd go back upstairs and go to sleep. But Spann and I would work for two hours down there every day. He learned me a lot, man. Muddy wouldn't even pick up a guitar while I was with him. And I played on his [1956] records "Rock Me," "Just to Be With You," "Got My Mojo Working." James Cotton was there too, so we got back together. I worked with Chuck Berry on some records too. I helped him out on "Deep Feelings" and "School Day." I played second guitar behind him.

I stayed with Muddy a year and we got along good, but what got to me was being on the road. Sometimes we'd drive a thousand miles to make it to the next gig. Get off at three, four o'clock in the morning, get right in the car and start to driving. One time when we were comin' back from Florida. Spann had stopped and bought him a pistol—Saturday night special. So we all bought them. I got me a little old gun, it just fit in my coat. Well, we had made it almost back to Chicago. Muddy was in front of us with his chauffeur; he always did drive separate. So he went on and just outside of Chicago the police pulled us over. He got Spann out of the car and come up with his gun, so then he hauled us all out. "Hands up against the car." They pulled a gun from every man in that car. They called for another car; kept their guns on us the whole time. They thought they had captured the black mafia or something. We all got thrown away in jail; we'd be there today without Muddy. He came down as soon as he found out and made them let us go. But they kept the guns.

Finally we had this set of one-nighters—40 one-night stands in a row. Then when we had just finished, we drove all the way back to Chicago and had to open up at the 708 Club the next night. After all these 40 one-nighters. That night I was playing on the bandstand, Muddy had got him a fifth of Old Grand Dad, and he was sitting out front with this young girl. Now we done played a whole set, Muddy hadn't been to the bandstand yet. When he did come, he sang two songs, and it was time for intermission.

Now, we had this fan to keep us cool sitting right in front of me. I had my hand on the guitar, and I pushed that steel fan with my other hand [and received an electric shock]. Fire come from my mouth; I couldn't turn it loose. So at intermission, I told Muddy I couldn't play out the night. He got mad at me, called me all kind of things, and raised his foot to kick me. I grabbed him. Here come Spann with a trace chain, gonna whip me about Muddy. I had ahold of Muddy, and every time Spann tried to get me with that chain, I put Muddy next to him. Every time he hit Muddy. I said, "Man, when you get right, I'll turn you loose." So finally, I turned him loose and jumped back; we went on to the bandstand and played the night out.

I called Wolf from the club. I said, "Hey, man, that's it. Whoever you got in there, they got to go. I'm coming back." He said, "No problem." After the gig, he met us at Muddy's house. He told Muddy, "Next time you do that, man, I'll kill you over him." Muddy didn't speak to me in a year, but we finally come back to being friends. Things were never right between him and Wolf, though. Ever since Wolf come to Chicago and started to taking over, Muddy didn't like him too well. A kind of rivalry started up between them about who was the boss of the blues. After I went with Muddy, Wolf didn't speak to him no more. When they'd get on the same bill together, like at Ann Arbor Blues Fest, Wolf would go up first and play so long that Muddy wouldn't want to follow him. Then Muddy'd get up and try to outdo him.

After that I never left the Wolf no more. I thought he'd be around forever, forever. Oh, we'd still have our fights and stuff. Sometimes we'd come to taking swings at one another. One time he threw me out of the studio. We was fixing to record "Smokestack Lightnin'," and something set him off. He threw me out, fired me, and sent me home. I left the Chess building; it was almost dawn. I went on home and didn't come back. Wolf sent to the West Coast and flew in all these guitar players, but couldn't none of 'em please him. He finally drove to my house and sent somebody in to tell me he wanted to see me. I said, "That's fine." But I didn't go nowhere. I just sat there in my living room. My wife said, "Don't you think you should go and see . . . " But I just sat there. Wolf sat out there in that car all night until finally I went out there to see him. He apologized to me and he asked would I come on to the studio. I told him to go on, I'd come when I got ready. So when I got there, all these guitar players were sitting, lined up along the wall, looking mighty unhappy. They weren't used to the Wolf. Oh yeah, they liked his music all right, but they never met nobody like him. So we got together and did it right on one take. And he turned to those guitar players and said, "That's the way it's supposed to be." So they all packed up and left.

After that, Wolf didn't have any other guitar player but me. I led the band, and we didn't use two guitars the way we used to. We got in the studio then and really started to workin'. We did "Wang Dang Doodle," "Back Door Man," and "Spoonful" [in Chicago, 1960]. Wolf had got to where he liked to wear overalls onstage. We all still dressed sharp in suits and such, but Wolf never knew when he might get a notion to start to crawlin' on the ground and rollin' around. When we played Tampa, Florida, this woman came up from the audience and gave Wolf this big old spoon. He put it in the overhauls like you might carry a hammer. That got me, man.

We did a session later with Buddy Guy playing second guitar, in the early '60s. That time we recorded "Shake It for Me," "Killing Floor," and "The Red Rooster," which had Wolf playing slide. He could play some mean guitar; his hand wrapped twice around the neck of the guitar. The Rolling Stones covered that tune and had a hit with it. When they came over here from England they played on the TV show, *Shindig*. The people said, "Who do you want to have on the show with you?" and they said, "Howlin' Wolf." So they put him on the show with those little guys sitting around his feet, staring up at him with those big eyes. I didn't play that date, though; they had Michael Bloomfield back up the Wolf.

So this guy, Horst Lippman, he came over to Sylvio's where we was playing, the old original band, and he asked Wolf, he said, "How would you like to go to Europe?" Wolf took his contract and studied on it and finally he agreed. Then he came to me and asked me would I like to go? I said, "Sure, why not." But I didn't pay him no mind. People used to ask you all kinds of funny things late at night in the club. He went all over Chicago, asking guys to go on this tour: Willie Dixon, Sunnyland Slim, Sonny Boy Williamson. They all agreed to go. So when he left, he waved at me and said, "So long, Hubert, I'll see you in Europe." I waved, "See you." I never thought I'd see him again, though.

I had three days to get my passport, and they still couldn't find it [Sumlin's birth certificate]. Ain't found it today. They sent down to Greenwood, but I was born by midwife and, at that time, they didn't have no birth certificates. We didn't take the band; the band stayed back in the States. Wolf and I got on that plane; it was my first plane ride. I just knowed good and well that was it. I put

Wolf in the window seat, and I just prayed that we'd make it. When we got there, I couldn't believe this, but they knew more about us than we knew about our own selves, almost. They had our whole life history, records—everything. So it really was a big deal. We was just like the Beatles was over there. We just didn't make the money.

They took us in the studio for about two weeks, and recorded this television show. Then we got on a bus and traveled everywhere—France, Germany, all over. Places I had never been. And I learned so much. What had done happened, Big Bill Broonzy had opened the door over there, so they were ready for us. They knew us everywhere, and we sold out everywhere we went. I didn't change nothing. I just played because Wolf was there—when he hit that bandstand, I knew what he was gonna do. We all did. So we made the band, blues all-stars. Sugar Pie Desanto, Lightnin' Hopkins, we all played together. I backed up everyone on guitar, with Sunnyland on piano, and Clifton James on drums. We had Willie Dixon on bass—some of the greatest musicians in the world, man. And we had this old guy, Sleepy John Estes, with Hammie Nixon, on the show with us. He didn't have a guitar, so I gave him mine, which was acoustic. He would play that onstage and Hammie Nixon would blow a jug. Those Europeans had never seen anything like that before. That was the great time of my life, man.

We had a great time traveling around together. Sometimes Sonny Boy would get up over the PA system, while everyone was trying to get some sleep, and blow his harp. Pretty soon they'd all be jammin' and carryin' on. I recorded my first record, solo record, on the bus. Our guide, a German dude, he recorded me playing on the bus, and the record company bought it. This same guy, Horst Lippman, who was running the tour, owned the record company—L+R. So he took me in the studio to record something to put on the other side of the record, with this instrumental. We went to the studio in East Berlin, on the other side of the wall. They had guards with machine guns and everything on the border. When I got there, I looked around for some other people, but wasn't nobody there. They said, "No, Hubert. We just want you—by yourself." So these women came out—the engineers and everybody were all women; there wasn't any men there. So they set down this fifth of vodka next to me, and they said, "Do you need anything? Is there something you would like?" I wanted to get out of that place, so I took a drink and did my first number. It was "I Love You," and they put it out with this instrumental from the bus, and it became a hit in Europe. My first record.

We traveled all over Europe for three months, the whole group. After that they auctioned me and Wolf off. Everybody else went back to the States, but we went on to England. Everybody turned out to see us: Rolling Stones, Beatles—I met 'em all. One night in walked Jimi Hendrix. Little old dude, come steppin' in. He said, "Hello, my name is Jimi Hendrix." I said, "Mine's Hubert." He said, "I know, I've been listening to you for a long time. You're my favorite guitar player, Hubert. I've been waiting all my life to play with you." Wolf said, "Let him play, let him play." He got up there onstage, man; he did good. He grabbed Wolf's guitar, and he put on a show—played with his teeth. And I said, "Oh, my!"

So the next time we went back to England was ten years later, to record the London Sessions [*The Howlin' Wolf London Sessions*]. So I knew all those guys, only they was grown up then. I had met them when they were still youngsters. Mick

Jagger, Eric Clapton—all these guys. So we got it together. Wolf had some bad experiences recording since Leonard Chess had died and Marshall Chess had taken over. He hooked Wolf and me up with all this wah-wah stuff. They did a record but Wolf didn't want to put it out. They released it as *Howlin' Wolf Doesn't Like This Record,* and he didn't either. "Dogshit" is what he called it. [*This Is Howlin' Wolf's New Album. He Doesn't Like It. He Didn't Like His Electric Guitar at First, Either.*] Later he did *The Back Door Wolf* for them. That record had a harpsichord on it. So they set us up with these British guys who wanted to get together with him. They had Charlie Watts and Bill Wyman there too. Wolf was really sick by this time, so we only could record about one song a day. After that he'd get tired and he would go back to the hotel. Then we all got together in the studio, shut the doors, and jammed. Sometimes we'd play all through the night. When that record [*The Howlin' Wolf London Sessions*] came out, it sold pretty good. We had already done recorded all those numbers, though, and a lot of people had already copied them too.

When we got to traveling with Wolf near the end, everywhere we went he had to check for the VA hospital, to see where he could go to get his dialysis treatments. He had always ridden with the band, but now he was so weak that he would fly to meet us at the date. He was a sick man, but he was still performing. One time when we were comin' from Toronto, Canada, on our way back to Chicago—this was about four months before he died—he told us, "I'm gonna get this club for you guys, and I want you guys to carry on working. Now, I don't want you to mess up my name, 'cause I ain't gonna be with you all the time, and I may not be with you too much longer. But I want you to carry my name on after I'm gone." And everybody agreed to stick together. Wolf bought the 1815 Club, and we played there a good while. Wolf got weaker and finally he collapsed onstage one night. They had to call the fire department, and they took him away in an ambulance. Nobody wanted to go onstage after that old man.

After he passed, I laid down the guitar. I said, "That's it. No more." I just couldn't imagine going on without him. Every time I'd look at my guitar I'd think about him. He seemed like he was everything, like Jesus Christ, to me. There wasn't any getting over that guy, man. They never made anyone else like him. Once you get in this field, man, it's hard to get out. I ain't never knowed nobody to make it. Oh, lots of people got big minds—"I'm gonna quit. I'm gonna retire." Fuck it! You retire for two days, a year, two years—you ain't retired yet. Because in your mind, deep in your mind, you playin' music, man. You doin' what you like, doin' what you love. Man, if you see an instrument, or you sing, and you love what you do, you been in this field all your life. Uh huh, no way you gonna retire. Finally after three months, I picked up my guitar again. I said, "Why not?" and I got together with Wolf's old band. Eddie Shaw took the band over, and he said, "I'm gonna call it Eddie Shaw and the Wolf Gang." And we all said okay. That worked for about four years, but it was hard because we had to start from scratch all over again. We did one record on Alligator in the *Living Chicago Blues* series, but it wasn't the same for me without the Wolf. After a while I decided to go out on my own. Eddie'd brought his son into the band to play guitar, and I stayed three weeks to show him my stuff.

I have, in my lifetime since I've been out here in this field, helped a lot of guys, youngsters comin' up, to play. But they're on their own now. Some of 'em doin' better than I'm doin'; some of 'em millionaires and so forth. But I don't think about that. What I think about, I'm gonna be out there doin' this stuff anyway. I'm gonna do just like Muddy Waters, Wolf, and the rest of them. I'm gonna die in this stuff, 'cause I'm dedicated.

When I first got out here, me and Wolf would sit down, and he told me, "Everybody gets the fuckin' blues sometimes. They say they don't, but they don't know what it is." For instance, we sittin' here, your girlfriend could be back there somewhere and you start to thinking, "I wonder what the devil is she doin'? I need to be catching up with her." All this shit, when it comes back to it, that's the reason people make records—the way they done been treated, the way they saw things. Fuckin' blues, man. Don't think they're going away. The blues are getting stronger and stronger. I don't care if you play jazz—how did you play jazz? Come from the fucking blues—it's just jacked up a little bit, got a funky sound. Rock and roll, same thing. They think Elvis Presley wasn't playing the blues? He played his ass off, man, and he know what it was all about.

It's bad to say, but what the people think about me ain't worth 15¢. You have to go and leave your wife, your home, and leave the city, and leave the state, to make your living. I don't mind, though, as long as I can make enough to eat and get by, and for my family; well, I'm all right.

I still like to go. I still love to go by bus and train and car and everything, but, old as I got, I started to takin' a plane. That way I can still work when I get where I'm going. I used to drive everywhere for the Wolf. Wolf didn't trust nobody. We used to load the equipment up, drive, sometimes a thousand miles, unload, tune up, play a set, then drive. I did it for 25 years. Sometimes I'd be drivin' all night, and these guys resting so easy back there. I'm up front tryin' to make out the road. I could have been dead so many times, man, but the Lord just blessed me, 'cause it was not my time. Still around.

OTIS RUSH

BY JAS OBRECHT During the mid 1950s, a tough
new breed of guitarists began to emerge from Chicago's West
and South sides. These twenty-something bluesmen had all
been raised in the South, and they played loud, hard, and
sure-handed. Master string-shakers, they framed their cathartic tales of heartbreak and woe with unforgettable riffs and

story-telling solos. Their ranks included Magic Sam, Freddie King, Buddy Guy, Joe Young, Luther Allison, Jimmy Dawkins, and the first among them to score a hit, Otis Rush.

Born on April 29, 1934, Rush was raised on a plantation-style farm near Philadelphia, Mississippi. A southpaw, he learned to play a flipped-over right-hand guitar, and to this day still strings "in reverse," with his bass strings nearest the floor. Seeing the Muddy Waters band during a 1949 visit to Chicago caused an epiphany: "All I could say," Rush remembers, "was, 'Whoa! I got to do that.'" He stayed in Chicago, immersing himself in records by Muddy Waters, Howlin' Wolf, Albert King, B.B. King, and T-Bone Walker—occasionally slowing down the turntable to play along—and took lessons with Reggie Boyd. Rush made his club debut circa 1953, playing to his own foot stomps. In '56, Willie Dixon spotted him playing at the 708 Club and arranged for his session debut with Eli Toscano's fledgling Cobra Records.

Rush's very first recording, a heartrending rewrite of Dixon's "I Can't Quit You, Baby" delivered with a fever-and-chills vocal performance, reached the Top 10 in *Billboard's* charts for "R&B Sellers in Stores" and "Most Played R&B in Juke Boxes." Hailed as one of Chicago's most brilliant performers, Rush was soon moving in progressive directions. His sultry moaning and groaning in Dixon's "My Love Will Never Die" foreshadowed '60s soul ballads, while his tormented "All Your Love (I Miss Loving)," "My Love Will Never Die," and "Double Trouble" became urban blues classics. With its visceral attack, beautiful phrasing, shimmering vibrato, and elastic bends, Otis' guitar approach was soon inspiring a generation of rock and blues guitarists—Eric Clapton, Jimmy Page, Peter Green, Magic Sam, Carlos Santana, and Stevie Ray Vaughan among them. On Rush's recommendation, Cobra recorded Magic Sam in 1957 and Buddy Guy in '58 (with Otis playing rhythm guitar on Guy's first Chicago recording).

Under Dixon's guidance, Rush signed with Chess Records and recorded another classic—"So Many Roads"—in 1960, but the association proved to be one of many unhappy experiences he'd have with record labels. Later in the decade he cut records with mixed results for Duke, Vanguard, and Atlantic's Cotillion subsidiary. His brilliant 1971 album *Right Place, Wrong Time* lived up to its name, staying on the shelf for a half-decade. Rush confessed to being "high as a kite" from alcohol while making 1975's *Cold Day in Hell* for Delmark, and his 1978 Sonet LP, *Troubles, Troubles,* would be his last studio album for 16 years. He played occasional dates and recorded live albums for Delmark, Black and Blue, Trio, and Blind Pig, but mostly stayed home drinking and "living off the land" by "hustling pool, trying to catch the lottery."

Rush ended his studio hiatus in 1993 to record *Ain't Enough Comin' In* for Quicksilver Records, using the same production team and core musicians as Buddy Guy's *Feels Like Rain.* But unlike Guy's album, with its airwaves-approved duets and star names, Rush carried the show alone, journeying from passionate pleas to gritty soul and sanctified screams. The title track was the album's sole Rush composition. I interviewed Otis twice in Chicago that summer, and an edited version of our exchange appeared in the November '93 *Guitar Player* as "Otis Rush—Right Place, Right Time." Here's the complete transcript of those conversations.

"RIGHT PLACE, RIGHT TIME"

We want to call our story "Right Place, Right Time," since your new album is so strong.

Sure thing! Well, thank you. Thank you. [*Laughs.*] I'll let you be the judge. I don't know too much. I just appreciate your sayin' what you're sayin'.

Plus all your Cobra material has recently come out in a box set . . .

Yeah, yeah. I heard about it. Look like it's open season on me. Everybody is releasing my old records.

Are you getting royalties?

Well, some of 'em. And some of 'em, no.

You're credited with starting the so-called West Side sound.

I've heard it, among me and some others.

Does that term have meaning to you?

Not really. I don't even know what they're talkin' about. [*Laughs.*]

It's used to describe your music, Buddy Guy's, Magic Sam's . . .

Well, I was playin' before Buddy and Magic Sam. Buddy, the first time he went onstage was on my show. He came by to sit in. Buddy always says, "Hey, you the first guy that let me get onstage"—that's what he tells me now.

And you played on his first Cobra records.

Yeah, and I got Magic Sam on the Cobra label. Magic Sam was a nice guy, man. Him and Buddy—they both nice guys. Buddy and Sam played different, but both of 'em was tough, man. We play on shows together, you know.

Did you do much playing together offstage?

No, we didn't jam together that way. It was just whenever we see each other, we'd go up and play.

How did you meet Magic Sam?

Sam came by where I was playin' at, and then he got a job down the street. I was playin' at 2711 Wentworth, and Sam was somewhere around 63rd and State. Now, I had made a record already, but Sam hadn't. Him and some other peoples was together, and they come out and sit in.

Were you impressed?

Oh, yeah! Him and Buddy were about the same way. Sam and I used to hang out together, you know. We was playin' at 4:00 [A.M.], and they got off at 2:00, and they would come by. We'd all sit around and drink and play music. I had my band, and sometime I'd go by to listen to them play, and sit in. So we knew each other for a long time. Sam had a special sound, but believe me, I don't know how he got that.

He had more reverb . . .

He liked gimmicks. He was messin' around with them gimmicks too—him and Earl Hooker.

Earl had a wah-wah early on.

Right.

Did you ever want to go that route?

Yeah. I didn't have the money to buy one at that time when they come out. I never did get one until a few years ago.

Were Telecasters and Stratocasters hard to get during the '50s?

Now, I don't really know about the Telecaster, but I knew it played good. Yeah, it does. It was hard to get a guitar because we was so poor, man, but I had scuffled and got enough money to buy me one. Everybody bought Fenders and Fender Bassmans. The first one Magic Sam had was a Telecaster, and then he bought a Stratocaster.

Was Sam a family man?

Yes, he was. He had a wife and some children.

What was he like offstage?

Sam was sort of a lively guy. He wasn't quiet—he was just lively! [*Laughs.*] He might walk up and say, "President, you got a bug on your head!" President, "Where?" "It's me!" [*Laughs.*] That's the kind of guy he were!

Was he much of a drinker?

Yeah, yeah. No need of me lying. You know, that's a shame. I drinked too, but he was *really* on it. Yeah, he was drinkin'. He just a good-time guy—he don't know when to go home, you know. No sleep, then you gotta work the next night. He'd go take a nap over in the corner, then get up and go play, nap, then get ready and go out again before he go home. That's the wear and tear. That'll get you. He was a good-time dude, and he had a lot of fun, far as I know. Hey, he was just an all-around great guy.

Do you know what killed him?

No, I don't. All I know, they say a heart attack.

Did your Cobra releases lead to any tours?

Yes. The very first record I made was "I Can't Quit You, Baby, I Got to Put You Down for a While," and I started travelin' behind that. That was the first work I ever had, behind that record.

What kind of a studio were your Cobra sessions held in?

No, no, no. I don't know what it were before I went there, but it was a building, two or three rooms together there. The amps was sittin' on the floor, and they had little shields and things up around the walls, little booths. The whole band recorded at the same time. Ike Turner was on one of the records we recorded in that same room. Sam recorded in there, Buddy. It was on Roosevelt Street. Now it's all torn down.

The Cobra box set credits Ike Turner with playing some of the guitar on "All Your Love."

Well, that's "Double Troubles." That was "Double Troubles" and "Keep Lovin' Me." That was the two he was on.

Did you teach him the parts?

No, I did not. Ike was playin' when I met him. I met Ike in St. Louis before he ever played on my record.

Were you aware of blues music when you were growing up in Philadelphia, Mississippi?

Yes, yes. You know, I was listening to a guy like Charles Brown, the piano player, and John Lee Hooker. Muddy Waters had some records out, and Howlin' Wolf. I was in Philadelphia then.

Were people performing blues in your town?

No. They was playin' those records on the jukebox. Philadelphia is . . . You can take a baseball and throw it all the way across it, you know. [*Laughs.*] That's the town—well, it's more like a county.

Your vocals seem to have a lot in common with gospel singing.

Yeah, yeah, yeah, yeah, yeah, yeah. I used to play guitar, matter of fact, in church—and sing. It was a Sanctified Baptist Church or something. I don't know how I was playin'. [*Laughs.*] I was a good guy, but hey, I didn't know what it was all about.

When you started playing clubs, was anyone especially inspirational?

Yes! That was Muddy Waters. He didn't do anything. He just sit there and play. My sister took me to listen to him at the Zanzibar, on the West Side here in Chicago. Okay. I'd just arrived, and I don't know nothin' about guitar. I just had one at home. So I'd come here to visit my sister and then go back to Philadelphia, Mississippi—that's my home. I came here and said, "Whoa. This is for me!" I heard Muddy, and I said, "Give me a guitar!" So I went and started practicin'.

Did he have Little Walter with him at the time?

Yes, he did. He had Little Walter. Junior Wells was sittin' in with him also, Jimmy Rogers on second guitar, Elgin on the drums, Muddy on lead guitar. Aw, man, it was so great! So I started listenin' to these guys, and I started off workin' for five dollars a night. I quit my day job here in Chicago.

Did any of the older musicians give you good advice?

No, no, no, no. I've always been out there by myself. No one helped me to get out here. I've always had my own band, just a guitar around me, and I would always choose a guy to come sit down and play with me. I just started out that way. It wasn't nothin' big or small. As far as bein' a leader, I just had to do it. Somebody had to do it.

So they never helped you.

Well, yeah, after I made a record. But damn, before I made a record, I'm catchin' hell! [*Laughs.*] You know, all this time they raisin' hell. They got a nice record out and they jammin', you know, but nobody helped me. It's just once . . . Well, Willie Dixon helped me out a little bit there. He wrote "I Can't Quit You, Baby," and I sit down and try to play it so many times. And it was a pretty nice record for me. Big Willie Dixon.

How did he teach you the song?

He just had it on paper. It's a blues, a 12-bar blues, so I choose the way I want to sing it. He can't sing for me. He'd hum, and I said, "Well, I'll try it this way." So I changed some of the words in it, but that's Willie's song. But I did it my way. Well, I saw Willie writin' 'em, you know, and I'm lookin' at these records and I'm listening at what peoples wrote. I said, "Well, damn, I can do this too," you know. [*Laughs.*] So I went at it. I'm lucky I had a few records out there.

Do you remember writing "All Your Love (I Miss Loving)"?

Yes. I was on my way to the studio for Eli Toscano [of Cobra Records], and I needed two songs. So I did "All Your Love" and that other one—what the hell was it? "Every day I" do somethin'—I forgot the title of it, and I wrote it! [*Laughs heartily.*] Oh, yeah—"Checkin' In on My Baby." "Every day I look for sunshine and know it rain, every time I check on my baby, she's out with another man," or something like that.

Do you compose songs on paper?

Yeah, yeah, yeah. You gotta put it down. Sometime you hear the music first, sometime you hear the words. Sometime you add the words to your music that you hear. Sometime you add your music to your words. Yeah.

Have you saved your song manuscripts?

Oh, no, no, no. I wouldn't know.

What are your favorite of your own songs?

Well, I like "Double Troubles," and I like "All Your Love." Some of the songs.

Right Place, Wrong Time—that was an album that I thought was pretty good. We recorded it in '71, and they didn't release it until '77 or '76.

What songs would have to go on a best of Otis Rush collection?

Oh, I'd have to get some new songs on there. That's one thing. I gots some new songs. Pretty soon you'll hear them. Some of them are on the new record, like "It Ain't Enough Comin' In to Take Care of What's Got to Go Out."

Your new album has the same production team and many of the same musicians as Buddy Guy's Feels Like Rain.

Yeah.

But you don't have a lot of famous people sitting in.

No. I didn't do it my way. That's the way the promoter/producer did it. That wasn't my idea. I thought Eric Clapton was gonna be on there, which was said many times. All these same peoples that was on Buddy's was gonna be on mine. It didn't happen. When I got to the studios, it was a different thing.

Your solos on the record seem to tell a story.

Yeah. Sometime, you know, you feel like playin', and it is a story. But it doesn't say any words. It's a feelin'.

Do you think out solos before recording them?

Yeah, you do have to go over it a few times.

Do you have ways of psyching yourself up to deliver an intense performance?

Well, yeah. I'm listening. Like if I'm going to work, I listen to tapes. I'm listening all day, most of the time. I listen to that guitar and singin'. Yeah.

Have you got a record collection?

Yes, yes. All kinds. I have a big stereo here.

What records could you recommend for aspiring blues guitarists?

Well, you would choose your favorite artist, who you love to hear play. You know what I mean? And if it's B.B. King, choose B.B. If it's Albert, choose Albert. If it's me, choose me. It's up to the individual, what he loves to play. It might be Kenny Burrell, if he like a little jazzy guitarin'. I like Kenny Burrell. Matter of fact, I play some of his stuff, but I didn't get a chance to put it on the records, because we're not tryin' to do too much at one time. Next record, maybe some of it may be on there.

Who are your favorite blues performers?

Well, I like Albert King. I like his playin' and his singin'. I like Bobby Blue Bland's singin', and I like B.B. I like Buddy Guy. I like all the guys, man! There's nobody I can't say I don't like, because you can always learn somethin' from anyone. Yeah! But if a guy wants to learn to play the blues, if he can, go around the guy that he really likes to listen to. And if he can't, get the records. Get him a record player and sit down and play it. Slow it down. In the beginning it's difficult.

Did you learn this way?

Yeah, yeah. This is what I'm tellin' you. They used to have 78s, 45s, and all that stuff. Say the notes is too fast for you, right? So you bring it down to 33. That's gonna put you in another key, but you learn it in the other key, and then you turn the speed back up and then play along. You learn your notes like that. I did a lot of that with Kenny Burrell. I usually play "Chili Con Carne" ["Chitlins Con Carne"] by him.

You also play country music.

Yeah, a little bit.

Do you enjoy playing guitar as much as you did when you were younger?

I can't say. I still enjoy playin'—when I think I'm soundin' alright. [*Laughs.*] 'Cause sometimes I like to take an elevator, you know, right through the stage to the basement.

Sounds self-critical.

That's just the truth. Sometimes you sound so bad! You got a bad amp or a bad speaker or something wrong with your amp. Sometime the weather change and you get these bad sounds. This is what I'm talkin' about. And then again, your backup band sometime is not playin' right. All that goes together.

Albert King used to have strong reactions onstage.

Yeah. Well, I understand his reaction. He might come down a little strong, from what I hear, but I feel the same way onstage when something is wrong and I'm lis-tenin' at it. Sometimes musicians are assing off, you know. Sometime a musician is not payin' attention.

What do you expect from the musicians who perform with you?

I have rules. You know, when show time come, go to the stage. I don't need to be lookin' for you. And don't get drunk onstage during the show. And be on time comin' to work.

Has new equipment changed the way you make records?

Yes, yes, my goodness, yes. Yeah, you know, hey, they got so much stuff, man, I don't know whether to scratch my watch or wind my head! [*Laughs.*] I'm telling you, it's a hell of a thing to look at all this equipment that they have—amplifiers, guitars. You really don't know what to do no more. You just pick up something—if it sound good, you keep it!

What's your all-time favorite setup?

Well, I like the old Fender Bassman. And I like the one I have now—I'm playin' on a Mesa Boogie now. For guitars, number one, I like Fender. But I like Gibson too.

You've played a number of Stratocasters.

That's right. Like the Cobra stuff? That was Fender. Some of my *Tops* LP was recorded alive with a Gibson 355—that real old one.

Is it easier to bend on either of these types of guitar?

Yeah, I think the Fender's got an edge. But Gibson is good for many things, man. You just can't explain it—like chords and jazz, stuff like that.

What guitar is on the new record?

You're hearin' Fender guitar. I just got a new guitar. John English gave it to me, and I want to give him all the credit that he deserve. The guy is a wonderful guy, and he don't know me and I don't know him. He just made me a guitar.

Is it like other Fenders you've owned?

No, it's different. It plays different. It's the best Fender I ever played—best guitar I ever played, really. It's got some special tone or something. It has the straight pickups, like the old Fender. It'd be good to talk to John English, 'cause I don't know one end of the guitar from the other.

Yeah, sure.

[*Laughs.*] But he knows about it. He made me a purple one, and he's sort of got these little Christmas tints in there, you know. And it changes colors under the lights—it changes green, gold, purple, then it looks black. It's a trip, man. It's really a trip-out! Hey, this might be some hell of an idea, you know. Yeah, he know what he doin'. This guitar look better than Christmas, I swear. Yeah!

Do you still have any of the gear you used during the '50s?

I got a couple of red guitars, which are Gibson. But I didn't have them at that time; they was given to me.

What happened to your old amps and guitars?

Somebody stole my guitar. I still got an old Fender Bassman in the closet.

Does playing a flipped-over guitar change your sound, since you're bending strings the opposite way from most players?

Yes, it's different. 'Cause you're pullin' down on it, and the right-hand guy got to push it up. It's got to be different there. Albert King play that way too. As a matter of fact, last time we did a gig was San Francisco, and he was checkin' my guitar out.

He used a different tuning on his own guitar, though.

He plays open tuning, yeah. But he play my guitar, and he played the way he play.

Do you ever use open tunings?

Yeah, sometime.

Which ones?

I can't explain that to you. [*Laughs.*] It's just a way to tune that guitar, though. Different ways to tune your guitars. Still learnin'. [*Laughs.*]

Have you played slide?

Yep. I have a slide, but I just try to play without the slide, so that's what I work on. I don't use the slide. I play just with my hands.

Sometimes with a pick and sometimes without.

Right. It's the sound. You pluck with your thumb, and then the pick is a different sound.

How can you tell a good amp?

Well, you cannot judge it, really. You can go in the store and play it all you want to, but you really got to take it to the gig and check it out with the peoples around you. You gotta have an audience just like you gonna play—that's the way you gotta check your amp. So, many of the stores will let you do that, let you take it and check it. By you playin' in a club with peoples in there, you can tell if it's good. You know if you got enough volume. You know how loud you got to go for distortion, so you know if the speaker is good or blowed. You can tell all kind of things.

Do you know of any great unknown blues guitarists in Chicago?

No, I don't. I really don't. I think just about all the guitar players is out here. I go to work at Kingston Mines and Blues Etcetera and Blues on Halsted—you know, the guys meet up around here.

Who would you go out of your way to watch perform?

I listen to anybody. Like I say, you can always learn somethin'. I'm always out here tryin' to learn somethin', and I'm still tryin' to learn.

Who's your favorite blues piano player?

I tell you, I listen to Charles Brown. As the blues, he strikes some nice chords and runs and notes for me. He's not a big jazz or he's not a hell of a damn piano player, but the way he plays notes, I like it. And I like Ray Charles, yeah.

I bet Charles Brown drove women crazy in the '50s.

I'm sure he did. You know, Ray Charles was tryin' to sing like Charles Brown there for a while. Yeah, some of those old tunes. Everybody was tryin' to sing like Charles Brown—even myself.

Have you had a chance to work with him?

Sure, he played with me in New York for a whole week—as a backup keyboard.

Oh, it were a thrill! Here this guy is sittin' with me for a whole week—playin' piano for me! Also, he had his own show in Europe and Sweden, and I had my own show. I had my own band, he had his own band over there. So hey, he's a swell guy, man.

Do you play acoustic guitar?

I can. It's about the same thing, except you can't squeeze the guitar strings on it. You can't go down there and hit them high notes.

How would you answer someone who says you have to be unhappy to perform blues music?

Who said that? You don't have to be unhappy to play blues. [*Laughs.*] I mean, I'm happy sometime. Sometime I'm not, no matter what I do. The blues is my livin'. I play 'em because it's a livin', just like a job. But I get the blues, yeah, more so than other times, like anybody does, man. I play the blues, but not because I'm sad—it's a livin'!

Do you ever play blues when you're home alone?

Yes. I been pickin' and playin' today and just about every day.

Do you need to practice?

Well, what I did is just sort of laid back for a while, because of the recordings. And now I'm beginning to go back into what I was doin'. Hopefully this record will work, and I can get straightened out on some good jobs. I don't have a personal manager right now. Me and my wife Masaki are doing it.

It seems like the perfect time for musicians like you and Buddy Guy to step forward.

You're absolutely right. I'm tryin' to make an effort, tryin' to make a start right here. And I intend to be consistent.

"BEEN SOME POWERFUL STUFF HAPPEN TO ME" Five years later, *Living Blues* editor David Nelson asked me to interview Otis Rush for his magazine. Rush had a new album to promote, *Any Place I'm Going,* co-produced with his wife Masaki and Willie Mitchell for House of Blues. Through the years, Rush had been characterized as a brooding, intensely guarded man who's extraordinarily reticent during interviews. This was not the case during our two-and-a-half-hour conversation, which took place in Chicago on August 8, 1998, in the lobby of Rush's upscale North Shore high-rise. Perhaps Otis' unflinching descriptions of the abuses suffered during his youth provide insight into the anguish that drives so many of his classic recordings. A lightly edited version of our conversation appeared as the November/December '98 *Living Blues* cover story, "Otis Rush: 'Been Some Powerful Stuff Happen to Me.'"

When you were beginning to play, did you solo right away or go through learning chords first?

I learned solos right away, because I was playing more like John Lee Hooker, Muddy Waters, stuff like that. I began to practice, and I learned as I go. I'm still learning.

Did you own an acoustic guitar when you were young?

Yes, I did. I didn't own it, but my brother did. I have a brother—he can't play, but he bought a guitar. I guess that was my big break. His name was Leroy.

Was this in Philadelphia?

Yeah, Philadelphia, Mississippi.

You once described that town as being so small you could throw a baseball across it.

Yeah. You can bat a home run, and it's over! [*Laughs.*] It's in Shelby County. It's forty-some miles from Meridian, a hundred miles from Jackson, Mississippi. Living there was a hell of an experience for me.

Why is that?

Just the things you had to go through. This was back in the '40s and '50s.

Was there a lot of racism?

Yeah, a lot of that too. I've had to go around the back to restaurants. When white people are having dinner, I must wait till they get through eating. After they eat, then we could eat. I'm not kidding. The rest rooms, they had signs up there— "White" and "Colored." You know I'm telling the truth. It was all over. You'd go to a restaurant, even on the highway, and it'd say, "Colored, go around the back." When we wanted some food, we can't order from the front. But I don't want to get into that. Like I say, it's been a hell of an experience.

You've said that your hard times started around the time you were five years old.

That's right. My mother didn't have a husband. There were seven of us—five boys and two girls, and she had to raise us by herself. I'm what they call a bastard. All my brothers had another father—they're half-brothers—and I have one whole sister, Odie Mae. There's also Leroy, Lorenzo, Eugene, and Wilmon. The other sister is Elizabeth. The seven of us had to support each other.

Did you ever work in a field?

Oh, yeah. Oh, yeah! From five years old. My mother and older brothers and sisters be out in the field picking cotton, pulling corn, or something. I'm lookin' at them workin', and I wanted my mother to compliment me. Every time I'd pull some cotton, I'd give it to her and let her put it in her sack—she used to drag the sacks. She said, "Boy, you're doin' great!" She kept on telling me how great I worked. I get tired and go sit in the shade, so at some point she said, "Come on, boy." I said, "What, Mom?" "You pick that cotton like you been pickin'." I didn't want to pick it. She said, "You better come on, boy, I ain't gonna tell you no more." So at six, seven years old, man, I'm working my ass off. I had to pick that cotton. At nine or ten years old, my goodness, I was plowin' the mule, turning this land over with the plow. No tractor—they had 'em, but not on this farm.

The white man let us go to school when the weather was so bad out there that we can't go to work. And we'd be prayin' for bad weather all the time! [*Laughs.*] We would hope for a storm, so today we could go to school. I went to school, man, but not like I should have. I'd be in school, I have all these plans for today—this is my great day—and [*knocks three times, then says in a loud, gruff voice*] "Junior in there?" They called me Junior and Bud then. "Is he in there? Send him out here." Then he'd say, "Come on, boy. I want you to go out here and cut them bushes and do that bottom over there." I come out of that school mad, man! I felt like kickin' my own ass. But, hey, you better get up and go—don't you be seein' that damn tree with that limb hangin' out like that with them ropes around it? Shit. I come out of there—and no argument! My teacher don't argue, just, "You got to go! You got to go, Junior!"

Were you aware of lynchings?

Was I aware of them?! I knew all the time what they'll do! I'm livin' there, man! I'm livin' in Philadelphia, Mississippi.

Nowadays most people are unaware that thousands were lynched in the South before World War II.

Hey, you don't be careful, they still do that shit down there. Okay? And you don't have to go so far south to run into one of these peoples. Right here in Chicago—you understand? You could go around a block, and you'll run into one of them. What do you call it—Klu Klux Klan? They everywhere, man! Look at what they just did to this man in Texas—drag a man behind a pickup truck until he's dead. That ain't happened no ten years ago. That just recently happened. So you know I gotta be right because they still doin' it! And who knows how many peoples is under the water or under the bushes and trees and leaves. We don't know they're there, but somebody know where they're at. A lot of peoples is missing.

When is the last time you went back to Philadelphia?

I went back eight or nine years ago. I played out there in Hollandale and went to see my brother.

When you were a kid, did you ever see anyone playing a one-string or diddley bow?

One-string guitar? No.

Did you know people who played blues music?

Not really. I used to listen to John Lee Hooker's records. He was about one of the oldest guys out there. John Lee Hooker and Charles Brown. Charles Brown played piano, and he had a great sound. And today, I can hits those notes on my guitar, and you can almost swear that it's a piano player.

That's spending some time with the music.

Well, I practiced. I didn't learn it overnight. Over the years I learned how to do this, but his songs always stuck in my mind—"Black Night," "Driftin' Blues." He had other tunes out there that I was crazy about. I thought he was the most fantastic singer and piano player that I ever met. I still think this today about those old sounds, them old records—you can't beat this, man! And you had piano players *everywhere* trying to sound like Charles Brown. I learned a lot of his stuff on my guitar, and you don't see a guitar player playin' piano on his guitar. But honest to God in heaven, I can hit it.

Did you get that from playing along while the record was running?

No, just listenin' and never forget them sounds. I learned a lot of stuff note-by-note. I hit this note [*frets an imaginary guitar*], and I says, "That don't sound right; I got to keep on practicin'." I kind of put it together at one point, and I do it onstage right now. I play a little of Kenny Burrell's stuff—"Chili Con Carne" ["Chitlins Con Carne"]. I do a little of Wes Montgomery [*hums a riff*]—that's "Bumpin' on Sunset." I used to play that. George Benson, man, but he came up late from these guys.

Did you ever hear of Charlie Christian?

Yeah, yeah, yeah, yeah. He was a monster on the guitar, you understand? And Wes just captured it all. I'm lookin' at him play with his fingers. I played next door to him—Wes was in one door, and I'm in the next door. He was playin' at the Plugged Nickel down on Wells, downtown Chicago, and I'm playing at Mother's Blues. You had all kinds of musicians coming through the Plugged Nickel—Kenny Burrell, everybody.

Did you copy any blues guitar records, like "Boogie Chillen"?

John Lee Hooker, of course. I can play that. I won't say note-for-note, but I did learn "Chili Con Carne" note-for-note, and that's a lot of scratchin'. I took me a month to really work it out. I can play it today. My son Tony, who's on my new

CD, we recorded this in Memphis, but we didn't put it on the record. My son play the guitar.

Did you teach him?

Some little things, I teach him. I carried him on the road with me one time in Canada, but he was a bit young, and he wasn't ready for the stage. But now he's a Chicago policeman, and the police station has got some kind of band, and they do shows. Tony's by my first marriage, and my two daughters is by Masaki. Lena's 18 years old, going on 19, Sophia's 15 going on 17. And are they bad! Ooh, my goodness. If I didn't love 'em . . . [*Laughs.*] I tell you what, I'd ditch 'em! But I love 'em, and, oh, man. How strong is love? Nobody knows. Because if I didn't love 'em, I don't know what I'd do. I know I wouldn't be foolin' with 'em! They wouldn't be around me if I didn't love 'em.

Are they hard-headed?

Oh, man, they got other words for it. I ain't gonna say it, because you're taping me. They nice children, but them teens, them teenagers. When I was comin' up, I don't think I was like this. I couldn't be.

Was your mother strict?

Shoot! [*Laughs nervously.*] I used to get my butt whooped. One time I went with my brother Eugene—he died—to a place where they gin cotton. I guess I was about eight or nine. My brother was a teenager. There was a pencil sharpener hangin' on the wall of this gin. We looked at it, and he tore it off the wall. "I'm gonna get this, Bud"—he called me Bud—"I'm gonna take this." I said, "Yeah, man, yeah!" I'm happy he took it.

When we get home, my mother could see it got some splinters on it from where it tore off the wall. So she says, "Where'd you guys get this pencil trimmer at?" And I jumped up and said, "He found it, Mama, I 'clare he did." We couldn't even say "swear"—hey, you say "swear," you gonna get that belt on you—so we'd say, "I declare, Mama."

She says, "You sure you find this?" Now my brother said, "Yeah, Mama, I found it." Again, I said, "Yeah, Mama, he found it, I 'clare he did." She said to me, "Boy, come here. How come this wood and nails hangin' here? Boy, you lied to me. I'll fix you up." She didn't whip my brother, but she told me to go take my clothes off. Meantime, she was humming and braiding together three peach tree branches, just like people do hair. She said, "You lied to me. You know you took that." I said, "I didn't take it—he took it!" "But you told me you find it, didn't you?" "Yeah, but Mama, what you gonna do with those branches?" She said, "I'm gonna give you the whoopin' of your life." I said, "You can't whoop me with that, you'll kill me!"

She whaled me and whaled me, and I hit the floor. I can't do nothin' but scream. I guess I'm jumpin' so fast and hard, it's hard to get hit, so she grabbed me by the legs and lift me up. She took me by my feets, held me upside down, and pounded my head on the wooden floor. [*Laughs nervously.*] She said, "Don't you lie to me again." I was glad when she turned me aloose. I'm tellin' you, she didn't play.

Was your mother churchified?

Yeah, yeah, until she got that belt. I got these whoopings like this, and ooh, I was careful about what went down from then on. She'd cut you. That old peach tree switch, it'd wrap around you. I got scars on me, and I'm not telling you all of it.

When I was a teenager, I wet the bed, and my mother tell me, "Every time you wet the bed, I'm gonna whoop your ass." So I'd get up in the morning knowing that automatically I'm gonna get a whoopin'. Sometimes I wet the bed two or three times a night. I slept with my brother, and he'd tell on me sometime. Sometimes I'd get up during the night and find the sheet and be dryin' the bed, but them pee circles tell the truth—it's there. Oh, man, I peed in the bed 365 days out of the year. She eventually took me to the doctor, and the doctor said, "Don't whoop the boy. His kidneys is bad." He gave me medicine, but it still didn't help me. I had to grow out of that.

Were you ever inclined to be violent toward others?

I suppose so. It made me angry. I can't help but to say you're right, because I begin to get angry. I get in a few fights, stuff like this. Later on, some of the musicians, something ain't right—I got in fights with musicians on intermissions.

After you moved out on your own, were you close to your mom?

I kind of kept my distance, but I love her so much. I'm glad she whooped my butt. She learnt me a lot. After she whooped me, I had respect for other peoples, most of all her. Like I say, she had seven children, and she wasn't about to let us rule her. She was disciplined, and boy, she whoop your butt.

Did your mother have any problems with your playing blues music?

Well, see, that's some of the reason I play. She used to go to town on a Saturday night, and every time she'd take me to a little cafe and feed me a hamburger and a pop—RC Double Cola. All these pins and needles would hit me in the head when I drank the pop, because I didn't know how to belch. They had a jukebox at that little cafe where I'd get my hamburger, and that's where I'd listen to Charles Brown and John Lee Hooker. Sometimes I'd buy my own bag of precooked hot dogs and go to the movies and watch Roy Rogers and Gene Autry.

Where did you learn about Eddy Arnold and the Blue Grass Boys?

Down there at the same jukebox. And it wasn't all jukebox, it was radio from Nashville, Tennessee—WLAC. Yeah! You could hear that station, man, no matter where you go. We didn't have no TV—wasn't no TV at that time. I grew up in the country on a farm.

Did you have electricity at home?

Later in my age, when I became teenage, we had electric. Other than that, it was a kerosene lamp. We didn't know nothin' about no electric.

What kind of church did you attend?

Baptist, up in the hills in the woods. That's where my church was.

Did you sing in church?

I sing, but to myself. That's when everybody was singing—the choir was singing, my mother was singing in the church. She'd sing and get happy and shout. Just like when preachers is preachin', she'd look like somebody was killin' her. She just went out of her mind and shout, I guess, from the hurt inside about life. And I know that we was botherin' her, but she had us under control because my dad was never around.

Are you the only professional musician in your family?

Yes. That's from watching my mother when we went to town and I get that hamburger. She went and bought one of them big, old wide records, a 78 by Tommy McClarence [McClennan], and Lightnin' Hopkins. She would say, "Listen to that fool play!" I heard every breath she breathed, you understand? My ears was inside of that record, listening. And John Lee Hooker—she kept buying up those records. There was a lady called Bessie Smith. And Memphis Minnie—hey, man, she was something else on the guitar. She was more like a modern singer and guitar player in those days. Louis Jordan.

We had a wind-up record player, and we'd wind that up until the spring get so tight, then we put that record on. It was spinnin'—sound good, you know? It had a little dog and said "RCA Victor." Anyway, we had the Soul Stirrers, Sam Cooke, the Five Blind Boys, just different records. We had these big records, and it was just like a nightclub to me. We wind that thing up and I'd listen to it, and I'd learn to find notes on my guitar. But they had a guy named Vaughan Adam. He had been to the Army, and he came back out of the war. He was slick on the guitar. He could play all them pretty chords. We live on the same farm. We was livin' on Otis Lewis' farm. I never will forget him. There was a bunch of houses on his plantation, and everybody live close together near the front office—bang, bang, bang—and as far as you could see was acres of farm fields.

At what point did you say, "I gotta get out of here, and maybe music's my way out"?

I ain't never thought I'm gonna be playing no music. When I came to Chicago, I was farmin'. I had my own little place by then—I had left home. I had my own little farm, five acres, and I was stayin' on a white man's farm. And I had the most prettiest field—it was just like a movie, and people stopped to take pictures of it. It was so rich, and I did it! They'd park their trucks, and every day, they lined up out there, looking at my work. I grew corn—got 14 wagonloads of corn—and I did about five bales of cotton, so I got a bale to the acre. I didn't have no stock.

Did you grow greens and other vegetables?

Yeah, we grew that, but there was so much of that around, you don't even think about that. I grew this on this white man's farm. I was sharecroppin'. Whatever I make on this farm, I have to give him half of it. God's truth. He put all the money up for my fertilizer and stuff. You got to have poison to keep the bugs and boll weevils off of the cotton. I worked by moonlight at night. I got a scar on my stomach right now from turning this thing that spread the poison—I turn that knob so many times, it rubbed it sore. I put it on when the dew falls. The poison looks like flour from the kitchen when you bake biscuits. It just land on that dew, and that's what made my cotton so special. I'd work from sunup to sundown. Then I'd go home, eat, get a little rest, and then about 10:00, 11:00, get up out of the bed, go out there and work by that moonlight until about 2:00 or 3:00 in the morning. Then I'd go back and get a little rest, then get up and go back out there.

That's a hard way to live.

I did it. Even when it was too bad weather for me to work in this field, he had a truck to haul logs from the woods and take them to town to the sawmills. That's where you get your lumber from to make houses. I knew how to load this truck with all them big logs—it had them big hooks—and if I wasn't workin' in the field, I'd take that. I'd get paid a little bit for that. I worked, I worked, and then at the end of the year, my crops was so rich.

Now, harvest time, he asked me in the field one day, "Otis, I want you to tell me something." I said, "Sure, if I can." He says, "What's six times six?" I said, "36." He said, "Damn!" You know, I'm not supposed to know these things. I just said it at the time, but I really didn't know what it were. I just guessed 36. I went back and started counting my fingers and said, "Damn! I was right!" So he didn't cheat me too much. That's what he was after. See, if I'd have said 46 or 26, he'd tear me up. Nobody had to tell me—he asked me that question to see if I could count. He gave me a pretty fair shake, okay? He still took lots—as a matter of fact, all my corn. But he gave me cash money for my cotton. I started counting, laying on the bed—I said, "Damn! I've got to go."

My sister had said she had met T-Bone Walker up here in Chicago, people like these. Muddy Waters. They had jobs up here, you know. I said, "Maybe I go up there and get me a job!" So I came to Chicago, thinkin' I might be able to get a job and stay awhile and work, and then go back. So I went, and eventually I did find a job. I stayed here two weeks with my sister, and she took me by to see Muddy Waters.

How old were you at the time?

I don't know. I was in my teens.

Where did you see Muddy?

Muddy was at Zanzibar. That's about 1400 West Roosevelt. That's where I saw my first musician alive onstage. It was Muddy Waters, Jimmy Rogers, Little Walter, L.C. McKinley, and Junior Wells was there. As we got out of the car, I heard this music. I'm thinking it's a record, a jukebox. And when I went in there and looked up on my left, they was up there playin' that stuff, and I flipped out, man! I said, "*Damn!* This is for me!"

I didn't meet Muddy Waters and Junior and all of them. I froze up in the seat and just look at 'em and drink me a beer. I got up and left when I was expired by them, man. I was froze. I had already been messing around with my brother's guitar, but I didn't know anything about it. I just liked to pick it up and nurse it. I went home to my sister's, and I didn't even have a guitar in Chicago. My brother kept his when I came to visit my sister.

I had planned to go back, but after I saw Muddy and these peoples onstage, I went downtown and bought me a Kay guitar—it was so cheap. I bought a little amp, and that was so light and cheap, when I play a note, it look like the amp danced. We was livin' up on the third floor at 3101 Wentworth—that's where my sister was.

I'm up on the third floor, and all the neighbors are saying, "Oh, Lord, this boy's up there again with this noise! Lord have mercy!" I was runnin' 'em crazy, you know what I mean? My stuff was so cheap, it really run you crazy. But I was *enjoyin'* the hell out of it, and I just played day and night. I'm sittin' up there at the time peoples' getting to bed. I get up early in the morning and wake 'em up, tryin' to play what I heard Muddy and them play onstage. I went out and bought his records. I used to sound *just like* him. I used to play all that stuff, like Little Walter, Muddy. I used to make my livin' doin' that after I got started—playin' like them.

Did you go back to Mississippi?

I stayed here. I worked hard. I went and got me a job at G.H. Hamilton Company at 47th and Racine. They had everything from a dead man casket to turnip greens. [*Laughs.*] That's a cold storage. They had stock—beef. They had all kinds of departments, and you'd work different places. This was while I'm up on that third floor at my sister's house, making all that noise. I had learned a few notes, and this is how it got started.

One night a guy by the name of Bob come by. He had a club at 2711 South

Wentworth—Club Alibi. He says, "Who is that guy that's been making all this noise up in the window? Where is he?" You could hear him talkin' outside. "Where is that guy? Somebody tell me where that guy is. I need somebody to play for me." I'm listening too, laying back across the bed. They point at my apartment. "He's right in that window up there." He came up and knocked on the door. He says, "You the guy that make all the noise?" "Of course. I'm him." I didn't know if he liked me or hate me. Anyway, he says, "Look. I want you to do me a favor. My band didn't show up tonight. Would you come and play for me? Come on, man. Just sit up there and play. I'll give you five dollars." Shit! I grabbed my shirt, my Kay guitar, my amp that dance when I play, and went down there, and he put me onstage. I pat my feet like John Lee Hooker, both feet goin', and I did a night. I never had a band, no way, so that was easy for me.

Like I say, I had this job at this G.H. Hamilton Company. I'm a good worker out there, and these people knew it. But after I did that five-dollars-a-night job, the guy says, "Man, you did so good, come back tomorrow night." Ooh-wee! Five dollars, for *my guitar?* And nobody even give me a sodie pop for playin'? [*Laughs heartily.*] Hey, lookee here: "Five dollars?" Then after that second night he says, "Tell you what. Come back tomorrow night too." For three nights. Four nights. I said, "That's twenty dollars—for *me?*"

Now, I'm up all night, right, getting five dollars a night. I was making at least seventy-five to a hundred a week on my job. But five dollars for my guitar? I done lost all my rest. By the time I got to work the next day, I'm out of it. My boss says, "Otis, you're sick." I said, "Ah, I'm alright." He says, "Something is wrong with you. I know you a good worker, and I never have any problem out of you. You got to be sick." He sent me to see the company doctor, so I play the game, just like I'm sick. "Well, yeah, I guess maybe something wrong with me," but I already know what's wrong with me.

Came back, I work a little better, but I get sleepy. I was drivin' a power-lift trac-tor-truck. I had to lift iron and stuff—tons of stuff—and load trucks with it. This man told me, "Otis, you gonna have to take some time off until you get straight-ened out. You sick." I went on home and said, "I ain't goin' back to that job." So my five dollars a night became ten. Ten became fifteen. Fifteen became twenty. I worked for twenty dollars a night, and I was enjoyin' it. Rent was twelve dollars a week. When I got thirty dollars a night, I said, "Damn! For *my guitar?*" By now I got the fever.

By the time I had quit my job, I had saved up. I had made good with my farmin' when I left from down there, and I had put all that away—I didn't waste it. When I worked at G.H. Hamilton Company, I was working there nights and some days. I worked hard, saved a little money. And I went and bought me a second-hand car off a parking lot. It was a '48 Buick Roadmaster Torpedo, and it was laying down just like a real torpedo would lay. And I said, "Damn! Look at me!" Now I can't wait to go home. I want the peoples to see me in this car. My car was dark green, almost black-lookin', and it had Cadillac hubcaps all the way 'round it. It had a big silver sun visor up in front, and then every window had its own visor. It had a radio, heater. I said, "Man! This is *me?!*"

I hop in the car—I'm goin' to Mississippi. I get me a map, and I mapped it out. Never before drived it, but after I got that map, I wasn't afraid. I see it, and I see how to get there. I'm drivin' and drivin'. I wanted to drive all the way without going to sleep, but I didn't know nothing about drinkin' no coffee or taking these pills to stay awake. After a while I had gotten sleepy, and I almost killed myself. It was two-lane highway, and I dozed off, went to sleep drivin'. I could hear a truck horn—[*moans twice like a blowing horn*]. I'm headed straight for it! I jerked my wheel to my right, and I just missed this truck head-on. My man was blowin' his horn, and he saved my life.

Sounds like you had an angel riding alongside you.

Yeah, 'cause that would have done it. I pulled off the highway and parked that car. I was kind of up in the trees now. Lay there, couldn't go to sleep now. I was so scared. But eventually I did lay there until I got me a nap. But while I was asleep, I hear this truck come by. It had such an impact—the noise, the wind—my car was shakin'. In my dream, I'm thinkin' I'm drivin' and went to sleep again, so as I wake up I was tearin' up my car inside, because I thought I was movin'. That learnt me a lesson. That told me not to be out there drivin' sleepy. Now I be drivin', I get sleepy—I pull the car over and park it. If I see somebody in the band tryin' to drive sleepy, I want to get out and whoop his ass. Right away, I want to whoop some-body's ass. I tell 'em, "Quit it. You drivin' sleepy, you can kill everybody. If you really want to kill yourself, just let us out. Then you just drive into a tree, or stick a match to you."

Did you make it down to Philadelphia?

I made it safe and was drivin' around down there. Of course, a lot of them want-ed my car. A lot of these white people say, "Where you get this car from, boy?" I say, "I bought it." After they kept tryin' that, I said, "They don't want me to have this car down here." It was kind of sharp, man, and freaked off whoever had it. I said, "It's about time for me to get the hell out from down here."

I'm getting ready to leave the next day or so, because things is getting too hot for me, and I went to a big picnic out in a pasture. These white peoples was sayin', "I want to buy this car, boy," just like that. I said, "Sure! I'll sell it." I know what time it is now. I let one guy know that he could buy my car if he wanted. But all the time, I know I'm not gonna sell him my car. I'm playin' for this time, because tomorrow he won't see nothin' but my dust. And that's what he saw—nothin' but my dust.

My brother decided to come up with me and visit because he didn't have to pay. I had a car full of peoples that wanted to come up to Chicago. But we ran out of money and almost ran out of gas. Now, I'm looking at that gas tank, and it kept get-ting lower and lower. I'm way out there somewhere, and the hand done got way over. I know it's about to go, and I'm so worried, I don't know what to do. Again, God provide for me. There was a guy thumbin' for a ride. You don't want to pick these peoples up, but I had said, "Maybe he can give me a few dollars, and I can get some gas and go on home." Sure enough, he said, "I'll get you some gas! Just give me a ride." What a blessing! He filled my car up. "Oh, man, fill my car with *gas*? Ooh-wee!" You're right—that was some angels watchin' over me. I made it back, and I wasn't wantin' too much to drive anymore because I almost had that accident.

Is this when you started putting a band together?

At first, it wasn't nobody but me playin' guitar. Then I added Poor Bob, who worked with Hound Dog Taylor, so there was two of us playin' guitar. I practiced with him, and we sit and pat our feet. Then I add Paytons [Earl Payton] on the harmonica, and that sounded so good. Then I went and got T.J. [McNulty], the drummer. He worked the same job out at the G.H. Hamilton Company, but he didn't know nothin' about no drums. I taught him how to play drums, what kind of beat I wanted. What I did, I got a bucket for him, put some rubber 'cross the top of it, and let him beat the bucket while we play. He eventually went and bought drums, and later on he got with Luther Allison. But I'm the one that put him in music. I used to carry a harmonica on the job with me, and blow that harmonica out there. That was my first instrument. See, I remember when a dime could buy you a harmonica. That's the kind of life I lived, and I used to blow pretty good, but I got interested in the guitar.

Back in the '50s, were there different blues scenes on the West and South Sides?

It was different. It's still different now. It's just the peoples. Some of 'em got attitudes from the South Side. Some on the South Side don't want to go to the West Side. Same vice versa.

Is it true that Muddy tended to play the South Side while Howlin' Wolf played the West Side?

No, they was playin' for Sylvio's. Sylvio's was West, out on Lake Street. The 708 Club was East 47th Street, real close to Cottage Grove, and that was South. I remember these addresses so well. So they playin' backwards and forwards. They play over there sometimes on the weekends, sometime over here. Just where they could get a gig at.

Were your Cobra sessions the first time you played with a decent band?

That was before the Cobra session, because me and Louie Myers and Dave Myers had started practicin' and playin', and that's when I started making fifteen dollars a night. We called ourselves the Four Aces—I named us. Junior Wells was playin' half-time with Muddy. Muddy had Little Walter playin' with him, but Little Walter had made "Juke," and that was a hot record. Walter went on his own.

What kind of guy was he?

Walter, they tell me, was rough. But let me tell you about Walter. Walter was a hell of a nice guy to me. I never find no faults in him. I sit there and talk to him just like I'm talkin' to you. He talk to me, he make all kind of sense. We made sense to each other. Howlin' Wolf was the same. I heard lots of peoples talk about him, but I never had no problem. I talk to these guys and give 'em respect, and I got it in return.

Did you know another of Muddy's harmonica players, Henry Strong, who was also known as Pot?

I know Pot, and he was a hell of a damn harmonica player. Nice kid, man. Pot got killed by a knife. Juanita killed him. She would hang around the clubs where we played. You know, she hang awhile, but I'm kind of movin' out, you know what I'm sayin' [*motions like he's moving away from someone, then laughs*]: "I got somethin' to do. I gotta go get me a beer right here. I gotta go to a wife someplace." I been knowin' the girl for a *long* time, man—for *years*—and wouldn't have thought that she'd do something like that. Pot went out, stayed a one-night stand, and she got that switchblade and tapped him, cut him two or three times. Bang, bang, bang—it was over. She hit that wrong spot. They locked her up—she got a record, but she did that shit and got out of it.

When was the first time you saw a record with your name on it?

That was "I Can't Quit You, Baby." I got copies from the record company.
What was your reaction?

I had flipped already. When I went in the studio, I know I'm making this record, right? I don't know if I had made 20 [years old] or not. Anyway, Willie Dixon helped me on that: "I can't quit you, baby, I gotta put you down for a while. Messed up my happy home, you made me mistreat my onliest child." Believe me, I didn't have no idea what I was getting into when I record this record. But Willie had some things written I didn't like, so I changed a lot of the words. And it was a hit! It was the biggest record for me for a long time.

Did you send copies home to Mississippi?

No. I was so excited, I don't even talk to them. I don't even call them. My head was so jammed up with the music: "I'm a artist. I can play. I made a record!"

Didn't Muddy give you some advice after your first hit?

Yeah, yeah. That was at the 708 Club, parked right out front. He said, "Otis, I want to talk to you." Him and Jimmy Rogers and all of 'em out there, sittin' in the car, drinkin'. Well, I had my share of drinks, and he was tellin' me, "You got a good record out there—I want to give you some advice." I'm listening, but it's goin' in one ear, comin' out the other. To me, he was meddlin', but I still listened. Just for respect, I held a conversation with him, but other than that, I didn't gave a damn about what he was talkin' about.

But what he said made sense, and I realized that he gave me these points, and I could see some of the musicians that's been out there already, how they act. He was tellin' me, "Don't get the big head. Be nice, don't treat peoples dirty." He was tellin' me to try to smile, practice—which I was doin' all that. It were all real good advice, and every word he was tellin' me was true. But I had already learned how to respect people, because my mother done whooped my ass. Muddy didn't have to tell me nothin'.

While older players like Muddy and Elmore James were still playing acoustic guitars with soundhole pickups, younger guitarists like you and Buddy Guy and Magic Sam were playing Fender Stratocasters. What attracted you to solidbody guitars?

This was something new came out. We wanted something *loud* and powerful. I told you my Kay was so weak. And the stronger the amp is, the better for us—that's why you'd hear a lot of loud music. The old Fender Bassman was a big seller and a strong amp. Peoples try to buy it now for collection. I still have mine upstairs, a tweed one. They's nice amps. But now I got all kind of amps—Mesa Boogie—and I got 12, 13 guitars.

What kind of amp did you use on the Cobra singles?

It was an amp called Challenge. I bought it at Lyon & Healy.

Were you playing with a guitar pick then?

Usin' fingers. But after a while, I began to use a guitar pick, then thumbpicks and all that stuff.

You once said that working for Eli Toscano at Cobra was "heaven," and working for Chess was "hell."

Yes. With Eli, I was able to do what I wanted to in the studio. Chess, he's runnin' everything, and I didn't have no freelancin'. I had to do everything his way. Eli at Cobra treated me the best.

Even though he gambled away your royalties?

He was a con man. He conned me out of "I Can't Quit You, Baby," which was a big hit. It was all in the *Cashbox*. It was nationwide, Tops Tens. And back in these days, man, you don't get this kind of record. I went on a tour and played with the guy that wrote for Elvis Presley—Carl Perkins—and Jimmy Rushing, Big Moms Mabley, the Drifters, and I ain't nothin' but a bluesman. I played with a lot of peoples, man. Chuck Berry, Bo Diddley. That's sayin' somethin' back in them days. That was in the '50s.

Were there a lot of hangers-on after you had a hit?

Oh, yeah. Everybody knows you, you know what I mean? Everybody want a piece of the pie.

What's the first popular song you wrote on your own?

After "I Can't Quit You, Baby"—and like I say, I put some words into that, because I didn't like the way Willie had everything—then he came up with "My Love Will Never Die." Then he had this "Groanin' the Blues" and "Jump Sister Bessie"—I said, "Man, this is some horseshit all over!" I didn't know whether to scratch my watch or wind my head by now. I said, "I can do better than this." So I started writin' my own material. I did "Three Times a Fool," "Checkin' on My Baby." Then we sittin' in the living room, playin' cards. Some lady had a hand. "Oh," she says, "trouble, trouble, trouble, trouble, double troubles."

And "Double Trouble" became one of your big records.

Yeah. That came just by people talkin'. You can say something, and I done clocked it up here [*taps forehead*]. And when I get home, I write it. I just put that initial [idea] down, and then I go back and pick it up later and write a song from it. I got songs now that I'm workin' on now, man, I wish I could tell it. But I got some lyrics that'll make you cry.

How did you write "All Your Love (I Miss Loving)"?

[*Hums the song's syncopated opening guitar pattern.*] Think about it now [*hums riff again, then sings the opening line of Gershwin's "Summertime" set to the same syncopation.*] Right?

What about that middle riff?

I put that in there from something I heard Jody Williams playin'. He had some kind of shit fouled up, man, and I said, "Shoot, I can do better than this." At that time Bill Doggett had "Honky Tonk" out, and some of them cats was playin'. And I begin puttin' my stuff together.

What did you think of Eric Clapton's cover of "All Your Love" with John Mayall's Bluesbreakers?

Yeah. I'm listening at the TV give them credit for my music. They doin' a story on John Mayall and Eric Clapton. They sayin', "Nobody sound like this guy"—they talkin' about John Mayall. But that's not John Mayall's music! That's my music. They didn't even know I'm the writer. All they know it was John Mayall or Eric Clapton. And it came from me.

Did you like Eric's version?

Eric plays nice, man.

And then he did "Double Trouble" later on.

Yeah, I can't say nothin' but they sound good. But they ain't me.

Have you ever met?

Yeah. He was supposed to help me record this CD [*points to a copy of* Any Place

I'm Going], but some kind of way he managed to not help me. He helped Buddy Guy, and he did a show for a week down at Buddy's club, and I went down there and talked to Eric to get him to help me. He sit there and told me he was gonna help me. Masaki was with me. But we called him up, and he got excuses—some tour or something. For some reason, he didn't want to help me. All excuses, which don't make sense—if you want to help somebody, you can help them. But I don't hold that against him, because as long as God give me my right mind, I'm gonna learn new stuff. And if I write new stuff, I ain't even gonna need his help. I'm gonna write some stuff that he gonna want to record.

Do you have any favorites among the songs you've written?

"Right Place, Wrong Time" was one of them. "Keep Lovin' Me Baby," "Double Troubles," "All Your Love," "Checkin' on My Baby." "Three Times a Fool," "It Takes Time," "Easy Go." This is my writing. I have a bunch of them, and some of them I can't think of.

Did your appearance on the 1966 Chicago/The Blues/Today! *anthology do you any good?*

Not really.

Were your Atlantic sessions in Muscle Shoals with Duane Allman a good memory?

Well, I had [co-producers] Mike Bloomfield and Nick Gravenites there.

It's been reported that Nick showed your song "Right Place, Wrong Time" to . . .

Dr. John. Yes. You talkin' about angry? I been angry at Nick. This is my shit, and he let this man come in there and hear it. I recorded "Right Place, Wrong Time" in '71, and it came out about five or six years later. Meantime, while mine's laying around, Dr. John go by and he see it. He got a gold record [for 1973's "Right Place Wrong Time"], and I got not a dime. But if you take out my phrase—"right place, wrong time"—he don't have a record, I don't have a record. The punch line is the phrase that sold everything. If you don't put that in the song, you ain't got no song.

If you could do your career over again, what's the first thing you'd do differently?

All these records that been stole from me—number one, I'd fix it where they couldn't can't do that to me. On this one [*points to Alligator's* Lost in the Blues] they put Lucky Peterson on piano. That was Bruce [Iglauer] at Alligator Records—I'll never record for him. Oh, man, you don't know how close I come to going to jail . . . Understand? Because this I die for [*points to song titles on CD insert*]—this is my music. I put this together, and I ain't gonna see nobody just run over me and take it from me. If you do, you gotta take me first. My mother bounced my head, trying to discipline me to learn to respect peoples, but she also taught me how to fight.

Do you consider this record disrespectful?

Of course it is! You know that. He went and bought the master from Sonet Records over there [in Europe]. When he come back here, he call up Lucky Peterson to put piano on this. I didn't have no piano on the record! He says, "Otis' favorite piano player, Lucky Peterson." Me, I didn't have no money—he had the money, you understand? So I went and got a writer. So all over TV, in Europe, Africa, America, he's known for having took my record. He don't like me for it today, because we got in a fight with the press. And he talked about me something terrible too. That's Alligator Records. He's everywhere. He's got a hand in those Grammy [Handy] Awards out of Memphis—nominations and all this stuff. Now, Koko Taylor, he tried to put her down before me. I said, "When the show come and they're on there, if I'm not the headliner, I don't even play." Son Seals—I don't open up no shows for these peoples. I'm out there playin' before they got into music.

Would you open a show for John Lee Hooker or B.B. King?

Yes. B.B., John Lee Hooker, I respect. But here's somebody here—Koko Taylor, Son Seals—I have no respect for them. Koko Taylor don't play no guitar. She just stand up there and sing. Shit. Me, I fight a bear about my music—I'd run from him, do something! I'd make him tired, man. [*Laughs.*]

If you could somehow magically put together your dream blues band, who'd be in it?

Well, when it comes to the piano, Charles Brown is the blues man, okay? You got to know that. If you went to the horns, the guy what blowed on "Chili Con Carne"—Stanley Turrentine. He blow like nobody else, man. You got all of these famous horn players, but when it come to my feelings, I listen to this man. As a bass man in my field, I would use James Green when he was young. He's an old bass player. And Ernie Gatewood had some great sounds. For rhythm guitar, Luther Tucker was a hell of a player. When it went to a guitar player with a slide, it would be Earl Hooker—you can't beat him with the slide. That's how I learned to play slide without the slide—I don't use it, but I make the sounds.

Earl was so clean.

He tried to show me how to play the slide. I put it on, but by me being left-handed, I got to reach up top to get my sound, but his [higher strings] were at the bottom.

You and Albert King both put your string sets on with the skinny ones nearest the ceiling. This must cause a different sound on bends, since you're moving the strings the opposite way from most players.

A right-hand man try to push the little *E* up, where I ain't got nothin' to do but just pull it down. And it's more easier to pull something down than to push it up. Just like this building—you can tear it down in a second, but to put it up takes a few months.

Did you ever try to restring a guitar with the skinny strings nearest your toes?

I have did it, but it don't make no sense to try to learn over again.

Whereas a lot of guys show off during solos, you tell a story with your guitar.

Mm-hmm. Well, I can play fast stuff, but I try to take my time and make you feel what I'm doin'. You can play a bunch of notes so fast, but then you turn around, and somebody out there listening says, "What did he play?" Sound good, but can't remember nothin'. Take your time and *play*. Measure it out enough where they got time to hear what you're doing. To me, that's important.

Do you know the names of all the notes on the guitar?

I do most of mine by ear, but I can read because I went to school and I learned how to play. I can read some music, but I can't play that shit fast and read it all.

Are you always aware of what key you're in?

Always aware of what key, my chords, my notes. I can make that guitar say what you sayin' right now. I can say the Lord's Prayer on my guitar, and you'll say, "That's every word of it."

The guitar is such an expressive instrument . . .

Just like you talkin' there? I can make my guitar say just what you said. And I ain't bullshitting. I can sing with my guitar, just like I sing with my voice. I did things by Aretha Franklin that's unbelievable. "Baby I Love You" is one thing I did already on a recordin'.

Among all your albums, which are your favorites?

I did a thing live in San Francisco with the Bobby Murray band behind me—*Tops,* I named it. That's my arrangements on all that stuff. We never played a note together before we got onstage, but I had sent the records to them to practice, because they were gonna back me up. So you hear us together right there for the first time, and it turned out nice. I'd been looking for that particular kind of sound.

Do you have positive feelings about Ain't Enough Comin' In*?*

Yeah. It could have been a hell of a record, but John Porter, he's greedy. He don't listen to me. He's the producer, but I put all this stuff together.

What are your feelings about managers?

Hey, look, they're hell, okay? I had Rick Bates for my manager for *Ain't Enough Comin' In,* and that was the biggest mistake of my lifetime—hirin' him. You make a record, and then they send this guy to you: "I want you to use this guy." You recordin' for them, so you're trying not to be hardheaded. They want me to use this guy, I'll go along for a while. So in the meantime, he gettin' deeper and deeper in your business and in your pocket. This son-of-a-bitch tried to get me to sign something that says if he do this particular thing for me, he wants to get paid *forever.* If I sign that, even if I'm dead, he still get that money! Hey, man, when a manager come to you like this, that show you he ain't no good. I don't sign nothin' forever for nobody. Oh, I know a few peoples this has been done to, but I don't want to talk too much. They done signed forever and they makin' big money, but my man's got his hand in their pocket, and he got it in there forever. And they gotta pay it. They gotta sign that.

What's the most stressful thing about today's music business?

People that don't care, man. People that don't care about you, people that take records from you. That put something on your mind. That ain't no good for no one, you understand? It just is trouble. It's just like somebody got the key to your door, and you don't want 'em in your house. You done told them, "Stay out," but they come back again. Takin' my music is takin' money from me. You know, who wants to be stuck up? My mother whooped my butt so much, I have nothin' but respect for peoples. She didn't have to whoop me this much, but I'm glad she whooped me. I work; I don't steal.

Do you believe in spanking kids?

Yeah, I tell you what: You hit 'em today, discipline 'em, and here come somebody with a police badge. You goin' to jail—you "abusin'." That's what's wrong with the world today: They need some abusin' goin' on around here. Some of these kids need their ass whooped, like Mama whooped mine. I know that, but me, I'm not gonna hit mines. Why? They done heard so much of this shit, they ready to call the police. It only take one call, a couple of calls, and you got a record, like you done killed some damn somebody. Somebody came here for me—I been havin' problems. I told you my kids is bad, but I'm gonna let 'em go the way they want to go. I done told them that I ain't gonna try to whoop 'em, but I ain't gonna let 'em whoop me, either. Father or no father, man, don't nobody hurt me. You know what I mean? I don't want to hurt nobody, but I don't intend to get hurt. So now I don't try to tell them too much. I tell them right from wrong, and if they want to go on, I say, "You go ahead on. But I told you how to do this. Are you gonna listen to me? If not, go to hell."

Is success hard on marriage?

Of course. Anything is hard on marriage. Marriage is a hell of a deal. I don't care if you're success or unsuccess, marriage is a mother, okay? You have to deal with what you think is best for you. Ain't nobody gonna treat you like you treat yourself. You got to kind of look out for yourself. But I've taken a lot of stuff that I shouldn't have took. Why I do it? I try to stay out of trouble.

What are your feelings about drinking liquor?

For me? I haven't been drinkin' nothin' for the last four years, but here lately I've been drinkin' a little wine. I damn well have been missing it. I'm not lyin'—when I first moved in this building, I wasn't drinkin', but I've drinken my share in my lifetime in music. But I had drinken so much, it was making me sick. Beer—I had to have it to go to sleep, wake up, whatever. I needed a drink. But now I can drink it or don't drink it. But it did make me sick. I had to go in the hospital. I got high blood pressure, and my man said to take it easy with that stuff.

Are you a happy or surly drinker?

I was happy, understand? I could make it, I thought. But what it was doin' was gettin' my insides. I used to smoke, but I put it down. For maybe four years, I ain't smoked. My wife, she just steadily smoke, smoke, smoke. I keep telling her, "Don't smoke," and she gets the habit. She'd tell me, "You go get you a drink. I'm gonna smoke as much as I want." She says that if smokin' kill her, she's ready to die. It's your privilege—keep smoking—but there's something to it. The lung can't take all this smoke. That's what kills peoples in these buildings—it's not so much the fire get them, it's the smoke. They can't breathe. What a way to go.

How do you deal with your anger?

Man, I go for a walk. I go around this park [*points across street*]. It's two miles around there, they tell me. Sometime I go twice. I go in the morning, and sometime I go in the afternoon. I do it now. And I run a little, so I feel pretty good too. I'm able to deal with a lot of my stress. I been out there just about every day this week. And I ain't just started—I been doin' this for months.

Playing music also takes a lot of stress away. When I go onstage, my stress is in trouble. It don't be gone long, but it ain't strong like it were before I went onstage. My stress get weak. I don't know what I be playin' on my guitar sometimes, and when I do play that way, I can play little things other than blues. I play different kind of guitar. But when you stress onstage—ooh, that's a hard road to travel. But if you ever get your stress feelin' and play it onstage, you can make a person cry. I have did it. I been playin' onstage and ladies would faint. They had the fire department come take 'em out on these stretchers. I was on a tour, and they did it. Took two or three peoples and carried them away. They wasn't dead or nothin', but emotionally they went out, and they don't know where they were, I guess. They took 'em to the hospital. Now, that's from me playin'. Been some powerful stuff happen to me that maybe one day I can tell you about it. But right here, I keep it the way we got it.

Do you believe in God?

Of course I do.

Is there a heaven and a hell?

Yeah. Sometimes I don't know, but I do believe there's got to be somethin' somewhere. You just can't come here and disappear. I have a feeling that my ashes or something been here before. I have some crazy dreams, you know what I mean? I've had a lot of strange dreams. I've had dreams that I've passed away, and I'm lookin' at myself pass away. I'm lookin' at the lights go out. But when it winds up, it's just like a question mark—why?—and the light goes out. That's as far as I'm goin'. I leave it alone.

I have had dreams that repeat over and over, I guess, for about thirty or forty years. I dreamed this dream that I could fly. I've been able to stand here, like I'm talking to you, and just barely go [*raises arms like spreading wings*] and fly. I say in my dream, "Look at me, look at me—I can fly!" As I'm dreaming this, it comes to me in my dream that I tell people, "I've been dreaming that I can fly, and really I can fly now—see?" I'm showin' people how I'm floatin' around, and I come down and land like a helicopter, easy. I've repeatedly dreamed this over and over for most of my life.

That flying dream must make you feel good.

I don't know if it's good or bad. But what I was so happy about was I could fly, man. I was worser than Superman!

Does playing music ever give that exhilarated feeling?

Best high you can get is off of just playin' music. When you drink and play, you feel okay. But when you get high just from playin', all of a sudden somethin' hit you. I have played to myself sittin' in the room and said, "Damn! How come I can't do this onstage?" But I find out the only time I can play that is when that spell hit me.

When you get high from your music, your knowledge is something different than it is when you just pick up a guitar and feel good. There's something special hit you, and you cannot play like that every day. You don't even think like it. Ideas won't come to you. Ideas come to you by spells, and most of the times you get ideas, you got to get up and write it down. And the biggest mistakes I ever made is layin' there sayin', "I'm *gonna* get up and write it down" or "I ain't gonna get up— I'll remember this." And then you wake up later, and [*snaps fingers*] it's gone. So when things come to you, get up and write it down.

Do you love the guitar as much today as you did at the start of your career?

Yeah. Yeah, I love it. I love a good-sounding guitar, because that's my work. That's my pride. I get paid for it, and I have to be very careful with it. I must respect it, because you don't get this every day. It's a gift.

MAGIC SAM

BY STEVE FRANZ
Promoter John
Fishel has never forgotten the night in Chicago
when he went looking for Magic Sam. Fishel
was lining up musicians for the upcoming 1969
Ann Arbor Blues Festival, and Bob Koester, head
of Delmark Records, had suggested booking
Magic Sam. With a contract in hand, Fishel and
Koester headed down Pulaski Avenue looking
for the L&A Lounge. When they got there,
Mighty Joe Young was onstage and Magic Sam
was relaxing at the bar, passing time before his
set. Big Bill Hill was doing a live radio broadcast

*This chapter on leg-
endary West Side
bluesmen Magic Sam
Maghett originally
appeared as "The Life
and Music of Magic
Sam" in* LIVING BLUES,
*January/February
1996. It begins with
an account of Magic
Sam's breakthrough
performance at the
1969 Ann Arbor
Blues Festival.*

from the almost deserted nightclub. Fishel recalls, "Sam and I adjourned to a near-by broom closet, which doubled as a dressing room. Sitting on a bucket, we discussed business, and a deal for Ann Arbor was consummated."

Afterward, Sam got up onstage to do his set. During the middle of the first number, Freddie King strolled in and struck up a conversation with Hill, who was running the broadcast. In an attempt to make the club seem busier than it actually was (for the benefit of the radio audience and Hill's sponsors), Hill prompted King to get a guitar and jam with Sam. As Fishel later wrote: "Freddie went into a dyna-mite version of 'Hide Away.' Sam followed with an even better 'Looking Good.' The battle of the blues was on. For the next 45 minutes, the radio audience and the few patrons in the bar were treated to a stunning display of one-upmanship. It's hard to say if there was a winner in this battle; to my ears Freddie King was the victor." It wouldn't be long, though, before Magic Sam had his chance to triumph.

"Magic Sam was scheduled to go onstage at approximately 3:00 on Sunday, August 3, in Ann Arbor," Fishel continues. "By 2:55, he was nowhere in sight. I was excitedly informed that Magic Sam had arrived with his bass player. When I went to greet them, I was shocked to realize that Sam had not brought a drummer. He excused himself and returned a few minutes later with Sam Lay. They took the stage to moderate applause, Sam Lay using Fred Below's drums. Magic Sam stepped forward and launched into 'San-Ho-Zay,' the Freddie King instrumental, while the sound crew struggled to get a balance. When the music ended, there was tumul-tuous applause."

What followed was an incomparable performance by Magic Sam—the quintes-sential "West Side" set. With Sam Lay pounding the hell out of Fred Below's drums and the able Bruce Barlow on bass, Sam's roaring guitar rode a knife-edge for the entire set (eliciting comparison to some of Jimi Hendrix's mid-1960s work), and he sang his lungs out on "I Need You So Bad" and other numbers. More than just a magnificent performance, Magic Sam's set was akin to the ultimate cutting contest. As Jeff Titon wrote in the October 1969 issue of *Blues Unlimited:* "Magic Sam seemed a bit dazzled by the crowd's response, especially as he is not an actor who gyrates or preaches to work the crowd to a fever. The music alone moved the peo-ple, who weren't expecting it from someone they'd never heard of, and they screamed for him the rest of the evening, embarrassing Freddie King and James Cotton." As the last notes of "Looking Good" faded into audience applause, it was obvious that Magic Sam "had arrived." The sad part was that the 32-year-old blues-man wouldn't be around much longer.

"ONE BIG BLUES PARTY" Magic Sam was born Samuel Gene Maghett on February 14, 1937, in Grenada County, Mississippi, just east of the county seat of Grenada. Relatives regarded him as a "music child" as he easily made the progression from a wall-mounted diddley bow to harmonica, guitar, bass, piano, and drums. Sam lis-tened to records by Little Walter and Muddy Waters, passing along pointers he'd pick up to schoolmate Morris Holt (later to become known as Magic Slim). In 1950, the Maghetts moved to Chicago—like so many other African-American fami-lies from Mississippi—and settled near 27th and Calumet.

Sam liked the freedom of city life, and he soon made friends with guitarist/vocalist Syl Thompson (later Syl Johnson) and his brother, bassist Mack Thompson. He enrolled at Drake School on the South Side, where he "often took his guitar with him," Bill Lindemann wrote in his liner notes for *West Side Soul.* "His classmates used to tease him about it, but one morning Sam played before all the students at assembly, caught the fancy of the girls, and went home with a pocketful of telephone numbers."

"When I came to Chicago, I saw Sam sitting on the front steps with the guitar," Syl Johnson told *Living Blues.* "He played like a hillbilly style. I taught him how to play the blues, what little I knew, and we became good friends, he and my brother, bunch of other guys, and we came through the years as friends." The late Mack Thompson recalled, "Really, it wasn't a band. Just sit around the house, you know. Just between the neighborhood guys. We all lived near each other." Sam also met James "Shakey Jake" Harris, a full-time gambler and soon-to-be part-time blues vocalist and harp blower. Shakey Jake was enamored of Little Walter's harmonica style, and once he knew how to play just one of Little Walter's tunes, Jake officially started his blues career. "I learned 'Juke,' because I didn't know nothing else to play but church songs," he told researcher Pete Welding. Jake encouraged Sam to sing while playing guitar, and the pair later recorded together on several occasions.

Sam began practicing regularly with Syl Johnson, Mack Thompson, and Shakey Jake, and he gained valuable vocal experience by singing in a gospel group, the Morning View Special. "This is when we started trying to work the clubs," Mack Thompson remembered. "Actually, the first gig I played was with Shakey Jake, me, and Magic Sam. Shakey was the leader of the band. We played on Madison near California, a place called the Wagon Wheel. I think I was making about eight dollars a night—or was it six? I don't know; I didn't care." Sam soon dropped out of school and in 1954 paid a visit to his home town of Grenada.

That summer, Otis Williams—would-be blues drummer and singer—was shining shoes in Grenada's Doak Street Barber Shop when Magic Sam happened by. Williams' recollections in *Living Blues* offer a picture of Sam at the very start of his career: "He was home from Chicago where he had lived for several years. I'll never forget this very pleasant young man with the guitar slung over his left shoulder. He had a ready smile as I asked questions while shining his shoes. He didn't display any of the phony hip cockiness that most fellows showed when they returned from the big city. Sam's friendliness seemed to be genuine as he readily obliged when we asked him to play and sing a few numbers. Sam talked about bright lights of swinging Chi-town nightclubs. He held his audience spellbound with stories about Shakey Jake, Big Bill Broonzy, Sunnyland Slim, and others. He made Jew Town seem like one big blues party on Sunday mornings."

By 1955, the 18-year-old Sam was determined to play the clubs in earnest. "I took Magic Sam out of a laundry where he was working," Shakey Jake told Pete Welding, "and put him in the musician's union, put Mack in the union." Now "legal," the young musicians were eligible for nightclub work. Jake brought Sam to see Muddy Waters one night at the 708 Club. Somehow, Muddy was convinced to let Sam sit in; after hearing the performance, the club owner hired Sam for a gig. Later that year, Morris Holt, Sam's childhood friend from Grenada, immigrated to the Windy City. After lying about his age, Holt began doing club work. He played bass behind Sam for a while and eventually hooked up with Mr. Pitiful and the Teardrops.

A short time after all this, Mighty Joe Young told *Living Blues,* he saw Sam and his band in Robbins, Illinois: "There was a jam session going on out there: Magic Sam, Mack, Syl Johnson. They was wailing away. I didn't know them, because I hadn't been in Chicago too long. They was playing pretty good guitar. Sam had a beautiful style at the time, like it was between his own and this tune about 'It's My Own Fault' by Lowell Fulson. Sam played it with the tremolo on the guitar, and it gave him a little bit different sound and put him in his own bag. I was lying in bed three weeks later and I heard a record come over the air on Bill Hill's program, 'All Your Love.' And the minute I heard that guitar, I recognized it and knew it was Magic Sam."

Besides Lowell Fulson, Sam was picking up musical ideas from Ray Charles, Junior Parker, and B.B. King. Syl Johnson claims that he introduced Sam to "boogies," and instrumental guitar solos became a steady part of Sam's repertoire from then on. The busy, three-piece "West Side" sound was becoming popular around this time, developing out of the necessity of making a small band sound full.

Like the other young players on Chicago's West Side, Sam favored Fender solid-bodies—first a Telecaster, then a Stratocaster—and eventually acquired 335-style Epiphones. He often used house amps, and it's likely he owned a Fender Bassman. Unlike most of his peers, he dialed in plenty of distortion and tremolo. He'd occasionally lick his picking fingers, explaining that this helped him "change the sound." Another West Side regular, Jimmy Dawkins, described in *Living Blues* how Magic Sam's "filling in so heavy with just his guitar sounding like double chords— that comes from playing with three pieces. It was the thing that we couldn't get no money to have a full band. There's a thing with most of the West Side boys. What we're doing is playing with a bass, drums, and guitar, but we're thinking of a horn or two horns, and when we throw those heavy chords, that's what we're doing. It's a creative thing. It makes us get this heavy sound, as we call it, substituting for a full band."

While Dawkins mentions a typical ensemble of guitar, bass, and drums, another lineup of two guitars (one lead, one rhythm) and drums had also become popular, as practiced by Hound Dog Taylor and the Houserockers. Elmore James played at times with a three-piece band, often with Homesick James on second guitar, and J.B. Hutto's Hawks used a similar lineup. Today, Magic Slim and the Teardrops— though they are a four-piece band—carry on the West Side style.

THE COBRA ERA Mack Thompson recalled making a demo of "All Your Love" at "this little jive-time hole-in-the-wall." After being turned down by Chess—who surely must have later regretted the decision—Sam followed Otis Rush's advice and took the dub to Eli Toscano's Cobra label in 1957. Toscano had only entered the record business the previous year, first with Abco (where Sam had made his recording debut playing backup on a Morris Pejoe single) and then several months later with Cobra, which had just scored its first hits with Otis Rush. Howard Bedno, partner with Toscano in the Cobra operation, described ABC TV & Repair Shop, which Eli and his wife Archie ran at 2854 West Roosevelt Road, to researcher Diana Reid Haig: "Eli's store was just a little makeshift one-stop that carried black records—all 78 rpm discs at that time. Archie Toscano worked behind the counter selling the records. After being in business a year or so, Eli opened a recording studio in the back of the shop. Eli did all the recording engineering in the little studio. He was one heck of a mechanic and, when he had spare time, he would repair TVs in the back of the shop."

The "All Your Love" demo caught Toscano's attention, and a session was quickly arranged. As a result, Sam became a labelmate of Otis Rush and Buddy Guy, who recorded for Cobra's short-lived Artistic subsidiary. Magic Sam explained to Bill Lindemann that for the recording session, handyman Toscano "had a way of sending the sound through some pipes in a back room and back again to get just the right amount of reverberation." Five Magic Sam sides were cut there in 1957: "All Your Love," "Love Me with a Feeling," "Everything Gonna Be Alright," "Look Whatcha Done," and "Magic Rocker." Accompanying him were Mack Thompson on bass, Little Brother Montgomery on piano, and Billy Stepney on drums. Willie Dixon, who was helping with A&R for Cobra at the time, also played some bass. It's likely Sam's tremolo-drenched guitar parts on "All Your Love" and "Everything Gonna Be Alright" were recorded through a Fender Tremolux or Vibrolux amp.

Until this session, Sam had been working under the pseudonym of "Good Rocking Sam," but Toscano needed another name for the release because several bluesmen were already using "Good Rockin'." Thompson recalled that they sat around the studio after the session trying to think of a new name for Sam. "Sad Sam" and "Singing Sam" were vetoed for being "old time." Then, Thompson says, he thought of "Magic Sam," a transposition of Sam's real name—Maghett, Sam: "'You gotta be stuck with this name for the rest of your days,' they told him. Sam thought awhile and said, 'Well, I don't want to be Sad Sam, Poor Sam, Black Sam, Dark Sam, or what have you. Okay—put Magic Sam on it.'"

Toscano released "All Your Love" and "Love Me with a Feeling" as Cobra 5013. "Southern blues with the authentic sound" is how *Billboard* described "All Your Love" in a June 24, 1957, review. "Magic Sam's vocal," the review optimistically continued, "with typical primitive guitar stylings in the backing, will appeal to all aficionados. Should do well regionally—wherever the idiom is appreciated." Magic Sam was definitely on his way. "All Your Love," with plenty of tremolo guitar and Willie Dixon's eloquent bass, was a fine slow minor-key blues. Sam's voice, however, sounded unsure, perhaps reflecting his late start as a vocalist. With its generic lyrics, "Love Me with a Feeling" fluctuated between a minor and major key and featured a busy lead guitar line. Researcher Mike Rowe noted that during this era, records by the "new young bluesmen" were generally released with a solid blues on one side and a "rock 'n' roll novelty or dire ballad" on the reverse. But this marketing technique was not necessary in Sam's case. As Mighty Joe Young recalls, "The record was a hot record. He really took on Chicago with that tune."

"Everything Gonna Be Alright" and "Look Whatcha Done" were paired for issue as Cobra 5021 in mid-January 1958, again to favorable industry reviews. But "Everything" was basically a reworking of the "All Your Love" theme, as were his subsequent recordings of "All Night Long" and "Easy Baby" for Cobra and "My Love Is Your Love" and "You Don't Have to Work" for Chief. The repetition prompted Mike Rowe to write in *Chicago Breakdown*, "While his tremolo guitar was distinctive enough, as a creator Sam was very limited." In his autobiography, Willie Dixon echoed Rowe's sentiment: "It seemed like Sam had just trained himself to that particular style and couldn't move easy. This is why I used that particular style with him, and it turned out to be pretty good because you could always tell him, even from his introduction to the music."

Among Sam's other Cobra sides, "Look Whatcha Done" was a tough blues and "All My Whole Life," recorded at Sam's second session for the label in 1958, contained the archetypal Chicago-style rhythm guitar riff and the earthy feel of the best Chicago blues records from the '50s. Shakey Jake's 1958 waxing of "Roll Your Money Maker" for Artistic, which featured Sam in a supporting role, was notable as well, as was the unreleased "Magic Rocker," from Sam's first Cobra session. The first of Sam's many guitar-wizard workouts, "Magic Rocker" was a catchy, finger-snapping instrumental with an unusual but effective drum riff. Why Toscano chose to release offal like "21 Days in Jail" instead of "Magic Rocker" is puzzling.

Sam's success on Cobra did not last long. Neither did Cobra itself. In July 1959 the label issued its last release; a short time later Eli Toscano's body was fished out of Lake Michigan. The official cause of death was a "boating accident," but many suspected foul play. That same year, Sam got his draft notice from the army. As Syl Johnson recalls: "Uncle Sam's old jive army took him away and that ruined his career. He didn't want to go, so he ran away. He deserted the army, you know, cause he didn't want to be there. He came back and they put him in jail for six months and he came back out and he hid for a while and then he wasn't Magic Sam anymore, like he used to be."

EVERY NIGHT ABOUT THIS TIME After the army fiasco, Magic Sam signed with Mel London's Chief label in 1960. Compared with Toscano's venture, Chief was a quiet operation that had managed to survive on the strength of offerings from Elmore James and Junior Wells. Sam first entered its recording studio around April 1960 and again early in 1961. His most significant issue for London was "Every Night About This Time" backed with the instrumental "Do the Camel Walk." Sam's other Chief sides ranged from the odd to the downright silly, some relying more on novelty than on good taste. These included "You Don't Have to Work," a reworking of "All Your Love" featuring the Four Duchesses on backing vocals, as well as the uptown, "dirty dancing"–oriented "Blue Light Boogie" and the bizarre, twangy country instrumental "Square Dance Rock, Pt. 1 and 2." "Every Night," however, was a beautiful blues graced by Johnnie Jones' piano and S.P. Leary's drumming.

In the fall of 1963, Peter Kroehler was attending Northwestern University in Evanston, Illinois. In his high school days, he had listened to Big Bill Hill's broadcasts over WOPA and developed an interest in the blues. One day, someone played Kroehler "My Love Is Your Love" on a cracked Chief 45, and after finding out that Magic Sam was still playing in Chicago clubs, he made a pilgrimage to the Alex Club at 1400 West Roosevelt. "Sam seemed to enjoy playing more than any other individual I had seen," Kroehler wrote. "Even after all these years, I can't recall many musicians who appeared to enjoy their work as much as Sam." Commandeering his father's Sony reel-to-reel recorder and a Shure mike, Kroehler recorded Sam on at least two occasions—in October 1963 and February 1964. He remembered going over to Sam's apartment on Sundays, hanging out with Sam's friends, playing the tapes, and drinking beer.

Kroehler had aspirations of making a live recording from his cache. If he had done so in the mid '60s, it would have been one of the earliest live Chicago blues albums. Unfortunately, nothing came of Kroehler's plans until the early 1980s, when he brought the tapes to Bob Koester, who then produced Delmark's first-rate *Live at the Alex Club,* which recaptures the sound and feel of a crowded Chicago blues club of the early 1960s. The release presents Magic Sam in his prime and in his natural environment. The din of the crowd can be heard over Sam's searing guitar and full band, while the emcee breaks in to make various announcements and work the crowd a bit. "The music would never have had the same impact on me if I had heard it anywhere else," Kroehler wrote. "And, above all, the experience opened my eyes to a whole part of the city I had never known, a part of Chicago where the blues seemed to be an integral part of everyone's life. There was nothing fancy—no gimmicks, no frills. The atmosphere at the Alex Club made me feel alive, and I'm sure everyone there felt the same."

After the Chief operation collapsed, Sam participated in an October 1963 recording session with Mack Thompson, keyboardist Johnny "Big Moose" Walker, and drummer Bob Richey. Four titles later appeared on the German L+R label. Sam recorded with the same personnel again the following February, resulting in the issue of a CBS promotional 45 sent to German radio stations.

After a two-year hiatus, Sam returned to the studio for Al Benson's Crash label. A veteran Chicago DJ and booking agent, Benson had earlier operated several notable Windy City labels, including Parrot, Blue Lake, and Old Swingmaster. With Otis Spann on piano, Sam cut "Out of Bad Luck" backed with "She Belongs to Me." While "Out of Bad Luck" revealed echoes of the familiar "All Your Love" theme, Sam proved that he had come into his own as a vocalist, switching with ease from a knife-edged delivery to gruffness. The record foreshadowed Sam's next recording venture with Delmark Records.

WEST SIDE SOUL Magic Sam's seminal album for Delmark, *West Side Soul,* was recorded in July and October of 1967. The album garnered widespread praise, including the only five-star rating awarded to a blues album by *Down Beat* in 1968. Peter Guralnick has called it a "perfect album," while Peter Lowry, reviewing it upon its release for *Blues Unlimited,* noted Sam's extensive borrowing of material. Sam's sources were diverse—the album features songs by Freddie King, J.B. Lenoir, Junior Parker, and Otis Rush, as well as "Sweet Home Chicago," originally recorded by Kokomo Arnold and Robert Johnson during the 1930s. Sam was proud of his repertoire, explaining to *Living Blues,* "I am a bluesman, but not the dated blues—the modern type of blues. I'm the modern type of bluesman. But I can play the regular stuff, and also I am a variety guy. I can play the soul stuff too."

Magic Sam's follow-up for Delmark, *Black Magic,* was recorded in the fall of 1968. Sam himself described it as "the best album I've heard—and I'm not sayin' it just because it's mine." Excellently engineered, both Delmark studio albums have aged very well. Koester did not limit Sam to under-three-minute cuts, which would have destroyed the groove on songs such as "I Need You So Bad," and Sam's rendition of "Sweet Home Chicago" set the standard for most subsequent covers.

If Sam lacked direction earlier in his career, he was now in full control of his musical vision. It was no mistake that "soul" was part of the title of his first LP, nor was it a mistake that his Delmark records were marketed to a largely white audience—he seemed to be on the verge of crossover success while retaining his popularity in the black community. Janis Joplin, John Mayall, and other rock stars praised his genius, while interviewers found him to be a warm and happy-go-lucky guy, with a ready smile and unabashed love of barbecue (Sam was fond of saying he was a spare ribs cook first and bluesman second).

Soon Sam was swamped with engagements all over the country, his touring schedule fueled by enthusiastic reviews in *Rolling Stone*. "Columbia Records wanted him bad," Syl Johnson recalls. (Reputedly the label made a $30,000 offer, but Sam was still under contract to Delmark.) Sam's health was declining, however. According to Bob Koester, a doctor told Sam he had a serious heart condition; others, including Syl Johnson and saxophonist Eddie Shaw, have implicated heavy drinking. Shakey Jake thought Sam had cancer but wouldn't let anyone know.

After his triumphant appearance at the 1969 Ann Arbor Blues Festival, Sam fainted at a show in Louisville, Kentucky. He took some time off to recover in Chicago, but was soon off again to Europe, where a tour had been lined up. He returned to the states, only to fly off to California for more engagements. Afterwards, Sam headed back to Chicago.

On the morning of December 1, 1969, reported Bob Koester in *Blues Unlimited,* "Sam complained of heartburn after breakfast and went to lie down in the bedroom. He collapsed before he got to the bed." At age 32, Magic Sam was dead. Ironically, *Black Magic,* whose packaging proclaimed him a "living legend," had been released just days earlier. Various benefits were held by local Chicago blues musicians and Sam's close friends, and he was buried a few days later.

Adding additional pallor to the grim proceedings were the details of his financial estate. "Magic Sam got into trouble once on account of a union man who took his money and didn't turn in receipts, and they fined Sam $1,000," Shakey Jake told Pete Welding. "At the time of his death, he was still paying the fine off. He had a hard time 'cause of that, really a hard time. And I had to get him back in the union; they didn't want him and, far as they were concerned, he could go work in a steel mill."

"I felt an enormous sense of loss when Sam died," Jim O'Neal wrote many years later. "Somehow it seemed that all of us—Sam, his fans, his fellow musicians, and friends and family—indeed, the very course of the blues—had been robbed. What would have become of Magic Sam and his music, we'll never know. But everyone just knew that Sam was on the verge of something monumental."

BUDDY GUY

BY JAS OBRECHT It's almost midnight at Legends, Buddy Guy's popular Chicago blues club, and our host is two-and-a-half hours into his set. He whoops, shouts, and sings with the passion of a country preacher faced with the fires of perdition. A quick jerk of his left hand, and his band drops to a *whisper*. He raises his eyebrows, grins charismatically, and careens into a solo like a runaway Mack. ¶ The crowd

Our first section presents a snapshot in time of Buddy Guy, February 1990, frustrated with his recording career and anxiously awaiting the big break that was soon to come. An edited version appeared as Guitar Player's *April 1990 cover story.*

roars wildly as Guy leaps from the stage to prowl the house. Surrounded by fans, he wails from the aisles, the pool tables and video machines, even from inside the ladies' room. His band pumps hard as he journeys outside the front door onto the icy corner of 8th and South Wabash, never missing a lick. A nearby El roars past, momentarily drowning out the band. Guy looks up and laughs: "That train is messing my time up!" He rushes back inside to finish his solo on tiptoe, his back against a wall as overhand runs and choked bends segue into a patented Muddy Waters lick.

Long before the sweat dries, you're sure of one thing: Like hurricanes, tornadoes, and earthquakes, there's no holding back Buddy Guy.

Jimi Hendrix sat at his feet. Eric Clapton insisted in *Musician* magazine that "Buddy Guy is by far and without a doubt the best guitar player alive. . . . If you see him in person, the way he plays is beyond anyone. Total freedom of spirit." Jeff Beck recalls the night he stopped by Legends with Stevie Ray Vaughan: "That was just the most incredible stuff I ever heard in my life. We all jammed, and it was so thrilling. That is as close as you can come to the heart of the blues."

Opened in 1989, Buddy Guy's Legends has become a mecca for rockers and bluesmen. During our visit, saxophone great A.C. Reed got up to sing a dirty blues, and B.B. Odom plowed through a set of his namesake's best-known tunes. Other famous drop-ins include Hubert Sumlin, Robert Lockwood, Jr., Eric Clapton, Bill Wyman and Ron Wood, Joe Walsh, Jimmy Vaughan, and Buddy's longtime playing partner, harmonica ace Junior Wells. (Blues-approved players preferred! Staffers still smirk about the night a batch of big-hair rockers from a nearby music industry convention stopped by and cleared the stage—and audience—with pyrotechnic blazing.)

What's going to happen on any given night is anyone's guess. Greg Rzab, a bassist who cut his teeth with James Cotton and Otis Rush before becoming the mainstay of Buddy's band, explains: "We've had this particular group about a month; Buddy just hires people and we play. I've seen him do this many times, like a snake molting. In fact, during the four years I've been with him, there hasn't been one rehearsal—ever. And with all the bands that have been here, I've never heard him direct any musician. There's no script. Buddy comes onstage and just starts playing. Sometimes it's like he's plugged into a 240-volt socket—all of a sudden, he'll burst into some stuff, and no one knows where it comes from! He plays some things with the same tone and feel, but there's no pattern in his playing, so we just wing it. I keep the groove happening, so he keeps me around. It's a great gig, and a lot of fun."

In his mid fifties, Buddy Guy still looks remarkably young. Face to face in Legends' small, bare-bulb back office, he sometimes bears an unnerving resemblance to Jimi Hendrix. Despite his supreme talent, he's criminally under-recorded. Raised in Louisiana, he cut his first sides in Baton Rouge in 1957; within a year, he was recording in Chicago with Otis Rush and Willie Dixon sitting in as his sidemen. He became a house guitarist for Chess Records in the early '60s, backing Muddy Waters and Howlin' Wolf, among others, but didn't release a full-fledged solo album until 1968's *A Man & The Blues*. His solo sessions escalated in the late '60s and early '70s, when he was frequently paired with Junior Wells. Since the mid '70s, though, he's been poorly represented on vinyl, except for portions of *Stone Crazy!* (recorded in France during the late '70s) and a few live tracks released by Antone's Records. His ambition at the time of this 1990 interview was to someday record an album of the *real* Buddy Guy.

IN SEARCH OF THE REAL BUDDY GUY

You're really a gentleman toward other players. You move to the side of the stage when they solo. You play great chords behind them.

[*Smiles.*] Yes. You know, I was taught by the greatest musicians that ever lived. And that was Muddy Waters and the Wolf and [Little] Walter and them. And they never did dominate, although they were, in my book, dominating musicians. I had a chance to come up there with them. Junior, James Cotton—we all taking lessons from those people. And in order for someone else to carry on, we have to just say, "Okay, here's your shot." I didn't get that. There's this young kid I got, Scott Holt; he's out of Tennessee, and his dad and his mama thanks me now, because I had to *fight* my way up. There was so many guitar players when I came to Chicago, you were just one out of the bucket. And there was so many places.

Your bandmates claim that you never try to cut other guitarists.

No, I don't, but I don't hold back. I was shy all of my life, up until I really got here in Chicago, and Muddy Waters slapped me in the face. Him and Wolf and Walter and them told me there ain't no such thing as that. I'm going to tell you exactly like they said: "There ain't no such thing as that shit." They said, "We know you can play, and you gonna play." Because I didn't want to get in their way. That's why I got a chance to make quite a few records with those guys. And I was so nervous at them asking me to play, I would lose a lot. I was afraid to even play what I knew, because I'd say, "How can I show who *I* am, sitting behind Muddy Waters, Wolf, or Walter," or any of the other greats that I played with—John Lee Hooker, Big Mama Thornton, just to name a few. And it all flashes back to me now when I'm playing onstage with these young kids. Sure, I feel proud letting them see what I'm doing, because I'm self-taught. It's a God-gifted talent that I have, because I've never been taught guitar by anybody.

John Lee Hooker says that a lot of young players can play flashy solos, but have trouble keeping a groove.

Music is just like the automobile: You get in it, you look for air conditioning, you look for heat, and you look for that thing to almost take care of you. These young people are saying, "I'm playing what's gonna take me to videos and MTV," whereas I suppose John Lee—and I'm not speaking for him—I suppose John Lee and myself and Muddy and all of us were just playing for what we like. When I learned how to play guitar, I wasn't looking forward to making a decent living at it, because there wasn't no such thing as that. We were playing for the love of blues. And the kind of blues that John Lee and I play, young people are going to take it and improve it. This is what they're doing. Our music don't take us into bigger spotlights as these young kids' music do. You know, the record companies are looking for young, good-looking, talented musicians doing something different, and the young people are record buyers. And the way they're playing those guitars is being sold to those young people, and that's what it's all about.

I would like to be commercially successful, but the love I have for blues sometimes makes me forget about how successful I could be—or wealthy, should I say—at my music. A lot of great friends have did a lot for me just by speaking about me, or speaking about my playing, which has helped me a lot. And I owe them a lot of big thanks for that.

Does having people like Clapton claiming you're the greatest living guitar player cause any pressure?

I feel good about him saying that, because it helped me with who I am. I don't have albums out that compare to Stevie and Eric and Beck and the rest of those people. My albums come seldom and *very* seldom, because I'm not with a company or anything now. I haven't had an album out in going on 12 years. And when someone like Eric makes a statement like that, it's great, but I don't want to pat myself on the back and try and live up to that. I don't let that cross my mind. I still just want to be Buddy Guy. I thank him for saying something like that, but man, you've got him for number one, Stevie, and quite a few more. That's a big question mark there—how good I am, or the best one alive. Now, I don't know about that. Because if you go catch him, he can make you almost forget about what he said, because he can play.

You own Legends, where you could control your sound. Why not tape a live album here?

I wish I could. I'd jump in Lake Michigan on a night like tonight and swim if someone would come say, "I want to do an album on you live." I just want to be treated right. I want to be Buddy Guy on an album. The closest I've ever come is *Stone Crazy!*, and I had to do that in France. The guy I did it for named the label after my mother, Isabel, and he said, "I want you to do what you've wanted to do all your life." I said, "What's that?" He said, "Be Buddy Guy." I said, "I'd be glad, then, to do an album for you."

I guess this is why I don't have a company giving me a shot at it now, because I really wants to be Buddy Guy. I wants to play the things that never came out of me that I know I have. And if I get that opportunity next time I go into the studio, I'm going to give it. If it sells, fine. If it don't, I will please myself inside because I know what I *can* do, and I'm not going to be shy with it anymore. I don't want anybody teaching me how to play when the tapes are rolling; I've had that happen to me a lot in the past. I've got to play what I already know.

You do have your own style. No one plays like Buddy Guy.

Thank you, but that leads back to being self-taught. I've got some bad habits in the way I play. That's the way I taught myself, and I can't get away from it.

What bad habits?

I play a stiff hand. My right hand is very stiff; it's not relaxed. My picking is very hard. I tears up a lot of my Ernie Ball strings at night. I have to keep them by the stack. I tears into my guitar with my whole heart, soul, and body. When I decided in 1967 to go professional, traveling as a leader, I left a day job driving a tow truck. And my boss told me, "Whenever you feel like coming back, you don't have to ask for a job. Just come in here and punch your time clock." And I do my guitar the same way. I feel towards my music just like I did when I was working. If I'm going to do it, I want to do it to death.

Was that your last day job?

Yeah. I went on vacation in 1967, and the manager I had then, Dick Waterman, told me, "The people love you out there." I said, "How could they love me? They don't know who I am. I just want to make sure I don't starve." My mother and father were living then, and I wanted to try to help them. I didn't trust myself on the road, as sometimes now I doubt my playing, even though Eric and them make those statements about it. But I think it's proven itself now. When I go places, quite a few people will be there saying, "I want to hear you." That lifts me a lot. And when I left on vacation that time, I went to Ann Arbor, Michigan. I had three pieces. I started playing some of my wild licks, and you could hear the kids between songs saying, "He's been listening to Hendrix." And then another guy would say, "No, that's who Hendrix got his influence from." So, they got to me and said, "You listen to Hendrix?" And I said, "Who is Hendrix?" And this kid looks like, "You've got to be crazy, if you don't know who that is." So I said, "I've got to find out who this is."

So I go to Toronto, my next stop, at an outdoor festival called Mariposa. There was about 30,000 people there, and naturally I got shaky nervous. A.C. Reed said, "Man, go burn them. If they don't know you now, they'll know you when you finished." So I said, "Okay, man, if you say so, I'm going to *try*." And I decided to jump off the stage. I thought there was a brace to brace myself back when I leaped off, but there wasn't nothing there but a curtain. But it so happened that I didn't fall; the curtain saved me. So I said to myself, "The best thing to do is don't stop playing." When I came from under there, there was 30,000 people hollering, "That's Buddy Guy! That's the real Buddy Guy."

Did you ever meet Hendrix?

Yes, I did. I've got a film of it now. The night Dr. Martin Luther King got assassinated, I saw a kid come in with a big hat on and ease up to the stage with a tape recorder. And some amateur cameraman was spotting his video on him. This was in New York City, and they were yelling about him being Jimi Hendrix. I was just doing what I had to do, and he said, "Pay them no mind. I've been trying to catch you. I canceled a show in London just to come see you play, because I'd never seen you. But I heard you, and I stole a lot of licks from you." As a matter of fact, a kid just came in the club and said, "I've got a tape I want to show you: Hendrix on his knees, taping your licks and watching you play with your mouth, with the guitar under your feets, and different things like that."

Did you get some of that from Guitar Slim?

I got all of it from Guitar Slim. I don't want to make a comment about what some other guitar players would say, but Guitar Slim and T-Bone Walker are some of the people I copied for *showmanship*. B.B. King, he don't have to do nothing but just shake his left hand and everybody will listen. But the first time I saw Guitar Slim, a guy brought him in on his shoulders like a little baby. And he had on a red suit—I got one back there now for tonight—with some white shoes. And when I heard him, I said, "My God! This is the way a guitar should be played."

If you're not going to give it all you've got, you shouldn't play anymore, because you owe this to the people. Your fans are your supporters. Don't hold nothing back from them. You owe them everything that they come to see. And strangely enough, since I've been professional, I haven't missed a gig yet. I had the flu last night enough for the average guitar player to say, "Get somebody in my place," and stay at home. But I think somebody was sitting there last night saying, "I wants to see Buddy. I wants to see him play." And I owe that to him. I'm going to come if I have to come on my knees and play.

What should a Buddy Guy solo be all about?

Muddy Waters, T-Bone, Guitar Slim, and B.B. King, and Eric Clapton. I could name them for an hour.

And yet you don't sound like any of them.

I guess that's the Buddy Guy coming out in me then, but I be hitting the same strings, the same fingering of the board, that they do. And the same thing goes for them. You know, I can't be a B.B. King. I can't be an Eric, even though I try a lot. I wonder a lot—what's my problem about not getting records out? So I try to be everybody up there at once—even John Lee Hooker and Lightnin' Hopkins. And please believe me, I'm not lying: Even before I go out tonight, all of these people will cross my mind just as I pick up my guitar. It looks like they're telling me, "Go get it, Buddy. Do it!" Because without those people, I don't even know if I would be playing. Yes, they were sending a message to me while they were alive, and I think they're still sending it to me now, saying, "You've got to play. We left this load on your shoulders, and you've got to carry on." Matter of fact, Muddy told me that two weeks before he passed. I heard he was sick, and Junior Wells and I called him. I said, "We're on our way to your house." He said, "Don't come, because I'm doing fine. Just don't let the blues die." And the next time I heard, it was the international press saying, "How do you feel about Muddy passing?" And I couldn't say nothing for a day. I just sat there. I just couldn't believe it. You know, those things are going to happen to all of us.

Do any conversations with Muddy stand out in your mind?

Yes. I was very shy when I started. I wouldn't sing, but I would play if you'd corner me off, and I'd play well. And Muddy went out there one night and said, "Gee, that guy can play," but when he called me out of the room, I just shied back in the corner and said, "Pay him no mind, man. He's just talking like that." And he just turned around and slapped me, man! And it was hard enough for me to say, "Why are you doing that?" He said, "I don't want to hear that from you. You gonna play." After that he just took over like a daddy to me, man.

As a matter of fact, Muddy was the one . . . I was going on my third day without eating in Chicago, trying to borrow a dime to call my mom to get back to Louisiana. And Muddy Waters bought me a salami sandwich and put me in the back of his 1958 Chevy station wagon. He said, "You're hungry, and I know it." And talking to Muddy Waters, I wasn't hungry anymore; I was full just for him to say, "Hey." I was so overjoyed about it, my stomach wasn't cramping anymore. I told him that, and Muddy said, "Get in the goddamn car." Yes, he's dead and gone, and that's exactly what he told me. This happened at the famous 708 Club, and he was parked in front of the club. And then he said, "Sit down and eat." I said, "Yes, sir!" [*Laughs.*] I wish he were here now. I thanked him many times before he passed away, and told him how much better I felt after he slapped me and made me eat that sandwich that night.

And then later he just walked up to Junior and grabbed him in the collar and went to slapping him. Junior said, "Why are you doing that to me?" And Muddy said, "Remember you used to stay at my house? And remember you pulled your knife on me?" Junior had pulled a knife on him because the whole band was staying at his house, and he found out that the drummer or somebody didn't pay him rent, so Junior felt that he shouldn't pay no rent. [*Laughs.*] Muddy said, "I got you where you don't have the knife now, and I'll whoop your ass!" And he starts spanking Junior all in the face. Junior wasn't saying nothing, just holding his head down. I said, "You going to fight back, Junior?" He said, "No, I ain't going to fool with that old man." [*Laughs.*]

Yeah, good old man. He could spank me now if he was here. I wouldn't say nothing but laugh and go drink me some beer behind that man. [*Laughs.*] Yeah, I deserve a spanking from somebody that great, man, because those people paved the way for the electric music that we play now. I don't know if anybody else would give them that credit, but them, and the Chess Records, left a great trail for us to follow. Yes, they did.

You recorded with Muddy early in your career.

Yes, I did. He had heard about me because I'd played a set or two with a horn player by the name of Rufus Foreman, and Magic Sam had seen me play. And the word was just getting around: "This little black guy from Louisiana can play, man. He's playing these Muddy Waters tunes." Naturally, that's what I was playing—B.B. or Muddy or Jimmy Reed. It just caught on, and they took me in like a kid. For instance, for one of Muddy's albums, Leonard Chess said, "I want to go way back and have an acoustic album," and I got to play on that [*Folk Singer*]. As a matter of fact, I'm fixing to do some things with Eric Clapton the first week in February [1990], and from then on I'm going to do two or three songs each and every night with my acoustic. Because it takes me back to the sound that you can't take away from the guitar.

Is Folk Singer *one of your favorite albums?*

Yes, but everything I did with Muddy Waters is my favorite. Everything I ever did with that guy, man, was like an experience to me. I often tell young people right now that those are some shoes that never will be fulfilled. I used to listen to that guy sing "Got My Mojo Working," and it was like my mother sewing on a sewing machine. She would make her feet make the stitches, and she never would stick her finger when she pushed under that needle. And that's just the way he would sing "Mojo Working." And whatever he sang, he could make me sit there all night. During those days, there wasn't hardly a club in Chicago that didn't stay open until 5:00 in the morning. And you better believe they had to kick me out of it, because I couldn't miss a lick of it. [*Laughs.*] My manager gave me an album of everything he ever recorded [*Muddy Waters* box set], and I can go lie down on my floor now and put them on one by one, and don't miss nothing he said or what he played.

Do you own a lot of records?

Not so much of the new stuff. Not much of my stuff. But him, and B.B. King, and the Wolf.

What records do you treasure the most?

"Sweet Little Angel" by B.B. King, and Muddy Waters' catalog. And I got everything Eric ever played, him and Stevie, and all of the guys. I think we listen to each other a lot. And when we meet, that makes us communicate better too.

Stevie Ray covered your "Leave My Girl Alone" during his tour with Jeff Beck.

Yeah, he's a great friend of mine. Matter of fact, he came here as a special guest on my birthday. He walks in the door, and these people just go crazy. And now he tells me just call him; anytime he's available, he will come sit in here with me to help keep the club going.

Your version of "Leave My Girl Alone" has one of your characteristic sounds—the double-stop with a constant high note over a hammer-on in the lower voice.

It's kind of like an octave with two fingers. You pick the two strings at the same time, but they're different notes. I could probably show you better than I could explain it to you. I don't have long fingers, but I can stretch over almost five frets.

I can play the *A* note on the *E* string, and take the *G* string and go five frets down and drag the little finger back up and play those octaves all the way back up until the fingers go together, plucking two strings at the same time.

What's the secret to playing those Buddy Guy wildman bends?

I use my third finger. It seems to be the strongest one. It's hard for me to explain what I'll be doing, but when I'm up there trying to please that audience, I can bend it from here to the front door of this place [*laughs*]. Eric mentioned something about that once. I just will bend it until it breaks. I'll make the little *E* kiss the big *E*. Yes, and if it sounds good, I'll keep getting it. And if it sounds bad, I just try to make it sound good.

Do you back that ring finger up with other fingers?

I don't have to. You just have to practice and get your fingers real strong. I'm not the best guitar player. I've got a lot I should learn, or could learn, but I always thought that other finger has to be ready for something else. I can't just depend on it on that string, because if you stay on that one string, you'll wear your welcome out. So I have to stretch it, make it kiss the *E,* and go grab another one and take it somewhere else. I try to make the best that I can out of it.

Describe how you add vibrato.

You mean with the left hand? It's similar to what B.B. King does, rocking back and forth with the hand, but I'm not as good as him. I don't think anybody can do that as well as he can, and we talked about that. As a matter of fact, last year [1989] was the first time I opened the show for him—twice—and you better believe I had to hurry up and get my front-row seat so I could try to get some tips on that man. This guy invented the squeezing. T-Bone was playing the neck of the guitar, but when B.B. started squeezing that guitar, we *all* started squeezing that thing. I have to give it to him, because I got more into guitar than I'd ever been. I was just so in love with playing blues, I would play Lightnin' Hopkins and T-Bone. And then when he squeezed the guitar, I said, "Jesus Christ! Who is this?" And when I saw him, I thought I had a lot to learn. And I'm still like that.

How far back does your knowledge of blues go? Are you familiar with players from the 1920s?

Yes. Strangely enough, I'm one of the luckiest blues guitar players alive in that respect, because I had a chance to play with Arthur Crudup in Australia. We went on tour together. I had a chance to play with Fred McDowell. And Son House, who just passed a year-and-a-half ago; I understand he taught Muddy. So what else can you ask for if you're a guitar player and had a chance to sit down with *this* guy and play? Those are the kind of things that keep us all going.

When do you play your best?

When I'm not trying to be my best. When I'm not pressing myself to try to make this audience get into what I'm doing. I feel like I'm not doing a good job if I don't see them smiling or saying, "Yes." For example, when we first started going to Europe playing blues, the Europeans were like, "We take this as a *serious* music, almost like opera." Nobody said anything or patted their feet—nothing. I was thinking, "Oh, Jesus. I'm not doing nothing right now. Maybe I got to flip out or do something." Then I got booed. I talked to Muddy again, and he said, "Don't feel bad. It happened to me." When Chris Barber took Muddy back to England for the first time, they booed him for playing this loud stuff through the amp! They invited him back the next year, and he left the amp and took the acoustic guitar, and they booed him for not playing the amp! [*Laughs.*] The same thing happened to me in Germany. I had to go stepping out in front of Roosevelt Sykes, John Lee Hooker, and Big Mama Thornton, and they would just boo every time they'd see me. I said, "Oh, my God!" Me being shy, man, I was just like going under the table. And then when I went back, I said, "I know what I'll do. I'll get me a chair and sit down like John Lee and them and play." I went back, and they got me the same way they did Muddy. They said, "No, no. You've got to get out there and move around. That's what we're looking for now." It takes you so long to figure out what they're saying, unless someone comes up and translates it for you.

You're said to be one of the first Chicago blues guitarists to play standing up.

When I came to Chicago, everybody was sitting down: Muddy, Junior, the Wolf, Walter, and all of them were in chairs playing this beautiful music that still is the best blues you ever heard of. And we used to have the Battle of the Guitars. I was the poorest, and I told them I needed the more-est [*laughs*]. Most of the band-stands used to be behind the bar, and Muddy, Wolf, or Walter would play in their chairs. So I said, "Oh, jeez, these guys is playing way more than I can play. I got to figure out something else to do to be a winner." The winner got a bottle of whiskey, and at that time I didn't drink whiskey. I had a little friend who weighed about 300, and he said, "I'll make you win this whiskey, because I don't have a nickel." It was snowing, and he said, "You remember that thing you told me Guitar Slim used to do?" I had this 150-foot lead wire, and he said, "I'm going to take this wire outside, and you sit in the car. I'm going to plug it in while you're in the car. You come out of this car playing and sliding in the snow, and we got the whiskey." I said, "That's not going to win it, but I'm going to do it."

And when they called me, I stepped out of the car. He opened the door and said, "You all want to see him, come out here." The place was packed, and I had the streets full. So when I walked in, there was Magic Sam and a few more guitar play-ers—including Earl Hooker, who is the greatest guitar player that I ever saw. They had the bottle of whiskey, and it was empty. They told me, "You won it, but we done drinked it all!" [*Laughs.*] The club owner came out and picked me up and stood me on the bar, and I walked straight down the bar. And then he said, "Here's another bottle of whiskey." And that little guy looked at me and said, "Let's go to the bath-room." And I went in the men's bathroom and played for about 45 minutes solo!

Wasn't that called "headcutting"?

Yes, but I don't think I would outplay anybody. It was just like a winner in a contest. We didn't have just one judge saying, "Buddy, you won it." The audience would clap, and it was kind of like something on TV a long time ago, when they'd show a gauge needle move according to how loud the audience clapped. After a while it got to the point where they'd say, "Well, I don't care who wins it, we're going to drink it anyway, because he doesn't drink!" [*Laughs.*] So I learned a lot from that, and I got a lot of experience from it. Those guys like Earl Hooker, man, they couldn't jump around and run up and down the bar like I did, and that's the advantage I took of them.

No one ever played slide like Earl Hooker.

No. I found one of Muddy's tunes in this collection I've got, and he had Hooker playing on it. As it struck, my guitar player said, "Listen to Muddy!" I said, "That's not Muddy; that's Earl Hooker. Nobody plays it that clean, and you don't hear nothing but the strings."

What did he use for a slide?

I got it! I got his slide in my pocket at home, and I sleep with that thing. It's just a piece of pipe like anybody else used.

You're not usually associated with slide guitar.

I learned a little of Muddy's slide, but it don't ever come out. I'm embarrassed to come out with it. After I heard Earl Hooker play slide, I put that thing I was using in my pocket—it was a bottleneck—and I said, "I don't even want to see that no more, the way this guy plays."

Did you ever play in open tuning?

No, I never did. When I finally met B.B. King, he took me to his hotel room—I didn't even use a straight pick then, I was using fingerpicks—and he told me, "If you want to get a little faster, you have to start practicing with a straight pick." And from him telling me that, I would have one ever since.

You hold the pick with your thumb and two fingers.

Because I can switch it into my palm, and you won't miss it. All of a sudden, I'm picking with my fingers. My pick's like a small triangle. I have to buy them by the thousands because I break them. [*Pulls a Gibson medium rounded-triangle from his pocket.*] That's a heavyweight; the thin is the one I use mostly. I also have a [coffee-colored] Buddy Guy pick that I give away to people as souvenirs.

Do you always know what you're doing in musical terms?

No.

Do you know the names of chords?

A few. F, F#, and flats, and so on like that. You learn that through the years.

Do you always know what key you're playing in?

Yes. You have to know that. But if you'd asked me what did I just play before I left the stage, each note—no, I couldn't tell you. But I could go back and get the guitar and find it and tell you what note I played.

If you're in the key of A, *for instance, will you automatically solo in a certain area of the fingerboard?*

Yes. I know exactly where I want to be. On all of the new guitars—except the acoustics—you've got several places you can play A. I play A in the middle of the neck on the 5th fret, and then you can go to the high A, which is *way* up there. You start all over again at E when you get higher [at the 12th fret]. It goes, E, F, the same as it is at the beginning of the neck. I don't run enough in the different positions on my guitar like a lot of people do. For instance, George Benson is one of the greatest I've seen; he can do that from top to bottom. I have a tendency to stay there and wear a hole in the neck of my guitar [*laughs*] and just play one sound. Oh, that sounds so good! Someone stole my first Strat from me, and Eric had asked me about buying it. I had wore that neck almost through, and I didn't want to get it redone because I wanted it to stay original, just like it was.

You're now endorsing Fender and Guild.

Yes. I started with a Strat in the beginning. Guitar Slim was tearing 'em up every time I saw him—that's just the kind of wildman he was—and I wanted to be like him so much, I just went into that. And that guitar was built to take it. I finally went to Newport in 1967, and the owner of Guild offered me an endorsement.

What else could I ask for? He walks up and says, "You come over to the factory tomorrow; we're going to give you a guitar." And I started playing the Guild guitar. Then B.B. King walked in in New York and said, "I see you got a little Lucille." [*Laughs*.] It was red, and that was enough to make me stick with playing that. It was a semi-hollow Starfire. Now I have a Nightingale. They made one for Eric and one for me. Mine is number 002.

I pop so many strings from playing so darn hard that I have to keep two or three guitars up there to make sure the few fans I got don't miss anything. When I break a string, I don't want to take that time in between and have them missing that note. My guy just hands me another guitar while he puts the string on the other one.

What's your favorite guitar?

The two I'm playing, the Fender and the Guild.

Does your tone change when you use a wireless?

Yes, a bit. Actually, a cord is as true as the acoustic guitar. It gives you the truer sound.

What's your favorite setup from the guitar?

I'm using a Marshall amp. Different clubs will call for you to do different sets on the amp. Sometimes you can be too loud, and normally I will ask the audience, "Am I too loud, or am I too soft?" because I do play very soft sometimes. And then you get the mixed emotions. Some will say, "You're too loud," and then the other half will say, "You're not loud enough." So then I just back up from the mike and tell a big lie, like, "I'm going to do it my way anyway!" I usually use a Marshall 800 amp, but they just sent me the new two-piece head. My soundman hooked it up for me last night and said, "Go for it!" I kind of liked it, but I've got to learn it and play with it for a while. Then I'll be able to get my different sounds and things that *I* like best out of that myself. I play for the people, and if it calls for it, I'll use a wah-wah or an octave [divider]. I'm not trying to be like anybody else.

Do you modify your Strats?

No, this one I have now is special-made for me. They made one for Eric Clapton, and they called me in there to pick out the neck and the kind I want. And without even knowing what he had, I just went for this. They said it was too close to put out a Buddy Guy model or something like that, but it's a bit different from what he picked out.

Some players insist that old Strats are the best.

Well, I've talked to quite a few of the engineers, and they will tell you it's just like the car now compared to the cars in the '40s and '50s. You could run one of those old cars into these things we got now, and that car out of the '50s is going to have a scratch and the one we're riding in now is going to have the grille knocked out because it's plastic. So what they told me is that it's the same thing as talking about guitars. The material's not the same. The wood that they're making them out of now is not the same. And why is that? I don't know.

Actually, I was in Africa in 1969 with my original Strat. We were riding in a station wagon, and it was tied on the top of the station wagon. They was driving 85 and 90 miles an hour, and the guitar flew off and fell out of the case. We backed up to get it, and a car was coming. I laid in the street to make sure the car would go around. The guy said, "African people will run over you, man! They don't care nothing about it." And the only string that was out of tune was the *E*. [*Laughs.*] It got scratched all up, but it was still in tune.

That guitar got stolen?

Yes, some kid broke into my house when I was living here in Chicago, and I guess I cried as long as I did when my mother passed. The lady next door was a nice old lady, which was the kid's mother, and I guess he was so embarrassed. I even asked him why did he sell it—I would've bought it again. I would even give the guy more than what he got for it. He left his mother's keys in the apartment, and the police said, "Whoever broke into here left the keys," and his mother said, "Those are my keys, and my son did it." Her husband was very sick, and I was loaning her money every month, and she owed me. She said, "Well, I'll have to pay you," and I cried more then. I said, "There's no way you could pay me." I wouldn't even accept it from her, because she didn't do it; she was a very nice lady. As a matter of fact, I talked to her a couple of days ago.

Do you have a guitar at home?

Yeah, a lot of them. I got one in the bed with me now, 12-string acoustic. I use heavier strings at home; that keeps the muscles in my fingers a little stronger.

What do you play when you're by yourself?

I will put the slide on sometimes. If you catch me practicing at home, I hit a few licks that I hit here onstage. And to be honest with you, a lot of stuff you see me do onstage, I've never done it before. Everything I do onstage comes to me right then. I just have this good feeling about blues music and what I'm doing, and I feel like I should *try* it, man, try it. Actually, a lot of the sustained notes that you hear us all doing now—and Hendrix said he was getting this from me—I was doing out in the public early on. Chess Records called it *noise;* they wouldn't let me cut it. They was telling me, "Who's going to listen to that noise?" And where did I get the idea from? Once I took a break and forgot to cut my guitar off, and this lady passed by with a wide skirt. The jukebox was going with a tune I liked—I had punched it—and her dress tail hit the *G* string, and this guitar just stayed there, humming in *G*, the whole time that record was going. I got the idea from that to just hold this sustained note. That had to be '59, or something like that. If you love it like I do, boom! I can just be sitting there listening, and all of a sudden somebody will hit something, and I'll jump and say, "What was that?" It's just like a good-looking woman will pass, and you can't keep your eyes off.

What's the best band you ever had?

If I had to name the best people that I ever played with in my life, I would name the guys traveling with me in about 1967: A.C. Reed, [tenor saxophonist] Bobby Fields, who passed away, a bass player named Jack Myers, and a drummer named Glen McTeer. But I would have to put Fred Below and Otis Spann in too. Those guys taught me a whole lot, just about being a musician. Below used to look up and curse at me, and he would be counting. You could hear him playing drums, "A-one, two, three. . ." And when I'd make a mistake, he would tell me right then [*laughs*]. A funny story: When we used to be recording at Chess, they built a pen to put Below in, because Below would interfere with the other musicians, telling them what to play! Oh, man, how I wish nobody had to die, when it comes to some-thing like Below and Otis Spann. Otis Spann would set a bottle of whiskey on a piano and tell me, "If you don't take a drink of this, you ain't going to let the soul out of you." Yeah, they was the best I ever seen, man. They corrected me in so many wrong things I was doing in my earlier days. If I was playing a bad time, they would tell me, "You got to clean that up."

Is that where your good sense of rhythm comes from?

I don't know if that's the case. I would listen to them. And right now, I listen to these kids if they tell me something. I've never gotten to the point of, "You can't tell me nothing!" In anything I do, I'm listening. There's people working for me in the club right now. If they tell me something, I don't jump up and say, "Oh, no, this is *my* club. I want it this way; I want it that way." They'll hear, and I've got to listen. That's the way it should be.

You never rehearse your band.

[*Laughs.*] You know, that's a bad habit. But I like for my guys to be free. I don't hold anybody *down* back there behind me. And tonight I'm going to do the same thing. Let them go, let them loose. On a given night, they're going to give me the best that they can. I didn't ever rehearse with Muddy or any of them. They would tell me, "Go get it, Buddy." Matter of fact, I was playing with B.B. King at Bill Graham's Fillmore West one night, and he said, "I'm going to play, but I want *you* to put on a show."

Do any of your children play guitar?

I got one son, 19 years old. He came to me about a year-and-a-half ago and said, "Daddy, give me one of them guitars. I'm going to play Prince." I gave him a big amplifier and a guitar, and two weeks later I went over, and this guy was playing this thing about the doves on Prince ["When Doves Cry"]. And he looked at me and laughed. He's as much shy as I was when I was a youngster. He said, "I got Prince, now who else should I listen to, Daddy?" I said, "Well, if you like Prince that well, you better find Hendrix. I'll look out for some stuff for you." And before I found anything, he had found a Hendrix show on an educational channel. He came back; he was crying. He said, "Daddy, you know the first thing Hendrix said?" I said, "What?" He said, "He said he learned something from you. I didn't know you could play that." I said, "You didn't ever ask me, son. If you had, I could've told you I gets wild." He never could just see me in person, and I don't have anything on television that he could see. I finally sneaked him in a club and he saw me play, and he cried a little more. I done wrote a song like that, too: My child don't know who I am, so how could I expect other young people to know who I am? That's because I don't have records out.

I just hope to hit something one of these days. Maybe somebody will get back to some record company and say, "You better listen to him, and give him another shot at another album." I don't know. If I knew what my problem was, I would correct it. I would like to do a little better financially, because I'm not getting any younger. I want to play as long as I'm alive, and there'll come a time when you need something to carry you as a musician. I've been lucky enough to buy a couple of raggedy buildings, and I pay a retirement-type insurance, because I don't want to be a burden on nobody if I live long enough to survive this. I don't want nobody to say, "We got to take care of him," make collections for me, and different things like that. And in order to do that, you have to make it while you're in good health and try to save some of it for a later day. My mother used to tell me, "Son, always put up a dry stick for a wet day." A blues player like myself has so many ups and downs—more downs than ups.

Despite this, you seem to love your work.

I love it so much, man, I even forgot what down is like. Even when I'm down, I think I'm up. If anybody in the business loves it better than me, they must eat it! [*Laughs.*] All my life, I've been doing what I love, and I'm not going to change that for nothing in the world. I'm having a lot of fun, and I've never been angry enough to do something to somebody in a way that would hurt them. All of my life, I've been in between people. When I'm in clubs and two people are disagreeing and it looks like it's going to get physical, I can get in between them and say, "Why? What do you gain by doing this to each other? Tomorrow you could be best friends. Tomorrow he could do something to save your life. But if you hurt him or kill him, who knows what he could have done? He's not there to do it."

The world is so tangled with so much craziness. I think we need to be loved a little more than we do. That's why I'm so thankful for my music. At least I draw people together and try to put smiles on their faces. I'm so tired of frowns and fighting. One day I hope the whole world could just look and smile. Yes, especially when I play a note on my guitar!

"THE HAPPIEST MAN ALIVE" Buddy Guy's fortunes changed considerably after the preceding interview. When we spoke again on a frozen winter's morning in 1993, his new album, *Feels Like Rain,* was ready to ship, following the most critically acclaimed release of his career, *Damn Right, I've Got the Blues*. At 57, Guy was lightning-quick to honor those who inspired him, beginning our conversation: "Whenever you hear me play, man, there's always a part of Muddy Waters, Howlin' Wolf, Little Walter, T-Bone Walker, and all those great musicians. Everybody comes out in me."

During our 1990 interview, you said you'd jump into Lake Michigan in exchange for being able to make the album you wanted to make.

Yeah, but don't make me jump in there this morning—it's zero outside!

Have you come close to that goal?

I think some of the things behind *Damn Right, I've Got the Blues* are. I won a Grammy with it, and I feel very proud of Silvertone Records for giving me the chance. Bonnie Raitt—she's on my next album—she felt the same way. Before that, people were coming up to me and saying, "You got it. I see it. What's *wrong?*" My late friend Stevie, Eric, Beck, Keith [Richards], and all of them, they was coming up to me and saying, "I can't understand. We come out and we play with you, and you're like blowing people off the stage, and won't nobody record you." I didn't let that send me down into the basement and forget about myself. I just kept saying that sooner or later, somebody gonna hear me. I'm just gonna keep on. You don't give up. My parents taught me to try, and I just been trying and trying. It's better late than never. It's very late in the day for me, but . . .

You're still a young man.

[*Laughs.*] Well, you know, you need glasses, I'll tell you that. Then you'll see what I'm talkin' about. But I'm enjoying it. I'm just very proud, thankful to God that I'm still around to see this thing finally happening to me at this late day and age, but I'm not looking at that. I'm just looking at the fun I'm having and knowing that I'm a part, hopefully, of trying to keep the blues alive. That makes me the happiest man alive.

Feels Like Rain has some nice covers, but the real guitar genius seems to be in the two songs you wrote.

[*Laughs.*] Ah, well, this is what we talkin' about. You know, throughout my whole musical career, I've always wanted to just cut loose. And I have been told from the time I came here to Chicago that didn't nobody want to hear that. But, as Albert King says, as the years go passing by, somebody was listening. And if it wasn't Eric, it was Stevie or somebody else who was selling enough records for somebody sooner or later to say, "What the hell they talkin' about? They keep talking about Buddy Guy, but I never heard him. I gotta check him out." I owe the biggest thanks in the world to Eric, the late Stevie, Keith, Beck, and all these people, because they was sellin' records and I wasn't. Finally Silvertone said, "I gotta check this out," and they came to me and said, "Listen, we want you to go in and make a record of Buddy Guy, and we gonna support you." I said, "This is what I been waiting for." At the time I signed, I had an offer from two or three more labels, and the first thing they asked me was, "What have you got new?" And I'm like saying to myself, "I don't need nothin' new. Whatever I got old will sell, if you let me do it." Yeah.

What's the story behind "Country Man"?

I left home with that, man. I had kind of written a song before *Damn Right, I've Got the Blues,* but I wasn't through with the song. It goes through your mind, and if it happens you're out there. I just wanted the fans and the people in general to know that I am a country man. I was born and raised on a farm [in Louisiana]. I'm a sharecropper's son. I know how to pick cotton, feed the chickens, and milk the cows. I want to be famous, but I don't want to be so famous that I forget the people who knew me before I was famous. And this is my expression of lettin' people know I'm gonna stay the same as long as I'm alive. Just come and see me or call me, even if it's early in the morning. I'm not gonna say, "To hell with you." I'm up. I'm walkin' the dog. I'm havin' coffee. I'm out here shovelin' snow, cuttin' grass, washin' the car. I'm no different from nobody else, man. And it's not gonna go to my head because I won a Grammy. Hopefully, if I can win another one it's not gonna change me at all. I wanna talk to you, I want you to come and see me, I want you to drink out of the same beer can with me, and we'll just have fun. You'll say "That's just another guy" after I leave the stage or before I get to the stage.

You've always seemed to be that way.

Yes, and I'm gonna stay that way. Because I got friends very famous, and it look like something happen to you when you can't just relax. I own the largest blues club here in Chicago, and I go set on the bar. Sometime I have to take my rings off because some people say, "I can't believe I'm shakin' your hand," but they be *breakin'* it. [*Laughs.*] So that's the way I want to live. Some people isolate themselves after they get to be known, but people make you. And people also can break you.

Your other blues original, "She's a Superstar," has a very positive attitude towards women.

That's the general idea of the song. The way I was raised was, "Without a woman, what would we do?" [*Laughs.*] With her, what do we do? That's one of those things: You can't get along with her, but you can't do without her. This song goes out to my sisters, my aunties, my wife, my family, my daughter, and every woman I know. I just want to let them know I got the respect and love for them that I wished everybody had. They stand out. You can't get along with 'em, you can't live without 'em, so what do you do, man? I just come out and let you know. They're superstars in my book.

That solo has some unusual tones.

Yeah, I was using an octave pedal and a wah-wah. That's it. You know, young people are record buyers. Blues records can't crash the big AM stations always, so I'm trying to get some licks. I'm trying to say, okay, if I can get one or two tunes on this album to make you play it, somebody go out and listen to it, they gonna get a taste of the blues right behind that. So I'm trying to get slick enough to trick somebody who's eight or nine or thirteen years old into saying, "Who the hell is that? I went to buy it for this effects he was givin', and he done hit me with this Muddy Waters thing behind it. Who was Muddy Waters?" So I'm trying to keep this music alive through my way of saying I'm gonna outsmart you with the blues. As long as I live, I'm gonna get it in that door one way or another.

Is that why you did a soul cover and some rock and roll?

Ah, no. In a way that could be the truth, but before you're Buddy Guy, before you're Muddy Waters, before you're B.B. King, you have to play everybody. You know, when they was throwin' songs at me, they was looking at me like, "You're a blues player, but look at this." And I said, "Let's cut it." They was looking at me: "You know how to do that?" I said, "Man, what you think I did before I was Buddy Guy?" I had to play everybody's music in Chicago to keep the little five-dollars-a-night gig in the club. I couldn't go in and play all of Buddy Guy's stuff. I didn't have nothin'. I had to play a large variety—Little Richard, Fats Domino, Guitar Slim, and maybe a country and western, which I never did learn that well—so the guy would say, "You can bring him in here on a Friday and a Saturday, because he's playin' what these people want to hear." And that's what made who Buddy Guy is today. And then you get in the studio, and you go for yourself.

You arranged Guitar Slim's "Suffering Mind" like a gospel tune. Have you performed gospel?

I tried to sing gospel. My family is very Baptist, and you know, I'm not a baby. Before the electric guitar, I was listening to Lou Rawls with the Pilgrim Travelers and Sam Cooke with the Soul Stirrers, stuff like that. They didn't have no drums or stuff like that. They was using four, five, six guys, and making that musical sound. Then they came upon the amplified guitars and things and put them into the churches and into the blues. Of course I was singing spiritual stuff, yeah. Not in the church, but I was walkin' in the streets. Not on the corners—it was on the road, where I come from—but I would take a walk and belt it out.

Besides Bonnie Raitt, does anyone else play guitar solos on the record?

Bonnie's guitar player on "Feels Like Rain" [Johnny Lee Schell], he was hittin' some of those notes there with me. Bonnie played the slide, and he was playing most of the rhythm guitar on there.

You're also paired with John Mayall.

[*Laughs.*] Yeah. Well, John is an old friend, man. You know, Eric got kicked out there with John as a very youngster. John is one of those old pros in blues, man. He's one of the originals that was diggin' that stuff up in England.

Were you aware of his music during the '60s?

Yes, I was, but only by records. My first trip to London was February of 1965, and every time I see Eric and Beck, they tell me they heard about me because they had one record, the record I had made live at the Copa Cabana with Muddy Waters and Howlin' Wolf. They shake this record at me every time I see 'em. I was going crazy with it [in England], and Eric said, "I was out there in the truck, about to give up. I didn't know a Strat would sound like that." That's the time him and John were fittin' to explode that music. Actually, I didn't know who I was. When I got to London, they were saying, "Buddy Guy!" And I'm saying, "How the hell do *you* know me as a musician, and I don't know me?" Next thing I know, they were saying Hendrix, Eric, the Cream, and all that, and they're coming to me saying, "I got this from you." I told Eric once, "'Strange Brew,' man, that note runs me crazy." He said, "It should. It's yours." Yeah.

It must have seemed strange the first time you heard British kids playing your music.

Well, not really. The strangest thing was I didn't know nobody was payin' attention to me. In a club, yeah, I'm gonna put on a show. But my records were just a lost cause. I was doing my biggest work *behind* Muddy, Junior Wells, and whoever else would ask me to come in and make a session with them. I was just happy, man, to be invited to a Muddy Waters session or Wolf session or Little Walter session or Sonny Boy session. See, my dream had come true. I didn't give a damn about no hit record. I didn't give a damn who hear me. I had achieved what I left Louisiana to do, which is meet these great blues musicians. Then when Eric and Beck or whoever say, "I got something from you," I said, "Hell, I didn't know it." Yeah. That's just how lost I was with that. I was just havin' fun.

When you worked with Muddy on Folk Singer, *did he give you directions on what he wanted you to play?*

No. He knew. Actually, I remember that very well. Leonard Chess and Ralph Bass, one of the producers, told Muddy to go in Mississippi and try to find somebody because the colleges was goin' for that acoustic blues. They wanted him to go back and find somebody who really could play the acoustic guitar with him. They wanted no band and no electric instruments. He said, "Set the session up tomorrow. I got it." And when I walked in the studio, Leonard Chess and them was lookin' at Muddy like he was crazy. He just told him, "Shut the fuck up. I got who I wanted." I went to playin', and man, they're sittin' there with their mouth wide open, saying, "Now how in the hell you know that?" I said, "What did you think I learn on?" Even Willie Dixon didn't know it, and he's on there. That was a morning I never will forget. Of course, I love that record. I got that record, and I'll keep it as long as I live.

Your new version of Muddy's "Nineteen Years Old" dives straight into the heart of the blues.

[*Laughs.*] Who wouldn't want to do something by Muddy Waters? Nobody can wear his shoes, but it's an honor to even try and do one of Muddy Waters' songs, man. They came up in the studio and said, "What do you got real bluesy?" I said, "Man, this 'Nineteen Years Old.'" And they just said, "Roll the tape." No rehearsal or nothing. I just wanted to play the blues the way he used to. Muddy didn't come in and say, "I wanna rehearse." He used to look at me and say, "If I rehearse it, I'm gonna mess it up. Let's just play the blues. That's all you need to do."

Your fingerstyle solo parallels Muddy's slide solo.

Well, I used to watch that guy, man, and happy tears used to fall out of my eyes when I'd see him do it. Oh yeah. When I came to Chicago I had a slide, and I think I got the late Earl Hooker's somewhere with me now. I saw them guys play that slide, man, and I gave it to them! [*Laughs.*] I said, "Ain't no sense in me even tryin'," the way they was playin' that slide—Muddy, Elmore James, Earl Hooker, and all these people. And the way Earl Hooker could make a slide talk, I said, "I'm through."

Do you ever play slide when you're alone?

No, but I'm thinking about now maybe I should just try it once in a while. But now you got people like Bonnie Raitt and that little kid in Florida. He's only about 11 years old, and when you hear this kid—man! They brought him on the stage with me in Florida, and I thought, well, okay, he's gonna hit two or three licks. That guy come out there, man, and I was cuttin' loose. Every time I played something, I heard somebody answering me. I looked down, and he just wasn't even paying me no attention. Man, he was playin' the hell out of his guitar. I said, "Hey, man, you got to be heard of." His name is Derek Trucks, and I'm trying to bring him to a few festivals. Another kid that plays straight fingers is down there in Austin [Guitar Jake], and I'm gonna try to have both of them at my club.

Who chose the title song of the new record?

That's a John Hiatt tune. I think this guy is the Willie Dixon of the last of the '80s and the '90s. This guy, man—I gotta meet him. I understand he's a guitar player, and I did one of his songs on *Damn Right, I've Got The Blues*. This guy is outrageous as a writer. Bonnie done did some of his stuff, and I'm lookin' to meet him, because I'm trying to gets ideas how he can come up with such great, great material. They sent me "Feels Like Rain," and I'm from Louisiana, and some of the lyrics are speaking about where the river pours into the sea.

What are your feelings about doing videos?

Well, it's almost like what's happenin' today is what's happenin' today. That's music now. We just finished a video for "Some Kind of Wonderful" with Paul Rodgers. I had a great time doing it. I made a video for *Damn Right, I've Got the Blues* with "Mustang Sally." I got a grandbaby, and he didn't know who the hell I was until I come out with the video. He saw it and said, "I wanna be like granddaddy. 'Mustang Sally'!" And he was only about three-and-a-half. But without the video, he wouldn't have come and told me that. So it's a good exposure for young people to see blues, because the average blues clubs where we been playin' all our lives, you gotta be 21 to come in there. You gotta wait till you turn 21 before you can find out who I was, or when Muddy was living, to see what he looked like. So this exposes a little bit for blues people.

Any chance you'll make a country video for "Change in the Weather"?

Whatever it calls for, man, I'm here. I'm like B.B. King—he's one of my great teachers. And he says, "Whatever opportunity you have to expose anything, don't ever take no." Whatever they want me to do, I'm for it.

Does your variety in tones come more from your guitars or amps?

No. I just stay with my guitar and my amps, man. I tried a few pedals on that album, and if this works, I'll try a few more. Actually, I think the amplifiers back in the '40s and '50s used to get all of this stuff we use; it didn't get the wah-wah, but we got a lot of different sounds out of amps without the effects. And now it seems the effects are being taken out of the amplifiers and being sold to you secondly. Because all the distortion and stuff—you've got to almost buy it now. I got an old Fender Bassman, and I can plug that up and people ask me, "Well, what are you using?" I say, "Just an amp."

That ferocious solo in "Country Man" has a penetrating tone.

It was the wah-wah with the octave pedal on it. What I'm trying to do is keep up with the times, and if that helps me, look out—I'm coming back with more.

You talk about keeping up with the times, but these devices often make guitarists sound like Jimi Hendrix 25 years ago.

Well, actually, I was going through that stuff before he really exploded with that stuff. Earl Hooker came up to me with the first wah-wah before I ever heard of Hendrix. We would go down to the music store and run people out with that. But Leonard Chess and them never would let me come in the studio with stuff like that. Aw, no.

What do you expect from your second guitarist?

When I came to Chicago, man, that second guitar took the place of a piano player. Besides my records, I use a second guitarist in most of my personal appearances. And I like to stand back sometimes and play rhythm. I just don't want to be a lead guitar player; I enjoy playing behind other people. When Scott Holt comes out there, man, I like to get back there and make a pretty sound. Music to me, man, is let's make it sound good. It don't have to be Buddy Guy out there in front. Let's make everybody happy when they go home, man. Let me see a smile on the faces of these people who thought enough to come out there and spend some time with us. Let's make 'em happy.

What do you tell the musicians in your band?

I have only one rule for the guys in my band: play. I've seen tough band leaders, but I don't do that, man. I figure men are men. They could probably get out of hand, and I'd have to say something. But all I tell my men is, "I hired you according to your ability—not because of who you are—and you know you got a job to do, and I got a job to do. Let's do it. Just play for me to the best of your ability, and I'm satisfied. If you're not gonna do it, then we can depart on a friendly basis."

What guitar do you play the most?

My personal signature model Strat. I got two of them, including a polka-dot one.

Did you have special requests when Fender built them?

Yeah. I had to go in there and feel around and give them what I was looking for, for which Eric had did the same. I come out so close to what he had, some minor changes gotta be made before they really put mine on the market. They can't put two identical guitars out there and call one Eric's model and one the Buddy Guy model. I guess him and I's taste is too close to call.

What's your amp?

I'm using reissue Fender Bassmans now. That's about as close as you can come to getting the original stuff from back during the '50s and '60s. I don't think you can ever reproduce that Leo [Fender] stuff no way, but they did a good job on this, and it's about as close as I can get to what I really want.

When you hit the stage, what's between your guitar and amp?

Just a wah-wah and an octave, that's all. Sometime I don't even use that. I think the octave is a Boss; the wah-wah is a Dunlop. I endorse for Dunlop too, and he's got one they're workin' on now. I don't know if you know it, but all wah-wah pedals came to me kind of left-handed, because of Hendrix. I told him, "You gotta stick my wah in the other side, because my wah-wah pedal is to my right." He looked at me and said, "You know, I never thought of it." Yeah.

Stacks of Buddy Guy CDs are now available—everything from Chicago Boss Guitars, *which has your first solo recordings in Chicago, to* Feels Like Rain. *Which of your own records would you recommend for struggling blues guitarists?*

It all depend. Some of my early stuff is a much slower blues, and I was a very slow learner. So when I got ready to learn, that's what I needed—the slow blues—so I could understand it. I picked up speed on the last several albums—*Stone Crazy!* and *Damn Right, I've Got The Blues.* But I would listen to all of 'em, because if you don't, you're gonna get set on one thing. Like when I was learning, I didn't just sit and listen to B.B., Muddy, and say, "That's all I want." I listened to Howlin' Wolf, Lightnin' Hopkins, T-Bone Walker, and a lot of jazz. I listen to a lot of jazz right now. When I get in my car and drive out today, I got it on a jazz station, trying to steal some jazz lickin' and convert it into blues. And that's what it's all about. So I would recommend a kid not only to listen just to Buddy Guy, but if you like Buddy Guy, listen to many more other great guitar players. Beck, Eric, the late Stevie, George Benson, and all these guitar players. You should listen to everybody.

FREDDIE KING

BY DAN FORTE Eric Clapton cites him as

This chapter was taken from two articles written by Dan Forte that appeared in Guitar Player *in January 1977 and October 1997.*

the first guitarist he tried to copy, and in his pre-Thunderbirds days Jimmie Vaughan paid him the ultimate compliment by touring the chitlin circuit as "Freddie King, Jr." He was arguably the first black blues guitarist to cross over to white rock audiences, and, although he passed away over two decades ago, on any given night it's a safe bet that on a bandstand somewhere in the world (most likely Texas), a guitarist will kick off "Hide Away," reverently playing each phrase as close to the original as possible.

Freddie King played with an air of authority, consistency, and utter confidence that seemed to match his imposing six-foot, 250-pound frame. As Vaughan stated in his July '86 *Guitar Player* cover story, "Everything he played, it sounded like he'd sat down and figured it out beforehand. But actually, that's just the way he played. That's the way you *want* to be; that's what style is all about." King definitely staked out his own style and identity; his was perhaps the last generation of bluesmen who didn't merely reinterpret the licks and lessons of their forebearers. Albert Collins, Magic Sam, Otis Rush, Buddy Guy, Freddie King—each was as distinct as the other.

THE TEXAS CANNONBALL Born Freddie Christian in Gilmer, Texas, on September 3, 1934, he later changed his last name to his mother's maiden name, King, and early in his career spelled his first name "Freddy." "I finished school at 16 and went to Chicago," he said in 1976, a few months before he passed away. "Carried a guitar on my back. I went there to live in 1954, but I'd been there back in '50 and in '49. Muddy Waters, that's who I was looking for. So I found him and Jimmy Rogers. Then I met Howlin' Wolf and all those cats."

He cut his first single, "Country Boy"/"That's What You Think," for the Windy City's El-Bee label in 1956, and was backed on the session by one of his mentors, Robert Lockwood, Jr. "I use a steel fingerpick on the index and a plastic thumbpick," Freddie said in his January '77 *Guitar Player* interview. "Jimmy Rogers and Eddie Taylor taught me how to play like that. Robert Jr. Lockwood can play with all three fingers." Videos of Freddie in the early '70s show him picking with a thumbpick, metal fingerpick, and bare middle finger.

Although he was always popular in his home state of Texas, where the "Texas Cannonball" is revered in the same light as Lone Star legends Bob Wills and Buddy Holly, King's style was far from the jazzy leanings of such Texas 6-stringers as T-Bone Walker, Gatemouth Brown, and Pee Wee Crayton. As producer Daniel Jacoubovitch points out in the liner notes to Modern Blues Recordings' reissue of *Freddy King Sings*, "In his own judgment, confirmed by the evidence of his recordings, his music owed more to Chicago than to Texas."

But King was also part of Chicago's new breed, along with his neighbor Magic Sam Maghett. "We'd go around and listen to each other," he explained. "Then we'd trade licks—me, Otis, Magic Sam, Jody Williams." He credited a Hound Dog Taylor slide boogie as the genesis of the instrumental "Hide Away," adding that "me and Magic Sam worked it out. I wish I could play slide, but I can't. My fingers are too heavy; I play too hard. I do some of the same licks, though, as Elmore James, Earl Hooker, and guys like that."

Bill Willis, the staff bassist at King Records, played on "Hide Away" and other landmark tracks Freddie recorded in Cincinnati. Willis, who learned organ from playing alongside Bill Doggett, now pulls double duty in Jimmie Vaughan's band, playing organ while supplying organ bass with his left hand. "King had four of us who played on everything—me, Philip Paul on drums, Sonny Thompson on piano, and Freddie Jordan on guitar," he says. "I had been there from about '58, and Sonny brought Freddie in from Chicago around 1960."

The combination of the Chicago-bred singer/guitarist and a jazz-seasoned studio band proved winning. "Well, they were kind of laid back," Willis says of the tunes. "I mean, nobody pushed. A lot of times you go into the studio now, and it's, 'We gotta get this done, we gotta get that done.' It wasn't done that way at King. When Freddie came in, we'd go over it a few times until he said, 'Yeah, that feels good. Man, let's do that again.'"A lot of times [label head] Syd Nathan would sit in there and just tape it without us knowing. He'd play it back and say, 'That's the feel. You guys had a good feel on that one; that's what you want.' Everything was live, so you had that spontaneous feeling going."

No matter what tempo or groove, Freddie and the rhythm section always had an uncanny swing feel—check out "Lonesome Whistle Blues" and especially instrumentals like "The Stumble." "Philip was a jazz drummer, and we kind of thought groove more than anything else," nods Willis. "And the thing is, none of us played together outside. The only time we played together was in the studio. Sonny always had nice, tasty things to play, so you almost automatically fell into a groove. When they'd bring in Freddie, our thinking was, 'Okay, what can we do to make this groove?' It was basically where the *artist* felt comfortable. We never told Freddie, 'Man, this should be a little faster.' It was, 'Do it the way *you* do it. We'll play with *you*.' That way the groove stayed there; we got into *his* groove. That's why a lot of the instrumental things, especially, had *such* a good groove to them.

"We were in a *big* studio, and they put baffles up to block out the sound. A lot of times I didn't hear what I was playing, like on 'Hide Away,' because I went directly into the board. They turned my bass amp off, and I very rarely used headphones. I wanted to hear everybody through the room and catch all the nuances."

Freddie co-wrote most of his tunes with Sonny Thompson, although Willis penned "You Mean, Mean Woman" on King's first album, 1961's *Freddy King Sings*. "Sonny, by being older than all of us, knew a lot of old blues," he offers. "I think they just got together and did what felt comfortable to Freddie. They would do the music and then get together with the words." "Hide Away," the flip side of "I Love the Woman," landed King on the radio and climbed as high as #29 on *Billboard*'s pop chart. In fact, despite Freddie's formidable vocal ability, the success of "Hide Away" led to an all-instrumental LP, 1961's *Let's Hide Away and Dance Away*, which would become even more of a primer for budding guitarists.

A BONANZA OF INSTRUMENTALS Freddie King's instrumental outings succeed where other blues artists failed because he peppered his 12-bar compositions with hooks, bridges, and arranged passages. These weren't jams; they were memorable, stand-alone dance numbers. "Well, that was Freddie," Willis smiles. "He would play, and it was kind of funny the way he would do it. He would say, 'Okay, I'm gonna fall off of this, and then I'm gonna fall off of that.' We were saying, 'Fall off? What is that?' Being a jazz musician, I had to change my whole way of thinking. But Freddie made it easy, because he would do these little hooks, so they weren't unfamiliar. It was never like a pressure thing. He and Sonny would go down to the studio the first day and go over whatever they were gonna do. We might just sit and listen to familiarize ourselves with what he was doing. Then the next day—we're talking like 8:00 in the morning—we would go into the studio. And we might not leave until 2:00 or 3:00 the next morning. We would just play. We wouldn't tape; we'd just play to get that feeling of playing with each other.

"Then when session day came, we just went for it. We all used eye contact. He would be playing—like when we did the 'Peter Gunn' thing in 'Hide Away'—and just before he started it, he would take his hand and point it like a pistol at us. 'Okay, we're going into "Peter Gunn."' It was just a little thing between the guys. Freddie was really a wonderful person, and if you made a mistake, instead of going, 'Damn, man, what happened?', he'd just stop and say, 'Uh-oh, let's go back and do that one over.' It wasn't an animosity-type thing; Freddie didn't let that enter into it."

It's no fluke that Freddie's instrumentals scored with the teen crowd around the same time that Duane Eddy and the Ventures were spearheading rock and roll's first instrumental age. King became a strong influence on the cresting surf crowd, but was no doubt influenced by both the music and the climate the guitar-driven singerless combos fostered. He was pushing the blues envelope to fit with what was current, as Willis confirms: "Freddie was like, 'I want to make good records. I want to make hit records.' Whatever it takes—if it sounds like the Ventures or whoever, 'I'm still gonna be me. My licks are going to be there.' That's what made his instrumentals go over. It was commercial enough to where it wasn't really lumped into blues, per se, but that's what it was. People hadn't really heard the Texas drum shuffle kind of groove, and that was what made 'Hide Away' and all those things good. When we first started it, Philip asked him what he wanted, and Freddie said, 'I want a shuffle.' 'Like a boogie-woogie shuffle?' 'No.' So we played around with different kinds of feels until that Texas shuffle came up."

In 1963 King Records repackaged and retitled the *Let's Hide Away* album as *Freddie King Goes Surfing,* and in 1965 he recorded *Freddy King Gives You a Bonanza of Instrumentals*—both now available on one CD, Modern Blues' *Just Pickin'.*

The Texan's style didn't rely on B.B. King's hummingbird-like vibrato or the megabends of Albert King; its most distinctive feature was Freddie's right-hand attack. His use of fingerpicks set him apart from the Gatemouth Brown/Johnny Guitar Watson school of bare-fingered string yankers. His attack was stinging, his phrasing staccato, but his tone had more shades than the icepick-in-your-forehead treble of Brown or Watson, particularly on his earliest recordings. Always a high-volume live performer, Freddie later incorporated heavy sustain into his arsenal.

Like many guitarists at the time, H.L. "Blues Boy" Hubbard, one of the elder statesmen of the Austin blues scene, picked up on the *Let's Hide Away* album. "I met him before he made that record," Hubbard recalls. "He would come through town with a manager and an old beat-up Buick with one side caved in. In fact, they had to get in and out of one door. My band, Blues Boy Hubbard and the Jets, were at Charlie's Playhouse on the East Side, and a disc jockey named Tony Vaughn brought Freddie there. We played a gig behind him, and he played 'Hide Away.' I had never heard it, but I liked it right off; I said, 'That sounds pretty good.' I asked him where he got that song from, and he said it was something he made up between himself and another black guy he'd met. Next thing I knew his record was on the radio. When he put his first instrumental album out, I learned *everything* on that album. Every note."

Hubbard and the Jets became Freddie's backup band whenever he'd come to

Austin. "He knew more about the guitar than any other blues player I know," Hubbard says. "Freddie King was all up and down that guitar. I thought 'The Stumble' was one of his nicest instrumentals. That didn't really stay in the 12-bar blues—he put so many passages and turns in it, it made you think. And everything he did came from the top of his head, listening to somebody else but not using that particular thing. Like that [*hums descending lick from "The Stumble"*], that's a church thing. And Freddie took those things and was able to make instrumentals out of them. If you listen to any one of those Freddie King instrumentals, you'll notice that the beginning and the ending are different, but in the middle they're all the same. After the melody, they're all pretty much 12-bar blues. But like [*hums opening to "Side Tracked"*], I asked him, 'How do you think of shit like that?' He said, 'Man, I just be ridin' along and think of that. Hell, I'll pull over, take my guitar out.' He couldn't write or read music, but he bought himself a recorder, and he'd pull over to the side of the road while he had this melody in his mind and tape it."

When they first met, Freddie was playing his Les Paul goldtop, but, Hubbard remembers, "After he had his hit record, the next time I saw him he had an ES-345, that red one. I never saw him use anything again but that 345. He was still playing it when he died." In '76 Freddie listed a 335, 355, Les Paul, and two Firebirds as others in his Gibson collection, and detailed his string gauges—Ernie Ball .010, .011, and .012 on the treble strings and Gibson medium-gauge on the remaining three. "I used to use Fenders, but not anymore," he said. "Fender is a good-sounding guitar, but for the way I play I think Gibson is the best."

Jimmie Vaughan, whose band Storm eventually backed King on occasion, recalls his gigs at Austin's Armadillo World Headquarters as "so powerful it was unbelievable—and I never heard anybody play louder, not back then." Hubbard concurs: "Freddie would play through the Showman, and Charlie would come to the bandstand and whisper, 'Tell Freddie to cut it down.' He'd turn the volume knob down, but after a while he was right back where he started. He had to have that volume to get the sustain through his amp. Freddie would have to play with a lot of volume because what he did was he would take all the bass tone off his amp. Man, he would take the midrange completely off, the bass completely off, and turn the treble wide open, and the volume wide open almost every time. I'd say, 'What the hell are you doing?' And he'd smile and say, 'Watch this.'" Years later, when songwriter/guitarist J.J. Cale was asked by Leon Russell to mix some live Freddie tapes from the Armadillo, he recalls King's only instructions: "Turn me way up and turn everyone else down."

GOING DOWN Having toured with rock and roll package revues following "Hide Away," Freddie was back on the chitlin circuit through the mid '60s. In 1968 he signed with Atlantic's Cotillion line, recording *Freddie King Is a Blues Master* and *My Feeling for the Blues*, both produced by R&B sax legend King Curtis and utilizing Curtis's band, the Kingpins, and New York session men with mixed results. But in 1970, Leon Russell and partner Denny Cordell signed King to their newly formed Shelter label and co-produced *Getting Ready*. Once again, Freddie was a major crossover success, wowing the rock ballroom crowd. Oklahoma-born drummer Chuck Blackwell, whose credits include Russell, Taj Mahal, and Joe Cocker's *Mad*

Dogs and Englishmen, played on all three Shelter LPs (the others being *Texas Cannonball* and *Woman Across the River*), supplying the pounding freight-train groove on the classic "Going Down." "Don Nix wrote that, and he usually just did acoustic guitar renditions on his demos, so most of that was arranged by Freddie and Leon," he surmises. "Our studio environment was pretty loose. We got in the studio, and there wasn't a lot of intense time spent. Of course, Freddie just pulls it right out. As I recall he sang and played guitar at the same time on the tracks. There wasn't much overdubbing."

The teaming of the Tulsa gang and Freddie was the best combination since the Federal dates in Cincinnati. "Well, we grew up with Freddie," the drummer says proudly. "The first album I ever bought was the one with 'San-Ho-Say' and all the good ones on it—the *Hide Away* album. It was *real* music back then. They was givin' us a bunch of poop back then, and then some *real* music started driftin' in. We all just locked in on it—Freddie King, Jimmy Reed, all that."

Getting over to the Fillmore audience seemed no obstacle to the self-assured Freddie. "I think that's what he'd always been doing," Blackwell states. "And we just put him in a place where the white kids could dig him. A good musician's a good musician, and Freddie just played his ass off every night, and everybody thought he was the greatest. He was a great individual, a very down-home person. I got along with him just wonderful—human being to human being."

On December 28, 1976, King died of pancreatitis brought on by acute ulcers. He was 42. September 3, 1993, the day the bluesman would have turned 59, was proclaimed Freddie King Day by then Texas Governor Ann Richards. But guitarists pay tribute to Freddie every night—every time they play "Hide Away," "The Stumble," and other King classics.

BLUES WITH A FEELING

JOHN LEE HOOKER

BY JAS OBRECHT More than a half-century after recording "Boogie Chillen," John Lee Hooker remains the world's baddest boogieman and one of the most idiosyncratic performers in blues history. While he has cut more than a hundred albums with some of the finest blues and rock musicians, the heartbeat of his music has always been his mesmerizing voice, propulsive guitar, and rhythm-driving foot taps. Like Lightnin' Hopkins, Muddy Waters and very few others, he's a musical law unto himself and a direct link to early blues. "With John Lee, there's a break in the continuity of styles," says Keith Richards, a lifelong fan who sat in on Hooker's *Mr. Lucky*. "What he picked up has got to come from one generation further back than anybody else, and John Lee can still make it work."

Hooker confirms August 22, 1917, as the date he was born to sharecroppers who raised him on a Mississippi Delta farm between Clarksdale and Vance. He sang gospel in his father's Baptist church and at age 13 began learning guitar from his stepfather, Will Moore, who never recorded. John Lee ran away to Memphis in his youth and was brought back home, only to leave again for good.

After a stay in Cincinnati, he moved to Detroit, determined to make his mark as a blues performer. He pushed a broom on the day shift in the Ford Rouge plant and spent nights prowling the clubs along Hastings Street. His earliest sessions at Allied Sound Studios produced a string of classic postwar blues, including "Hobo Blues" and "Boogie Chillen," an infectious piece of "get up and go," as B.B. King calls it, that became Hook's breakthrough R&B hit. "I wrote that song in Detroit when I was sittin' around strummin' my guitar," he says. "The thing come into me. It was just a old funky lick I found. I heard Will Moore do a song like that when I was a little kid down South, but he didn't call it 'Boogie Chillen.' But it had that beat."

Hooker's second hit, "Crawling King Snake," came out in '49, followed by "In the Mood" two years later. Recording alone or with a single sideman during the early '50s, he produced dozens of tough 78s that he considers some of his best records: "Back when I was younger coming up, I was playing more hard blues by myself. I could play more guitar and do more by myself. I had no band to inter-fere. I could do what I wanted to do when I wanted to do it." He played bare-fin-gered at these sessions, with the soundhole pickup on his Stella acoustic running into an Ampeg or Silvertone amp. Like his stepfather, John Lee kept time with his feet, patting quarter-notes with one foot and eighths with the other, and retuned his guitar from standard to open *A* to play boogies.

While undeniably his own, Hook's music was perceived by some as a fond mem-ory of Mississippi. "John Lee plays the blues like I heard 'em when I first started to play," details B.B. King. "The way Lonnie Johnson, Robert Johnson, and Blind Lemon played, they were so themselves. Well, in the modern times—and what I call modern times is the time I started to play—John Lee Hooker was one like that. Lightnin' Hopkins was like that. You know who they were the minute you hear 'em play. When John Lee Hooker plays, it's like writin' his name: 'I'm John Lee Hooker.' I don't necessarily think of it as Delta or city or any other type of blues. I just think of it as John Lee Hooker playin' the blues. But it takes me home—of course!"

Like Hopkins, Hooker did a lot of label-hopping in the early '50s, using the pseudonyms Texas Slim, Delta John, Birmingham Sam, Johnny Williams, and Johnny Lee to avoid contractual problems. (It's estimated that between 1949 and '53, he made some 70 recordings on 24 different labels, using a dozen different names.) In 1951 Hooker began recording with Eddie Kirkland, a scrappy guitarist whose slashing rhythms and savvy bass lines helped him keep a downhome feel while forging a more disciplined, commercial sound. Signing with Chicago's Vee Jay Records in 1955, Hooker began cutting with a four-piece featuring guitarist Eddie Taylor. "Dimples," cut in March '56, became his first British hit a few years later. Hooker returned to his old style for his 1960 and '63 performances at the

Newport Folk Festival, recording solo or with a bassist for the tracks released by Vanguard. He regards his Newport '60 appearance with the Muddy Waters band as an important turning point.

When John Lee Hooker paid his first visit to Europe with the 1962 American Blues Folk Festival, he was floored by the reaction in England: "It was just like God just let Jesus go over there. That's all you could hear: 'John Lee Hooker!'" The Animals' 1964 cover of "Boom Boom," a British Invasion hit, helped Hooker cross over to rock and roll audiences. He soon signed with ABC, releasing albums on its Impulse and Bluesway subsidiaries. His *House of the Blues,* a collection of early-'50s Chess sides, reached #34 in the British charts in '67, while 1971's *Hooker 'n' Heat* charted in the U.S. As the '70s progressed, he made albums for Atlantic, Tomato, Stax, and various European labels, with dwindling returns. Finally, Hooker recollects, "I got so disgusted, I said, 'I'm not gonna record no more.' The record companies, they rob you blind." He stayed out of the record business for about eight years, and then hired manager Mike Kappus, whom Hooker has consistently credited for revitalizing his career: "Mike worked hard, got me a record deal, got me pulled together. And that's how I come to be where I am today."

Hooker revitalized his career with 1989's *The Healer,* featuring guest appearances by Carlos Santana, Bonnie Raitt, Robert Cray, Canned Heat, Los Lobos, George Thorogood, Roy Rogers, and Charlie Musselwhite. Reminiscent of Hook's early days, "Rockin' Chair" was a spine-chilling four minutes of ferocious solo guitar and haunting voice. The album's commercial success led to dozens of CD collections of past works, as well as the Point Blank albums *Mr. Lucky, Boom Boom, Chill Out,* and *Don't Look Back.* John Lee continues to make guest appearances on albums by John Hammond, Van Morrison, B.B. King, and other friends, and for a while in the late 1990s his Pepsi ad was a staple of prime-time TV.

Our first interview, originally published in the November '89 issue of *Guitar Player* as "John Lee Hooker: 'Blues So Deep, It Sends a Chill Up and Down Your Spine,'" took place on a sunny fall afternoon at Hooker's comfortable home in Vallejo, California. His walls were decorated with gold records, music awards, concert posters, letters from governors, and snapshots posed with George Thorogood, Jerry Garcia, Carlos Santana, and promoter Bill Graham. His modest collection of about 50 albums included titles by Clifton Chenier, Wayne Cochran, Albert King, James Brown, Junior Parker, Champion Jack Dupree, Muddy Waters, Charles Mingus, and a few of his own albums. In his garage, the license plate of his white Cadillac read "Doc Hook," while his sporty red Toyota was registered as "Les Bogy." *The Healer* had just come out, and Hook was thrilled to be on the comeback trial. Our conversation took place in the shade near his hot tub.

"BLUES SO DEEP, IT SENDS A CHILL UP AND DOWN YOUR SPINE"

While The Healer *features many well-known musicians, the strongest tracks are the ones where you're by yourself, especially "Rockin' Chair."*

That's my favorite tune! The others is good for dancing, some of them, but getting right down to the nitty gritty and the real funk, this is it. Just playing the guitar, sittin' there in my old-time rockin' chair. A lot of people like that too. It is *the* closest to my heart. It, and another one on there—I can't think of the name of it, but it's with Musselwhite. Oooh!

"Rockin' Chair" seems to be in the oldest style you play in.

Oh, boy! Whew! That's *direct* to my heart. That's a funky blues. People can just sit there and just *meditate* and think about how it feels sometimes. It'll send a cold chill up and down your spine. It chills you, it's so deep. Sometime when I play stuff like that, tears come out my eyes.

When you were working in Detroit in the early days, you often played like that, with just your guitar, a small amp, and your feet keeping the beat.

That's the way I used to play. No band, no nothing. Just John Lee Hooker and his feet.

Did that style develop from playing by yourself a lot when you were young?

No, it come from my stepfather, Will Moore, from whom I learnt to play. He taught me how. I used to listen to him. My real father, he didn't care for that kind of music in the house, because he was a minister. My real father and my mother, they wasn't together. They separated or divorced or whatever. My mother, she got remarried.

How much of your style today is similar to Will Moore's?

As the years went by, just a little bit changed with new, young musicians around. Well, maybe my basic style have changed a lot. I listen to my old records, way back, and look at my new stuff, and it's a difference. What I'm doing now is still funky, but my old style was just nothing but me by myself just playing the hard, hard blues. Now with a band, it changes quite a bit.

If someone wanted to hear John Lee Hooker's best guitar work, where should he begin looking?

I would tell him to start lookin' at the years gone by. Back when I was younger coming up, I was playing more hard blues by myself. I could play more guitar and do more by myself. I could do the same thing now if I went on and started playing by myself. But to get the best hard stuff I did, you want to go back to the Detroit days when I was playing by myself in coffeehouses. I played more guitar. I had no band to interfere. I didn't need to give no band no breaks and solos. I could do what I wanted to do when I wanted to do. With the band, it gets in the way a lot.

A band restricts you to playing in a certain format.

Yeah! Now you said it. When you got a band, you got to concentrate on what to do. When I'm by myself, I just do it when I want, change when I want, not change when I don't want. I can sit there and play a whole lot of guitar and just go to it.

Do you see a similarity in your approach and Lightnin' Hopkins'?

Oh, yeah. Lightnin' did it all the time. That's where he was comin'. He didn't believe in all them bands and things.

Are there certain blues albums that you like to listen to a lot?

Oh, yeah. I would start with Albert King and Jimmie Ray Vaughan—well, Stevie Ray Vaughan. Jimmie, too, is nice. Layin' these blues on you. And Muddy Waters and on and on. The great ones have stood here and then have gone, but they still live on in my memory, whom I love so much. Just a great memory.

Right now, it seems like there are tens of thousands of blues guitar players.

Whoo! Well, I hate to say it, but it seems like there's *too* many. And a lot of them is really good! They are good ones, but if you look around, a lot of 'em sound alike. You hear one, you just about done heard them all. So in your mind, they all are good, but if you go in to record with them, you just say, "Hey, this guy sounds like so-and-so. He sound like B.B. He sound like Stevie Ray." They don't have a unique style all to themself, like I got. Some of them play a tremendous lot of guitar—they play much more guitar than I do—but what I play is with a solid drive, a funky beat, and nobody got it but me! That's what make me stand out. In fact, all of them sound almost alike—*do do do do do* [*mimics stratospheric wailing high on the fingerboard*]. It's good, but . . .

You know how some guys try to copy another player exactly?

Yeah!

What would you have someone learn from you?

That's a good question. What would I have them learn from me? Just learn to stop trying to make all the fancy chords and a whole lot of guitar all the way down the neck real fast. Forget about the fancy chords and concentrate on just a funky beat and something with a lot of soul and just a feeling to it.

You've played with dozens of great guitarists, from Eddie Kirkland on down to the musicians on your new album. Which of them could send chills up and down your spine?

Albert King [*laughs*]. I don't know why, but there's just something about his guitar. He got a outstanding style of his own, and a lot of people try to copy him too, but they don't get it. I don't know, there's something about Albert—I hear his voice and his guitar, and it just chills me.

He's one of the last guys you'd want mad at you.

[*Laughs.*] He sure as big as this house! He's the *last* guy I want mad at me! Yeah. Well, you know, me and him good buddies. I respect him; he respect me. We're always glad to see each other. B.B.'s the same way. Me and him are really good friends. He's a tremendous guitar player. A lot of 'em try and sound like him. I think he changed over the years too. He's gone to the big-band style, the Las Vegas style. But he can play some hard blues when he just want to. But he don't do too much of that now. He's on the Vegas trip and circles. That's where you make a lot of money, but with me, I just like to please myself.

Throughout your career, you've seemed to remain true to your own vision of music.

Yeah. We all like money, you know, but the main thing is, I want to please myself. I'm doin' alright money-wise, but I want to play what pleases me. I don't want to play Vegas circles. I want to please the other people, but I want to please myself too. And so I just stays in what pleases me. When I was making this record, I had all these good people on it, but it was an entirely different style, like "The Healer" and Los Lobos. But I said, "Hey, I got to play some funky blues on here. I want to play some funk." Now, this other stuff will sell real fast, like Los Lobos and Carlos Santana—I'm sure they're going to go AM—but I wanted to please myself. I wanted to play some deep funk!

When you were growing up in Mississippi or working in Memphis, did you ever dream about someday being one of the greatest bluesmen in the world?

No, it didn't never occur. I know I had the know-how. I know I had the stuff to do it with. I know I had the voice. I know I had the unique style. But I never would have thought that I would have come to get my foot in the door where I had a chance to prove what I could do. I never knowed that I would come to be this great, this popular on this planet, enjoying these things as one of the greatest bluesmen in my field that is. But I always thought I could be if I had the chance.

Did you work in the Ford Rouge plant after you moved to Detroit?

Yeah, I was a janitor. I pushed a broom. I was so into my music, but I had to work to survive. I always did like to be independent. I wanted to be on my own. I didn't want handouts, and I had to work to support myself. And I didn't want to be doing it in the factory. I would play my guitar at night, be up late, and they would catch me asleep, wake me up. They wouldn't fire me, because at that time it was so union, and then they wanted help so bad, they did give me all kind of chances. They'd wake me up if they found me asleep [*laughs*]: "Little John"—they used to call me Little John—"Little John, get up! Wake up."

Back then, you recorded under a lot of different names—Texas Slim, Delta John, John Lee Cooker, John Lee Booker. Did the record companies give you those names, or were they your idea?

That was me. I want to say this very slowly [*looks carefully around the yard, tips his hat back, and leans forward*]. I was the hottest blues singer when I got my foot in the door with, like, "Boogie Chillen," "In the Mood," "Hobo Blues," "Crawlin' King Snake." Everything I did [*snaps fingers*] just turned to gold. I had this manager, Elmer Barbara, and all these record companies would come to him. They said, "This kid got something so different." And I was under contract with Modern Records in L.A., and they was crooked—some of the biggest crooks ever lived. So Barbara would come to me late at night and say, "Man, I got a deal! This record company want to do something with you. I know you under contract, but we can change your name." I said, "I don't care," and this kept going on. Every different little record company would come to me, and I'd say, "Call me what you want to—as long as you got the money." They did give me a name, and I went in the studio late at night.

Would you change your style?

Sometime, but the company knew. There wasn't nothin' they could do about it.

How would you record guitar back then?

I had an old Stella with a pickup in it. I thought at that time it was a great, great sound. Tremendous sound that was really good until the electric come along. T-Bone give me my first electric guitar. Then I thought that was the best I ever seen. It was a Fender—no, no, it was Epiphone.

Given your choice of any amp, what would you choose?

Fender. I love Fenders and Gibson guitars. I thought two or three times about endorsing Fender amplifiers—get 'em free, 'cause that's all I use. I love the sound of the Twin.

What's your favorite guitar?

A Gibson. I got two Gibsons and two Epiphones. [Rich Kirch, backup guitarist in Hooker's band, details: "The Gibson ES-335 that John uses now—serial number 26201—was given to him by Carlos Santana on his birthday several years ago. He plays that one all the time. His blonde Epiphone is his favorite one; it's on a lot of the old records. I'm not sure what year it is, but it's a semi-hollowbody with a single cutaway. He also has a Lucille guitar—the Gibson B.B. King model—and another 335. He gave one of the 335s to Junior, his son."]

You're holding a Les Paul on one of your early albums.

Yeah, that's when I first started out.

Do you ever use picks?

No.

How do you tune your guitar?

Regular tuning and open tuning. Open *A* and open *G*. [Kirch adds, "John plays most everything in *E*, except to boogie, when he usually tunes three strings up so he's in open *A*."]

Have you ever been interested in playing slide?

No.

Why?

No reason. I just never did care for it myself. I love to hear it, but for myself, I wasn't into it. I didn't want to do it. It wasn't the sound that I wanted, which is good. Oh, I love Bonnie Raitt's slide; she's one of the best slide players I ever heard in a long time. She's one of the unique ladies I ever seen. I love her voice, I love the style of guitar. She can do that slide.

Your cousin Earl Hooker was great too.

Oh, yeah. Well, he was number one. Bonnie Raitt got her style from Fred McDowell. She used to go out there [to Como, Mississippi]. I knew him real well.

If you could put together an all-star blues band, who'd be in it?

That's a good, big, big question. The famous people, like? Well, you can only get so many guitars in one band, so I would say Albert King—the Big Man, I call him. The others, right now I really can't put my hand on it, but number one, I really would pick Albert King to be one of them. There are many, many more that's good—tremendous good. Of course, I don't copy him; I don't do none of his stuff. But I don't do none of nobody's stuff but mine. So I'd get him first, and all the rest of it I'd fill in. If I could pick one who's gone, I'd pick Otis Spann. He was one of the greatest piano men that ever lived. Drummer, I don't know. There's some funky bass players. The guys that I'm used to playing with—and I heard a lot of 'em—one of them's gone, Geno Skaggs. The young kid I got now, Jim Gayette, I never thought he was that good until I really take a good listen to him. He's a funky little bass player—he play funk, play rock, play it all.

Did you know any of the early bluesmen, or were you familiar with the work of, say, Robert Johnson or Blind Lemon Jefferson?

I didn't never know any of those gentlemens; I only know them through my stepfather, so I don't have too much to say. I don't know their background, but all the blues today—they was the root of all that music. It come from them. It come up progressive from those guys, and it could rise and rise and rise, but it was still from them. They was the one who created all of that.

When you began performing, did it seem almost impossible that a blues performer could play to a white audience?

Right. No, you couldn't imagine it. But I had a feeling that it was comin', but when? I know it would come sooner or later. Now it's here in the full. I know back then that the blues was only for the older black people in just a certain area. You get a hit record then, it wouldn't be half of the hit it is now. Just a half a big hit now is *big,* but back then the #1 record didn't make a lot of money 'cause it only went to a certain people, the older black people. But down through the years it all changed.

Is right now a good time for the blues?

Oh, yeah. All over the world. To the non–English-speaking people, Japanese, France, Russia, the Communist countries, the blues have just cut their way into every country in the world, all over the world. Young, old—they found out the true identity of music that is the blues. It is the first music was here. It is the one tells the story. It is the one to tell the life story of a human being or a man and a woman. Who started this? Eve and Adam in the Garden. When the blues was born, it was born with Eve and Adam. Over years and years and years, they beginning to find out the roots of this stuff and what it means to people. The rich, the poor—they all have the blues. No matter how much money you got, when your woman or the one you love have left you or you can't get along with her, all the money in the world cannot fill the place of happiness in your home. Because money can't talk to you. So that's the reason the rich people, they get the blues. They get worried and upset, and then they can't talk to that money at night. They can only spend so much, but they cannot buy happiness. So everybody realizes that now. The young, they study the blues. It's in the library. They read about it.

See, what they call rock and roll haven't been around over 35 or 40 years. What is rock and roll? That was all taken from the blues. Everything that we are saying, they are saying: "My woman done left me [scat-sings a solo]." The blues was saying all along, "My woman done left me heartaches," or, "My baby gone, she won't be back no more." Well, rock and roll say the same thing, but they got the really up-to-date form and they call it rock and roll. It's the blues!

Johnny Shines tells of how a guy could walk up to a bus stop and tell people how his house just burned down and his kids died, and most people would walk away.

Right.

And yet that night those same people might spend $10 to hear him sing about it in a club.

Right. Oh yeah! Yeah, you know, that's the blues. The blues is here to stay. That's all I can tell you. And they stronger than ever. I have to admit that when I first started playing the blues and first started making a record, I wasn't making that much money. Just a little bit, but at that time I thought it was big money. You know, you make $1,000 for a week or $500 a night—that was *big* money to me. But now I consider $500—I go out for dinner a couple of times, it's nothing. But back then that was a lot, a lot of money. Now all the kids, especially the young white kids, oh, they eat the blues up. They love 'em. And they playing them too. The young kids, they can play them. It first got big in England. The blues got *real big* in England before it got big here in the '60s. The Stones and Animals and things like that—ooh, boy!

The Animals' cover of "Boom Boom" is probably where most white kids in the '60s heard of you for the first time.

It was! It was! And when I went overseas, it was just like God just let Jesus go over there. That's all you could hear: "John Lee Hooker!" But they had never saw me. But everybody over there was playing my stuff.

Was the audience very different from what you were used to?

Oooh wee! You know, this is the truth: Before I got to the concert hall—even if it was rainin'—the place be full with a line around the block. They had to start puttin' on two shows a night to accommodate those people. Before I got there, the guys was playing all my music—Eric, Jimi, Georgie Fame, Spencer Davis, they all was doing it. John Lee Hooker. And then on the radio it was big over there. When I went over there, oh boy, it was just like the President coming. It made me feel good, you know. That's where it started from, and then I come back over here, and it started catching over here real big. Then everybody in the world got it—the white kids, the black kids.

When the white kids became interested in your music, did you lose some of the black audience?

No. With dedicated fans, no matter who come in, they still are gonna like who they like. Just like a baseball team. I live here and I like the Giants, but I'm a strictly Dodger fan. Although they ain't doin' nothing, but I still like 'em and I'm still with 'em. Oh, I love baseball.

What else do you like outside of music?

I love being home. I'm a regular home person. I like just to lay back.

Do you play guitar much when you're home?

Oh, yeah.

During concerts, it often seems that you compose songs on the spot.

Sometimes, yeah. Sometimes, no.

Do you have a good memory for songs?

I've got a hell of a memory. I don't forget nothing. Once I get it in there [*taps forehead*], I just [*snaps fingers three times*]. I can lay down at night and think of a song, get up, and sing it word by word and don't forget nary a word.

Do you sing songs that aren't blues?

Yeah. Like *The Iron Man* with Pete Townshend. And I was surprised I did that. He kept telling me I could do it, and I cut it in New York. That was completely out of my style, but it don't sound bad.

You also contributed a version of "Red House" to a Jimi Hendrix project, Variations on a Theme—Red House.

Oh, yeah. I did it real bluesy and funky. That's really nice. Mr. Jimi Hendrix, one of my favorites. He was one of my idols, and I was glad to do it. The guy that used to manage him [Alan Douglas] said Jimi would talk about me a lot, and he was the one who had me do this. It's going to be in music stores for people who like Jimi Hendrix and stuff like that.

Did you know Hendrix at all?

No, I wished I had, because I was a great fan of his.

You seem to have a very smart business sense.

Oh, yeah. I'm very deceptive. Money ain't anything, but I just don't run through it. I know I'm not going to be doing this all my life, and I know that if I live on, I'm going to retire and just have a good life, a good home, and have money to kick back and do what I want to do, go where I want to go. Some of them live so fast when they're making big money, they run right through it. And when they can't do this . . .

Did you learn that lesson the hard way?

Yeah [*laughs heartily*]. Yeah, yeah, I did. I learned it the hard way. But now I'm very well set. I got a pretty nice home. I'm into real estate. I got three more homes in Oakland that I leased out. But like I said, I learned it the hard way. I could have run through partying, women, whiskey, living the fast life, and I wouldn't have had nothing. You get through, and it's just a dream. It's a dream you went through, and you got nothing—all that stuff's behind you. And then when you're old, that's gone. When all your money and success is gone, all your so-called friends are gone. They ain't friends; they leeches that hangin' on as long as you got something. I learned it the hard way. I *love* people—don't get me wrong. Oh, I love people. Friendship is the best thing in life. I go out of my way to help people. I'm a kindhearted person. I have a lot of people; I know some of them appreciate it, some of them don't. I hate to say it: Some of them are leeches. *I* know they are, but I don't tell them. I know what they're thinking before they do it. I *know.* I can look right through people, but I still love 'em.

And you've always got your guitar.

Yeah, always got that! When the women gone, I always got my guitar. My woman can leave me, but my guitar ain't gonna leave me. Always got that. Remember that song "Red House" that Jimi did—"way back yonder 'cross the hill"? He say, "I still got my guitar!" [*Laughs.*] Yeah, I still got my guitar.

"THE FUNKIEST MAN ALIVE!"   Once again on assignment from *Guitar Player*, I revisit-ed John Lee Hooker during the spring of 1992, this time at his house in Redwood City, California. Shooing two attractive young European ladies who were keeping him company that morning, the 74-year-old Hooker received me with a rascally smile and warm handshake. He was in the mood to play, so he sat on his couch, tuned his electric guitar to open *A*, and launched into an instrumental version of "Boogie Chillen," each foot tapping to a different beat—a terrific way to begin our interview, which appeared as the magazine's August '92 cover story, "John Lee Hooker—The Funkiest Man Alive!"

Watching you play "Boogie Chillen" close up, it seems like what you're doing is very simple, and yet it's very difficult for others to get it right.

For me, it's simple, but . . . [*Laughs.*]

That was one of the first songs you recorded.

Uh-huh.

Did you write it when you were a young man in Mississippi?

[*Nods yes.*]

How are you counting time with your feet?

[*Laughs.*] I couldn't tell you. It just boogie. Just go on with it. I don't need drums.

You often played that way in Detroit, using your feet instead of a rhythm section.

Yeah. That first come from my stepfather, Will Moore, from whom I learnt to play when I was 13. John Hammond do it too.

Do you usually keep your guitars tuned to a chord?

Not really. But I use open tuning. "Boogie Chillen," that's in open *A*. For "Boom Boom," I got to rekey [retune] it.

What do you look for in a tone?

I look for a deep, gutty feelin'. I don't use picks, so I can get that deep gut feel-in'. People ask, "How you get that?" It's just there. There's a lot of people try to play real fast chords—*da da da da da*—that's not the blues. It's synthetic. It ain't the hard, solid blues. It's a lot of speed and everything. It's got no feeling to it. You sit down and play some [*whispers*] funky, funky guitar. Take your time! Don't rush it. Just let it come flowin' through you. I can play guitar so funky, until it bring teardrops to your eyes. It got that funky, funky tone. I'm just me.

While most musicians stick to 12-bar blues, you seldom follow that format.

That's for the birds. People just feel—that's the way the blues supposed to be played. The way you feel those notes or scales. Shut your eyes, and then you'll know what you're doing. I know what notes to hit. I know what notes not to hit. I can do a 12-bar perfect—*perfect.* Oh, yeah. If I did then, I wouldn't be known for John Lee Hooker. See, I'm known for not doing it. When I'm just playing to myself I do it: 8, 12, 4, 16, 24. But ordinarily I don't do it, because it would take away a lot of my feelin'. You cannot learn this in a book. You feel it here [*points to heart and head*], not by what you got writing on a piece of paper. Throw that paper away! When I walk into a studio, I don't need all that stuff. I can go into a studio and in two hours' time I can record five or six songs. Sometimes it take some people three or four weeks to record one or two songs!

Sometimes it takes a band years to make one album.

[*Laughs.*] Yeah! It do! I can make ten albums in a year, and they come out perfect too.

Can you make up songs on the spot?

Yeah. They're on the spot. I get that good feelin'. But one thing I don't like—what really bugs me—is anybody tellin' me how to play. What to do and how to do. Don't do that.

Has that been a problem on your recent Chameleon and Charisma albums, since so many of the songs feature guest bands? When you recorded with Santana, for instance, you were working in a pretty straight format.

Heavy duty. We get together on it. They know how I do it. With "The Healer" we did two takes—it come out perfect. "Strip Me Naked." [*Laughs.*]

What were you thinking when you wrote that?

Well, I got stripped naked once. She took the house, the Cadillac. And the money in the bank—she took that too.

Did Carlos come to you with the music for that song?

He come to the house, and we set around. Like, he talked and we go with things. Just me and him. I go to his house, we lay the foundation, and then he pass it on to the guys. And it come out perfect every time. "Strip Me Naked," that took just about two takes.

Have your recent albums had a big impact on your career?

Very, very big impact, because it was all-stars. But this one I got comin' out now [*Boom Boom*], I'm not gonna have all-star everyone—just me and my band and some local people. Carlos will probably be on it. We already got a thing called "Chill Out" on the shelf, so we'll probably use that. I'm in the studio now workin', gettin' some pretty good stuff. A lot of the stuff I did a long, long time ago, which is new to the kids now. Some of my classic stuff, but the kids never heard it, so I'm doing it over. I always did want to do it that way. Now that I got a chance, I'm gonna do a lot of it all over, like "Sugar Mama," "Boom Boom," "Dimples."

Those songs turned a generation of kids on to your music during the 1960s.

That "Boom Boom," that "Dimples"—turned a *whole* generation. It went to Europe and told Europe, and then come back here and turned the whole universe on. Then different artists took to doing that song, "Boom Boom"—Bruce Springsteen, all them. Big Joe Turner, he was doin' "Dimples."

Is it a compliment when people try to play like you?

Yeah, it is. Because I know I'm doing something to be loved. If he didn't like it, he wouldn't try to do it! So it's very complimentary to me.

Some guys feel very protective . . .

Not me. I love people that do my stuff. Robert Plant, he did "Dimples." He sing it all the time. He's one of my favorite people. Nice guy. Every time he come over, he try to look me up. He flew me out to New York once to meet him. Paid for my hotel and everything. Had a lady with him called Big Maggie Bell, from Scotland. Met her. But my hero is Bonnie. Me and her just like this [*holds two fingers together*]. I guess you know that. We real close. I've known Bonnie Raitt over the years, and I'm a guest on her tour in L.A.

A lot of your old material has recently come out on CD.

Yeah, you know they comin' out now because we're doin' big things. They just throwin' out everything now—boom. Rhino Records did one.

That has many great tracks, but it's missing "Mad Man Blues."

Yeah. Ohhh, I love the "Mad Man Blues." [*Claps time and sings "I love the Mad Man Blues" and "I'm gonna kill somebody" to the original melody.*]

Do you play blues when you're alone?

Yeah, around the house I do. Yeah. Sit down in my room and just go with things I want to do, some of that old stuff that I'm trying to revive again and bring back.

Do you work on your own guitars?

No. The little light stuff I do, like adjusting the bridges and raising the saddles. You get beyond that, no.

Why do you play semi-hollowbody guitars?

Well, I like 'em. You got to do that now because the generations come and go, and the young generation, they like to dance and they want it loud. But you still can make it funky loud.

You could play a Fender.

I could, but I don't want to. I'm plainspoken, and I don't want that. This is what I like. You don't got to bring me around the bridge. This is what I like—boom. I like the tone. I always did like Gibson. Even the old style, I did.

Why do you have a guitar with B.B. King's name on it?

I saw it, and I went and bought it. He's a old buddy of mine. I said [*to the salesman*], "Give me that one." He give me a price—he said, "It's a lot of money." I said, "I don't care! Just give it to me." He said, "Who are you?" I said, "I'm John Lee." He said, "Oooh," and he come down on the price when he found out who I was. I was signing stuff in his store.

What's the greatest amplifier?

I know who got the greatest name—Fender. I got one sittin' right there [*points to an old Concert*]. I got another one back there, man, a Bedrock—boy, that thing is powerful! Whoo. It's not famous, but oh, it's powerful. But Fender is a brand name, and it's the name that sells, and that's what people go for.

How do you set the amp controls?

Different songs, different settings. I don't like it real sharp. I like it kind of medium. Not too much bass, not too much sharp. I get different settings.

Do you like reverb?

Not really. On some of my new stuff I did. About two weeks ago, I got reverb on a couple of my really funky tunes, like "Sugar Mama."

Carlos Santana says a man's tone is his face.

He know.

Albert Collins' tone, for instance, is spiky and sharp. . . .

It is. Oh, it's a thousand miles apart from mine. It's good, but it's his thing. You talkin' in a different world.

Do you like B.B.'s tone?

Whoo! Yeah! Are you kiddin'? Oh, yeah. My old buddy. And Albert King is funky. That old man is funky! He put that pipe in his mouth and rear his head back. He's a good man, and he gonna do things his way or no way! [*Laughs.*] He be workin' on his own bus right now.

You've used some of the same backup musicians for many years now.

Oh, yeah. My guitar player Rich is nice, nice. Whoo, he's a good guy! Boy, that guy loves me and I love him. I'm the one that brought him to California. He'd been in Chicago all his life. I been knowin' him about 12 years along. I got the guy a ticket, brought him out—he been with me ever since. I talk to him every day. He's a heck of a nice guy and good guitar player. Jim Gayette—oh, he is funky! He's a funky bass player, and funny too. He keep the band laughin' all night.

When you were starting out, would you play for a long time at night?

Before I become famous? When I was a kid? If my parents would let me I would.

You hear about guys playing in Delta juke joints from nightfall until morning. . .

No, I didn't do that. No. I would've, but I didn't. [*Laughs.*]

What was Hastings Street like when you first came to Detroit?

That was the best street in town. Everything you wanted was right there. Everything you didn't want was right there. It ain't no more now. It's a freeway now, called Chrysler Freeway. But that was a good street, a street known all over the world. But I didn't just play on Hastings—I'd play any club on Russell, Chene, Jefferson. In them days, I was so into my music, but I had to work to survive. I was a janitor. I pushed a broom.

What do you remember of your sessions at United Sound Studio in Detroit?

On West Grand Boulevard and Second? Still there. I would always use my amp, just plug into my old funky amps. It was a Ampeg or a Silvertone.

Was your first electric guitar the Les Paul you're seen with in some of the early pictures?

Really, it was. Really good one. Before that I had some round-hole pickups [for amplifying an acoustic guitar]. No, T-Bone Walker give me my first electric guitar. Then I thought that was the best I ever seen. It was a Epiphone.

Did you use an acoustic for early sides like "Mad Man Blues"?

Yeah, that's acoustic. I had an old Stella with a pickup called DeArmond, and it fit across the round hole. You slide it in. I thought at that time it was a great, great sound.

Was Newport '60 your first big concert?

Never been so scared! My first big concert, yeah. Couldn't get my body to stop shaking!

You appeared with Muddy Waters there.

Yeah. I was good friends with Muddy.

Do you have any favorite memories of him?

Yeah, I do. I got so many I couldn't tell 'em all. He'd come to Detroit, he used to stay at my house. I had a big house in Detroit. Matter of fact, I own property there now. He never would stay in a hotel. Him and Genny, his wife, would stay at my house. Little Walter would be with him. He was a sideman then, one of the greatest harmonica players ever lived. I think so. We would go on tour together sometimes, me and him and Little Walter, Jimmy Rogers. Remember Jimmy Rogers? He had this old Oldsmobile, brand new. And Little Walter was crazy, and he used to drive. Speedin' in it. He'd be boogeyin'! And he'd be laughing 'cause I'd be nervous. Just a lot of good remembrances. Things I cannot ever forget. Muddy was a really good man. And he was just beginnin' to come into it really on, like I am now. Just beginnin' to climb up the ladder really high.

His last four albums were terrific.

They was. He was beginnin' to climb up to the top, and it's a hard climb. But, you know, you get there somehow. Some get there and some don't. I be one of the few giants at the top of the ladder. In my travelin' and living in God's world, I love people. My heart go out for people. I'm just a softie. I just give my heart to people, and how can I say no to the people that I know I should? I don't like hurting people. We all like money, don't get me wrong, but it's not the greatest thing in the world, but we have to have it. Friendship, love, peace of mind, and health is the greatest thing in the world. You have to have money to survive, but—and a lot of us do—we can't let money get in the way of friendship and love and the people that put you where you at today. People put me where I'm at today. Weren't for those people, John Lee wouldn't be sittin' on top of the ladder. I'd be sitting down below.

And who put me there? The workin' people, the poor people go out and work five or six days a week, and come out to see me and go out and buy my albums, and stuff like that. Young kids. Old people. Them the people that got me there. Some stars seem to forget—well, they don't forget, but when you get to the high, they say you forget the people that blazed the path for them, the people that put them there. Wasn't no people, you wouldn't be there. So them the people I love. I love to go in them little small clubs, funky bars, get up there singing. I walk into a lot of little clubs, and they surprised to see me in there. Say, "What're you doing in here?" And I say, "I'm just like you. I'm here to have some fun and get down with you." I don't think about I'm a big star, or I got money. I don't think about that. I'm out there at a place I like, get down and have a beer with you. I don't look at me being a big star. I really don't. I really don't.

Who were some of the other bluesmen that you enjoyed playing with?

There's so many of them I enjoy. You sure got me on the spot there. But really I enjoyed it with Muddy when we did the Cafe Au-Go-Go in New York, me and Otis Spann and Muddy Waters. Oh, so many it's hard to say.

What's your opinion of Otis Spann?

One of the greatest piano players of the blues ever. He had the name of the greatest piano player, and he was great. And a good man too. Loyal, friendly, no ego, no nothing. Just a perfect gentleman.

Who would you consider the great slide players?

Whoo! Well, I would say Ry Cooder. He's one of the greatest. Yeah. Right on. I had a cousin, he gone. He's was pretty great—Earl [Hooker]. He was a monster. Nobody could beat him. I got some of his stuff here now, man. We used to work together a lot over the years. Boy, he used to make a wah-wah talk and slide along with it. [Fred] Below's on drums. I got that album here now. We sits around and we play it—it's really funky.

Have you ever played slide guitar?

Nah. I have messed around with it. I could, but I won't be very good. I used to play a little harmonica and drums.

Did you ever see Elmore James?

Once. I was in Chicago. I went to the hotel where we sit there and talk. He was a nice man. A lot of people copied him too. *Lot* of people.

Out of the younger generation of the blues singers, who was my pride and joy? Stevie Ray. I know that kid—I used to go around Austin, Texas, before didn't anybody know about Stevie Ray and Jimmie Vaughan. Every time I go there, he sit in and play. We used to talk. He used to come to the dressing room, come to my hotel room. Those days he used to wear a cap. To me, he was one of the greatest young blues singers. He could do anybody, probably—Albert King, Jimi Hendrix—do anybody's thing. George Benson. He played jazz. I sit down and watch him do that. He had his own style—he did, definitely—but he could play anything else anybody could play. He'd say, "I'm gonna play you now," and he play me. And if he can play me, he can play anybody!

Who's come closest to playing like you?

Let's see. Eddie Taylor is *real* close. He can do it. Buddy Guy pretty close. He can play "Boogie Chillen" real good. He plays it on every show. Buddy Guy is playin' so well, and I'm so happy for him. He gettin' a lot of recognition that he should have had a long time ago, like us all should have got. He's such a beautiful person.

Do you admire John Hammond's playing?

Whoo! Who don't? Me and him together over the years a lot too. Now, he can play like me! [*Laughs.*] Yeah, he can. He say, "I'm gonna play like you now, just like you," and then he goes to playin' it and starts laughin'. I say, "If you was outside and you walkin' up, you think it's me in here playin'." He's a really nice gentleman. He's another easygoing person too. He love people. He's a softie. He talk to me about it a lot. We sit down together [*imitates Hammond's voice*]: "John, you know, you love people. We let 'em get away with things we shouldn't, but we don't want to hurt them." That's the way he talk. I said, "They think John Lee don't know any better, but I do. I just love people." You help people. You take 'em in. It all come back to you.

Perhaps the true measure of a man is how he treats people day in and day out.

Right! The little things in life, the love. I always believe in "it comes back to you if you do something good." That's the whole thing I believe in. I was taught that, and I think it do too. You do good deeds, somewhere in life it's gonna come back. You can do wrong so long, you gonna get it in some kind of way. That's my belief. So I'm happy with my life. I had a good life, and I had a rough life—I've had both. I don't try to live in the past. I can't bring back those little things. I can't change the rough things that come through, so I look for the future. You can't live in the past—a lot of people try to live in a memory. I live for today and for people today. This is a different world. This world changes all the time.

SPINNING THE BLUES On assignment for *Blues Revue Quarterly,* I journeyed back to John Lee Hooker's Redwood City home on December 29, 1992. The cover story was to be entitled "Spinning the Blues with John Lee Hooker," so I brought along a stack of records that included the earliest 78s made by T-Bone Walker and B.B. King. In some cases, Hooker's comments were made while the discs were spinning.

Other times, he spoke at length following a song's completion. We began by listening to a 1929 T-Bone Walker 78.

T-Bone Walker, "Trinity River Blues"

Old one there. Oh, yeah. Is that T-Bone? He's one of my favorites. Real favorites. He was the first man to give me my electric guitar—an Epiphone. He was easy to get along with. He was very friendly, very loving, very romantic with the ladies— yeah, like most men, including myself. I can't say enough good things about him. [*Listens intently.*] I didn't know him that far back. What label is that one?

Columbia.

It sure sound different—his voice. Yeah. It sound like old Blind Lemon, almost. T-Bone was such a gentleman.

Did you ever hear him play an acoustic guitar?

I never did. When I knew him, he was playin' electric. He was the first man that made the electric guitar popular around back East in Detroit. Everybody was trying to sound like T-Bone Walker. The guitar players, you'd hear that fancy electric style. It's very up-to-date. That sound he was doin' then would be up-to-date right now in these late years. But this [song] doesn't sound like him to me.

It's a beautiful arrangement.

Yes, it is.

Albert King, "Personal Manager Blues"

Albert King. Yeah. He was a great man. Boy, now he played *the blues!* He's my favorite guitar player.

Why?

He plays the funky blues. He don't go fancy. He stay right where he at. Stevie Ray sound just like this. Oh, I love Stevie Ray! He sound just like Albert, though, when he want to. Albert had a heart attack, and that was a big loss to me. I loved him.

He sure was a character. Did things his own way.

Yeah, his way and no other way! Well, that's the way he was. He didn't let no manager tell him what to do. He'd tell the manager to go fuck off! He'd fire 'em in a minute. He went through managers like rain. That's the way he was. He was a trip! [*Laughs.*] He was right up front. He didn't hold back no punches.

B.B. King, "Miss Martha King"

Is that B.B.? Yeah, yeah, yeah. One of the nicest men in the world now. Yeah, you can tell that's him. Different style, but it's him. I admire that man so much. I always have admired him. I knowed him when he was a little skinny guy, weighed about 120 or 130 pounds. He's bigger than that now! Yeah, he is. That's what the age and good livin' will do for you, you know. [*Laughs.*] He is a sweetheart man. He love people like me. He don't have special people he love and some he don't— he love 'em all. He got something for everybody. He always friendly, he always ready to talk to people. He's just a hunk of love.

I admit I like his older stuff better. It was more bluesy. I like everything he do now, but go back and get that old stuff he used to do, which he can do now if he really want to. Them hard blues. I guess we all tryin' to update for a while—you got to keep up with the time and what the people want. Like in the race—you got to keep up with this race. So that's what I try to do, and that's what he's doin'.

During the 1940s, why did bluesmen like B.B., T-Bone, and Gatemouth Brown want an orchestra?

Well, why you wanted to have them was some of them little nightclubs was noisy. People drinking. If they sit in there by theyself with just an acoustic guitar, they couldn't be heard unless they playin' a coffeehouse where people don't drink while you performin'. Coffeehouses—that's what I did. Just playin' guitar, and nobody talkin' while I'm performin'. And you could be heard.

I never knowed B.B. or T-Bone Walker to play coffeehouses. They played night-clubs where people were noisy, dancing, and they had to have the big band. I don't know if that was their choice or not, but they didn't do what I did by myself at coffeehouses. When I was playin', they just quit servin' food and sandwiches until after my show was over. It was quiet, and they could be just sittin' and they could hear me. But bars wasn't like that, you know. Some of 'em come there to drink and lookin' for women and loud. They like the music, but they ain't payin' it much attention. They just lookin' for what they want, and with the drinkin' they get wild. So they got to have a band to cover that. You follow me?

Sure.

You got to have a band. Come right back to myself: The coffeehouses are gone now, and I have to play with a big band at these clubs and concerts, or I wouldn't be heard sometimes. I do it sometimes by myself with the electric guitar—me and Ry Cooder—but mostly for people listening in the concert hall. But nightclubs, you can't do that. They want the music loud, they want to dance, they want to boogie, so you got to have a band. But it used to be you could play by yourself at coffeehouses like the Chessmate in Detroit, where the people would sit and listen. But now you don't have a choice. All that stuff is gone. But that's the real music. Once you listen to it, you want to hear more and more and more of it. That's the history of American music, because everything come from there. But here lately people get to hear it a lot; they used to sweep it under the carpet. They wouldn't play it on the radio, but now they playin' it. All the young kids, all the young folks love it now. They love it all over the world. But at one time, they didn't know what it was. But when they hear it, they love it.

This next song was recorded by Blind Blake in 1929, and he sings about addresses in Detroit.

I heard of him.

With Charlie Spand on piano. I don't know anything about him.

Me neither.

Blind Blake, "Hastings St. (Hastings St. Boogy)"

Sound like Blind Lemon a little bit. Yeah. This sound like up-to-date music, don't it? [*Laughs at the line "they're doing the boogie, very woogie."*] I never knew where he was from—it sound like he used to live there. I didn't know that. Detroit was jumpin' then. Good piano player. "169 Brady"—yeah, Brady was right off of Gratiot. Brady Street is gone now; I don't think it is no more. Hastings Street is gone, yeah. Jefferson is still there, Gratiot is still there. Chene, St. Auburn, Grand River, and the big main street, Woodward Avenue. When I got to Detroit, Hastings Street was the best street in town.

Do you like Blake's guitar playing?

Yeah, that's the old sound here. Yeah, I do. That's the real blues. You know, it don't take fancy chords. See, all these fancy chords is not real blues. It's just a lot of fast fingers, you know, just sort of 80-, 90-mile-an-hour speed. Which I don't do that. I play the real funky blues in my own style.

And you've got the big beat driving right down the middle of your music.

Driving big beat. Don't get me wrong: These guitar players, they really good in they own way, they own style. They really like just a lot of fancy pickin'—they do—and maybe I couldn't do that. And I don't want to do it. But I don't call it the real blues, though. It's just a lot of speed. What they doin' is good, but not for me. It's the real funk that I play. There's a heck of a lot of fancy guitar players out there, but comin' out of the real blues, it ain't there. I got my own style that ain't nobody else got but John Lee Hooker, and I wouldn't change if I wanted to.

My sound what I got, I don't go by a certain time—8, 12, and 16 [bars], which I can do it *perfect* if I want to—but I'm known not to do it, and I don't do it. I'm allowed to jump here and jump there, because that's the way the blues is. Just lower your head and play the blues—it come from the heart and soul. And then you feel it. And when you feel it, somebody else is feelin' it too. I could play perfect on everything if I wanted to, but then there wouldn't be John Lee Hooker any more: "Oh, he gone to the fancy style" or "He gettin' fancy perfect." I do that on some of my songs—perfect intention—but then I do it unperfect when I don't want to do it perfect. Some of 'em I do perfect, like "Boom Boom." Some of 'em I don't go about perfect changes—I just play my guitar.

Let's hear another famous guitar player—Lonnie Johnson in 1930.

Lonnie Johnson, "No More Troubles Now"

Oh, boy. I love that man. Oh, I wish I had that. Send me some of that. I knowed him personally. Nice man. Like he just said [on the record], he like women, wine, and song. He lived in Toronto. That's where he died. I knowed him real good.

It was said that in the early days, he was the most sophisticated blues guitarist.

He is! He got that style, man. He's blues and he's pop. There's some of everything, the way he plays it. He loved everybody. He was a hero to everybody. When he lived in Canada, I'd go see him play, and everybody loved that man. He was so friendly. Always smiling. Nice personality. Everybody loved him—black and white, wherever you are, they loved Lonnie Johnson.

Did you know about him when you were young?

Well, not real young. I knew him when I was pretty young—I was around 30. I used to follow him. Oh, I just can't say enough about the man. He was genius. And he had his own style too; he didn't sound like everybody that pick up a guitar. Nobody sound like Lonnie Johnson. You could tell it was Lonnie Johnson every time he picked it up. Oh, he could play a lot of notes, but you know who he was because he had his own style. [*Listens intently.*] Whoo. Oh, so sad when I hear that.

Memphis Minnie, "Ma Rainey"

Oh, yeah. Memphis Minnie. I knowed her real good.

Why weren't there more female blues guitarists back then?

That's a question I can't answer. Men is just ahead. Millions of men guitar players, just a few women. I guess it just wasn't . . . I don't know. That one I can't answer.

Would it have been harder for them to travel around to play?
Yeah, I'm sure it would have been. Memphis Minnie played guitar.
Johnny Shines thought she might have been the first blues performer in Chicago to have an electric guitar.
Could have been. I knowed her when she live in Detroit—her and Son Joe, what played with her.
Can I play you an old song that's really dirty?
I don't care. Get funky. I don't care what it said—pussy, whore, or anything!

Lucille Bogan, "Shave 'Em Dry"
[*Laughs at opening verse.*] "Make a dead man come." Who is that?
Lucille Bogan, 1934.
I never heard of her. [*Laughs uproariously at the line, "Say, I fucked all night and all the night before, baby, and I feel just like I want to fuck some more."*] I like that!
Have you heard people play this kind of music?
Yeah.
What about "The Dirty Dozens"?
Yeah. That's a song they used to play, "The Dirty Dozens." "Dozens" means bad—something's bad, bad. But playin' "The Dirty Dozens"—I really never did know what they meant by that, but I heard the word a hundred million times.
Was that music around when you were a child?
Oh, no. My parents didn't allow it, no. If I'd heard it, they would kill me! [*Laughs.*]

Robert Johnson, "Preaching Blues"
Oh, yeah. Famous man. And he got to be famous since he been gone. He more famous now than he was when he was alive.
He played around Clarksdale in the 1930s.
I never seen him.
Had you heard his records?
I heard his records when I come to Detroit. I got up to Detroit when I was about 14. I left Mississippi when I was 14.
Were you playing already?
I wasn't famous, but I was foolin' around with the guitar.
Does this Robert Johnson record sound like Mississippi music to you?
It could be any country or any state, and over the years, I guess it would be. Nowadays, he could be any state or any country. But then that was the kind of music in the South.

John Lee Hooker, "Shake Your Boogie"
That's me. That ain't me singin', though, is it?
It's supposed to be you in 1948. Sounds like you're 14 years old.
Yeah. It's got my name on it, but I think it's somebody else singin'.
You sound like you're bashing your guitar pretty hard.
Yeah, I do that.

John Lee Hooker, "Good Business"
Yeah, that's me. "You got good business, and I like to trade with you." Yeah.

Do you have a collection of your own old records?

Not that old [*points to the one on the turntable*].

Your latest album, Boom Boom, *covers some of your early hits.*

Some of my classic stuff, but the kids never heard it, so I did it over. I always did want to do it that way. Just me and my band and some local people doing the stuff I did a long, long time ago, which is new to the kids now, like "Sugar Mama," "Boom Boom," "Dimples."

Your career seems more happening now than ever before.

It is. And it hit me by a shock—it was strong, fast, and quick. I'm able to handle it. It don't bother me, success. I'm just a normal person. If you didn't know me as a star, you'd never know it just to see me out in the streets, the way I act with people. I'm really down to earth. I'm more into poor people than I is to people that got a lot of money, rich people. I love 'em all, but my father was just everyday people, just down to earth people. Small nightclubs—I go in and jam and talk to the people. That's the way I am. Success hit me by surprise, but it didn't change me at all. I never thought I would come to be one of the greatest musicians alive, you know. I never thought that. But hey, it happened, and I can't change it, the way people feel about me and love me, which is good. And I give love back to 'em. I really love people, and it shows.

It's just a shame that some musicians don't feel the way I feel. They're real famous, you know, but that's where we come from. The people made us what we are. If it wasn't for the people, we wouldn't be what we are, ridin' in these fine cars and nice homes. The people bought this for us, and I love these people for that. But there are some people I don't associate with. Don't say I hate them, but I don't like what they stand for. As a body and flesh and blood, I love them. But I don't love what comes out of that body, the action and what they stand for. But my door is always open for the right people, because I really love people.

"BOOGIE ALL THE TIME" A half-decade later, *Living Blues* magazine asked me write "John Lee Hooker: Boogie All the Time" for their May/June 1997 cover. We did the interview over two days in his Redwood City home, where the confirmed homebody and avid Dodgers fan now spends most of his days. Our first conversation took place in his small bedroom, where John Lee was dressed in a silk three-piece suit while sprawled across his bed. The second, five weeks later on January 20, 1997, was in his living room, surrounded by music posters, a Duke Snider–signed Dodgers jersey, Grammy Awards, a large portrait of his daughter Zakiya, snapshots with his many children and grandchildren, and a photo of John Lee with President Bill Clinton. At the time, his Pepsi ad was a staple of prime-time TV and John Lee was retired from touring, but still played occasional dates.

Stacked side by side, there have been at least two feet of different John Lee Hooker CDs released in the past decade.

Oh, yeah, it's a lot. My pile's higher than that.

Only a few others have written as many blues songs as you—Lonnie Johnson, Tampa Red, Blind Lemon, Lightnin' Hopkins . . .

Oooh, yeah! Maybe Lightnin' Hopkins. He wrote a lot. He wrote 'em all the time.

Did you have that songwriting gift as a child?

Yeah. Since I was about 11 or 12 years old. I sang in the church, and I just had this gift.

Were you making up songs before you played guitar?

Yes, sometimes.

Were they blues songs or spirituals?

Blues-type songs.

While you were growing up in Mississippi, who were you closest to?

It wasn't no musician. It was my mother and father.

What kind of a woman was your mom?

Wonderful woman. Her name was Minnie Ramsey. She was a church woman, made me go to church. My mother and father, they separated—divorced or whatever—and she got remarried to a guy they called Will Moore. This happened when I was just a kid, and then I went with my stepfather after that. My dad was a Baptist minister. I couldn't play guitar in his house. And my stepfather was a musician.

Did you like Will Moore when you first went to live with him?

Yeah! He was a good man. I liked him very much.

Did he work a day job?

Yeah. He had a farm.

Was your mom affectionate with you?

Very. She was affectionate with all of us.

What did she call you?

Johnny. Everybody call me "John Lee," but my real name is "Johnny Lee."

Were you a rebellious kid?

No. I always was kind of a Christian, because I was raised that way with Sunday school. You may not believe this, but I *never* had a fight since I been born. I never been in trouble, never been involved in violence. Never. I don't believe in fightin'. I'm a lover, not a fighter. If I find out anybody ain't right, I just cut 'em loose. I try to stay away from trouble. People have tried to get me in trouble, but it didn't happen. I never been sanctified and holy, but I been a good person. A very good person. I help a lot of people.

What drew you to the guitar?

I used to see Will Moore play. He had a guitar, and he give me one—old Stella. I started off from there.

Did he show you any guitar parts?

Yeah, sometime he did. Will Moore taught me what I know. The things that I'm playing now, that's what he taught me. I got a lot from him.

Did he teach you to beat your feet in rhythm?

No, no. I did that myself! [*Laughs.*] But I seen him do that.

Was there any special place you liked to play?

Well, several places. I liked to sit on the porch, or I liked to go out in a little park in the woods and sit there to myself and play.

Were you out in the country?

Yeah, I sure was. I was in between Clarksdale and Vance, Mississippi. Clarksdale was a pretty good-sized city, and I used to go there all the time. They had everything around Clarksdale. More going on there than Vance. After I got out of the country, I lived in Clarksdale at one time on Isaquena Street. It was a nice city. A lot of people integrated in there.

Did Clarksdale have a blues scene?
Yeah, but not no big one.
Were guys playing on the streets or in jukes?
Probably. I don't know about now, but they used to.
Did you have jamming buddies?
In the country? No.
Were you by yourself a lot?
Yeah.
Did you have brothers and sisters?
Oh, yeah. They all gone now, though.
Were there other kids in the house when you were young?
No. Just me.
Did you listen to music a lot?
Oh, yeah. I loved it. I loved Charley Patton, Blind Lemon, Blind Blake, Leroy Carr. I didn't see these people, but I heard their music. My stepfather had all those records.
Did you play along to records?
When I listened to them, yeah, sometimes.
Have you ever learned another person's solo note-for-note?
Sometimes, yeah. Not too much. I liked my own stuff. I always leaned on myself. I never was a person for copyin' people. I like to be John Lee Hooker.
Did any of your brothers or sisters take up music?
No. I was the only one.
Did your mother ever hear any of your records?
No. Dad neither. I left them when I was young, come to Detroit. I left there when I was about 14 or 15, and I never did see them any more. Well, I went to Memphis once and they come and got me, but I didn't stay long—about a week— and left again.
So you weren't that close to them later on?
I loved them, but I wasn't close to them. I wasn't there.
Did your mom pass away before you made records?
[*Very quietly*] Yeah.
How did you make it up to Detroit?
When I left home Memphis was my first stop. I worked there for a little while at the New Daisy Picture Show, a movie place. I left there and come to Cincinnati, stayed in Cincinnati for about a year, and then I come up to Detroit. I worked at the Phillips Tank & Pump Company in Cincinnati. I did general stuff.
Was there much of a blues scene in Cincinnati?
There was some, but not a whole lot.
What brought you to Detroit? Most musicians from the Delta wound up in Chicago.
Too much competition there. Too many blues singers was there. I wanted to go to Detroit where there wasn't no competition between blues singers. I went there, and that's where I grew up. I never lived in Chicago.
Did you know people when you first got to town?
In Detroit? No.
How'd you get by?
I had a little money. I went to a place called Mom's, a rooming house. I played my guitar, and she told me to come on in. I sit around and play. They just liked to

have parties, you know, and she took a real liking to me, and I stayed there. Fond memories.

Did your blues change after you got to Detroit?

No. Same thing.

Do you remember the first time you saw somebody with an electric guitar?

Mm hmm. T-Bone Walker. He was my idol. He give me my first electric guitar. It was a Epiphone.

What stood out about his playing?

He was so good. Had a different style and an electric guitar too. He was nice. He loved to take me with him everywhere he went. He called me "The Kid." This was in Detroit.

There's that scene in The Blues Brothers *where you're playing on the street.*

Yeah.

Did you ever do that in real life?

No, I really didn't. People asked that a lot of times, and I really didn't. It was just something they filmed—boom, boom—right there on the street.

Once you started making 78s in Detroit, you recorded about 80 songs in the first year for various labels.

Yeah. There wasn't that many different labels. Modern and Crown were the same label.

What was their studio like?

Oh, it was nice. It didn't have all this stuff they got now, but it was good. The old United Sound Studios there in Detroit on West Grand Boulevard.

Were you cutting in a small room?

Sometime big, sometime small. They had sound rooms, and sometimes I'd be in a big studio, but they put a booth around me to keep the sound in. Not all the time, but most of the time. They put a ply board under your feet, and your feet would just tap it.

Would your amp be set up near you?

Behind me.

Were you cutting with one mike at first?

Yeah. One mike. They didn't have all that stuff they got now. The records was good quality, though.

Were you surprised hearing yourself on playback?

Oh, yeah. [*Laughs heartily.*] Felt good, yeah. Sure did.

Can you remember the first record that came out with your name on it?

On a big [78 rpm] record? I would say "Hobo Blues." It wasn't as big a hit as "Boogie Chillen," but I think that was the first record.

Do you recall writing that song?

I used to hear a lot of blues singers sing it years and years before I recorded it. I just did it.

What record changed your life the most?

"Boogie Chillen." It was my first hit.

Were you playing it before you recorded it?

Yeah. Played it around in clubs, right there in Detroit. That became a big hit. Everywhere you went, you could hear that. It was number one throughout the country, right up there with "In the Mood"—that was number one too.

Did the success ever cause you trouble?

People be jealous, some of them. I know some people hate to see you doin' good.
Isn't that something?

It sure is! [*Laughs.*] They hate to see you doin' good! I never did understand
that. I was makin' money, doin' good. Quit a job. I was playin' music, buyin' cars.
They jealous! I never could understand that—I don't think I ever will. They want
to see you down so they can have pity on you.

Among all the musicians you've worked with, who was your closest friend?

Well, it's pretty hard. The musician I worked with that was the closest, he's not
real famous. He tried to be. Eddie Burns. You heard of Eddie?

He started playing harmonica for you in Detroit around '49.

Yeah! He could play harmonica. Oooh! He is *so* good. We was so close, good
friends, and he listened to me a lot to get a lot of his stuff. But later he wasn't
playing guitar as good as he was then. He adopted my style, and he could also
play a different style, but it was still the blues. I liked him because he was such a
nice person. Me and him was just like brothers. Still is. I never see him, but once
in a while I talk to him. We were real close. When we come to Detroit, I was just
starting out, you know. And Eddie Kirkland. You ever heard of Eddie Kirkland?

The records you made with him really kick.

It kicks butt, doesn't it? Yeah, the stuff I made with him was kick-butt, kick-butt.
Oh, yeah. I got one on there now [on *Don't Look Back*] me and him wrote called
"You Ain't No Big Thing, Baby." It's on that new record.

*Whose idea was it to team you with Eddie Kirkland? In those days cutting with a
second guitarist was something different.*

Bernie Besman. You heard of him?

An executive at Modern?

Yeah. He was no connection with me—I was just on that label—but he knowed
Eddie. Bernie had a big distributing company. Distribute the records all over the
world—Modern and almost anybody else. So I met Eddie Kirkland. My first record
was with him on the Sensation label. Then "Boogie Chillen" got so big Bernie
couldn't handle it, so he threw it over to Modern.

How did your studio setup change when you started bringing in a second guitarist?

Eddie Kirkland and I used different amps in the studio, different mikes.

Did he play slide on any of your early tracks?

No. I never known Eddie to. He wasn't a slide person.

*Were the two of you aware of what Muddy Waters and Jimmy Rogers were doing on
two guitars?*

Later on, yeah.

When you hooked up with Kirkland, which of you was the better guitar player?

I never say I'm better than anybody, you know. That's a word I wouldn't use—I'm
"better" than you or he's "better" than me. Different styles. You just play. I never say
I'm better than Eddie, and Eddie never say he's better than me. I just got a bigger
break than he got. He never did get the break he should. He still ain't got it.

Muddy said you can never be the best musician—you can only be a good one.

Right. That's true. You can be a good one, but you can never be the best one.
Who is the best one? I don't know.

It could change from night to night.

It can. I don't like a lot of fast pickin', loud music. [*Imitates a shred solo.*] That ain't music. That's a lot of fast notes. Showin' off—that's all it is! A lot of fast notes and loud too! If I'm there with people like that, I gets up and go. I says, "Let's go. Take me to my car." A lot of loud music ain't got no feelin'. It's fast, but that's all it is. I like it so funky. When I play the boogie, I play with a funky beat, but not [*imitates a shred solo*]. I go [*sings a walking bass line*]—that's it. This fast stuff, that's for the birds. That's not the real blues. You can't play really hard, deep blues really fast.

Few people can do an effective one-chord song like you or Muddy.

They don't do that. That's the real, real blues. Deep, deep blues. It ain't a lot of fancy notes—you don't need a lot of notes—although I can do that if I want to.

That seems like something white rockers brought to it.

Yeah. A lot of black kids doin' it, but not as many as white kids doin' it.

Do you feel closer to the electric guitar than the acoustic?

Now I do. I'll tell you why I love acoustic: That's all I used to play. I loved it. Still do. Now everybody plays the electric guitar because you got to because of the clubs you play in. There is no more coffeehouses. Everybody drinkin', they loud. You got to have electric guitar to be heard—not real loud, but so people can hear you without drowning their ears out. Playing acoustic guitar, if people talk they can't hear you. In the old days in the coffeehouses, you'd sit there and just play the acoustic guitar and people enjoy when you playin'. They'd just sit there, and the waitress don't even serve till you get through playin'. Dead quiet. They wanted to hear. Now people don't want to hear. They want to be dancin' and jumpin'. So you got that, but I still don't play too loud. I had a guy with me who was so loud, I had to let him go. I couldn't get him to slow down. He was good too.

When you were cutting at Chess with Eddie Burns, did you work parts out in advance?

Sometimes, yeah. Eddie, he liked to work out things, which is good.

Would you take turns soloing?

No, I really didn't do that. I did mostly rhythm. I'd do it sometimes though.

It must be tough to find rhythm players who can do your style right.

Yeah. Rich Kirch can. [*Snaps fingers*] Like that. He's a nice guy. Oh, he's my buddy.

In his autobiography B.B. talks about how tough it was to cross over to the mainstream audience in the '60s.

Yeah! It was tough! I was the first who did it.

Was that because you were lucky, or because Lonnie Johnson was gone?

Yeah. Well, Lonnie Johnson did it. He was the first that did it.

When he went over to Europe in '59.

Oh, boom! He was right there. And I was the next one. Muddy asked me. He said, "God-damned motherfucker, how you get over there? All those god-damned white kids love you." He said, "Yeah, those white kids love John Lee Hooker. How in the hell you get that?" I said, "I don't know, Muddy. They all like me there." B.B. told me one time, "John, I'm out there with all them white kids, and they all be asking me about you." "They do?" "Yeah!" So I said, "Well, B.B., I don't know. They just like what I do."

Didn't T-Bone play piano on a record you made in Germany in '62?

You talkin' about "Shake It Baby." Whoo! He was good on piano. He could rock away.

Did you ever play piano?

No. I wanted to, but I didn't.

Have you learned any instruments besides guitar?

Harmonica. I play it once in a while around the house.

Who did you like among the harp players?

Little Walter. I like his style. He brought harp up to date. He could make it sound like a saxophone or do anything he wanted to do with it. Everybody tryin' to be like Little Walter. He was a mean guy, but he was nice. He didn't take no stuff off of nobody. He was a fighter, but he didn't pick fights, though. He just didn't back down.

Who's the meanest bluesman you ever met?

That's a good question. [*Long pause.*] Everybody was nice to me. They say Sonny Boy [Williamson], but I never knew Sonny Boy.

The first one or Rice Miller?

The old one [John Lee Williamson].

He had a tough sound.

Yeah, he did. I know the other Sonny Boy Williamson real good. I liked him, but he was a mean one when he got to drinking.

Do you have good memories of your years in Detroit?

Very good! I grew up there. I got a son back there now. Robert's back there. Got a lot of memories there, but I don't want to live there any more.

What made you leave Detroit in the '70s?

After me and my wife broke up—I divorced her—there was nothin' there for me no more, so I come out here [to California]. I'd been out here a few times and I liked it, so after my divorce I come back.

Have you been married more than once?

Four times. I ain't never gonna get married again. I mess around some now, you know, but not like I used to. I may shack. When you're shackin', you do wrong and you can get the hell out! No, I ain't gettin' married no more. That's a big responsibility, and you might get a woman you don't know. You think you do, but she starts running around, cheating and going on—I don't want that. Just come in, stay awhile and get out. Sometimes a woman thinks she wants to marry you, and after she gets married to you, she gonna find different and want to start trouble. And if God call you today, you want someone that's gonna take care of your kids.

In his new book, B.B. King writes of having 15 children.

Is that what he said? I don't believe that.

He had most of them in the '50s.

That's new to me. Fifteen kids—hmmh!

How many kids do you have?

Eight.

Are you in touch with all of them?

Yeah. They're all grown up. Sometimes they ain't always right, but you still love 'em. They do little things you don't appreciate, but you love 'em.

Were you a strict dad?

Well, you know, I didn't go overboard, but they lived according to my rules. My rules wasn't hard rules: Do the right thing. Be home at a decent hour. When kids do some things that you don't approve of, you talk to 'em. You tell them what you don't like and what you do like, and hope that they don't do that anymore.

Did you raise your kids to believe in God and Jesus?

Oh, yeah, because I do. I'm a Jehovah's Witness.

Were you that most of your life?

No. I was a Baptist. My family was too.

What led you to become a Jehovah's Witness?

God is Jehovah. I come to believe in that. You don't have to be sanctified, but you do the right thing in life and love people and believe in him. I always do.

Do you think there's a heaven?

I believe in paradise. It's here on earth. "He will clean the wicked and save the righteous." You don't believe in God, do you?

Sure I do. And I believe in treating people right.

You're right. God will never destroy this earth. He'll destroy the evil on this earth, but he invented this earth. When, we don't know. It's been here forever. He's not gonna destroy this earth. He'll destroy the people that are on it and do evil. He will clean this up, and the righteous will survive. That's what I believe in. I could be wrong.

Once you pass away, will your spirit know other spirits?

That I don't know.

Have you ever been visited by a spirit?

Oh, yeah. My mother. I have seen her in my dreams and in my sleep. I've seen her vision walk into my room as a spirit.

Do you believe in the power of prayer?

Yes. May be wrong to believe it, but I believe in prayer. I was taught to believe in prayer. What do you go to church for? You just pray in the church. I believe there's a God, but can he hear you? I don't know. I hope he do.

Did God give you your special talent for blues?

Yeah, I believe he did. Nobody can tell me different. I don't read and write that good, so God give it to me. See, God gave you your talent. God give you everything you got. I don't think he gave you evil, though. I think the devil put evil in you, and God put the good things in you—the prayer, the gift, the talent.

What I got, it's not in a book. The blues is not in a book. It's here [*taps forehead*] and here [*taps heart*]. If it's in a book, it's fictitious. Oh, you can write the lyrics down as you think of 'em, but it comes from here [the head] and here [the heart], and then you put it in the book so you don't forget it. I can go into a studio [*snaps fingers*] and just write on the spot. The talent that I got is a natural-born gift from God.

People say, "How you do it?" I say, "I can't tell you how to do it. You got to have a talent and a gift." When people get it out of a book and study for days to make a song, it takes the feeling away. It can't come from there. You got to feel it. Sometimes when I get so deep into it, teardrops come into my eyes. I get so commotion from the blues that the good feeling make me so sad that I feel the teardrops.

Are there times it makes you happy?

All the time, yes. Real happy. Sometimes I'm so happy that that's what cause the tears—feelin' so good. They not hurtin' tears. They happy tears.

Being able to express yourself with blues songs is a good way to let go of stress.

Very easy. That's what I do. You can pick up a guitar and sing—it heals you. There's a song called "The Healer"—"blues is a healer." You play that song, and it heals your mind. Just keep on doin' that, and it takes away a lot of the evil and the stress, because you know you can't change nothin', but you can try to forget it or live with it through your music.

The name of my new album is called *Don't Look Back*. Don't look back to the things that happened to you in the past—the bad, the ugly. Leave it behind. You can't change it. When you think of some of the good things you did, you hope that you keep on doing good things in life, like lovin' people. I believe in one race—that's the human race. God made us all. We's all different colors and different languages, but we all God's children. He created us all. Everyone.

Why have so many women been attracted to blues music?

Well, it tells the story about women and men. That's what music is all about. It's about being human and love and hate. You hear the blues talk about "my woman have left me." "I love you baby." "Honey, don't go." "Come on back." You talking about a woman, you talking about a man. They feel different things. Every song I write says something about a human being, just like a man write about a woman. I don't write about no man! [*Laughs.*] I wrote about a woman for a song called "Dimples," you know. [*Sings "She got dimples in her jaw."*] She says, "Well, I like that," because it saying good things about her. "She got dimples in her jaw." "I like the way she walk." "She wiggle when she walks." You know, they like stuff like that. You ain't gonna write a song called "I Hate You—You're No Good." They wouldn't like that! So you got to say good things about women—they love it then.

Are any of your songs closest to your heart?

Yeah. "In the Mood," "Dimples," "Boom Boom," and "Boogie Chillen," I would say.

Have you ever had a hard time writing songs?

Yeah. I write it one way, I don't like it. I try to change it, do it another way, then I don't like that. Try to do it another way, and it still not what you want.

Have your most popular songs come quickly?

Yeah. "Boom Boom," "Boogie Chillen," "Dimples."

Are there songs where the only time you ever played them was when you recorded them?

Yeah, a few. Not too many of them, though. Most of them I played. Like you said, once you record them, sometime you don't do them again. You got so many to pick from when you're playing nightclubs, you pick the best ones that you like and people like. Some songs you do on record just to fill the record out.

What do you think when people want you to sound like you did decades ago?

I don't ever play it. Them days are gone. You don't ever sound like that again. You sound kind of like that, but you don't sound altogether like that. B.B. don't play that stuff anymore, although I love it. I love that downhome feeling of "Rock Me Baby"—that's my favorite of what he played. Every time I see him, when I walk into the room, he says, "Uh-oh. I gotta play 'Rock Me Baby.' Here's my man! I gotta play that song or I can't get out of here!" I like that and "The Thrill Is Gone."

Is it safe to say you're making more money off your Pepsi commercial than you made all during the '50s?

Ooh-wee! Oh, man, *five* time more. *Ten* time more! That one commercial [*snaps fingers*], they owe a million. A hundred thousand up front, and every time they show it I get a royalty. I'm ready for another one! That's better than the studio, and it didn't take that long.

Are you happy with the way your life has gone?

Yeah. I'm doin' better than ever with money and success and stuff like that—just got older. I still got six houses in California, and I'm set for life. But I don't care about being rich.

What do you care about most of all?

People. People, people, people. Love and friendship. People getting along—that's what I like. I don't believe in who is you—God made us all. I want to love people.

Are you a peace maker?

I try. Sometimes it work, sometimes it don't. I usually have a peace of mind and give a peace of mind.

What's the best reason for becoming a blues performer?

Some of them do it for the money, some of them do it to be famous. Some get into it and be serious, some get into it and want to be a star and be heard. I'm not in it for the money. I'm in it because I love it. I *love* it! I'll never retire from music, 'cause it's in my blood. Sometime I'm not able to play—sometimes I'm sick and I can't play—but it's always here [*thumps his heart*]. Always here.

LIVING WITH GOD, MEETING THE PREZ, AND GETTING THE GIRL Our next interview took place in October 1998, when the Clinton–Lewinski scandal was dominating the news. Great Britain's *Mojo* magazine requested a short interview for their January '99 issue, "10 Questions for John Lee Hooker on Living With God, Meeting The Prez, and Getting the Girl." John Lee returned to his spiritual beliefs and thoughts of the afterlife.

You've advised many musicians—especially guitarists—to slow down and play half as many notes. But what's the best playing advice someone's given to you?

Well, the best advice given to me was from my stepfather, Will Moore, and T-Bone Walker. Both of 'em told me, "Once you start, don't stop. If you really want to do it, don't let people dis-encourage you. Don't let people tell you that you ain't gonna make it. If you're determined to do it, just keep on pluckin'." I found that really paid off for me. Sometimes things don't go like you want to, and you get kind of disgusted and say, "Oh, I'm gonna quit. I'm gonna hang it up." But don't do it. Keep on pluckin'. If you really want it, you'll have it. I found that was the best advice.

A lot of time when you're tryin' to start off, people dis-encourage you. "Oh, you ain't gonna do it. Waste of time." That's what happened to me—people tell me I wasn't going to make it. But I'd look at 'em and laugh, because I know what my stepfather and T-Bone told me: Keep on pluckin', you know. And that's what I did.

You've raised several children. What's the most important thing for a father to teach his kids?

That's a good question! Teach your children to be obedient, to love and be with other people. And keep your mind occupied on something that's not trouble. Keep busy and do the right thing. Learn how to get along with people. That's what I teach 'em, and so far it paid off. I tell them not to get out in the street and get with the gang and run around. There are plenty of good places they can go. They can study their music or stay in school or go out with people that are quality and want to live a good life. Stay home. That's what I tell them. And stay away from drugs! Drugs are runnin' this world now. They run kids and grown-ups too. I teach them to keep their minds occupied on the good things in life. My mind is occupied on music and women, my mind is.

For many years now, you've been renowned for being a ladies man. Even Keith Richards bows to you in that department. What's your secret?

I'm nice to 'em. Respect them. And good women, they respects that—they watch that, they notice that. I'm not the kind that runs around with anything with a skirt on. Yes, I am kind of a ladies' man, and there's really nothing wrong with it. I don't think so. I would be a one-woman man if I had one that was really true, but right now I'm not a married man. When I was a married man, I was a one-woman man.

I notice you have a picture of yourself with President Bill Clinton above your fireplace and a framed letter from him on the wall. What do you think about the scandal?

I feel sorry for him. I met him, and we talked. He loved me, loved my music. His wife did too. I like the man when we met. Many others did the same thing that he did, but they didn't get caught. They did worse than what he did, and they didn't get caught. He might have done some wrong things—probably did—but I still don't dislike him. And I know they shouldn't throw him out of office! What happened is between him and his wife and God. But they're trying hard to throw him out, and I don't think it's right. The ones they put in there judging him, they ain't God. The man did a damn good job for the country. What's that girl's name? Monica? He didn't make the girl do that. He didn't rape her—she chased him around, and she might have even set him up. He run the country, and this other thing is his personal, private life. But he got his hand caught in the trap. But I like him. He's very warm. He flew in to Moffett Field Air Force Base, and when he got off the plane, we were waiting for him. He pointed at me and said, "There's John Lee Hooker!" He knew who I was. Him and his bodyguards walked up to me, and we hugged each other and stood there and we talked. He play a little music, you know. I gave him a CD. A very gentle man, he was. Then I played for him at a fund-raiser, so I saw him again. I really like him a lot. There's nothin' I can do to save him, but it if was up to me, I'd leave him alone.

See, God's looking down watching you. You can't see God Jehovah, but he sees you. He knows every move you make and what you do—I believe that! He the one that created you, created woman. I believe that, and can't nobody tell me different. I'm not an angel, but I live a good life. But I'm not perfect—there's only one man perfect, and that's God. He's perfect.

You always keep a guitar here at home. What do you play when you're all alone by yourself?

Just messin' around with the blues, just whatever come to me. Try to find different ideas and stuff like that. Nothin' special. Sometimes at home I sit down and play my old songs—the old ones are really the best songs.

What's the difference between singing the blues and saying your prayers?

Well, not much. When you sing the blues, you're sincere from your heart. It's a gift that the higher power gave you. The higher power is God, if you believe in God. Some folks don't believe in the higher power of God, but I do. I think it is a gift from God Jehovah that enables you to do that. He created you and gave you the talent. Everybody can't sing—they can sing, but they don't have my talent.

That's a good, good question you asked. When you're sayin' your prayers, you're praying to God to forgive you and to help other people. You pray for other people, to be obedient, to be loyal to people and forgive them. There's bad people, and you pray that they will be a better person. You pray that yourself will be a better person. And when you sing, you hope people catch on to your singin' and it will soothe their mind if they got a worried mind or something is really botherin' them. The singin' will pick them up. There's a song called "The Healer." That was meant to heal people's soul and mind. You don't find many people like John Lee Hooker—I don't think you do—and I sing for the people, to bless the people, to heal their mind. There are people I wouldn't associate with, but I don't hate 'em. I really don't. I pray for them to get over that thing.

You've loved and lost a lot of people in your life—your mother and father, fellow musicians, friends. Who do you miss the most?

I lost a lot of people—I lost my whole family. That's a hard question. I'd have to say my mother and father. I knowed them well, and I knew they wasn't gonna live forever. I know they long gone by now, but I still think about 'em. I don't worry about it now that people have come and gone. I miss 'em, but life must go on and life must end. I don't let it get me down. I don't let it stop my life, because life must go on. No matter how much I love you, you are not going to live always.

What do you think happens when your time is up? Does your spirit go somewhere?

Yeah. Where, I don't know. But that's what the Bible says. I study the Bible. We have Bible study all the time. We go to church, Jehovah Witnesses. We have Bible study in our home, to pray and bless people and ourselves and talk to God Jehovah. We have the Bible. I'm not good on readin', but people read the Bible to me and it soaks in. I'm not braggin' on myself, but I know I'm a good person—a very good person. I care for people. Sometime people get greedy over money and different things, but I don't.

Do you think you'll see your mom again?

That's what I'm hoping. I'm hoping to see her in some beautiful place—and my father. That's a dream and a hope. Nobody never found that out yet, but where you go, I hope that's true. We pray and study the Bible and hope that we come back again as a person. If you pray to God Jehovah, you will relive. This earth is made for paradise. See, God made this planet, and it will never be destroyed. But the filth and the trash and the sin will be destroyed. But not the earth, not the ground, but the bad people and the filth and the evil will be cleaned up. It will become a new world, and new generations will live on with no sadness, no grief. It will be a beautiful place for people.

You're pushing eighty now, and people talk about the "golden years." But are the golden years so golden?

I don't feel any differently. I feel real active. I feel real blessed to be here, to enjoy the younger generation and the older generation, all of it. I'm here for a purpose, I know. For God hasn't taken me away, so I believe that. And I get out here and go about my way. Oh, I have my aches and pains. I know I'm not gonna live forever. I don't think so, being that Armageddon will come. That's the end. You may be here when Armageddon come. You may live through it. Who knows? But that's when the earth be cleaned up, and then only the righteous will survive, through the God Jehovah. They the only ones will survive. If you're a Christian and believe in the God Jehovah, I believe you can live through that. But people against each other and fighting over wealth and doing evil—that's a sin, and I think they'll be destroyed away. That's a sin. I believe in that. But where and when, we don't know. But right now we're living in a world of doubt; it's full of good and it's full of evil. People are evil over money, love, sex, everything.

This is the truth, from my heart: I really don't believe in chasing money. I have enough to survive and live, but I don't go crazy over money. I have just enough to survive like I am now. I'm set. And I don't look to be a double-millionaire or billionaire. I am very generous with money. I'll give you a lot with no regret. I ain't looking for that back, because I give from my heart and soul. I'm not greedy over money. I don't take what don't belong to me. I just live an easy, peaceful life and love people. That's what I want.

You've recently worked on a book about your life. As you were reliving your life, did you think of things you wished you'd done differently?

Yes! But you can't. If I could change things, one thing I would change is for the good. The things I did in my young life—18, 19, 20—I wouldn't do. If I could change that, I would. I'm not sayin' I was an angel in my younger days, but I wasn't bad. But I was just wild and would do things that was kind of dangerous then. I wouldn't do that any more. I used to be a wild person—I'd drink and party, whole lot of women. I don't do that anymore. If I had to live it over again, I would reach back and get one lovely woman in my life and stick with her. But back then I didn't do that. I just got a bunch of 'em, screwin' around. I wouldn't do that now. If I had a good wife, a good woman, I'd be like an angel to her—just that one, one woman. I really would, if I could relive that. But I can't find her now.

This is the 50th anniversary of your recording "Boogie Chillen." Did you ever imagine your music would carry you for so long and so far?

I really didn't! I didn't thought I would get this far. I rarely talk about it or brag about it, but I never know I'd be one of the biggest blues singers in the world. The music carried me so far, everything I touch would turn to gold. I never figured that. But back longer than 60 years ago, when I was in Mississippi, I run into this woman at a circus. I was about 10, 12 years old. I'm at this circus, and out of all the young people, the kids, she come straight to me. I never will forget. I was singin' around a little bit then, but there was nothin' to it—just hummin' around in the church and whenever I could. She walk up to me and said, "Young man, one day you will be a great musician—you will be real famous and a very rich man." I looked at her, and I kind of laughed. Then she said, "I read people. I'm a fortune teller." That's what she said. She also said, "You ain't got no money," and I didn't! I didn't have a dime, so I said, "No." Then she said, "You gonna be very famous, young man," and I said, "Yes, sure." Then she walked away, and I never seen her since.

I didn't pay much attention then, but then it dawned on me for years and years and years, and it done happened. I did become famous and a very loving person and very successful with money. This woman looked to me like a living angel— and she could have been an angel, because out of all those people, she came straight to me. I know this woman been long gone, because she was kind of an old lady then. But I still think about it a lot, because it's true what she told me. That's why I believe in certain things—people can read your life's story.

B.B. KING

The first B.B. King section, written by renowned guitar journalist Tom Wheeler, was originally published as the September '80 GUITAR PLAYER cover story, "B.B. King: 'Playing the Guitar Is Like Telling the Truth.'"

BY TOM WHEELER AND JAS OBRECHT

"PLAYING THE GUITAR IS LIKE TELLING THE TRUTH"

Riley B. King is the world's preeminent blues guitarist. There is hardly a rock, pop, or blues player anywhere who doesn't owe him something, although because much of his influence has been indirectly transmitted through rock stars, more than a few may be unaware of that debt. His dedication is as inspiring as his talent, and it's hard to imagine someone working harder at music, or anything else. For decades Riley, better known as B.B., has worked a staggering 300 nights a year or more, in part because he feels that he must live up to a long-held title. They call him King of the Blues.

"There are days when I don't feel like going onstage," he admits, "but whether I want to go on or not, I *must* go on. Usually when I'm up there, I try and do like an electric eel and throw my little shock through the whole audience, and usually the reaction comes back double-force and pulls me out of it, because the people can *help* you entertain; they become a part of it. It's something like radar: You send out a beam, and it hits and comes back with even more energy."

Sweating in the spotlight, working on the fretboard, B.B. seems like a string-bending surgeon with his deft and confident left-hand technique. Unlike many self-taught guitarists, he plays very efficiently, without the wasted effort that comes from using the wrong fingers. He takes a breath. From his expression you know that in a split second Riley B. King will lay himself bare. He extends an irresistible invitation to share in the simple transfer of joy and pain which he has perfected: He stings Lucille; Lucille stings you. David Bromberg recently put it this way: "Usually in a good concert you'll hear people say 'ooh' or 'aah' at various times, but when B.B. plays they all go 'ooh' at the same time and 'aah' at the same time. He doesn't just play his guitar; he plays his audience."

Many of the post-Beatles guitar stars were of course technically accomplished and innovative, but in most cases, beneath the arrangements and the special effects were guitar licks unmistakably attributable to B.B. King and other American bluesmen who, in the U.S. at least, were then known only to limited numbers of blues buffs. Aside from phrases and blues scales, the dynamics of rock guitar as a communicative vehicle also owe much to the originality of B.B. King. He can make Lucille talk in an almost literal sense, with screams, sassy put-downs, cute little tickles, or an unabashed plea for love. He can articulate the hopelessness of poverty or a love gone wrong with a poetic subtlety rarely matched by mere words.

When he was developing what has become one of the world's most readily identifiable guitar styles, B.B. borrowed from Lonnie Johnson, T-Bone Walker, and others, integrating his precise, vocal-like string bends and his patented left-hand vibrato, both of which have become indispensable components of rock guitar's vocabulary. His economy, his every-note-counts phrasing, has been a model of taste and style for thousands of players. Mike Bloomfield was awestruck upon hearing Eric Clapton in the mid '60s. Later describing his impression, he groped for superlatives: "He was as good as . . . *B.B. King.*" For Bloomfield, an ardent musicologist, it was the ultimate tribute.

According to one prevalent view, there is some quantum of suffering that must be endured before an entertainer "qualifies" as a blues artist. Under anybody's standard, B.B. King has qualified many times over. He was born on a Mississippi plantation and earned 35¢ for each 100 pounds of cotton he picked; he once calculated that he had walked thousands of miles behind a plow during his years as a farmhand. It was only during the rainy season that he was allowed to leave the farm to attend school, and he walked ten miles to join his 85 classmates in their one-room schoolhouse. For two decades he took his music to scores of obscure and often sleazy bars throughout the South, where isolation crushed the dreams of many a performer.

At age 24 King was performing in a bar in Twist, Arkansas, when two men started a fight, kicking over a barrel-sized kerosene lamp. The building erupted in flames, and the panic-stricken crowd scrambled into the street. Not having enough money to replace his $30 guitar, B.B. raced back in to save it. The man who was later to acquaint much of the world with the blues was almost burned to death, and just after his escape the building collapsed, killing two other men. When he learned that the fight had been over a woman named Lucille, he gave that name to his beloved instrument and its many successors "to remind me never to do a fool thing like that again." The story is the stuff of legends, but legends sometimes spawn stereotypes, and B.B. King is a complex man, one who in the interview that follows disavows several popular images of blues entertainers.

The young B.B. King spent countless hours in the small recording facilities used by Kent (later Kent/Modern), Crown, and Blue Horizon, turning out regional hits in the early '50s. He estimates that he's recorded over 300 sides in all, although because of poor distribution and low retail prices he never reaped much profit on many of them.

He cut more LPs after signing with ABC-Paramount in 1961, one of the best of which is *Live at the Regal*. He was transferred to ABC's now defunct Bluesway label in 1967, and he made the R&B charts a year later with "Paying the Cost to Be the Boss." Producer Bill Szymczyk contributed much energy to *Live and Well* in 1969, and it was hailed in *Down Beat* as "the most important blues recording in many years."

Finally in 1970, over 20 years after cutting his first record, B.B. scored a nationwide hit with "The Thrill Is Gone." Though it employed a string section and thoroughly modern production, he is suspicious of the emphasis so often placed on elaborate recording techniques, noting that many early blues classics were cut in garages or mobile facilities. In fact, his first major R&B hit, RPM's "Three O'Clock Blues," was recorded in 1950 in the Memphis YMCA. It stayed on top of the regional charts for four months, and as he discusses below, it changed his life.

B.B. has been acclaimed in virtually every music poll, and his affection for music of almost all types continues offstage. In his hotel room, a bed or table is usually covered with mounds of cassette tapes, perhaps 50 of them, "just for my own listening enjoyment." He often practices long into the morning hours, even during periods of grueling roadwork, and spends much of his free time listening to the records in his mammoth collection at home.

B.B.'s approach to his art is not only the cornerstone of a distinguished career but also a metaphor for a remarkable philosophy of self-improvement and universal brotherhood. In 1973 he and Fayette, Mississippi, mayor Charles Evers co-sponsored a memorial festival commemorating slain civil rights leader Medgar Evers. B.B. was a founding member of the JFK Performing Arts Center and has received public service awards from B'nai B'rith and many other organizations. He co-founded the Foundation for the Advancement of Inmate Rehabilitation and Recreation. He has played many prison benefits and been cited for his service by the Federal Bureau of Prisons. He is a licensed pilot and an accomplished player of several instruments other than guitar. He received an honorary doctorate from

Mississippi's Tougaloo College, and his hometown renamed a park after him and painted a guitar on the street near the corner where the King of the Blues used to play for dimes. The town turned out to see him put his large hands in the wet cement, and the tribute was a highlight of B.B. King's life.

In the following interview B.B. reflects upon his professional standards, his guitar techniques, and his more than 30 years as a bluesman. He rejects certain public perceptions of blues performers and explains the evolution of his relationship to his art. B.B. King is witty, gracious, independent, and significantly more eclectic than his contemporaries. At the core of his career is a dedication to his ideals, to his fans, and to his belief that music is a social tool, a vehicle for bringing people together. *—Tom Wheeler, 1980*

When were you born, and where did you grow up?

I was born in 1925 in the country outside of Itta Bena, Mississippi, which is not too awful far from Indianola. My parents separated when I was around four, and I spent some time in the hills of Mississippi, up around Kilmichael. That's where I lost my mother, when I was nine. I was a farmhand all of my life, until I was inducted into the Army and sent to Camp Shelby near Hattiesburg, Mississippi, in 1943. I was plowing, driving tractors and trucks, chopping cotton—everything that one does on a farm, I did some of it.

When did you first encounter music?

The first music was in church. From that time until now, that certain something was instilled into me. I had been baptized as a Baptist, then I was in the Holiness— the Church of God in Christ—and the singing and the music in the churches was something that a small boy, even in his fifties today, will never forget.

What did your family think of you playing the blues when you started?

I couldn't play them at home. I was formerly a spiritual singer, and they wouldn't go for the blues, not around the house [*laughs, shakes his head*], not then. That's one thing about the early days of the blues. A few of the spiritual people *liked* blues, but they would play *their* blues after 12:00, when they were in their room and nobody could hear them. But you always had a few devils like myself and a few others that would listen to *anything*. You played it and it sounded good, we would listen to it. I was singing spirituals in my first group, the Elkhorn Singers, but I'd love to go to juke joints at that time.

What made you choose the guitar?

I think that a lot of that has to do with the Sanctified Church, because this preacher played guitar in the church, and that was one thing. But also, guitars were kind of available. The average home had a guitar and a harmonica, usually; you could always find them around. But saxophones, trumpets, pianos, and things like that were rare. Only the middle class families would have a piano. Sometimes a lot of us would like to sneak in the church to play with the piano, and many of us got jobs as janitors, because this enabled us to be near it. We'd be cleaning up the church or something like that, and get a chance to fool with a piano a little bit.

Do you remember your first guitar?

My first one was a Stella, about two-and-a-half feet long, with the big round hole in it, and it was red, one of their little red guitars. I was making $15 a month, so I paid $7.50 the first month and $7.50 the next one. I kept it for a long, long time.

It was stolen, but I don't remember when. The next one was a Gibson I bought in Memphis with the help of my cousin, Bukka White. It was an acoustic, but we had just learned about DeArmond pickups. I didn't have enough money to buy the regular electric, so we bought that and put a pickup on it that cost $27. The very first Fenders—I had one. I used it when I first went out on the road, '49 or early '50. I also had a little Gibson amplifier that was about a foot wide, and about half a foot thick [*chuckles at the recollection*], with a speaker in it of about eight inches, I suppose, and that was my amplifier, and I kept it for a long time.

When did you begin playing professionally?

In the middle 1940s, in Indianola, on the corner of Church and Second Street. Second Street is like the main part of town, and Church Street crossed it and went into the black area, what we called "across the tracks." I never passed the hat, but the people knew that I'd appreciate a dime if I played a tune they'd requested.

Why had you picked that particular corner?

I was afraid to sit in the square near city hall, because I probably would have been run out of there. I forget the name of the sheriff that we had then [*laughs*], and on my corner both the blacks and the whites would see me. It wasn't something I planned; it was just like a good fishing place—it seemed like a nice spot to be. You'd find me on that corner on Saturdays, and sometimes after I got off work I'd take my bath, get my guitar, and hitchhike to other little towns like Itta Bena or Moorhead or Greenville. Most times I was lucky. I'd make more money that evening than I'd make all week driving tractors. I'd probably have enough money for a movie. Next day, go to church, then back to work. At the time I was making $22.50 a week with the tractors.

Do you remember your first paying job as a musician?

I don't remember my first paid gig, but I remember the first gig where I started working for like a week at a time—1949 that was, in West Memphis, at a place called the 16th Street Grill. That lady was paying me $12 a night, room and board. I was 24 years old, and that was more money—I didn't know there was that much money in the world. So that's how that started. That was me alone up there—sing, and then play, as I normally do. Sing and play. Working there made me think about going on the radio as a disc jockey, because the lady at the grill told me that if I could get my own show like Sonny Boy Williamson and Bobby Nighthawk and quite a few of the guys, she would give me a steady weekly job, and I *loved* that idea.

How did you acquire the name "B.B."?

The idea came from the local radio station where I was working, WDIA. I was singing some advertisements for Pepticon, one of these cure-all patent medicines. Later, when I became a disc jockey with my own one-hour show, they would call me "the blues boy," or "the boy from Beale Street." A lot of times they'd shorten it to B.B., and I liked that, and it stuck with me all this time.

Before you were nationally recognized, was there much contact between you and your contemporaries such as Muddy Waters? Were you aware of each other; did you have each other's records and so forth?

No. I had *their* records, but see, Muddy Waters and John Lee Hooker and all of those guys were playing *before* me, and they didn't know me from Adam. I was *plowin'* when they was *playin'* [*laughs*]! I liked them, and I imagine that they were aware of each other. But they didn't know anything about me, no. Like Ike Turner was about 14 years old when I first met him, in Clarksdale, Mississippi. I had this great big band at that time, which consisted of my guitar, a set of drums, and a saxophone. That was a *big band,* wasn't it? When Ike saw me [*laughs*], he said, "Oh, *man,* you need *help!*"

What was it like gigging for years in small, segregated clubs all over the South?

Well, you hear this term "chitlin circuit." That's not one of my terms, but they're talking about the joints where we used to play before we started to play the white establishment. These clubs were small, most of them, and always across the tracks, in the black area. A lot of the promoters couldn't afford to pay you very much money, and if they didn't have a pretty good crowd, sometimes you didn't get paid at all. I only have about $180,000 owed up to me from my playing during my career. I'd say 90% of the promoters were for real, just like they are today. But then you had the other 10%—the young promoter, probably his first time to give a dance or concert. If he didn't make it, that was it, because he had thrown in everything he had to do this one concert, which he felt would be a gold mine. He'd say to himself, "Well, if I can get B.B. King or Junior Parker or whoever, *this* night they're going to pull me through," and a lot of times that didn't happen, and when it didn't happen for that promoter, you didn't find him. He wasn't around afterwards.

When you started entertaining, did you think of yourself mainly as a singer, as opposed to a guitar player?

When I first started, couldn't nobody tell me I couldn't sing. See, if you told me I couldn't sing then, I would have an argument with you. Later on, I found out how little I really knew, how bad it really sounded. I then found out that my guitar playing wasn't any good either [*laughs*]. It's funny how this happens, because at first, you believe that you *really* have it, like you're God's great gift. I mean I felt like that, I really did, and had someone told me I wasn't, well, I would just ignore them because I figured they didn't know what they were talking about. My singing was more popular in the early years than my guitar playing. I was crazy about Lonnie Johnson, Blind Lemon Jefferson, Charlie Christian, Django Reinhardt, T-Bone Walker, Elmore James, and many, many others, and if I could have played like them, I would have, but I've got a thick head that just don't make it, and my fingers—they don't work either. Therefore, I think my playing was very, very, very limited, more so than my singing, because I did have a kind of style of singing at that time.

Compared to many electric guitarists, you play few notes.

I was at the Apollo Theater one time, and there was a critic there, and to me what he said was one of the great compliments that people have given me. The critic wrote: "B.B. King sings, and then Lucille sings." That made me feel very good, because I do feel that I'm still singing when I play. That's why I don't play a lot of notes maybe like some people. Maybe that's the reason why most of my music is very simple—that's the way I sing. When I'm playing a solo, I hear me singing through the guitar.

How did people like Django Reinhardt and T-Bone Walker influence you?

In the way they phrase. They still do it today. Even though they may be in different categories, even though some are jazz and some are blues, when I hear them *phrase,* each note to me seems to say something. And it doesn't have to be 64 notes to a bar. Just one note sometimes seems to tell me a whole lot. So that's one of the reasons why I like them. Same thing with Louis Jordan; even though he plays saxophone, the way he phrases seems to tell me something, and that can just stop me cold when I listen.

Did you play rhythm guitar first?

No, I never accompanied myself, still can't. I *cannot* play and sing at the same time; I just can't do it. I've always been featured from the very beginning. I still can't play rhythm worth anything, because I never had the chance to really play in a rhythm section. But I know a few chords.

Did you invent the fingerstyle, perpendicular-to-the-neck vibrato?

Let's put it this way: I won't say I invented it, but they weren't doing it before I started [*laughs*]. I will say that I'm still trying. Bukka White and quite a few other people used bottlenecks. As I said, I got stupid fingers. They won't work. If I get something like that in my hand and try to use it, it just won't work. So my ears told me that when I trilled my hand, I'd get a sound similar to the sound they were getting with a bottleneck. And so for about 32 or 33 years I've been trying to do it, and now they tell me that I'm doing a little better.

What about the idea of hitting the fret a step lower than the intended note and bending it up—were people doing that before you?

Yes, but I'd never heard anybody do it the way I do it. My reason was that my ears don't always hear like they should. I'm always afraid that I might miss a note if I try to hit it right on the head, so if I hit down and slide up to it, my ears tell me when I get there. But also it's more like a violin or a voice; you just gliss up to it.

Were there any milestones in the evolution of your technique, specific experiences or events that made you alter your approach?

I don't think so. It was like this cancer that got hold of me and started to eat on me. Like when I heard T-Bone Walker play the electric guitar, I just had to have one. I had to play, but it's been a gradual thing, and it still goes on. In fact, if you went to my room right now you'd find a Blind Lemon tape that I've been listening to whenever I'm lying around.

Do you take many cassettes on the road?

I take quite a few in order to hear the old things. I listen to the radio to hear the modern music, but I like to go back to some of the old things so that I can keep the same feeling. I like contemporary things with slick changes, but even if I play them I like to put in the feeling of yesterday. You're lost with either extreme, so I try to make a happy medium and do them together.

Your record collection is something of a legend.

Well, I've got over 30,000 records now. You won't believe this, but even though they're not alphabetized I can always tell if one's missing. One day I plan to get me one of these home computers and enter them all into that. Every time I go home I just tape, tape, tape. [B.B. has since donated his record collection to the Blues Archive at the University of Mississippi.]

Do you play visualized patterns on the fingerboard, or do you hear a note or phrase in your head before you hit it on the guitar?

I hear it first, sure do. It's like some guys use an electronic tuner and just look at the needle on the meter, but I can't buy that; I have to hear it, and it's the same with a phrase. No one else can set your hat on your head in a way that suits you. I don't think I've ever seen anybody that when you put their hat on their head they didn't take their hand and move it, even if it's just a bit. Well, I'm like that with the guitar. Do it your own way. When I play it's like trying to describe something to someone; it's a conversation where you say something in a certain way. A lot of times I play with my eyes closed, but in my mind I can still see the people paying attention to what I'm doing. I can see them as if they're saying, "Yeah, okay, I get it." Playing the guitar is like telling the truth—you never have to worry about repeating the same thing if you told the truth. You don't have to pretend or cover up. If someone asks you again, you don't have to think about it or worry about it. To me, playing is the same way. If you put yourself into it, instead of something else, then when you get out there on the stage the next time, you don't have to worry, because there it is. It's you.

Today you're doing things on guitar that sound different from what you were doing only six months ago. Your style seems to continue to grow.

Well, I hope so, because I do study. People hold it against me sometimes. They say, "You're not playing the same thing that you played the last time." But I don't *want* to play the same thing I played last time. That would get boring. I always try to add something, or maybe take something away, to give it a little twist.

Do you play instruments other than guitar?

I try. I was doing pretty good on clarinet before I got ripped off for one. I got to where I could read faster on clarinet than I could on guitar. I know a few scales on the violin, and I fool with that a bit. I'm a little better with piano, and better than that with bass. Drums—I did some time with them too. Also harmonica.

Does working with other instruments alter your approach to guitar?

Yes, it affects my phrasing, and it makes me a little more fluent. It's something for me to do when I'm not practicing like I should. I usually practice mentally, but when it comes to physical practice, I'm a little lazy. I don't know how it is with other musicians, but with me sometimes I don't play like I want to, and then I get a little bit disgusted and lay off for a while. Then one day, something happens, and I can't wait to get back to it.

You mentioned mental practice.

Sometimes I hear something—someone will walk by and whistle, or I'll hear it on the music in a restaurant—and I'll start to look at the fingerboard in my mind to see how I'd do it. I visualize the different ways to do it. That's a good thing to do; it helps you learn the guitar. Just don't do it too much when you're driving, or you'll forget where you're going [*laughs*].

Do you ever stick your neck out onstage, or do you usually reassemble a series of notes, a scale perhaps, the structure of which is already known to you?

In my room, you'd be surprised at all the things I try, but I never go out on a limb, not onstage, no, no, no. I make enough mistakes without it. The guys in the band always tease me. But if you're in the key of *C* and really don't want a *Cmaj7*—that *B* note—if you should hit it, you can flatten it and get the dominant 7th, which sounds all right, and if you make a mistake and hit the *A*, it's the 6th, so it's still relative. I learned through these many years of being out there and hoping to get everybody working with me that if you make a mistake, *please* work something into it, so that it's *not* a mistake.

There's a very unusual melody line near the end of "Chains and Things" on Indianola Mississippi Seeds, *where . . .*

I made a mistake. Now you're getting all the secrets. My bandleader and I have laughed about it many times, but I made a mistake and hit the wrong note and worked my way out of it. We liked the way it sounded, so we got the arranger to have the strings follow it. They repeat the phrase the way I played it. If you've got a good take going and then hit one wrong note, you don't want to stop, so I was in the key of $A\flat$, and when I hit [*hums E, D$\flat$, E$\flat$, E$\flat$*], which is #5, 4, 5, 5, we just got the rest of the band to follow right along.

Do you read music?

Reading music is what I call spellin'. I *spell*; I read slowly. If the metronome is not goin' *too* fast, I can do it pretty good.

"Three O'Clock Blues" was your first major R&B hit. How did it change your life?

I could go into the important theaters. As far as the black people were concerned, when you were getting into show business there were three places you *had* to go through to be acclaimed: the Howard Theater in Washington, D.C., the Royal Theater in Baltimore, and the Apollo Theater in New York. "Three O'Clock Blues" enabled me to go into these places, and it opened other areas, like one-nighters. I had been making about $85 a week with my playing and being on the radio and everything else I could do—$85 total—and when I recorded that first big hit, I started making $2,500 a week. I didn't get to keep all of it, but that was the guarantee.

In the early years, how widespread was racial prejudice in show business?

In the *early* years—you mean right now?

Well, I was talking about . . .

Well, *I* do. It still happens. A lot of things are not happening for us as blacks as they do for the whites. It's a fact. It's a *natural* fact. I've been one of the lucky few. A lot of things have happened for me, yes; a lot of things have happened for a lot of blacks. But when you compare it to what's happening for the whites, it's a big difference, a great big difference. Fortunately, though, it has gotten much better over the past few years. Blacks get better breaks. We're getting there.

Does racism exist predominantly in one field—radio, recording, club work?

You find it in all of them. I can't say which is more, one or the other. But the problem is never with the musicians themselves; it doesn't matter to them. Even when it was very segregated down South, the players always got together and had a good time. Still do. The trouble's been more with the companies, the establishment. Being a blues singer is like being black two times—twice. First you've got to try to get the people to dig the blues, and then to dig you. As a blues singer today, yes, I'm very popular. The FM radio is usually very fair with us, but you won't hear B.B. King or blues very often on AM radio. And I'm not only talking about the white stations. I'm talking about the black ones too.

Your music is kept off of some white stations because you're black, and off of some black stations because it's blues?

Yeah, of course! I remember once I went to a black dude, a disc jockey that had a program in the South, and he said, "You know, every day we have an hour of blues." I said, "Really? Who do you play?" He said, "Well, I play you, Bobby Bland, Junior Parker, Albert King," and so on. I said, "What about Jimmy Reed, or John Lee Hooker?" "No," he said, "they don't fit my program." And that really got me uptight, you know. This guy is lord and master. He knows what everybody wants. I guess by being a Virgo, I'm a little sarcastic sometimes, so I said, "Well, how long is your station on the air?" He said 12 hours. And I said, "And you play a *whole hour* of blues?" He says, "Yeah." I said, "Well *look* [*laughs*], why be so nice to us blues singers and give us a whole hour? Why not play a record or two during them *other*

11 hours?" He didn't like what I said, but I didn't really care, because that's the way I felt and that's the way I feel today.

Have the attitudes of black people toward the blues changed over the years?

They're chang*ing*. Today they're not ashamed of it. We've always had black people who like blues, but if I had to try and put it into categories, we had the people that were down here with me, that did the work, you know. Then you had the middle and upper classes, as we called them in Mississippi. The people that worked on the plantations, the regular working class people—*they* understood. They were never ashamed. About 90% of them were a part of it in the beginning; they knew what I was doing. A lot of them could do it even better than I do. But then you had that middle class. A *few* of them would be down with us, and then the others would play our records, but like I said before, they'd only play them after 12:00, you dig? They felt that blues was kind of degrading a bit. They were made to be ashamed of it. They liked blues, but they weren't particular about everybody knowing about it. It's just like me. I like to eat sloppy, and I'd rather eat in my room rather than let people catch me. Among the upper class, the college graduates and the ones who had money, only a precious few would acknowledge my kind of music in the early days. That is changing today, and they're listening.

Early on, were you more popular among younger listeners?

Some of the people have stood up and been counted all along, of course. This is a funny thing to say, but it's the truth: When I was young, young people as a mass didn't dig me. When I was, say, like 20 years old, it was always people my age and older. But today, we are gaining ground because black kids will come up to me and say, "Hey, I don't dig the blues, but I dig *you*." So I think we're making progress. At some concerts we'll have all ages and colors. That I like. Lately we're starting to have not just blacks and young whites, but older whites too. I'm surprised, but we have them.

You once complained about the notion that in order to be a blues singer you have to be in torn clothes, you can't be successful, and you've got to be high on something. Do you still encounter that attitude?

I think that that's the one thing that has been *the* big mistake about people in the blues. They seem to think that you have to be high or just completely smashed or stoned out of your head to be able to play blues, and that's *wrong*. And then I don't think that a guy has to be in patched trousers. That image that people seem to put on us is wrong. Blues music is like any other kind of music. Some of us excel, and some of us don't. Some of us are really able to please people, and some of us are not. But we all have the blues. Red, white, black, brown, yellow—rich, poor—we all have these blues. You can be successful and still have the blues. I have been fortunate, and yet now I have more to sing about than I ever did before.

You're referring to the world situation?

Yes. I look around me and I read the papers, and I see what's happening in this country and all over the world. Here, there are money troubles. Food's running low in other places. There's been price fixing, and oil problems. I go to the prisons, and I see what's happening there. Look at what's happening with the people that we pay our taxes to. Look at Asia, at Cambodia. There was bombing going on for years after the Vietnam War was supposedly over. They weren't bombing trees. They weren't bombing ditches. I think of my people, the ones I left behind in Mississippi, and *all* the people in *all* the Mississippis. We are a part of each other, you know. Those problems used to affect me individually, directly, and now they affect me indirectly. When one person is hurt, it hurts me too. When I see their condition, I know what they feel, and I feel it, and it hurts.

Comparing the earlier years when you were playing to limited blues audiences in the South and in the black theaters in the North to your present success when you are known all over the world, have the blues taken on any new meaning for you? Do you feel the same when singing and playing as you did then?

My blues mean *more* to me now than it did then, because in the early years, sure, I wanted other people to like what I was doing. But at times, I was singing for my own personal amusement. A lot of times I'd get it in my mind that nobody understood me, to be honest with you. A lot of times, the people were there, but they really *weren't* there. The *bodies* were there, but I didn't think they were *with* me. And whenever I felt like that, I would go ahead and sing to amuse myself. I'd close my eyes and visualize all of those beautiful people out there enjoying themselves. But as I kept playing and years started to pass, I started thinking a little different from that. I started to feel that it was my *job* to make people interested in what I was doing, to make them be *able* to understand what I was doing, to make them see that I wasn't just teasing, that I was really for real, you know. And this took a while to do, and it takes time today too.

In purely artistic terms, do you relate to your music any differently?

Yes, it's more of a creative art form now. Before, when I made a record I really didn't think that that's exactly what it is—a record of what you're doing and who you are on that day. And once it's out, it stays. I'm much more conscious of that.

What do you do differently?

It's not just music. It's kind of like a selling job, public relations. Sometimes audiences don't pay attention unless you present it a certain way. No matter how good it is, you seem to need to put a catchy title on it. A lot of people, especially blacks, won't like it if you call it blues, but if you go ahead and play it and call it a different name, they'll like it. That's the truth. So the blues are more important artistically, and also because I feel that I've got a message that should be heard.

What's your message?

Well, here I am. I'm trying to work. I'm trying to bring people together. I'm trying to get people to see that we *are* our brother's keeper. So there are many, many things that go along with it. I still work at it.

You once deliberately chose a spot to perform that was located between black and white neighborhoods of a small Mississippi town so as to draw a racially mixed audience.

Yeah, I got 'em all. We never would have had any segregation if people would've had enough music around. If musicians from all around the world could get together, country to country, that would be a good thing. Like when I toured the Soviet Union in March of '79, the other people who got together thought about politics, but the American and Russian musicians didn't think about anything but music. It was a tremendous experience.

Do you find that your goal of using music in order to bring people together is a common attitude in the entertainment business?

Yeah, I think most of us are doing it. As musicians we feel that if we can get people together just on a social level, having fun, then they can go ahead and get to know each other in other ways too. They can discuss their differences. We get them together and then something good can come from it, because that's when people start communicating.

What brought about your recognition on an international scale?

That has to do with many things, like the changing of times, like the marching, and like the people getting together and trying to stamp out prejudice and all of the many, many things. It seemed to bring people together. It started out to make people think, to see that everybody had something to offer, and that if you listen carefully you could learn something from others. People started searching for the truth . . . while I've been diggin' all this time. Black awareness—there was a time if you called me black, it was insulting [*nods*], oh yeah, insulting. In Mississippi we always did call white people white people but we, as a whole, really didn't want to be called black. We felt that at the time it was degrading, because it seemed that the person calling you black was really saying *more* than what they said. But later on we started to think about it. If the Indian is a red man, and the Chinese is a yellow man, and you're a white man, then why *not* be a black man? Everybody got aware and became proud of the fact that we are what we are. We began to feel that we *did* have something to be proud of. Like when James Brown made "I'm Black and I'm Proud," this really hit a lot of us, and I think all of this has to do with the blues. There was a time when we felt that nobody else had dirty clothes in the closet, you know—the troubles of life. We were sort of made to feel like we were the only ones that had dirty clothes in the closet, and anytime somebody said something to us or about us, we always felt that we should close the door and not let 'em know what we had in the closet.

And that finally began to change?

Yes. After the early '60s and all that, it's a funny thing, we come to find out that *everybody* has dirty clothes in the closet, and if the people in Nashville and Kentucky can be proud of bluegrass music—which is real music about the way they live, and about their problems, and their happiness and all—why *not* be proud of the blues? This kind of transition caused people to recognize the blues singers. Even the people who don't dig blues come up to me and say that they respect what I'm doing.

Many guitar players discovered you by reading comments by Eric Clapton, Mike Bloomfield, and your other musical descendants.

I talked in terms of black people. Now, as far as the white part of it is concerned, when the Beatles came out, they started people to listening again. See, when Elvis came out in '54, they'd scream—*yaahhh,* you know. They never did hear half of the lyrics. If you could move or shake a bit, if you could twist a bit, rock and roll, that was it. Even though the Beatles' fans used to yell their heads off, their songs said something. People listened again for lyrics. All of this seemed to come back, to be re-imported, in a manner of speaking, because I heard many Beatles tunes that had been recorded by some of the blacks over here. They were re-imported with a different sound. Then Michael Bloomfield, Elvin Bishop, Eric Clapton, and quite a few of the other guys had been listening to myself, Muddy Waters, and many others. *Their* followers started getting inquisitive about their playing, and they said that they had listened to me. That's when the white youth started listening to us. And then another thing: The white youth never did have to feel, say, inferior when they were listening to blues, because they never did have to go through the thing that a lot of the young blacks did—things that made them feel that blues was real-ly degrading to them.

Do you ever get a chance to jam with some of the younger musicians whose careers you've influenced so greatly?

Jamming is something that I rarely do, but we have done it, yes. I have jammed with some of the guys that say they idolize me, but most times I'm rarely around them, or if I am it's just for a short time, like playing the same job. But who knows about the future?

Did you ever jam with Jimi Hendrix?

Yes, we all jammed together at a place called the New Generation in New York City. Any guitar player in town would usually get off work long before us, so they'd come by to see if I was really like someone had told them I was. Everybody would have their guitar out, ready to cut me, you know [*laughs*]. Jimi was one of the front-runners.

Do you ever listen to any of the guitarists who have become famous by playing a style that was originally derived from you? Do you ever find that you are influenced by their playing?

Actually, I'm influenced by anybody that I hear. I don't think that I've ever heard anybody play something that didn't intrigue me at one time or another. If they have been influenced by me, I still find that they have put *their* feelings into what they did, and my things which have influenced them sound different when they come out again. There's only been a few guys that if I could play just like them I would. T-Bone Walker was one, Lonnie Johnson was another. Blind Lemon, Charlie Christian, and Django Reinhardt: Those were the only guys I ever heard—well, there's Barney Kessel, and Kenny Burrell [*laughs*]. If I could have played just like them—not today, but when I first heard them—I would have. And there are also things that they do today that if I *could* do, I probably would, but not the way that they did it. Instead of playing it A, B, C, D, I'd probably play it A, C, D, B—not the exact same thing, because I think that there are very few people that play the same ideas identically as you would feel it yourself.

How long have you been using semi-solid, thin-body guitars?

Since the first one I saw, about '58. I have been using Gibson ES-355s for a long time because they're stereo and I like the highs. I can't hear lows too well—my ears don't tell me much—but highs I can hear very well. My new guitar, which Gibson is planning to release as the Lucille model, is sort of like a 355 but with a few changes.

How has it been modified?

It has a closed body with no f-holes, so you don't get the feedback. I used to have to put towels in my 355 to cut down the resonance, but with the new Lucille I can crank right up. Also, I can tune the tailpiece [a Gibson TP-6] at the back. I usually wear sleeves most of the time, and on the other tailpiece, because of where the strings were wound, I always snagged my sleeves, or I'd wind up hurting my hand a little. With this one, my sleeve doesn't get caught, and when I cup right on the bridge, it doesn't hit the end of the windings, so I don't hang up my sleeve and I don't hurt my hand. Also, the neck is a little bit thinner.

What kind of circuit does it have?

There's a Y cord that lets me bypass the stereo.

Which pickup do you use?

I usually go through the stereo circuitry, with both pickups working against each other. With just a quick shift of the hand I can set the volume or change the tone. To tell you the truth, I'm not even sure which pickup does what. I just put them both on and use my ear.

Did you ever use the vibrato tailpiece on the 355?

No. I think the reason people came out with vibrato tailpieces was because they were trying to duplicate the sound that I was getting with my left hand, and they forgot that I don't need it [*laughs*]. I always took the handle off. The new guitar is really something. I can't put it down, and it has really got me wanting to play again, just like when I started.

Have you had many guitars over the years?

Yes. I was in an accident once, and the insurance company gave me a Gretsch, and then I was in another accident and that one got busted up, and they gave me an Epiphone. Somebody stole that. Then I got some Gibsons, and about four of them got busted up. I've been in about 16 accidents. On the thirteenth or fourteenth one, an accident right outside of Shreveport, Louisiana, I remember seeing the bone in my right arm. They took me to the hospital and sewed it up, and the doctor told me that I nearly lost the use of the arm because of some nerve in there. But we drove to Dallas, and I played that night with my left hand. I still made the job.

Weren't you also injured in Israel?

Yes, I fell about nine feet and messed up the side of my face and my shoulder, and busted a blood vessel in my left hand. My teeth went right through my lip—seven more stitches. But I went swimming that evening in the Dead Sea. I couldn't miss it, man, because we were sold out in Jerusalem. The Holy City—I *had* to make that!

What kind of strings and picks do you use?

I use Gibson's 740XL set, with the .009 for the first string. I use a fairly stiff pick. Sometimes it's hard to get good amplifiers, and since I almost always play only with downstrokes, I find that I don't have to hit the strings quite as hard with a stiff pick to get the volume I want.

What kind of amplifiers do you prefer?

Whatever the promoters set up for us ahead of time on the road. I used to request Gibson SG amps, and the second choice was a Fender. Lately I've been try-ing the Gibson Lab Series amps, and I think we'll be using them from now on.

Of your own records, which ones do you think are the best? Any favorite solos?

I've never made a perfect record, never. Although I'm not ashamed of any of them, there's always something that I could have done better. I know the critics always mention *Live and Well* or *Live at the Regal,* but I think that *Indianola Mississippi Seeds* was the best album I've done artistically.

How seriously were you criticized for using strings and pop songs and more sophis-ticated chord progressions on some of the recent albums?

I have had some people that weren't thinking. They'd come up and say some-thing about it, but they didn't realize that I was using strings in the early '50s, with things like "My Heart Belongs to Only You," "How Do I Love You," "The Keys to My Kingdom," and quite a few things like that. We were using strings long before "The Thrill Is Gone," many years before. But those critics didn't say much about that. They thought that you were being Mr. Big or you were being jazzy. My answer is this: If the song needs just a guitar and me singing, we use that, and if you need something else to make it, then you should use that. Whether it be a full orchestra or just a harmonica and guitar—whatever's needed, that's what you should use, though I don't think that one should put a lot of stuff in there just to put it in there.

Were you criticized when you decided to have a large stage band with nine or ten pieces?

I have been criticized, yes, but again, a lot of the people who are criticizing didn't know that I had a big band back in the early '50s. It's a great thing to have a big sound from time to time. Years ago, Blood, Sweat & Tears and Chicago showed that if you've got a good band, a band that shouts and plays well, you can get a great thing going. Count Basie and them—that's all they did. They'd swing you to death, man, they'd swing you crazy, and I've always liked that.

What do you look for in a musician who comes to work for you?

A man. I look for a man first, and a musician second. I must respect what he has to offer. I wouldn't say that a guy that can really blow the roof off a building is necessarily the best musician. He may be fiery; he's the type of guy that can really move an audience in a hurry. But an audience don't like to stand on its nose all the time. They want to get down and be something else from time to time. Then you've got another guy that has a touch when he's playing that can really move people, like in a slow groove. Well, you don't want *that* all night. Each guy is good for his one particular thing. Everybody in my group is behind me to push me. I need their cooperation. But I look for someone who's 100% man. If he's only 50% musician, that's okay; we'll turn him into 75% musician after a while. But if he is not 100% man, there's nothing I can do.

Do you have much of a problem with discipline, members not showing up on time and so forth?

I've had guys in the band that screwed up from time to time, but I feel kind of like their father or uncle, and unless they do it very bad I won't do anything to them. I may fine them today and give it back tomorrow. They can tell you such fantastic lies: "Man, the *train*, like, came by, and one of the cars ran off the track, man, and they wouldn't *allow* nobody to come across." So I laugh, and if he doesn't screw up tomorrow I don't say anything about it. All of the guys are very good musicians and very dependable. I've been fortunate to have dependable men. But I got a thing: Three days of screwing up in a week's time, and you're out. No more fines. So these guys are cool. I tell them that if I can make it, so can they.

You've toured the world and worked 300 nights a year for over three decades. What is the source of your strength and energy?

You've asked me a hard question. I guess one thing is that when I first became popular and started going to many, many places, I always felt kind of bad about stopping school in the tenth grade. I always felt that I wanted to be able to talk to people everywhere I went, to really participate in whatever was around. As I moved about, I found then that my education was really far off. I started learning how much I didn't know. That was one of the reasons why I *really* started to push myself, and I've done it through the years. Sometimes a lot of people wouldn't expect a blues singer to know certain things, and I *do* know them. I won't mention them, being a Virgo, but it just knocks me out for people to cut me short, thinking that I may not know. I work a lot of times just to have that little bit of pleasure. That might not sound like very much, but to me it kind of knocks me out for people to think, okay, the B. didn't go to college or he didn't do this or he didn't do that, and certain things they don't expect me to know—I know *about*. I pay attention, and if I hear something played or hear somebody say something, I'll put it on the tape recorder and listen to it and work with it. I wouldn't say it as he did, but I liked what he was doing and I would do it *this* way, *my* way.

How do you maintain your health and keep up the pace?

It's part of my job. It's like this story about the snake who's lying by the road all cold and muddy. This guy sees him, picks him up, and takes care of him. He gets home, around the fire, and the snake warms up and pokes his head up and says, "You know what? I ought to bite you." The guy says, "You wouldn't do that. I took care of you." And the snake says, "Yeah, but I'm a snake, and that's my job—I'm *supposed* to bite you!" [*Laughs.*] It's the same with being on the road and keeping up with the schedule. Sometimes it's a part of your job to eat, and sometimes it's a part of your job to get some sleep.

Many people call you the King of the Blues. Does that change your outlook on your work or make you feel obligated in some way?

Well, I guess I look at it both ways. First, I never think of myself as King of the Blues; I happen to be a guy named B.B. King, and he plays the blues. Of course, I think I know my job pretty well. What keeps my feet on the ground is that there are people who haven't had the popularity that I've had who are just as talented, or even more so, some of them. But I have so many young fans now, white and black, that come up to me. They trust me; they have faith. You know how it is when you do something and it's appreciated by your girlfriend or your father or mother or whoever it may be. You can see it in their eyes. I can't explain it; it's a feeling that I can't tell you about. You have to see for yourself to know. Maybe like your little brother or your daughter or your son, maybe even like your pet, your little puppy or something. When you look at them, there's something that *tells* you— I know it seems a little deep, and it's hard to explain—but you know that this pet or this person or whoever is really serious about what you've done.

I wish I knew the words—now I'm really at a loss. You're hurting when you can't say what you really want, but there are times when no one else can tell you that they dig you like this special person can. This feeling has happened to me as a musician through the years. It's made me think a lot of times when I go out on the stage and guys come up and want to play guitar with me. You can look in their eyes, the young musicians, and know that you have been something that's going to help them go much further than probably what they would have without you. It's like seeing your own children or your neighbor's children. You don't want to mess up, and this makes you really buckle down and try to do it a little better. I look at my own kids sometimes, and my nephews and nieces. They won't say it around me, but I can tell that they've been whispering, "That's *my* daddy! That's *my* daddy!" That within itself is enough to make me really go out and try to do better. I try and live and be a certain way so that each day I meet a person, they can't help but say, well, he's just B.B. King. And that's all.

B.B. KING: MEMPHIS AND THE EARLY YEARS A decade after Tom Wheeler's B.B. cover story, Billy Gibbons flew up from a break in his ZZ Top tour schedule to join me in interviewing B.B. King for *Guitar Player*'s July '91 cover story, "Billy Gibbons and

B.B. King: Memphis and the Early Years." Our meeting ground was the Embassy Suites in Indianapolis, Indiana. On hand was a cassette of early B.B. King guitar highlights from Ace Records' *The Memphis Masters* and a copy of Stefan Grossman's *Bottleneck Blues Guitar* instructional video, cued to a scene of Bukka White playing a lap-style "Poor Boy" with a metal rod slide. Bedecked in a splendid silk three-piece, B.B. shook our hands warmly and settled into a chair. —*Jas Obrecht*

Word's out that you're opening a nightclub on Beale Street.
KING: Yes, it's called B.B. King's Blues Club. I'll be playing at the opening soon.
What led you to choose that location?
KING: I started from Memphis. Beale Street was very good to me in the beginning. When I came to Memphis from Mississippi, the first place I thought of, because of hearing so much about it, was Beale Street. I come to find out that Beale Street was like a college of learning. You had *everything* goin' on [*laughs*]. Beale Street was like a little town all of its own. Good musicians in the park playing various styles of music. In fact, the first time I ever heard a black guy play a Hawaiian steel guitar was there in Beale Street Park. He was playing the steel like a lot of the country people. It drove me crazy!
GIBBONS: Let's show that little piece of film we peeked at, which shows someone you know playing lap-style slide. [*Starts video.*]
KING: Bukka White! That's my cousin. [*Laughs heartily.*] Thank you! Old traditional blues song. I sure appreciate this. You don't know what you're doin' to me.
GIBBONS: He's got some real power in his forearm; the way he's shaking that thing takes some strength.
KING: He was a big guy. Not just fat like I am, but *big*.
Had you seen people in the Delta playing that style?
KING: Yeah, that's what I grew up with. That's why I feel that I've got stupid fingers, because I could never do it. I could *never* do it. It's sort of like trying to play the piano—my right hand, pretty good. The left hand, it just seems like the only reason I've got it is to help the other one out.
When you first moved to Memphis, you reportedly lived with Bukka for ten months.
KING: Yeah, I suppose so. He was working over at Lauderdale and Vance at a place called Newberry Equipment Company. He got me a job working with him. We used to make tanks that they used in service stations, what they put the fuel in down underneath the pumps. Yeah, that's what we were doin'. These big transfer trucks that carry fuel from place to place—we made those too.
GIBBONS: You were playing on the evenings or weekends?
KING: Mostly weekends. I would go out with him sometime [*nods to Bukka*]. When I first came to Memphis, I kind of left in a hurry because [*laughs*] . . . This is a funny story. I was a tractor driver in Mississippi, and there was nine of us that drove the tractors on the whole big plantation. I was considered pretty good. See, if you were a slow learner, you was choppin' cotton—you'd pick cotton by hand. But if you a pretty fast learner or you want to advance, first you plow the mules and then you learn to drive the tractor. Once you drive the tractors, man, you *in*; that's doin' it. You're kind of pampered a little bit when you're a tractor driver. You big stuff. Well, I wanted to be a tractor driver, so when I was about 14, man, I was a regular hand at it.

At the beginning in that part of the Delta, the old houses was way up off the ground because the Mississippi River would flood around there. So the boss' house was way up, and when he moved to town, that left this building to be something like a tractor barn, and we'd put the noses of all nine tractors underneath it. The tractor has a big muffler, and exhaust comes up through the top of about the center of the engine.

GIBBONS: The pipe's sticking out.

KING: Right. When a tractor has been running a long time, usually it's hot. So you use magnetos on it for your fire. You have a battery to start it, but the magneto runs it. Well, when you cut it off after it's been running a long time, a lot of times it will backfire. It'll do two or three times back or forward. If it's in *gear* . . .

GIBBONS: Oh, no. I know what's coming.

KING: [*Laughs.*] I thought you'd get it. This particular evening, boy, I'd been flyin' all day, man, and everything was cool. I'm thinking about a lady I'm going to go see that night, ran the tractor up like we usually do, cut it off, get off there, and that sucker turned over a few times more. And when it did, under the house it went! That broke off the exhaust. Scared me so bad—I knew my boss was going to have a fit! His name was Johnson Barrett, I love him, but I knew he was going to have a fit. I didn't go to see the girl. I got me a bus, and I left and went to where Bukka was that night. Now, that was the first time I went to Memphis. I stayed away for about ten months, you're right. But then I started to thinking about it, because I missed my family and I missed everything. So I went back down there and told him what happened. He laughed then. I told him, "I'm sorry, and I came back to pay for it," which I did. I stayed there a year. I left legitimately the next year, which was the last of '47. I went back to Memphis, and *that's* when I started living on my own.

I'd been listening to Sonny Boy Williamson [Rice Miller], the harmonica player on the radio. He used to be on a station in Helena, but at this time he'd moved to West Memphis, Arkansas. He had his little program on KWEM, I believe. I felt like I knew him. You know how we are with entertainers—you meet a person that you heard so much about . . .

GIBBONS: You know him.

KING: Yeah. So I went over that day, and I begged him to let me go on the radio with him. He made me audition, so I sing one of Ivory Joe Turner's tunes called "Blues at Sunrise," and he liked it. I didn't know anything about chords—still don't. But I had a good loud voice, strong, and I could keep a good beat. But if you thinking in terms of the changes and everything, I was terrible. Still is. [*Laughs.*] But he liked it. And that day, as fate would have it, he had two jobs. One what was payin' him a couple of hundred dollars, maybe, where he was making $15 or $20 down at the 16th Street Grill. The lady's name was Miss Annie. He had 15 minutes, and when he was off the air, he called Miss Annie and asked her did she hear me. She said yes, and he said, "Well, I'm gonna send this boy down in my place tonight, and I'll be back tomorrow." He hadn't asked me anything! She said fine, and when I went there to play for Miss Annie that night, I found that West Memphis was then like a mini Las Vegas. Wide open.

In the front of her place they sold sandwiches, burgers, and stuff like that, but in the back of it they gambled, shoot dice. My job was to try to entertain the people that was up front. Me being young, slim, and crazy about the girls. And I could holler real loud then, man. So she said, "You know, the people seem to like you. If you can get on the radio like Sonny Boy is, I'll give you this job. You play six nights a week, you have a day off. $12 a day, room and board." Well, man, I didn't know there was that much money in the world! Drivin' a tractor, when I thought I was big stuff, you made $22.50 a week. But she was gonna pay me *$12 a night?* And them girls?

GIBBONS: That's why we got into this business!

What were you playing?

KING: I was playing anything you mention, but nothin' right. During that time Louis Jordan was very popular, Dinah Washington, Roy Brown. I could mention a lot of people that was popular in the vein of stuff that I could do. I never did any of it right, but my way of doin' it was me, and it came off pretty good.

Were you performing by yourself?

KING: Yeah, I had a guitar with a DeArmond pickup.

GIBBONS: Just the add-on kind, wasn't it?

KING: Yeah, you just put it on. I had me a Gibson amplifier and an old black Gibson guitar, the first one I ever had with the f-holes in it. And, man, that was the thing at that time.

Not long after that, you started to record.

KING: Yeah. After Miss Annie telling me that if I could get on the radio like Sonny Boy was that she would give me the job, that's when I first heard about WDIA in Memphis. That was the first all-black-operated station. So I went over there a couple of days after I had talked with her, and I saw Nat Williams on the air. I actually had started off singing as a gospel singer, so I was pretty up on radio stuff. So I asked for Nat Williams, this black disc jockey in the picture window. His question was, "What can I do for you, young fella?" I said, "Well, I'd like to make a record, and I'd like to go on the radio." So he said, "Maybe we can help you with one; I don't know about the other." So he called Mr. Ferguson, the general manager, and Mr. Ferguson said, "Yeah. I think we can." So that *very evening* they put me on the radio, doing ten minutes with just me and the guitar. Now, that's without the amplifier. And would you know, they was gonna start a competitive product to what Sonny Boy was advertising over in West Memphis.

GIBBONS: Flour?

KING: No, no. See, when he left Helena, that was the end of the *King Biscuit Time.* When he came to West Memphis, he was advertising for a tonic called Hadacol. Well, Mr. Ferguson was starting a new tonic called Pepticon. And that's what I was introducing.

What exactly was it?

GIBBONS: A little of everything.

KING: Yeah. I never did really find out what Pepticon actually was until about eight years ago; somebody sent me a bottle of it. But I know we used to sell it like there wasn't gonna be no more. Come to find out it was 12 percent alcohol! [*Laughs.*]

GIBBONS: Somebody was feeling good!

KING: Some of those church people were having a good time with it. I used to go out on the truck with the salesmen on the weekends, and man, they'd give me like $100, $150 sometimes, according to how much they sell. I'd be on the top of the truck singing:

Pep- ti- con   sho' is go- oo-od

Pep- ti- con   sho' is good. You can

get it any where in your neigh-bor-hood.

    That's how it started, really.

GIBBONS: Going back to West Memphis, I had heard stories about the wildness. I mean, West Memphis was it, man.

KING: Yeah, it was really good. I loved it. I really did.

GIBBONS: There are still guys today that talk about it. In fact, you can drive down that old main street, and it hasn't changed too much. You can pick up the feeling. There's still something about it.

KING: Memphis was a bit conservative. They didn't believe in having racetracks and all that, so they put it right over in West Memphis, and all the money and everything would go over there on the weekends. So they had gambling and all that, as long as they had a particular sheriff that they kept in there for a long time.

GIBBONS: Was there other live music?

KING: Yeah. See, it wasn't just this particular little place. Anybody that was all right with the sheriff and the city government was okay, okay? That make sense? And there was a big white place out there where they really had good music all the time because they could afford to have the best—black, white, or any type of entertainment you could bring. What you have to remember, though, was that during this time it was still segregation, but when we went to that club, there was no segregation. You couldn't get out on the floor and dance, but you could have all the fun you could playing the music. Everybody get together and you talk, spin yarns as we usually did. The people out there was doing their thing, and we did ours in the back. But a few of the better clubs were black clubs where whites would come to them.

GIBBONS: That's so peculiar. Try as you might to keep a lid on a good time, you can't do it. When people want to have a good time . . .

KING: They will have a good time.

GIBBONS: It's gonna be there.

KING: And I'll tell you, had it not been for that, my life would have been very slow—very, very slow. I loved it.

GIBBONS: In fact, there is still a faction of people who, if they had their choices, would relive those times in West Memphis, particularly the '40s up to the '50s.

KING: Oh, yeah.

    Was Beale Street similarly wild?

KING: Not really. The guys would have what we called little turn-row crap games or something like that, but if a cop caught you, you were in big trouble! But it was always something going on. You had the One Minute Cafe where you could go in and eat for 15¢, man. I mean, *really* eat: bowl of chili, nickel's worth of crackers [*laughs*], and what we call a bellywash—something like an Orange Crush drink. Man, you could live, I mean, really *live*. Sunbeam Mitchell's was one of the established places for music, so you'd have the best traveling musicians coming through. Let's assume that we were going through town: We'd go to Mitchell's, because we'd have a chance to see the best and find out what's goin' on in the city. That's where you get your information. Kind of like when I used to come to Houston, I'd go to the Fifth Ward and go to Club Matinee.

Well, Memphis was like that. You had several pawnshops. You used to keep a couple of good rings, a good tie pin, and a pair of good shoes, so if you got broke, you go down and pawn them. They know you coming back, because ain't nobody else gonna wear your shoes! Clothing and food and good music of all kinds. You had gospel, find a little spot over here where a guy's preachin', find another over here where some guy's sittin' on the stool playing his guitar, over further some guy's gambling. You may have a few pickpockets. You had some of *everything* going on in the area of three blocks.

GIBBONS: Correct me if I'm wrong, but I've been told that in comparison to West Memphis, which was a different scene, Beale Street was wide open too, but in a stricter sense. There was a police department keeping everybody in line.

KING: Yeah.

GIBBONS: You didn't want to act up. Beale Street was controlled.

Did old-time country blues mix with electric blues on Beale Street?

KING: Well, see, I didn't know the difference at that time. You had a chance to see people that you'd never seen before; you'd just hear about them. But on Beale Street, he was just another person. It's kind of like if we walked in a room now with Bruce Springsteen or the Beatles or U2 or the Rollin' Stones—we all people. You don't see them as if you're out there and don't get a chance to rub elbows with them. On Beale Street, guys like me was lookin' up, but the other guys were just, "Hey, there's old so-and-so. How you doin', man?" But it was a big thing for guys like myself that just came from Mississippi. I had a chance to see Muddy Waters, all the guys that was big then—Sonny Boy Williamson. And then you got a chance to see guys with big bands, like Duke Ellington coming through. Count Basie. And all these people would patronize or fool around on Beale Street.

During that time it was segregated, with the exception of certain places. Now, in the radio station where I worked at, there was no segregation. None. When you came in there, your title was whomever you were. If you was an elderly person, it was Mr. So-and-so or Mrs. So-and-so, but other than that, you were who you are and you was treated with respect. But when you walked out, it was like leaving the Embassy [*laughs*]. It was a different story.

Beale Street was similar, because everybody—white and black—that lived and worked there was accustomed and used to the people being there. Duke Ellington and Count Basie or Louis Armstrong was known not only to the blacks, but to the whites as well. They had the Hippodrome and a few other places where the slick black promoters would bring in one of the big artists, and they would play two shows—one for whites and one for blacks, and they made money. Those were the days, though, man. If you were a little entertainer, you could always stand in the background. Like when the big guys be on the stage, you'd be in the wings lookin'. So it was some beautiful moments, some moments that I'll cherish and forever love.

You think that you got drug problems today, but it was there too. Most of the people would say, "If you want to make it, don't do that there. See what that dude doin' on the corner? Leave it alone," like that. It was sort of controlled, but people did do it.

Some of the jug band musicians fell into that.

KING: There was several great jug bands there. You know, in each society of music or whatever, you always got what I call the hierarchy, the people at the top that's the best at what they do, whether it be a boxer or a singer. So whenever one of these guys came around, like the great jug bands, everybody move over there where they can check that one out. I remember, for instance, Lightnin' Hopkins. When I first met Lightnin', it was in Memphis, met him there on Beale Street.

Was there something called headcutting?

KING: Well, you could call it that [*laughs*]. People do this now. When a great musician would come to town, like a jazz musician, well, all of the guys would be laying around him trying to cut his head. Well, we had some giant musicians there. The Newborn family was terrific. The old man, which was Phineas [*pronounced fine-us*] Newborn, played drums, and his son Phineas [*pronounced fin-ee-us*], they called him, played the keyboard. And he was *bad*—when I say bad, I mean terrific. And then he had a brother named Calvin, who's still around and plays back in Memphis. Terrible, man, I mean, he plays some guitar! And then you got Fred Ford, Bill Harvin, Herman Green—a lot of people that would be waitin' on you when you come to town. You supposed to be a musician, they want to get you on that stage up at Sunbeam's, and then they started calling Gershwin tunes and stuff like that.

GIBBONS: Oh, lord, look out! The tough stuff.

KING: So if you wasn't trained or didn't know tunes pretty well, you'd see a guy start taking his horn down—something was wrong with his horn—and the other guy breaks a string on his guitar, and they move. A guy came to town named Charles Brown. I'm still crazy about Charles even today. The guy who made "Merry Christmas, Baby" is the one I'm talking about. Well, they knew Charles was a blues singer and a blues player, but they didn't know that Charles had been to college and majored in music. Nobody knew that.

GIBBONS: Whoa!

KING: So Charles came to town. He had Wayne Bennett playing guitar, and a few other people. That night after the show they kept begging Charles to come up to Sunbeam's. They get him to get on the stage, and then they started calling "Lady Be Good" and any of the good jammin' Gershwin tunes, because those were the real jazz standards. That night when Charles Brown finally figured out what they was trying to do to him, he called "Body and Soul," which has got *a lot* of changes. When he called the tune, all the guys figured they really gonna cut him now. But then he started to modulate chromatically.

GIBBONS: Giving it to 'em!

KING: So a guy done learned it in one key, and now Charles is taking them through it all chromatically. Then I started seeing guys who had something wrong with his horn and such. Finally it wound up with Charles Brown, the bass, and the drums [*laughs*]. That's the best example I ever seen, and it was really fun to see that happen.

You recorded with some of the Newborns early on.

KING: My very first record, the whole family was on it. I made my first record for Bullet Recording Company out of Nashville. I had old man Phineas on the drums, his son Phineas Newborn, Jr., was on keyboard, Calvin was on guitar, and a lady was playin' trombone—I can't think of her name now [Sammie Jett]. It had Ben Branch on tenor sax, Thomas Branch on the trumpet, and Tuff Green, bass. It was four sides, and we did them at the radio station in the largest studio, Studio A. "Take a Swing with Me," "How Do You Feel When Your Baby Packed Up to Go," "Miss Martha King," and "I Got the Blues"—the first four sides I ever recorded.

Let's play another one of your early sides, "Mistreated Woman."

KING: [*Laughs.*] That's on Modern Records—or RPM, really. That's me. [At this point the solo starts.] Yeah, that's the old guy.

GIBBONS: Gibson guitar?

KING: Yeah. Crazy about T-Bone Walker. Crazy about Lowell Fulson.

Charlie Christian?

KING: Oh, yes. God, yeah. Well, Charlie Christian, Django Reinhardt—those are my jazz players. I don't know, this is going to sound a little weird to you, maybe, but I've always been conscious of being put down as a blues player. So I've had one thing that I always tried to keep in mind: It's always better to know and not need than to need and not know. I always like to know more than people think I know, so I practice hard trying to be able to do things that nobody would expect me to do. That's how I learned to fly airplanes; nobody ever thought that I could be a pilot, so I learned to be a pilot. I learned to do many other things simply because coming from Mississippi usually was the first downer, you know: "Yeah, man, this dude from Mississippi, still got clay mud on his shoes," stuff like that. It's still that way. So I started to say, "Yeah, I'm from Mississippi, and I'm proud of it." And today I'm very proud to be a Mississippian—very, very proud. Because I've been put down for trying to be something else. It wasn't a matter of just being something else—I just wanted to do what I did better than it had been done before. I felt that if I could do it there, I could do it at the White House, do it in New York, do it anyplace, and it could be thought of as being artistically well done.

GIBBONS: Through your graciousness over the years, you've become a cornerstone for so many people by knowing more than what people thought you knew.

KING: Well, it was satisfactory to me, in a way of speaking. All right, I don't speak English well, but if I go to Spain, I'll try to learn a couple of words. Any different country, I'll try to learn a couple words. So when I hear people talking in Japan and they say a few things, I'll pick it up. It's the same thing musically. If I hear you play [*indicates Billy*], I may not be able to play what I hear you play, but I'll know a little something about it because I'm *listening*. Got my ears on it. Same thing with him [*indicates Jas*] or whoever. Well, that is a peace of mind for B.B. King—maybe not to anybody else, but to me. And this is not something you do once in a while. Each day I've got my ears kind of cocked, learnin'. If I could do what you do or what somebody else do, I'd find myself saying, "You sound so good like that, but I wouldn't sound that good, so I better try it *this* way." But it's still your idea.

GIBBONS: Let me indulge in a little complimentary flattery by pointing to the single-string soloing on that track we just played. So many have cited the B.B. touch; so many people have made references to the B.B. King influence. I would say that it's your sound and approach to soloing that has made the guitar such a lead instrument. It's really inspired a lot of people to learn how to improvise and solo.

Wouldn't you say that was just developing for the guitar around the time you recorded that track in '50?

KING: It's a funny thing. During that time, guitars hadn't really come into being, if you will. Excuse the word, but it was a bitch to try to get a good guitar at that time—just to try and *get* one. And when you did get one, you better hold onto it—don't loan it to nobody. If you did, they didn't come back, most of 'em. So yes. Nobody had any idea that the guitar would become what it is today. Where I grew up at, there was no other instrument that was available to you, really, but maybe a harmonica. And everybody don't want to blow everybody's harmonica. In my area, they couldn't afford keyboards of any kind. You couldn't afford no pianos or organ. I guess I've only seen an organ in maybe three or four homes in an area of 150 homes, and those was what we called—an old word down there—*uppity* [*laughs*]. They had the uppity blacks as well as the whites, see. So very few people had those. Only time I ever seen a piano or organ was when I went to church. So when I would go over to somebody's house, there usually was an old guitar laying on the bed. And the only strings I ever knew about at that time, we bought them at a drugstore, and they was called Black Diamonds.

Red packs.

GIBBONS: Or the glass jar, if you really want to go back.

KING: Yeah. And your *E* string, man, was about as big as my *G* string is today. I use a .010 for my *E*, a .013 for my *B*, and a .017 for my *G* string. And those *E* strings then had to be close to .014.

GIBBONS: At least. Somebody gave me a set of Black Diamonds, right out of the box—wires!

KING: Now, when you break one of those strings, then you would take baling wire—the wire that you bale hay with or the wire they used to wrap broomsticks—and we would use that for strings. You take that and tie it onto the string. Once you tie it on, you put that wire on your tuner, so from here to here [*indicates from about the fifth fret to the bridge*] you got string.

GIBBONS: You couldn't play down below that? Oh, man!

KING: You could never play down low. But a lot of people didn't do it anyway—in fact, my friend Gatemouth still don't! So you take a clamp [capo]—when you could afford one—and put it on between the end of where the string is broke, so you got good clear string. And if you couldn't do that—in most cases, we didn't—you get a pencil or a piece of stick that's straight across, and you put it on there, take some string, tie it down, and that's your clamp.

A homemade capo.

KING: Yeah. It's like the nut of your guitar.

GIBBONS: Hope that you sing real high for the rest of the week!

KING: [*Laughs.*] Well, we learned to do things. We let [tuned] it down!

As a child, did you ever make a one-string?

KING: Yeah. We take the same cord from around that broom, and you put a big nail up there [*points about five feet up the wall*]. Take another one and put it down there [*about three-and-a-half feet lower*], and you put the string on the nails. Then you take something like a brick—we always found that a brick was really good for sustaining tones—put it in down there between the string and the wall, tighten it, put another brick up there on top, tighten it, and then you bang on it.

Would you play with a slide?

KING: I can't play slide on my guitar today! [*Laughs.*] Still can't. Another thing we used to do is take an inner tube—you don't find 'em often now, but most of the cars at that time had inner tubes inside of the tire. So when one of those would blow out, you'd take the rubber and stretch it. You'd make a board and put small bricks or pieces of wood on it, just like you do your guitar, and you could play that. You could also take a stick and wet it, put it across, and it sounds similar to a violin. You leave it to kids, boy—we'd find a way to make music!

Was there a moment when it became clear that you were destined to play the blues?
KING: Yeah. It was after I had been in the Army when I was 18. Working on the plantation where we lived, we was growing produce for the Armed Forces. You was compelled, you was drafted, as you became 18 during World War II. There wasn't no ifs and ands—you went and signed up for the Armed Forces. Well, in our area they claimed we was doing things for the Armed Forces, and they needed us there. So we went and took partial basic training, and then they reclassified you and sent you back home. You couldn't leave; you had to stay there. If you left, then you was reclassified again and went back in. But even if I die tomorrow, I couldn't get a flag, because we didn't complete the basic training. I came back home—I was driving a tractor at this time—and I started to go on the street corners to sit and play on a Saturday evening after I got off work.

I would always try to sit on the corner of main streets, where we get blacks and whites coming right past us. I would sit and play; I didn't ask nobody for anything—I would *hope!* Now, I was singing gospel with a quartet; we were pretty good. We were like an opening act for groups like the Soul Stirrers, Spirit of Memphis, and like that. But for some reason, the guys never seemed to want what I wanted. I wanted to move up a little bit with it, and everybody was very conscious of their families, which I can understand. But I guess I wasn't as family-orientated as they were. I kept thinking that we could go off and do like the Golden Gate Quartet and many of the other groups. Every autumn, after our crops was gathered, I would say, "Hey, now is the time to go," and we'd make plans to leave and go to Memphis or someplace where we could record. But every time that would happen, they'd say, "No. We didn't do too well. The crops didn't . . . So we won't do it."

Anyway, while sitting on the street corners playing, people'd ask me to play a gospel song. And when I'd play it, they'd always pat me on the shoulder or something and compliment me very highly: "Son, you're good. If you keep it up, you're gonna be all right one day." But they never tip. But dudes who would ask me to play a *blues* song would always tip, man, give me a beer. Man, they'd yell at everybody else: "Don't you see this boy playin'? Give him something!" Instead of making my $22.50 a week on the plantation, I'd sometimes make, gosh, maybe $100— at least $50 or $60.

GIBBONS: You're speaking of the war years now?
KING: Yeah. So these people would always give me nice tips, man. That's when the motivation started. That's when I started deciding I would play the blues.

What were the first blues 78s that knocked you out?
KING: My aunt used to buy records like kids do today, and some of her collection was Blind Lemon, Lonnie Johnson. She had Robert Johnson, Bumble Bee Slim, and Charley Patton. I could just go on and name so many she had. But my favorites turned out to be Blind Lemon Jefferson and Lonnie Johnson. I liked Robert and all the rest of them, but those were my favorites.

What's the appeal of Blind Lemon?

KING: I wished I could tell you, because if I could, I'd do it! [*Laughs.*] He had some-thing in his phrasing that's so funny. He had a way of double-time playing. Say, like, one-two-three-four, and then he'd go [in double-time] one-two-three-four, one-two-three-four. And the time was still right there, but double-time. And he could come out of it so easy. And then when he would resolve something, it was done so well. I've got some of his records now—I keep them on cassette with me. But he'd come out of it so smooth. His touch is different from anybody on the guitar—still is. I've practiced, I tried, I did everything, and still I could never come out with the sound as he did. He was majestic, and he played just a regular little 6-string guitar with a little round hole. It was unbelievable to hear him play. And the way he played with his rhythm patterns, he was way before his time, in my opinion.

Which of his songs would you recommend for guitarists?

KING: [*Sings in a gentle voice*]

"See that my grave be kept clean,
See that my grave be kept clean,
See that my grave be kept clean,
See da-da-da-da-da-da"

That's one of them. Lightnin' Hopkins did it, and many people have done it since. But that's where it came from. [*Resumes singing*]

"It's a long road ain't got no end,
Long road ain't got no end,
Long road ain't . . . "

Oh, one other part:

"Three white horses in a line,
Three white horses in a line,
Three white horses in a line,
Gonna take me to my burying ground"

Something like that.

GIBBONS: Since this interview is centered around Memphis and the early years, I'd like to cite a personal favorite vision that has recently come out. The two B.B. King albums that come over from England that have the picture of you . . .

KING: Wearin' shorts, huh? [*Laughs heartily.*] Well, you know, I used to think that I was kind of hot stuff. My cousin Bukka White told me something that has stayed with me over all these years. I mentioned how we used to be put down as blues singers. I've quite often said if you was a black person singing the blues, you black twice. And if you a white person, you black once. Because people usually will put you down. Like, if you from the country, people was, "Aw, look at the little coun-try dude." And if you from the city, country people won't talk so much about it, but they say, "Well, he from the city, he think he's something." Well, my cousin Bukka White used to say, "You see how I dress? [*Tugs lapels of his suit.*] When you dress like this, it's like you're going to try to borrow some money. The banker don't know who you are, and the people that you're talkin' to don't know what you are. So you always dress like that, and people don't know, because you look clean and neat, and they may loan you the money. But if you come up and you're not dressed nice, you look like you're a beggar. But dressed up, the white people see you, and you look like a preacher or something like that, so you get by a little easier." I started to do it, and I started to notice that made a difference—always. After that I started a trend for my own band, and we sort of set a pace like that. I got used to doing it, and I like it. Anyway, there was something else I started to tell you a little while ago . . .

GIBBONS: About the Bermuda shorts.

KING: Yeah! Thank you. Well, I thought at that time that this was kind of slick, you know.

GIBBONS: It was slick. To this day.

KING: Yeah, but if I had realized what my legs looked like then, I probably wouldn't have done it. I had seen guys from Australia wearing short pants, and I thought it was cool.

GIBBONS: In fact, in that photo you're playing a Gibson—it could have been a Switchmaster or the ES-5. Big-bodied.

KING: Yeah, I think I had what they called the 400.

GIBBONS: Did the big bodies give you much trouble with feedback?

KING: I didn't think of it so much at that time. T-Bone Walker had one that had three pickups, and I was crazy about it. Crazy about him. Well, as I said, during that time it was hard to get and keep a good guitar, so the early '50s is when the Fenders first came out. So I had one of the early Fenders. I had the Gretsch, I even had a Silvertone from Sears, Roebuck. So I had any kind of guitar you can probably think of. But when I found that little Gibson with the long neck, that did it. That's like finding your wife forever. This is she! I've stayed with it from then on. Now, a lot of times you may buy a guitar just to keep at home, but to play—for me, that was it. They had the ES-335, and then they had a new idea for the 355, and I've been crazy again. So that's the one I've held onto. But I've tried guitars through the years—you name them, I've probably had one.

GIBBONS: You've been credited with starting so many fads, trends, crazes, and things that have gone way beyond that now because they're carved in stone as just the way to do it. And people keep digging up relics of the past: Just recently a friend of mine sent me a postcard that's a reprint of a publicity shot of the B.B. King Orchestra. The band members are lined up, and you're leading the pack, standing in front of the bus. Everybody is just natty, neat as a pin. It's the definitive vision of the way an outfit should look. And it's coming back around to this.

KING: Yeah, I remember that. We took that picture in front of my first old bus. That was a pretty big band then, about 12 or 13 pieces. I thought myself big stuff because we could play the blues like I thought we should, and then we could venture into other little things from time to time. This was '55.

GIBBONS: Well, you had the strength to be that leader.

KING: I've enjoyed doing what I've done. I've had so much happiness from so many people.

GIBBONS: It shows.

KING: If you'd ask me 40 years ago—this is 41 years I'm into it now—would I even be living today, I would have bet you odds no. But so many good things have happened. I'm happier today, this very day, than I've ever been in my life. I've had so many wonderful things happen. And I'll tell you what, you've made me happy just sitting here talking with you. This is a real treat. I never dreamed this would ever happen. I really thank you. I've been asked before if there was anything I would do differently if I had this life to start again. And there are only two things I can think of that I would change: I would finish high school and go to college and try to learn more about the music, and I wouldn't marry until after 40!

B.B. KING: DEUCES WILD—RECREATING THE CLASSICS The following interview took place a few days before the release of B.B. King's *Deuces Wild* album, which reaffirmed King's ability to make his guitar Lucille transcend stylistic boundaries. It ran in the January '98 *Guitar Player* as "B.B. King: Deuces Wild—Recreating the Classics with Eric Clapton, the Rolling Stones, David Gilmour & Bonnie Raitt." Van Morrison, Tracy Chapman, Mick Hucknall, Dr. John, D'Angelo, Joe Cocker, Marty Stuart, Willie Nelson, and rapper Heavy D also appeared on the project. At home in Las Vegas, the 72-year-old bluesman was in a jovial mood during the conversation.

We like your new record.
Thank you very much. I'm glad to hear that.
I notice you're not alone on it.
[*Laughs.*] Oh, no.
You have Lucille with you.
Oh, yeah. I got my girl on there with me, yes. I'm using Lucille the 16th at this time.
Have you worn out any of the previous ones?
No. Never wear 'em out. Sometimes you wear the neck down a little bit or something like that, but I send them back to the company. I usually always request another one, and they usually send me another one. And guess what? I never send it back! [*Laughs.*] I play the first Lucille that Gibson made for me. It's sort of special. That's the one used throughout the record.
Are the differences in your tone from track to track due to changes in amplification?
Yes, and it's due to John Porter, the producer. John set my amplifiers on each recording date, and I was pleased with it. It sounded good, so I would never change it. I'd just leave it like it was.
It's wonderful to hear you on a rap tune!
[*Laughs heartily.*] Well, that just goes to show you: You can never tell what an old guy may do! Well, let me put it this way. This is a project that I've wanted to do ever since I been recording—that is, record with great people like the Rolling Stones, Eric Clapton, Bonnie Raitt, and so on. I'd been on my manager Sid [Seidenberg] about doing this—and we been together over 30 years—and he had been in the sides of MCA, kind of like . . . Are you married?
Yes.
Alright. I've been married too, so I know how ladies can get you to do things when you maybe thought you were not gonna do 'em. They bring you a cup of coffee when you don't expect it. They'll fix you a nice dinner when you don't expect it. [*Laughs.*] They do many nice things for you, and then they pop that question! "When you gonna do so-and-so?" So that's kind of the way we were with MCA until they finally decided to do it, and I'm very, very happy that they did.
Are you particularly close with any of the guest artists?
Some I know very well, like Eric Clapton. Bonnie Raitt is one of my best friends. Dr. John is one of my dear friends. Willie Nelson is one of the greatest people I know on this planet. Oh, I love the man. He done things for people, and nobody

give him credit for a lot of it! Like the Farm Aid and all that—this was from the bottom of his heart. He didn't have to do that. He hadn't been in trouble or nothing at that time. He was just trying to help people, and then later it seem like some rapped on him. But to me he is an angel on this earth. He is a great, great man. Not only that, he is a hell of an artist and one of the nicest people I know.

Isn't that some guitar he's got? The classical with the extra hole in the top . . .

Oh, man! I just love it. He wore a hole in it, yes, and he can really play it, man.

How did you choose Heavy D for "Keep It Coming"?

I did not know Heavy D, but I knew about him. I had a chance to meet him through John Porter.

Had you listened to much rap music?

Oh, yeah. I listen to some rap music, and I love it. I think that most of the rappers are very, very talented. Try, if you will, to rhyme everything you do to a beat—you'll find that these people are very talented. The only thing I didn't like—and I was so happy that Heavy D chose not to do it, although I didn't ask him not to do it—was the use of certain words that they use sometimes—the four-letter words, and I don't mean "golf." But he was so nice.

How did Lucille feel about having a rap song written about her?

Oh, she loved it. Lucille love them young men, you know.

Several of your solos are like a sweet conversation.

Well, let me tell you this, and I'm being honest: I don't think I've ever enjoyed recording more.

Were any of the tracks done without your guests in the studio?

No, no, no, no, no. Every track except one, I was there and playin' on it with the artist when we were laying it down. Yes, sir—the Rolling Stones, everybody. The only person that I didn't work with on it was Joe Cocker. I worked with everybody else, including Eric Clapton. He laid the track down, but he and I worked to it.

Did anyone impress you with his or her studio savvy?

Well, most of them didn't change my impression of them. I was in awe of them before they came to the studio, and loved everybody's work and respected them highly. Working with them in the studio just enhanced that.

How long have you known Clapton?

I met him before I went to Europe the very first time, and that's been 20 years ago, I guess. I remember getting into Great Britain, and I saw in the paper that he had been interviewed. He said that one of the things that he enjoyed while in the U.S. was meeting me, and that really knocked me out, man. He has done many things to help me. I remember we were doing a celebration of the Apollo Theater, and he flew over to be with me. Even before that, we did a video called *B.B. King and Friends,* and he flew over and came with me to do that. He's done several things, and I owe him so much. And I've thought his playing was fantastic from day one.

It's fun hearing the two of you solo toe-to-toe.

[*Laughs.*] He cut me up!

You play with a lot of conviction in "Please Send Me Someone to Love."

Yes. I knew [songwriter] Percy Mayfield very well. He was one of my dear friends.

What was he like?

He was very easygoing, liked a drink now and then, loved people, loved to joke with them. A beautiful, very talented man.

Tracy Chapman was an interesting choice for "The Thrill Is Gone."

Yeah, right! We just submitted songs, and she decided that she would do that one. The day we recorded it was the day I met her. We recorded that in L.A., and she was superb. A beautiful young lady. Seemed to be shy, but when she get in the studio, she ain't shy no more!

Did Bonnie play the rhythm guitar on her track?

And the slide, yeah. I think she was playing her Strat.

Which of the Stones soloed with you?

Keith. I think Ronnie played some too, but Keith was the one that cut me up. [*Laughs.*] Yeah, that was Keith. And he was not drinking at all that day. He was himself, a beautiful man and a hell of a guitar player. And that's Mick playing the harmonica as well. He was great. We had a good time—it was like an old home-coming, friends getting together.

What's on tap for the near future?

Well, I'm going to be doing some concerts. I'm going over to see the pope. We've got an audience with the pope, and we're going to do a Christmas show for him, and hopefully I'll get a chance to be blessed by the Holy Father. And we just finished some work with Jon Landis on his new movie *Blues Brothers 2000*. I play a used car dealer named Melbourne Gasparon. I have a used car lot, and I sell Dan Aykroyd his first car when he gets out of prison. Then we have a jam session later on in the movie, and my band consists of Eric Clapton, Bo Diddley, Travis Tritt, and Jimmy Vaughan on guitars. My singers are Koko Taylor, Lou Rawls, Isaac Hayes, Eric Clapton, and me. It's funny!

Do you ever play acoustic?

Yeah. I have two or three at the house, and I play at home on them sometimes.

Any chance you'll record with one?

Yes, I think I will. You know, that's all I had in the early parts of my career. I didn't have an electric guitar, because where we lived we had no electricity. So that's all I played for at least 17, 18 years.

One last question. What are the first steps a young musician can take toward getting his own style?

You don't want to play like B.B. King, you don't want to play like Jas Obrecht or somebody else. You want to be you. So what you do is listen to Jas, listen to B.B., listen to anybody else you like. I don't use the word "steal," but try to "borrow" a little bit from each guy, if you can. You apply that to yourself, like learning to read or write. You hear words that you like, and you add that to your vocab, but you don't try to always sound exactly like the other one. And like that you become you.

If I came to town and I wanted to hire somebody, I wouldn't want to hire some-body that sounds like Jeff Beck, Eric Clapton, or George Benson. If I wanted to do that, I'd hire George Benson or Eric Clapton! So try to be yourself. Study scales. I'm lazy—I never practice as much as I should have. If I had, my style would have been better. But practice. That's one thing you do. It's just like the old saying about the young man who was on his way to Broadway and saw a few old musicians. He asked him, "How do you get to Carnegie Hall?" And one smart aleck said, "Practice." So practice and try to be yourself.

ALBERT KING

BY DAN "BOB" FORTE One of the occupational
hazards of being a dyed-in-the-wool blues fanatic is that you
become attached to performers who inevitably pass on. One
can be philosophical, of course, and realize that "the records
will live on forever," but in recent years the blues ranks have
narrowed so many times that even the most philosophical
buff can't help but feel a bit numb, even jaded, as yet another in an already dying breed leaves with no suitable replacement on the horizon. But the loss of Albert King, who suffered a massive heart attack on December 21, 1992, hit me
especially hard, on both artistic and personal levels. ¶ You
see, I first met Albert King under what can only be described
as unique circumstances. One night in 1969 my father came
home from his job as an inspector on the Oakland Police
Department and said, "Guess whose trailer full of equipment

got stolen?" Albert had been playing in San Francisco, and while parked at his hotel—this was during the days when he still toured in a station wagon with *Albert "Born Under a Bad Sign" King* painted on the side—a thief with a trailer hitch simply unhooked the guitarist's U-Haul, attached it to the rear of *his* station wagon, and drove off, not even knowing what he'd stolen until he got home.

That particular modus operandi was all the OPD needed to home in on the crook; the next task was locating the guitars, amps, drums, and organ at pawnshops throughout the East Bay. Once that was accomplished, I got a call one summer afternoon while mowing the lawn. "If you want to meet Albert King," my dad said, "get up to the police station as soon as you can. He's flying up from L.A. to reclaim his stuff."

As quick as you could say "I'm a crosscut saw, baby, drag me 'cross your log," I was pulling up to the station house, armed with copies of *Born Under a Bad Sign* and *Live Wire/Blues Power.* The 6'4", 250-pound bluesman finally lumbered into my dad's office, wearing a black fedora (with the front brim flipped up, as always) and a lime green, pin-striped suit over a lavender shirt with a diamond stickpin. For the next several hours I pumped my idol with questions about Robert Nighthawk, Little Junior Parker, and T-Bone Walker, and he obliged with anecdotes about each. I rode along with Albert and my dad, from hockshop to hockshop, recovering the fenced property one instrument at a time. I'll never forget the look on Albert's face when the last pawnbroker brought out a rectangular guitar case held together with a brown leather belt. "That's my Lucy," he beamed, cradling his trademark Gibson Flying V as though it were his baby daughter.

When we said our good-byes, Albert promised to put me on the guest list the next time he played the Fillmore. A nice offer, I thought, but one that will never come true. And, at any rate, I was already in blues heaven, inspecting my copy of *Born Under a Bad Sign,* now inscribed with a printed "A.B. King."

At a time when most of the select group now known as Guitar Heroes were jockeying for king of the hill, this self-taught southpaw was already *my* guitar hero. One of the advantages of growing up in the San Francisco area in the late '60s was KMPX, the country's first underground FM radio station, and shortly after its release in 1967, *Born Under a Bad Sign* was getting near-constant airplay. With backing by Booker T. & The MG's and the Memphis Horns, the Stax album was a milestone, the hippest thing the blues or rock world had seen in ages. Songs like "Crosscut Saw," "The Hunter," "Laundromat Blues," and "As the Years Go Passing By" were peppered throughout the time slots of Abe "Voco" Kesh, Larry Miller, and "Big Daddy" Tom Donahue.

I first saw Albert perform on February 2, 1968, at San Francisco's Winterland, where he shared billing with England's Soft Machine, John Mayall's Bluesbreakers, and the Jimi Hendrix Experience. That weekend was in fact Albert's first exposure to the hippie throng that underground radio and Bill Graham nurtured, but he played the crowd as skillfully as he played Lucy—as though he knew precisely what to do before even taking the stage. And what he did, wisely enough, was just *be himself,* Albert King. Some accounts actually credit King with stealing the show from Hendrix; I would prefer to call it a draw. I'm not going out on a limb when I state that onstage Jimi Hendrix was quite possibly the most overwhelming phenomenon any rock audience had ever witnessed. But Jimi played *at* the audience;

Albert played *to* it. While thousands stood with mouths open and eyes glazed over as Jimi extracted unheard-of guitar sounds from his Stratocaster, they laughed and hollered and danced and *participated* in the dialogue that Albert carried on from the stage. As Jerrold Greenberg of *Rolling Stone* wrote, "The least contrived, certainly the most 'old-fashioned' of the three, Albert King was nonetheless the only consummate artist among them, the only one who could play on the full emotional range of his audience with as much facility as he used to sustain a note on his guitar." (No fool when it came to PR, Albert would later recall the bill as himself, Hendrix, and Janis Joplin, since Big Brother & The Holding Company replaced Mayall on the last night of the stint.)

Albert was soon "a permanent member of the Fillmore family," to quote his introduction on *Live Wire/Blues Power,* headlining shows with younger bands like Creedence Clearwater and recording the aforementioned LP at Graham's new site, Fillmore West.

And after our first meeting he indeed remembered his promise of putting me on the guest list, and my parents held up their end of the bargain, inviting him out to the suburbs for fried chicken or his favorite, Chinese food (with, in Albert's case, plenty of white bread accompanying both). I became Albert's unofficial valet whenever he hit town. Some of you ex-hippies might remember a hyper little redhead carrying a suit bag and a guitar case with no handle, leading the way for a larger-than-life black man—probably saying something very peace-and-love like "Get outta the way, Albert King's coming through!"

There was always a lot of voodoo surrounding Albert's pickless, backwards-strung, oddly tuned technique, but one of his most memorable displays, for me, was when I showed him the '61 Les Paul/SG I'd gotten for my seventeenth birthday. After tossing the case unceremoniously on his hotel bed, he examined the right-handed Gibson, flipped it over left-handed and mashed down on one of his patented perfect-fourth bends. My guitar, standard tuning, no amp. Sounded exactly like—you guessed it—Albert King.

Albert was terrible with names but had a great memory—a combination that resulted in him calling me Ted (never Dan) for several years. Then one day I was no longer Ted; for most of the next decade I was Bob.

Although Albert was perhaps the first bluesman who teamed with a symphony orchestra, in St. Louis in 1969, and played at the historic WattStax concert in 1972 and on *American Bandstand,* he will probably be best remembered as the "Flower Power Blues Guitarist," thanks to his success in the late '60s and the rapport he established with that audience. But he was simultaneously one of the few bluesmen scoring hits on contemporary black radio. As Mike Bloomfield told me in 1977, "Between Al Jackson's production, the Booker T. & The MG's rhythm section, the choice of material, the Memphis Horns, and Albert's playing, he was the only bluesman I know of who had a completely comfortable synthesis with modern black music—R&B, so to speak—and sold copiously to a black audience as well as the white audience. He was the only singer who had clever, modern arrangements that would fit in with the black radio market and with the white market and in no way compromised his style. That's sort of amazing, in that B.B. King never did it, except once with 'The Thrill Is Gone,' but Albert did it time after time."

THE "ALBERT KING SOUND" As with most "overnight successes," Albert's glory days came after years on the chitlin circuit. He was born April 25 in Indianola, Mississippi, and although the liner notes to *Bad Sign* listed the year as 1924, reports at the time of his death put it at 1923; he was 69. (A good rule of thumb when interviewing Albert, a notorious embellisher, was to double- and triple-check all facts and take any declarations with several grains of salt. For instance, his desire to get out of music and go back to driving a bulldozer, quoted extensively in later years, was a yarn he'd been spinning since arriving on the Fillmore scene.)

He was first attracted to the guitar through his stepfather, Will Nelson. "He had a guitar," King recalled, "but I couldn't play it. I used to climb up on a chair and hit the box hanging upside the wall. Sounded good to me." Because he was left-handed but played right-handed instruments, even picking up licks from watching other players was difficult, let alone any type of formal instruction. (To clear up the mire that often surrounds unorthodox lefties, Jimi Hendrix would restring right-handed guitars so as to be standard for a southpaw—the chassis he was working on may have been right-handed, but his playing was all lefty—while Albert literally played upside-down and backwards, with the lowest strings closest to his toes.)

After fooling with a one-string "diddley bow"—essentially a wire connected to a wall and played with a bottle as a slider—Albert graduated to a homemade guitar. "It was a wooden cigar box for the body," he explained, "and a little tree that I cut off and shaved up to make the neck. And I used wooden pegs for the keys, with holes in them to wrap the wires around. Years ago they used to make whisk brooms that had real thin stainless steel on them. Sounded good. I had all of the strings tuned different, but I had to use the same grade wire on all six. I kept that guitar for a long time, but it got burned up in a fire."

As a boy, King was exposed to two giants of country blues. "The first one was Blind Lemon Jefferson," he stated. "Later I heard him on records, but I used to see him in these parks, like on Saturday afternoons in these little country towns around Forrest City, Arkansas. We'd work till noon on Saturdays, and then my stepdad would hook up the wagon, and sometimes my sister and I and the other kids could go to town. This one particular day he was playing acoustic guitar, and he had his cup. He sounded something like that folk singer, Richie Havens—something on that order. He had a crowd of people around him, and we'd put nickels in his cup, and he'd play a song. It was amazing to me to see him count his money. He could feel the face of the coin and tell you what it was. Then he'd put it in his pocket and play some more. I also heard this lady Memphis Minnie. She used to come to town and sing to the electric piano—they called it the 'self-play-ing' piano. Not the kind you pump with your feet; the kind you just turn on and it goes to playing the sheet music on a spool. She brought her music with her that would fit right in that. I was a little boy, and I used to sneak and peep in the door before they'd run me away."

Albert's first legitimate guitar, a Guild acoustic, didn't come until he was 18. "See, this guy had a guitar," he recalled in 1977. "He'd paid two dollars for it. Well, he had a girl, and they wanted to go to the afternoon movie show, but he didn't have the money. I didn't have a little girl, but I had my allowance that my mother gave me. So it was getting close to show time, and this girl was really get-ting upset to get in to see the movie. I offered him my $1.25 for it. 'No, I ain't gonna sell my guitar. Give me $1.50.' I said, 'You just wait around; that girl's gonna be ready to go to the movies soon.' It was really funny. All the guys who didn't have nobody were gathered around waiting to take her. Well, I had my mind on that blasted guitar. She was getting ready to go in with another guy, and he couldn't stand that, so he came over and said, 'Give me that $1.25, man; you can have the guitar.' So that's how I got my first guitar, and I just started rapping on it from the left side."

The upside-down approach may have presented its share of obstacles, but as a result one of the blues' most distinctive sounds was born. "I knew I was going to have to create my own style," he conceded, "because I couldn't makes the changes and the chords the same as a right-handed man could. I play a few chords, but not many. I always concentrated on my singing guitar sound—more of a sustained note."

Steve Cropper, who played rhythm guitar on many of King's Stax sessions and appears on *Jammed Together* with Albert and Pops Staples, points out that the lefty also had his own tuning. "He tuned to an *E* minor chord, with a low *C* on the bottom. That's a low son of a bitch, like a tuba, but he didn't play it that much; that string got overlooked a whole lot. He mainly concentrated on the top three strings, the highest ones. We were in the studio once, and I said, 'Boy, that sure would sound good if it had Albert King playing on it.' He was out of town, so I took one of my old guitars and strung it backwards and tuned it to his chord and tried it. And it worked, because I'd been around Albert, and I knew how he played—I'd picked up his guitar and goofed with it a couple of times. So I set one up with that action, and it sort of got the Albert King sound."

The "Albert King sound" was almost on a different instrument. After working on construction crews in Osceola and Little Rock, Arkansas, and occasionally singing in a gospel quartet called the Harmony Kings, Albert moved to Gary, Indiana, in 1953. "I stopped playing guitar [an Epiphone electric] and got a job playing drums with Jimmy Reed. We were playing them little small joints, and it got to where Jimmy wouldn't stay sober and wouldn't work half the time, so I said, 'Hell, I'm going to make a record myself.' Al Benson in Chicago had a label called Parrot, so I went over and auditioned for him. He said, 'Okay, be in the studio tomorrow night.' We recorded 'Bad Luck Blues' and 'Be On Your Merry Way.' He said, 'I've got to see if it's going to sell, then I'll give you a contract later [*laughs*]. I didn't get no contract, I didn't get no statement—the record sold about 350,000 copies. I didn't get any money out of it, but it kind of helped make a name for me, you know."

Following a handful of singles for the Bobbin label, Albert scored his first bona fide hit in 1961. "Don't Throw Your Love on Me So Strong," cut in St. Louis with Ike Turner on piano and released by King Records, went to #14 on the R&B charts. A collection of his King and Bobbin sides was released as Albert's first LP, *The Big Blues.* "Sam Lay, who played drums in the Butterfield band, used to be his drummer, and he gave me that record," remembered Mike Bloomfield. "I'd never heard of him before. I was knocked out; the guy was just a fabulous lead guitar player. His style was superb, comparable to Otis Rush or Buddy Guy or any modern blues guitarist, but it wasn't as well-formed as when his first Stax record, *Born Under a Bad Sign,* came out years later. I could hear that the way he played guitar was different than the other guitarists, but I couldn't figure it out until I saw him in person. Then I realized that he played backwards.

"He was a huge, immense man, and his hands would just dwarf his Flying V guitar. He played with his thumb, and he played horizontally—across the finger-board, as opposed to vertically. And he approached lead playing more vocally than any guitar player I ever heard in my life; he plays exactly like a singer. As a matter of fact, his guitar playing has almost more of a vocal range than his voice does—which is unusual, because if you look at B.B. or Freddie King or Buddy Guy, their singing is almost equal to their guitar playing. They sing real high falsetto notes, then drop down into the mid-register. Albert just sings in one sort of very melliflu-ous but monotonous register, with a crooner's vibrato, almost like a lounge singer, but his guitar playing is just as vocal as possible. 'I Love Lucy' is a good example of that. He makes the guitar talk.

"His attack, the timbre, the tone—it's always right," Bloomfield continued, obvi-ously enjoying a chance to talk about one of his favorite subjects. "I can listen to ten minutes of him playing the same licks over and over and never get bored. He can take four notes and write a volume. He can say more with fewer notes than anybody I've ever known."

As with all of the truly great blues stylists, Albert's influences are virtually indiscernible in his totally individualistic style. Although he mentioned Lightnin' Hopkins, Lonnie Johnson, Elmore James, and Howlin' Wolf as influences (in addition to Blind Lemon), T-Bone Walker topped King's list of favorites. "When T-Bone Walker came," he told me, "I was into that. That really gave me an idea of what I wanted to do; that opened it up. That was the sound I was looking for, because he had an incredible blues sound. But all those licks and things he was making, I couldn't do. I said, 'I'm gonna have to try to do something with these strings.' So I developed that string-squeezing sound." In other words, Albert's style developed as a result of *not* being able to emulate his favorite guitarist—which is why T-Bone relied on chords, linear lines, and half-step bends, while Albert would, to quote Bloomfield again, "bend the guitar seven frets," if that was the note he was shooting for.

As Bloomfield noted, Albert's trademark sound finally jelled on *Born Under a Bad Sign*. Music critic Robert Palmer wrote, "Its impact was as inescapable among blues players as John Coltrane's influence was in jazz." MG's bassist Donald "Duck" Dunn explains, "We took a blues artist and put a few different rhythms behind him; it wasn't just that shuffle type of stuff. You've got to attribute a lot of that to [drummer/producer] Al Jackson and his drum patterns." Cropper adds, "Al gave it a little bit different flavor. Like 'Crosscut Saw' has a sort of bloopy, crazy kind of lick, and that was Al's innovation—which consequently made everybody else play a little different. The only one who didn't play different would be Albert King, who played like Albert King."

Working on the 1977 *Guitar Player* cover story, I found it wasn't difficult to find people eager to sing Albert's praises. As Elvin Bishop said, "Everybody in the world that I know of who plays any kind of blues guitar was affected by him to a small degree at least. A couple of his little pet licks are just part of the language." Johnny Winter pointed to one of Albert's early singles, "I'm a Lonely Man": "I learned that and played it for about five years every night, note for note, man. I got every sin-gle record he made." Bill Graham even granted a rare interview, doubtless his only one for a guitar magazine, to talk about the Fillmore's bluesman-in-residence. "In the mid '60s, once the Fillmore got started, I began to speak to a lot of the musicians I respected and ask them where they got whatever they did. I decided to track down some of these artists to see if I could expose their talents to people who didn't know they existed. It may sound corny, but it's almost like dealing with your child. If your child says, 'I want the ice cream,' you say, 'Well, you've got to finish your meat first.' I'd look at the headliner and say, 'Who would I like to expose their audience to?' When you had a Jimi Hendrix, the Hendrix fan, who was into guitar, would listen to a John Mayall or an Albert King. So Albert was the meat, even though they got to enjoy it.

"Albert was one of the artists I used many times for various reasons," Graham continued. "He wasn't just a good guitar player. He had a wonderful stage presence, he was very congenial and warm, he was relaxed onstage, and he related to the public. Also, he never became a shuck-and-jiver. One of the sad things that happened in the '60s—it's not a nice thing to say, but it happens to be true—was that the blues artists began to realize that anything they did onstage, white America would accept. And a lot of them became jive. But Albert remained a guy who just went onstage and said, 'Let's play.'"

Bloomfield concurred: "I've never seen him once when he wasn't vital, exciting, and not shucking. I've seen every blues singer there is shuck at one time or another, but I've never seen Albert do it once. He's always giving 100% of himself—much more than I would."

As indelible as his influence was on white blues-rockers, equally significant was his effect on the black bluesmen who were his contemporaries, many of them, such as Otis Rush and Albert Collins, already distinctive stylists in their own right.

The impact Bishop spoke of is as pervasive today as ever. Compare the Eric Clapton solo on Cream's "Strange Brew" to the source, Albert's break on "Oh, Pretty Woman." Or listen to Mark Knopfler's uncharacteristic tone and phrasing on Dylan's *Slow Train Coming* or Stevie Ray Vaughan's work on David Bowie's *Let's Dance*. In his 1984 cover story Stevie didn't deny the similarity. "I kind of wanted to see how many places Albert King's stuff would fit," he told me. "It *always* does. I love that man."

THE ULTIMATE GUNSLINGER But Albert was fiercely protective about his signature licks and was the ultimate gunslinger when it came to jamming, as Stevie later found out. "When that album *Let's Dance* first came out, Albert heard it. He said, 'Yeah, I heard you doin' all my shit on there. I'm gonna go up there and do some of yours.' We were doing this TV show outside of Toronto, and during the lunch break Albert went around to everybody in there looking for an emery board. I didn't think anything of it. We were jamming on the last song, 'Outskirts of Town,' and it comes to the solo, and he goes, 'Get it, Stevie!' I started off, and I look over and he's pulling out this damn emery board, filing his nails, sort of giving me this sidelong glance. I loved it! Lookin' at me like, 'Uh huh. I got you swinging by your toes!'"

One of the ever-quotable Bloomfield's best lines on the subject of Albert King referred to the unenviable position he found himself in one night—jamming with Jimi Hendrix. As he related to Tom Wheeler, "Oh, my God, I was up there just wishing I was Albert King."

I can't imagine who B.B. King wished he was one night in 1970 when he got himself into an onstage battle with his namesake at Fillmore West. There was a lot of anticipation about the double bill, but Albert shook off any queries about a possible jam as we walked through the crowd. Albert's and B.B.'s dressing rooms were on the opposite sides of the hall, and the two didn't cross paths, let alone discuss a super session, so I'm sure Albert was as surprised as I was to see B.B., guitar in hand, standing at the side of the stage at the end of Albert's second set. "I'm looking for an amp for B.B.," he ad-libbed, as the crowd rushed the stage.

An amp was wheeled out and B.B. plugged in as Albert and his seven-piece band kept cranking out "I Get Evil." Known for playing a few essential notes rather than complex, high-speed runs, Albert nevertheless played over, under, around, and through B.B.'s more subtle licks, until B.B. decided that the answer to his dilemma might be a little showmanship and dropped to his knees. Unaware that the crowd was now screaming for more than just his double-stop bends, Albert continued to play until he noticed his rival on the floor next to him. In an instant, 250 pounds of purple, lime green, and black landed on the floor, knee-to-knee with B.B., and the Kings slugged it out like two gladiators. Bloomfield may have been referring to the same show when he said, "I remember seeing him and B.B. King jam at the Fillmore, and Albert cut B.B. to death, man. He had that big Acoustic amp, and it sounded like bombs exploding."

Regrettably, in later years Albert became as famous for bad moods as for great playing, and too many fans who only saw him once or twice, and only in the past ten or 12 years, might remember him more as the curmudgeon/bandleader who fired his bassist in mid-song or berated the house soundman for an entire set. Diagnosed as diabetic, Albert did curtail his touring schedule in recent years, although he headlined the 1992 Memphis Arts Festival.

Ultimately, we *are* left with the artist's work, which in Albert King's case is, thankfully, a formidable legacy indeed. *Born Under a Bad Sign* remains a classic, and *Live Wire/Blues Power* is a veritable textbook of licks. Fantasy Records recently added two very welcome discs, *Wednesday Night in San Francisco* and *Thursday Night in San Francisco,* recorded during the same stint as *Live Wire,* as well as his 1973 live set at Montreux, *Blues at Sunrise.* In 1972 Albert teamed with the Bar-Kays and effectively reinvented himself on *I'll Play the Blues for You,* the title emblazoned across the side of the Trailways bus he now took on the road and drove personally. And his pre-Stax work for the King and Bobbin labels has been reissued on Modern Blues Recordings' *Let's Have a Natural Ball.*

Of all the encounters I had with Albert King over the course of 23 years, the anecdote that sticks in my mind involves a show that I didn't even attend. My two older brothers went to see Albert play San Francisco while I was away on assignment. Exchanging pleasantries after the show, Albert looked around a couple of times and wondered, "Where's Bob?" "You mean Dan," they tried to explain. "He's out of town." "No, Bob," a confused Albert said again, "the little one, the baby." "Yeah, that's Dan. You call him Bob, but his name's really Dan." Albert sat back and paused for a second and said, "Well, who's Bob?"

Years later, Albert would correct himself ("Bob—I mean Dan") whenever we spoke, until my real name was at last ingrained into his head. After that, deep down, I always kind of missed Bob. But not like I, and the whole blues world, will miss Albert.

EDDIE "GUITAR SLIM" JONES

BY JEFF HANNUSCH More than three decades after his death, Guitar Slim's extroverted, passionate blues guitar playing can still send chills down one's spine. His highly personal compositions, including the R&B standards "The Things That I Used to Do" and "The Story of My Life," are staples in the repertoires of blues, rock, and even Zydeco bands. And anyone who ever saw the man perform, be they player or listener, has vivid memories of one of the most colorful figures in the history of New Orleans rhythm and blues.

Fellow New Orleans guitarist Earl King remembers seeing Guitar Slim at the peak of his all-too-short career: "Gatemouth Brown, T-Bone Walker, Lowell Fulson, and Guitar Slim were all performing one night at the White Eagle in Opelousas. Slim was headlining, because 'The Things That I Used To Do' was a scorcher. They were all sitting in the dressing room, and Guitar Slim walked up to 'em all and said, 'Gentlemen, we got the greatest guitar players in the country assembled right here. But when I leave here tonight, ain't nobody gonna realize you even been here.' Well, they all laughed, but that's exactly what happened.

"Slim came out with his hair dyed blue, blue suit, blue pair of shoes. He had 350 feet of mike wire connected to his guitar, and a valet carrying him on his shoulders all through the crowd and out into the parking lot. Man, he was stopping cars driving down the highway. No one could outperform Slim. He was about the performinest man I've ever seen." King's description coincides with that of virtually everyone else who saw Guitar Slim onstage or knew him personally. Though he's been dead for over two decades, Guitar Slim's legend continues.

When I was researching the Guitar Slim story, I got the telephone number of a guy who supposedly had been his tailor—because Slim was famous for the outlandish suits he wore. I called the number, an older black lady answered, and I told her I wanted to ask her husband about Guitar Slim. He got on the phone, and I introduced myself, and he proceeded to tell me this story about taking the bus downtown in New Orleans. They got in front of the Dew Drop club on LaSalle Street, and traffic was lined up on both sides of the street. So he got out of the bus to see what was going on, and Guitar Slim was playing out in the neutral ground on the boulevard, walking over the tops of cars while his valet was spooling out his big, long guitar cord to him. Then I asked the guy to tell me about the suits he made for Slim, and he said, "No, I'm no tailor; I'm a carpenter. You must have the wrong number." In New Orleans, even the wrong numbers have at least one Guitar Slim story.

"NEW ORLEANS' NEWEST GIFT TO THE SHOW WORLD" Even though his music has remained popular all these years, many details concerning his life are still shrouded in mystery, so much so that putting together a concise biography is like completing a complex jigsaw puzzle. Guitar Slim was born Edward Jones on December 10, 1926, and he's known to have at least one sister. Though Slim claimed in his Specialty Records biography that Greenwood, Mississippi, was his birthplace, Hollandale, Mississippi, has also been suggested. No matter, Slim was raised in the Greenwood area, a rural region of intense cotton production in the heart of the Mississippi Delta. Times were probably tough, and likely Slim did his fair share in the fields, visiting Greenwood on weekends.

The first mention of Guitar Slim (he was six feet tall, 160 pounds, so he easily fit the colorful alias) in the *Louisiana Weekly* was during September 1950. It stated: "New Orleans' newest gift to the show world is Guitar Slim, held over at the Dew Drop. The New Orleans blues sensation has made a terrific impact on blues fans in New Orleans. Acclaimed to be an exact carbon copy of Gatemouth Brown, the singing guitarist includes 'My Time Is Expensive,' 'Gatemouth Boogie,' and several other performances made popular by Brown."

The comparison between Guitar Slim and Gatemouth Brown is indeed apt; it is interesting to note that he would draw his greatest influence from the Texas guitar school, rather than the guitar players from his own state, Mississippi. "Gatemouth's 'Boogie Rambler' was Slim's theme," adds Earl King. "He listened to all of them and compiled bits of their style—Gatemouth, T-Bone, B.B. King. But he took a different approach; he had a lot of melodic overtones in his solos. He used to play a solo that had a marriage to the rest of the song, rather than just play something off the top of his head."

Earl also chafes when others suggest Slim was a poor instrumentalist and unable to even play without the aid of a capo, or, as Slim referred to it, "a choker." "Slim tuned standard, but he used that capo to get the effect of open strings. You can't do that without a choker. I've seen Slim play many a time without it. He just used it for effect."

Percy Stovall, who booked Slim during his early career, remembers: "I used to worry him sometimes and hide his choker. He'd be runnin' around saying, 'Stove, where's my choker at? I can't find my choker.' I'd say, 'I ain't seen it, Slim,' and he'd be running around trying to find it everywhere. Then just before he would go on, I'd pull it out of my pocket and hand it to him, and he'd say, 'Stove, I knew you had it all the time.'"

Stovall is the first to admit that Slim was his favorite artist, but also points out he had his share of headaches with him. "Man, he loved to drink," says Stovall, shaking his head. "If I didn't watch him all the time he'd miss his job. If he had a job over in Florida, I'd have to ration him. I'd make sure the valet gave him only a fifth of wine when he left New Orleans, another fifth in Biloxi, and one more by the time he got to Mobile. And don't nobody fool with Slim's wine or he'd be in trouble."

One of Stovall's favorite stories concerning his early days of booking Guitar Slim took place in Monroe, Louisiana. "Fats Domino and Slim played a Battle of the Blues," he recalls, "at the Monroe Civic Auditorium. Man, the place was packed. Slim had told Fats before the show, 'Fats, I'm gonna run you offa that stage tonight.'

"So Slim went on first because Fats had hit records out. Slim just tore 'em up. The place was goin' wild. Slim walked off the stage with his guitar and went out the back door of the place and got in a car, still playing. Everyone wondered where Slim had gone. When it came time for Fats to come on, Fats just told the people, 'Ain't gonna be no battle tonight. You just saw it.' So Fats just played his regular show."

By 1951, the record companies had been hearing about this wild guitar player in New Orleans. Imperial approached first, and Al Young produced four sides by Eddie Jones at the J&M Studio. The session was rather chaotic, originally producing "Bad Luck Is on Me" and "New Arrival," which sold poorly. Imperial wouldn't ask Slim back to the studio, but still issued the remainder of the session when Slim hit the big time, using his alias instead of Eddie Jones.

Slim's next record was a different story. Percy Stovall arranged a session with Jim Bullet in Nashville, producing the popular "Feelin' Sad" in 1952. David Lastie played sax on the tune and remembered the circumstances that surrounded the session: "We was working at the Kitty Cat Club in Nashville, and me, Huey Piano

Smith, Little Eddie Lang, and Willie Nettles did the session with Slim. 'Feelin' Sad' was a good little record; it had a church sound to it. We worked pretty good off it."

When Slim came in off the road, he stayed upstairs at the Dew Drop. "Slim liked to be where the action was," chuckles King. "In fact, you knew Slim was back in town, because early in the morning, around seven or eight o'clock, if he was tanked up, you'd hear them amps and PAs going off. People'd be calling the police because you could hear Slim three blocks away! And here's Slim up in his room with his shorts on, going through his stage routine.

"And Slim's room was something else, man. If you went up there, there'd always be about seven or eight different women up there. He'd have his songs written with eyebrow pencil on pieces of paper tacked to the wall."

King also recalls that Slim bought the first Les Paul guitar in New Orleans: "Slim was playing one of those big hollow-boxes like T-Bone had. But when the solid boxes came out he got one right away. Slim said the hollow-boxes were too big, and they didn't give him enough room on the stage. He couldn't control the feedback that was coming out of them. So he dealt with the Les Paul."

"THE THINGS THAT I USED TO DO" By 1953 Guitar Slim was one of the biggest draws on the southern R&B circuit. The responsibilities of managing and booking reverted to Slim's landlord, Frank Pania, who owned the Dew Drop, while Percy Stovall concentrated on building up a larger roster of performers. Pania also took it upon himself to find Slim a new band. He hired the Lloyd Lambert band from Hosea Hill's Sugar Bowl in Thibodaux, Louisiana. Hosea was a friend and business associate of Pania, and paired Slim with the band for a series of road dates. Bassist Lambert claims that Pania was responsible for introducing Slim to Johnny Vincent, then a Specialty Records A&R man. Vincent was impressed enough to convince his boss, Art Rupe, to sign Slim to a recording contract. "Slim was supposed to sign with Atlantic," Vincent recalls, "but this was one artist I just had to get. He was fantastic. Slim wouldn't let anyone outperform him. I wouldn't let him out of my sight until he signed with Specialty."

On October 16, 1953, Slim entered the J&M Studio to record what was to be the biggest record of his career, "The Things That I Used to Do." According to Lloyd Lambert, the personnel on the session was pianist Ray Charles, Gus Fontenette, Charles Burbank, and Joe Tillman on saxophones, Oscar Moore on drums, Frank Mitchell on trumpet, and Lambert on bass, with Jones playing his gold-top. Vincent claims he had to bail one of the musicians out of jail to play on the date.

When Vincent says, "Slim was hard to record," he has lots of support. Tales of Slim's recording sessions are many. Vincent claims that it took "all night" to record "The Things That I Used to Do." Engineer Cosimo Matassa says "all day," and Lloyd Lambert reports it took "two days." Nonetheless, the musicians were obviously gratified when it was over, because Ray Charles is clearly audible yelling "Yeah!" in relief in the last bars of the song.

According to Earl King, the idea for the tune came to Slim in a dream. Slim related to King that in the dream he was confronted by a devil and an angel, both of whom held the lyrics to a song. Naturally, Slim chose the devil's song, and it turned out to be "The Things That I Used to Do."

Vincent sent the tapes of the session to Rupe, who was less than impressed with the result. According to Vincent, "He told me it was the worst piece of shit he'd ever heard. He said, 'I'm gonna put it out, but if it don't sell, you start looking for a job.'"

The public disagreed with Rupe, to say the least. Immediately after its release, both *Billboard* and *Cash Box* made it the pick of the week. *Cash Box* called it "a slow Southern blues rhythmically chanted by the blues shouter . . . great vocal with the proper blues styling, and this side is headed for sales. Top notch."

"The Things That I Used to Do" stormed the charts. It topped the R&B roster for six solid weeks and ended up the biggest-selling R&B record of 1954. The lyrics, sung in Slim's impassioned gospel-like style, struck a chord in the public's imagination. For many, the real appeal of "The Things That I Used to Do" was the novel guitar approach that Slim took. As Earl King explains: "Slim was gettin' a fuzztone distortion way before anyone else. Believe it or not, Slim never used an amplifier. He always used a PA set, never an amplifier. He was an overtone fanatic, and he had those tiny iron-cone speakers and the sound would run through them speakers, and I guess any vibration would create that sound, because Slim always played at peak volume. That's why it was hard to record him—because of the volume he was accustomed to playing at. Let's face it, if Slim was playing you could hear him a mile away."

Lloyd Lambert agrees that Slim played as loud as he could. "He had this tinny sound," says Lambert, "that he'd get by turning all the bass controls as low as they would go, and turning up his treble controls as high as they'd go."

Although Slim was most associated with his gold-top Les Paul (after switching from his hollowbody electric), some pictures show him playing a white Fender Telecaster. The piercing tone Slim achieved was similar to that of Clarence Gatemouth Brown and Johnny Guitar Watson, and derived in part from the fact that he, like the others, played guitar with his fingers, pulling at the strings. ZZ Top guitarist Billy Gibbons concurs: "Eddie Jones definitely played with his thumb and his fingers. A lot of people could never figure out why R&B had such vicious guitar tones. They forget that most of the rooms that they played in were so loud anyway. I mean, can you imagine going into a black blues joint in 1954 and having it quiet and sedate? They'd just turn those old Fender amps up all the way, man, just to be heard. Slim would, like, aim for 'patent pending' and just blow!"

New Orleans songwriter Al Reed, who backed Slim, Earl King, Smiley Lewis, and others, also credits Jones with pioneering the distorted electric guitar sound. As he told John Broven in *Rhythm & Blues in New Orleans* [Pelican]: "A lot of the electric guitar sound has been attributed to Chuck Berry, but many people aren't aware of the type of guitar that Guitar Slim played. Guitar Slim was a most profound musician. He had an electric sound like you never heard. They would open the club doors wide so that the sound could just go in and out of the club, and he would draw people off the street. Big passing automobiles would stop, and the people would just listen to this guy play and watch him walk. I think he had a greater impact on the electric guitar sound than any other guitarist because he used the electric sound very much as it is used today. And Chuck Berry was not using that sound at the time. Guitar Slim was the finest and about the first. He was a great guy to be around. He was a man you could learn from—not what you heard, but what you saw. Because he could exhilarate you. Man, he would lift you above and beyond the clouds as he played. He could create sensations within your body that really played tricks with your mind. He was the first man to do this."

With the #1 record in the country, Frank Pania booked a full itinerary for Slim through the South, and bought him a brand new Olds Delta 88. Slim promptly got drunk one night and ran into a parked bulldozer, wrecking the car and ending up in the hospital. "Slim weren't too good a driver," laughs Lambert. "He didn't hurt himself too bad; the doctor just told him to take it easy for a month."

Pania decided to send Earl King out to impersonate Slim on a number of dates, and apparently got away with it. Even though King went along with the charade, he admits he was scared to death: "When I got back to town, the first person I saw was Guitar Slim," laughs Earl. "He was walking down LaSalle Street with a hospital gown on, a guitar under one arm and an amp under the other, yelling 'Earl King, I heard you been out there imitatin' me. If you wreck my name, I'm gonna sue and I'm gonna kill you!'"

Slim was soon back on his feet and ready to hit the road for a tour of the Northern theater circuit. Since Lambert's band already had Lawrence Cotton on piano, Slim had to split with Huey Smith, an event which likely saddened both of them.

"THE STORY OF MY LIFE" Eventually Slim's popularity became too much for Frank Pania to deal with, so he turned over Slim's management to Hosea Hill, who ran his own popular nightspot in Thibodaux, the Sugar Bowl. Consequently, Slim spent a good amount of his time in Thibodaux, which nestles Bayou Lafourche, Louisiana.

Guitar Slim's next release, "The Story of My Life," was a powerful follow-up and came from his initial Specialty session. Once again *Cash Box* spotlighted it by giving it its weekly award and calling it "another powerful item. His mournful tale is accentuated by the chanter's stylings and impressive guitar work."

His guitar work was indeed impressive, less lyrical but more visceral than his solo on "The Things That I Used to Do." Frank Zappa, one of Guitar Slim's biggest fans, ranks it as one of his favorite guitar solos of all time. In the February '82 *Guitar Player* he elaborated: "It's got that 'I don't give a fuck about nothin', I'm gonna play whatever I want in here, and you guys can hang it in your ass' kind of primitive abandonment. And Guitar Slim's solo on 'The Story of My Life' is one of the best early distorted guitar solos; it really sounds like he's mad at somebody."

Lambert still relishes the days of the mid '50s, barnstorming the country. "We had the best band out there," he affirms. "Fats, B.B. King, even Lionel Hampton— we could cut 'em all. We had trouble following Slim at first, because he'd always jump meter, but it got to where we'd just jump right with him and it would sound fine. Slim was a showman and a musician. He'd have purple suits, orange suits, green suits, with shoes and hair to match. He'd make motions and faces that would drive people berserk. You couldn't hardly get into the place when he was playing."

Earl King agrees: "Slim could play at the Dew Drop and get a mob of people, and the next night play in Shrewsbury [in adjacent Jefferson Parish] and get the same mob. Even the people who knew him to say 'hi' in the streets would think nothing of driving a hundred miles to go see him that same night."

When the first electric Fender basses came on the market, Slim wanted one for his band and talked Lambert into buying it. Although Lambert became one of the first electric bass players, Earl King says that it took a lot of convincing on Slim's part to prod him into buying the new bass. "When he saw that B.B. King's band had one, that was it. Slim wanted everything electric. If Slim would have seen all the gadgetry that's out today, it would be ridiculous. When the Cadillacs came out with all that gadgetry he was just like a little kid. He just marveled over that—seats moving, water shooting." Slim stayed so busy that Specialty had to arrange to record while the group was touring. Lambert recalled that the second Specialty session took place at Chess Studios in Chicago, and produced "Sufferin' Mind" in 1955, with Art Rupe flying in from L.A. to produce.

Rupe, however, took it upon himself to bury Slim's guitar way down in the mix, and even added a Hammond organ. The session lost a little of the New Orleans feel, but it was identifiable Slim just the same. His final Specialty session took place in early 1956 and was recorded in Los Angeles, before he switched to the Atlantic/Atco label.

Even though Slim's record sales began dipping, he was still a top attraction. He and the band criss-crossed the country, playing to overflow houses. When he came in off the road, he would spend the days in a lazy manner, usually drinking with friends at the Dew Drop or the Sugar Bowl.

Atlantic recorded Slim both in New York and at Cosimo's in New Orleans, according to Lambert. There was little departure from the last Specialty sessions (although voices were occasionally added and the horn section beefed up), largely due to the strength of Lloyd Lambert's tight band. However, on a previously unissued track, "Along About Midnight," Slim is backed by a host of New York jazz heavyweights, including bassist Percy Heath, saxophonist Johnny Griffin, pianist Elmo Hope, and drummer Philly Joe Jones.

Atlantic must have been somewhat disappointed, though, in their attempts with Slim. They had visions of crossing his records into the teenage market on the same scale Chess had done with Chuck Berry, but had little success. As it would turn out, his last Atco session in 1958 would produce the prophetically titled "When There's No Way Out" and "If I Had My Life to Live Over."

"I LIVE THREE DAYS TO Y'ALL'S ONE" Despite doctors' warnings about his heavy drinking, by 1958 Slim was really sick and getting weaker, so much so that he was unable to travel and forced to stay in Thibodaux. "I wouldn't say he was a pretty good drinker," says Lambert. "He was the best! Slim just wouldn't take care of himself. He lived fast; different women every night. I'd try and tell him to eat good and get his rest, but he'd say, 'Lloyd, I live three days to y'all's one. The world won't owe me a thing when I'm gone.'"

Earl King gives some insight into the last days of Guitar Slim: "Slim got ruptured [from riding the guitar onstage], and I think that's what caused him to drink more than he ever had. Man, when he came in off that last tour, he almost had to wear a truss. I went over to visit him in Thibodaux when he was sick, and he had empty 100 proof bottles laying all over his room. The doctor told him to stay off that hard liquor, but what are you gonna tell a guy who drinks a pint of gin and chases it with a fifth of black port every day?"

Strangely enough, Slim had quit drinking the last months of his life, according to some. "Slim was getting ready to go on another tour," continues Earl. "Slim sat in the Dew Drop one night and was talking very straight and serious. He told me, 'Earl, all this liquor I been drinkin', all the wrong things I been thinkin', you know my body's been slowly sinkin'.' That's when I went over and asked Hosea Hill, 'Is there something wrong with Slim?' He said, 'No, he's fine. He just got out of the hospital, and he's not even drinking. Why do you ask that?' I said, 'Because Slim talks too straight tonight; he's not funny. He's never under the weather about anything.' That was the last time I saw him."

In February 1959, the group embarked on a tour of dances and nightclubs in New York State. "We went up to Rochester," recalls Lambert, "and Slim came up to me and said, 'Lloyd, I'm tired, I don't think I can make it no more. Y'all got a good band; you can get another singer.' I said, 'Come on, Slim, you can make it. You just been with a broad or something.' He said, 'No, Lloyd, my time is up.' So we played the dance, and when it came time for Slim to come on, he could only do part of the first song and couldn't finish.

"We drove to Newark to play the next night, and Slim played the gig but he collapsed right after. One of the valets ran and got a doctor, and the doctor looked at Slim and said, 'Check this man into a hospital; he's really sick.' We were gonna stay in New York, because that's where our next date was. So we drove up to the Cecil Hotel, and I sent the valet across to take Slim to the doctor while I checked into the hotel. When I got to the desk, there was a telephone call waiting for me from the valet. He said, 'Lloyd, Slim's dead.' I didn't believe it, because I'd seen him not more than five minutes before. We got in the station wagon and drove 'round the corner to the doctor's. But sure enough Slim was layin' up on the table, gone."

Word of Slim's death on February 7, 1959, was slow getting back to New Orleans. The *Louisiana Weekly* was a full week late in its announcement. "Somebody knocked up on my door and said 'Slim's dead,'" remembers King. "I said, 'Man, that can't be true. People like Slim don't die. They're still here when I'm gone.'"

"It wasn't liquor that killed him," specifies Lambert. "The doctor said it was bronchial pneumonia. Today, they might have saved him, but all that drinking and hard living brought his resistance down."

Slim's body was kept in New York by authorities to see if drugs were involved in his death. Hosea Hill eventually paid the fare to fly Slim's body back to Thibodaux for a massive funeral at the Mt. Zion Baptist Church. Guitar Slim now lies in an unmarked grave next to his benefactor, Hosea Hill. He was buried with his gold-top Gibson Les Paul.

So ended the all-too-short life of the 32-year-old Guitar Slim. He is survived by several common-law wives, and a number of children, one of whom plays guitar in the small clubs around New Orleans and who keeps Slim's name alive. Hardly a year has passed since his death that someone hasn't re-recorded one of his songs. Earl King's 1982 version of Slim's anthem, "It Hurts to Love Someone," only reinforces the timelessness of his work.

Almost everyone is adamant about what would have happened if Slim were alive today. "He'd have been on the scale of a B.B. King or a Ray Charles," says Earl King.

Lloyd Lambert states simply, "No question about it. Guitar Slim would have been the biggest."

MISSISSIPPI
FRED MCDOWELL

BY TOM POMPOSELLO Mississippi Fred McDowell
was one of the most important rural guitarists to come out
of the 1960s blues revival. Undiscovered until 1959, Fred
was first recorded by Alan Lomax on one of the folklorist's
many field trips to the South. McDowell's specialty was bottleneck slide, with an eerie, vocal-like tone. In '69 the blues
singer switched from acoustic to electric, which, if anything,
only added intensity to that subtle, whining quality.
McDowell's playing influenced numerous rock and blues
slide guitarists, including Keith Richards and Bonnie Raitt,
who remembers: "He thought it was really funny, meeting
this 18-year-old girl playing guitar, but he was flattered at
my interest, and he taught me." ¶ Fred would take the time

to show his music to anyone who would ask. Unlike so many artists who are reluctant to explain the intricacies of their styles for fear (often with good reason) of being ripped off and receiving no recognition, McDowell's philosophy was, "Well, that might be true; that's just what they may do. But I do know that in their hearts, after I'm dead and buried, they're always gonna remember that I was the one that showed it to them, even if they don't tell nobody else."

"THEY CALL ME MISSISSIPPI FRED" Fred McDowell was born somewhere between 1903 and 1906. No one seems certain, because back then if you were black and living on a plantation, no one kept accurate documentation of such things. He was born in Rossville, Tennessee—a fact that always used to bemuse him: "They call me Mississippi Fred, but really my home is in Rossville, Tennessee.

"When I was a boy," he continues, "I think the first blues record I ever heard was Blind Lemon Jefferson singing 'Black Snake Moan.' 'O-oh, ain't got no mama now.' Man! I tell you, I thought that was the prettiest little thing I'd ever heard." He became interested in guitar when he was in his late teens. By this time, music was all around Fred. His uncle Gene Shields was a guitarist and the leader of a trio. He credits Shields with being the first person he saw play in the bottleneck style, using a smoothed beef rib bone on his little finger.

The harmonica player in Gene's trio, Cal Payne, showed Fred "John Henry." Cal's son Raymond, who was about the same age as Fred, recalls, "He was a real good guitar player—regular style, not bottleneck." But Raymond would never show anyone anything. "If you'd walk into the room when Raymond was playing," Fred recalled, "he'd right away put the guitar down so you couldn't see what he was doing. Then he'd make some kind of excuse—'I'm tired now,' or 'My fingers hurt.' No one could show me nothing anyway. Everyone could play 'cept me. All the boys. But I had to learn things my own way. Even if you'd be showing me, I'd have to go off on my own and get it my way. They'd all be playing ball or something, and I'd be practicing on Booster Green's guitar." (An older friend, Eli "Booster" Green taught McDowell his celebrated tune "Write Me a Few Lines." In 1966 the musicians were reunited for a couple of tracks on Arhoolie's *Fred McDowell*, Vol. 2.)

The first song Fred ever learned was Tommy Johnson's "Big Fat Mama (With the Meat Shakin' on Your Bones)." "I learned it on one string," he explained, "then two, note by note. Man, I about worried that first string to death trying to learn that song." This note-by-note method became an intricate part of Fred's latter-day technical approach. While McDowell experienced his share of obstacles on guitar, he was always sought after as a vocalist. He would sing along with other guitarists at old-time Saturday night suppers, and then take over on guitar when they got tired.

Tired of plowing fields with a mule, Fred left Rossville when he was about 21. During a trip to Cleveland, Mississippi, in the late 1920s, he heard the legendary Charley Patton perform at a juke joint. He was quite impressed, and consciously adapted several of Patton's tunes to his own style. His "Gravel Road," for instance, was adapted from Patton's "Down the Dirt Road Blues."

McDowell lived in Memphis during the 1930s, working as a laborer. He tried to master the guitar, but was hampered by not owning his own instrument. Finally, a white man from Texas named Mr. Taylor, whom Fred remembered quite fondly, presented him with one. This was 1941, and soon afterwards Fred decided to move south to Mississippi and settle down near his sister. While living in Como, Fred McDowell refined the style that would lead to his becoming one of the greatest postwar country bluesmen.

In 1959 folklorist Alan Lomax came to Como and asked if there were any local bluesmen that he should hear. Among the first names given was Fred McDowell's. Lomax found Fred at home that evening and proceeded to record him. Fred played well into the night—from 8:00 until almost 7:00 in the morning, as he recalls it. Before departing, Lomax promised that these recordings would bring McDowell fame and fortune. Well, he was half-right. Despite the fact that the payment was nominal, the recordings were met by much enthusiasm in folk and blues circles. They established the 55-year-old as one of the great "new discoveries" in the blues world. Fred had the opportunity to play and record for a whole new audience.

Arhoolie and Testament issued solo albums, and Fred was a sensation at the 1964 Newport Folk Festival. He toured Europe with the American Folk Blues Festival in 1965 and '69, going over especially well in Germany and Great Britain. Keith Richards heard Fred's version of the spiritual "You Got to Move" and rearranged it for the Rolling Stones' *Sticky Fingers*.

"JUST THE STRAIGHT AND NATCH'L BLUE" In 1969 Fred recorded a solo album for the Transatlantic label, using an *electric* guitar. It seems odd today, but the reaction at the time among purists was mixed. Everyone was used to Chicago blues played electrically, but Delta blues? One critic observed that much of the subtlety, especially in McDowell's fills, was lost, but nothing could have been further from the truth. One listen to "Amazing Grace" performed on the electric instrument, and you were a believer. The instrument proved very appropriate for the spirituals Fred loved to perform, intensifying his shimmering tone and sophisticated vibrato. His blues numbers, particularly the percussive, driving rhythmic patterns of songs such as "Shake 'Em on Down" and "Drop Down Mama," were also greatly enhanced. And the electric instrument undoubtedly made Fred's music more accessible to a new generation of blues enthusiasts. He was well aware of this, and used to caution his admirers: "I do not play no rock 'n' roll, y'all. Just the straight and natch'l *blue*."

Prior to 1968, the majority of McDowell's recordings were performed on his old wood-bodied National or his acoustic Hofner. His first electric was a red, dual-pickup imitation of a Gibson ES-335. He then found a good deal on a mid-'60s Gibson Trini Lopez Standard, which he used until his death. His only modification was to slightly raise the action by installing a small metal shim just above the nut. He used light-gauge Black Diamond Electric Strings, but didn't care much about the brand or the gauge, so long as the set included an unwound G string. (Whenever purchasing a new set, he'd always check for that unwound string before laying down his money.)

To get the necessary clarity on acoustic, Fred would pick with his bare right-hand thumb and index finger. For electric guitar, he used a standard plastic thumbpick and a plastic fingerpick on his index finger. His style of picking ranged from simple note-to-note to highly complex rhythmic and heavily syncopated brush strokes, or any combination of the two.

Most of McDowell's touring during the late '60s and early '70s was done by Greyhound bus. He hated to fly unless it was absolutely necessary. Consequently, he carried only a small practice amp with him, hoping that when he arrived at a club or festival, he could plug into whatever better equipment was available. Sometimes a well-meaning producer would want to record the bluesman through his own amp, insisting that it would be inaccurate to record a blues artist using someone else's equipment, or a club would close-mike his amp through the PA system. Unless this was done absolutely right, the result was a very muddy sound, which is why many of Fred's recordings leave the listener with a false impression of his tone. Judging from his reaction to good amps, he was after a clean, clear sound with a good amount of top end.

The first time Fred tried to play bottleneck guitar, he used a pocketknife to emulate Uncle Gene's style. But it didn't take long for him to realize that in order to get the volume and clarity he wanted, he had to switch to a glass bottleneck. Since his style did not utilize full chords barred with a bottleneck, he chose to use a short slide (about an inch long) made from a Gordon's Gin bottle. First, he scribed the bottle with a sharp object along the lines where he wanted it to break. Then he ran it under hot water in a bathtub, then under cold water while he gently tapped it along the scribed seams. It worked on the first try. (It's funny how a musician can get attached to something like a bottleneck. One evening I saw Fred nervously rummaging through his guitar case, and then breathing a sigh of relief upon finding his treasured Gordon's bottleneck. "Tom, if I'd have lost that," he said, "I might as well turned around and went back home.")

Where he wore his bottleneck depended on his tuning—standard, open *A*, or open *E*. On his earlier acoustic records, he often used the open-*A* tuning, wearing the bottleneck on his little finger. In standard tuning, he'd usually play in the key of *E* and wear the bottleneck on his little finger. For open *E*, Fred wore the bottleneck on his ring finger. He preferred to use his bottleneck more often in the *E* tuning, because it lends itself more toward melodic playing. (It's important to note that Fred's tunings were relative, since he tuned to his voice—rather than a piano or tuner—before performing.)

Most of Fred's playing was based in the tonic. He would often thumb the open bass strings while picking slide melody lines with his fingerpick. In songs such as "You Got to Move," he might depart from that procedure and simply play the melody line on the bass strings alone. His guitar part often echoed his vocal phrasing almost exactly, such as in "Baby, Please Don't Go," where his voice would trail off while his bottleneck finished the vocal line: "When you hear me play, if you listen real close, you'll hear the guitar say the same thing I'm saying too." He was very flattered one time by a perceptive fan who said, "You know, that's the first time I ever heard a talking guitar."

Fred returned home during the winter of 1971, canceling his tour because of severe stomach pains. Undergoing an operation, he was not to leave his home again. I visited him in Mississippi the following spring, and found him in good spirits as he showed me the time of my life. A few days later, he was back in the hospital. He never complained, but it was obvious he was in great pain. In July 1973 Fred McDowell died from abdominal cancer.

I have never heard anybody play or sing like Mississippi Fred McDowell, and I am convinced that what made Fred great as a musician was what made him great as a man. That "Mississippi mystique" of his, that undefinable something, is the spirit of the real blues.

LITTLE MILTON

BY JIM O'NEAL Little Milton Campbell ranks as one
of the most successful bluesmen of all time. In terms of
longevity, maintaining popularity, recording quality product,
and putting on a professional show year after year, all the
while taking care of business first, Milton has simply been a
marvel. ¶ His journey began as a teenager in Sam Phillips'
studio in 1954, and after those debut sides on the Sun label,

Milton continued to affiliate with legendary record labels with rarely a respite in between signings. From Sun he went to another Memphis label, Meteor, then to Bobbin in St. Louis, where he recorded highly influential though not chart-topping singles; his songs such as "I'm a Lonely Man" and "Same Old Blues" would influence the whole modern Chicago blues school, from Magic Sam and Otis Rush on down. A move to Chess Records' Checker subsidiary brought him national success as Milton began to incorporate more soul ballads and R&B arrangements into his repertoire.

One of Chess' best-selling artists of the '60s (when labelmates like Muddy Waters and Howlin' Wolf could no longer find their records on the charts), Milton had a No. 1 R&B hit in "We're Gonna Make It" and stayed with the label even after Leonard Chess sold the company. In 1972 Milton began another productive association back in Memphis, this time with Stax, scoring a few more hits before Stax hit the skids. At Glades, a label owned by T.K. of Miami (famed for disco-era K.C. & The Sunshine Band), the story was repeated: good records (produced by Milton himself), a few chart singles, and the company goes under. Milton held back on another major deal for a few years, and just when it looked like he was primed for the big time with MCA, his producer Al Perkins was murdered, leaving Milton with one album on the label but no connections at the company.

Finally he hit his stride again with Malaco in Jackson, Mississippi, and has satisfied his soul-blues audience time after time with a fine series of albums dating back to 1984. Among the Malaco hits was a song that has become an anthem now played by hundreds of blues bands: "The Blues Is Alright."

Despite his successes, Little Milton is not a household name, and much of the reason is that he has remained primarily a "chitlin circuit" act, touring and recording mostly for the black blues audiences in the South and Midwest. Always claiming to be a businessman first and an entertainer second, Milton has long been keenly aware of the white crossover audience for blues, but until recent years most of his moves have been made to ensure that he doesn't lose his substantial base of black support (thus the continuing mix of soul and ballads with harder blues).

Though little publicized in the media, the top chitlin circuit acts (especially those who record for Malaco, such as Little Milton, Denise LaSalle, Shirley Brown, and Johnnie Taylor) do considerably better in terms of record sales and touring income than do the vast majority of their counterparts who are playing the white blues bar and concert circuit. But Milton and Malaco finally decided to take on the crossover challenge with 1999's *Welcome to Little Milton,* featuring guest appearances by Dave Alvin, Lucinda Williams, Gov't Mule, and other white rock and country performers. If the guest star gambit succeeds, as it has with John Lee Hooker and B.B. King, Milton may soon be seeing his name in entirely different lights.

The following interview, first published in *Living Blues,* April 1994, was compiled from two sessions which, though 16 years apart, were remarkably consistent in terms of Milton's assessment of his career and his audience. The first was conducted at Milton's home in Chicago on January 24, 1978. (Milton moved to Chicago during his tenure with Chess and kept his house there until 1997, when he relocated to Las Vegas.) Since much of his touring activity is in the Southern states, he has also kept a small apartment in Memphis over the years. The second interview was done there on January 18, 1994.

Where did you get your first guitar?

From Sears, Roebuck. No. I'm wrong. Walter Field [Marshall Field] catalog. I had schemed and worked and saved and ordered the guitar without my mother knowing. And my mother don't read or write—very, very little. We were so used to ordering things for her from the catalog, you know, and when it came, I told her about the notice. I knew what it was. She said, "Well, baby, you go to the post office and see what it is that you all ordered for me." And I came back with this guitar. She hit the ceiling! And told me that I was gonna take it back. Mind you, now, she didn't even know I had the money!

How did you get the money?

I like picked cotton or chopped cotton or whatever, and I'd save like 50¢ here, a dollar, you know, whatever the hell I could get. And it took me best of a year almost to save it. It was 14 dollars and 40-some cents, was what it cost. I called it a little ol' Gene Autry–type guitar. With the hole in it, you know. So anyway, man, she was raisin' hell about it, and finally my stepfather came home and he was the boss. So he took her in the house and I'm sittin' out on the porch with it, lookin' sad. And he had a talk with her, and when he came out he winked his eye at me, you know. He say, "You can keep it." And she never mentioned it again. So that was it. I have asked her in the past, "Well, suppose I had taken that guitar back?" She says, "Boy, I'm glad you didn't." [*Laughs.*] She lives in East St. Louis, Illinois. Yeah, I'm a mama's boy. She's 87 years old.

You were living on the plantation then? Was that Inverness, Mississippi?

Not Inverness. My mother moved from Inverness when I was a baby in her arms. We lived on Old Highway 82, which they call the Old Leland Road now, between Stoneville and Greenville. Nothing exists out there anymore, but at that time, used to be a store there. They called it Magenta, Mississippi.

Were you born in Inverness or was it out on a plantation?

Yeah. Well, out on the plantation, of course. Geeez. Come on, Jim! [*Laughs.*]

Which one?

It was a place called Duncan's Plantation. When you're goin' into Inverness on 49, just before you get into the city limits, it's that area over to your left—you look all out across that field. That was part of the Duncan Plantation at that time. I'm sure it was vast, you know. I had a uncle and a aunt that was still living out there, and my mom used to take me out to visit them. And my father, my real father, lived further down on the other side of it.

Were you the only musician in your family?

No. I've got a nephew, Joe Campbell—he's a musician. He's an arranger and a producer. I think he's currently helping or whatever, producing artists like Lowell Fulson, for Rounder. He was my music director for years. He's originally from Greenville.

But your father didn't play, or any of the older people in your family?

No. Nobody. It was just me, figuring, being in love with the guitar music. And in love with the guitar.

Some of your old records have your name as James Campbell on the songwriter's credits. Is that your real name?

Yeah. Well, what happened was, that was a name given to me. Some kind of way it got mixed up at birth. Then I discovered that I had a brother on my father's side named James. So I immediately, years, years ago, had it legally changed. They gave me James Milton Campbell. So I eliminated the James. But back then, we used it as the writin' name, you know, like for the tunes and what have you.

When you first started out, didn't you go with Eddie Cusic?

Yeah, well, the first professional musician that I ever worked with was Eddie Cusic, who lives in Leland there.

What kind of band did he have?

Well, he had two or three pieces, you know. Two guitars and a drum. That was basically it. I think maybe once he might have had one horn or somethin'. But you know, little guys playing around the little joints like that, there were no big bands, man. Maybe one horn, see, 'cause like Bill [guitarist Little Bill Wallace] and Lonnie [guitarist Lonnie Holmes] and then Willie Love, when they were playin' together, they had Otis Green [on saxophone]—call him the Big Bear. It was just four of 'em, you know. That's all. I was just a little dude peepin' in then, tryin' to get in to hear 'em, standin' on the outside, too young to get in. The only big bands you had then, they call themselves the Re-Bops [Red Tops], out of Vicksburg. They used to come up through Greenville a lot, and they were very popular in the early '50s. They played all the better dances, see. We didn't get any of those. [*Laughs.*] 'Cause they had all of the horns and the vocalists and what have you. And they were mostly schoolteachers, and they did this thing as an outside thing, you know. So they knew all of the people that was supposed to be in the know. And they got all the better gigs, all the proms and things like that.

Was Houston Boines playing around Greenville too?

During the time that I knew Houston, he was mostly around Leland, 'cause he was the harmonica player with Eddie Cusic and me. Him and I played with Eddie Cusic at the same time. We shared a room in Leland. Times were hard then, man. So we had a room together—we paid six dollars a week. That was three dollars apiece, and there was some times we barely was able to come up with that three dollars a week to pay the rent.

Were you working on another job in addition to playing music?

Yeah, off and on. I worked at a service station. Sometimes when I just had to, I would go to the cotton fields, you know. Pick cotton, chop cotton, whatever the season was. But other than that, I worked the service station around there in town, in Leland.

Were you and Moose Walker playing together in a band?

Yeah, we used to get together and play in the same band. There was one guy named Cleanhead Love out of Greenville, Mississippi. Moose played piano for him, I played guitar. He was a drummer, and then there was some other guys around there that got bands together off and on, you know. They never did really last too long, but we were basically I guess the most thought-of young musicians around there at that time. And we'd always get the gigs if there were any.

What was it like in Greenville? Was it a good town for music?

Yeah. At that time it really was. Lots of work. Little honky tonk joints, I guess you would call 'em, but at that time you didn't have all of the changes that you have now, 'cause it was totally segregated—well, the parts that I knew about, anyway. If you got a gig at a white joint, it was all white. And naturally, the blacks' clubs were all black. So between the two race things there you had pretty good little scratchin' for pennies.

So you could play at the white joints?

Yeah, you could play there. That's all you could do, is play, but they liked the music, and that's about it.

Did you play the same music or did you have to change it around some?

Well, you'd have to change. It all depends on where you was, but back then they were goin' for some of the standard tunes, and you had to be able to do a little country and western. Would you believe I played country and western? In fact, it wasn't hard for me to do because I fell in love with country and western by just listening to that Grand Ole Opry back when we didn't have a TV. Just a radio, you know. And I used to play in this place in Greenville they called the Broadway Playhouse, up on North Broadway. It's not there anymore, but then I had to play country and western and standard tunes. Did a little of all of it, but basically back then the whites were strictly hung up on the boogie woogie thing. So if you could play that you could get away anyway. [*Laughs.*]

So were the boogie woogie piano players pretty popular?

Oh, yeah, yeah. They could slide the fingers across the keys, you know, would be playin' the boogie woogie and they'd run that little slide 'cross there, man. Actually during those times the tips were way greater than the salary you would get. You might would get maybe seven or eight, ten dollars a night. But usually it'd be two or three of us. Maybe piano player and a drummer and a guitar. And heck, man, the tips would be $35 or $40 a night, so split that three ways, plus your salary, you would be doin' pretty good. Even right now, when you're speakin' of playin' in the black clubs and the white clubs, we have to be honest about it: If you ever break that barrier and get into that white club thing, you definitely gonna make more money. It paid off more then and it pays off more now. Just for a very few of us. It's not that we're not qualified, but for some reason or the other, man, if you don't know the right people or make the right move, be in the right place at the right time, you just may never make it there.

What were some of the blues clubs in Greenville?

Well, you had a couple of clubs out in the country at that time. They called one Leroy Grayson's Place and one they called Bay Jennings', and you had other little joints up like around Metcalfe, Mississippi, maybe about two or three miles out of Greenville. You had the VFW Club, which is still in Greenville, and you had a Elks Club. And you had Henry T's Pool Room down on Nelson Street. That was one of my first endeavors, I guess, that I thought I really was doin' somethin'. We used to have a packed house. And then they had the Blue Note Club on Nelson Street back in those days. 'Cause now you got one or two clubs down there, one that's the Flowing Fountain. It was about the largest club in Greenville. People don't go down on Nelson Street too much anymore like they used to back in those days. 'Cause like now, the doors are open, they can go anywhere they want to go. But then it was segregated, and blacks didn't have anyplace else to go, so there was just a big crowd down there.

Who were the top blues acts around Greenville?

During that time? Well, I'm sure you would have to say Willie Love. Every so often Sonny Boy would drift in there and stay maybe two or three months. Sonny Boy Williamson, you know, him, Rice Miller. And then there was another guy that still lives in Leland, Mississippi—Bill Wallace. We call him Little Bill. And he had a group then. He was a big man then. And as I mentioned before, Cleanhead Love. What a hell of a name he had: Cleanhead Love and the Chocolate Drops! [*Laughs.*]

Oh, yeah, one more guy. I sure must mention him—Mack Simmon. He's passed.

We called him King Mack Simmon. He was a trumpet player. He was a guy that could talk you into doing damn near anything he wanted you to do, like, you know, playing. He would take you out and promise you maybe $15 or $20 per man, and that was big money then. So naturally all of the young musicians wanted to go work with him. And he could really get jobs. He was a good talker, and he had a nice personality until he'd have a few too many. And he liked to party. So while you'd be playing, he'd be up at the bar drinkin', invitin' all the ladies, you know. So when time come to get paid [*laughs*], he'd owe all the money, man. And sometime there'd be a big fight with the cats in the band with him. And everybody would vow that they were never gonna go out and play with him anymore. He'd get another gig, and he'd go around. His little gimmick was that he'd come to one guy and say "I just talked to blah-blah-blah, and he said he would go if you will go, so I got him to go," and then when he got through doin' it he'd have the whole band back together again. He'd have, I guess, maybe ten or 12 pieces. And then that was considered a big band. Sometime he might would have more than that. We were like the younger guys and playing the kind of things that the people really wanted to hear at that time. What was most popular was the shuffles, all those old shuffles and stuff.

What about Charlie Booker?

Yeah, I remember him. He had a few records goin' there too. He was pretty popular around there, 'cause I guess maybe anybody that had records out, you got to be all right for a while. Well, for a while there he was, but, mind you now, all of this was basically local.

Did you ever play much with Sonny Boy?

Yeah. Rice Miller, now. Well, that's one of the guys that I really learned a lot from. And it was through Willie Love and Joe Willie Wilkins that I was able to play with Sonny Boy. At the time that I got involved with him, it was Willie Love, Joe Willie, Sonny Boy, and myself. I guess maybe I was hooked up with them for a couple of years, in and out. Sonny Boy would do more traveling than Willie Love because he was the major name.

So you were goin' on the road with him.

Yeah, but we didn't go anywhere but Mississippi, Arkansas, Louisiana, you know. He lived in Mississippi, so we'd go from Greenville to Jackson or from Greenville to Helena, Arkansas, stuff like that. And Monroe, Louisiana. So if you call that on the road, I guess it is. [*Laughs*.]

What was Sonny Boy like to work with?

To me, he was a great person, a great, great entertainer. And a very talented musician. This is my opinion, of course. He was a person that was in total control of himself and what he was gonna do, how he was gonna do it, when he was gonna do it, and when he wasn't gonna do it. He was very firm. If he told you that he was gonna do somethin', he would do that. If he said he wasn't, there was no need to keep askin' him. And he didn't mind being very abrupt with you. A lot of people say harsh, but I didn't see it that way. He'd just speak his mind and that was it, and he'd go on and get a drink and it's all forgotten, you know. But he was very respectable, and he taught me that.

In fact, the three of them taught me the importance of being your own man but not to be snotty with people, you know, with your nose in the air, because it was the people that support you that make you. And that's where I got that from—that without the people, you're nothin'. And it's true, it's very true. I pity a lot of these artists of today. They get some success in their careers, and they get to be a little too busy or too good for anybody. Well, that same road that takes you there, most cases is the same one you have to come down, and if you burn the bridges, it's a little rough. You got to wade or swim, you know. It's a very refreshing thought to know that I was able to learn somethin' that has been such a meaningful thing to me in my lifetime, in my career, to know what it means to just be yourself. You know, be decent if you are decent. Some people can't be decent because they're not decent from jump. And some people gonna be nasty regardless whether they have success or not. But I know that success don't make you. If you're blessed by the grace of God and work at it, you might be successful. And they instilled that into me. I'm sort of proud of that.

How much of an influence was Joe Willie Wilkins?

Oh, tremendous. Tremendous. He was quite talented. He never really got the recognition that I think he should have gotten for his unique style of guitar playing. He had it down to perfection—make the guitar sound like two guitars at one time. And I'm not talkin' about just playing a part now and then switchin' and runnin' back to the bass part. He could play both parts at the same time. I never could do that. I never could understand that, you know. But he did it. He was very artistic, and he was a very good soul.

He shared a lot of ideas, knowledge, and personal experiences with me—not only to motivate me, but to give me an insight of what you might run into out here in this business. You know, they [some musicians] were their own person and was in total control of themselves, but they were not timid. They were real, real men, and if you were kind to them, they were kind to you. If you got rough with them, they could be rough with you. They didn't take nothin' like that, you know, but they tried to compromise if possible.

It just makes me feel good to sit back and reminisce about the things that people like that taught me. Back then I don't guess a bunch of the entertainers, which I'm happy to say, was into the drug thing, which is somethin' I've never wanted to be involved with. It was just steak-and-potato-eatin', whiskey-drinkin' people that had fun. And to me, that was the highlight.

Did other guitar players you knew influence you a lot?

Well, yeah, in the beginning I have to probably mention Eddie Cusic—so many things. I still remember some of the licks that he was doing, and I wanted to know. There's a little ol' thing that you do in the key of A natural. "A natural" means that the A string is open. I wanted to learn how to do that, and he showed me how to do it, and I still can. It's your regular country blues.

But I've always wanted to be versatile, and even though at that time I couldn't play too much of the other type songs, I could sing them and I'd play at them, makin' wrong notes and missin' the chords and what have you. But evidently the audience that we were playing for didn't know the difference. Now maybe the voice was just somethin' they wanted to hear. So I found myself gettin' off into other things other than just 12-bar blues stuff. And mainly I guess I learned that from the fact that I have always been a fanatic for country music. So I learned different little shortcuts and different things.

Other than Eddie Cusic, there was another guy, James Peterson. He was a local entertainer down in Stoneville, Mississippi—that's between Leland and Greenville.

We played together for some time, did a lot of gigs together—on the weekends, of course. He'd work every day. I thought I was too good a musician to work—damn near starvin', but I was hangin' in there. [*Laughs.*] Other than that, I guess I listened to mainly T-Bone Walker. I listened some to Lonnie Johnson, of course, and to Lowell Fulson.

Did Little Bill help you with the guitar?

No! [*Chuckles.*]

He claims you're one of his students.

We're real good friends. Now, he mean it in another sense. 'Cause I liked the way he played the guitar. I liked his approach, the one-string type pickin', one string at a time. But I was most influenced by T-Bone Walker, 'cause I idolized him. And Bill was one of those kind of guitar players that just plays one string. So I liked his style, the way he approached it, his playing ability. But he didn't take time, talkin' about teachin' anybody guitar. So he probably meant in essence of me listening to him.

Was Bill playing more like B.B. King?

I don't think so, 'cause you know everybody talk about B.B. King's style, but all you need to do . . . I'm takin' nothin' from B.B.—to me, he's one of the greatest guitar players and he's the greatest blues singer that's around today—I'm not just sayin' it because we're good friends. But if you just think back and compare, his style thing kind of started from Lonnie Johnson. Really.

But, back to whether Bill played like B.B.: Even today, the guys that don't have records and things going for them, they'll have a tendency to sound like what's happening today. So I guess Bill and everybody else that was playing guitar at least tried to sound like a B.B. King or a T-Bone Walker or whoever things were really happening for. That includes me, you know. Some of the guys were able to pull from certain ruts and some wasn't. Bill probably gave it up on makin' a career out of it a long time ago. But when I got into that thing and I discovered that it wasn't really helpin' me any, I had to discover Milton. And that's what I set out to do, and I'm grateful to God that I was able to do that. But some guys just get into that rut of sound-alike. To me, that's really bad, 'cause you're always gonna be a second [best] or sound-alike, and that's not gonna help you. You know, since the passing of Elvis, you talk about all of the look-alikes and the sound-alikes, but hey, man, it doesn't do anything really but glorify more of a memory of Elvis. And when you get through, they're still just gon' be a look-alike or a sound-alike, 'cause there was only one.

Did you get to see T-Bone?

Finally got the chance to meet my idol. Met him, played several gigs with him, and we got to be good friends. And that was one of the greatest things could have happened to me, because very seldom you'll get to meet your idol. If you do, it's hardly ever any times that you can think of that you'll get to be friends. In the same business, of course, you might wind up playin' some gigs on the same show or even with him, but to get to be friends and that, to me that was a completed segment of my life. One of the things that I had always wanted to do was meet T-Bone Walker. So we exchanged ideas. He showed me so many different little things, 'cause I was very inquisitive and I wanted to know how he felt when he did certain little runs and squeezed the strings a certain way and did the ad-libbing the way he would do it—you know, the guitar would like accompany what he was singin'. And that's the way I learned how to do it.

Where did you meet T-Bone?

Met him in what used to be called Chambers, Mississippi—now it's Winstonville—at the Harlem Inn. That's where I first met him. I had gotten to be a pretty decent little name as a local, had a little band, those Playmates of Rhythm, and I had been playing several gigs for Hezekiah, the owner of the Harlem Inn. At that time I think T-Bone had given up his band, or was just movin' around without a band, for whatever reason. And Hezekiah hired me and my band to back T-Bone Walker. I must have got up there about 11:00 that day.

You went early!

Yeah. I went early. Waitin' for T-Bone to come in. Every car pull up out front, I'd run to the door to see, and finally he showed, him and his driver, in this long two-door green Cadillac, like a coupe. I remember distinctively. And he came in and he was very pleasant, and Hezekiah introduced us, and we had to rehearse behind him and what have you. And I had a bass player that wasn't too cool, couldn't play too well, and he really didn't know how to tune his bass up correctly. T-Bone listened to him for a while, and then he said, "I tell you what you do, Milton. Let me tune the bass. I'll play the bass some, and you play the guitar." He'd sing and play with me, and we put it together. Man, my chest was stickin' out—couldn't have ran a train across and blocked me.

And then the years went on and I moved from Mississippi to St. Louis and started playing Chicago quite a bit—this was in the late '50s or early '60s. And the late Big Bill Hill, he was the top disc jockey far as the blues was concerned in Chicago, especially on the West Side and the South Side. He had live broadcasts and then he had a couple of joints that he would book shows in all the time. One was called the Roosevelt Ballroom on West Roosevelt Road. So he started bookin' T-Bone in there occasionally, and we did a lot of those shows together. So then we talked durin' the days, 'cause I was there and he was there. After that, I think he got a little sick. He started doin' a lot of European stuff, and I think his health started failin' on him and I didn't hear from him anymore.

What about Howlin' Wolf?

Howlin' Wolf I loved dearly. I never played with him, never. But we've been on the same bill, and I want to tell you, he was an artist that nobody wanted to go on behind. He just tore the crowds up. Nobody wanted to go on behind Wolf because, believe me, he'd leave the stage so hot. Man! What a performer. And he had such a unique style. It was different. You hear some of the guys now try and imitate him, you know, like Wolfman Jack. But Wolf was just one of a kind. He was a two-fisted, good-livin' but raw-livin' person, you know. He believed in what he believed in, and he did what he wanted to do. But he was a good guy as well. I don't ever really remember running into too many of the older guys that was just stuck on themselves. They didn't have those kind of attitudes.

I remember one time Wolf was playing a picnic at a little place up in Missouri, Wentzville, about 40 miles west of St. Louis, and I went. He had on some beautiful cuff links—cuff links was in then, big flashy cuff links. So I said to him, "Gee, Wolf, damn, those are some beautiful cuff links." And he said in his inimitable voice [*imitates Wolf*], "Yeah, you like 'em?" So I said, "Yeah, man. I really love 'em." "Okay." So he went on and did his show, and when the show was over we was hangin' around behind the stage drinkin' and talkin', and he said, "Milton, come here!" So I went over to him. He say, "I'm gonna give you these. 'Cause you like 'em." And he pulled those cuff links off and gave 'em to me. I think I still have those cuff links in one of my old briefcases there at home in my basement. I was just overwhelmed, and I said, "Gee, Wolf," you know, 'cause I didn't really mean for him to give 'em to me. I said to him, "Man, I know these are kind of expensive and they're so beautiful. You, you really gonna give 'em to me?" He said, "Well, I'm gonna give you them, but next time you see me with somethin' on, don't tell me you like 'em." [*Laughs.*] His thing was that when you tell somebody you like somethin', they're supposed to give it to you if it's possible. Materialistic thing like that, you know.

You were one of the pallbearers at his funeral, weren't you?

Well, it was honorary pallbearer, yeah. If there's such a thing as a beautiful funeral, I think that was. All this sadness and stuff, hey, I guess maybe people have their own way of expressing whatever, but I just don't see it. I don't want that to happen when I'm gone, 'cause I didn't live sad. Lived happy, you know. And I think the leaving should be a happy occasion, 'cause you don't have to worry about any more problems and not bein' able to pay your bills and somebody gonna come and repossess your car. [*Laughs.*] Hey, you're laughin', but believe me, it has happened to me! [*Laughs.*] Yes, indeed. Take your car and hide it, man. Keep the dude from findin' it, so he can't take it back.

You started recording as a sideman with Willie Love. When you were with Sonny Boy or Willie Love at Trumpet Records in Jackson, was Elmore James on any of the sessions?

Yeah, he did several sessions with them and vice versa, because all of these guys were friends. But I really wasn't even on the scene, you know. I was never on a session with him. Willie Love did "Nelson Street Blues" two different times. The first time they did it Elmore was playing guitar. And the second time they did it I'm playing the guitar.

How many sessions did you do with him?

Oh, now that would be hard to recall, 'cause you just stay in there until you figured you had recorded enough. Sometime we'd be there for two or three days. Sometimes maybe a day, you know, just whatever. Whatever time it took for him to get as many songs as the people that owned the studio figure he needed. By the way, we cut in a furniture store. They had this room in the back part of it, and what she [Lillian McMurry] did to make it sound decent, they would like take the mattresses and stand 'em up around the walls so that would catch some of the sound to keep the acoustics from just bouncin' around. Man, now you talkin' about primitive days of recording! Ah ha! That was really somethin'. And you listen to some of the stuff, believe it or not, and it really didn't sound too bad. It's not like the sophisticated stuff that you hear today, but hey, it was tolerable, and it was successful too. So it sold. That beats some of things that Leonard Chess did with the little suitcase recorder, where you go around and set up anywhere and run a microphone up there, guy sing. Hey, man, but look at the success it was. And it brought so many people to the attention of the public, to the ears of the public to make them a star of whatever magnitude. Those were those days. You can make a studio out of anything.

Did you do any sideman sessions back then with anybody besides Willie Love?

No, I don't think so. Now I might be forgettin' some of that stuff. 'Cause some gigs would come up, and there was a few bucks involved, so we just went. I believe I did some more sessions too with John Walker—I think they call him Big Moose now. He played piano. I don't think any of his stuff was ever released from down there, though, at that time. This was down in Jackson on the Trumpet label. As I said, they'd throw you that little money, you'd go in there and do your little thing and get on out. No questions asked.

How did you get with Sun Records? Was it through Ike Turner?

Yeah, through Ike Turner. In fact, Ike was basically the influence, I suppose I could say that very safely, in getting me started into the recording. He was gathering up the local talent in the Delta part of Mississippi, takin' 'em into Memphis, and gettin' 'em recorded. And the cats were just tickled to death because really, nobody else would do it, you know. Nobody thought about it, or I don't guess they probably had the initiative or the connections or what have you. But Ike was always kind of a businessman, a wheeler and dealer.

How did he hear about you?

Well, you know, basically in there everybody kind of knows about everybody. 'Cause my home town, like Greenville and Leland, is about 65 miles from Ike's home town, which is Clarksdale. So by us playing all around, sometimes you'd bump into each other. I was with different guys like Willie Love, Sonny Boy Williamson, some of the oldies like that. I was just a kid, but I was still with 'em. I had lied about my age even to get with Willie Love and them, 'cause I was really too young. If they had known how old I really was, I'm sure they would have kicked me back out. But I was just as tall as I am now—almost six feet—at that time. So I was able to get away with it.

And then later on after I got my thing going and Ike had his group, we'd sometimes run across each other. I think the first time that I met him, though, it must have been in Leland, Mississippi. And they had Jackie Brenston, and Raymond Hill playin' saxophone. They had "Rocket 88." That was a big, big record for them durin' that era. And naturally if you got a hit record and you're young and inexperienced, you're a little cocky. So we was sort of like runnin' around lookin' up to them. Which nothin' was wrong with that. We was proud of them. We used to say that we knew somebody that really had had a hit record, that was popular. 'Cause with all of the major big artists of that time—like Roy Brown, Big Joe Turner, Fats Domino—we was in the wrong part of the country to really get to know them, especially on a personal basis. And Ike was always one to say, like, who he knew and what he could do for you. "You wanna record a record? I know somebody." And then being around each other, we got to be pretty decent friends, and we remained that way for a long time. And we still are, good association.

I saw him last year for the first time in a while. We toured California. And when he and Tina were at their peak as a team, I went and spent some days with 'em a couple of times. Once in California, went by the studio, and another time when they were playing the Hilton, Las Vegas. I was on a vacation break, went and spent a few days at the hotel. They were playing the Casino Lounge—not the big room, where the Elvis and Ann-Margret people were—but it was real great, real nice. That was the good era then. You go in there now, the best you can find is maybe some music that's piped in or what have you. It's not the same Vegas, I tell you.

Elvis was recording for Sun at the same time you were. Did you know him?

I remember seeing Elvis one time in Marks, Mississippi. I was playing at Tippy's little ol' club, set right there on the highway. I think Tippy's dead now. His name was Willie Hill, but he had that hotel that set there. I'm sure he would just let these white boys in if they wanted to come, you know. I don't know if he knew some of their people or what have you.

So Elvis came to see you in Marks?

Yeah. But I never knew him on a personal basis. I met Carl Perkins. His thing, they first started out callin' it rockabilly and rock 'n' roll. I don't think he ever really got over into that country and western thing, so to speak, not near as well as Jerry Lee Lewis and most certainly not as well as Johnny Cash or Charlie Rich. Well, that's what they were playing till they decided they wanted to try to sound like some of the black artists, you know.

How did the black artists feel about that at the time?

I don't really know. But they were so big at that time, and these guys weren't any threat, and to tell you the truth, they're not a threat now. They're just gonna do whatever they wanna do and accept who they wanna accept. Unfortunately, the way it has to be is the exposure. If you get accepted and get the exposure, then you'll be just about as big as anybody else. And who's to say who gets that? It comes back to that they take care of their own.

What it was like to record for Sun?

I just started reminiscing about when Ike Turner first carried me to Sun Records, a little studio right there on Union. We just glad to record records. Sometimes if we got in there around 1:00 or 2:00 in the evening, we subject to be there all night. Possibly part of the next day. And have a few drinks, get hungry and get some food, eat, possibly go to sleep, and wake up and start all over again! Nobody worried about the time, because you didn't have to pay for studio time and stuff like that. They had a smooth way of rippin' you off.

Was Sam Phillips in charge of the sessions?

Yeah, of course he was. He'd be runnin' the board. Ike Turner at that time was more or less the producer. He'd be playing piano and showin' you different things if you make mistakes, how to correct 'em. But you really wouldn't make too many mistakes 'cause you'd just be ad libbin', in a sense. You didn't really do like we do nowadays. Like me now, as a producer, what I have to do is I write my lyrics, or if by chance I solicit some lyrics or somebody'd send some to me, then I'll sort out some of the best material. And we sit down and we'll arrange it, put the music and stuff to it. And then you go in the studio and you rehearse a little and you record, see. It's done professionally now. But back then, you didn't really make too many mistakes, 'cause you just kept goin', doing things over and over. And that's why a lot of the tunes got the same lyrics [*laughs*]—you didn't write out anything. You'd start singing somethin' and then maybe he want to change the beat, and you run out of things to say. You remember somethin' you said in a take or two on somethin' you did maybe half an hour or 45 minutes ago.

So you didn't really rehearse before the session?

No, no. You didn't do any rehearsin'. You know, I just got kind of halfway sophisticated with the recording just before I stopped recording for Meteor Records. Then we went into St. Louis, and I got hooked up with Bobbin. Then we started writing things. We kind of knew what we were gonna do before we went in the studio. But up until then, we just more than glad, man, just to get in there and start singin' somethin'. You'd pick out a pretty good beat, or somebody in the band would come up with a melody or somethin', and you'd start off playin', and then you'd try to put some lyrics to it.

So was this the first time that you'd been in the studio for yourself?

Yeah, the very first time, speaking of me recording for myself. I tell that with a little pride. The very first record, very first time in a studio. With Ike Turner. A lot of people get everything confused when we do interviews, and I've noticed when I read 'em, a lot of time they say that Ike Turner and I worked together, like I worked in his band or he worked in my band—that's not true. It never happened that way. Ike has always been the guy up front that knew everybody and had all of the connections. He took me into Sun Records to meet Sam Phillips. And he had a little three- or four-piece band at that time. Himself, Junior [Jessie Knight], whom was his nephew, and Willie Sims, which we called Bad Boy, and I took the saxophone you hear on there, C.W. Tate. So when we went into the studio, we had piano, guitar, bass, drums, and one saxophone. That is what you hear on there.

So we went in there and Ike introduced me to Sam Phillips: "You want to cut a record?" "Yeah." So, "Start playin' and singin'." We had not rehearsed anything. I think maybe two or three of those tunes I had wrote already and was doin' 'em on the regular gigs with my group, which was Little Milton and his Playmates of Rhythm. [*Laughs.*]

I think Ike must have taken me into Sun Records more than once—maybe at least two or three times—so we did a little bit here and there. Some of the stuff, I don't even know if it was worth keeping, 'cause I never seen it again anyway. And then with some of the things I recorded, some songs of mine, later on Ike took Billy Gayles in and recorded the song on Billy Gayles, so I imagine he probably took somebody else in and did 'em on them too. Go in the studio and they run out of material, they just pick up whatever, you know.

Have you seen the Rounder CD compilation of the 1953–'54 Sun sides?

Yeah. This is the very beginning, basically. There's some stuff on here was the very beginning. "Beggin' My Baby," "Somebody Told Me." This was like the Sun debut stuff. It's a long time ago, man. If I knew then what I know now . . .

What would you do different?

I'd probably do the same thing, but I probably would do it a little different, you know. It's some different routes that you would change. I don't really regret anything that I've done, speaking in the musical profession part of it. It's been pretty good.

So you used Ike's band on the first session?

On the first records, yeah. I had a little group, but Ike had the best group. I'm sure it meant more to him too to record with his group. It was a little more prestigious, I'm sure. Everybody got that little $10 or $15 or whatever. [*Laughs.*] It was fun, though, man.

Had you ever played with Ike's band before the session?

Well, not really played, but there had been occasions that I had gone around where him and his group was performing, you know, as musicians usually do. We'd have somethin' like a jam session, or maybe I'd sit in sometime—it all depend. But that was about the extent of my playing with him.

Who played in your band?

James Carr played tenor, and he also was with this guy that I mentioned, Mack Simmon. He was a hell of a tenor player. He's dead now. His brother, Drew Carr, played alto. Lawrence Taylor was a drummer at that time. He later switched to saxophone. And they played around with Little Wynn. He was a music teacher that worked at the school. [Drummer] Lonnie Haynes, we used to call him "Cool

Breeze." When he'd get wrapped up in his playing, he'd be *whooh* [*whistles like wind*]. So we called him Cool Breeze. Lonnie is in Belzoni, Mississippi. Old Willie Dotson—that was my bass player. Willie Dotson started out playing saxophone, and somethin' happened to his pipes. Doctors told him he had to leave the saxophone alone, so he had started playing bass. So he made him[self] an electric bass—cut it out like the Fender and bought the pickups and put 'em in there. That's what he played with me for a long time, a homemade bass. And it sound pretty good. The only thing was the strings—he could only adjust 'em down so far because he didn't have anything in the neck, like that steel [truss] rod. You have to have that to keep 'em from buckling. So the strings would be a little high sometimes, but he did pretty good. He was like a little lightweight electrician then. He fixed radios. I think he got that trade while he was in service.

Oliver Sain was around there too.

Yeah. 'Cause, see, Willie Love was married to his mother. Willie Love was Oliver Sain's stepfather. So when Oliver got out of service, he came to Greenville. That's when I first met him. That's how we got together.

You remember those records that Houston Boines did?

Not all of 'em. I can recall one that we had a lot of trouble with, 'cause he had a tendency to cloud his lyrics when he'd be tryin' to sing. And he had a heck of a tune, man—it was somethin' about the whiskeys. He'd put all the names of the whiskeys together ["Carry My Business On"], and we couldn't finish it 'cause it never would come out clear. Couldn't understand exactly what he was sayin'. I carried him to Sun Records. I was big then, I thought. [*Laughs.*] You know that's gotta be the biggest joke in the world.

Were you doing any radio broadcasting?

Yeah, I was a disc jockey there for a minute. In Greenville, I had a program on radio station WGVM. I had a sponsor out of Memphis, Lucky Hearts Cosmetics. And I did that, I guess, for a couple of years.

Was this after you'd started making records?

Yeah, yeah. I was into that even then. A lot of times I'd have to go do gigs out of town and we'd tape the show. I did a pretty good thing as a DJ there. Radio was good. One of the reasons I did the show was because I could put the band on. I'd have like an hour per day. Be some time in the evening, always in the afternoon. Maybe I'd play records for half an hour, then the last half an hour I'd put the band on. I'd set 'em up right there in the studio, and we'd do requests. Read the request and do the tune. That was fun too, man. Really was. That way I got a chance to broadcast where I was gon' be playing, you know. All that was free. [*Laughs.*]

What was the name of the show?

Just *The Little Milton Show*. That's all. So that was in the '50s too. I didn't get no salary, by the way, from Lucky Hearts. All I got was that free time and the exposure. You'd hustle a little on the side. If somebody wanted you to broadcast somethin' on your show, they'd throw you a few bucks and you did it. That was the only pay.

How did you get started on the radio?

Well, I would be broadcasting as a side musician with Willie Love. He had a show. And so then I got to meet the owner of the station and the disc jockey, and on Willie Love's show I would do the reading of the requests most of the time, and they liked my voice. Instead of a lot of stumbling . . . You know, for black people as

a whole, education was somewhat on the very bottom of the totem pole. I was a
little fortunate. I had learned a little, and I could read pretty good then. So they
chose me to do all of the reading of the requests. I did a fairly decent job, and they
kind of liked that. This company was looking, and they was really projecting to
blacks to buy their product.

What was Willie Love's show?

He bought his own time. And he was a little more business about it. I just wanted to be on the air, I guess. He would solicit the local merchants, around their
stores, and he'd do those commercials, and that's where he got his money from. So
he made a profit out of it. You could go in and buy you an hour. Maybe a hour
cost you, heck, I guess, $10 or $20 or less. And we talkin' about a whole hour
now—can you imagine? Lot of times, while his show was on, I'd go in, 'cause a lot
of time wouldn't nobody show up but him. He'd just sit down and play the piano
and sing. Sometime I'd go in and help him out. And then sometime if my drummer didn't show up, he'd sit in and help me out or play piano with us, you know.
We were kind of gettin' away from his regular straight 12-bar blues thing then,
though. There was so much he could play, and certain things he couldn't do.

Did any other people have radio shows like that?

Anybody that wanted it could buy time. Cleanhead Love and the Chocolate
Drops. And Charlie Booker. Little Bill and them had a show. He was with Willie
Love and then, when they split, he and Lonnie Holmes had a show.

What was Willie Love like as a person?

In his heart he was a beautiful person. Good guy, you know. He was very tem-
peramental at times, but deep down within he'd give you the shirt off his back. He
raised a little hell sometimes. Maybe he drank a little too much every once in a
while. But when it was all said and done, if you really needed him and he had it,
you could get it. If he didn't have it, he'd go and try to get it for you. You don't run
into too many people like that anymore. I don't guess any of us are without faults.

Was he ever working with the King Biscuit Boys during that time?

I think it was before he came to Greenville that he worked with them. When I
was a little kid, I used to listen to the radio sometime and catch that show comin'
out of West Helena, Arkansas, I believe.

Then when you went to Meteor Records, how did that come about?

I really don't know how it came about, to tell you the truth. But some kind of
way I met Les Bihari, one of the Bihari brothers. It might have been through some
of the associating or somethin' that I was doin' with somebody else, or from Sun
Records. I don't really know. But I met him, and he had a record company and I
wanted to record records, so that was that.

Were you still based in Greenville?

Yeah, but not all the time now durin' that time, 'cause I left Greenville in 1955
and moved to East St. Louis, Illinois, when I was still with Meteor Records. And I
stayed with 'em for another couple of years. It must have been around '56 or '57
that I got into this Bobbin thing, out of St. Louis. So it was just okay for little local
stuff, you know. It helped me along the way. You can't just overlook that kind of
stuff, 'cause everybody have to pay their dues. And it was just more of a eye-opener.

At the time you left Greenville, was there much racial tension?

In Greenville? No. And I'll tell you somethin': That's strange. Greenville has always been very liberal, very liberal, as far back as I can remember. Greenville had the first black policemen [in the Mississippi Delta]. But they had a little gimmick—he couldn't arrest any white folk. A white person come down in the predominantly black part of town and act up, he would pre-arrest him and hold 'em and go to this special telephone line—I think it was direct to the police station. He'd hold him there until the white cops come by and pick him up.

So his beat was the black district.

Black area. That was it. Burl Carson was the very first black policeman, which is Willie Carson. We all called him Burl. He's also a ex-musician, a pretty fair guitar player. He wanted to sound like T-Bone Walker. He played with Little Wynn—that's when I first met him. George Davis was the second black policeman. Then the next black cop that I remember, in the Delta, was in Indianola, dude named Slim—big, big dude. Ugly. Mean. Vicious. Oh, but he's a nice guy.

How was Greenville different from other towns in the Delta?

To be honest with you, I really don't know. People have been integrated in the Southern states for so long. They lived next door to each other; they did a lot of things together. They wasn't goin' to school together and goin' to church together, but other functions, you know. And then all of a sudden somebody said, "You're livin' next door to a black person." Or "A black person's livin' next door to me." And they got conscious of the fact that they'd been integrated, and they was talkin' about segregation. Hell, they'd been integrated for years and years. And then they were made aware of the fact, and a lot of 'em changed and a lot of 'em didn't.

And you got a lot of good, sensible people that really don't give a damn what race you are. If you treat them right and you're a respectable person, then they treat you as a respectable person, and they respect what you do, and I think that's really the way it should be. So Greenville was like that. You go to Leland, then it might be a different thing, or any of those little outlining areas, you know. But I don't ever remember too much major racial catastrophes happening in and around Greenville and Leland durin' that time. You know, I'm talkin' about somebody lynchin' somebody or police beatin' up on somebody to the point that they couldn't walk somewhere or what have you. I'm not sayin' that it didn't happen, now, but I wasn't aware of it.

Did you hear talk about other towns where that did happen?

Well, yeah, you would hear of some miscarriage of justice here and there—like the Emmett Till situation, stuff like that. And then there was the guy that had been going with this white woman for years, and then they fooled around and got caught together. She screamed rape, and they electrocuted him. That was a big case. It's really hard when you think about stuff like that. And you know, everybody talks down about the Southern states, but you'd be surprised what goes on in the Northern states. So I don't think it has to do with one particular state. It's about people and where their hearts are. And it's a damn shame because we all are here together, and we're goin' to have to make it here. Together. On this earth. And we could make it so much more pleasant for each other if we just had the capacity to respect each other as individuals.

What difference did you notice when you moved to East St. Louis and then to Chicago? How was life different there?

Well, number one, it was more modern 'cause you had a lot of industry and back then times were better, economically speaking. People had more jobs, everything was more plentiful. And far as the music scene was concerned, if you had a record out there, you had plenty of radio stations that were programming your music—rhythm and blues, rock 'n' roll, what have you. And its difference was that you could make more money, you could gain more popularity in the Northern areas, and, naturally, popularity meant success, success meant more money, so that's the reason I went. That's why I made my move.

But racial problems, you had 'em in Illinois, you had 'em in Chicago, had 'em in East St. Louis, had 'em in St. Louis, Missouri—look at the Chuck Berry situation. That was durin' that same time. I'm not sayin' that it was wise for him to be doin' the things that he was doin', but, after all, he was grown. I think the tension was focused on him because he was black and who he was, and they wanted to make an example of him. But you find it everywhere. And not only back then, you still find it now. But I was lookin' at the money and a better way of life for my family, for myself, and that's why I went. And it worked out pretty good!

So you took your whole band with you when you moved to East St. Louis?

Yeah, I took the whole band. Guys followed me up there. We did all right. In fact, that was my first major break. It was in a much more of a metropolitan-type atmosphere, and we got more exposure. I moved my mom and stepfather from Leland up there. I might have been up there maybe four or five months, couldn't stand it any longer without the girl, so I came and got her and moved them up there.

What inspired you to take your whole band and move to another town?

Well, what had happened, this guy Henry T, from Henry T's Pool Room, he had a cousin up in East St. Louis that had a nightclub. Some kind of way somebody had heard us. And this guy, Virgil McNeese, was willin' to finance the trip up there and pay us and give us a regular steady gig workin' at his club as a house band. So I took that. However, it didn't last very long, 'cause we discovered that he didn't have any money. I can't even think of the club now. Such a bad experience.

Did you go to East St. Louis with the intention of staying there?

Yeah, because the offer made sense, and we were supposed to be gettin' paid more money than we'd been gettin'. So we got there at that time Ike Turner had it sewed up around there. Back in that time, if you had a good group and you was really doin' somethin', you could make it. And we had a good group. So it wasn't very long that that whole area belonged to Ike Turner and Little Milton.

Ike had already been there.

Oh, yeah. He was there maybe a year and a few months before I was. He had a good group—Johnny O'Neal and Billy Gayles were his main singers there. Johnny was off and on, and Billy Gayles got to be more of a permanent thing with him. Clayton Love played the piano. Ike always had a damn good group, so he was really set. But he didn't have too much competition till we got in there, you know. But we, him and I, used to have 14, 15 gigs per week. Yeah, we'd be doin' doubles and triples and things. We had too many gigs—more than we could really handle. Because on Saturday we'd do a matinee, and then we'd do a show that Saturday night in Missouri, and then come over to Illinois.

At that time, see, Illinois was open 24 hours. So in St. Louis, the Missouri side, they closed up like around one, maybe two. Then we'd start playing over in Illinois like around three and go to six, seven, whatever. Then we'd do a matinee on

Sunday, same thing. So on Friday and Saturday and Sunday, you're talkin' about nine gigs. And then we'd work every night the rest of the week, and sometimes certain nights of the week we'd do a thing in St. Louis and come over in East St. Louis and do somethin' else. It was really jumpin' then. What they call the heyday of that era. We were able to keep together a six-, seven-, eight-piece band all the time.

Did you have an agent getting bookings for you?

No. Didn't need no one. It was just me. What you'd do is get you a phone number, and you'd be on the radio all the time when they had live broadcasts from the clubs and what have you. So anybody that wanted to get you, they could get you. They called the club, asked for your number. A lot of times the gigs that paid more money would be like some big money-making social clubs, sororities, and organizations like the Elks or Masons. They'd get you for some of their big annual affairs. Sometime, if you had a good group and the guys could read, they'd bring in a name artist, and you'd be the backup band. I've done lots of those things too. We played behind Roy Hamilton, T-Bone Walker, and Percy Mayfield. Oh, man, there were just a whole bunch of 'em.

What station were you on when you'd do that broadcast?

Well, at that time they had two main stations in St. Louis that was projecting strictly—basically, I should say—to blacks. That was KATZ and another station. I can't recall the call letters, but George "The G" Logan was on that station. That live broadcast thing got to be very popular around that area.

What was more important, radio broadcasts or the records?

You know, even then, I think it would be safe to say, the records need the radio station, the radio station need the records, and the artists need both. That's about as sensible as I can put it.

Did all the guys you took to St. Louis stay up there?

Yeah, I believe. Oliver Sain, he's still there. Lawrence Taylor and Willie Dotson. As I said, James Carr passed a few years back. Jerry Walker, the drummer, he's still there. He's originally from Parkin, Arkansas. That's right out of West Memphis. Leon Bennett ["Turkey Red"], he died. He was from around West Memphis. But we needed a piano player. Either Oliver or Jerry brought him to me.

After you moved to East St. Louis, would you go to Mississippi to play?

Yeah, occasionally. Well, I really didn't have the time, you know, and all that was good 'cause the name of the game is makin' money, and I was pretty well satisfied at doing what I was doing where I was.

So Ike Turner and you were the main two around that area?

Yeah, durin' that time. Then came Albert King. He came into pretty good prominence after a while, and we had another guy had a band there, Roosevelt Marks. Then you had a few more around there. George Hudson was a music teacher who had like the big band like Count Basie's band, but then they was in a different bag.

Where did you do the Bobbin sessions?

The beginning of them, we did 'em in the radio station after closin' hours. He [Bob Lyons] was the manager of KATZ, and he started Bobbin Records.

Then you went to recording studios later?

Yeah, we went to one there in St. Louis. I can't think of the name out there, but we did some out there.

Did you play guitar on records by any of the other Bobbin artists?

No more than what we'd do with Oliver [Sain] and Fontella [Bass].

You were on Fontella's records?

On some of the earlier things, yeah.

Remember a record by the Earthworms on Bobbin? The credits on the songs are to Sain and Campbell. I thought maybe that was a little group that you were in.

That name sound familiar. Yes, that had to be Oliver and me.

It was just a couple of instrumentals, one called "Mo' Taters" [b/w "Fishtail"].

Yeah. [*Laughs.*] Yeah, that's us. Boy, man, you all don't miss nothin'! Well, see, we thought of the Earthworms 'cause it was my group, and that's Oliver, by the way, saying "mo' taters." [*Laughs.*] Yeah, I had forgotten all about that.

Who else was in that?

All of us, the group. Jerry's on drums, Willie Dotson on bass, and the saxophone was James Carr, Lawrence, and Oliver, and we probably had Larry Prothro or somebody on trumpet, I imagine. Might have had Fontella Bass on piano, 'cause she was part of the organization at that time. That's somethin'. "Mo' Taters." That's a funky little old tune too.

Did Bobbin do much material on you that was unissued?

Everything we did basically was released. Because we wasn't really doin' a lot of different things at that time. There was some tunes kind of hung up there somewhere, but in the transition from Bobbin to Chess, I was able to bring most of the stuff that we were doing. So he had some kind of deal goin'—they were kind of like leasing me to Chess, some kind of way it got all screwed up. But I wound up with Chess.

When did you leave St. Louis?

For good, 1967.

And you came to Chicago?

Yeah. See, I left Bobbin and came to Chess around that time. So then all of the major interest was here—the studio, and I had better musicians and everything for recording with. And my wife and I, we separated around that time, so other than my kids that were there, I really didn't have too much to hang around there for. My mom still lives there.

At the time you left, was there still a lot of work for you in the nightclubs?

Yeah, but then what had happened, see, was when I got with Chess, well, we did several tunes, but we finally really did good when we did "Blind Man." It came out in November of 1964, October or November. And that kind of put me into a different thing. And I got in demand, I should say, nationally. So then we came back, our next release was "We're Gonna Make It" in 1965, and then I was in demand throughout the country. So then I couldn't stay there.

So by the time you moved to Chicago, it wasn't like a local band anymore anyway?

No, no, it was a national band.

Since you've been touring, I don't guess there have been any clubs in Chicago that you ever played steadily.

No. Ever since 1964, always been club dates and one-nighters for me, you know. Hadn't always wanted it to be that way, but unfortunately—or fortunately, in some cases—it turned out to be that way.

How far back did you start handling your own production in the studio?

Just before I left Chess Records. Right after Leonard died. 'Cause we had Billy

Davis. The very first, the *We're Gonna Make It* album, we had done. The second album was *Little Milton Sings Big Blues.* I produced that one. That was my first producing endeavor, for Chess Records. I had done all the other stuff for Bobbin Records, the independent label out of St. Louis. That's where we did "Lonely Man," where I say I was just comin' into myself. But after that, we were havin' such problems with the [Chess] producers. Calvin Carter, Gene Barge, they was all into it with each other, you know, all the time, jealousy and what have you. So I said, man, you know. When I left the Chess organization, I went to Stax in Memphis. *Waiting for Little Milton,* that was my first major production with all of the horns and strings and voices and everything. The background voices on it, if you didn't know it, was the Soul Children. [*Laughs.*] Yeah. So that's how far it goes back. Between '71 and '72, somewhere like that. Yeah. And I've been doin' it ever since.

Every record since then you've essentially done yourself?

Yeah. Until I got to Malaco. And then, this is the truth—and I really don't give a damn who like it, but it's true—they don't really produce me. I can't speak for the other people now, but they assist me in producin'. Fortunately, I've come up with good material. We're still sellin' a few.

When you recorded for T.K., you were doing the same thing basically?

Yeah.

Producing the tapes and sending them to them, or going down to Florida to record?

I would take 'em. I never recorded down in Hialeah, Florida, where the studio and the company was. I did my stuff in Chicago and some of it in Memphis. And when I'd finish it, then I'd take it down there to them. That was really total control then, because I only would take the songs that I wanted them to hear. You know, when you're in the studio and everybody's there, especially if there's some executives that's come through while you're doin' your session, they gonna see if somethin' they like is in there, whereas I only would package what I wanted them to hear. So I'd have two or three tunes left over. That mean my burden would be lighter the next album. [*Laughs.*]

There was a period beginning in the late '70s, after T.K. and before you'd signed with Malaco, when you weren't signed with anybody.

That period that you're talkin' about, you're right. I wasn't signed with anybody, and I was just sort of coolin' out, waiting till somethin' decent came along. We had had some bad experiences. Leonard had died, so Chess had gone. They went out. I got with Stax, they folded. Got with T.K., they folded. So I was sort of floatin' and that stuff sort of leaves a bad taste in your mouth. Stax went under owin' me a bunch of moneys, my production company as well as myself. So did T.K. So I was just coolin'. And Al Perkins and I, we've been good friends for years, he approached me and asked that we should try and do somethin'. You know albums were not a big, big thing then. They were just beginning to come in, so we didn't really want to get into a big production deal, so what we did, he had some tracks and I went and overdubbed my voice on those tracks, and it turned out real good.

Unfortunately, his thing at that time wasn't near what it was supposed to be and not near what it did finally get to be. As far as his connections with MCA, and then producing and getting the stuff distributed and exposure-wise, he didn't have that deal with them on the very first thing that we did. And we did that one record, "Real Love" and "Survivors of Love," that one 45 [on Perkins' Mier label], and from that Jimmy Vanleer at Golden Ear. He had some tracks, so I went in and overdubbed the guitar and my voice, and we came up with the album *I Need Your Love So Bad*. And that was just more or less somethin' to let everybody know that Little Milton was still around, alive and well, you know. So finally Al Perkins' thing got right with MCA. He called me to let me know that he was ready now and it was straight, so we did the project of *Age Ain't Nothin' but a Number*.

You went into a studio and did that one?

Yeah. We did tracks on that one. And that was during the same time of his most untimely, unfortunate death. That album was sittin' on his desk, finished product, and I was to meet him that Tuesday in L.A. to take the pictures and all of that. And he got killed sometime that Sunday. And he'd called me Saturday all day. Every time I'd turn around, the phone rang. He's sittin' there in the office, playing *Age Ain't Nothin' but a Number*. He was highly up in the air about that, you know. He just loved it. Lucky Peterson was my keyboard player and bandleader then, and when his mother told me Al had died, I felt like a ton of bricks had hit me. Not only that we were friends, real good friends, but here I am right on the threshold of probably one of the biggest record deals that I had ever had, with MCA.

MCA never followed up to try to get you another album?

Well, I got scared, because I didn't know anybody over there. And when he died, I knew that his sister, she didn't have the expertise or the know-how to handle a deal of any size, 'cause she didn't know anything about the business. So, they [MCA] released it, and we knew that without him it just wasn't gonna be that thing from the sky. So I felt that my best bet would be to get out of that as fast as I possibly could. So I talked to my lawyer, and we got the balls rolling and they let me out of the contract. And I went with Malaco, and that's where I've been ever since.

Did you approach Malaco or were they looking for you?

I approached them. I did it through [Malaco promotion man] Dave Clark. I was tellin' him that I wanted to get away from MCA because I was afraid that I would just become a number in a big conglomerate company. So he said, "Well, why don't you call my company?" So he suggested the idea, and I did. And they were interested. I went down and talked with 'em, and we worked out a deal.

Now my problem was to get free from these [MCA] people. In the beginnin' they were somewhat reluctant to do so. I don't know if I really made the right move or not—you know, you can't really be sure. It might have been a good thing to stay there and take my chances, or get in there and try to get to know somebody. But now that I think about it, maybe I did do the right thing, because they had B.B. and they had Bobby Bland from when they purchased that other company, ABC Dunhill. B.B., naturally—I'm sure he's not sufferin' for anything one way or the other, but I know from where I sit his popularity as far as sellin' a lot of records is not happenin'. And with a company that big, if the emphasis, half the emphasis, was put on B.B. King what they put on some of these country and western artists with them, I think it would make a hell of a difference.

You like country music a lot.

My opinion is that country and western is nothing but the blues. I think it's just white man's blues presented in the white man's form. What makes it so for real is because the lyrics are for real. They're singin' about things that's actually happening. They're singin' about reality. So are the blues singers. They're singing about everyday life, the sadness, the happiness, the hurt, the pain, the disappointments. So what's the difference? I mean, really, what's the difference? It's strange how nobody never says it's a racial music. 'Cause somewhere in there I get a funny feelin' that maybe they could say that, you know, without sounding prejudiced or envious or anything. Just maybe. And the reason I say that is because country and western artists could take "Hey, Hey, the Blues Is All Right" right now and do it. Say, a George Strait or Vince Gill or somebody. I would hate to hear Vince Gill doin' it, though. With that little beautiful voice that he got, that high soprano or tenor or whatever. And it would be a whole different concept, see?

That's one of the problems about this. That's how they characterize: It ain't so much the music, basically, as who does it. And that's what keeps the hindrance there, towards the so-called blues that's predominantly black-owned. That's what keeps it settin' on the back burner. But it's better. And who knows? Just one day, it might finally get the recognition that it so rightfully deserve, because it's such a rich, meaningful music. It's a damn shame that so many people ignore it, and without really listening to it and gettin' into it, because a lot of 'em have the wrong concept about blues. They think blues is all about ignorance, black, poor, illiteracy, and some of our black so-called blues artists don't do anything to help that image. You know, they go to work, to the gig, with clothes that they've been wearin' for two or three days. They perform in 'em, show after show. I wasn't taught that way about entertainers. I was taught that an entertainer was supposed to look professional, not just sound professional. Be proud of what you're doing. Be proud of yourself. Be proud of your image.

You know, to each his own—they do what they want to do. But it's a shame that when a lot of these big, huge crowds come to see a black performer, especially if he's a raw, country-type blues artist, they expect to see him with a big hat on and sittin' down with a bottle of liquor in front of him and a snuff can or tobacco can over here to spit occasionally, and that's it. But to me that's false representation of the blues. It's false representation of what Little Milton is about. You will never see me like that. I could be at your house just layin' around partying, but you ain't gonna see me like that—all smelly and what have you. To me that's a false representation. But then we get hooked into that, and people get hooked into it. A lot of times, I'll come onstage and it scare people to death. They don't know: "What? Oh, what did he do?" So, I don't know. As they say, it's hard but it's fair.

You've managed to stay commercial throughout the whole period you've been recording. I can only think of a couple of other people who have been able to do that in the blues, like B.B. and Bobby Bland maybe. What's the reason for it?

Well, I think it's because of doing only the type of material that you can really get into. In other words, I only do material that, to me, makes sense. It's gotta be a good, strong lyric that makes sense; it's gotta be a melody that I can really bite into. And when I say bite into, what I'm talkin' about is to really get into it yourself, the total you. And I think when you do that, then you can get somethin' out of it. And as you get somethin' out of it, you project what you feel to other people, your potential buyers or what have you. And if you're true to the code of what you are about, then whatever you sing, you gonna still come out sounding like you. And that's somethin' that a lot of people can't do. You got a lot of people that got helluva voices, can really sing, but that personal identity sometimes is missing. And my thing is, once I'd found myself, when I discovered me, I have never wanted to sound exactly like nobody else. Even if I covered a tune that they did.

Did you used to?

Oh, yeah. A long time ago. And you listen to some of that stuff on that Rounder CD, you'll hear me soundin' like Chuck Willis, Fats Domino. You hear some of that on there. You hear some B.B. King on there, you know. "Somebody Told Me," that's the same style, melody thing, of B.B. King's "Woke Up This Morning." And these were people that were there. And it's hard to be not influenced by great talent around you when you don't have that personal identity of your own. You have a tendency to try and sound like anybody that's successful. So, no exception for me.

But once I discovered me, what has been partially responsible for my longevity in the business is I've tried to be true to the code—true to me, true to what I feel. And you still can enjoy it. You know, it's strange: I guess maybe it's just human nature, but people can tell when you are enjoying what you're doing. You kind of hear that little tingle thing in your voice, and that has a lot to do with it. And I think you need those kind of combinations now in order to stay here like this. But if you jump from pillow to pillow, somewhere in between you could get caught out there, and in that space, if you fall, you ain't got nothin' to fall back on. And I'm just a true believer of that.

So you might not have a million-seller every time, 'cause you're not movin' around and what have you, but at least you'll have a good track record. And I've always wanted to have it said about Little Milton that regardless of how many songs I record or how many albums I have, all of them were good. I've always wanted 'em to be put together properly. I take my time and choose the material that I know I can feel, that I know I can deliver, even though I've been able to be flexible as I felt, but I still think choosing the right material a lot of time is the key. And I've tried to do that. It's been successful. As I've said, I haven't had all them great million-sellers, but if they go buy a Little Milton record, they know that it's gonna be some good material and I'm gonna give it my level best to perform it the way it should be, at least the way I feel it should be.

At what point did you develop the identifiable Little Milton style, so people could tell it was you they heard and not you trying to sound like somebody else?

I think that started to happen for me when I left the little stint that I had with Meteor Records, when I left Mississippi and moved to East St. Louis, Illinois. When we did tunes like "I'm a Lonely Man," that started it, 'cause I wrote that. I really got into it, and I could just feel that. From that I started writin' a lot. And Oliver Sain—he's a hell of a writer, a hell of a musician—he was my bandleader at that time, and we started writin' a lot of stuff together, and I started feelin' like a force. When you do it from the gut, from the heart—what you really feel—it just starts happening. I wasn't doin' anything that I didn't feel. When I started doin' that, I just graduated a step at a time, and pretty soon I had that force. And I had good control. Then what I had to do was box it: If you got a product, once you get everything worked out in it, then you have to set it out there to sell it. I had the control, had the force, had the voice, and the know-how. And I had to learn how to present it to get it accepted and presented in a proper way, professionally. That takes time. And that takes a lot of doing. As I say, you got a lot of people with a lot of beautiful voices, but they come out and they just don't know how.

You took the time then to learn the business of music.

Oh, yeah. Well, every artist should do that if they're capable of doin' it. It'll keep you from being a total fool. You're not gonna be the smartest person in the world, ever, 'cause there's always somebody out there that knows a little bit more than you. But if you're quiet and listen, you can learn a lot. But you have to know that it's more to this than just jumpin' in front of the microphone, recordin' a record, or jumpin' in front of the microphone, gettin' onstage, while you leave everything to somebody else. Well, it's good to have management and agencies and all of that, but you should stay in touch with yourself, with what you are doing. I like to go and say, "Let me see that bank book or let me see the deposit thing. I wanna see this or let me look at the itinerary. Let me . . ."

Being just a puppet—you gotta be told when to get up in the mornin', what you gonna do, somebody else has laid out everything for you—to me, that's the wrong way. Because if somethin' goes wrong with that person, you could be totally lost. Or if they decide they wanna screw you out of whatever you've accomplished, that can be totally lost. Or if you decide that you want to make a change in somethin' and you don't know which way to go, then you are automatically lost. So I wanted to learn business end, and it can be very productive financially as well, so when you say somethin', you know what you're talkin' about. You can be more convincin' when you know what you're sayin'.

Nobody can sell you better than you.

Well, it shouldn't be. But sometimes that don't work either. But it's just knowing what's going on with yourself, with your business. I think that's important.

Is that one of the reasons that you and your wife, Pat, formed Camil Productions?

I formed it before she got into the picture. Then I trained her to handle it. But, yeah, that's one of the reasons. And that was some of Leonard Chess' teaching, from Chess Records. We were very close, and he wanted me to know about these things—publishing and all of that stuff. As soon as you get to be a old man, you won't be able to be up on the stage all the time forever. Which, I am. [*Laughs.*] But he said usually, unless you are very unfortunate, you're gonna always leave somebody behind. And with the things that you have accomplished, there can be somethin' left there that can have everything to continue to roll on when you gone. Said, it won't do you any good, but it'll do them some good. So he was talkin' about the publishing and stuff like that, and he was right.

So basically you have control of your own management and productions?

I have total control. Total control. Even though I don't take the credit for producing my records—Tommy Couch and Wolf Stephenson, they take the credit for that. It don't bother me because basically what Wolf does is sit behind the control board. And Tommy Couch might come in every once in a while. Nobody tells me what to do, how to do it, and I don't think they're qualified to do that anyway. But we don't have any problems; we got a beautiful understanding. It's a good relationship. And I tell them what I want to do, what I'm gonna do, and that's what we do. If they got some suggestions, I'll listen. If I think it's a good idea, we'll try it. If I don't, we won't.

What's the basic process when you start to record a new album now?

The basic process is gettin' the tunes together first. If I even solicit some songs, or, naturally, if I write 'em, I know exactly what they're about. And once I get my material together, I've made up my mind about what I'm gonna record, then I go in to the studio and sit down with the musicians and we work out the rhythm, the arrangements, for the tracks.

Do you make a cassette of the songs first?

Sometimes we have cassettes of 'em. But usually I have all of the cassettes when I go in. I'll do that basically myself, especially if it's somethin' I write. See, I take the guitar and put it on tape and we go in and then I always basically have ideas of how I want the lines to go for what the keyboard and bass is gonna do, and the tempos and what I want the drummer to do. And you've got good musicians down there. They are great musicians in Jackson, and the ones in Muscle Shoals as well. So you don't really have any problem with gettin' the arrangements. And once we get it down, we'll put it on tape. And if we need to make some adjustments or some changes, we do that, and once we get our tracks together, then I'll put demo versions of my voice on the tracks. Then I'll take a tape with me and live with it for a few days. Then I go back in by myself, overdub the master vocal.

When do you do the guitar?

I usually do the guitar durin' the same time we do the [basic] track. Or if it's somethin' I want to add, like this time I'm gonna do a few changes, I'll go back in and just do the guitar. But I'm basically finished. Everybody takes a month, month and a half, to do an album. And when I go in to do my overdubbing, I give myself two days. And I'm finished. I may go in and I do four or five songs, we take a break, go and relax, get somethin' to eat or whatever, come back in, I do three or four more songs, and then the next day I come in and do the other, three or four more. And that's it. And I'll take that tape with me, so we got a rough thing of what we got, and I listen to see if there's anything I need to make adjustments on. I was just talking to Tommy a little while ago about the next album, and Harrison [Calloway] is doin' the horns, workin' on the arrangements. So I guess maybe next week or somethin' they might put the horns on there, and then we got some back-ground voices to put on there. Then we're through with it.

Do you hear those arrangements, the voices and the horns?

Oh, yeah. Yeah, before they do anything with 'em. See, this is what I was talkin' about—control. If there's anything needs changing, I'll tell 'em that I think should be changed. They don't give me no problem. We've got a good understanding and mutual respect. They know that I know what I'm talkin' about. And I'm my worst critic. But I'm always aware of the fact that sometimes you can overproduce stuff. It's a very thin line there, and I try to watch that, 'cause you can try to make it too perfect and you lose that inner feeling of it. Sometimes that first take . . .

Is the one.

Yeah. And a lot of times if it's finished, I say, "Let's take another one, but don't erase that one. Just leave that one over there." And sometimes you go right back and do it maybe two or three more times, but you go back and listen to that first one and sometimes it's the best one. I did that with the album *Waiting for Little Milton,* with Stax. "How Strong My Love Is"—that was the semi-audition tape. I was showin' the guys, Bobby Manuel and Al Jackson and all, exactly how I wanted it to go. So we played it a while before I started singin' it, before I started doin' the monologue. Then I motioned to Dave Purple, the engineer with Stax, and we start-ed doing it. I did the monologue and did the vocal, and I said, "Now, this track is good, so I know I'm gonna come back later and do the master vocal." And when I came back in the studio to do the master vocal, I couldn't come close to that one. It just didn't work. So I just let it alone.

I understand you had the chance to record on B.B. King's Blues Summit.

Uh-huh, I did.

And that Bobby Bland did too, but neither one of you did it.

Well, I can't speak for Bobby, but the reason I didn't do it was because of the arrangement. The deal wasn't right. B.B. and I are good friends, but he don't own a record company. You know what I'm sayin'? So friendship goes so far. I've always tried to be businessman first, entertainer second. I hope it does be tremendously successful for him, but those slavery time deals—it don't faze me anymore just to say you're recording a record, just to say you were with B.B. King or whoever else is gonna be on there, without the proper residuals the way they're supposed to be. You know what I'm sayin'. So I declined, unless we could get a better deal, and they informed me what the other artists were doin', but I don't know if they was— maybe they were. Maybe that's good for them.

So that was just basically between you and MCA, then?

No. It wasn't no thing with MCA. It was with Sid Seidenberg [B.B. King's manager], his people. They put that together. So they were tryin' to look out for B.B. and themselves, which is fine, 'cause he's their artist. But I'm me—I got to try and look out for Milton. And you're not gonna tell me that you're gonna give me a flat fee to do nobody's album like that, unless you gonna give me a million dollars. Just go and give me the million, yeah, okay, go ahead. Then you don't worry about it. I'll take my chances now. But then they start talkin' about a few bucks here, and nothing ever to come forth from anything that happens, you sign away all your rights, all of your everything—to me, that's not good business. I just didn't think that was a good deal. You know, I didn't get upset with them. I hope they didn't get upset with me. And B.B. and I talk. He said, "Well, you know, it just couldn't be worked out. Maybe next time." I said, "Maybe next time." I would love to, but, we tried to work with 'em every way that we possibly could, and we just couldn't get together. Even Malaco had got involved in it, trying to get some sort of arrangement where, if we did a thing with him, he would in turn do a thing with us. And that didn't work out either, so I don't know. Everybody's tryin' to look out for themselves, which is nothin' wrong with that. But I deserve the right to look out for myself.

Camil Productions books Artie White, and you've done some recording on some of his albums too, haven't you?

Yeah, I've sort of made a semi-guest appearance as far as guitar player is concerned on some of his stuff. All of the stuff that I did guitar appearances on was stuff that I wrote for him, or one song in particular that I had done. Speaking of writing, have you heard the latest thing that I did for Koko Taylor? "Mother Nature." That's my song. She's doin' a helluva job on it too.

Have you played guitar on anybody else's albums?

You know, we was talkin' about people in the family, musicians. Well, there's only two musicians, but we do have another entertainer in the family—Charles Wilson. He had an album with Ichiban [*Blues in the Key of C*]. That's my nephew, my oldest brother's son. And I helped him on that album a little, played on a couple of tunes. Had the Angels at that time, let them do background vocals on it for him.

Do you have more than one band now? You spend part of the time in Chicago and part down South.

No. I only got one band. The All-Stars.

Where are they from?

Basically from Tennessee. Four of them is from Jackson, Tennessee. Tony Brown lives in Memphis now—that's the bandleader and the drummer. But Joe McKinney, keyboard player and vocalist, he lives in Jackson, and Al Wiler, the bass player, lives in Jackson, and Ron Hurt, he's a guitar player, he lives in Jackson, Steve Mayl the trumpet player, he lives in Memphis. So do Danny Worth—he's originally from Amarillo—and Lynette [Love], female vocalist, and the world-renowned Scrap Iron, road manager. Scrap been with me about 15 or 17 years, he say. So I don't know if it's exactly that long, but maybe so. Time moves so fast, man; it really does. So that, with the bus driver, John Gray, that's my unit. We cut it down some, you know—it was much bigger. But the economy got so bad, man, and when you talk about goin' overseas, you know, they cry so, and I can understand it because those tickets are extremely high. It was better for me to cut back. So we eliminated three people. We did use from nine to ten pieces.

How do you divide your time now between Chicago and Memphis and Greenville?

Well, I go home to Chicago—naturally I have to go home. I get home maybe two or three times a month, if I'm not too busy. If I'm real busy, then I get there when I can. And Memphis basically has been the same way. With the apartment in Memphis, I got my privacy and my comfort. This is like a second home for Pat and myself. So it's pretty convenient. I just might move here as a home one day. I had planned on doin' this one time right just before Martin Luther King was assassinated. And that set Memphis back, way back, so I just sort of froze that idea. 'Cause Stax was goin' big then, you know, all my business connections and everything, dealings I should say, was there.

Is Memphis a better place for you to work out of as far as your live performances go, the circuit that you tour?

Well, yes and no. It's good because basically my stronghold is in the South and the Midwest, so Memphis is more or less like a central located area. It's sort of easy for me if we're gonna play in the Midwest, if we're gonna play St. Louis or Chicago or Milwaukee or New York or Nashville or Washington, D.C. You notice how it's sittin'—it's basically centrally located. So it's pretty easy. I would hate to have to be living in California or Vegas somewhere and have to come out.

Do you ever play Las Vegas?

I never played the Las Vegas Strip. When we play Las Vegas, which we do every year, as close as we've gotten to the Strip would be Moulin Rouge. And it's black-owned. Other than that we play Town Tavern, which is black-owned. But no Strip. I played Bally's in Reno, once, and that was more or less a special function. We did one night, but they were very nice to us. It was great. But who knows? I guess it's been every artist's dream to become accepted across the board. And that would be one hell of a step for any artist to play the big rooms, like a Caesar's Palace or the Dunes. Other than Caesar's Palace, I think the Hilton was bringin' in probably more top names than anybody, and B.B. was hooked up into that at one time. One time on vacation, I went and spent a week out there with him. He introduced me to these people, supposingly the right people, and, you know, you get promises, but you don't have that inside connection. They're very polite, but they sort of like take care of their own. If you not in that clique, then your chances of gettin' in is kind of slim.

And now there's a whole new strip of casinos coming to Mississippi.

Yeah. Well, you got Las Vegas in Tunica. [*Laughs.*] But, really, it's just surprising to see Tunica. That'll blow your mind. Anybody had told me even four or five years ago that the ol' home state of Mississippi would be boomin' like this as far as the casinos are concerned, there's no way I would have believed it. Speaking of casinos, on the new album of mine that's coming out, we got a tune that a guy wrote and gave it to me to record, and out of all my experience of songs and this business, I think it's an instant hit. It's by Eddie Rolling, in Clarksdale, Mississippi, from the City Auditorium. And it's called "Casino Blues."

When you were playing in the Delta in the 1950s, Tunica was a gambling place already, wasn't it?

Well, it was somewhat of a semi-private type gambling thing, you know. Some of the counties in the state of Mississippi have certain people that were willing to bend the rules a little, for whatever reason. I wouldn't even want to comment on why or what was happening, but you had some places that you could do basically whatever you wanted to do as long as it wasn't too far out of step. And then other places was more or less like a mausoleum. But, yeah, the sharp, hustlin'-type gamblers would come from miles around, goin' to Tunica to gamble. There was a gentleman—unfortunately he's not with us any longer—called Hardface [Harold Clanton]. He was very popular, nice guy. I got a chance to meet him several times—real good people. But I understand he would like have these functions, and the people would come from miles around. They called 'em "skin balls" and "kotch balls" and different stuff.

Did you ever play for him? He hired a lot of bands.

I don't know if we ever really played for him, but it seem like I can vaguely remember maybe once—that's been so, so long ago, though.

Do you still have much of a following down where you came from, in Greenville?

No. In Greenville, it's a funny thing, but you can get too big for your former surroundings. People, without knowing it, put you on a pedestal themselves. But naturally you get the blame for it. You know what I mean. Sometimes we do pretty good, but I don't even know about playing too much around in my home town. We get more support anywhere around Greenville than we do in Greenville. Yeah. You get people that'll come out to another town—for instance, Indianola, B.B. King's home town—they'll come from Greenville to Indianola to catch my show. But if I play Greenville, they won't come out.

Have your bookings remained pretty steady through the years? Are you getting as many gigs now as you used to?

Well, we do all right. It could be better. But I work a lot, and I do a lot of hustling, you know. There's an old saying that I truly believe in: If you want your prayers answered, get up off your knees and hustle. So I do a lot of that, instead of just waiting for the promoters to call. We'll call a promoter or sometimes we'll use the company to back some of my shows. You just win some and lose some. Some get rained out.

So sometimes when you play an auditorium or hall in a little town like Clarksdale, you actually finance the whole show.

Most cases, yeah. A lot of times I'll be financin' the show. I'll get the services of other artists, you know. And it's just an investment. And sometimes you can be successful, sometimes you lose. I'm one that knows that. It's good to want to win all the time, but it's foolish to expect to win all the time. So that's another side of the business that you have to be willing to accept.

What do you think about what's happening with Beale Street in Memphis? Has the music scene improved there?

Yeah, for a lot of musicians that wasn't workin'. Because they didn't have nowhere to work. They can say what they want to say, but Beale Street has been extremely helpful for the musicians and for the city. It brought back the atmosphere of that tourist attraction. You know, there's more there now than to just come and look down on the river. You got entertainment, and that's basically what that area has been noted for, and I think it's great. And I know it's a lot of musicians that's working that wouldn't be workin' if there was no Beale Street.

Have you benefited from it?

Not really. Not other than seeing other musicians being able to earn some money, you know. It's good to know it's happening. But I've never been a local entertainer since the Mississippi days and the East St. Louis days. And even when I was livin' in East St. Louis, we still went out, and we really did go out on the road. So I never was depending on just the local gigs to survive. And a lot of people say, well, "You've lived in Chicago since '67?" But I never was local. I've lived in Chicago for years, but there are people that don't even know I live in Chicago right now, 'cause we just don't play the local clubs. I'm not sayin' that they can't afford us, but they just don't pay the kind of money that we ask for. So we don't play.

What's the audience that you appeal to the most?

I think it's more or less middle-aged. At one time that's all it was—middle-aged and the older people, you know. But now we've been able to accumulate some of the younger folk, white and black. But my audiences are still predominantly black, all over the country.

And it's predominantly women.

Oh, definitely so. In the audience you'll have 75 or 80 percent females. I love that, because they don't mind screaming and lettin' you know. Guys, they want to be macho and they don't say too much. Yeah, my ladies. I count on my ladies.

Do you think the ladies are the ones who buy the records too?

The most? I really would think so. I don't have any proof of that, of course, but I would think so.

So many blues artists today are playing predominantly for white audiences. Have you thought of going in that direction?

Well, they just have to accept me doin' what I do. If I'm to go in that direction, I'm not gonna change what I'm doing. I can't go onstage and play 12-bar blues, fast, slow, and medium, all night just because I'm gonna get paid for it. I'm cheating myself, then. I'm not sayin' that I won't do it, now, but I'm talkin' about constantly—I just can't do that. Then the joy of doing what I do would go out of it. Then I would get bored, and I just don't want to become a puppet-type artist. I want to enjoy what I do, and I would love for them to accept my music and my shows the way I present it.

For people who haven't heard you, how would you describe your music and your shows, other than the 12-bar blues?

It's a variety. I do some rhythm and blues, I do some pretty songs, we do standard stuff sometimes. It all depends. And the stuff is well put together. For instance, "Wind Beneath My Wings," stuff like that—to me, that's refreshing. And a lot of people might criticize you; they say, "Well, a blues artist ain't got no business singin' somethin' like . . ." Well, to me that's bullshit. You sing what you feel, what you can sing. Being versatile keeps you refreshing. I don't get bored with myself, I don't get bored with my music. But I think boredom is gonna set in eventually if every time you hit the stage you know you gonna do exactly the same stuff, over and over and over again. You might be makin' a lot of people happy out there, but what about yourself? Then nothing is a challenge anymore. And when you don't have a challenge, you're bored. And when you're bored, all sorts of crazy things happen to you. I truly believe that's why a lot of the entertainers get hooked into the drugs. They lookin' for some outlet of some kind, and somebody come along with just a little persuasion, and they always say that they can handle it. Nobody can handle it.

What are your favorite records of the ones you've done?

That's easy. Basically, all of them. And the reason I say that to you, and I'm not trying to be facetious or anything, is because, again, I flatly refuse to record anything that I don't like, and you know as well as I do, if you like somethin' then you can put all you got into it.

What more would you want to accomplish with your career before you're finished?

I would like to be accepted across the board. I would like for all people to hear my music. It's up to them whether they like it or not, but I would like for my music to be exposed, my talent, for people to know Little Milton. Then it's up to you whether you want to hang over there with him or not, musically speakin'. But at least I would have had that chance to let you sample what I got to offer. That's what I would like.

CONVERSATIONS WITH THE BLUES

B.B. KING AND JOHN LEE HOOKER

BY JAS OBRECHT John Lee Hooker and B.B. King, the world's preeminent bluesmen, met at Fantasy Studios in Berkeley, California, during March 1993 to record together for the first time. The session was for B.B.'s *Blues Summit* album, a star-studded affair featuring duets with Ruth Brown, Robert Cray, Albert Collins, Lowell Fulson, Buddy Guy, Etta James, and Koko Taylor. No track comes closer to celebrating B.B.'s Mississippi roots, though, than his mesmerizing "You Shook Me" with the Hook. ¶ While B.B. King and John Lee Hooker have similar backgrounds—both were raised in the Mississippi Delta, idolized the same musicians, migrated north, and began recording in the late '40s—their styles are remarkably dissimilar. A master of single-note solos punctuated with his signature hummingbird vibrato, B.B. has typically worked with a jumping, well-rehearsed big band. Much more of a lone wolf, John Lee tends to perform solo or with a small, hand-picked band, matching his deep,

deep voice with propulsive, trance-inducing rhythms or raucous boogies. Performing together, though, the bluesmen easily found common ground during the "You Shook Me" session.

A few weeks later, on April 4th, the B.B. King Band played the Circle Star Theater in San Carlos, California, just a few miles downhill from one of Mr. Hooker's homes. We had just 35 minutes between sets to score the interview and photo shoot. After a thrilling performance before a packed house, B.B. cooled down for a few minutes and then settled into an easy chair alongside the couch where John Lee Hooker was holding court. Their exchange began with a hearty handshake, and first appeared in print as *Guitar Player*'s September 1993 cover story, "B.B. & The Boogie Man: An Historic Conversation."

KING: John, you did me a great favor. I owe you one.
HOOKER: Look, B.B., there ain't nothin' in the world . . . I could never give enough to do what I did with you.
KING: Same here.
HOOKER: All my life, I wanted to sit down with one of the great masters.
KING: Oh, listen to that! [*Hitches up pants legs and pretends he's wading.*] Now go ahead, John. [*Both laugh uproariously.*]
HOOKER: He's a genius. I been on the stage with him a lot, but this is the first time I recorded with him. That was a pleasure too. I never will forget it as long as I live. We did "She Shook Me, Like the Hurricane Shook the Trees." We played the hell out of that tune.
   Was B.B. hard to work with?
HOOKER: Just like takin' candy from a baby. I been talkin' about wantin' to do that for years and years. We come up together—I don't want to say how far back—but we were youngsters. We would party, go out together. But something I dreamed of was wantin' to sit down with this man, side to side, face to face, and just play. It was such a tribute, to me, and I just felt it will be with me until the day that I go, tryin' to be with one of the greatest musicians alive, one of the most famous persons alive, and one of the nicest persons. He just like a lamb, he's so easy for people to talk to. He's such a nice gentleman. He'll talk to anybody, anywhere. He's not the kind of person that run, duck, and hide from his fans. That's what I like about him. I said, "Well, here's two *mah-sters.*" You know what a *mah-ster* is? Like two great men.
   The two of you have probably made more blues recordings than any other pair of artists in history.
KING: I would think so. I think John has made many more than I.
HOOKER: Oh, yeah, I have. I did a lot before he did.
KING: See, John was playin' when I was plowin'. I was still on . . .
HOOKER: What is a plow? [*Both laugh uproariously.*] You down there in Indianola.
KING: I was still in Indianola. Just come to Memphis, and John was makin' records then.
HOOKER: You know who I met you through? [Promoter] B.B. Beaman.
KING: B.B. Beaman, Atlanta, Georgia.
HOOKER: He was *thin* [*points to B.B.*]—weighed about 125, 130 pounds.
KING: Yeah.
   Is that before you had a hit with "Three O'Clock Blues"?
KING: Yeah. That was about the time of [1952's] "Three O'Clock Blues." I'd made about six or seven records before "Three O'Clock Blues." The first four sides I made

was for Bullet Record Company out of Nashville. It's funny—when I made those four sides, they went out of business. So I was that bad!

HOOKER: You know the first thing I heard from you? "C'mon, Baby, Take a Swing with Me."

KING: That was one of the first four sides.

HOOKER: [*Sings "C'mon, baby, take a swing with me."*]

KING: Yeah! Then after that I recorded several other tunes. I'd been listening to Lowell Fulson. I got his "Three O'Clock Blues," and when I did that, that was the one that did it.

HOOKER: Yeah, I love that Lowell Fulson. Still do. "Everyday I Have the Blues"—he really did a good job on that.

KING: Yeah. You know, a lot of people don't know it, but after Memphis Slim wrote it and recorded it, Lowell Fulson was the first one that ever made a hit on it. 'Cause I don't think Memphis Slim called it "Everyday I Have the Blues." He called it something else, but it was the same lyrics.

HOOKER: It was the same, same thing.

Do you hear traces of the Delta in John Lee Hooker's music?

KING: I don't think of John as a lot of people do. I think of John Lee Hooker as John Lee Hooker. And he play the blues like I heard 'em when I first started to play. And he *still* plays 'em. He plays the blues like John Lee Hooker does. It was two or three people that I knew before—in other words, that was older than John—and that was Lonnie Johnson, Robert Johnson, and Blind Lemon. I didn't know them all personally, but I did get a chance to meet Lonnie before he died. But these people, the way they played, they were so themselves. Well, in the modern times—and what I call modern times is the time I started to play—John Lee Hooker was one like that. Lightnin' Hopkins was like that.

HOOKER: Oh, yeah.

KING: You *know* who they were the minute you hear 'em play. When John Lee Hooker plays, it's like writin' his name: "I'm John Lee Hooker." So I don't necessarily think of it as Delta or city or any other type . . .

HOOKER: No, me neither. It's just blues.

KING: I just think of him as John Lee Hooker playin' the blues. It takes me home, of course. Yes!

HOOKER: You know people ask me about Mississippi blues, jump blues, big city blues, Mississippi boogie—it's all the blues to me. The blues is all over the world now. People that don't speak English love the blues. I'm so happy for myself and other blues singers out there that the blues is beginning to get so popular.

Is it better now than during the 1950s and '60s?

HOOKER: Oh, yeah! Are you kidding?

KING: Yeah, because nowadays people don't class you so much. It's not always thumbs-down, as it used to be. It used to be back in that time, in some places, the minute you say you a blues singer, it would be thumbs-down.

HOOKER: Yep.

KING: It was just like, "Oh, he's a nice guy, but he's a black."

HOOKER: Yeah, yeah.

KING: "He's a nice guy, but he's white." Nowadays there's not so much of that. You do find it, but . . .

HOOKER: It's very rare.

KING: The only thing I kind of take issue with a little bit is when people say, "Oh, that's city blues, that's Delta blues, that's Mississippi, that's Chicago," and so on. Muddy Waters, for example, is to me the first of the so-called Chicago blues.

HOOKER: That's right.

KING: Muddy left Mississippi, went to Chicago. John left and went to Detroit. I left and went to Memphis. We was still migrating, and wherever we went, our identity was pretty strong, like Muddy's was and the people surroundin' him. So you had a lot of the new guys to be born and started to play later. But to add to that, to me, blues is that label again. For instance, when John Lee made "Boogie Chillen," that wasn't blues. That was get up and get it!

HOOKER: Get up and go! That was the first rock!

KING: That's right!

HOOKER: You get rock and roll from that.

KING: So when people say blues and you say "Boogie Chillen," how in the heck could he be blue? He's havin' a ball! He's havin' a good time.

HOOKER: That's right.

KING: If I sing "I got a sweet little angel," I'm not blue at all.

But when you were growing up, wasn't blues used as party music in the Delta?

KING: It still is. You didn't only just hear it in the roadhouses. You could hear it on the streets of Indianola, Sunflower. You could hear it in most of the places around. Even in Memphis, you could find it on Beale Street then. When I first went to Beale Street, there was . . .

HOOKER: Look, B., okay, I want to say something now. The blues was here when the world was born and man and woman got together. That's called the blues. Rock and roll sayin' the same thing that me and this man are saying: "My woman gone, she left me." See, rock and roll, you have the same thing, you just cut 'em in a different form. Cut 'em hopped up and shined and polished up. You sayin' the same thing. You talkin' about a woman that left him. You could make it a ballad. [*Croons "My woman have left me, she gone away."*] You wouldn't call that blues, but we all sayin' the same thing. But I'm gonna tell it in a different way. You understand that, B.?

KING: Yeah. Another thing, see, like they use words today that if I'd have used them around home comin' up, I'd get smacked in the mouth.

HOOKER: Oh, you get you teeth knocked out!

KING: Like, for instance, if a guy say, "Man, make it funky!" If I said "funky" around home, my mother would knock the hell out of me! [*Both laugh.*]

HOOKER: [*Like he's talking to his mom*] "I wasn't makin' funky!"

KING: Now you hear guys quite often, and nobody pay any attention: "Here, make it a funky beat, man. Put a funky beat." Well, now we accept it. But during the times I was growin' up, man, that was a bad word. That was like a kid swearin' in the house.

HOOKER: It sho was. You say "funk" around my mother [*laughs*] . . .

KING: Smack you! "Boy, what are you saying?" Bam!

What can someone gain by listening to B.B. King play guitar?

HOOKER: Well, I'll tell you what he just told you about me. There only one B.B. There's a lot of imitations, lot of people pick up the guitar and follow this man— many, many of 'em. Used to be everybody that pick up a guitar try to sound like B.B. King. But you can tell when the *main* person, the main man, hit it. You know it's B.B. There was a boy in Chicago called Little B.B.

Andrew Odom?

HOOKER: I think so. Tried to sound just like B.B., but I know it wasn't B.B. He be playin' with my cousin a lot, Earl Hooker.

KING: Yeah! That's a bad man. Ain't been but one other person play slide like Earl Hooker. You know who that is, for me?

HOOKER: What, Bonnie Raitt?

KING: Bonnie Raitt. She is the best that is today, in my opinion.

HOOKER: Yeah. So let me finish. So you can tell in a minute if you hear B.B. from an imitation—I can. What they don't know, maybe—and I think you know this, B.B., you know it [*points to Jas*], and I know it—anybody can sound like John Lee Hooker, but it ain't the real John Lee Hooker. He make it real good, but I can come along and just *hit it,* and they gone. They'd rather see me. Like King: Lot of B.B.s out, but it ain't like the real one. You can tell it's B.B. King. He had one song I never will forget, but everything he do, I love it. Come to my house, I got stacks of B.B. I've got his six-pack. What they call it?

KING: The box set.

HOOKER: I got that. And he got one in there: "You breakin' my heart, and there ain't anything I can do."

KING: "There ain't nothin' I can do," yeah.

HOOKER: Boy, people used to play that thing!

It's interesting that both of you play Gibson's B.B. King guitar.

HOOKER: Yeah, I went and bought one.

KING: John has played so many different guitars through the years, though. So many different ones, and they all sound like John.

HOOKER: I got my identity. I got my style. I got nothin' to regret. I got nothin' to try to gain. I got nothin' to try to change. I wouldn't change for all the tea in China and all the money in the world. Who else you gonna sound like?

KING: It's just like one piano that sits over in the corner. If John go and play it, he gonna sound like himself, 'cause that's the way he play. If I go play it, I'm gonna sound like myself, 'cause that's the way I play. Now, if you don't believe it, you can hear Ray Charles play it or Pinetop [Perkins] or Elton John—they gonna sound like themselves. That's just one of the things that we're lucky we were blessed to be able to do—to be ourselves and do our own style. Like, when I heard John, I know it was John. If I hear Jimmy Reed, I know it's Jimmy Reed. My cousin Booker White—know it's him. Even in jazz and rock and roll, *certain* guys—not all—have that identity.

It's just like you as a journalist—certain styles people have of writing, singing, whatever they do. Like an architect or some of the Old Masters painters, da Vinci and all these guys that was doin' whatever they did. You *knew* the way that they did it. Same with the classical musicians—some of 'em you *knew.* Well, that's what I think of John. John couldn't change if he wanted to.

HOOKER: No.

KING: I couldn't change if I wanted to.

HOOKER: I'm like in the old way. I couldn't change if I wanted to. But *if,* like B.B. said, if I did it, it wouldn't be me.

KING: It's just like a way of talkin'.

Is it a waste of time for someone to try to play like you?

HOOKER: I would think so.

KING: Well, not really, John. Think about it. 'Cause when we first started—I know I did—when you first started, you heard somebody you liked.

HOOKER: Oh, all the time. I did, I did.

KING: So I liked somebody when I first started. We had our idols then, just like kids do today. So there's nothing wrong, I don't think, with listening to or trying to play like someone—*in the beginning.* But then as you learn, you start to think that there's already one of those. So you try to play as you play.

HOOKER: Don't play like Jimi Hendrix or B.B. King or somebody else. Play . . .

KING: As you feel yourself. Put you in it. We all like somebody. Everybody did. John, who was your idol? Who did you like when you first started to play?

HOOKER: Well, when I first started to playin', T-Bone Walker was my idol.

KING: Me too. [*Both laugh.*]

HOOKER: Boy, I used to follow him like a little puppy followin' his mama.

KING: Yeah, me too. I tell ya somebody else I liked—I was crazy about Lowell Fulson.

HOOKER: Whooo weee! "Everyday I Have the Blues," and then "Blue Shadows Fallin'."

KING: Even before that, Lonnie Johnson.

HOOKER: Oh, man!

KING: I was crazy 'bout him. Lonnie Johnson and Blind Lemon. Those were my people, along with T-Bone Walker.

HOOKER: Lonnie Johnson, he sing, but it didn't sound like deep blues. What would you call that?

KING: I don't know. He was so versatile, he did some of all of it. Lonnie Johnson. Now, most of the kids today are crazy about Robert Johnson. Now, I think Robert was great. I think he was really great, but he wasn't my idol.

HOOKER: No, he wasn't mine, either.

Why did Robert Johnson have a gold record in 1990?

KING: Well, that's from the same thing I just got through sayin'. Johnny Winter *swears* on him. [*Laughs.*] He says he's the greatest thing ever happened—that's what he told me. And a lot of the kids are crazy about it because they say it's authentic.

HOOKER: It's authentic. Let's put it like this: The man has been out of existence so long that they really built him up a lot just talkin' and writin' about it. Then when they did put it out, everybody went for it. He get so much publicity.

KING: There you go. You just hit it.

Publicity?

KING: Of course!

HOOKER: So much publicity!

Do you like Robert Johnson's music?

HOOKER: Some of it, yeah. I'm like B.B. I'm not a fan of his, though. But I listen to it.

KING: And I like some of the things he did. I just didn't idolize him like I did Lonnie Johnson.

HOOKER: Lonnie Johnson and T-Bone Walker. I would have dust his feet if he'd have said so.

KING: Here's what happens in a lot of cases. We'll take John as an example. John has been great since I first heard him. He was doin' great things all the time, but he couldn't get the publicity . . .

HOOKER: That's right.

KING: Until he got this manager he have today and Bonnie Raitt.

HOOKER: This man right there [*points outside the room to Mike Kappus of San Francisco's Rosebud Agency*].

KING: So that was the same thing with me. My manager's name is Sid Seidenberg.

So when Sid and I got together, that's when things started to change. Gosh, as great as Bonnie Raitt is—I've known her all her career—and as great as Robert Cray and Roy Rogers and a lot of the people we hear today are, John has been like that since before they were *born*.

HOOKER: It's true.

KING: You understand? But, thanks to John's manager and other people that know how to package it, the people that knew Robert, that knew Roy, that knew Bonnie—many of the people—now can hear John. Like a guy told me not long ago: He said his son came home and says, "Daddy, you got to hear this guy I just heard!" And his father say, "Who is it, son?" He said, "Oh, you wouldn't know him. You wouldn't know anything about him." Said, "Well, who is it, son?" He says, "You got to hear B.B. King! You just got to hear it!" [*Laughs.*] So his father said, "Son, long before you was thought of, I was listening to him." He said, "Yeah, but Dad, you don't know about things like that! This is new!" So it's the same thing. John and myself and a lot of us that's been playing for a long time just never got the break.

HOOKER: Never got the breaks, and then they just didn't push the blues like they should. They still don't, like they really should right now. But they pushin' more than they used to. They used to just push it under the cover.

Does recording with rock stars make that big a difference?

KING: Oh, yeah. Of course, of course! That's why I mentioned Bonnie Raitt. It's like U2 and myself. Had it not been for U2, a lot of people wouldn't know. But thanks to Sid, we were able to have this happen.

HOOKER: The same thing I say about my manager. Thanks to Mike. You know, I had give up recordin'. I said, "I'm not gonna record no more." The record companies, they rob you blind. Like Modern Records and Vee Jay and them—they just robbed you. You know they was takin' everything you had. Well, I think you know that too. [*B.B. nods and laughs.*] They were! I said, "I'm gonna get out of the business." And I had been out for about eight years. I was still with Mike. Mike says, "Let's get you a record deal." He worked *hard,* got me a record deal. Got me pulled together. And that's how I come to be . . . I never was forgotten, but I got disgusted. I said I wasn't gonna record anymore.

KING: See, Mike's a very good man, as Sid is to me. They always lookin' out for things that'll help us, that will get the publicity that we . . .

HOOKER: Never was able to get.

KING: Now, don't misunderstand me. Nobody gave Bonnie nothin'. Nobody gave Robert Cray anything. They earned it. But today they are superstars. What I'm trying to say is that had people known John in the beginning as they have known him now, he would have been a superstar years ago.

HOOKER: Right. Just wasn't gettin' that push.

Like Muddy Waters, you're both making very good records during the second halves of your careers.

HOOKER: Well, Muddy gone now, but he . . .

KING: But he was makin' them then, man!

HOOKER: Yeah, he was makin' them, but they wasn't bein' pushed.

KING: Even today—take it from me—if I wasn't on the record with U2, nobody would have played B.B. King.

I don't know about that.

KING: Can you take my word for it?

Yes, but I'd listen to your record even if it were just you and an acoustic guitar.

HOOKER: *You* know he's a monster. You know how good he is. But you're just one.

KING: Look, I'm not trying to be false modesty or anything of that sort. But today listen to the radio. Watch the TV. And every time that you hear a new B.B. King record play . . . Of course, I don't think it will be like that with this album John and I just got through doin'. I think this is gonna be played.

HOOKER: I think so too. I'm prayin'.

KING: But prior to that and prior to John and Bonnie Raitt—understand?—I bet you wouldn't hear a John Lee Hooker record played.

HOOKER: I don't think so either, B.

KING: I have to eat my words. I said that if I ever had a record played on MTV, I would eat the cover. [*Both laugh.*] So I had to eat my words because they did play me with U2. We did "When Love Comes to Town," and they played it. I said, "Well, I'll be darned. I might as well go start eatin' covers." [*Laughs.*]

HOOKER: Gettin' back to Bonnie Raitt. She was on about 20 years that nobody ever knowed her. Remember that?

KING: Yeah. Used to be an opening act for me.

HOOKER: Me and her used to party together. She used to drink liquor like water.

KING: One of the nicest people I ever met, though. One of the nicest.

HOOKER: Oh, she's nice. Whoooo wee.

KING: She's a great person. Nobody gave her anything. She earned it. I was so happy to see it.

HOOKER: Nobody give her nothin'. She earned it. Like this man here, nobody give him nothin'. He earned it. Nobody give me nothin'. I earned it. But they just beginnin' to play us now, but not like they should.

KING: I think what we're talkin' about now is, today the blues is known better. One of the things I take issue with quite a bit, you hear people say, "Oh, the resurging of the blues."

HOOKER: Resurgin'! It ain't never went nowhere!

KING: It never left, as far as I can tell. I've worked on an average of 300 days a year since '56, many concerts every year. What they fail to realize, though, is that when you have superstars like Eric Clapton or Robert Cray or Jeff Healey or Stevie Ray Vaughan, when they came on the scene, they had their new thing goin' *and* they played the blues, so that made a difference. But they hadn't left nowhere. It's just each time we got a new disciple.

Does it seem like there's something fundamentally wrong with this?

HOOKER: No, it don't bother me. Not at all. I don't know what about B.

KING: No, the only thing that bothered me is that we didn't have nobody like that at first.

HOOKER: That's right.

KING: That was the thing that bothered me. We wasn't recognized. So today, to find that we have some people that's playin' the blues and not ashamed to say it . . .

HOOKER: Right. Then they had the right people to push it.

KING: That today makes me happy. Very happy.

HOOKER: Me too.

KING: So today we got superstars. John's a superstar today.

HOOKER: B.B. I know could have been. . . That older stuff we did? It should have been . . .

KING: There was a lot of good stuff done. When you did "Boogie Chillen," man, everybody should have known about it.

HOOKER: Yeah. And "Boom Boom," "Dimples," and stuff like that.

Do you remember creating "Boogie Chillen"?

HOOKER: Yeah, I do. I used to hear my stepfather, when I was a kid. My style—I got it from him. He'd do stuff like that [*sings "boom-da-boom, boom-da-boom, boom-da-boom" while snapping fingers*], "Boogie Chillen," different things. I do remember that. I got people to do something like what rested in him. Everything I do is direct from Will Moore, my stepfather. He play just like I'm playin' today. I learnt from him. He played that kind of stuff—foot stompin'.

Open G?

HOOKER: Yeah. "Mama don't allow me to . . ."

KING: "Stay out all night long."

HOOKER: "Boogie Chillen" and all that kind of stuff. It used to be "Boogie Woogie," and I changed it to "Boogie Chillen." I didn't know it was gonna . . . You know, it was just a old funky lick I found.

KING: But it was a monster hit.

Were you writing about your own mom?

HOOKER: Nah, it's just a song. There's so many kids, their mama don't allow them to stay out all night long, you know. I couldn't just be talkin' about my mama. Lot of people have kids don't stay out all night long, but they gonna stay out anyway. [*Sings "Mama didn't allow me to stay out all night long."*] I didn't care what she didn't allow, they would stay out anyways! They knew they would get a beatin' when they get home, but they still stay out.

Does playing guitar bring you as much joy and satisfaction as it did when you were younger?

KING: Yes. I think it brings even more today . . .

HOOKER: It do.

KING: Because I'm more concerned about what I'm trying to do. Then, I was just havin' fun.

HOOKER: Havin' fun, drinkin', stayin' out.

KING: [*Laughs.*] As you said, stayin' out all night long. But now today I'm concerned about it, because if I get out there now and I hit something that don't sound right, I know that there are a lot of people that are listening to me.

HOOKER: Critics.

KING: Well, not only that, but a lot of the kids that are listening to me. Reminds me of a story I heard once. There was a trumpet teacher teachin' trumpet to his class. And one little boy, the teacher was tryin' to teach him to play non-pressure, where his jaws wouldn't balloon out. So the teacher was talkin'. So there's one little smart egg in the class [*laughs*], and the teacher say, "Why are you playin' like that? I keep tryin' to tell you that when your jaws pop out like that, that's not good." So the little smart egg, he said, "Well, Dizzy Gillespie plays like that!" So the teacher thought about it for a moment, and he says, "Yeah, but there's only *one* Dizzy Gillespie." So I think about it a lot of times now when I'm playin', that the kids out there idolize me, like me. And not just kids, but people that are starting to

play or the people that's already playin' and maybe came out to admire what I do
or be critical of what I do. And if I make them wrong notes or put them in the
wrong way or hit something I don't intend to hit . . .

HOOKER: B., I have never heard nobody as true as you, man. Nobody.

KING: Well, thank you. But I make mistakes, though. So when I make 'em now . . .

HOOKER: Everybody do.

KING: Yeah. To answer your question, when I make a mistake now, it hurts [*thumps
chest*]. Oh, yes. It hurts.

HOOKER: You're right.

KING: Because, see, I'm supposed to be professional—that's what I think to myself.
I'm supposed to entertain. I'm supposed to rehearse, practice enough to not do that.

HOOKER: But some people, when you look out into the audience, they don't even notice
what you did, they so excited about lookin' at him. But he know it [*points to B.B.*].

KING: Yeah, and that hurts, don't it?

HOOKER: Yeah, that's right. They may not know, but you know you made that mistake. And you lookin' back at the fellows, and some of them look like they kind of
smile, you know, because they know I did.

KING: But when you're able to run it into something else . . .

HOOKER: To cover up.

KING: Yeah, like you and I, say we talkin', and we got a male conversation goin' on
and all of a sudden a lady walked in, you gotta change it into something else!
[*Laughs.*] That's the way it is with playin'. Here's another thing: When guys start to
gettin' to be our age, John, they're not quite as fast as they used to be.

HOOKER: I know.

KING: And as you get a little older, you think more about it. Remember when you
was young and somebody said, "Come here," you get up and start running? Now
you think about it—do I really want to run, or will I just walk on over there?

HOOKER: Yeah, walk to the car!

KING: And a lot of the youngsters that come around can play rings around me—
this is not false modesty!—but what they do, they think of what I did that gave
them a chance to think beyond that. You think Graham Bell thought of what his
work would be doin' today? There was that first foundation. I was able to go and
see one of my idols, Lonnie Johnson, and I was able to shake his hand and thank
him. Because he was one of the people that made me want to play. I don't know.
Here I am, still doin' somethin' with it.

HOOKER: Well, B., time for me to go.

Is this the first interview you've done together?

KING: Yes. The very first.

HOOKER: I've did it with a lot of people, but this is the first I ever did with B.B. And
I couldn't wait for tonight to come!

KING: It's an honor to me. What you are doing for us will even help it to go further. We
appreciate it. Thank you. And thanks to a couple of other guys named Mike and Sid.

MUDDY WATERS
AND JOHNNY WINTER

BY TOM WHEELER Muddy Waters and Johnny
Winter were friends. As onstage performers and studio col-
laborators, the Mississippi blues bossman and the Texas rock
star were also partners. But there were additional bonds perhaps even more profound than their deep, mutual respect as
fellow professionals. Johnny's unbounded admiration for his
mentor was matched by the appreciation that Muddy felt for
his follower's efforts on behalf of the blues. This 1982 interview covers the Waters/Winter Grammy-winning album projects, as well as Muddy's techniques, tunings, equipment, and
recordings. Throughout the conversation the interplay
between the two guitarists reveals a glimpse of their unique
relationship, and outlines the historical impact of Muddy
Waters' blues odyssey from the Mississippi Delta to Chicago's
South Side.

WINTER: Well, the first thing that you've got to understand is
that I taught Muddy how to play guitar [*laughs*].

WATERS: Hey, that's right; don't laugh. You're still teaching me now. You play eight notes to my one!

When did you first get together?

WINTER: We met in Austin, Texas. We were on the same bill at a club called the Vulcan Gas Company, which later turned into the Armadillo. I can't tell you how excited I was to be on the bill with Muddy Waters. He's been my idol since I was 11 or 12, so I was there with my camera and my tape recorder. I was so honored just to meet Muddy, I wasn't about to ask to sit in.

WATERS: I asked to sit in with *him* [*laughs*]. I said, "That guy up there onstage—I got to see him up *close*." We didn't play together on the show, but we got together afterward and jammed a little and talked. Johnny had this old National, and I explained that I had played one kind of like that, so right off we had something in common.

WINTER: The first time we ever worked together was in 1974 or '75 on a TV show called *Soundstage*, in Chicago. It was a tribute to Muddy, with a lot of people that

Muddy had influenced—Junior Wells, Dr. John, Buddy Miles, me, Mike Bloomfield, Koko Taylor, and a few others. It was then that Muddy and I realized that we could definitely work together. When I finally got a chance to produce records with him, my whole thing was to make the record that Muddy wanted to make, with the musicians he wanted to work with. If Muddy gets pissed off, things change. He's the boss. My job as producer is to get things sounding right to him. And it's been very special and unusual, because we don't disagree.

WATERS: Our first album together was *Hard Again*. I was leaving the Chess label, and my manager went to CBS, and just like that they said, "Well, you should go to Johnny Winter's label, Blue Sky."

WINTER: Epic is part of CBS. They wanted Muddy, but they weren't sure exactly how to produce him. They distributed Blue Sky, so they asked me if I was interested. I said, "Hell yes! Let's do it!" It was that easy.

WATERS: And we didn't practice. We just got in there, and we'd run over a song and put it down. We caught it. The whole album took two days. We would've been done before, but Johnny would get tired and say, "Well, let's come back tomorrow" [*laughs*].

WINTER: I couldn't believe how he was running me ragged. The studio was downstairs and the control room was upstairs, and I was running back and forth saying to myself, "God *damn*, Muddy, you're gonna kill me." I figured we'd play about four hours, take a break, and work some more. But Muddy said, "No, I don't want to take no break, man!" [*Laughs*.] It was one song after another, and they kept getting better and better. They'd run it down once just to go through it, but I'd go upstairs and listen to that first take and know that there was no reason to do it again. That's so rare, when everything's *right* the first time.

And Hard Again *was a Grammy winner in 1977?*

WATERS: All of our records were Grammy winners, all three of them. *I'm Ready* was in '78, and then came *Muddy "Mississippi" Waters Live* in '79. *King Bee* is our fourth one together.

You've mentioned that your guitar style was influenced primarily by two people.

WATERS: Son House and Robert Johnson. I can tell you a little bit more about Son House than Robert Johnson. Robert's records were out in 1937, like "Terraplane Blues" and "Walkin' Blues." I was already doing my thing then, and I never followed him around to hear him or anything like that. But Son House I did follow around and listen to. And I do believe that the way Robert played, you could hear some of Son House in him. Robert was putting in more notes. It was about three notes to one. Robert was one of the greatest of the slide players.

WINTER: Muddy's told me that there were a lot of players to learn from in the Delta— not just the ones you've heard of, but many who never got recorded for whatever reason. Being even as great as Muddy is just isn't enough by itself. He's also very stable and very intelligent, and he held it together for many, many people, always working towards making it. Some good musicians were real itinerant, never worked at the same place twice, just didn't care, couldn't hold a band together . . .

WATERS: Not with Krazy Glue [*laughs*].

WINTER: But Muddy knew he was damned good, even among all those others. When he was coming up, that music was everywhere.

WATERS: All over the place. Great people you never heard of who just didn't take it for a career. They'd just pick up the guitar and play it like heck and then put it down and forget it. I'd listen, and maybe I'd do some things a little different, maybe learn a few notes to add, and then other people would do it different ways and add more notes till you get up to this boy here—Johnny will stick about 18 notes in there instead of three [*laughs*].

Before you went up to Chicago, were you playing acoustic exclusively?

WATERS: Yes, starting with a Stella, and I had a Silvertone when I came North. First electric I got was in 1944. That's when I hooked into it, and it was a very different sound, not just louder. I thought that I'd come to like it—if I could ever learn to play it. That loud sound would tell everything you were doing. On acoustic you could mess up a lot of stuff and no one would know that you'd ever missed. So electric was really rough.

WINTER: What made you get into electric?

WATERS: People were talking louder in the neighborhood taverns around Chicago, where I'd be sitting and picking my guitar. The people would be drinkin' a little booze and talkin' loud, and you couldn't get your sound over them.

WINTER: Hasn't changed much [*laughs*]. You just have to get bigger amps. Back in Chicago, were they amplifying harps before guitars?

WATERS: Where I was playing, they did it just about the same time. Rice Miller had a little microphone for his harmonica even before Little Walter was doing it.

WINTER: Rice Miller was one of the Sonny Boy Williamsons, the second one.

WATERS: And when I first got to Chicago, the first Sonny Boy [John Lee Williamson] would blow over the house mike sometimes. So the electric thing had started a little bit.

What was the Chicago club scene like when you arrived in 1943?

WATERS: It was going already, with people like Tampa Red, Memphis Slim, Big Maceo, Lonnie Johnson, and Big Bill Broonzy. Those people were heavy in Chicago.

WINTER: But boy, they didn't sound *nothing* like the blues Muddy started up there.

WATERS: No, it was different from what I do. I recorded for Columbia early on, and did a thing for Decca, even before I started recording with Chess. But I had a hard time trying to get it through.

Why was it difficult at first?

WATERS: Because I brought up the *deep-bottom Mississippi Delta blues,* and blues like Big Bill Broonzy's was entirely different. Mine was a rustier sound, a grittier sound. Big Bill and Memphis Slim and some of the others was singing very clear, and maybe they'd use a saxophone.

WINTER: It's funny that one little area of the Delta would have a sound all its own, but you could go just a few hundred miles one way or the other, and it wouldn't sound the same at all. You can't exaggerate how distinctive Muddy's playing is. In my band, if I stop playing, the main feeling keeps on going, but when Muddy stops, the whole feeling can change, because he's got that Mississippi thing and the Chicago sound all wrapped up together. It's pure style. Muddy Waters is Chicago blues, which is electric and has that group sound to it. But he's always kept the feeling of the Delta. And he's a very smart player. He'll do this one hot lead, sort of an Elmore James type of lick that you hear a lot, but Muddy will do it differently and put it in where you don't expect it, and it's just perfect and really grabs you in a new way. Many bluesmen overdo it, but Muddy never does.

What about his impact aside from influencing guitarists?

WINTER: One of the most important things Muddy did was to set up a particular instrumentation—piano, two guitars, bass, drums, and harp. And it became a model, with variations, for many who followed. So this was all part of the thing he did in Chicago. I read in a book once where down in the Delta Muddy asked his sister if she thought anyone would like his kind of music up in Chicago, and she said. "No, they don't want to hear that."

WATERS: When I got up there I had to keep feelin' around, testing out Aristocrat, which became Chess. Before, I had done some things for the Library of Congress. They weren't going to bring it out, but Pete Welding brought it out on his own label, Testament. It's called *Down on Stovall's Plantation* [later reissued by MCA as *The Complete Plantation Recordings*.]

WINTER: That's a great record, just amazing.

WATERS: That was made when I was in Mississippi with Son Simms, Louis Ford, and Percy Thomas. We had mandolin, violin, and two guitars. Then I recorded for Aristocrat in '46. I made "I Can't Be Satisfied" and "Feel Like Going Home," and they came out in '47 and went over good and quick. And I was with Chess all the way until I got over with Johnny at Blue Sky just a few years back.

WINTER: We tried to capture the feeling of some of those old sounds on the records that we did together.

Of all your records, which ones stand out, particularly for the guitarist?

WINTER: The first one I ever bought was *Best of Muddy Waters*. That's good, and you can hear him in a small group setting.

WATERS: That record, and the first one I did with Johnny—*Hard Again*—are the two best albums I ever did.

WINTER: *Muddy Waters at Newport* is a real good live one from 1960. But there aren't any bad ones.

WATERS: I got some good stuff even on some bad ones [*laughs*].

WINTER: You can't go wrong with a Muddy Waters album. The only thing I didn't care for as well was when they added all that brass.

WATERS: When I did *Brass and the Blues*? Well, I liked that better than that *Electric Mud* record I did.

Wouldn't you consider Electric Mud *a rock and roll album?*

WATERS: I don't know what to consider it [*laughs*]. We ain't even going to get into it.

When it came out about 12 years ago, it made a lot of waves and people took notice, but your own opinion was, "Man, that's dogshit."

WATERS: That's what it was! But you're right—when it first came out it started selling like wild. It got up to around 80,000, and then they started sending them back. They said, "This *can't* be Muddy Waters with all this shit going on—all this wow-wow and fuzztone."

WINTER: It's worth buying just for the picture on the inside, though. See, the business people thought it'd work, because it had that hippie thing. Those people don't think the same way. They thought they'd take the blues and make it *modern.* You know: "Hey, if Muddy Waters is the big influence behind the Rolling Stones and all these people, all we gotta do is get the real man and put these hot modern players on there." They didn't understand the blues.

WATERS: I think Johnny knows more about my music than I do. When we went to do *Hard Again,* he was bringing up things I had forgot all about, and he was play-

ing them just like they're supposed to be played, and I sat back and said, "*Well!*"
He wanted to go back to the old sound, but I didn't know he went so far back. He
knew about the tunings, phrasing, slide, picks, and everything.

WINTER: One thing I always wondered was how you got into thumbpicks.

WATERS: It was after I came to Chicago and was having that problem of getting
myself heard. I was banging my hand all up, so I went to a thumbpick. That still
wasn't loud enough, so I started playing electric. I used to play with a metal
thumbpick, but the sound is too tinny to me, so I use a plastic one. No way could I
use a regular flatpick.

When you switched to electric, did you change your style?

WATERS: No, no. But I did have to learn how to put that style into an electric guitar.
Even today it hasn't changed that much. Only now I play with a band, and I give
everybody a chance to play. I tell them, "I'm not going to hold you back. You go
out there and make the people love you. *I* love you, but I can't make the people
love you. *You* do that."

WINTER: Muddy's a lot different than many leaders. He's proud of his musicians,
and he goes out of his way to help them. That's just one of the reasons why he's
the father, one of the reasons I just glow when I talk about him. He gave Otis
Spann his chance, plus James Cotton and Little Walter, Luther Johnson, and just so
many others.

WATERS: Back in Mississippi it was usually just me, or maybe two of us.

WINTER: His style was already worked out by the time he got to Chicago. You did
have somebody show you how to fret a little bit, didn't you?

WATERS: Yeah, Blue Smitty [Claude Smith]. See, I was mostly playing slide. When I
started working with Blue Smitty and Jimmy Rogers, I learned a few note things. It
didn't change my style, just improved it a little by putting some finger work on
there. Smitty couldn't slide good, but he showed me how to go up there and do
something else, and I put them together. I thank him today for it, because it was a
very, very good improvement he did for me, because I didn't have to try to do
everything with the slide by itself.

WINTER: A lot of the older guys never would use those other fingers, just the slide.

Did you try actual bottlenecks before you began using a metal slide?

WATERS: Yeah, I learned how to break my bottle. First I'd get me a bottle that I'd
think was going to fit my finger. I had the slide in the wrong place at first, on my
second finger, and later I put it on my little finger. So I had to get the right pop bottle to fit. Then I'd wrap some string around the neck and soak it in kerosene and
light it and let it burn till it go out. Then you just rap it, and it breaks off just right.

WINTER: Every time *I* tried doing it like that I'd make the biggest mess [*laughs*].
There's a real trick to it.

WATERS: It's a short slide, because I don't play as many strings at once as Johnny. I
play single strings mostly.

WINTER: I was so amazed to hear Muddy on record, because I couldn't see how in
the world he could play slide and then be fretting it at the same time. I thought he
was going back and forth between a regular guitar and a steel guitar on his lap or
something. As much as I got off his records, I learned a lot more just sitting across
from him and watching. It just knocked me out to see these things up close.

Can you tell us some of those things you picked up?

WINTER: Hell no! I don't want nobody else learning them [*laughs*]! No, really, there's a lot, but the main thing is hard to put into words, and that's feeling. And besides, there are some things that you can't learn.

WATERS: No matter what you do, some things come out all different, just your own. It's like singing. Your face, and what you're doing on your face, will change the tone of your voice. That's where my tone is. It's like Johnny will go [*singing, with an ascending melody*], "Goin' down walkin', walkin' through the park." But I'll go way *down* at the end there, because my voice will go down there and Johnny won't go that deep down.

WINTER: Out of all the blues singers, I don't think anyone can do more with one note than Muddy. And every note is blues—whether voice or guitar. Every time I hear him, it's like the first time.

Do you consciously play vocal-style lines on guitar?

WATERS: Yes. I can't make the guitar say as much as my voice, but I try to get it as close as I can. I'm no hell of a guitar player, not the best guitar walkin' around the streets, but one thing I have tried is to make the guitar sound like my voice. See, I could never do like what Johnny does. But the *feeling* that I put into my guitar—a lot of players can't put it there.

WINTER: A typical guy now will play so many notes.

WATERS: That one note of mine will say something that the other guy can't say. The tone that I lay in there, the other guy can't get it out with 12 notes.

WINTER: Muddy will sing a line, and then he'll answer on guitar, almost like a second voice.

WATERS: That's from the Delta style, definitely. Me and my guitar, we have a conversation and talk together.

Is the guitar's tone as important as your vocal tone?

WATERS: Oh yes, it *has* to be there. I think on any guitar, if I could make a note on it, you could still know it's Muddy. But I really can't do nothing with other people's guitars. A lot of the sound is the amp. I'd rather always use my own amplifier. It's the Fender with the four ten-inch speakers, the Super. Even if I forgot my own guitar and had to borrow one, I could make the sound come out of that amplifier. I don't like the Twin—different sound. I like some of Johnny's amps. They're Music Mans, and them little guys is *tough,* man.

Do you ever pick up your acoustic anymore?

WATERS: I got two or three around the house, but I don't even hardly pick them up. You get lazy when you get up in age.

Do you remember your first electric?

WATERS: I really can't remember the name, because I bought it secondhand. It was one of those off brands. Jimmy Rogers and me were playing a club, and I left it there overnight. We got back and Jimmy's amp was gone and so was my guitar. So we couldn't work. When I actually started making records, I had a Gretsch with a DeArmond pickup on it.

WINTER: What was the archtop you were playing on the cover of *Muddy Waters at Newport*?

WATERS: That was John Lee Hooker's, and I just grabbed it for the picture. My own guitar was up onstage, the same red Telecaster I got now. I got that one in 1957 or 1958.

WINTER: That's Muddy Waters' guitar, and it won't let anyone play it but him. You pick it up and it just says, "No!" You can't believe the action. My own action stays real high, but it's nothing compared to Muddy's.

WATERS: Yeah, I got a heavy hand. Everyone says, "Oh man, the strings are too high! What're you doing?" [*Laughs.*] A lot of guys want to squeeze and bend their strings up, like B.B., so they have the strings real low. My strings are *heavy*, like a .012 or a .013 for the first one. I don't need to worry about bending, because I can slide so high up there. But don't let Johnny talk about that slide—he's a dangerous man with a slide!

WINTER: My strings aren't so heavy, so I can't quite get that biting sound like Muddy. The heavier the strings, the better your chance of getting a good sound, definitely.

Are you playing mainly in standard tuning now?

WATERS: Mostly standard, 'cause it's tough if you're waiting in between songs to tune to G or A. And I'm too lazy to carry two or three guitars around like Johnny [*laughs*]. He's still a young boy—he can pull that stuff around. What would I look like with two or three guitars like these kids? I don't need to be bothered with that. I got my one old guitar.

WINTER: I ain't heard no one complain.

Have you ever modified your Telecaster?

WATERS: Yes, in the '50s a guy in Chicago made me a neck for it, a big stout neck with the high nut to raise up the strings for slide. I needed to strengthen it up because of the big strings, and I think that the big neck has a lot to do with the big sound.

WINTER: You switch that thing on the front pickup and it's got so much bass it'll just about blow the amp up.

Sometimes during a verse—maybe just going into the turnaround—you'll switch the toggle from the bass or middle position to full treble and just let 'em have it.

WATERS: Yeah [*laughs*], I like to do that alright.

WINTER: I've never seen anyone do that so effectively, so dynamically. Sometimes he'll go the other way—like from a solo to backing up his voice, and he'll go from the brightest treble to the bass. He'll do it anywhere it works, going back and forth real quick, man, sometimes a couple times in one solo. One thing I always wondered, Muddy— there's a clicking sound you make, like the sound of the slide hitting the frets.

WATERS: I know what you mean. People don't know that I do a lot of this [*pats the strings against the pickup with his right hand*]. I do a lot of *pattin'*.

WINTER: And a lot of times I'll mix it up louder—because it just fits in there perfect. Those little things make a difference.

You've seen the blues go through many changes. Where do you see it going from here?

WATERS: I've seen it go up and down many times. Everything's improved over the years, and it's still changing. But if you're an old standard blues singer like me, my changed sound is still the same basic Muddy Waters style. If you change it too much, it's not blues no more. You can send it into rock and roll or even disco. You don't want to get too far away from it.

WINTER: I think people are moved by the blues because it's communication and emotional expression more than just music. Some people think it's about everybody sitting around and feeling bad together, but it's not at all. We have common problems, and you feel *better* by hearing that other people also have them, and hearing what they think about it and what they're doing about it: I don't have enough rent money, and neither does this guy here. Anybody can understand the blues if they halfway try. It might be braggin' blues about how cool you are, or down-and-out blues. No matter what kind, talking to people is more important than how many notes you play. John Lee Hooker is no Chet Atkins, but he gets up there and gets the point across.

Johnny, you've done a lot to help the blues continue.

WINTER: Well, a lot of people have been working their butts off all their lives, and the major record companies don't seem to care. So my commitment is to help make sure that people out there who want to play blues music will have a label and a way to be heard. I want to make sure that someone's not just playing great at home by himself because he can't get anyone to record him.

WATERS: And that's a heck of a move Johnny's making, because the big companies forget about the old blues singers, don't care. "What do we want with him? He can't sell enough records. We ain't got time." They look for somebody else.

WINTER: The younger guys can get out there and hustle, like Muddy and I did and everybody else. But you get *tired* of hustling when you're 60 or 70 years old, and people who might have started rock and roll or based their whole careers on what you did just don't even seem to remember. It pisses me off. You see someone who's still great, and during certain periods no one's interested in recording him. There's no excuse for it.

What kind of shape is the blues in right now?

WATERS: It's in good shape.

WINTER: It just keeps going. People say sometimes that they think the blues is dying. But it ain't going to die.

WATERS: It may change around a little bit, but it won't die. See, the groove was here [*long pause*] before time.

WINTER: During the '60s with all the hippie stuff, when the Rolling Stones and all the younger white musicians were acknowledging their gigantic debt to the older blues musicians, kids were listening to the blues. Their idols were telling them how great it is—guys like Eric Clapton and Mick Jagger. In a way it's more real now. They buy it because they really know who Muddy Waters is, not because Mick Jagger recorded a Muddy Waters song. I feel better about it now, but it did help in the '60s—anything to make people aware of where it came from, that's important. Muddy's the father. It's a debt that'll never be repaid in full. Lately I've felt great because he's finally starting to get the kind of recognition he's deserved for so long.

WATERS: Thanks to you.

WINTER: No, no, no. I ain't done anything. [*Johnny leaves the room to get his guitar.*]

WATERS [*whispering*]: That's my son.

BUDDY GUY AND
JOHN LEE HOOKER

BY JAS OBRECHT It was too good an opportunity to pass up. John Lee Hooker, for nearly a half-century the driving force in boogie blues guitar, and Buddy Guy, the baddest of the Chicago sharpshooters, were coming to L.A. to perform at a star-studded NARAS benefit honoring Carlos Santana. After several phone calls, both bluesmen agreed to do an interview together an hour before the show. ¶ At the concert, John Lee sat down with his Epiphone for a mesmerizing version of "The Healer" with Carlos Santana, who produced and played on Hook's hit record of that song. Hooker then handed his guitar to Santana, walked to the edge of the stage, and brought the crowd to its feet with a hand-raising, hip-shaking boogie. Later in the show, Buddy Guy floored Santana and everyone else with a version of "Blues for Salvador" that began with Buddy copping Carlos' recorded version note-for-note. Grandstanding, Guy then improvised gloriously while entertaining the crowd with theatrics such

as playing one-handed, bringing his glass-clear tone from a boom to a whisper, and making huge intervallic leaps. The entire time he remained completely relaxed and locked in on the song.

Later that week, Buddy's *Slippin' In* won the Grammy Award for Best Contemporary Blues Recording, while John Lee's *Chill Out* took Best Traditional Blues Recording.

Our interview, which originally ran as the June '96 *Guitar Player* cover story, "John Lee Hooker & Buddy Guy: The Baddest Blues Alive," took place at the Hilton across the street from the Universal Amphitheater. Buddy Guy showed up five minutes early, eagerly anticipating John Lee Hooker's arrival. "John and I work together a lot," Buddy said, "but I don't remember doing an interview with him before. He can make you laugh, I'll tell you that. If doing an interview is like anything else I've experienced with him, it'll make me laugh." A knock on the door moments later signaled John Lee's arrival. His helper, Steve Lee, pushed John Lee into the room in a wheelchair. Hooker's face lit up the instant he saw Buddy.

HOOKER: Yeah!

GUY: What kind of voice is that I hear?

HOOKER: That of a cripple.

GUY: Oh, you ain't a cripple. You not crippled at all. I know what's wrong with you. How you feel?

HOOKER: Pretty good. I got arthritis.

GUY: You gotta leave them young women alone.

HOOKER: I wouldn't last long without them. Hey, Buddy, you gained some weight there. You're as big as B! [B.B. King].

GUY: No, I can't get that big, John. That's a little too much for me.

HOOKER: How's the club?

GUY: It's good! I gotta get you down, man. Some of them gals, they been sayin', "Buddy, if you bring John Lee in, we gonna make him the happiest man . . ."

HOOKER: Yeah, the old ones.

GUY: You know I don't fool with nothin' old! You taught me that when I met you in '65! [*Laughs heartily.*]

What was Buddy like when you met him?

HOOKER: He was a gentleman. He was young, wild. He did things different. He backed me up on a few things in the studio. He did "Motor City Burnin'" with me, which I ain't got a copy of. You got that?

GUY: I ain't actually never heard it. They never did give me one. I still gotta get it.

HOOKER: You never did hear it? Whoo, that's a good one. Remember the time they had the riot in Detroit? "The Motor City burnin', and there's not a darn thing I can do but pack my bags and go."

GUY: We cut that in Chicago with Al Smith, you remember?

HOOKER: Uh-huh. For Vee Jay, I think. Oh, you got the guitar hummin'.

Why do blues records from the '50s and '60s sound so good?

HOOKER: I guess it's quality. They wasn't puttin' on all this stuff like they do today—fictitious stuff. It was just the real stuff then. You go in the studio, and we didn't have 24 tracks then, 8 tracks. You'd just go on in and do it, and the records really sounded good. They sound pretty good now, but the old stuff, to me, sounds better. I got some old stuff on you too, Buddy.

Did overdubbing hurt the sound of records?

HOOKER: I think so. I really do. It takes away something.

What were guitars like when you first started out?

HOOKER: When I first started it was Stella, Silvertone, things like that. They didn't have the fancy guitars they got now. They had Gibsons, but they wasn't fancy like they is now. I didn't even see a Gibson. I saw old Stellas and Silvertones, just things like that.

GUY: I was born so far in the country, man, I didn't know what a damn guitar was when I first saw one.

HOOKER: [*Laughs.*] Don't make it funny. You're getting interviewed.

GUY: No, I'm serious. When I first saw Lightnin' Slim with electric guitar, I wanted to pull the wires off it, because I thought it was a joke that he sounded like that. It was a Sunday evening, the sun about to go down in Louisiana, and this guy just came and plugged up with a little amp that looked like a radio. I said, "What the hell is that?" Then he start playing "Boogie Chillen," and I said, "Well, that's the way it sounds, but I don't think the guitar's supposed to be that loud."

HOOKER: That was recorded with just a roundhole [acoustic] with an old DeArmond pickup.

Some of your early records, like "Mad Man Blues," have a ferocious guitar tone.

HOOKER: It was the acoustic with the electric pickup.

Do you think bluesmen down South played slide a lot because acoustic guitars would warp in the humidity and the action would go bad?

GUY: I don't know about that. Since I've met the great slide players of Chicago, I've never heard any of them say that that's what made them play slide. Because I understand they used to play the guitar with a knife before they came up with all the slides and things. They would lay it down across their laps.

HOOKER: Yeah. That's right. Like he said, people would play with a knife.

In open tuning?

HOOKER: In whatever tuning he was in!

GUY: There wasn't no such things as pitch forks or things like that. You just wind the string up until you said it sounded good, and you'd go to work on it.

HOOKER: Fred McDowell could play really good slide.

You're also both fans of the late Earl Hooker.

HOOKER: Yeah, my cousin. He was my dad's brother's son. I knew him when we were kids. He did his own thing. He was a hell of a guitar player.

GUY: I don't think I ever heard anybody like him, not when it come to slide.

HOOKER: The slide and the wah-wah.

GUY: Actually, Muddy had him play slide on a couple of things, and you know Muddy could play slide himself.

HOOKER: But nobody play like Hooker.

GUY: No. Hooker was the only man that didn't change his guitar into a slidin' tuning. He would come get my guitar or anybody else's and run you outta there with a slide. I went to Chicago with the slide, and when I saw him, I gave it to him.

HOOKER: He stayed with me about four months there in Detroit, and he tried to show me how to play slide. I said, "No, no. Not with you around." I never was a slide person anyway.

Who's the first blues guitarist you saw in person who knocked you out?

HOOKER: Good question. I saw T-Bone Walker, and he really knocked me out. He was a big influence on me. Like Buddy Guy, he got his own sound.

What set T-Bone apart?

HOOKER: What stuck out was he had his own style. Nobody sounded like him. He really was a really good guitar player. Everybody wanted to play like T-Bone. He was the first person I saw playing the electric guitar. He was so good, that's when I started playing electric guitar.

Was he clean?

HOOKER: Whooo! Clean as a whistle. He played with his teeth, behind the back of his head. He did all that stuff. There was more, but he was the only one that really stood out to me, and I used to follow him around. Detroit had local guys back then, like Eddie Burns and Eddie Kirkland. There were some more, but I can't think of them right now.

GUY: When I got to Chicago, there were so many great guitarists around that I went to work a regular job. When I saw these people play, I just knew that there was no way I had a chance. I just wanted to *meet* these great musicians, and I woke up and they was askin' me to play with them.

One thing helped me a lot was I was a good listener, and if they would ask me to play with them, I didn't go tell John Lee or Muddy Waters or the Howlin' Wolf or Walter what to play. But so many great guitar players would get that chance to be with them and say, "Here's my chance to show off," and Muddy and them never would use them much anymore, and that was their downfall. When I went into the studio with them, I got in the corner and said, "I'm at school now. It's time for me to learn my lesson, not teach."

HOOKER: Like Buddy say, there was *so* many good guitar players in Chicago. Whoo!

GUY: Oh, man. I used to walk along and just go in and listen, trying to find Muddy, Wolf, Walter, or some of these people. A lot of times I never made it because every three doors there was a tavern with a three-piece in there, and they were sounding so good, if I stopped I never made it to where Muddy and them was that night. Most of these guys never became famous. Some of them just went to drinkin' and had wives, and you couldn't take care of family working for a dollar and a half a night when half a pint of whiskey was $2.50, so you had to be in the red. Matter of fact, when I first met Walter, the Wolf, and all of them, I was in the red every night because they'd come by and tab on me.

HOOKER: You know, I never did live there because there was too many good musicians. I was up in Detroit.

GUY: Jazz, blues, whatever you want, man. Back then there wasn't any cover charge, and in the summer there wasn't any air conditioning, so all these bars had the door open. And the crime wasn't like it is now. You could walk anywhere at night and you could hear it before you get there. You'd say, "Mm, let me see who this is." For three years I lost track of when the weekend was, because *every* night these clubs was packed.

HOOKER: He ain't kiddin'. Every night.

Did you ever put on someone's 78 and play along with it?

HOOKER: You mean other people? No. I'd listen to it and get ideas from it.

GUY: I had to copy records. I never been taught by no one. Nobody in my family— neither one of my grandparents or anybody—was musically inclined, so . . .

HOOKER: He had to copy somebody.

GUY: I got a chance to start buying those 78 records, which I'm sure you know if you drop one, that's the end of it. So I couldn't let anybody fool with that. That's how I learned how to move my right and left hands—by listening to other people.

What records really grabbed your attention?

GUY: "Boogie Chillen," man, of course. That grabbed a lot of people's attention back then, because in those days, you couldn't turn your radio on and find a guitar player every time you changed the dial. If you was comin' up when I came up and you wanted to hear a guitar player, if you didn't listen to the country and western coming out of Texas at night, you had to listen to John Lee, Muddy Waters, T-Bone, Lonnie Johnson, and those people like that. There was only a handful of guitar players, because there wasn't a lot of money being made by a guitar player, especially if you were black. You were just a guitar player. We learned to play guitar for the love of the guitar, not for the love of money.

HOOKER: That's right.

GUY: Now you can pick up a guitar and say, "If I be good, I can get rich." We didn't see that. There was nothing like that.

HOOKER: No, no. It was love of the guitar.

GUY: When we came up, you were one of a kind if you could play the guitar. Young people doin' it now, they got the television, they can see John Lee or B.B. whenever they get ready and get ideas from it. We were so far back up in there, if you *heard* a thing on the radio, you were lucky. The radio was scratchy, and if it was rainin' you had to cut it off because the lightning might hit it and blow it up or whatever. [*Everyone laughs.*] You would be different if you could play, because there wasn't as many playin' as there is today. Today, you're looked at as just another guitar player.

HOOKER: You ain't kiddin'. Too many of 'em. Everybody playin' guitar.

GUY: Right. But back then, if you was a guitar player they'd walk *miles* to come see you, because you was the only one.

Did you think playing guitar was something you could ever do for a living?

GUY: No. My parents was like, "Yeah, you can learn how to play, but you gotta go to school to be a doctor or lawyer so you can survive." You're talking about the time when we still had to ride in the back of the bus. You had a hat there, and if somebody would throw a dime in it, that's what you got for playing John Lee's "Boogie Chillen." That was about the end of that up until the '60s, when the British explosion come through, and then they started going to arenas and being on television. Music exploded, and we knew how to play. These kids come over and said, "I learned this from John Lee." There was the Rolling Stones, Jeff Beck, Cream, and all those people, and people started paying money to see 'em.

When the British guys first started bringing your music back over here, packing arenas and making a whole lot of money, did that make you mad?

HOOKER: No, it didn't.

GUY: No, it did something for us! To be honest with you, Santana, the Stones, Eric Clapton, and other people who went to stardom have done a lot for myself, B.B. King, Ike and Tina Turner, and others. Back in the '60s, they had to tell white America who John Lee Hooker and Muddy Waters were, and these great musicians was already here. There was a television show once called *Shindig*, and they asked the Rolling Stones to be on it. The Stones said, "We'll do this show if you bring on Muddy Waters," and they asked who was that. Mick Jagger and them got offended by this. "You mean to tell me you don't know who Muddy Waters is? We *named* ourselves after one of his famous records." So these people have done as much for us as any record company just by saying, "This is where I got it from. This is John Lee Hooker, Muddy Waters, and Little Walter music we're playing."

HOOKER: I was happy when they came over, and then when I went over to Europe, I was king over there.

GUY: Yes, sir! That's where I met you at. I met John in 1965 at the American Folk Blues Festival. And when I saw what he was doing in Europe, I said, "Hey, wait a minute, maybe I should move over here."

HOOKER: Blues music is more popular over there than it is in America, and more people recognize you over there.

GUY: Quite a few blues musicians left here to live there.

HOOKER: I don't want to live there.

GUY: We got a point to prove here. I want to prove to America that we were here.

HOOKER: You know, Buddy, why it's more popular over there than it is here? Because we got so much of it here. Everybody plays the blues guitar, but you don't find too many good ones over there. When you find them over there, they really appreciate it.

GUY: Oh, yeah.

What does it take for a modern blues guitar player to really stand out?

HOOKER: Have his own style and be good at it. There's a lot of blues guitars out there, so do your thing like you want to do. Don't try to be like me. If you want to play like me, it's up to you, but try to play your own kind of blues. Do the style that's something different than everybody got. If you sound like Buddy or me, the public will say, "He's a copycat." If you want to buy something, you gonna buy Buddy Guy. You ain't gonna buy no copy—you gonna buy the real thing. So you want to get something different that nobody else got, a sound all to yourself. Like me—I don't play no fancy guitar, but I'm different.

GUY: The bottom line is there'll never be another John Lee, Muddy Waters, Howlin' Wolf, and people like that. Those people only come along once in a lifetime. Musicians are like boxers, man. There's only one Muhammad Ali, there's only one Joe Louis, and there's only one Rocky Marciano. Everybody got their own thing, and that's something God gave us. I don't think you or your son or grandson can pick up a guitar and say, "I'm gonna be John Lee Hooker." Those shoes will be vacant once he's gone, because nobody's feet gonna fit those shoes. You're better off thinking, "I just want to play."

HOOKER: Yeah, right.

GUY: And just play. You're not going to be Willie Mays as a baseball player, you're not going to be Johnny Unitas as a football player. You're just going to be a player. And with the media, if you're at the right place at the right time and you're good, you might get more publicity than we do or whatever, but those shoes there are still under that bed and you can't wear 'em.

HOOKER: And you can't fill 'em. You cannot fill 'em.

What do you look for in a guitar tone?

GUY: What it originally was, which was a guitar and an amplifier with not so much technology on it. If you could just take me back and get me the guitar that I heard John Lee make "Boogie Chillen" with, or the one B.B. King used on "Three O'Clock in the Morning" or Muddy Waters played on "Louisiana Blues," I would collect them all right now. I'm like this: I want to hear what come out of it. The looks of a guitar don't mean nothing to me . . .

HOOKER: Don't mean a thing.

GUY: Right. The sound makes the difference.

HOOKER: The tone.

Can you play an unplugged electric guitar and know whether it's going to sound good?

GUY: I don't think so. You gotta hear it come through the amp. See, it's not only the guitar, it's the amplification too.

HOOKER: You gotta hear what comes out of the amp. Otherwise it's just a piece of wood.

What's the best-sounding blues amp you've owned?

HOOKER: Good question. It used to be the old Silvertone, but now I use a Fender.

GUY: My favorite's the Fender Bassman. That's the one Leo came out with along with the Strat, and they just had that natural Otis Rush, Little Walter, Muddy, and John Lee sound. You just plugged it in, and you didn't have to go through all of this stuff trying to find which number to put the controls on to get it. My first amplifier stayed at the same position so long the controls froze there from Otis Spann or someone spilling wine or beer on it. It just locked there, so all I had to do is turn it on. It's had the same tone wherever I've taken it.

Have you noticed variations among the sound of various Bassmans?

GUY: The original Bassmans are different than what they got now. I've talked to engineers, and I don't think they could reproduce that thing. People can't get that tone that it had.

How would you describe that sound?

GUY: That's kind of hard to say. You probably could do a better job of it if you would hear Otis Rush play "I Can't Quit You, Baby" through that original amp and then hear him today playing the same thing through what looks like the same amp. The tone's just not there.

HOOKER: It's not. It's really not.

GUY: They just don't have those transformers and other material to make that amp like that anymore. It's almost like when you lose your loved ones—you bury them, and that's that. It's not coming back.

John Lee, have you ever played through a wah-wah or a fuzztone?

HOOKER: Wah-wah? Yeah, I played it. I don't like it.

GUY: Takes the blues out of it. Wah-wah, wang-wang the blues.

Is there a place in blues for effects pedals?

GUY: John might know more about that than me, but you never know what's gonna sell records. What record companies be looking for now, man, is good looks and sales. They're looking for that from John and me and everybody else. They don't care nothing about what me and him are talking about now, because it's a business. They just say, "If you put a record out and make a lot of money, John, I'm gonna keep recording you and keep giving you money."

HOOKER: Right.

GUY: But if you don't, you know, you just John Lee and Buddy, once was.

HOOKER: Let me put it this way. They're so far advanced now in this world, slick and polished up, that they ain't lookin' at your sound. They lookin' to sell a lot of records, and if not, they don't want you.

Do you feel pressure from the label to have famous people on your records?

HOOKER: I don't feel pressure now, but maybe a long time ago I used to. Now, with the name John Lee Hooker, they figure they can sell a certain amount of records no matter what it sound like. It may not be full of production, but they figure if it's John Lee Hooker, people will buy it.

Were guys bending strings when you were young?

HOOKER: I guess some people was; I wasn't. Buddy was. I heard him, and he could bend the notes. Some things I bend notes, but it's not too much. But Buddy— oh, boy!

GUY: Yeah, but I stole all that, some from John, B.B., T-Bone, and all them. I think we all have gotten something from somebody.

HOOKER: Yeah, we all got something.

GUY: I didn't just pick up a guitar and people say, "Yes, there he is, a country boy that has something new." No. I heard B.B. squeezin'. I met him and said, "Where did you get it from?" He said, "I couldn't learn to play with the slide, so I had to come up with the next best thing that was as close to the slide as I could get." I couldn't bend strings when I first started, because if I broke one, I couldn't get me another one. Every time I tried, it made me break my strings. You'd loan somebody the guitar and say, "Watch out, man! You'll break my string!"

HOOKER: "Don't break my damn string! I ain't gonna bend it any, so don't you bend it." [*Everyone laughs.*] I be breaking lightweight strings now. What gauge you play?

GUY: I've gone back to a little heavier now, John. They was breakin' so fast, and I had a guy couldn't change 'em fast enough. That's a little too thin.

HOOKER: I play light, but I don't bend 'em that much.

Did you hear a lot of boogie music before you did "Boogie Chillen"?

HOOKER: Well, yeah. I heard people like my stepfather Will Moore and Charley Patton.

It's too bad Will Moore never made a record.

HOOKER: No, he never did. I saw Charley Patton around Clarksdale. He was just about the only one of those guys I did see.

What is it about your boogie that brings entire audiences to their feet?

HOOKER: That boogie just ride on. It got no end. It just go higher, higher, higher. That get people up. They can't sit down. They can't sit still. When I play, people boogie all over the place—just *zoom.* I says, "Let's boogie—get up."

That's been happening all your life.

HOOKER: Yeah, it is. All my life. I'm very fortunate, very lucky. I'm very talented. God give me that talent, and I put it to good use through the people that love me and I loves them. I really gets them up.

What do you look for in the second guitarist in your band?

HOOKER: I ask them to play. They don't play, I ain't gonna pay 'em. I'm paying them to play, not to hold the guitar. I watch Buddy, and he makes his second guitar play.

GUY: Yeah. You know, I did a lot of playing for other people, and actually I really enjoy playing behind someone else. Oh, yes. That was my first love, because I don't really have a singing voice. When I first met John and Muddy and all of them and got a chance to play with 'em, I said, "This is it for me, the top. My goal is just to play behind them." The way these guys could sing, I didn't want to open my mouth anyway. See, God made John Lee and Muddy and Wolf to sing. When you talk to these people, they sound like their singing. Really, I'm being honest with you. I don't even consider myself in the same room with them, so far as vocals go.

HOOKER: Shoot, you can sing too, man. You know what song I *love*? "Damn Right, I Got the Blues." I play it all the time.

GUY: I knew I couldn't sing that good, so you're damn right that give me the blues.

HOOKER: Let me ask you something, Buddy. Was that the hit song on your record?

GUY: Yeah.

HOOKER: I thought it was.

GUY: Actually, John, it's almost like Koko Taylor's "Wang Dang Doodle." We had finished recording the record, and they asked me did I have anything else. I said, "Yes. 'Damn Right, I Got the Blues.'" The guy come over, said, "That's the title of the album." I said okay. I think we cut that in one take too.

HOOKER: It sure is good.

GUY: Thank you. Took me long enough to try to get one before somebody recognized me. I been out there for years. Remember when we used to say "scufflin'"?

HOOKER: Yeah.

GUY: Yeah, I'm scufflin' like hell trying to get something for somebody to listen to me.

John Lee, why do you wear sunglasses when you sing the blues?

HOOKER: Sometimes I get so emotional. I hear my own voice soundin' good, but it's so sad when I get to singing deep down, the tears run out of my eyes. The dark glasses hide my teardrops.

What's your approach to writing songs?

HOOKER: It's just a talent. It's a gift to write. It didn't come out of a book. I can hear you speaking words and make a song out of it.

Do you remember writing some of your famous songs, such as "Maudie," "Boom Boom," and "Tupelo, Mississippi"?

HOOKER: Yeah, "Maudie," "Boom Boom," "Boogie Chillen," "Dimples."

Did you have a guitar in your hand when you wrote all those songs?

HOOKER: Sometimes yes, sometimes no. Sometimes the songs just come to me here [*points to his head*] and here [*points to his heart*], and I just get my guitar after I get it like I want it, and I phrase it in there.

Can you name a song that you sang a cappella before you figured it out on guitar?

HOOKER: Yeah, "Boom Boom." I come in the club that night—they called it Apex Bar, there in Detroit. It was a small nightclub, and I was playing there every weekend before I got real famous, you know? I was famous, but not as I am now. And every night there'd be a girl in there. Her name was Willa. She was a bartender. I never would be on time; I always would be late comin' in. And she kept saying, "Boom, boom—you late again." Every night: "Boom, boom—you late again." I said, "Hmm, that's a song!" I put it together and I was playin' in there in the club before I recorded it. I played it around in the clubs, and people would really get up and go wild when I played that song. They would get on their feets and holler, "That's a great song, man." I recorded it, and it just took off like wildfire.

Did you play "Boogie Chillen" in clubs before you recorded it?

HOOKER: Yeah, I did. I wrote that song in Detroit when I was sittin' around strum-min' my guitar. The thing come into me, you know? I heard Will Moore done it years and years before. I was a little kid down South, and I heard him do a song like that, but he didn't call it "Boogie Chillen." But it had that beat, and I just kept that beat up and I called it "Boogie Chillen."

Did Will Moore tap his foot like you?

HOOKER: Oh, yeah. He did.

Where did you learn about open-tuning your guitar?

HOOKER: From him. He called it Vastopol [open *D*] and Spanish [open *G*].

Did Will Moore play slide guitar?

HOOKER: Not that I know of, no.

Carlos Santana says that when you recorded "The Healer" and "Chill Out" with him, you made up the lyrics on the spot.

HOOKER: Yeah, sure did. I do a lot of 'em like that. It comes out right too—one take. Yeah, it come *boom*, right out. I'd had the words on my mind—I thought I wanted to do that—but I had never did it. I tried it out, and it come out quick. I said, "Leave it right here, and don't try to put no changes to it. Take the first take." I had had that title on my mind—"The Healer" was Carlos' title—and I just put the words to it right there. I love Carlos, man. He's one nice, good man, and he love to play that boogie.

Is it easier for you to play a boogie in regular or open tuning?

HOOKER: Either way.

Have you ever played with guitar picks?

HOOKER: I used to try to thumbpick, but I didn't like it. Just the natural hand [*holds up his right hand, simultaneously crossing his index finger with his middle finger and his pinkie with his ring finger*]. That give me the real, real thing.

Are you still learning things about playing the blues?

HOOKER: You never learn it all. You always learnin' something different. Always learnin'.

Do you feel you're at the peak of your career now?

GUY: I wouldn't say that. I would like to see John Lee exposed more than he has been because of what he has contributed to this music throughout his lifetime. We're still behind the curtain in a certain respect. They don't want to see older men like John and myself on television. They wants to see good-looking young people up there. You know, record buyers are between seven and 14 years old—that's who makes records platinum. Our blues record buyers keep us recording, but if we'd get exposed a little more, I'm sure that little kid next door would say, "Wow! I can see where whoever got this from. They got it from John Lee Hooker. That's original stuff he's playing—they just modernized the music." They don't give us that chance, but we're still fighting. We didn't give up, and that shows you the love we got for the music we have lived with.

HOOKER: Like ZZ Top. Billy Gibbons told me, "We got the boogie from you."

What's the best reward in your line of work?

HOOKER: Money. [*Everyone laughs.*]

GUY: That's soulful, huh?

HOOKER: That's number one, but there's a lot of other good things.

GUY: You keep all of the trophies, huh?

HOOKER: Keep the trophies—give me some grease!

GUY: The reason he's saying that is we played so long for nothing, man, the trophies can wait.

HOOKER: You can't pay rent with no trophy. Give me that green stuff, dead presidents. You know what dead presidents is?

Sure, man. I got some in my pocket. [*Everyone laughs.*]

HOOKER: Dead presidents—that's the best reward!

GUY: I guess you're right, John.

HOOKER: You know I'm right.

Does winning a Grammy mean anything to you?

HOOKER: Yeah, it means a lot to me. There's no money in it, but fame, you know. It helps your career. It makes more people known to you. They recognize you and look up to you more, as far as that goes. It's nice to know that you're a winner.

It must feel good to know that people all around the world love your music.

HOOKER: All over the world. I lay in my bed and think about that: all around the world. I say, "When I'm gone, I won't be gone. They won't see me in person, but I will forever be here in the hearts and minds of people." That's the way I look at it. I'll never be forgotten.

OTIS RUSH
AND BUDDY GUY

BY JAS OBRECHT During the summer of 1994, Buddy Guy and Otis Rush were both on the comeback trail, with successful new albums and tours in the works. After a flurry of phone calls, Guy and Rush, two of the prime innovators of Chicago's West Side Sound, agreed to collaborate on their first joint interview. We met at Legends, Buddy Guy's Chicago nightclub, around noon on June 8th. Buddy's face lit up when he saw Otis come in the door, and the bluesmen greeted each other with a handshake and a hug. This story first appeared as the November '94 *Guitar Player* cover story, "Buddy Guy and Otis Rush: Chicago Blues—The Inside Story."

RUSH: Hi there! How are you? Sorry I'm late.
GUY: Oh, don't worry about that! This guy can be late any time! C'mon, make yourself at home.

RUSH: Let me run to the bar, if that's the case. [*Both laugh and Otis gets some white wine on the rocks.*]

I understand you gentlemen go way back together.

RUSH: Yes, yes, yes, yes. Way back there in the '50s, I think.

GUY: 1958. I came to Chicago on September the 25th in '57, and then I finally had learned my way how to catch the 47th Street bus and come to the South Side. Otis is the man that first let me come up on the stage and play a tune in one of the clubs that you would want to get in, the famous 708 Club on the South Side—708 East 47th Street. They had Muddy Waters there on Mondays, Howlin' Wolf on Tuesday, Little Walter on Wednesday, and, aw, man! Otis Rush, Junior Wells, the Four Aces. It was just the place. And he called me up and I played a tune with him. When I came off, I was tellin' everybody how stranded and hungry I was, because people were saying, like, "Blah, blah, who are you and why are you . . ." and all that stuff. Man, all I wanted to do was get home. Somebody went and called Muddy, and Muddy came down. And that's when he give me that famous slap in the face and the famous salami sandwich. [*Smiles.*]

Every time I hear Otis play, man, it makes me think about the very particular day he called me up there, man. I'm like sayin', "I don't even have no business onstage with this guy," 'cause Otis is the guy with the Albert King, left-handed style sound. He deserves all the credit for that, because Otis was playin' "I Can't Quit You, Baby" when I had never heard of Albert King, you know.

Otis, how old were you when you made that record?

RUSH: I don't really know. Does it make a difference? [*Chuckles.*] I was, maybe, 19 or something like that. 'Cause I was in my teens when I came here to visit my sisters. I'm a farmer. I'm from Philadelphia, Mississippi. I was down there. I wasn't playing any music. I just came to visit my sister, and she took me to hear Muddy Waters at the Zanzibar. There was Muddy, Little Walter, Junior Wells, Jimmy Rogers, Elgin on the drums, L.C. McKinley. And I sit there in the corner, and I don't even speak to 'em. I don't know 'em. So I sit there like a block of ice and just look at 'em. "Damn," I said, "this is for me." I didn't have a guitar. I went and bought me a Kay and a small amp. The amp was so weak and light, it looked like it danced with the notes. [*Everyone laughs.*] And I sit in the window for months and months. People begged me to get out of the window or they were gonna call the police.

They couldn't sleep?

RUSH: I don't know what it was. I know I had to play guitar. That's where I got my start. Muddy Waters. And then later on I recorded a record in '55 and '56. That's when it really catchin' on, '56.

The Cobra records?

RUSH: Yeah. "I Can't Quit You, Baby." Like Buddy said, I met him a couple of years later.

Buddy, was Otis involved with your recording for Cobra?

GUY: Uh huh. Otis has got some licks on my first 45 with Cobra!

RUSH: That was Eli's idea. He was at Cobra.

What kind of location were your Cobra records cut in?

RUSH: It was a little hole in the wall. I don't know if it was a garage. It could have been, but it must have been a five- or six-car garage. It wasn't big, but he had a little living quarters in there, him and his wife.

Did Eli treat you with respect?

RUSH: Ah, yes and no. Yes meaning when I go in there to record, he listened to me. I call that respect. But when the time come to pay off and check those royalties, he said I didn't have nothin' comin'. He was a big gambler, him and [harmonica ace] Shakey Jake, oh, way back. You remember who Shakey Jake is.

GUY: [*Smiles.*] Yeah, I do.

RUSH: Boy, he'll tame a elephant, Shakey Jake will. [*Laughs.*] So he tamed Eli, you understand? Took all his money gambling. And Eli was borrowin' money from peoples, gambling, and Jake just loadin' up, you know. I'm real upset, because this record was a hit record, and he say I didn't have no royalties comin'. So, okay, I begin to don't want to record records from the very beginning. That's why I don't record. All of the bullshit. I can't take it no more.

You reportedly went 16 years between recording albums.

RUSH: It might have been more. I had a record out, *Right Place, Wrong Time*. I recorded it in '71, and they didn't release it until '77, something like that. And then the record was nominated for a Grammy Award. How come they didn't release the record around '71 or '72, at least? And so I'm goin' through all this bull, you know, and people askin' me for a record. That's why I quit for two years. Buddy, you got the floor. I think I said all mine.

GUY: I met Otis and Magic Sam, and they was such nice people. We used to have those Sunday afternoon guitar battles. A lot of the blues clubs would call it the "guitar battle," and they'd give you the bottle of whiskey if you win the guitar battle. Whoever win the whiskey never did hardly get a drink of it because all your friends was sittin' out there watchin'. It was like, maybe, Luther Allison, myself, Otis Rush, Magic Sam, Earl Hooker—we was all doin' that stuff. But every once in a while, when Muddy and them would come by, it was, like [*in a serious voice*], "Okay, man, the jam session is over. Now it's time to listen to the teacher."

Did you consider it disrespectful to go toe-to-toe with them?

GUY: In my book it was. I think that's why I got a chance to record with them a lot, because they know when I went in to play behind Muddy, I didn't want nobody to even know it was me. All I wanted to do was make the hair stand on my head to say I was on a record with Muddy or Wolf or Walter, Sonny Boy, some of those people like that. Music then was a lot of love instead of a lot of money. When I learned how to play guitar, I couldn't look up and see a Prince or a Eric or a Beck or a Keith, makin' all this money playin' the guitar. You just had to love this thing to play it. But I had also met some entertainers that you can't say how nice they was. Because if they didn't have to say, "Hey, Buddy, I'll play with ya. . . ."

RUSH: They didn't want you on the stage. They ain't got time to let no one else play. They want to hog everything theyself.

GUY: Right, right. And that's how we got together—Otis, Magic Sam, Betty Everett, and Harold Burrage was the main people there at Cobra.

RUSH: That's some pretty nice peoples right there. [*Chuckles*.]

GUY: Yeah. And I said, "Forget the Chess or whoever else," because I went to Chess first, and they like closed the door. I never saw them. I made a demo tape to be brought to Leonard Chess, and they never did listen to the tape no way. 'Cause, see, I didn't get into Chess [until 1960]. I left and just followed Magic Sam and Otis Rush over to Cobra Records. And these people was always there, and they was like, "I'm not gonna hide behind a door." They was all out there sittin' and talkin'. I said, "If I get a new family, this is it."

Otis, Leonard Chess reportedly thought you sounded too much like Muddy Waters when he heard you.

RUSH: Well, that go to show you, Chess don't know music in the first place. A lot of these companies don't know music. I mean, I was trying to sing Muddy to make a livin'. I'd have been singing like Screamin' Jay Hawkins, if that's what it took! [*Laughs*.]

GUY: Put food on the table.

RUSH: "I Put a Spell on You." Anything to put the food on your table.

What can young players benefit from listening to Magic Sam?

RUSH: Well, they learn a lesson, for one thing. He's a magic Sam—that's what he is. He got his style when he hit the guitar. The way he played and phrased his songs, you know that's Sam. He played a guitar well. Very well. So did he [*points to Buddy*].

What impressed you about young Buddy Guy?

RUSH: Hey, man, I said, "Damn, I wished I'd knew that! I have to put that in my collection." No shit!

GUY: [*Laughs.*] I don't know, Otis.

RUSH: And I never did get it! [*Laughs.*]

GUY: After I saw these guys play, man, I said, "Well, Buddy, you gotta cut the bull out. You gotta play." 'Cause they were *playin'*. I had watched Guitar Slim, and he was like puttin' on a show. It wasn't as much guitar playing as Otis or Sam or Earl Hooker were playin'. When I came here and saw them, I said, "Well, you gotta start all over again." These guys would sit down in a chair and just play the guitar like it was supposed to be played.

RUSH: We'd sit down, that's for certain.

GUY: A lot of people was sittin' down then. And a lot of people was listening to the blues. You'd find a few people would dance, but places like the 708 Club didn't have dance space. You would go in, the police were in there, and you'd just sit and listen to Otis or Muddy, whoever was playing there. And we had to play 40-20. You play 40 minutes and off for 20—our union had it like that. By the time you got really into Otis or Muddy, they'd take this 20-minute break. I'm like saying, "Hurry up, 20 minutes, so I can watch Muddy!"

Did any of the older players offer advice that's served you well?

RUSH: Yes. Muddy Waters did. It's when I recorded my first record. He came by the 708 Club, and we was all sittin' out in the car, talkin' and laughin', shootin' the bull. And he says, "I want to talk to you. You have a good record, and don't get the big head!" [*Laughs.*]

Did he ever slap you?

RUSH: No. [*Everyone laughs.*] Yes, he did. With music. He slapped me good with the music. Yeah! You know it.

GUY: Yeah, he did that. It seems like back in those days we were more closer than we are now. I mean, there wasn't no going to bed for me if I heard Otis was play-ing somewhere. The only time I would miss him or Muddy or Earl Hooker was when I had to play. And vice versa. You would look up, and there was a Magic Sam or Freddie King or Otis. We just followed one another. I learned a lot from that. I just said, "I gotta follow these people so I can learn more than what I know." Right now young people comes to my show, and some of them have the attitude that they already know this. And I would recommend them to go and sit down night after night and listen to Otis play.

RUSH: They could get some of them old records and listen to all them old guys at the time we started.

GUY: Right, right.

RUSH: Because we was sorta all out there rockin' in the same old boat. You know what I mean? I had a little record out, but I wasn't doin' nothin' neither. I had a lit-tle jump ahead of Buddy and Magic Sam—a couple of years—but I'm sufferin' too.

GUY: It was that circle. Everybody was playin' the same clubs. You'd go round and round here in Chicago. I know I didn't travel to the Mississippis and Alabamas and places like that.

RUSH: That's right, man. I didn't.

So you didn't do any of the station wagon tours?

GUY: No. Maybe once, very . . . Matter of fact, the first one I ever did, with Willie Dixon on my first record, Willie Dixon took the first deposit and bought a car, and I never did see the car anymore.

RUSH: The granddaddy of 'em all—that's what I call Willie Dixon.

Did any labels give you complete freedom to play what you wanted?

GUY: I just got like that after *Damn Right, I Got the Blues*. Before then they handed me stuff and told me the same thing Otis is telling you: "You sound too much like B.B. King. You sound too much like John Doe," or whoever they wanted to say. And I'm like saying, "Well, I don't have nothin'." And that's what I was afraid of every time I went in the studio.

RUSH: It's just like the man put a brand on you [*thumps table*]—a stamp. That's what he done. Because he got the money, he can talk bullshit. You understand? But to me, that's hell. But with Eli, that was heaven to me. With the Chess, that's hell to me. Duke is hell to me. On down the line was hell to me.

GUY: I didn't know what to do until this label, Silvertone, came and said, "Listen. Everybody talks about your playing. We want to support you and let you play." I said, "Yeah!" Because everything I got, nobody never really listened at what I had to offer. 'Cause I'm just gonna give you what I got, and if that don't go, then I have myself to blame.

Let's talk about songwriting.

RUSH: All the records have a punch line.

GUY: Some of 'em it be the first thing you said or the middle thing you said, and everything else is based around that.

RUSH: Right. Like, say, "Double Troubles." I wrote that song around two ladies. My lady and another lady sittin' there playin' cards, and they was mad at each other. One win and the other one didn't. And she said, "Damn! I'm havin' nothin' but double trouble!"

GUY: Grabbed you, right?

RUSH: Grabbed me right there. And as bad as I write, it took me about a half hour, but I got "Double Trouble" down. And the next day, when I was feelin', like, music, I go back and pick that up. I do that all the time. I'm doing that now. If you don't get up and write it down . . .

GUY: [*Nods in agreement.*] You lose it.

RUSH: Really. You think, "Oh, I can remember! I can remember!" Then all of a sudden, "What was that?"

GUY: Yeah!

RUSH: I want to back up to my electric ass-kicker when I do that! [*Laughs.*] I plug it in the wall and just back up to it—slow, medium, and fast! Because I lost a lot of good tunes because I didn't get up and write 'em down.

GUY: If I don't jot lines down the same way, I'm like saying, "I know I had a hell of a punch line the other day," and I can't get it for nothin'. Maybe a week or so, it come back.

RUSH: It'll come back. It does. It comes and go, it comes and go.

What about guitar riffs?

RUSH: It works pretty much the same thing. I've dreamed some notes when I'm in the bed, but I didn't get up and play 'em. Then again I dreamed some notes and I *did* get up and check the guitar, and then I know the next day I can play it. But if I don't and go to sleep, I forget what I dreamed.

When does your best playing happen?

RUSH: Man, sometime at home you get off in a bag to yourself and you sound *good.* Right, Buddy?

GUY: Yeah, yeah.

RUSH: Sometime you just don't get into it out on the stage.

GUY: Mm hmm [*nods in agreement*].

RUSH: The best kind of music, to me, is just plain playin' off of nothin' high. No high—no whiskey. And then you get the feeling to play. Man, that's mighty ni-i-i-i-ce!

GUY: That is the best stuff. Actually, when I want to learn something, I don't want nothing to effect my ability to learn. And then when I come out here to go on the stage, I'm like saying, "I gotta have a beer or a shot of cognac," because I'm shakin' when I go up there. And I don't care where or who or when and what I'm play-ing—it's just there. It's that stage fright.

RUSH: It's here too. Every word you said. Welcome to the club! [*Buddy and Otis smack their fists together.*] It's just like he said.

What can you tell musicians about mixing drinking and playing?

RUSH: Don't get me wrong. I didn't say anything was wrong with drinking. My point is get high off of just playing and no drinkin'. If you ever get high off of just playin' and no drinking, it's a hell of a sound!

GUY: Nothin' like the natural stuff. It's like Otis says. If you really wants to make yourself feel good, just grab that darn thing and be at home by yourself with a cup of coffee or glass of water. That natural high is there. And you don't need nothin'. You don't need no one. You don't need anything to do it. It's just an automatic high.

Do you sometimes find a tone that really inspires you, but then later on it just isn't there?

RUSH: Yes, I do. [*Points to Buddy.*] He do too. Buddy knows. You go to a place to play, and it doesn't sound the same every night. Your amp don't sound the same. The weather changes the speakers and everything. When they get cold, they change. You know, the moon play a hell of a part in the weather too. For all of us, and those instruments.

GUY: I think it's just me. Otis is telling you exactly right, but I've figured out my playing is like an athlete. You know, you go see a football player or a boxer or base-ball player, and that day he don't do nothin'. As soon as you don't go, this guy just turns to Superman. And I think guitar playing is the same way. I'm not at my best every time I go to the stage, and I get angry at myself. . . .

RUSH: You be tryin'! You're tryin' *real* hard.

GUY: Yes! I try too hard sometime. But you should realize they don't look at an entertainer like that. They think he supposed to be at 100% all the time. You're not supposed to have a headache; you're not supposed to say, "I don't feel well tonight." But the average guy from the media looks at you and says, "Oh, shit. He

stinks. I went to see him, and he didn't sound right *at all.* Blah, blah, blah, blah."
But he don't know you was tryin' to do your best at that particular time, but it's
just one of those bad days.

RUSH: And then again, you could be playin', and you say, "Damn, I'm not playin'.
Damn! What's wrong with me?" And the public come up: "Oooooh! I never saw ya
play so good!"

GUY: Right!

RUSH: I'm sayin', "Oh, where's my hat!" [*Pretends he's hiding his face under a hat.*]
Catch a cab! [*Everyone laughs.*]

GUY: Yeah. That's so true. Yes it is.

What brings you closest to the heart of the blues?

RUSH: My roots, man, from childhood. When I'm born—ever since I can remember—I been having hard time. It all started right around when I was five years old. I
remember pretty good. It's been happening to me ever since. Still happenin' to me.

Is playing blues music sometimes an expression of your anger?

RUSH: Yeah! Sometimes. But let me clear this up so you don't get a misunderstand-
ing. See, I get angry like you do. And if I happen to have a guitar in my hand, I'm
sorry. I don't have to be mad at my guitar; I can be mad at somebody out there.
And then again, I can get mad at my guitar. Yeah.

GUY: It's just a human. I be onstage sometimes and say, "Shit!" You know, there's a
note I've missed or my voice wasn't right. It's just like your tapin' [*points to tape
recorder*], if it doesn't work right. You say, "Well, I got Buddy and Otis here to this
interview"—and today you got the first one we ever done together—and the battery
gone. You put a battery in it, and it still doesn't work. And it just frustrates you.
Well, we human the same way. And our work is the same thing. You know, we just
not a superhuman that ain't nothin' gonna happen to us or we not gonna ever feel
bad or we don't get tired or we don't need sleep, we don't need to eat or we don't
need a bath. We're just guitar players, but we still the same human being as you are.

*You have very different playing styles, but you both play Stratocasters. What's the
appeal of that particular guitar?*

GUY: I saw Guitar Slim play one first in Louisiana before I came to Chicago. And
when I got here, I saw Otis had one and a few more people. I guess it was Otis,
Magic Sam, Freddie King, and myself's type of guitar compared to what Muddy and
Son House and the rest of those guys played with, which was acoustics. A lot of
them had put the pickup on their acoustic guitar—Elmore James with the big box
and stuff.

First of all, I liked what I heard in the Strat. I found out that if I dropped it or it
fell, it stayed in one piece. And that made me love it more than anything else,
because half of the time I didn't have a case no way, so I needed something to take
the wear and tears as well as it would last me to play, because I couldn't afford
strings, I couldn't afford another guitar. At that point I wasn't gonna let you steal
it, because I slept with it. You'd have to steal me with it.

RUSH: I got a Strat 'cause Earl Hooker had bought one. Just lookin' at him play, he
was magic to me. He was something like a leader with instruments. Nobody in
Chicago I knew of had instruments like Earl Hooker. He had a Fender Bassman, he
had the wah-wah, he had the echo chambers. When something come out, Earl
Hooker had it already. Earl Hooker was a *great* guy, man.

GUY: [*Laughs*.] Man, that guy was somethin' that I don't think I will never see in my lifetime again. Hopefully, somebody else will see somebody like that. As a blues guitarist, I've never seen anybody could play the way he played it, and especially the slide guitar. I remember once he made me and B.B. King cry in Joliet, Illinois. B.B. said, "There's no way a man can play no slide that clean." Earl wouldn't never hardly sing that much, but everything would come out with the slide. He could play the melody, and it sound like somebody singing.

He was the first one stole the long cord from me that I learned from Guitar Slim out of New Orleans. Earl Hooker would steal his tubes out of my amplifier. If we'd leave our amplifiers in the clubs 'cause we be back here tomorrow night to jam again, he would go down there in the midday, and you'd think he's over there messin' with his guitar, but he would change the speakers out of your amp if you sounded good to him. Then somebody that'd seen him there would say, "Well, Hooker been over there." And I would just go by his mother's house and say, "Open the door, man. Give my speakers and my cord back." And he would give 'em back. He stammered a lot, kind of like John Lee [*imitates Hooker*]: "You-you-you-you sounded so good, I wanted to see what you had that I didn't have." Yeah, we was the best of friends when he passed away. From the time I met him, I never did see him drink or do nothin'. He didn't have no bad habits other than stealing your stuff.

RUSH: He's slick. Earl Hooker. I paid a lot of attention. He's another one of my heroes.

What was the best blues amp for your sound?

GUY: After I heard Otis and them play, man, the Bassman. And I still use 'em. The first time I heard Otis, he was getting a snappy sound out of this Strat and this Bassman, and I'm like sayin', "What is he doin'?" I was at 708 Club, and I heard this man play with Willie D. Warren, who had tuned his guitar strings way down. And the people was goin' crazy, the way they was playin' that stuff. I think Otis had [drummer Fred] Below, that guy [Warren], and himself, and I said, "Man, wait a minute!"

RUSH: You're talking about the bass now. See, Willie D. and somebody around Arkansas, where he was born, they knew about the strings bein' run down.

Would you explain what that means?

RUSH: Like a Fender bass wasn't in Chicago, okay? It was two guitars—Little Walter had two guitars and Muddy Waters had two guitars.

GUY: Wasn't no bass.

RUSH: That's what I'm trying to tell you. I took Willie D. Warren and had him tune his strings down. I kept listening to the sound, and I said, "I'm gonna stick with this guy." I went and bought a better amp for him, okay? That made the guitar sound a little more stronger and deep. And then everybody from every direction came to see what we was doin'. Muddy Waters, the Wolf, you name 'em—they was comin' by to see how we was gettin' the sound. After they learned what was happenin', they didn't ask who or where it came from. They found it, and *gone*. That's how it went all over Chicago. And then after this, I took Dave Myers too. He'd been a bass player for many years with Little Walter, and I told him, "We got to get you a Fender bass." Why, I went to St. Louis, where Ike Turner had this Fender bass. There wasn't no Fender bass in Chicago. Willie Dixon was the man, and sometime I didn't like the way he played bass.

And he used a stand-up bass.

RUSH: Yeah. And when I came back here, I took Willie D. and made it work. And after this, everybody started buying Fender bass. Fender ought to cut a lot of guys like him and me in on some kind of a stake. These peoples, I don't want to say too much about them.

Let me show you something. I been playin' Fender guitar for many years, and they've gave me two or three guitars, okay? I play Gibson guitar for maybe 25 years. I bought the Epiphone, my first guitar that looked like a Gibson, and now Gibson make Epiphone. Now, just since this new record been out, I told this guy at Gibson, the owner, I said, "Fender gave me two or three guitars. I been advertising your guitar. Even in that GHS Strings [ad], that Gibson guitar is right up there. I want you to give me a guitar. Give me the *original* Gibson, not some phony Gibson." But the original cost a hundred-and-some thousand dollars.

An original 335?

RUSH: Yeah. They just gave some guy one, but my manager is telling me, "I don't think they gonna give you one." Don't give it to me. I'll just hang the Gibson up on the wall and play the Fender, you know. That's what I'll do.

What does your Fender endorsement deal mean to you?

GUY: That finally, I guess, someone is giving me the respect that myself, Otis, or whoever should get. Because I open magazines, and I'd see other people in there that's overnight guitar players. When they finally come and say, "Okay, here's your chance," I think, better late than never. But I'm not mad, because that's Fender.

RUSH: Fender make him feel like, "Hey, I am somebody." That's nice. How come Gibson can't do these things?

Is there as much racism in the music business today as there was in 1960?

RUSH: You know that stands today. You know it's always gonna stand. You got to know that. That'll never go away. The racism is part of civilization. That's the way it is.

Doesn't your playing music to such a broad audience help to ease some of that?

RUSH: Yeah! Well, we all can help do this, you know. The first step is be kind to each other. Don't rob each other, kill each other. We start it right here, and on and on. There's a billion ways to go, and we all got a role to play, just like makin' a movie.

What would you most like to change about the business?

RUSH: Well, I'd like to have the company, and I'd like to own a studio! [*Laughs.*] Do I need to say any more? That's heaven to me.

GUY: I would like for my music to go beyond what it is now in order for it not to die. Because the blues at one point was frightening. Before *Damn Right, I Got the Blues*, before John Lee Hooker's *Healer* and a few more records, I was frightened. I wasn't gonna quit playin' it, but it just look like my grandbabies didn't know who I was, my next door neighbor didn't know who I was. Now I can walk out of my house and somebody will say, "Hi, Buddy! Yeah, I heard you with Eric or Otis," or whatever they want to say about it.

It's interesting how you've helped promote each other's careers at various times.

GUY: Well, I think that's the religious part in us. And we hope a lot of people still be like that today. It would be a better place to live, because that's what it's all about. Actually, somebody did something for me. I told B.B. when I first met him after my first two little records, I said, "Man, I don't know what to do. Everybody tell me I sound so much like you." He said, "Pay that no mind, because if anybody know who I was watchin', I was soundin' like them. But they didn't make a name for themself like I did. Whatever you can do, go for it, and I'll pat you on the back and help you if I can." All these guys said, "Man, just go ahead and play. We sounded like somebody too."

RUSH: Do your thing.

GUY: Yeah. Everybody sound like somebody, because nobody popped in breathing the next day playing guitar. It's all a learning thing. It's almost like learning walking, talking, and everything else.

RUSH: Guitar don't belong to no one person, man. You take that son of a gun up and hit on it! Play it, man. A guitar don't care who play it. It sit there and wait faithfully for you, like a car does. And I named my guitars, Buddy. I got three.

GUY: You done give 'em names?

RUSH: Yes, sir. "Check Me Out and if I'm Wrong I Don't Want to Be Right." [*Buddy laughs.*] I also got "C'mon, Smooth, and Let Me Live." What lets you live? A pretty guitar hangin' on your shoulder. What lets you live? Your guitar lets you live! Huh? It bring you the money, man. If you don't have it, they might not pay you. [*Laughs.*] My other guitar is "I'm Gonna Take 'Em to Meet Lucy and Lucille and See if We Can Make a Deal." [*Laughs.*]

GUY: Guitars brings a lot of joy, man.

Photo Credits

INDEX

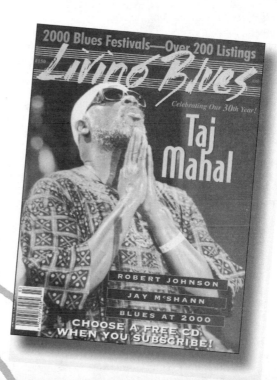

When It Comes to Music, We Wrote the Book